Physical Science

interactive SCIENCE

Go to **MyScienceOnline.com** to experience science in a whole new way.

Interactive tools such as My Planet Diary connect you to the latest science happenings.

MY PLANET DIARY

- **Search Earth's Journal** for important science news from around the world.

- **Use Earth's Calendar** to find out when cool scientific events occur.

- **Explore science Links** to find even more exciting information about our planet.

- **Visit Jack's Blog** to be the first to know about what is going on in science!

PEARSON

Glenview, Illinois • Boston, Massachusetts • Chandler, Arizona • Upper Saddle River, New Jersey

Program Authors

You're an author!

As you write in this science book, your answers and personal discoveries will be recorded for you to keep, making this book unique to you. That is why you are one of the primary authors of this book.

✏️ **In the space below, print your name, school, town, and state. Then write a short autobiography that includes your interests and accomplishments.**

YOUR NAME

SCHOOL

TOWN, STATE

AUTOBIOGRAPHY

Your Photo

Acknowledgments appear on pages 636–639, which constitute an extension of this copyright page.

ISBN-13:   978-0-13-320926-6
ISBN-10:   0-13-320926-1
            16 18

ON THE COVER
Thermogram
The thermogram on the cover uses "warm" colors (red, orange) to show warm regions and "cool" colors (green, blue) to show cool regions. This color mapping matches our common association of the color red with warmth and the color blue with coolness. However, the color choices for this image are arbitrary, and other colors could have been chosen for the thermogram.

Program Authors

KATHRYN THORNTON, Ph.D.
Professor and Associate Dean, School of Engineering and Applied Science, University of Virginia, Charlottesville, Virginia
Selected by NASA in May 1984, Dr. Kathryn Thornton is a veteran of four space flights. She has logged more than 975 hours in space, including more than 21 hours of extravehicular activity. As an author on the *Scott Foresman Science* series, Dr. Thornton's enthusiasm for science has inspired teachers around the globe.

DON BUCKLEY, M.Sc.
Information and Communications Technology Director, The School at Columbia University, New York, New York
A founder of New York City Independent School Technologists (NYCIST) and long-time chair of New York Association of Independent Schools' annual IT conference, Mr. Buckley has taught students on two continents and created multimedia and Internet-based instructional systems for schools worldwide.

ZIPPORAH MILLER, M.A.Ed.
Associate Executive Director for Professional Programs and Conferences, National Science Teachers Association, Arlington, Virginia
Ms. Zipporah Miller is a former K–12 science supervisor and STEM coordinator for the Prince George's County Public School District in Maryland. She is a science education consultant who has overseen curriculum development and staff training for more than 150 district science coordinators.

MICHAEL J. PADILLA, Ph.D.
Associate Dean and Director, Eugene P. Moore School of Education, Clemson University, Clemson, South Carolina
A former middle school teacher and a leader in middle school science education, Dr. Michael Padilla has served as president of the National Science Teachers Association and as a writer of the National Science Education Standards. He is professor of science education at Clemson University.

MICHAEL E. WYSESSION, Ph.D.
Associate Professor of Earth and Planetary Science, Washington University, St. Louis, Missouri
An author on more than 50 scientific publications, Dr. Wysession was awarded the prestigious Packard Foundation Fellowship and Presidential Faculty Fellowship for his research in geophysics. Dr. Wysession is an expert on Earth's inner structure and has mapped various regions of Earth using seismic tomography. He is known internationally for his work in geoscience education and outreach.

Instructional Design Author

GRANT WIGGINS, Ed.D.
President, Authentic Education, Hopewell, New Jersey
Dr. Wiggins is a co-author with Jay McTighe of *Understanding by Design, 2nd Edition* (ASCD 2005). His approach to instructional design provides teachers with a disciplined way of thinking about curriculum design, assessment, and instruction that moves teaching from covering content to ensuring understanding.

UNDERSTANDING BY DESIGN® and UbD™ are trademarks of ASCD, and are used under license.

Planet Diary Author

JACK HANKIN
Science/Mathematics Teacher, The Hilldale School, Daly City, California, Founder, Planet Diary Web site
Mr. Hankin is the creator and writer of Planet Diary, a science current events Web site. He is passionate about bringing science news and environmental awareness into classrooms and offers numerous Planet Diary workshops at NSTA and other events to train middle and high school teachers.

ELL Consultant

JIM CUMMINS, Ph.D.
Professor and Canada Research Chair, Curriculum, Teaching and Learning department at the University of Toronto
Dr. Cummins focuses on literacy development in multilingual schools and the role of technology in promoting student learning across the curriculum. *Interactive Science* incorporates essential research-based principles for integrating language with the teaching of academic content based on his instructional framework.

Reading Consultant

HARVEY DANIELS, Ph.D.
Professor of Secondary Education, University of New Mexico, Albuquerque, New Mexico
Dr. Daniels is an international consultant to schools, districts, and educational agencies. He has authored or coauthored 13 books on language, literacy, and education. His most recent works are *Comprehension and Collaboration: Inquiry Circles in Action* and *Subjects Matter: Every Teacher's Guide to Content-Area Reading*.

Reviewers

Contributing Writers

Edward Aguado, Ph.D.
Professor, Department of Geography
San Diego State University
San Diego, California

Elizabeth Coolidge-Stolz, M.D.
Medical Writer
North Reading, Massachusetts

Donald L. Cronkite, Ph.D.
Professor of Biology
Hope College
Holland, Michigan

Jan Jenner, Ph.D.
Science Writer
Talladega, Alabama

Linda Cronin Jones, Ph.D.
Associate Professor of Science and Environmental Education
University of Florida
Gainesville, Florida

T. Griffith Jones, Ph.D.
Clinical Associate Professor of Science Education
College of Education
University of Florida
Gainesville, Florida

Andrew C. Kemp, Ph.D.
Teacher
Jefferson County Public Schools
Louisville, Kentucky

Matthew Stoneking, Ph.D.
Associate Professor of Physics
Lawrence University
Appleton, Wisconsin

R. Bruce Ward, Ed.D.
Senior Research Associate
Science Education Department
Harvard-Smithsonian Center for Astrophysics
Cambridge, Massachusetts

Content Reviewers

Paul D. Beale, Ph.D.
Department of Physics
University of Colorado at Boulder
Boulder, Colorado

Jeff R. Bodart, Ph.D.
Professor of Physical Sciences
Chipola College
Marianna, Florida

Joy Branlund, Ph.D.
Department of Earth Science
Southwestern Illinois College
Granite City, Illinois

Marguerite Brickman, Ph.D.
Division of Biological Sciences
University of Georgia
Athens, Georgia

Bonnie J. Brunkhorst, Ph.D.
Science Education and Geological Sciences
California State University
San Bernardino, California

Michael Castellani, Ph.D.
Department of Chemistry
Marshall University
Huntington, West Virginia

Charles C. Curtis, Ph.D.
Research Associate Professor of Physics
University of Arizona
Tucson, Arizona

Diane I. Doser, Ph.D.
Department of Geological Sciences
University of Texas
El Paso, Texas

Rick Duhrkopf, Ph.D.
Department of Biology
Baylor University
Waco, Texas

Alice K. Hankla, Ph.D.
The Galloway School
Atlanta, Georgia

Mark Henriksen, Ph.D.
Physics Department
University of Maryland
Baltimore, Maryland

Chad Hershock, Ph.D.
Center for Research on Learning and Teaching
University of Michigan
Ann Arbor, Michigan

Jeremiah N. Jarrett, Ph.D.
Department of Biology
Central Connecticut State University
New Britain, Connecticut

Scott L. Kight, Ph.D.
Department of Biology
Montclair State University
Montclair, New Jersey

Jennifer O. Liang, Ph.D.
Department of Biology
University of Minnesota–Duluth
Duluth, Minnesota

Candace Lutzow-Felling, Ph.D.
State Arboretum of Virginia & Blandy Experimental Farm
Boyce, Virginia

Joseph F. McCullough, Ph.D.
Physics Program Chair
Cabrillo College
Aptos, California

Heather Mernitz, Ph.D.
Department of Physical Science
Alverno College
Milwaukee, Wisconsin

Sadredin C. Moosavi, Ph.D.
Department of Earth and Environmental Sciences
Tulane University
New Orleans, Louisiana

David L. Reid, Ph.D.
Department of Biology
Blackburn College
Carlinville, Illinois

Scott M. Rochette, Ph.D.
Department of the Earth Sciences
SUNY College at Brockport
Brockport, New York

Karyn L. Rogers, Ph.D.
Department of Geological Sciences
University of Missouri
Columbia, Missouri

Laurence Rosenhein, Ph.D.
Department of Chemistry
Indiana State University
Terre Haute, Indiana

Sara Seager, Ph.D.
Department of Planetary Sciences and Physics
Massachusetts Institute of Technology
Cambridge, Massachusetts

Tom Shoberg, Ph.D.
Missouri University of Science and Technology
Rolla, Missouri

Patricia Simmons, Ph.D.
North Carolina State University
Raleigh, North Carolina

William H. Steinecker, Ph.D.
Research Scholar
Miami University
Oxford, Ohio

Paul R. Stoddard, Ph.D.
Department of Geology and Environmental Geosciences
Northern Illinois University
DeKalb, Illinois

John R. Villarreal, Ph.D.
Department of Chemistry
The University of Texas–Pan American
Edinburg, Texas

John R. Wagner, Ph.D.
Department of Geology
Clemson University
Clemson, South Carolina

Jerry Waldvogel, Ph.D.
Department of Biological Sciences
Clemson University
Clemson, South Carolina

Donna L. Witter, Ph.D.
Department of Geology
Kent State University
Kent, Ohio

Edward J. Zalisko, Ph.D.
Department of Biology
Blackburn College
Carlinville, Illinois

Museum of Science.

Special thanks to the Museum of Science, Boston, Massachusetts, and Ioannis Miaoulis, the Museum's president and director, for serving as content advisors for the technology and design strand in this program.

Table of Contents

 Enter the Lab zone for hands-on inquiry.

△**Chapter Lab Investigation:**
• Directed Inquiry: Making Sense of Density
• Open Inquiry: Making Sense of Density

△**Inquiry Warm-Ups:** • How Do You Describe Matter? • What Is a Mixture? • Which Has More Mass? • Is a New Substance Formed?

△**Quick Labs:** • Observing Physical Properties • Modeling Atoms and Molecules • Separating Mixtures • Calculating Volume • What Is a Physical Change? • Demonstrating Tarnishing • Where Was the Energy?

my science ONLINE.com

Go to MyScienceOnline.com to interact with this chapter's content. Keyword: Introduction to Matter

> **UNTAMED SCIENCE**
• What's the Matter?

> **PLANET DIARY**
• Introduction to Matter

> **INTERACTIVE ART**
• Conservation of Matter • Properties of Matter

> **ART IN MOTION**
• What Makes Up Matter?

> **VIRTUAL LAB**
• How Do You Measure Weight and Volume?
• Will It Float? Density of Solids and Liquids

 Enter the Lab zone for hands-on inquiry.

△ **Chapter Lab Investigation:**
• Directed Inquiry: Melting Ice
• Open Inquiry: Melting Ice

△ **Inquiry Warm-Ups:** What Are Solids, Liquids, and Gases? • What Happens When You Breathe on a Mirror? • How Can Air Keep Chalk From Breaking?

△ **Quick Labs:** • Modeling Particles • As Thick As Honey • How Do the Particles in a Gas Move? • Keeping Cool • Observing Sublimation • How are Pressure and Temperature Related? • Hot and Cold Balloons • It's a Gas!

my science online.com

Go to MyScienceOnline.com to interact with this chapter's content.
Keyword: Solids, Liquids, and Gases

▷ **UNTAMED SCIENCE**
• Building a House of Snow

▷ **PLANET DIARY**
• Solids, Liquids, and Gases

▷ **INTERACTIVE ART**
• Gas Laws • States of Matter

▷ **VIRTUAL LAB**
• Solid to Liquid to Gas: Changes of State

 Lab zone Enter the Lab zone for hands-on inquiry.

Chapter Lab Investigation:
• Directed Inquiry: Copper or Carbon? That Is the Question.
• Open Inquiry: Copper or Carbon? That Is the Question.

Inquiry Warm-Ups: • What's in the Box?
• Which Is Easier? • Why Use Aluminum?
• What Are the Properties of Charcoal? • How Much Goes Away?

Quick Labs: • Visualizing an Electron Cloud • How Far Away Is the Electron? • Classifying • Using the Periodic Table • Expanding the Periodic Table • Finding Metals • Carbon—A Nonmetal • Finding Nonmetals • What Happens When an Atom Decays? • Modeling Beta Decay • Designing Experiments Using Radioactive Tracers

MY SCIENCE online.com

Go to MyScienceOnline.com to interact with this chapter's content.
Keyword: **Elements and the Periodic Table**

> PLANET DIARY
• Elements and the Periodic Table

> INTERACTIVE ART
• Periodic Table • Investigate an Atom

> ART IN MOTION
• Types of Radioactive Decay

> VIRTUAL LAB
• Which Element Is This?

 Enter the Lab zone for hands-on inquiry.

△ **Chapter Lab Investigation:**
• Directed Inquiry: Shedding Light on Ions
• Open Inquiry: Shedding Light on Ions

△ **Inquiry Warm-Ups:** • What Are the Trends in the Periodic Table? • How Do Ions Form? • Covalent Bonds • Are They "Steel" the Same?

△ **Quick Labs:** • Element Chemistry • Ion Formation • How Do You Write Ionic Names and Formulas? • Sharing Electrons • Properties of Molecular Compounds • Attraction Between Polar Molecules • Metal Crystals • What Do Metals Do?

my science online.com

Go to MyScienceOnline.com to interact with this chapter's content.
Keyword: Atoms and Bonding

> **UNTAMED SCIENCE**
• The Elements of Hockey

> **PLANET DIARY**
• Atoms and Bonding

> **INTERACTIVE ART**
• Periodic Table • Investigate Ionic Compounds • Table Salt Dissolving in Water

> **ART IN MOTION**
• Bonding in Polar Molecules

> **VIRTUAL LAB**
• Will It React?

Enter the Lab zone for hands-on inquiry.

△ **Chapter Lab Investigation:**
• Directed Inquiry: Where's the Evidence?
• Open Inquiry: Where's the Evidence?

△ **Inquiry Warm-Ups:** • What Happens When Chemicals React? • Did You Lose Anything? • Can You Speed Up or Slow Down a Chemical Reaction?

△ **Quick Labs:** • Observing Change • Information in a Chemical Equation • Is Matter Conserved? • Categories of Chemical Reactions • Modeling Activation Energy • Effect of Temperature on Chemical Reactions

my science online.com

Go to MyScienceOnline.com to interact with this chapter's content.
Keyword: Chemical Reactions

> **UNTAMED SCIENCE**
• Chemical Reactions to the Rescue

> **PLANET DIARY**
• Chemical Reactions

> **INTERACTIVE ART**
• Physical or Chemical Change?
• Conservation of Matter • Balancing Equations

> **ART IN MOTION**
• Activation Energy

> **VIRTUAL LAB**
• Energy and Chemical Changes

 Enter the Lab zone for hands-on inquiry.

Chapter Lab Investigation:
• Directed Inquiry: Speedy Solutions
• Open Inquiry: Speedy Solutions

Inquiry Warm-Ups: • What Makes a Mixture a Solution? • Does It Dissolve? • What Color Does Litmus Paper Turn? • What Can Cabbage Juice Tell You?

Quick Labs: • Scattered Light • Measuring Concentration • Predicting Rates of Solubility • Properties of Acids • Properties of Bases • pHone Home • The Antacid Test

my science ONLINE.com

Go to MyScienceOnline.com to interact with this chapter's content. Keyword: Acids, Bases, and Solutions

> **UNTAMED SCIENCE**
• What's the Solution?

> **PLANET DIARY**
• Acids, Bases, and Solutions

> **INTERACTIVE ART**
• Table Salt Dissolving in Water • Classifying Solutions • The pH Scale

> **VIRTUAL LAB**
• Acid, Base, or Neutral?

 Enter the Lab zone for hands-on inquiry.

△ **Chapter Lab Investigation:**
• Directed Inquiry: Stopping on a Dime
• Open Inquiry: Stopping on a Dime

△ **Inquiry Warm-Ups:** • What Is Motion?
• How Fast and How Far? • Will You Hurry Up?

△ **Quick Labs:** • Identifying Motion • Velocity
• Motion Graphs • Describing Acceleration
• Graphing Acceleration

my science online.com

Go to MyScienceOnline.com to interact with this chapter's content.
Keyword: Motion

> **UNTAMED SCIENCE**
• The Adventures of Velocity Girl

> **PLANET DIARY**
• Motion

> **INTERACTIVE ART**
• Speed and Acceleration • Graphing Motion

> **ART IN MOTION**
• Relative Motion

> **VIRTUAL LAB**
• How Can You Measure Acceleration?

 Lab zone® Enter the Lab zone for hands-on inquiry.

Chapter Lab Investigation:
• Directed Inquiry: Sticky Sneakers
• Open Inquiry: Sticky Sneakers

Inquiry Warm-Ups: • Is the Force With You?
• Observing Friction • What Changes Motion?
• How Pushy Is a Straw? • What Makes an Object Move in a Circle? • Why Redesign?

Quick Labs: • What Is Force? • Modeling Unbalanced Forces • Calculating • Around and Around • Newton's Second Law • Interpreting Illustrations • Colliding Cars • Which Lands First? • Orbiting Earth • Using Scientific Thinking • How Close Is It? •

MY SCIENCE ONLINE.com

Go to MyScienceOnline.com to interact with this chapter's content.
Keyword: **Forces**

> UNTAMED SCIENCE
• Sir Isaac Visits the Circus

> PLANET DIARY
• Forces

> INTERACTIVE ART
• Balanced and Unbalanced Forces
• Conservation of Momentum

> ART IN MOTION
• Types of Friction

> VIRTUAL LAB
• Investigating Newton's Laws of Motion

 Enter the Lab zone for hands-on inquiry.

Chapter Lab Investigation:
• Directed Inquiry: Angling for Access
• Open Inquiry: Angling for Access

Inquiry Warm-Ups: • Pulling at an Angle
• Is It a Machine? • Inclined Planes and Levers
• Machines That Turn

Quick Labs: • What Is Work? • Investigating
Power • Going Up • Mechanical Advantage
• Friction and Efficiency • Modeling Levers
• Building Pulleys • Machines in the Kitchen

my science online.com

**Go to MyScienceOnline.com to interact with this chapter's content.
Keyword: Work and Machines**

> UNTAMED SCIENCE
• Remodeling Stonehenge

> PLANET DIARY
• Work and Machines

> INTERACTIVE ART
• Types of Pulleys • Work

> ART IN MOTION
• Levers

> REAL-WORLD INQUIRY
• Bicycle Racing and Efficiency

 Enter the Lab zone for hands-on inquiry.

Chapter Lab Investigation:
• Directed Inquiry: Can You Feel the Power?
• Open Inquiry: Can You Feel the Power?

Inquiry Warm-Ups: • How High Does a Ball Bounce? • What Makes a Flashlight Shine? • What Would Make a Card Jump?

Quick Labs: • Mass, Velocity, and Kinetic Energy • Determining Mechanical Energy • Sources of Energy • Soaring Straws • Law of Conservation of Energy

my science online.com

Go to MyScienceOnline.com to interact with this chapter's content. Keyword: Energy

> **UNTAMED SCIENCE**
• The Potential for Fun

> **PLANET DIARY**
• Energy

> **ART IN MOTION**
• Kinetic and Potential Energy

> **INTERACTIVE ART**
• Types of Energy • Energy Transformations

> **VIRTUAL LAB**
• Exploring Potential and Kinetic Energy

CHAPTER 11

Thermal Energy and Heat

 The Big Question **370**
How does heat flow from one object to another?

Lab zone® Enter the Lab zone for hands-on inquiry.

△ **Chapter Lab Investigation:**
• Directed Inquiry: Build Your Own Thermometer
• Open Inquiry: Build Your Own Thermometer

△ **Inquiry Warm-Ups:** • How Cold Is the Water? • What Does It Mean to Heat Up? • Thermal Properties

△ **Quick Labs:** • Temperature and Thermal Energy • Visualizing Convection Currents • Frosty Balloons

my science online.com

Go to MyScienceOnline.com to interact with this chapter's content. Keyword: Thermal Energy and Heat

▷ **UNTAMED SCIENCE**
• Why Is This Inner Tube So Hot?

▷ **PLANET DIARY**
• Thermal Energy and Heat

▷ **INTERACTIVE ART**
• Heat Transfer

▷ **ART IN MOTION**
• Temperature and Thermal Energy
• Conductors and Insulators

▷ **VIRTUAL LAB**
• Temperature or Heat? What's the Difference?

 Enter the Lab zone for hands-on inquiry.

Chapter Lab Investigation:
• Directed Inquiry: Making Waves
• Open Inquiry: Making Waves

Inquiry Warm-Ups: • What Are Waves?
• What Do Waves Look Like? • How Does a Ball Bounce?

Quick Labs: • What Causes Mechanical Waves? • Three Types of Waves • Properties of Waves • What Affects the Speed of a Wave? • Wave Interference • Standing Waves

my science online.com

Go to MyScienceOnline.com to interact with this chapter's content.
Keyword: Characteristics of Waves

> **UNTAMED SCIENCE**
• Extreme Wave Science!

> **PLANET DIARY**
• Characteristics of Waves

> **INTERACTIVE ART**
• Wave Interference • Properties of Waves

> **ART IN MOTION**
• Wave and Energy Movement

> **VIRTUAL LAB**
• Bouncing and Bending Light

 Enter the Lab zone for hands-on inquiry.

Chapter Lab Investigation:
• Directed Inquiry: Changing Pitch
• Open Inquiry: Changing Pitch

Inquiry Warm-Ups: • What Is Sound?
• How Does Amplitude Affect Loudness?
• What Is Music? • Hearing Sound • How Can
You Use Time to Measure Distance?

Quick Labs: • Understanding Sound
• Ear to the Sound • Listen to This • Pipe
Sounds • How Can You Change Pitch?
• Design and Build Hearing Protectors
• Designing Experiments

my science online .com

**Go to MyScienceOnline.com to
interact with this chapter's content.
Keyword: Sound**

> **UNTAMED SCIENCE**
• Was That a Whale I Heard?

> **PLANET DIARY**
• Sound

> **INTERACTIVE ART**
• Musical Instruments • Exploring
Sound Waves

> **ART IN MOTION**
• Observing the Doppler Effect

> **REAL-WORLD INQUIRY**
• How Can Sound Solve a Problem?

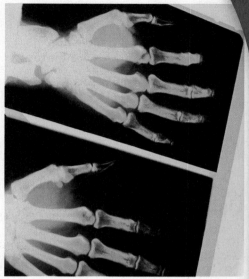

 Enter the Lab zone for hands-on inquiry.

Chapter Lab Investigation:
• Directed Inquiry: Build a Crystal Radio
• Open Inquiry: Build a Crystal Radio

Inquiry Warm-Ups: • How Fast Are Electromagnetic Waves? • What Is White Light? • How Can Waves Change?

Quick Labs: What Is an Electromagnetic Wave Made Of? • Waves or Particles? • Differences Between Waves • Parts of the Electromagnetic Spectrum • How Cell Phones Work • How Does GPS Work?

my science online.com

Go to MyScienceOnline.com to interact with this chapter's content. Keyword: Electromagnetic Waves

› UNTAMED SCIENCE
• The Day the Waves Died

› PLANET DIARY
• Electromagnetic Waves

› INTERACTIVE ART
• Electromagnetic Waves • Modulating Electromagnetic Waves

› ART IN MOTION
• Invisible Information • Global Positioning System (GPS)

› VIRTUAL LAB
• Wave or Particle? Exploring the Properties of Light

CHAPTER 15

Light

 Enter the Lab zone for hands-on inquiry.

Chapter Lab Investigation:
• Directed Inquiry: Changing Colors
• Open Inquiry: Changing Colors

Inquiry Warm-Ups: • How Do Colors Mix?
• How Does Your Reflection Wink? • How Can You Make an Image Appear? • Can You See Everything With One Eye? • How Does a Pinhole Camera Work?

Quick Labs: • Developing Hypotheses
• Observing • Mirror Images • Bent Pencil • Looking at Images • True Colors • What a View!

my science online.com

Go to MyScienceOnline.com to interact with this chapter's content.
Keyword: **Light**

> **UNTAMED SCIENCE**
• Why Is the Ocean Blue?

> **PLANET DIARY**
• Light

> **INTERACTIVE ART**
• Mirrors and Lenses • Refracting and Reflecting Telescopes

> **ART IN MOTION**
• Refraction, Reflection, and Rainbows

> **VIRTUAL LAB**
• Color in Light

 Enter the Lab zone for hands-on inquiry.

△ **Chapter Lab Investigation:**
• Directed Inquiry: Build a Flashlight
• Open Inquiry: Build a Flashlight

△ **Inquiry Warm-Ups:** • Can You Move a Can Without Touching It? • How Can Current Be Measured? • Do the Lights Keep Shining? • How Can You Make a Bulb Burn More Brightly?

△ **Quick Labs:** • Drawing Conclusions • Sparks Are Flying • Producing Electric Current • Conductors and Insulators • Modeling Potential Difference • Ohm's Law • Calculating Electric Power and Energy Use • Electric Shock and Short Circuit Safety

my science online.com

Go to MyScienceOnline.com to interact with this chapter's content.
Keyword: Electricity

▷ **PLANET DIARY**
• Electricity

▷ **INTERACTIVE ART**
• Series and Parallel Circuits • Current Flow

▷ **ART IN MOTION**
• Static Charge

▷ **VIRTUAL LAB**
• Discovering Ohm's Law

▷ **REAL-WORLD INQUIRY**
• Energy Conservation

Lab zone® Enter the Lab zone
for hands-on inquiry.

△ **Chapter Lab Investigation:**
• Directed Inquiry: Detecting Fake Coins
• Open Inquiry: Detecting Fake Coins

△ **Inquiry Warm-Ups:** • Natural Magnets
• Predict the Field • Electromagnetism • How
Are Electricity, Magnets, and Motion Related?
• Electric Current Without a Battery

△ **Quick Labs:** • Magnetic Poles • Spinning
in Circles • Earth's Magnetic Field • Electric
Current and Magnetism • Magnetic Fields
From Electric Current • Electromagnet • Can a
Magnet Move a Wire? • How Galvanometers
Work • Parts of an Electric Motor • Inducing
an Electric Current • How Generators Work
• How Transformers Work

my science online.com

Go to MyScienceOnline.com to
interact with this chapter's content.
Keyword: Magnetism and
Electromagnetism

▷ **PLANET DIARY**
• Magnetism and Electromagnetism

▷ **INTERACTIVE ART**
• Magnetic Fields • Motors and Generators

▷ **ART IN MOTION**
• Maglev Train

▷ **REAL-WORLD INQUIRY**
• Exploring Electromagnetism

Video Series: Chapter Adventures

Untamed Science created this captivating video series for interactive SCIENCE featuring a unique segment for every chapter of the program.

Featuring videos such as

Physical Science

interactive SCIENCE

PEARSON

Interactive Science

Interactive Science is a program that features 3 pathways to match the way you learn.

- The write-in student edition enables you to become an active participant as you read about science.

- A variety of hands-on activities will not only engage you but also provide you with a deep understanding of science concepts.

- Go to MyScienceOnline.com to access a wide array of digital resources built especially for students like you!

 Interact with your textbook.

 Interact with inquiry.

 Interact online.

interactive SCIENCE

WHAT MAKES THESE SNOWBOARDERS "FLY" DOWNHILL?

How is energy conserved in a transformation?

These women are competing in the sport of snowboard cross. They "fly" down a narrow course, filled with jumps, steep sections, and ramps. Disaster looms at every turn. If they don't crash into each other or fall, then the first one across the finish line wins.

Develop Hypotheses What do you think makes these snowboarders go so fast?

_____

_____

_____

_____

> **UNTAMED SCIENCE** Watch the **Untamed Science** video to learn more about energy.

342 Energy

MY SC

 ## Get Engaged!

At the start of each chapter, you will see two questions: an Engaging Question and the Big Question. Each chapter's Big Question will help you start thinking about the Big Ideas of Science. Look for the Big Q symbol throughout the chapter! ......

Start with the Big Question

Energy

CHAPTER 10

Energy | UNTAMED SCIENCE | THE BIG QUESTION 343

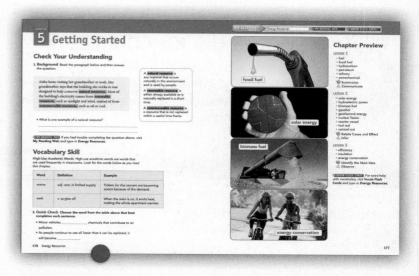

Build Reading, Inquiry, and Vocabulary Skills

- In every lesson you will learn new Reading 🔄 and Inquiry skills △ to help you read and think like a scientist.

- Go online to MyScienceOnline.com and click on My Reading Web to get additional reading at your level.

my science online.com

Go Online!

At MyScienceOnline.com, you will find a variety of engaging digital resources such as the Untamed Science videos. Follow the Untamed Science video crew as they travel the globe exploring the Big Ideas of Science.

Unlock the Big Question

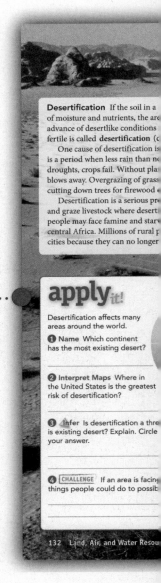

Desertification If the soil in a
of moisture and nutrients, the are
advance of desertlike conditions
fertile is called **desertification** (c

One cause of desertification is
is a period when less rain than no
droughts, crops fail. Without pla
blows away. Overgrazing of grass
cutting down trees for firewood

Desertification is a serious pre
and graze livestock where desert
people may face famine and starv
central Africa. Millions of rural p
cities because they can no longer

MY SCIENCE online →

Go to MyScienceOnline.com to access a wide
array of digital resources such as Virtual Labs,
additional My Planet Diary activities, and
Got It? assessments with instant feedback.

Explore the Key Concepts

Each lesson begins with a series of Key Concept
questions. The interactivities in each lesson will
help you understand these concepts and Unlock
the Big Question.

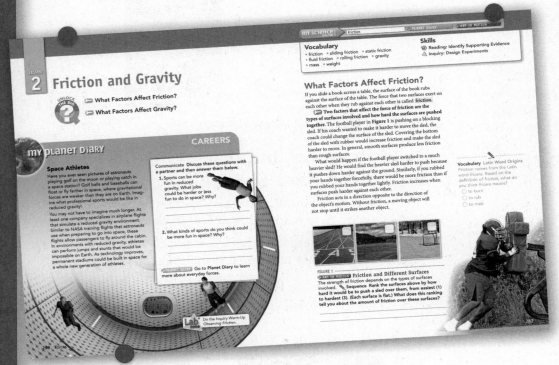

LESSON 2

Friction and Gravity

UNLOCK THE BIG

☐ What Factors Affect Friction?
☐ What Factors Affect Gravity?

my planet diary   CAREERS

Space Athletes

Have you ever seen pictures of astronauts
playing golf on the moon or playing catch in
a space station? Golf balls and baseballs can
float or fly farther in space, where gravitational
forces are weaker than they are on Earth. Imagine what professional sports would be like in
reduced gravity!

You may not have to imagine much longer. At
least one company specializes in airplane flights
that simulate a reduced gravity that astronauts
use when preparing to go into space. Similar to NASA training flights, these
flights allow passengers to fly around the cabin.
In environments with reduced gravity, athletes
can perform jumps and stunts that would be
impossible on Earth. As technology improves,
permanent stadiums could be built in space for
a whole new generation of athletes.

Communicate Discuss these questions with
a partner and then answer them below.

1. Sports can be more
fun in reduced
gravity. What jobs
could be harder or less
fun to do in space? Why?

2. What kinds of sports do you think could
be more fun in space? Why?

▶ PLANET DIARY Go to Planet Diary to learn
more about everyday forces.

Lab zone Do the Inquiry Warm-Up
Observing Friction.

---

my science → Friction   PLANET DIARY   ART IN MOTION

Vocabulary   **Skills**
• friction • sliding friction • static friction   ◉ Reading: Identify Supporting Evidence
• fluid friction • rolling friction • gravity   △ Inquiry: Design Experiments
• mass • weight

What Factors Affect Friction?

If you slide a book across a table, the surface of the book rubs
against the surface of the table. The force that two surfaces exert on
each other when they rub against each other is called **friction**.

☐ **Two factors that affect the force of friction are the
types of surfaces involved and how hard the surfaces are pushed
together.** The football player in **Figure 1** is pushing on a blocking
sled. If his coach wanted to make it harder to move the sled, the
coach could change the surface of the sled. Covering the bottom
of the sled with rubber would increase friction and make the sled
harder to move. In general, smooth surfaces produce less friction
than rough surfaces.

What would happen if the football player switched to a much
heavier sled? He would find the heavier sled harder to push because
it pushes down harder against the ground. Similarly, if you rubbed
your hands together forcefully, there would be more friction than if
you rubbed your hands together lightly. Friction increases when
surfaces push harder against each other.

Friction acts in a direction opposite to the direction of
the object's motion. Without friction, a moving object will
not stop until it strikes another object.

Vocabulary Latin Word Origins
Friction comes from the Latin
word *fricare*. Based on the
definition of friction, what do
you think *fricare* means?
○ to burn
○ to rub
○ to melt

FIGURE 1
◀ ART IN MOTION **Friction and Different Surfaces**
The strength of friction depends on the types of surfaces
involved. **Sequence** Rank the surfaces above by how
hard it would be to push a sled over them, from easiest (1)
to hardest (3). (Each surface is flat.) What does this ranking
tell you about the amount of friction over these surfaces?

---

apply it!

Desertification affects many
areas around the world.

❶ **Name** Which continent
has the most existing desert?

❷ **Interpret Maps** Where in
the United States is the greatest
risk of desertification?

❸ **Infer** Is desertification a thre
is existing desert? Explain. Circle
your answer.

❹ **CHALLENGE** If an area is facing
things people could do to possibl

132 Land, Air, and Water Resou

---

my planet diary

At the start of each lesson, My Planet
Diary will introduce you to amazing events,
significant people, and important discoveries
in science or help you to overcome common
misconceptions about science concepts.

apply it!

Elaborate further with
the Apply It activities.
This is your opportunity
to take what you've
learned and apply those
skills to new situations.

Lab zone

Look for the Lab zone triangle. This means that it's time to do a hands-on inquiry lab. In every lesson, you'll have the opportunity to do a hands-on inquiry activity that will help reinforce your understanding of the lesson topic.

fertile area becomes depleted
become a desert. The
reas that previously were
rt uh fih KAY shun).
ate. For example, a **drought**
falls in an area. During
er, the exposed soil easily
by cattle and sheep and
ause desertification, too.
. People cannot grow crops
on has occurred. As a result,
. Desertification is severe in
there are moving to the
ort themselves on the land.

Key
■ Existing desert
■ High-risk area
■ Moderate-risk area

y in areas where there
a on the map to support

rtification, what are some
its effects?

Land Reclamation Fortunately, it is possible to replace land damaged by erosion or mining. The process of restoring an area of land to a more productive state is called **land reclamation.** In addition to restoring land for agriculture, land reclamation can restore habitats for wildlife. Many different types of land reclamation projects are currently underway all over the world. But it is generally more difficult and expensive to restore damaged land and soil than it is to protect those resources in the first place. In some cases, the land may not return to its original state.

FIGURE 4
Land Reclamation
These pictures show land before and after it was mined.

✐ **Communicate** Below the pictures, write a story about what happened to the land.

🖿 Assess Your Understanding

1a. Review Subsoil has (less/more) plant and animal matter than topsoil.

b. Explain What can happen to soil if plants are removed?

c. Apply Concepts Wha
that could prevent
land reclamation?

got it?

○ I get it! Now I know that soil management is important because

○ I need extra help with

Go to **MY SCIENCE** 🔵 **COACH** *online for help with this subject.*

Lab® zone
Do the Quick Lab
Modeling Soil Conservation.

got it?

Evaluate Your Progress

After answering the Got It question, think about how you're doing. Did you get it or do you need a little help? Remember, **MY SCIENCE** 🔵 **COACH** is there for you if you need extra help.

Assess the Big Question

Explore the Big Question
At one point in the chapter, you'll have the opportunity to take all that you've learned to further explore the Big Question.

Pollution and Solutions

What can people do to use resources wisely?

FIGURE 4
▶ REAL-WORLD INQUIRY All living things depend on land, air, and water. Conserving these resources for the future is important. Part of resource conservation is identifying and limiting sources of pollution.
✎ Interpret Photos On the photograph, write the letter from the key into the circle that best identifies the source of pollution.

Land
Describe at least one thing your community could do to reduce pollution on land.

Air
Describe at least one thing your community could do to reduce air pollution.

Water
Describe at least one thing your community could do to reduce water pollution.

Pollution Sources
A. Sediments
B. Municipal solid waste
C. Runoff from development

Lab zone Do the Qu Getting C

▭ **Assess Your Understan**

1a. Define What are sediments?

b. Explain How can bacteria help clea spill in the ocean?

c. ANSWER What can people do to use resources wisely?

d. CHALLENGE Why might a compar to recycle the waste they produ would reduce water pollution?

got it?

○ I get it! Now I know that water can be reduced by

○ I need extra help with

Go to MY SCIENCE COACH on with this subject.

Answer the Big Question
Now it's time to show what you know and answer the Big Question.

Review What You've Learned

Use the Chapter Study Guide to review the
Big Question and prepare for the test.

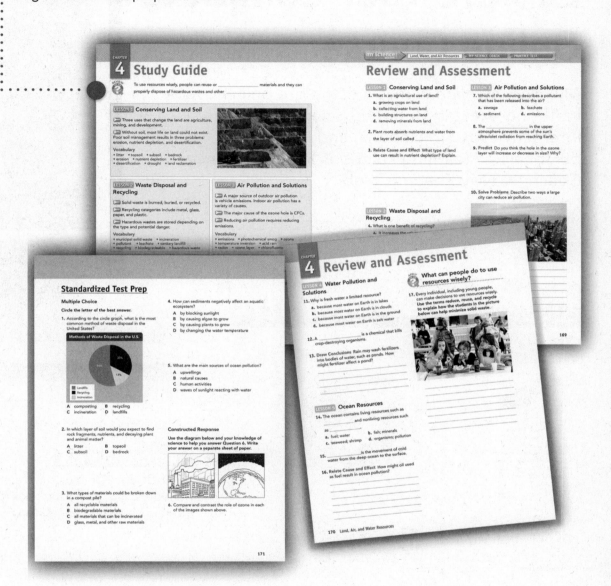

Practice Taking Tests

Apply the Big Question and take a practice test in
standardized test format.

Explore Your Complete Online Course

MyScienceOnline.com is a complete online course featuring exciting Untamed Science Videos, Interactive Art Simulations, and innovative personalized learning solutions like My Science Coach and My Reading Web.

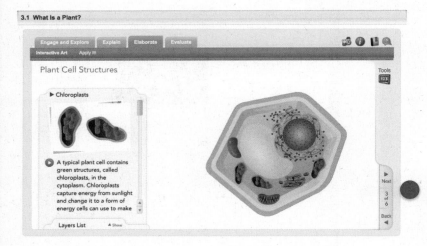

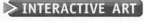

> INTERACTIVE ART

At MyScienceOnline.com, many of the beautiful visuals in your book become interactive so you can extend your learning.

> VOCAB FLASH CARDS

Practice chapter vocabulary with interactive flash cards. Each card has an image, definitions in English and Spanish, and space for your own notes.

o you know a plant when you see it?

Tools

▶ Next

1 of 4

Back

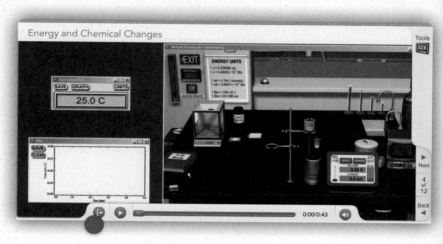

Energy and Chemical Changes

Tools

25.0 C

▶ Next

4 of 12

Back

0:00/0:43

> **VIRTUAL LAB**

Get more practice with realistic virtual labs. Interact with
on-line labs without costly equipment or clean-up.

Your Online Student Edition

Create an online notebook! Highlight
important information and create
sticky notes. Notes and highlights
are saved in your own personal
Online Student Edition.

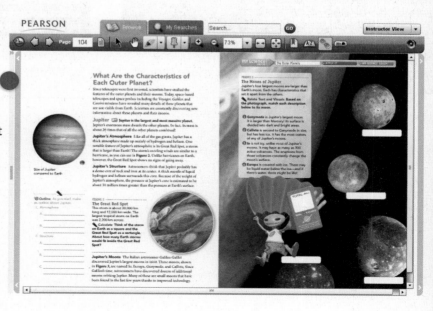

? BIG IDEAS OF SCIENCE

Have you ever worked on a jigsaw puzzle? Usually a puzzle has a theme that leads you to group the pieces by what they have in common. But until you put all the pieces together you can't solve the puzzle. Studying science is similar to solving a puzzle. The big ideas of science are like puzzle themes. To understand big ideas, scientists ask questions. The answers to those questions are like pieces of a puzzle. Each chapter in this book asks a big question to help you think about a big idea of science. By answering the big questions, you will get closer to understanding the big idea.

✎ **Before you read each chapter, write about what you know and what more you'd like to know.**

BIGIDEA

Scientists use scientific inquiry to explain the natural world.

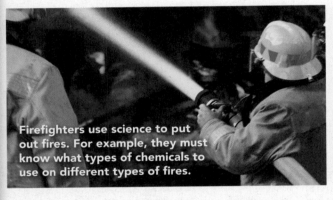

Firefighters use science to put out fires. For example, they must know what types of chemicals to use on different types of fires.

What do you already know about how science affects your everyday life? ✎ **What more would you like to know?**

_____

_____

_____

_____

_____

_____

_____

_____

_____

_____

BIGIDEA

Scientists use mathematics in many ways.

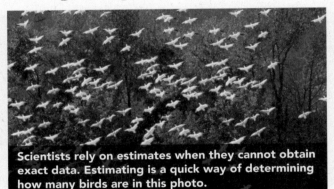

Scientists rely on estimates when they cannot obtain exact data. Estimating is a quick way of determining how many birds are in this photo.

Which math skills have you used to study science? ✎ **Which math skills do you need to practice?**

_____

_____

_____

_____

_____

_____

_____

_____

_____

_____

BIG IDEA
Atoms are the building blocks of matter.

Many ionic compounds form crystals. Some crystals have a cubic shape, like these crystals of halite, or sodium chloride.

Na⁺

Cl⁻

If the building blocks of matter are the same, then what makes everything different?

✏ **What more would you like to know?**

_____

_____

_____

Big Questions:

❓ How is matter described? Chapter 1

❓ How is the periodic table organized? Chapter 3

❓ How can bonding determine the properties of a substance? Chapter 4

✏ **After reading the chapters, write what you have learned about the Big Idea.**

_____

_____

_____

BIG IDEA
Mass and energy are conserved during physical and chemical changes.

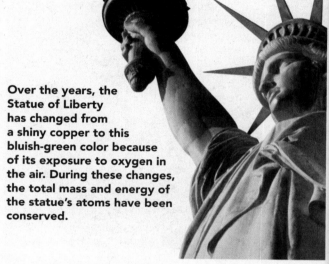

Over the years, the Statue of Liberty has changed from a shiny copper to this bluish-green color because of its exposure to oxygen in the air. During these changes, the total mass and energy of the statue's atoms have been conserved.

If you burn a candle, gradually the candle becomes smaller. What happens to the part of the candle that burns away? Does it cease to exist?

✏ **What more would you like to know?**

_____

_____

_____

Big Questions:

❓ Why does a substance change state? Chapter 2

❓ How is matter conserved during a chemical reaction? Chapter 5

❓ What determines the properties of a solution? Chapter 6

✏ **After reading the chapters, write what you have learned about the Big Idea.**

_____

_____

_____

A net force causes an object's motion to change.

By hitting the soccer ball with her head, this athlete changes the direction of the soccer ball.

What do you already know about how the force of one object can affect the movement of another object? ✏️ **What more would you like to know?**

_____

_____

_____

_____

Big Questions:

❓ How do you describe the motion of an object? Chapter 7

❓ How do objects react to forces? Chapter 8

✏️ **After reading the chapters, write what you have learned about the Big Idea.**

_____

_____

_____

_____

Energy can take different forms but is always conserved.

As these snowboarders fall, they don't lose any energy—the energy just takes different forms.

What do you already know about what happens to the mass and energy of a candle as it burns? ✏️ **What more would you like to know?**

_____

_____

_____

_____

Big Questions:

❓ How do machines make it easier to do work? Chapter 9

❓ How is energy conserved in a transformation? Chapter 10

❓ How does heat flow from one object to another? Chapter 11

✏️ **After reading the chapters, write what you have learned about the Big Idea.**

_____

_____

_____

BIGIDEA

Waves transmit energy.

What do you already know about waves and how they travel from one place to another?

✎ **What more would you like to know?**

_____

_____

_____

_____

Big Questions:

❓ What are the properties of waves?
Chapter 12

❓ What determines the pitch and loudness of sound? Chapter 13

❓ What kinds of waves make up the electromagnetic spectrum? Chapter 14

❓ How does light interact with matter?
Chapter 15

❓ How does an electric circuit work?
Chapter 16

❓ How are electricity and magnetism related?
Chapter 17

✎ **After reading the chapters, write what you have learned about the Big Idea.**

_____

_____

_____

The light and heat that lightning gives off travels in the form of electromagnetic waves.

WHAT ARE ALL OF THESE THINGS MADE OF?

How is matter described?

Imagine a warm day at Waikiki Beach on the island of Oahu, Hawaii. You can feel the warm breeze, the hot sand, and the cool water. Palm trees, hotels, shops, and the volcanic crater called Diamond Head are all a part of the scenery around you. People swimming, surfing, and sailing are enjoying the ocean.

Classify Categorize the items found at Waikiki Beach by what they are made of.

_____

_____

_____

_____

_____

_____

▶ UNTAMED SCIENCE Watch the **Untamed Science** video to learn more about matter.

Introduction to Matter

1 Getting Started

Check Your Understanding

1. **Background** Read the paragraph below and then answer the question.

On a hot day, Jorge decides to make a pitcher of cold lemonade. He combines **pure** water with lemon juice in a **ratio** of six to one. He adds sugar and ice and stirs all the ingredients together. The **properties** of the lemonade are that it is cold, yellow, and sweet.

A **pure** material is not mixed with any other matter.

A **ratio** tells you the relationship between two or more things.

A **property** is a characteristic that belongs to a person or thing.

- How would the properties of the lemonade change if the ratio of pure water to lemon juice were three to one? Assume the amount of sugar is the same.

_____

_____

> **MY READING WEB** If you had trouble completing the question above, visit **My Reading Web** and type in *Introduction to Matter.*

Vocabulary Skill

Prefixes A prefix is a word part that is added at the beginning of a root word to change the word's meaning. The prefixes below will help you understand some of the vocabulary in this chapter.

Prefix	Meaning	Example
endo-	in, within	endogenous, *adj.* describes something that arises from inside an organism's tissues or cells
exo-	out	exoskeleton, *n.* an outer shell or outer skeleton that protects animals, such as crustaceans

2. **Quick Check** The Greek root *therm* means "heat." Predict the meaning of the term *endothermic change*.

_____

_____

substance

mixture

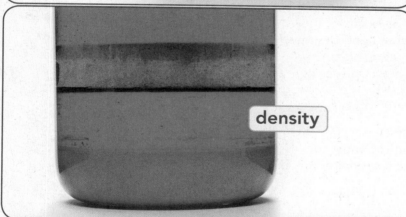

density

chemical energy

Chapter Preview

LESSON 1
- matter
- chemistry
- substance
- physical property
- chemical property

🔄 **Summarize**
△ **Classify**

LESSON 2
- element
- atom
- chemical bond
- molecule
- compound
- chemical formula
- mixture

🔄 **Compare and Contrast**
△ **Infer**

LESSON 3
- weight
- mass
- International System of Units
- volume
- density

🔄 **Identify the Main Idea**
△ **Calculate**

LESSON 4
- physical change
- chemical change
- law of conservation of mass
- temperature
- thermal energy
- endothermic change
- exothermic change
- chemical energy

🔄 **Relate Cause and Effect**
△ **Draw Conclusions**

▶ **VOCAB FLASH CARDS** For extra help with vocabulary, visit **Vocab Flash Cards** and type in *Introduction to Matter.*

3

1 Describing Matter

UNLOCK THE BIG ?

🔑 **What Properties Describe Matter?**

my planeT DiaRY

CAREER

Art Conservation Scientist

Science and art may seem like two very different interests, but they are both part of the job for an art conservation scientist. Over time, art can fade, decay, or get dirty. Conservation scientists find ways to restore art by examining its properties. They look at texture, color and age of the paint, the condition of the canvas, and materials used to make the paint. Then, the scientists can determine chemical properties of the painting. For example, they can predict how the painting will react to light, changes in temperature, and the use of chemicals for cleaning. Thanks to art conservation scientists, masterpieces of art can be enjoyed for many years.

Before

After

Write your answers to the questions below.

1. Why is it important for an art conservation scientist to study the properties of a painting before it's repaired?

_____

_____

_____

_____

2. Name another career that combines science with another interest.

_____

_____

▷ **PLANET DIARY** Go to **Planet Diary** to learn more about matter.

Medusa by Caravaggio, about 1598. Uffizi Gallery, Florence, Italy

Lab zone® Do the Inquiry Warm-Up *How Do You Describe Matter?*

Vocabulary
- matter • chemistry
- substance • physical property
- chemical property

Skills
↺ Reading: Summarize
△ Inquiry: Classify

What Properties Describe Matter?

You have probably heard the word *matter* used many times. "As a matter of fact…" or "Hey, what's the matter?" In science, **matter** is anything that has mass and takes up space. All the "stuff" around you is matter, and you are matter too. Air, plastic, metal, wood, glass, paper, and cloth are all matter.

Even though air and paper are both matter, you know they are different materials. Matter can have many different properties, or characteristics that can be used to identify and classify it. Materials can be hard or soft, hot or cold, liquid, solid, or gas. Some materials catch fire easily, but others do not burn. **Chemistry** is the study of matter and how matter changes.

Substances Some types of matter are substances and some are not. In chemistry, a **substance** is a single kind of matter that is pure, meaning it always has a specific makeup, or composition. For example, table salt has the same composition and properties whether it comes from seawater or a salt mine. **Figure 1** shows two examples of water that appear to be very different. Water is a substance. Pure water is always the same, whether it comes from a glacier or from a geyser.

↺ **Summarize** How are matter and substances related?

_____

FIGURE 1 ·········
Properties of Matter
✎ **Compare and Contrast** Complete the Venn diagram with the properties of water from a glacier and from a geyser.

Glacier   Geyser

5

Physical and Chemical Properties of Matter

Matter is described by its properties. 🔒 **Every form of matter has two kinds of properties—physical properties and chemical properties.** A **physical property** is a characteristic of a substance that can be observed without changing it into another substance.

Some properties of matter can't be seen just by observation or touch. A **chemical property** is a characteristic of a substance that describes its ability to change into different substances. To observe the chemical properties of a substance, you must try to change it into another substance. Physical and chemical properties are used to classify matter.

Basketball Hoop Two physical properties of metals are luster, or shine, and the ability to conduct electric current and heat. Another physical property is flexibility, which is the ability to be bent into shapes.

Mark all the objects that are flexible.
- ⃝ Aluminum can
- ⃝ Copper sheeting
- ⃝ Brick house
- ⃝ Glass window
- ⃝ Silver spoon
- ⃝ Wood drumstick

What do all of the flexible objects have in common?

_____

What physical property makes metal pots good for cooking?

_____

Water A physical property of water is that it freezes at 0°C. When liquid water freezes, it changes to ice, but it is still water. The temperatures at which substances boil and melt are also physical properties.

Rusty Metal Chain A chemical property of iron is that it combines slowly with oxygen in the air to form a different substance, rust. Silver reacts with sulfur in the air to form tarnish. In contrast, a chemical property of gold is that it does not react easily with oxygen or sulfur.

Frozen Fruit Bar Hardness, texture, temperature, and color are examples of physical properties. When you describe a material as a solid, a liquid, or a gas, you are describing its state of matter. State of matter is another physical property.

Describe three properties of a frozen fruit bar, including its state of matter.

_____

_____

Will any of these properties change after a couple of hours in the sun? Explain.

_____

_____

Charcoal Briquettes Fuels, like charcoal, can catch fire and burn. When a fuel burns, it combines with oxygen in the air and changes into the substances water and carbon dioxide. The ability to burn, or flammability, is a chemical property.

How do you know that flammability is a chemical property?

_____

_____

_____

Lab zone® Do the Quick Lab *Observing Physical Properties.*

apply it!

The wax in a burning candle can be described by both physical and chemical properties.

❶ Describe What are the physical properties of the wax in a burning candle?

_____

_____

_____

❷ CHALLENGE Why is melting a physical property of the wax, but flammability is a chemical property?

_____

_____

_____

_____

_____

_____

_____

🔑 Assess Your Understanding

1a. **Classify** The melting point of table salt is 801°C. Is this a physical or chemical property?

_____

b. **Draw Conclusions** Helium does not usually react with other substances. Does this mean that helium has no chemical properties? Explain.

_____

_____

got it?

○ **I get it!** Now I know that matter is described by its _____

_____

○ **I need extra help with** _____

_____

Go to **MY SCIENCE COACH** *online for help with this subject.*

Classifying Matter

UNLOCK THE BIG Q?

🔑 What Is Matter Made Of?

🔑 What Are Two Types of Mixtures?

MY PLANET DIARY

Smaller Than Small

What's the smallest thing you can think of? A grain of sand? A speck of dust? If you look at these items under a powerful microscope, you'll see that they're made up of smaller and smaller pieces. All matter is made up of very tiny particles called atoms. Atoms are so small, there is a special unit of measure used to describe them called a nanometer (nm). A nanometer is equal to 1/1,000,000,000 or one-billionth of a meter!

At least 50,000 of these tiny compounds called nanobouquets could fit on the head of a pin.

SCIENCE STATS

Write your answers to the questions below.

1. A nickel is about 2 millimeters thick, or 2/1,000 of a meter. How many nanometers is this?

_____

_____

2. Imagine being the size of an atom. Describe how something like a red blood cell might look to you.

_____

_____

_____

> PLANET DIARY   Go to **Planet Diary** to learn more about atoms.

Common Objects in Nanometers (nm)

Object	Approximate Size
Compact disc diameter	120,000,000 nm
Grain of sand	3,000,000 nm
Grain of pollen	500,000 nm
Human hair diameter	100,000 nm
Red blood cell	7000 nm
Length of 3–10 atoms lined up	1 nm

Lab zone® Do the Inquiry Warm-Up *What Is a Mixture?*

Vocabulary
- element
- atom
- chemical bond
- molecule
- compound
- chemical formula
- mixture

Skills
- Reading: Compare and Contrast
- Inquiry: Infer

What Is Matter Made Of?

What is matter? Why is one kind of matter different from another kind of matter? Around 450 B.C., a Greek philosopher named Empedocles attempted to answer these questions. He proposed that all matter was made of four "elements"—air, earth, fire, and water. Empedocles thought that all other matter was a combination of these elements. The idea of four elements was so convincing that people believed it for more than 2,000 years.

Elements In the late 1600s, experiments by early chemists began to show that matter was made up of many more than four elements. 🔑 Scientists know that all matter in the universe is made of more than 100 different substances, called elements. An **element** is a substance that cannot be broken down into any other substances by chemical or physical means. Elements are the simplest substances. Each element can be identified by its specific physical and chemical properties. You may already be familiar with some elements such as aluminum or tin. Elements are represented by one- or two-letter symbols, such as C for carbon, O for oxygen, and Ca for calcium.

apply it!

The elements make up all the matter in the universe.

1 Explain How can you tell one element from another?

_____
_____
_____

2 △ **Infer** Match the pictures on this page of items containing common elements to the element's name.

A) helium   B) gold   C) copper
D) iron   E) neon

3 [CHALLENGE] Choose another element that you are familiar with and describe its properties.

_____
_____

9

Atoms Imagine tearing a piece of aluminum foil in half over and over again. Would you reach a point where you had the smallest possible piece of aluminum? The answer is yes. The particle theory of matter explains that all matter is made of atoms. An **atom** is the basic particle from which all elements are made. An atom has a positively charged center, or nucleus, containing smaller particles. The nucleus is surrounded by a "cloud" of negative charge. The elements have different properties because their atoms are different.

Molecules Atoms of most elements are able to combine with other atoms. When atoms combine, they form a **chemical bond,** which is a force of attraction between two atoms. In many cases, atoms combine to form larger particles called molecules. A **molecule** (MAHL uh kyool) is a group of two or more atoms held together by chemical bonds. A molecule of water, for example, is made up of an oxygen atom chemically bonded to two hydrogen atoms. Two atoms of the same element can also combine to form a molecule. Oxygen molecules are made up of two oxygen atoms. **Figure 1** shows models of some common molecules.

✏️ **Compare and Contrast** How are atoms and molecules the same? How are they different?

_____

_____

_____

_____

_____

_____

FIGURE 1 ···

Atoms and Molecules

Molecules are made up of groups of atoms.

✏️ **Use the molecule models to complete the activities.**

1. **Interpret Diagrams** Count the number of atoms of each element in the molecules and write it on the lines below.
2. **CHALLENGE** On the bottom line, write a representation for each molecule using letters and numbers.

Key
C = Carbon
H = Hydrogen
O = Oxygen
N = Nitrogen

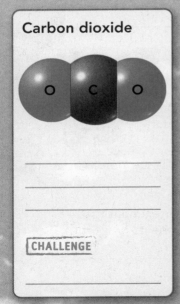

Carbon dioxide

_____

_____

_____

CHALLENGE

_____

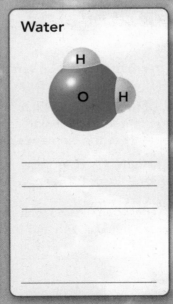

Water

_____

_____

_____

_____

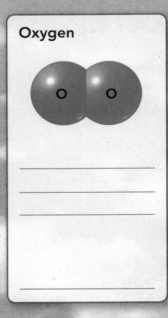

Oxygen

_____

_____

_____

_____

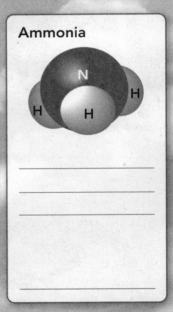

Ammonia

_____

_____

_____

_____

Compounds Water, ammonia, and carbon dioxide are all compounds. A **compound** is a substance made of two or more elements that are chemically combined in a set ratio. A compound is represented by a **chemical formula,** which shows the elements in the compound and the ratio of atoms. For example, the chemical formula for carbon dioxide is CO_2. The 2 below the O for oxygen tells you that the ratio of carbon atoms to oxygen atoms is 1 to 2. If there is no number after an element's symbol, it is understood that the number is 1. A different number of atoms in a formula represents a different compound. For example, the formula for carbon monoxide is CO. Here, the ratio of carbon atoms to oxygen atoms is 1 to 1.

When elements chemically combine, they form compounds with properties different from those of the elements. **Figure 2** shows that the element sulfur is a yellow solid and the element copper is a shiny metal. When copper and sulfur combine, they form a compound called copper sulfide. The new compound has different properties from both copper and sulfur.

FIGURE 2 ···

> ART IN MOTION **Compounds From Elements**
When elements combine, the compound that forms has different properties than the original elements.

✎ **Describe** List the properties of copper, sulfur, and copper sulfide.

Copper

Sulfur

Copper Sulfide

Lab® Do the Quick Lab *Modeling* zone *Atoms and Molecules.*

⊙ Assess Your Understanding

1a. Review What holds the hydrogen and oxygen atoms together in a water molecule?

_____

b. Identify Table sugar has the chemical formula $C_{12}H_{22}O_{11}$. What is the ratio of carbon atoms to oxygen atoms in this compound?

_____

_____

c. Draw Conclusions Two formulas for compounds containing hydrogen and oxygen are H_2O and H_2O_2. Do these formulas represent the same compound? Explain.

_____

_____

_____

_____

_____

got it? ···

○ I get it! Now I know that all matter is made up of _____

_____

○ I need extra help with _____

Go to MY SCIENCE ⑤ COACH online for help with this subject.

11

What Are Two Types of Mixtures?

Elements and compounds are substances, but most materials are mixtures. **Figure 3** shows some common mixtures. A **mixture** is made of two or more substances that are together in the same place, but their atoms are not chemically bonded. Mixtures differ from compounds. Each substance in a mixture keeps its own properties. Also, the parts of a mixture are not combined in a set ratio.

Think of a handful of sand. If you look closely at the sand, you will see particles of rock, bits of shells, maybe even crystals of salt.

Heterogeneous Mixtures   There are two types of mixtures. 🔑 **A mixture can be heterogeneous or homogeneous.** In a heterogeneous mixture (het ur oh JEE nee us), you can usually see the different parts and they can easily be separated out. The sand described above is a heterogeneous mixture. So is a salad. Think of how easy it is to see the pieces of lettuce, tomatoes, onions, and other ingredients that can be mixed in countless ways.

Homogeneous Mixtures   The substances involved in a homogeneous mixture (hoh moh JEE nee us), are so evenly mixed that you can't see the different parts. It is difficult to separate the parts of a homogeneous mixture. Air is a homogeneous mixture of gases. You know that oxygen is present in the air because you are able to breathe, but you cannot identify where the oxygen is in the air. A solution is another example of a homogeneous mixture. Solutions can be liquids, gases, or even solids.

....

Vocabulary Prefixes The prefix *homo-* comes from a Greek word that means "the same or alike." Predict the meaning of the prefix *hetero-*.

◯ more than one
◯ different
◯ equal

FIGURE 3 ·····················
Mixtures
Many foods are mixtures.

✎ **Interpret Photos** Label each food as a heterogeneous or homogeneous mixture.

Honey

Guacamole

Soy sauce

Ketchup

[CHALLENGE] Is ketchup a heterogeneous or homogeneous mixture? Explain your reasoning.

_____

_____

_____

_____

Separating Mixtures

Since the substances in a mixture keep their properties, you can use those properties to separate a mixture into its parts. Methods used to separate the parts of a mixture, including distillation, evaporation, filtration, and magnetic attraction, are shown in **Figure 4**.

FIGURE 4 ··

Separating a Mixture

Different methods can be used to separate mixtures.

✎ **Identify** Name the type of separation method being used in each photo.

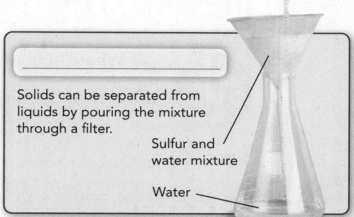

Solids can be separated from liquids by pouring the mixture through a filter.

Sulfur and water mixture

Water

Iron objects can be separated from a mixture using a magnet.

When left in the open air, liquid solutions can change to gas, leaving solid components behind.

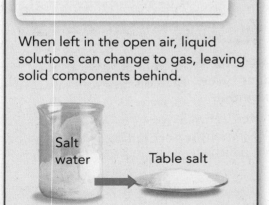

Salt water → Table salt

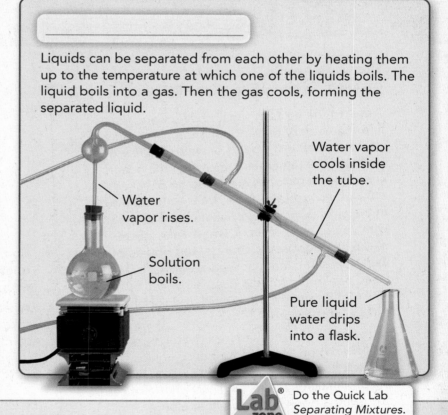

Liquids can be separated from each other by heating them up to the temperature at which one of the liquids boils. The liquid boils into a gas. Then the gas cools, forming the separated liquid.

Water vapor rises.

Solution boils.

Water vapor cools inside the tube.

Pure liquid water drips into a flask.

Lab zone

Do the Quick Lab *Separating Mixtures.*

🔑 Assess Your Understanding

got it? ···

○ **I get it!** Now I know that the two types of mixtures are _____

_____

○ **I need extra help with** _____

Go to **MY SCIENCE** 🄢 **COACH** *online for help with this subject.*

Measuring Matter

🔑 **What Units Are Used to Express Mass and Volume?**

🔑 **How Is Density Determined?**

UNLOCK
THE BIG
?

Site: Lake Assal
Location: Djibouti, Republic of Djibouti

Travel to the eastern coast of Africa and you will find the country of Djibouti. There, you can visit one of the saltiest bodies of water in the world. Lake Assal is ten times saltier than the ocean. Its crystal white beaches are made up of salt. While on your visit to Lake Assal, be sure to take a dip in the clear blue waters. Take a book or magazine with you to read. Wait … what? Take a book into a lake? It might seem strange, but bodies of water with high salt contents, like Lake Assal or the Dead Sea in the Middle East, allow you to float so well that it's nearly impossible to sink below the surface of the water.

Salt water is denser than fresh water. Less-dense liquids float on top of more-dense liquids. You, too, will float on top of the salty water. In fact, it will be difficult even to swim, so what else can you do? Read a book while you float along!

Floating in the Dead Sea

Communicate **Write your answers to the questions below. Then discuss your answers with a partner.**

What water activities might be easier to do in Lake Assal's salty water? What activities could be more difficult?

_____

_____

_____

▶ PLANET DIARY Go to **Planet Diary** to learn more about density.

Lab **Do the Inquiry Warm-Up**
zone **Which Has More Mass?**

Vocabulary
- weight • mass
- International System of Units
- volume • density

Skills
- Reading: Identify the Main Idea
- Inquiry: Calculate

What Units Are Used to Express Mass and Volume?

Here's a riddle for you: Which weighs more, a pound of feathers or a pound of sand? If you answered "a pound of sand," think again. Both weigh exactly the same—one pound.

There are all sorts of ways to measure matter, and you use these measurements every day. Scientists rely on measurements as well. In fact, scientists work hard to make sure their measurements are as accurate as possible.

Weight Your **weight** is a measure of the force of gravity on you. On another planet, the force of gravity will be more if the planet is more massive than Earth and less if the planet is less massive than Earth. On the moon, you would weigh only about one sixth of your weight on Earth. On Jupiter, you would weigh more than twice your weight on Earth.

To find the weight of an object, you could place it on a scale like the ones shown in **Figure 1**. The object's weight pulls down on the mechanisms inside the scale. These mechanisms cause beams or springs inside the scale to move. The amount of movement depends on the weight of the object. From the movement of the beams, the scale displays the weight to you.

Identify the Main Idea
Underline the sentence(s) that describe how weight can be affected by location.

FIGURE 1 ·······················
Measuring Weight
✎ Complete the tasks below.

1. **Estimate** Use the weight of the first scale to estimate the weight of the fish on the other scales. Draw in the pointers.

2. **Describe** How would their weight change on a small planet like Mercury? Or a large planet like Neptune?

_____

_____

_____

_____

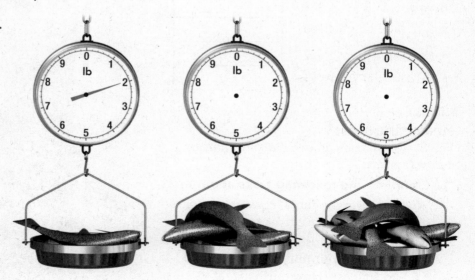

With 10 seconds left on the clock, John makes the play at the 9.144-meter line.

9.144

If we always used the metric system

Mass How can you weigh less on the moon than on Earth when nothing about you has changed? Your weight is dependent on the gravity of the planet you are visiting. The amount of matter in an object is its **mass,** which does not change with location even if the force of gravity changes. If you travel to the moon, the amount of matter in your body—your mass—does not change. You are the same size. For this reason, scientists prefer to describe matter in terms of mass rather than weight. The mass of an object is a physical property.

To measure the properties of matter, scientists use a system called the **International System of Units** (abbreviated SI for the French name, *Système International d'Unités*). 🔑 **The SI unit of mass is the kilogram (kg).** If you weigh 90 pounds on Earth, your mass is about 40 kilograms. Often, a smaller unit is used to measure mass, the gram (g). There are 1,000 grams in a kilogram, or 0.001 kilograms in a gram. The table in **Figure 2** lists the masses of some common items.

Mass of Common Objects

Object	Mass (g)	Mass (kg)
Nickel	5	0.005
Baseball	150	_____
Pineapple	1,600	_____
Full can of soda	390	_____
Inflated balloon	3	_____

FIGURE 2 ···
Measuring Mass
The SI system uses grams and kilograms to measure mass.

✎ **Complete the following tasks about mass.**

1. **Calculate** In the table, convert the mass of each object from grams to kilograms.

2. **CHALLENGE** Suppose you are taking a flight to Europe. You are only allowed a 23-kg suitcase. How much is that in pounds? (*Hint:* 1 kg = 2.2 lbs.)

   ○ 50.6 lbs   ○ 46.2 lbs   ○ 10.5 lbs

Volume

All matter has mass and takes up space. The amount of space that matter occupies is called its **volume.** It's easy to see that solids and liquids take up space, but gases have volume, too.

🔑 **The SI unit of volume is the cubic meter (m³).** Other common SI units of volume include the cubic centimeter (cm³), the liter (L), and the milliliter (mL). Common plastic soda bottles hold 2 liters of liquid. A milliliter is 1/1,000 of a liter and is exactly the same volume as 1 cubic centimeter. A teaspoonful of water has a volume of about 5 milliliters. In a lab, volumes of liquid are often measured with a graduated cylinder.

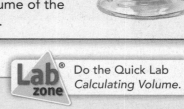

Calculating Volume

Suppose you want to know the volume of a rectangular object, like one of the suitcases shown in **Figure 3.** First, measure the length, width, and height (or thickness) of the suitcase. Then, multiply the measurements together.

Volume = Length × Width × Height

When you multiply the three measurements, you must also multiply the units.

Units = cm × cm × cm = cm³

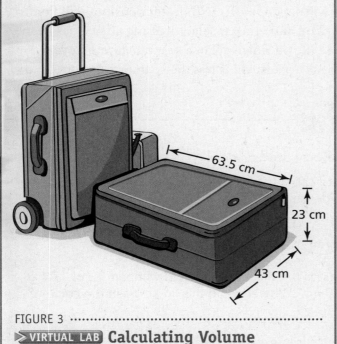

FIGURE 3 ....

⬧ VIRTUAL LAB **Calculating Volume**
△ **Calculate** Find the volume of the suitcase.

63.5 cm

23 cm

43 cm

_____

_____

Measuring Irregular Objects

How do you measure the volume of an irregular object, such as a key or a raspberry? One way is to submerge the object in a liquid in a graduated cylinder. The liquid level will rise by an amount that is equal to the volume of the object in milliliters.

Lab® zone Do the Quick Lab *Calculating Volume.*

🔑 **Assess Your Understanding**

1. Explain Why is mass more useful than weight for measuring matter?

_____

_____

_____

_____

_____

got it? ....

○ **I get it!** Now I know that the SI unit for

mass is _____

and the SI unit for volume is _____

_____

○ **I need extra help with** _____

_____

Go to **MY SCIENCE** 🅂 **COACH** *online for help with this subject.*

How Is Density Determined?

Remember the riddle about the sand and the feathers? Although they weigh the same, a kilogram of sand takes up much less space than a kilogram of feathers. The volumes differ because sand and feathers have different densities—an important property of matter.

Calculating Density **Density** is a measure of the mass of a material in a given volume. Density can be expressed as the number of grams in one cubic centimeter (g/cm^3). For example, the density of water at room temperature is stated as "one gram per cubic centimeter" ($1\ g/cm^3$). Recall that volume can also be measured in milliliters. So the density of water can also be expressed as 1 g/mL. **You can determine the density of a sample of matter by dividing its mass by its volume.**

$$\text{Density} = \frac{\text{Mass}}{\text{Volume}}$$

Sinking or Floating? Suppose you have a block of wood and a block of iron of equal mass. When you drop both blocks into a tub of water, you see that the wood floats and the iron sinks. You know the density of water is $1\ g/cm^3$. Objects with densities greater than that of water will sink. Objects with lesser densities will float.

Watch a bottle of oil and vinegar salad dressing after it has been shaken. You will see the oil slowly form a separate layer above the vinegar. This happens because oil is less dense than vinegar.

apply it!

Liquids can form layers based on density.

❶ **Apply Concepts** Label the layers of colored liquid in the column according to their densities.

Water: 1.00 g/mL   Honey: 1.36 g/mL   Dish soap: 1.03 g/mL
Corn syrup: 1.33 g/mL   Vegetable oil: 0.91 g/mL

❷ **Calculate** What is the density of a liquid with a mass of 17.4 g and a volume of 20 mL? Where would this liquid be in the column?

_____

_____

❸ **CHALLENGE** In which layer(s) would a solid cube with 6-cm sides and a mass of 270 g float? Explain.

_____

_____

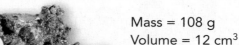

Using Density

Suppose you are a gold miner in the 1800s, like the men in **Figure 4.** One day, while panning through the sediment in a stream, you come across a shiny golden rock. How do you know if the rock is real gold? Since density is a physical property of a substance, it can be used to identify an unknown substance. You can measure the mass and volume of the rock and find its density. If it matches 19.3 g/cm^3, the density of gold, then you have struck it rich!

FIGURE 4 ··

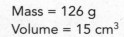 **Using Density**

Density can be used to identify substances.

✎ **Estimate** Hypothesize which rock sample is gold. Then, calculate the density of each sample. Circle the rock that is real gold.

My hypothesis is that the gold rock is:

◯ A   ◯ B   ◯ C

A

Mass = 108 g
Volume = 12 cm^3

Density = _____

B

Mass = 126 g
Volume = 15 cm^3

Density = _____

C

Mass = 386 g
Volume = 20 cm^3

Density = _____

 Lab zone® Do the Lab Investigation
Making Sense of Density.

🔑 Assess Your Understanding

2a. Identify Maple syrup will (float/sink) in water because its density is greater than 1 g/cm^3.

b. ◢ **Calculate** What is the mass of a sample of a substance with a volume of 120 mL and a density of 0.75 g/mL?

_____

c. [CHALLENGE] Liquid water and ice are the same substance, H$_2$O. How would you explain why ice floats in water?

_____

_____

_____

_____

got it? ···

◯ **I get it!** Now I know density is calculated by _____

_____

◯ **I need extra help with** _____

Go to **my science** 🔵 **coach** *online for help with this subject.*

UNLOCK THE BIG ?

🔑 **What Happens to a Substance in a Physical Change?**

🔑 **What Happens to a Substance in a Chemical Change?**

🔑 **How Are Changes in Energy and Matter Related?**

my planet diary

BLOG

Posted by: Dylan
Location: Fountain Valley, California

Whenever I go to the beach, I spend a majority of my time building a sand castle. I try to build it after a high tide comes. That way I have a lot of time to build up the walls and they will not be destroyed as quickly by the water.

Even though the waves will eventually destroy the castle and take the sand with them back to the ocean, the sand could be easily separated from the ocean. At the end of the day when I leave and kick and stomp on my sand castle, it is still sand. Only its appearance changes.

Write your answers to the questions below.

1. Describe the differences in the ways the sand castle is changed by an ocean wave and by Dylan stomping on it.

_____

_____

_____

_____

2. Dylan changed a formless pile of sand into a sand castle. What other natural materials can be changed into art?

_____

_____

▶ **PLANET DIARY** Go to **Planet Diary** to learn more about changes in matter.

Lab zone® Do the Inquiry Warm-Up *Is a New Substance Formed?*

Vocabulary

- physical change
- chemical change
- law of conservation of mass
- temperature
- thermal energy
- endothermic change
- exothermic change
- chemical energy

Skills

- Reading: Relate Cause and Effect
- Inquiry: Draw Conclusions

What Happens to a Substance in a Physical Change?

How can matter change? A **physical change** alters the form or appearance of matter but does not turn any substance in the matter into a different substance. In **Figure 1,** a butter artist has changed a formless block of butter into artwork. Although it looks different, the sculpture is still butter. **A substance that undergoes a physical change is still the same substance after the change.** Many physical changes, such as snow melting into water, occur in nature.

Changes of State As you may know, matter occurs in three familiar states—solid, liquid, and gas. Suppose you leave a small puddle of liquid water on the kitchen counter. When you come back two hours later, the puddle is gone. Has the liquid water disappeared? No, a physical change happened. The liquid water changed into water vapor (a gas) and mixed with the air. A change in state, such as from a solid to a liquid or from a liquid to a gas, is an example of a physical change.

FIGURE 1 ·······························
Change of State
Changes between solids, liquids, and gases are physical changes.

✎ **Predict** Describe the changes the butter sculpture will undergo in a few hours if it is left out in the sun.

_____

_____

_____

_____

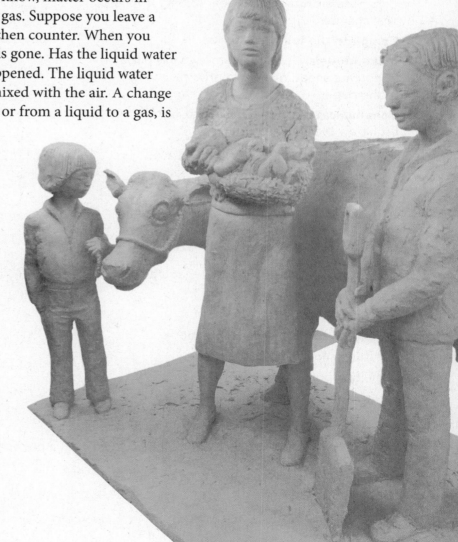

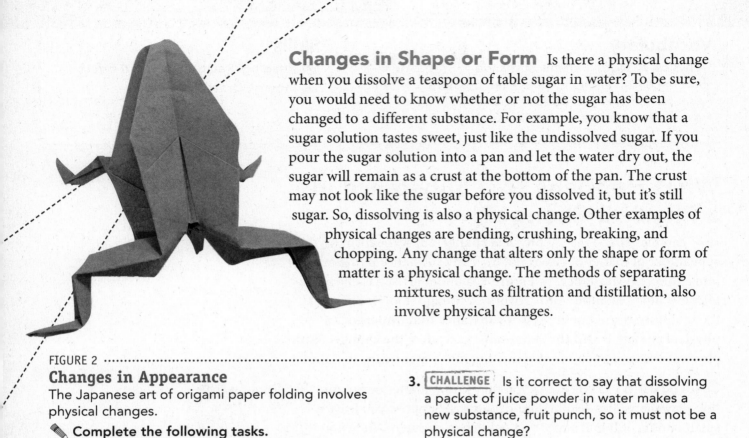

Changes in Shape or Form Is there a physical change when you dissolve a teaspoon of table sugar in water? To be sure, you would need to know whether or not the sugar has been changed to a different substance. For example, you know that a sugar solution tastes sweet, just like the undissolved sugar. If you pour the sugar solution into a pan and let the water dry out, the sugar will remain as a crust at the bottom of the pan. The crust may not look like the sugar before you dissolved it, but it's still sugar. So, dissolving is also a physical change. Other examples of physical changes are bending, crushing, breaking, and chopping. Any change that alters only the shape or form of matter is a physical change. The methods of separating mixtures, such as filtration and distillation, also involve physical changes.

FIGURE 2 ....

Changes in Appearance
The Japanese art of origami paper folding involves physical changes.

✎ **Complete the following tasks.**

1. **Make Models** Using the corner of this page or a separate sheet, make two physical changes to the paper.

2. **Communicate** Ask a classmate to identify and list below the changes you made.

_____

_____

3. [CHALLENGE] Is it correct to say that dissolving a packet of juice powder in water makes a new substance, fruit punch, so it must not be a physical change?

_____

_____

_____

_____

_____

_____

> **Lab** zone® Do the Quick Lab *What Is a Physical Change?*

🔑 **Assess Your Understanding**

1a. Classify Mark all the processes that are physical changes.

○ drying wet clothes

○ lighting a match from a matchbook

○ cutting snowflakes out of paper

○ melting butter for popcorn

b. Apply Concepts Describe three physical changes that occur in nature.

_____

_____

_____

_____

got it? ....

○ **I get it!** Now I know that a substance that undergoes a physical change is _____

_____

○ **I need extra help with** _____

Go to **MY SCIENCE** ⓢ **COACH** *online for help with this subject.*

What Happens to a Substance in a Chemical Change?

Another kind of change occurs when a substance transforms into another substance. A change in matter that produces one or more new substances is a chemical change, or chemical reaction. In some chemical changes, a single substance breaks down into two or more other substances. For example, hydrogen peroxide breaks down into water and oxygen gas when it's poured on a cut on your skin. In other chemical changes, two or more substances combine to form different substances. Photosynthesis is a natural chemical change. Several compounds combine with energy from the sun to produce new substances.

Figure 3 shows chemical changes that are used in forensics to collect evidence. To make fingerprints more visible, a chemical found in super-strong glues is heated. Vapors from the glue react with sweat or other body chemicals in a fingerprint to form a white powder making the print visible. Luminol is a chemical that reacts with blood. It combines with traces of blood that are too small to see with the naked eye to form a new substance that glows in the dark. The footprint in Figure 3 has been treated with luminol. Unlike a physical change, a chemical change produces new substances with new and different properties.

FIGURE 3 ....
Chemical Changes
The prints are visible because of chemical change.

apply it!

You are a detective investigating a robbery. When you arrive at the scene, there are not many clues that you can see to help solve the crime. You're able to write down a few observations.

Solve Problems
Determine how you would use chemical changes to gather evidence at the crime scene.

An empty jewelry box is knocked over on a table.

Chemical treatment: _____
_____
_____

An open box of bandages is on the floor. Bandage wrappers are found nearby.

Chemical treatment: _____
_____
_____

Shattered glass from a window is scattered across the floor.

Chemical treatment: _____
_____
_____

Copper: before

Copper: after
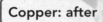

Examples of Chemical Change One common chemical change is the burning of natural gas on a gas stove. Natural gas is mostly made up of the compound methane (CH_4). When it burns, methane combines with oxygen in the air and forms new substances. These new substances include carbon dioxide gas (CO_2) and water vapor (H_2O). Both of these substances can be identified by their properties, which are different from those of methane. The chemical change that occurs when fuels, such as natural gas, candle wax, or wood, burn in air is called combustion. Other processes resulting in chemical change include electrolysis, oxidation, and tarnishing. The table in **Figure 4** describes each of these types of chemical change.

FIGURE 4 ····················
Types of Chemical Change
The copper in the Statue of Liberty is exposed to oxygen in the air.

✎ **Observe** What chemical change did the Statue of Liberty likely undergo? Describe the properties before and after the chemical change.

_____
_____
_____
_____
_____
_____

Examples of Chemical Change

Chemical Change	Description	Example
Combustion	Rapid combination of a fuel with oxygen; produces heat, light, and new substances	Gas, oil, or coal burning in a furnace
Electrolysis	Use of electricity to break a compound into elements or simpler compounds	Breaking down water into hydrogen and oxygen
Oxidation	Combination of a substance with oxygen	Rusting of an iron fence
Tarnishing	Slow combination of a bright metal with sulfur or another substance, producing a dark coating on the metal	Tarnishing of brass

Conservation of Mass Water may seem to "disappear" when it evaporates, but scientists long ago proved otherwise. In the 1770s, a French chemist, Antoine Lavoisier, measured mass both before and after a chemical change. His data showed that no mass was lost or gained during the change. The fact that matter is not created or destroyed in any chemical or physical change is called the **law of conservation of mass.** This law is also called the law of conservation of matter since mass is a measurement of matter.

Suppose you could measure all of the carbon dioxide and water produced when methane burns. You would find that it equals the mass of the original methane plus the mass of the oxygen from the air that was used in the burning. **Figure 5** demonstrates that during a chemical change, atoms are not lost or gained, only rearranged.

FIGURE 5 ·········

> INTERACTIVE ART

Conservation of Mass
✎ Interpret Diagrams Count the atoms of each element before and after the chemical change. Is mass conserved in this reaction? Explain.

_____

_____

_____

_____

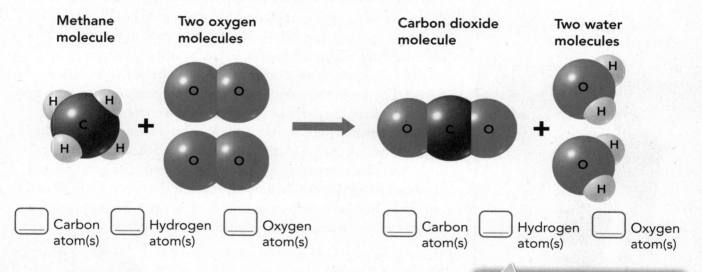

| Methane molecule | Two oxygen molecules | | Carbon dioxide molecule | Two water molecules |

☐ Carbon atom(s)   ☐ Hydrogen atom(s)   ☐ Oxygen atom(s)   ☐ Carbon atom(s)   ☐ Hydrogen atom(s)   ☐ Oxygen atom(s)

Lab zone Do the Quick Lab Demonstrating Tarnishing.

Assess Your Understanding

2a. Name A chemical reaction is another name for a chemical (combustion/change).

b. Predict What kind of chemical change do you think occurs when a banana peel turns brown in the open air? Explain.

_____

_____

c. CHALLENGE Assuming no mass escapes, explain why the mass of a rusted nail is greater than the mass of a nail before it rusted.

_____

_____

_____

_____

got it? ···

○ I get it! Now I know that when a substance undergoes a chemical change, _____

_____

○ I need extra help with _____

Go to MY SCIENCE ⬤ COACH online for help with this subject.

How Are Changes in Energy and Matter Related?

Do you feel as if you are full of energy today? Energy is the ability to do work or cause change. **Every chemical and physical change in matter includes a change in energy.** A change as simple as bending a paper clip takes energy. When ice changes to liquid water, it absorbs energy from the surrounding matter. When candle wax burns, it gives off energy as light and heat.

Like matter, energy is conserved in a chemical change. Energy is never created or destroyed. It can only be transformed from one form to another.

Temperature and Thermal Energy Think of how it feels when you walk inside an air-conditioned building from the outdoors on a hot day. Whew, what a difference in temperature! Temperature is a measure of how hot or cold something is. It is related to the energy of motion of the particles of matter. The particles of gas in the warm outside air have greater average energy of motion than the particles of air inside the cool building.

Thermal energy is the total energy of the motion of all of the particles in an object. Usually, you experience thermal energy when you describe matter as feeling hot or cold. Temperature and thermal energy are not the same thing, but the amount of thermal energy an object has is related to its temperature. Thermal energy naturally flows from warmer matter to cooler matter.

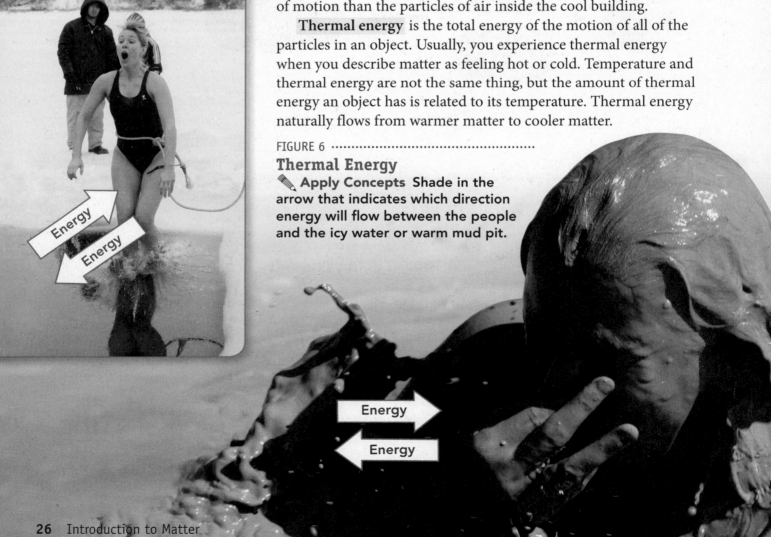

FIGURE 6 ···
Thermal Energy
✎ Apply Concepts Shade in the arrow that indicates which direction energy will flow between the people and the icy water or warm mud pit.

Energy

Energy

Energy

Energy

Thermal Energy and Changes in Matter

Thermal energy is a form of energy that is often released or absorbed when matter changes. For example, ice absorbs thermal energy from its surroundings when it melts, leaving the surroundings feeling cold. That's why you can pack food and drinks in an ice-filled picnic cooler. The melting of ice is an **endothermic change,** a change in which energy is absorbed. Changes in matter can also occur when energy is given off. An **exothermic change** releases energy. Combustion is a chemical change that releases thermal energy and light.

Transforming Chemical Energy The energy stored in the chemical bonds between atoms is a form of energy called **chemical energy.** Chemical energy is stored in foods, fuels, and even the cells of your body. Animals, like the bear in **Figure 7,** gain chemical energy from food.

Burning fuels transforms chemical energy and releases some of it as thermal energy. When you ride a bike up a hill, chemical energy from foods you ate changes into energy of motion. Chemical energy can change into other forms of energy, and other forms of energy can change into chemical energy.

FIGURE 7 ···

Transforming Chemical Energy
Chemical energy from food can be transformed into other types of energy needed for activity.

Relate Cause and Effect
Underline the sentence that describes how your hand would be affected if you made a snowball or held a frozen treat.

do the math! Analyzing Data

A student records the temperature of two reactions once per minute. Her data are plotted on the graph.

❶ **Calculate** What was the change in temperature for each reaction after 10 minutes?

_____

_____

❷ **Draw Conclusions** On the graph, label each reaction as exothermic or endothermic. How can you tell?

_____

_____

_____

_____

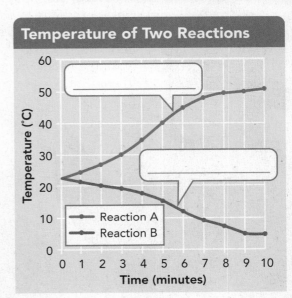

Temperature of Two Reactions

Reaction A
Reaction B

Temperature (°C) vs Time (minutes)

INDIANA JANE AND THE INVESTIGATION OF MATTER

EXPLORE THE BIG ?

How is matter described?

FIGURE 8 ·····················
> INTERACTIVE ART Indiana Jane is hunting for lost treasures of matter. Join her in following clues to describe different types of matter.

✏️ **Review** Answer questions about Indiana's findings along the way. Then, complete the logbook with information you've gathered about the properties of matter.

Tarnished coins I found these coins near the opening of a foul-smelling cave. I believe they were a shiny metal at one point, perhaps silver, platinum, or aluminum. I've determined the mass of each coin to be 315 g and the volume to be 30 cm^3.

What element are the coins made of?

○ Aluminum (density = 2.7 g/cm^3)
○ Silver (density = 10.5 g/cm^3)
○ Platinum (density = 21.5 g/cm^3)

Arrowhead This arrowhead, most likely carved by an ancient hunter, was discovered in a pile of rocks. **Describe the type of mixture the arrowhead was found in.**

_____
_____
_____
_____
_____

Mummy The mummy we found today is badly decayed, probably because its sarcophagus is not sealed airtight. I translated a scroll found nearby that says the mummy and case originally had a mass of 200 kg. The mass is now 170 kg. **Explain how the mummy and its sarcophagus decreased in mass if the law of conservation of mass must be obeyed.**

_____
_____
_____
_____
_____
_____
_____
_____
_____

Yellowed, torn map
Field notes: The paper of this ancient map has suffered from changes over the years making it nearly impossible to read.—IJ

Indiana Jane has to bring all the artifacts back to the museum. Describe each object's properties and the physical or chemical changes it underwent.

Object	Properties	Changes Undergone
1. Clay pot		
2. Coins		
3. Map		

Broken clay pot Field notes: I've come across some clay pots. Many have been broken or cracked over time.—IJ

Wax statue I believe we have found the remains of the famous Carved Dove wax statue. It would have been a valuable artifact, but all that's left is a puddle of liquid.
Describe at least two changes the wax has undergone over time.

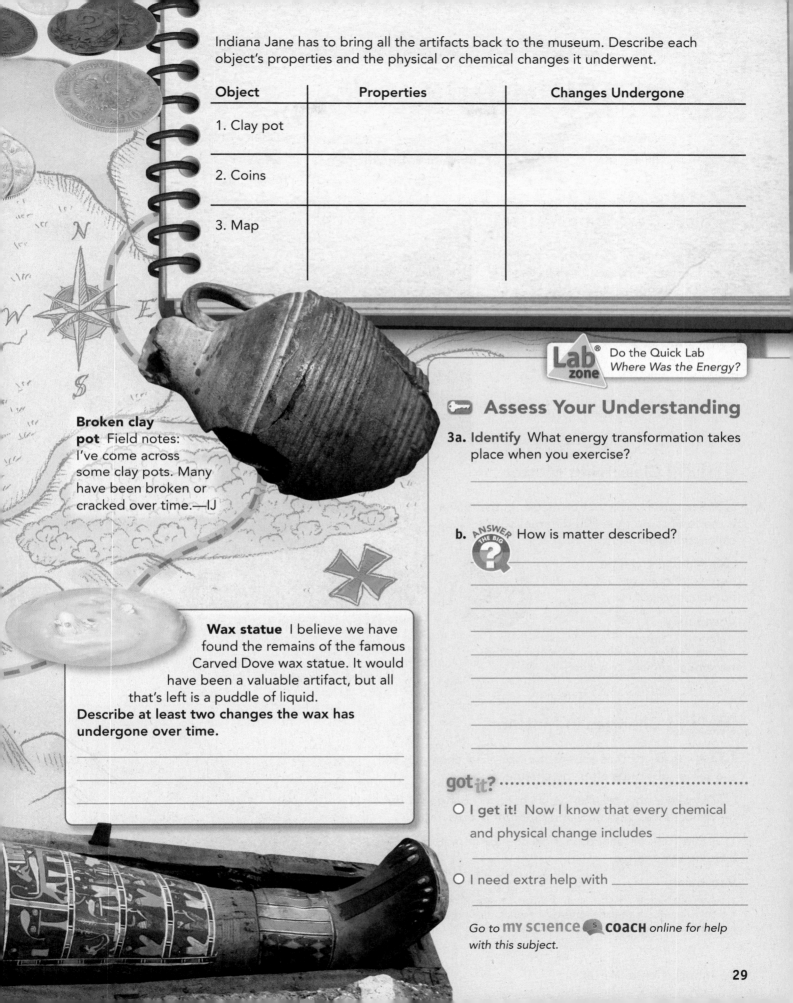

Lab zone® Do the Quick Lab *Where Was the Energy?*

🔑 **Assess Your Understanding**

3a. Identify What energy transformation takes place when you exercise?

b. ANSWER THE BIG ❓ How is matter described?

got it? ∙∙∙∙∙∙∙∙∙∙∙∙∙∙∙∙∙∙∙∙∙∙∙∙∙∙∙∙∙∙∙∙∙∙

○ **I get it!** Now I know that every chemical and physical change includes _____

○ **I need extra help with** _____

Go to MY SCIENCE COACH *online for help with this subject.*

REVIEW THE BIG ?

Water is a _____ . A _____ property of water is that it boils at 100°C. The _____ of water is 1 g/cm³.

LESSON 1 Describing Matter

🔑 Every form of matter has two kinds of properties—physical properties and chemical properties.

Vocabulary
- matter
- chemistry
- substance
- physical property
- chemical property

LESSON 2 Classifying Matter

🔑 Scientists know that all matter in the universe is made of more than 100 different substances, called elements.

🔑 A mixture can be heterogeneous or homogeneous.

Vocabulary
- element • atom
- chemical bond • molecule • compound
- chemical formula • mixture

LESSON 3 Measuring Matter

🔑 The SI unit of mass is the kilogram (kg).

🔑 The SI unit of volume is the cubic meter (m³).

🔑 You can determine the density of a sample of matter by dividing its mass by its volume.

Vocabulary
- weight • mass • International System of Units
- volume • density

LESSON 4 Changes in Matter

🔑 A substance that undergoes a physical change is still the same substance after the change.

🔑 Unlike a physical change, a chemical change produces new substances with new and different properties.

🔑 Every chemical and physical change in matter includes a change in energy.

Vocabulary
- physical change • chemical change • law of conservation of mass
- temperature • thermal energy • endothermic change
- exothermic change • chemical energy

Review and Assessment

LESSON 1 Describing Matter

1. Which of the following is an example of a chemical property?

   a. density   **b.** flammability

   c. hardness   **d.** luster

2. A substance can be classified by its physical properties, which are properties that

_____

_____

_____

_____

_____

3. Classify Which of the following is a substance: table salt, seawater, or sand? Explain how you know.

_____

_____

_____

_____

4. Interpret Tables Write a title that describes the table below.

Helium	Colorless; less dense than air
Iron	Attracted to magnets; melting point of 1,535°C
Oxygen	Odorless; gas at room temperature

5. **Write About It** Write an e-mail to a friend explaining why the melting point of a substance is a physical property but flammability is a chemical property. Use examples to explain.

LESSON 2 Classifying Matter

6. Which of the following is an element?

   a. water   **b.** carbon dioxide

   c. oxygen   **d.** ammonia

7. Four methods that can be used to separate

mixtures are _____

_____

_____

Use the diagrams to answer Questions 8–10. Each diagram represents a different kind of matter. Each ball represents an atom. Balls of the same color are the same kind of atom.

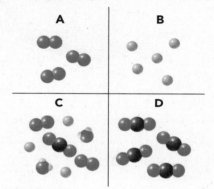

8. Interpret Diagrams Which diagram or diagrams represent a single element? Explain.

_____

_____

9. Compare and Contrast How do the atoms in Diagram A differ from those in Diagram D?

_____

_____

_____

10. Apply Concepts Which diagram or diagrams represent a mixture? Explain.

_____

_____

_____

LESSON 3 **Measuring Matter**

11. What is the SI unit of mass?

a. milliliter   b. kilogram

c. pound   d. cubic centimeter

12. The density of a substance is calculated by

_____

_____

13. Make Judgments Which measurement shown in the diagram is not needed to find the volume of the box? Explain.

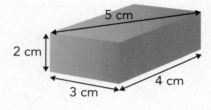

5 cm

2 cm

3 cm

4 cm

_____

_____

_____

_____

14. math! A piece of metal has a volume of 38 cm³ and a mass of 277 g. Calculate the density of the metal and identify it based on the information in the table below.

Density of Common Metals	
Iron	7.9 g/cm³
Lead	11.3 g/cm³
Tin	7.3 g/cm³
Zinc	7.1 g/cm³

LESSON 4 **Changes in Matter**

15. Which of the following is a physical change?

a. burning   b. rusting

c. freezing   d. oxidation

16. The law of conservation of mass states that

_____

_____

_____

17. Solve Problems How could you prove that dissolving table salt in water is a physical change, not a chemical change?

_____

_____

_____

_____

_____

_____

APPLY THE BIG

How is matter described?

18. Choose a substance you're familiar with. What are its physical and chemical properties? How would you measure its density? What are some physical and chemical changes it can undergo?

_____

_____

_____

_____

_____

_____

_____

_____

_____

_____

_____

_____

Standardized Test Prep

Multiple Choice

Circle the letter of the best answer.

1. Each diagram below represents a different kind of matter. Each ball represents an atom. Balls of the same size and shade are the same atom.

   Which diagram **best** represents a mixture of two kinds of molecules?

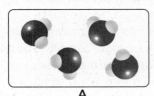
A

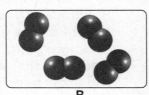
B

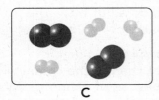
C

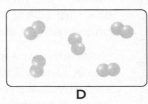
D

   A Diagram A   **B** Diagram B
   C Diagram C   **D** Diagram D

2. The fact that matter is neither created nor destroyed in any chemical or physical change is called the

   A law of exothermic change.
   B law of endothermic change.
   C law of thermal matter.
   D law of conservation of mass.

3. The density of a substance equals its mass divided by its volume. The density of sulfur is 2.0 g/cm³. What is the mass of a sample of sulfur with a volume of 6.0 cm³?

   A 3.0 g   **B** 4.0 g
   C 8.0 g   **D** 12 g

4. The abilities to dissolve in water and to conduct electric current are examples of

   A physical properties.
   B chemical properties.
   C physical changes.
   D chemical bonding.

5. Which two pieces of laboratory equipment would be the **most** useful for measuring the mass and volume of a rectangular block?

   A a metric ruler and a stopwatch
   B a balance and a metric ruler
   C a graduated cylinder and a metric ruler
   D a balance and a stop watch

Constructed Response

Use the graph below and your knowledge of science to help you answer Question 6. Write your answer on a separate sheet of paper.

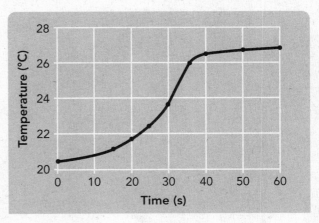

6. A student mixes two liquids of the same temperature together. The graph above shows the change in temperature after the liquids mix. Did the reaction absorb thermal energy or release it? Explain your answer.

Science and History

Long Ago in a Faraway Land...

In an old German tale, a strange little man named Rumpelstiltskin spins straw into gold. Sounds far-fetched, right? It wouldn't have sounded that strange to someone in the fourteenth century. Hundreds of years ago, alchemists searched for a way to turn metals, like lead, into gold. They also tried to make medicines that would cure all diseases and allow people to live for a long time. They thought they needed just one ingredient to do all of this—the philosopher's stone.

Nowadays, we know that a magic ingredient will not change the chemical and physical properties of elements. We have learned that different elements have different properties. But alchemists did make valuable contributions to people's understanding of the physical world. Alchemists discovered alcohol and mineral acids and recorded their observations of how these acids reacted with other substances. They worked in laboratories heating base metals and observing interactions and changes in color. They recorded their conclusions about these experiments. Their goal may have been impossible, but their research helped build the foundation of chemistry today.

Research It Throughout history, scientists have increased our understanding of the natural world by learning from those before them. Research how the fields of chemistry and medicine have developed from the experiments of alchemists. Write an essay describing the progression.

An Antiuniverse?

What if the entire universe had a mirror or negative image? Would everything happen backward? Or, would there be an opposite you? Scientists working in the field of particle physics think there just might be a mirror universe, but they don't really expect it to be the stuff of science fiction movies.

A little over a hundred years ago, scientists thought that the smallest part of matter—a part not made up of anything else—was the atom. That wasn't true. An atom is made up of a nucleus that contains protons and neutrons, surrounded by electrons. A physicist named Paul Dirac added an interesting twist to this knowledge. He correctly predicted that the electron might have a reverse twin, which he called a positron. (He won the Nobel Prize for this leap of genius back in 1933.) The positron has the same mass as an electron but the opposite charge—it's the antielectron.

Electrons, neutrons, and protons all have these antiparticles, or at least they did when the particles formed. Scientists have been able to study them in the laboratory. Inside particle accelerators, scientists can even use positrons and electrons to form entirely new atoms. But outside of the controlled laboratory environment, where are these antiparticles? Are they now part of an antiuniverse somewhere? Physicists are hoping to find the answers in the twenty-first century—your century!

Research It Write down three questions you have about particle physics and antimatter. Research to find out the answers. Articles about the CERN laboratory in Switzerland would be a good place to start. Answer your questions in one or two paragraphs.

Paul Dirac predicted that positrons might exist as the opposites of electrons. ▼

◄ Inside a special chamber, two invisible photons enter and produce a pair of electrons (colored green) and antielectrons (colored red).

35

HOW DID THIS BUILDING TURN TO ICE?

Why does a substance change states?

Firefighters sprayed water on a blaze in this historic building in Maine. The air temperature was −14°F, which was uncomfortably cold. This made it difficult for firefighters to battle the flames. The building was in danger of falling down because it was covered in ice 6 to 10 inches thick. **Infer How did this building get covered in ice?**

_____

_____

_____

_____

_____

_____

> UNTAMED SCIENCE Watch the **Untamed Science** video to learn more about changing states.

Solids, Liquids, and Gases

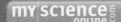

2 Getting Started

Check Your Understanding

1. Background Read the paragraph below and then answer the question.

> The air **temperature** outside has been below freezing all week. The local pond has frozen over and is ready for ice skating. Ronnesia is excited just thinking about all the things she can do on the **ice.** She eats a good breakfast to get the **energy** she needs for ice skating.

> **Temperature** is a measure of the average energy of random motion of particles of matter.
>
> **Ice** is water in the solid form.
>
> **Energy** is the ability to do work or cause change.

- Why is the pond ready for ice skating?

_____

_____

> **MY READING WEB** If you had trouble completing the question above, visit **My Reading Web** and type in **Solids, Liquids, and Gases.**

Vocabulary Skill

Suffixes A suffix is a letter or group of letters added to the end of a word to change its meaning and often its part of speech. In this chapter, you will learn vocabulary words that end in the suffixes -ation, -ine, and -sion.

Suffix	Meaning	Example
-ation	State of, process of, act of	Vaporization, evaporation, condensation, sublimation
-ine	Consisting of	Crystalline solid
-sion	State of, process of, act of	Surface tension

2. Quick Check *Vapor* is another word for gas. Use the table above to predict the meaning of *vaporization*. Revise your definition as needed.

_____

_____

liquid

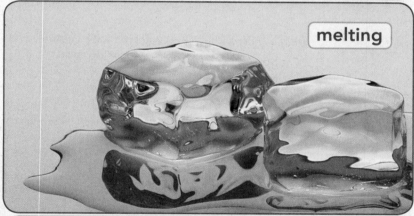
surface tension

melting

sublimation

Chapter Preview

LESSON 1
- solid
- crystalline solid
- amorphous solid
- liquid
- fluid
- surface tension
- viscosity
- gas
- pressure
- ↺ Relate Cause and Effect
- △ Infer

LESSON 2
- melting
- melting point
- freezing
- vaporization
- evaporation
- boiling
- boiling point
- condensation
- sublimation
- ↺ Compare and Contrast
- △ Predict

LESSON 3
- Charles's Law
- directly proportional
- Boyle's Law
- inversely proportional
- ↺ Identify the Main Idea
- △ Graph

▸ VOCAB FLASH CARDS For extra help with vocabulary, visit **Vocab Flash Cards** and type in *Solids, Liquids, and Gases.*

States of Matter

UNLOCK THE BIG ?

🔑 **How Do You Describe a Solid?**

🔑 **How Do You Describe a Liquid?**

🔑 **How Do You Describe a Gas?**

MY PLANET DiARY

Liquid Crystals

Have you ever wondered why some television sets are referred to as LCD TVs? *LCD* stands for "liquid crystal display." An LCD is a thin, flat screen. LCDs have replaced the picture tubes in many computer monitors and television sets because they are lighter and use less power. LCDs are also found in cell phones and clock radio faces.

Liquid crystals are neither solid nor liquid—instead they fall somewhere in between. But it takes just a small amount of thermal energy to change a liquid crystal to a liquid. As a result, LCDs tend to be very sensitive to heat.

FUN FACTS

Communicate Discuss these questions with a classmate. Write your answers below.

1. List some things that contain LCDs.

_____

_____

_____

2. Why might you not want to leave a cell phone or a laptop computer outside on a hot day?

_____

_____

_____

_____

_____

▷ PLANET DIARY Go to **Planet Diary** to learn more about solids, liquids, and gases.

Lab zone® Do the Inquiry Warm-Up *What Are Solids, Liquids, and Gases?*

LCD display with crystals cooling (background)

Vocabulary
- solid • crystalline solid • amorphous solid • liquid
- fluid • surface tension • viscosity • gas • pressure

Skills
↻ Reading: Relate Cause and Effect
△ Inquiry: Infer

How Do You Describe a Solid?

Look at the bowl in **Figure 1.** It contains the metal bismuth. Notice that the shape and size of the piece of bismuth are different from the bowl's shape and size. What would happen if you took the bismuth out of the bowl and placed it on a tabletop? Would it become flatter? What would happen if you put it in a larger bowl? Would it become larger? Of course not, because it's a solid. A **solid** has a definite shape and a definite volume. Your pencil is another example of a solid. If your pencil has a cylindrical shape and a volume of 6 cubic centimeters, it will keep this shape and volume in any position in any container.

Particles in a Solid The particles that make up a solid are packed very closely together. Also, each particle is tightly fixed in one position. ⌸ **This fixed, closely packed arrangement of particles in a solid causes it to have a definite shape and volume.** Do the particles that make up a solid move at all? Yes, but not much. The particles in a solid are closely locked in position and can only vibrate in place. This means that the particles move back and forth slightly, like a group of people running in place.

Place a check in each category that describes a solid.		
	Definite	**Indefinite**
Shape	_____	_____
Volume	_____	_____

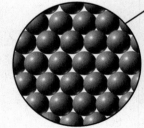

Particles in a solid

FIGURE 1 ·······························

Solid

A solid does not take the shape or volume of its container.

✎ **Interpret Diagrams** Describe the arrangement of particles in a solid.

_____

_____

_____

41

FIGURE 2 ·····································

Types of Solids

Solids are either crystalline or amorphous. Butter is an amorphous solid. The mineral fluorite is a crystalline solid.

✎ **Compare and Contrast** Use the Venn diagram to compare the characteristics of amorphous and crystalline solids.

Types of Solids   In many solids, the particles form a regular, repeating pattern. These patterns create crystals. Solids that are made up of crystals are called **crystalline solids** (KRIS tuh lin). Salt, sugar, and snow are examples of crystalline solids. The fluorite crystal shown in **Figure 2** is an example of a colorful crystalline solid. When a crystalline solid is heated, it melts at a distinct temperature.

In **amorphous solids** (uh MAWR fus), the particles are not arranged in a regular pattern. Unlike a crystalline solid, an amorphous solid does not melt at a distinct temperature. Instead, it may become softer and softer or change into other substances. Glass is an example of an amorphous solid. A glass blower can bend and shape glass that has been heated. Plastics and rubber are other examples of amorphous solids.

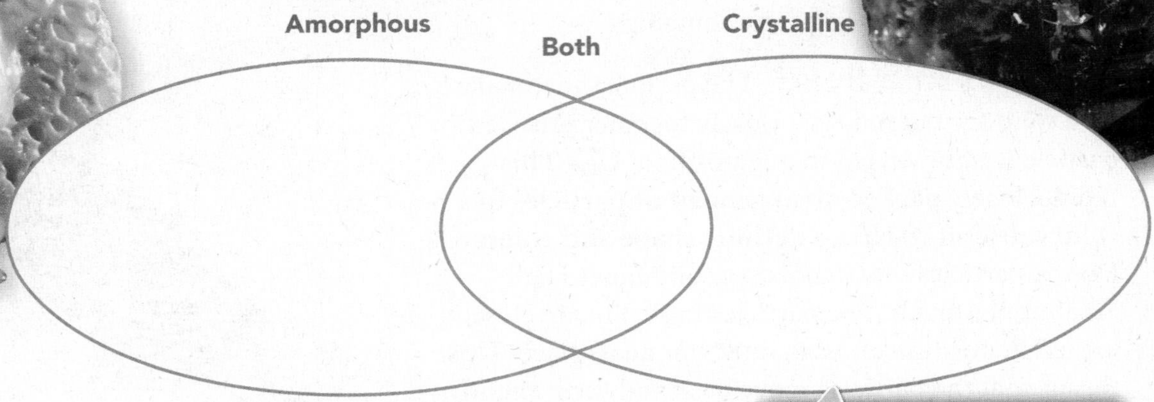

Amorphous   Both   Crystalline

Lab ® Do the Quick Lab
zone *Modeling Particles.*

🔑 **Assess Your Understanding**

1a. Identify The two types of solids are

_____ and _____.

b. Explain Are the particles in a solid motionless? Explain your answer.

_____

_____

c. Draw Conclusions Candle wax gradually loses its shape as it is heated. What type of solid is candle wax? Explain.

_____

_____

_____

_____

got**it?** ··

○ I get it! Now I know that a solid has a definite shape and volume because_____

_____

○ I need extra help with _____

Go to **MY SCIENCE** 💬 **COACH** *online for help with this subject.*

How Do You Describe a Liquid?

Without a container, a liquid spreads into a wide, shallow puddle. Like a solid, however, a liquid does have a constant volume. A **liquid** has a definite volume but no shape of its own. **Figure 3** shows equal volumes of iced tea in two different containers. The shape of a liquid may change with its container, but its volume remains the same.

Particles in a Liquid   In general, the particles in a liquid are packed almost as closely together as those in a solid. However, the particles in a liquid move around one another freely. You can compare this movement to the way you might move a group of marbles around in your hand. Like the particles of a liquid, the marbles slide around one another but still touch. 🔑 **Because its particles are free to move, a liquid has no definite shape. However, it does have a definite volume.** These freely moving particles allow a liquid to flow from place to place. For this reason, a liquid is also called a **fluid,** meaning a "substance that flows."

✏️ **Relate Cause and Effect**
Underline the cause and circle the effect in the boldface sentences.

Place a check in each category that describes a liquid.

	Definite	Indefinite
Shape	_____	_____
Volume	_____	_____

FIGURE 3 ·····················

Liquid
Each container contains 300 cm³ of iced tea. The iced tea takes the shape of its container, but its volume does not change.

✏️ **Interpret Diagrams** Describe the arrangement of particles in a liquid.

_____

_____

_____

_____

Particles in a liquid

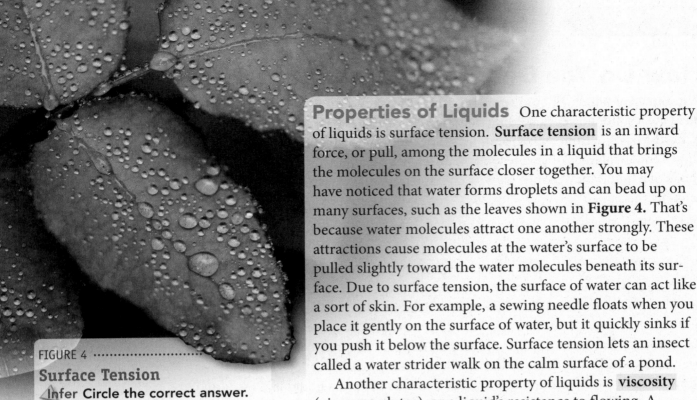

Properties of Liquids One characteristic property of liquids is surface tension. **Surface tension** is an inward force, or pull, among the molecules in a liquid that brings the molecules on the surface closer together. You may have noticed that water forms droplets and can bead up on many surfaces, such as the leaves shown in **Figure 4.** That's because water molecules attract one another strongly. These attractions cause molecules at the water's surface to be pulled slightly toward the water molecules beneath its surface. Due to surface tension, the surface of water can act like a sort of skin. For example, a sewing needle floats when you place it gently on the surface of water, but it quickly sinks if you push it below the surface. Surface tension lets an insect called a water strider walk on the calm surface of a pond.

Another characteristic property of liquids is **viscosity** (vis KAHS uh tee), or a liquid's resistance to flowing. A liquid's viscosity depends on the size and shape of its particles and the attractions between the particles. Some liquids flow more easily than others. Liquids with high viscosity flow slowly. Honey is an example of a liquid with a very high viscosity. Liquids with low viscosity flow quickly. Water and vinegar have relatively low viscosities.

FIGURE 4 ·······················
Surface Tension
Infer Circle the correct answer.
Water beads up on the surface of the leaves because water molecules (attract/repel) each other strongly.

 Do the Quick Lab *As Thick as Honey.*

🔑 Assess Your Understanding

2a. Name A substance that flows is called a

_____

b. Describe Why is a liquid able to flow?

_____

_____

c. Compare and Contrast How do liquids with a high viscosity differ from liquids with a low viscosity?

_____

_____

_____

got it? ···

O **I get it!** Now I know that a liquid has a definite volume but not a definite shape because _____

_____

_____

O **I need extra help with** _____

Go to MY SCIENCE ⓢ COACH online for help with this subject.

How Do You Describe a Gas?

Like a liquid, a gas is a fluid. Unlike a liquid, however, a **gas** has neither a definite shape nor a definite volume. If a gas is in a closed container such as the flask in **Figure 5,** the gas particles will move and spread apart as they fill the container.

If you could see the particles that make up a gas, you would see them moving in all directions. 🔑 **As gas particles move, they spread apart, filling all the space available. Thus, a gas has neither definite shape nor definite volume.** When working with a gas, it is important to know its volume, temperature, and pressure. So what exactly do these measurements mean?

Volume Remember that volume is the amount of space that matter fills. Volume is measured in cubic centimeters (cm^3), cubic meters (m^3), milliliters (mL), liters (L), and other units. Because gas particles move and fill all of the space available, the volume of a gas is the same as the volume of its container. For example, a large amount of helium gas can be compressed—or pressed together tightly—to fit into a metal tank. When you use the helium to fill balloons, it expands to fill many balloons that have a total volume much greater than the volume of the tank.

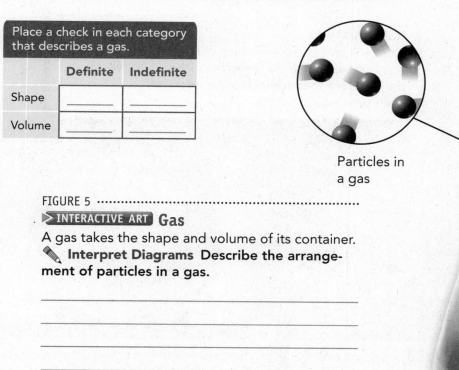

Place a check in each category that describes a gas.		
	Definite	**Indefinite**
Shape		
Volume		

Particles in a gas

FIGURE 5 ·····················

➤ INTERACTIVE ART **Gas**

A gas takes the shape and volume of its container.

✎ **Interpret Diagrams** Describe the arrangement of particles in a gas.

_____

_____

_____

_____

_____

do the **math!**

Calculating Pressure

When calculating pressure, force is measured in newtons (N). If the area is measured in square meters (m^2), pressure is expressed in pascals (Pa), where 1 Pa = 1 N/m^2. Suppose a gas exerts a force of 252 N on a piston having an area of 0.430 m^2. What is the pressure on the piston in Pascals?

$$\text{Pressure} = \frac{\text{Force}}{\text{Area}}$$

$$= \frac{252 \text{ N}}{0.430 \text{ m}^2}$$

$$= 586 \text{ Pa}$$

Practice Problem A gas exerts a force of 5,610 N over an area of 0.342 m^2. What pressure does the gas exert in Pa?

____

____

____

Pressure Gas particles constantly collide with one another and with the walls of their container. As a result, the gas pushes on the walls of the container. The **pressure** of the gas is the force of its outward push divided by the area of the walls of the container. Pressure is measured in units of pascals (Pa) or kilopascals (kPa) (1 kPa = 1,000 Pa).

$$\text{Pressure} = \frac{\text{Force}}{\text{Area}}$$

The firmness of a gas-filled object comes from the pressure of the gas. For example, the air inside an inflated ball has a higher pressure than the air outside. This higher pressure is due to the greater concentration of gas particles inside the ball than in the surrounding air. Concentration is the number of gas particles in a given unit of volume.

Why does a ball leak even when it has only a tiny hole? The higher pressure inside the ball results in gas particles hitting the inner surface of the ball more often. Therefore, gas particles inside the ball reach the hole and escape more often than gas particles outside the ball reach the hole and enter. Thus, many more particles go out than in. The pressure inside drops until it is equal to the pressure outside.

FIGURE 6

Gas Pressure

Photos A and B show a beach ball being inflated and then deflated. **Interpret Photos Circle the answers that complete the description of each process.**

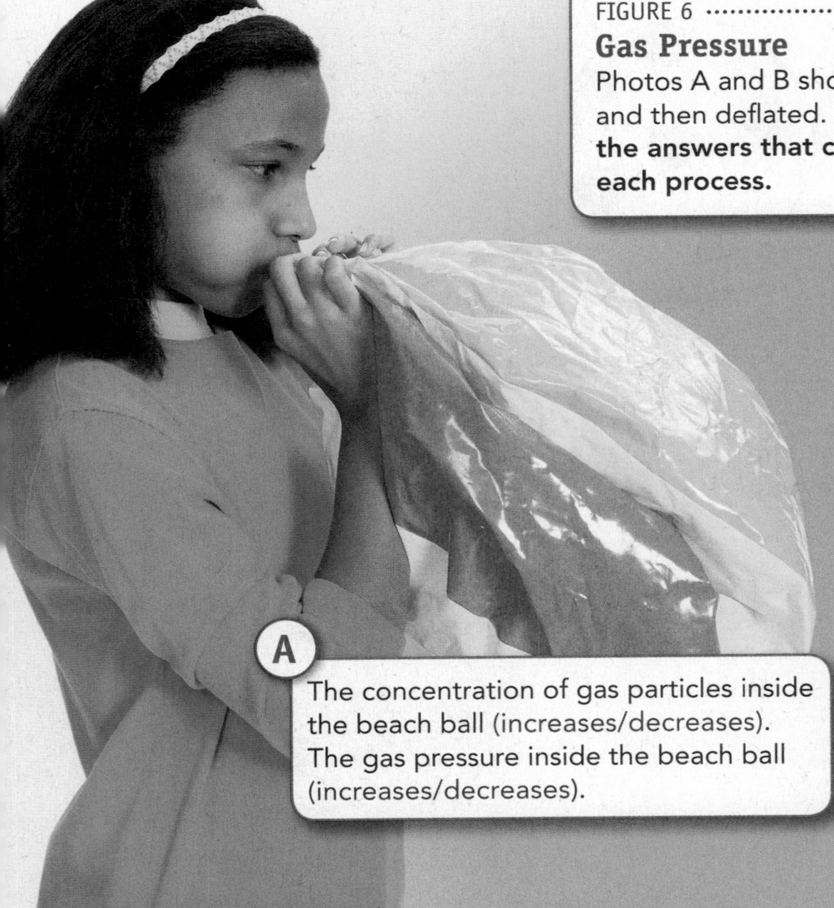

A The concentration of gas particles inside the beach ball (increases/decreases). The gas pressure inside the beach ball (increases/decreases).

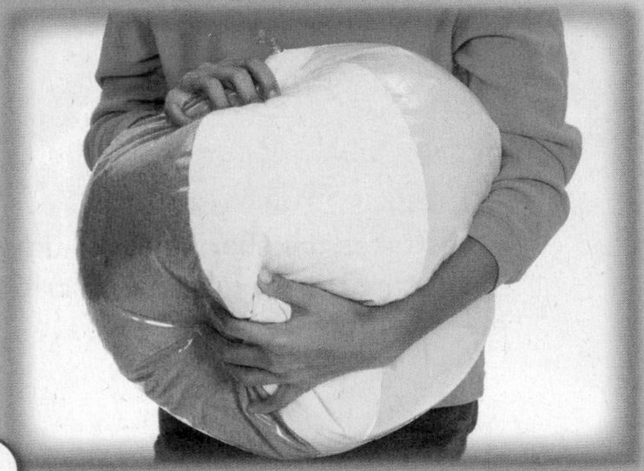

B The concentration of gas particles inside the beach ball (increases/decreases). The gas pressure inside the beach ball (increases/decreases).

Faster-moving, hot gas particles

Slower-moving, cool gas particles

Temperature

Temperature The balloonists in **Figure 7** are preparing the balloon for flight. To do this, they use a propane burner to heat the air inside the balloon. Once the temperature of the air is hot enough, the balloon will start to rise. But what does the temperature tell you? Recall that all particles of matter are constantly moving. Temperature is a measure of the average energy of random motion of the particles of matter. The faster the particles are moving, the greater their energy and the higher the temperature. You might think of a thermometer as a speedometer for particles.

Even at room temperature, the average speed of particles in a gas is very fast. At about 20°C, the particles in a typical gas travel about 500 meters per second—more than twice the cruising speed of a jet plane!

FIGURE 7 ·
Temperature of a Gas
✎ **Explain** Why are the hot gas particles moving faster than the cool gas particles?

_____

_____

_____

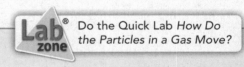 Do the Quick Lab *How Do the Particles in a Gas Move?*

🔑 Assess Your Understanding

3a. Describe Describe how the motions of gas particles are related to the pressure exerted by the gas.

_____

_____

_____

_____

_____

b. Relate Cause and Effect Why does pumping more air into a basketball increase the pressure inside the ball?

_____

_____

_____

_____

_____

got **it?** ·

○ **I get it!** Now I know that a gas has neither a definite shape nor definite volume because_____

_____

○ I need extra help with _____

Go to **MY SCIENCE COACH** online for help with this subject

Changes of State

UNLOCK THE BIG **?**

🔑 **What Happens to the Particles of a Solid as It Melts?**

🔑 **What Happens to the Particles of a Liquid as It Vaporizes?**

🔑 **What Happens to the Particles of a Solid as It Sublimes?**

MY PLANET DiARY

SCIENCE STATS

On the Boil

You might have noticed that as an uncovered pot of water boils, the water level slowly decreases. The water level changes because the liquid is changing to a gas. As you heat the water, the thermal energy of its molecules increases. The longer you leave the pot on the hot stove, the more energy is absorbed by the water molecules. When the water molecules gain enough energy, they change state from a liquid to a gas.

The graph shows the temperature of a small pot of water on a stove set to high heat. The starting temperature of the water is 20°C.

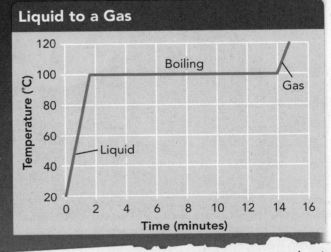

Liquid to a Gas

Answer the following questions.

1. How long does it take for the water to start boiling? At what temperature does the water boil?

_____

_____

_____

2. Does it take more energy to heat the water to 100°C or to boil it?

_____

_____

_____

> PLANET DIARY Go to **Planet Diary** to learn more about changes of state.

Do the Inquiry Warm-Up
What Happens When You Breathe on a Mirror?

Vocabulary
- melting • melting point • freezing • vaporization
- evaporation • boiling • boiling point • condensation
- sublimation

Skills
↻ Reading: Compare and Contrast
△ Inquiry: Predict

What Happens to the Particles of a Solid as It Melts?

Particles of a liquid have more thermal energy than particles of the same substance in solid form. As a gas, the particles have even more thermal energy. A change from a solid to a liquid involves an increase in thermal energy. As you might guess, a change from a liquid to a solid is just the opposite: It involves a decrease in thermal energy.

Melting The change in state from a solid to a liquid is called **melting.** In pure, crystalline solids, melting occurs at a specific temperature, called the **melting point.** Because the melting point is a characteristic property of a substance, chemists often compare melting points when trying to identify an unknown material. The melting point of pure water, for example, is 0°C at sea level.

What happens to the particles of a solid as it melts? Think of an ice cube taken from the freezer. The energy needed to melt the ice comes mostly from the air in the room. At first, the added thermal energy makes the water molecules vibrate faster, raising their temperature. ⚷ **At a solid's melting point, its particles vibrate so fast that they break free from their fixed positions.** At 0°C, the temperature of the ice stops increasing. Any added energy continues to change the arrangement of the water molecules from ice crystals into liquid water. The ice melts.

FIGURE 1 ··
Melting
✎ **Relate Diagrams and Photos** Draw a line matching each illustration of water molecules to either ice or liquid water. Then describe how ice and liquid water differ in the arrangement of their molecules.

_____

_____

_____

_____

_____

Freezing The change of state from a liquid to a solid is called **freezing.** It is just the reverse of melting. 🔑 **At a liquid's freezing point, its particles are moving so slowly that they begin to take on fixed positions.**

When you put liquid water into a freezer, for example, the water loses energy to the cold air in the freezer. The water molecules move more and more slowly as they lose energy. Over time, the water becomes solid ice. When water begins to freeze, its temperature stays at 0°C until freezing is complete. The freezing point of water, 0°C, is the same as its melting point.

apply it!

In metal casting, a liquid metal is poured into a container called a mold. The mold gives a shape to the metal when it cools and hardens.

1 Explain How does metal casting make use of the different characteristics of liquids and solids?

_____
_____
_____
_____
_____
_____

2 CHALLENGE The melting point of copper is 1084°C. How does the energy of the particles in a certain amount of liquid copper compare to the energy of the molecules in the same amount of liquid water? Why?

_____
_____
_____
_____
_____
_____
_____

Lab® zone Do the Lab Investigation
Melting Ice.

🔑 Assess Your Understanding

1a. Identify The change in state from a solid to a liquid is called _____

b. Compare and Contrast How does what happens to the particles in a substance during melting differ from what happens in freezing?

_____
_____
_____
_____
_____

got it? ···

○ **I get it!** Now I know that melting occurs when the particles in a solid_____

_____
_____

_____

○ **I need extra help with** _____

Go to MY SCIENCE ⬤ᔆ COACH *online for help with this subject.*

What Happens to the Particles of a Liquid as It Vaporizes?

Have you ever wondered how clouds form or why puddles dry up? To answer these questions, you need to look at what happens when changes occur between the liquid and gas states.

Evaporation and Boiling The change in state from a liquid to a gas is called **vaporization** (vay puhr ih ZAY shun). **Vaporization occurs when the particles in a liquid gain enough energy to move independently.** There are two main types of vaporization—evaporation and boiling.

Vaporization that takes place only on the surface of a liquid is called **evaporation** (ee vap uh RAY shun). A shrinking puddle is an example. Water in the puddle gains energy from the ground, the air, or the sun. The added energy enables some of the water molecules on the surface of the puddle to escape into the air, or evaporate.

Vaporization that takes place both below and at the surface of a liquid is called **boiling.** When water boils, vaporized water molecules form bubbles below the surface. The bubbles rise and eventually break the surface of the liquid. The temperature at which a liquid boils is called its **boiling point.** As with melting points, chemists use boiling points to help identify unknown substances.

Compare and Contrast
Compare and contrast the two types of vaporization.

_____
_____
_____
_____
_____
_____
_____

FIGURE 2

Types of Vaporization

Liquid water changes to water vapor by either evaporation or boiling.

Interpret Diagrams Label the type of vaporization occurring in each flask. Then draw arrows to indicate the paths of water molecules leaving each flask.

Suppose there is the same amount of water in both of the flasks. **Predict** Which flask does water vaporize from first? Why?

_____
_____
_____
_____

Condensation Condensation is the reverse of vaporization. The change in state from a gas to a liquid is called **condensation.** You can observe condensation by breathing onto a mirror. When warm water vapor in your breath reaches the cooler surface of the mirror, the water vapor condenses into liquid droplets. 🗝 **Condensation occurs when particles in a gas lose enough thermal energy to form a liquid.**

Clouds typically form when water vapor in the atmosphere condenses into tiny liquid droplets. When the droplets get heavy enough, they fall to the ground as rain. Water vapor is a colorless gas that you cannot see. The steam you see above a kettle of boiling water is not water vapor, and neither are clouds or fog. What you see in those cases are tiny droplets of liquid water suspended in air.

.... ✎ ....
Vocabulary Suffixes Complete
the sentences using the correct
forms of the word *condense*.

_____ is
the change in state from a gas
to a liquid. Clouds form because
water vapor _____

FIGURE 3 ··························
Foggy Mirror
✎ **Explain Why does a mirror fog up
after a hot shower?**

_____
_____
_____
_____
_____
_____

🔺**Lab** Do the Quick Lab
zone *Keeping Cool.*

🗝 Assess Your Understanding

2a. Identify The change in state from a liquid to a gas is called _____

b. Apply Concepts How does the thermal energy of water vapor change as the vapor condenses?

_____
_____

c. Relate Cause and Effect Why do clouds form before it rains?

_____
_____
_____
_____
_____

got it? ···

○ **I get it!** Now I know that vaporization occurs when the particles in a liquid _____
_____

○ **I need extra help with** _____

Go to **MY SCIENCE** 💬 **COACH** *online for help with this subject.*

What Happens to the Particles of a Solid as It Sublimes?

In places where the winters are cold, the snow may disappear even when the temperature stays well below freezing. This change is the result of sublimation. **Sublimation** occurs when the surface particles of a solid gain enough energy that they form a gas. **During sublimation, particles of a solid do not pass through the liquid state as they form a gas.**

One example of sublimation occurs with dry ice. Dry ice is the common name for solid carbon dioxide. At ordinary atmospheric pressures, carbon dioxide cannot exist as a liquid. So instead of melting, solid carbon dioxide changes directly into a gas. As it sublimes, the carbon dioxide absorbs thermal energy. This property helps keep materials near dry ice cold and dry. For this reason, using dry ice is a way to keep the temperature low when a refrigerator is not available. Some fog machines use dry ice to create fog in movies or at concerts, as shown in **Figure 4.** When dry ice becomes a gas, it cools water vapor in the nearby air. The water vapor then condenses into a liquid, forming fog near the dry ice.

did you know?

Mosquitos are attracted to the carbon dioxide gas you exhale during breathing. A mosquito trap baited with dry ice can attract up to four or five times as many mosquitos as traps baited with a light source alone.

FIGURE 4 ·········

Dry Ice

A fog machine uses dry ice to create fog at this rock concert. ✎ **Explain** Why does fog form **near dry ice?**

_____

_____

_____

_____

_____

Dry ice subliming

The Changing States of Water

Why does a substance change states?

FIGURE 5 ···

> **VIRTUAL LAB** Four examples of how water changes states—by melting, freezing, vaporization, and condensation—are shown here.

✎ **Review** Use what you have learned about states of matter to answer the questions.

FREEZING

This lake has frozen over due to the cold weather. As liquid water freezes, its molecules (gain/lose) thermal energy. How does the motion of the water molecules change during freezing?

_____

_____

_____

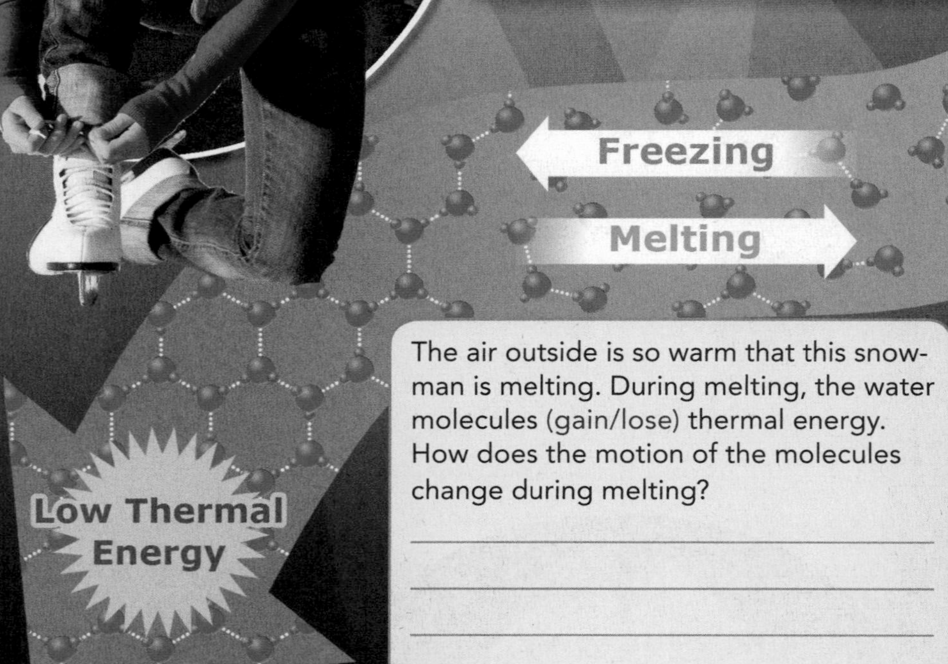

← **Freezing**

Melting →

MELTING

The air outside is so warm that this snowman is melting. During melting, the water molecules (gain/lose) thermal energy. How does the motion of the molecules change during melting?

_____

_____

_____

_____

Low Thermal Energy

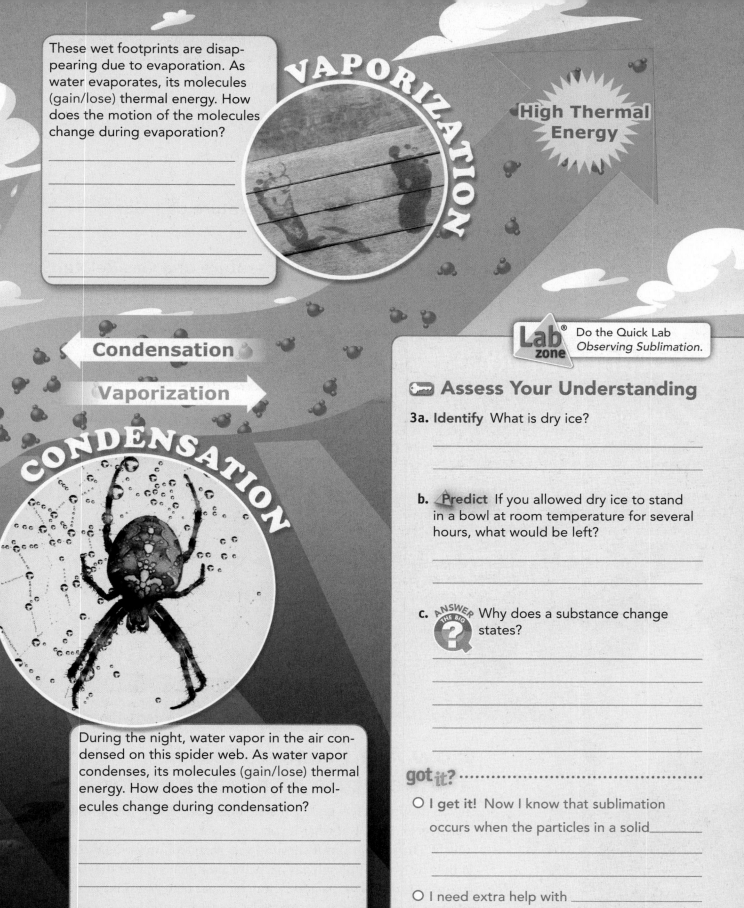

These wet footprints are disappearing due to evaporation. As water evaporates, its molecules (gain/lose) thermal energy. How does the motion of the molecules change during evaporation?

_____
_____
_____
_____

VAPORIZATION

High Thermal Energy

Condensation

Vaporization

CONDENSATION

During the night, water vapor in the air condensed on this spider web. As water vapor condenses, its molecules (gain/lose) thermal energy. How does the motion of the molecules change during condensation?

_____
_____
_____
_____

Lab zone® Do the Quick Lab Observing Sublimation.

Assess Your Understanding

3a. Identify What is dry ice?

_____
_____

b. Predict If you allowed dry ice to stand in a bowl at room temperature for several hours, what would be left?

_____
_____

c. ANSWER THE BIG ? Why does a substance change states?

_____
_____
_____
_____
_____

got it?..

○ **I get it!** Now I know that sublimation occurs when the particles in a solid_____

_____
_____

○ **I need extra help with** _____

Go to MY SCIENCE S COACH *online for help with this subject.*

55

3 | Gas Behavior

UNLOCK THE BIG ?

🔑 **How Are Pressure and Temperature of a Gas Related?**

🔑 **How Are Volume and Temperature of a Gas Related?**

🔑 **How Are Pressure and Volume of a Gas Related?**

MY PLANET DIARY

BIOGRAPHY

Jacques Charles (1746–1823)

French scientist Jacques Charles is best known for his work on gases. But he also made contributions to the sport of ballooning. On August 27, 1783, Charles released the first hydrogen-filled balloon, which was about 4 meters in diameter. This balloon, which did not carry any people, rose to a height of 3,000 feet. Charles also improved the design of hot-air balloons. He added a valve line that allowed the pilot to release gas from the balloon. He also added a wicker basket that attached to the balloon with ropes. Charles was elected to the French Academy of Sciences in 1785.

Communicate Discuss this question with a classmate. Write your answer below.

What sport or hobby inspires you to want to know more about science? Why?

_____

_____

_____

_____

▷ **PLANET DIARY** Go to **Planet Diary** to learn more about gases.

Lab zone® Do the Inquiry Warm-Up *How Can Air Keep Chalk From Breaking?*

How Are Pressure and Temperature of a Gas Related?

If you dropped a few grains of sand onto your hand, you would hardly feel them. But what if you were caught in a sandstorm? Ouch! The sand grains fly around very fast, and they would sting if they hit you. Although gas particles are much smaller than sand grains, a sandstorm is a good model for gas behavior. Like grains of sand in a sandstorm, gas particles travel at high speeds. The faster the gas particles move, the greater the force with which they collide with the walls of their container.

Vocabulary
- Charles's law
- directly proportional
- Boyle's law
- inversely proportional

Skills
- ↻ Reading: Identify the Main Idea
- △ Inquiry: Graph

Consider a gas in a closed, rigid container. If you heat the gas, its particles will move faster on average. They will collide with the walls of their container with greater force. The greater force over the same area results in greater pressure. 🔑 **When the temperature of a gas at constant volume is increased, the pressure of the gas increases. When the temperature is decreased, the pressure of the gas decreases.**

On long trips, especially in the summer, a truck's tires can become very hot. As the temperature increases, so does the pressure of the air inside the tire. If the pressure becomes greater than the tire can hold, the tire will burst. For this reason, truck drivers need to monitor and adjust tire pressure on long trips.

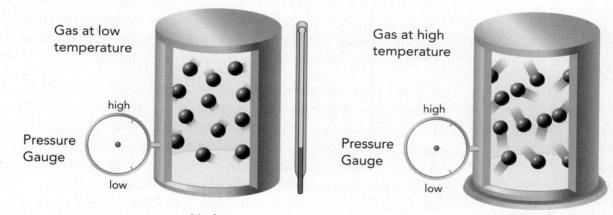

Gas at low temperature — Pressure Gauge — high / low — No heat

Gas at high temperature — Pressure Gauge — high / low — Heat added

FIGURE 1 ·······
Temperature and Gas Pressure
When a gas is heated in a closed, rigid container, the particles move faster and collide more often.

✎ **Infer** Draw an arrow in each pressure gauge to show the change in pressure of the gas.

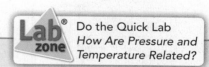

Lab zone Do the Quick Lab
How Are Pressure and Temperature Related?

🔑 Assess Your Understanding

got it? ··

○ **I get it!** Now I know that when the temperature of a gas at a constant volume increases, _____

_____

○ **I need extra help with** _____

    Go to **my science** ⓢ **COACH** *online for help with this subject.*

A gas-filled balloon is at room temperature, 20°C.

The balloon is lowered into liquid nitrogen at –196°C.

The balloon shrinks as gas volume decreases.

When the balloon is removed, the gas warms and the balloon expands.

The balloon is again at room temperature.

FIGURE 2 ···
Cooling a Balloon
The volume of a gas-filled balloon decreases as temperature decreases and then increases as temperature increases.

How Are Volume and Temperature of a Gas Related?

Figure 2 shows what happens when a balloon is slowly lowered into liquid nitrogen at nearly –200°C and then removed. As the air inside the balloon cools, its volume decreases. When the air inside warms up again, its volume increases. The pressure remains more or less constant because the air is in a flexible container.

Charles's Law French scientist Jacques Charles examined the relationship between the temperature and volume of a gas that is kept at a constant pressure. He measured the volume of a gas at various temperatures in a container that could change volume. (A changeable volume allows the pressure to remain constant.) 🔑 **When the temperature of a gas at constant pressure is increased, its volume increases. When the temperature of a gas at constant pressure is decreased, its volume decreases.** This principle is called Charles's law.

FIGURE 3 ·····································
Charles's Law
A gas in a cylinder with a movable piston is slowly heated.

✎ **Predict** Draw the piston and gas particles when the temperature reaches 200°C and 400°C.

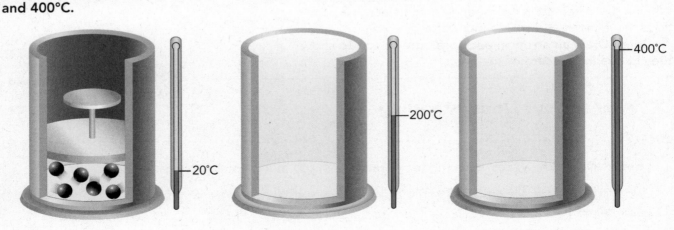

No heat

Some heat added

More heat added

Graphing Charles's Law Suppose you do an experiment to test Charles's law. The experiment begins with 50 mL of gas in a cylinder with a movable piston similar to the one in **Figure 3**. The gas is slowly heated. Each time the temperature increases by 10°C, the gas volume is recorded. The data are recorded in the data table in **Figure 4**. Note that the temperatures in the data table have been converted to kelvins, the SI unit of temperature. To convert from Celsius degrees to kelvins (K), add 273.

As you can see in the graph of the data, the data points form a straight line. The dotted line represents how the graph would look if the gas could be cooled to 0 K. Notice that the line passes through the point (0, 0), called the origin. When a graph of two variables is a straight line passing through the origin, the variables are said to be **directly proportional** to each other. The graph of Charles's law shows that the volume of a gas is directly proportional to its kelvin temperature at constant pressure.

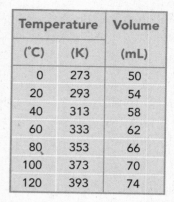

Temperature		Volume
(°C)	(K)	(mL)
0	273	50
20	293	54
40	313	58
60	333	62
80	353	66
100	373	70
120	393	74

FIGURE 4 ···

Temperature and Gas Volume

✎ In an experiment, a gas is heated at a constant pressure. The data shown in the table are plotted on the graph.

1. **Draw Conclusions** What happens to the volume of a gas when the temperature is increased at constant pressure?

_____

2. CHALLENGE Suppose the data formed a line with a steeper slope. For the same change in temperature, how would the change in volume compare?

_____

_____

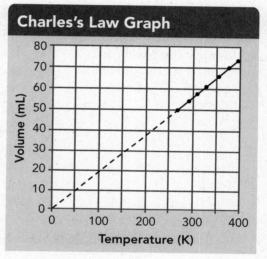

Charles's Law Graph

Do the Quick Lab
Hot and Cold Balloons.

🔑 **Assess Your Understanding**

1a. **Identify** The graph of Charles's law shows that the volume of a gas is

_____ to its

kelvin temperature at constant pressure.

b. **Predict** Suppose the gas in **Figure 4** could be cooled to 100 K (−173°C). Predict the volume of the gas at this temperature.

_____

got it? ···

○ **I get it!** Now I know that when the temperature of a gas is decreased at constant pressure _____

_____

○ **I need extra help with** _____

Go to my science ⓢ COACH online for help with this subject.

How Are Pressure and Volume of a Gas Related?

Suppose you use a bicycle pump to inflate a tire. By pressing down on the plunger, you force the gas inside the pump through the rubber tube and out of the nozzle into the tire. What happens to the volume of air inside the pump cylinder as you push down on the plunger? What happens to the pressure?

Boyle's Law In the 1600s, the scientist Robert Boyle carried out experiments to try to improve air pumps. He measured the volumes of gases at different pressures. Boyle's experiments showed that gas volume and pressure were related. **When the pressure of a gas at constant temperature is increased, the volume of the gas decreases. When the pressure is decreased, the volume increases.** This relationship between the pressure and the volume of a gas is called **Boyle's law.**

Boyle's law describes situations in which the volume of a gas is changed. The pressure then changes in the opposite way. For example, as you push down on the plunger of a bicycle pump, the volume of air inside the pump cylinder gets smaller, and the pressure inside the cylinder increases. The increase in pressure forces air into the tire.

Identify the Main Idea
Underline the main idea in the text under the red heading "Boyle's Law."

FIGURE 5 ··

▷ **INTERACTIVE ART** **Boyle's Law**

As weights are added to the top of each piston, the piston moves farther down in the cylinder. **Interpret Diagrams** First, rank the pressure in each of the cylinders. Then rank the volume. A ranking of 1 is the greatest. A ranking of 3 is the lowest.

 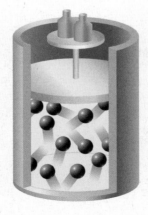 

1a. _____ pressure   1b. _____ pressure   1c. _____ pressure

2a. _____ volume   2b. _____ volume   2c. _____ volume

do the math! Analyzing Data

In an experiment, the volume of a gas was varied at a constant temperature. The pressure of the gas was recorded after each 50-mL change in volume. The data are in the table below.

1 Graph Use the data to make a line graph. Plot volume on the horizontal axis. Plot pressure on the vertical axis. Write a title for the graph at the top.

2 Control Variables The manipulated variable in this experiment is _____. The responding variable is _____.

3 Make Generalizations What happens to the pressure of a gas when the volume is decreased at a constant temperature?

_____

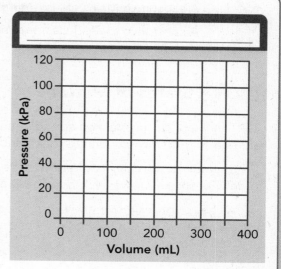

Volume (mL)	Pressure (kPa)
300	20
250	24
200	30
150	40
100	60
50	120

Graphing Boyle's Law Look at the graph that you made above. Notice that the points lie on a curve and not a straight line. The curve is steep at lower volumes, but it becomes less steep as volume increases. If you multiply the two variables at any point on the curve, you will find that the product does not change.

$$300 \text{ mL} \times 20 \text{ kPa} = 6{,}000 \text{ mL·kPa}$$
$$250 \text{ mL} \times 24 \text{ kPa} = 6{,}000 \text{ mL·kPa}$$

When the product of two variables is constant, the variables are **inversely proportional** to each other. The graph for Boyle's law shows that gas pressure is inversely proportional to volume at constant temperature.

Do the Quick Lab
It's a Gas.

🔑 Assess Your Understanding

2a. Identify The graph of Boyle's law shows that the gas pressure is

_____ to volume at constant temperature.

b. Read Graphs Use the graph that you made in Analyzing Data above to find the pressure of the gas when its volume is 125 mL.

_____

got it? ....

○ **I get it!** Now I know that when the pressure of a gas at a constant temperature is increased, _____

_____

○ **I need extra help with** _____

Go to MY SCIENCE ⓢ COACH online for help with this subject.

Study Guide

A substance (gains/loses) thermal energy when it melts or vaporizes.

A substance (gains/loses) thermal energy when it freezes or condenses.

LESSON 1 States of Matter

🔑 The fixed, closely packed arrangement of particles causes a solid to have a definite shape and volume.

🔑 Because its particles are free to move, a liquid has no definite shape. However, it does have a definite volume.

🔑 As gas particles move, they spread apart, filling all the space available. Thus, a gas has neither definite shape nor definite volume.

Vocabulary
• solid • crystalline solid • amorphous solid • liquid
• fluid • surface tension • viscosity • gas • pressure

LESSON 2 Changes of State

🔑 At a solid's melting point, its particles vibrate so fast that they break free from their fixed positions.

🔑 Vaporization occurs when the particles in a liquid gain enough thermal energy to move independently.

🔑 During sublimation, particles of a solid do not pass through the liquid state as they form a gas.

Vocabulary
• melting • melting point • freezing • vaporization • evaporation
• boiling • boiling point • condensation • sublimation

LESSON 3 The Behavior of Gases

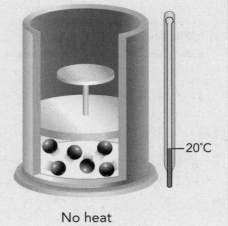

🔑 When the temperature of a gas at constant volume is increased, the pressure of the gas increases.

🔑 When the temperature of a gas at constant pressure is increased, its volume increases.

🔑 When the pressure of a gas at constant temperature is increased, the volume of the gas decreases.

Vocabulary
• Charles's law • directly proportional • Boyle's law
• inversely proportional

—20°C

No heat

Review and Assessment

LESSON 1 States of Matter

1. A substance with a definite shape and definite volume is a

a. solid   **b.** liquid

c. gas   **d.** fluid

2. Rubber is considered a(n) _____ solid because it does not melt at a distinct temperature.

3. Compare and Contrast Why do liquids and gases take the shape of their containers while solids do not?

_____

_____

_____

_____

_____

4. Predict What happens to the gas particles in an inflated ball when it gets a hole? Why?

_____

_____

_____

_____

_____

_____

5. math! Earth's atmosphere exerts a force of 124,500 N on a kitchen table with an area of 1.5 m². What is the pressure in pascals?

_____

_____

_____

6. Write About It Write a short essay in which you create an analogy to describe particle motion. Compare the movements and positions of people dancing with the motions of water molecules in liquid water and in water vapor.

LESSON 2 Changes of State

7. A puddle dries up by the process of

a. melting   **b.** freezing

c. condensation   **d.** evaporation

8. When you see fog or clouds, you are seeing water in the _____ state.

9. Classify Label the correct change of state on top of the arrows in the diagram below.

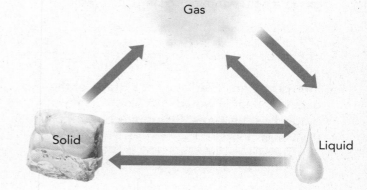

Gas

Solid

Liquid

10. Draw Conclusions At room temperature, table salt is a solid and mercury is a liquid. What conclusion can you draw about the melting points of these substances?

_____

_____

_____

_____

11. Apply Concepts When you open a solid room air freshener, the solid slowly loses mass and volume. How do you think this happens?

_____

_____

_____

_____

_____

_____

LESSON 3 The Behavior of Gases

12. According to Boyle's law, the volume of a gas increases when its

   a. pressure increases.   **b.** pressure decreases.

   c. temperature falls.   **d.** temperature rises.

13. According to Charles's law, when the temperature of a gas is increased at a constant pressure, its volume _____

14. Relate Cause and Effect How does heating a gas in a rigid container change its pressure?

_____

_____

15. Interpret Data Predict what a graph of the data in the table would look like. Volume is plotted on the *x*-axis. Pressure is plotted on the *y*-axis.

Volume (cm³)	Pressure (kPa)
15	222
21	159
31	108
50	67

_____

_____

_____

_____

_____

16. Relate Cause and Effect Explain why placing a dented table-tennis ball in boiling water is one way to remove the dent in the ball. (Assume the ball has no holes.)

_____

_____

_____

_____

APPLY THE BIG ? Why does a substance change states?

17. A fog forms over a lake. What two changes of state must occur to produce the fog? Do the water molecules absorb or release energy during these changes of state? What happens to the motion of the water molecules as a result?

_____

_____

_____

_____

_____

_____

_____

_____

_____

_____

_____

_____

_____

_____

_____

_____

_____

Standardized Test Prep

Multiple Choice

Circle the letter of the best answer.

1. The graph below shows changes in 1 g of a solid as energy is added.

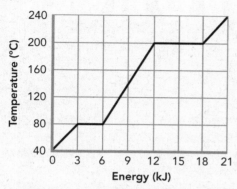

What is the total amount of energy absorbed by the substance as it completely changes from a solid at 40°C to a gas at 200°C?

A 3 kJ	**B** 6 kJ
C 12 kJ	**D** 18 kJ

2. Which of the following correctly describes a solid?

A The particles do not move at all.

B The particles are closely locked in position and can only vibrate in place.

C The particles are free to move about independently, colliding frequently.

D The particles are closely packed but have enough energy to slide past one another.

3. Which of the following changes of state is exothermic?

A freezing

B melting

C evaporation

D sublimation

4. A gas at constant temperature is in a cylinder with a movable piston. The piston is pushed into the cylinder, decreasing the volume of the gas. The pressure increases. What are the variables in this experiment?

A temperature and time

B time and volume

C volume and pressure

D pressure and temperature

5. A student is studying water. The sample has a definite volume, but no definite shape. Which state of matter is the student examining?

A gaseous water vapor

B a sublimed solid

C liquid water

D solid ice

Constructed Response

Use the diagrams to help you answer Question 6. Write your answer on a separate sheet of paper.

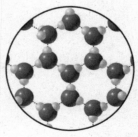 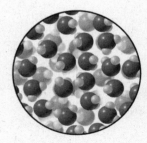

Before   After

6. The diagrams represent the molecules of water before and after a change of state. What change of state has occurred? Explain.

SCUBA DIVING

When you swim to the bottom of a pool, you can feel the pressure of the water around you. That pressure increases rapidly during a deeper dive.

To make really deep dives, people use SCUBA (self-contained underwater breathing apparatus) gear. The SCUBA tank is filled with air at very high pressure. Boyle's law states that as pressure increases under conditions of constant temperature, the volume of the gas decreases. In other words, more air will fit into the tank when the pressure is high.

Breathing air straight from the tank could damage the diver's lungs. The pressure of the air entering the diver's lungs needs to match the pressure of the gases already inside the diver's body. Valves on the tank adjust the pressure of the air as it is released to match the pressure of the water around the diver, so that when it enters the diver's body, it matches the pressure of the gases in the body.

Write About It Make an instruction card for new divers explaining that it is dangerous for divers to hold their breath during a deep dive or ascent. Use Boyle's law to explain why this is true.

◀ The regulator adjusts the pressure to match the surrounding water pressure.

A Shocking state

You touch a plasma globe, and lightning crackles. *Zap!* A plasma globe is a glass globe filled with partially ionized gas (that's the plasma!) and pumped full of high voltage power.

What's the Matter?

Plasma is different! In plasma, the electrons have been separated from the neutral atoms, so that they're no longer bound to an atom or molecule. Because positive and negative charges move independently, plasma can conduct electricity—causing the shocking light displays in a plasma globe. Plasma is its own state of matter. Like a gas, it has no shape or volume until it is captured in a container. Unlike a gas, it can form structures and layers, like the bolts in a plasma globe, or a bolt of lightning. It's shocking!

Find It Research and make a list of plasma objects. Compare your list with a partner, and discuss how plasma changes state to become a gas.

Growing Snow

You may have heard that no two snowflakes look the same. Writers use the unique structures of snowflakes as a metaphor for things that are one-of-a-kind, and impossible to reproduce. And it's probably true! A snowflake forms when water begins to freeze around small particles of dust inside a cloud. The exact shape of the crystal depends on humidity and temperature, and because there are tiny variations in both of these factors, each snowflake will differ slightly from every other snowflake.

All snowflakes share a common shape, though. The hexagonal shape of a snow crystal forms as molecules come together during the phase change from liquid to solid. The oxygen atom has a partial negative charge and the hydrogen atoms a partial positive charge, so the atoms are attracted to one another.

Graphing Research to find out how the exact shapes of snow crystals change as temperature and humidity change. Draw a line graph that illustrates your findings.

The most stable arrangement of water molecules occurs when six molecules form a ring.

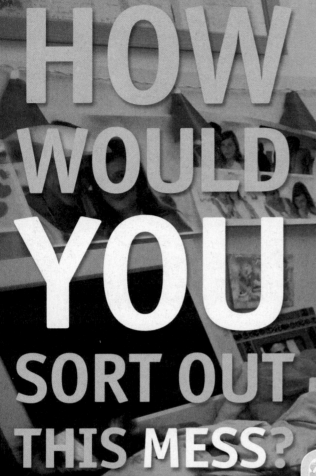

HOW WOULD YOU SORT OUT THIS MESS?

How is the periodic table organized?

Maybe you know someone with a messy room like this one. Imagine how difficult it would be to find things that you need. For example, what if you had misplaced your homework in this room? Where would you look for it? You might have to search for a long, long time! **Classify If this were your room, how would you organize the things inside it?**

_____

_____

_____

_____

_____

> UNTAMED SCIENCE Watch the **Untamed Science** video to learn more about organizing matter.

Elements and the Periodic Table

Check Your Understanding

1. **Background** Read the paragraph below and then answer the question.

> Katherine and her family are having a barbecue. They are burning charcoal in the grill to provide heat to cook their food. Charcoal is one form of the element carbon. As the charcoal burns, it reacts with oxygen molecules in the air. Each oxygen molecule contains two atoms.

- How can oxygen be both an element and a molecule?

_____

_____

> An **element** is a pure substance that cannot be broken down into any other substances by chemical or physical means.
>
> A **molecule** is a group of two or more atoms held together by chemical bonds.
>
> An **atom** is the basic particle from which all elements are made.

> **MY READING WEB** If you had trouble completing the question above, visit **My Reading Web** and type in *Elements and the Periodic Table.*

Vocabulary Skill

Greek Word Origins Many science words in English come from Greek. For example, the word *autograph* comes from the Greek words *auto*, meaning "self," and *graph*, meaning "written." An *autograph* is one's name written in one's own handwriting. Look at the Greek origins and their meanings below.

Greek Origin	Meaning	Key Words
atomos	Cannot be cut, indivisible	Atom, atomic number, atomic mass
di	Two, double	Diatomic molecule

2. **Quick Check** Predict the meaning of *diatomic molecule.*

_____

_____

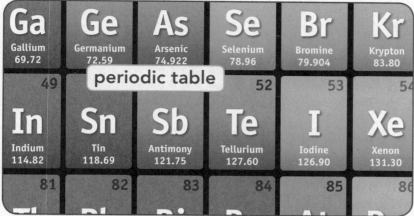

Ga	Ge	As	Se	Br	Kr
Gallium 69.72	Germanium 72.59	Arsenic 74.922	Selenium 78.96	Bromine 79.904	Krypton 83.80

periodic table

49			52	53	54
In	Sn	Sb	Te	I	Xe
Indium 114.82	Tin 118.69	Antimony 121.75	Tellurium 127.60	Iodine 126.90	Xenon 131.30
81	82	83	84	85	86

corrosion

semiconductor

noble gas

Chapter Preview

LESSON 1

- atom • electron • nucleus
- proton • energy level
- neutron • atomic number
- isotope • mass number

↻ **Compare and Contrast**
△ **Make Models**

LESSON 2

- atomic mass • periodic table
- chemical symbol • period
- group

↻ **Relate Text and Visuals**
△ **Predict**

LESSON 3

- metal • luster • malleable
- ductile • thermal conductivity
- electrical conductivity • reactivity
- corrosion • alkali metal
- alkaline earth metal
- transition metal

↻ **Ask Questions**
△ **Infer**

LESSON 4

- nonmetal • diatomic molecule
- halogen • noble gas • metalloid
- semiconductor

↻ **Summarize**
△ **Classify**

LESSON 5

- radioactive decay
- nuclear reaction • radioactivity
- alpha particle • beta particle
- gamma ray • half-life
- radioactive dating • tracer

↻ **Relate Cause and Effect**
△ **Calculate**

> VOCAB FLASH CARDS For extra help with vocabulary, visit **Vocab Flash Cards** and type in *Elements and the Periodic Table.*

Introduction to Atoms

🔑 **How Did Atomic Theory Develop?**

🔑 **What Is the Modern Model of the Atom?**

my pLANeT DiaRY

Nanowhiskers

What's more than 16,000 times thinner than a human hair, and, when added to fabric, able to repel spills, stains, and the smell of the sweatiest of socks? It's a nanowhisker!

Nanowhiskers are tiny threads that measure about 10 nanometers (nm) in length and 1.5 nanometers in diameter (1 nm equals 0.000000001 m). They are often made of carbon or silver atoms. Scientists have found a way to bond nanowhiskers to individual threads of cloth. The nanowhiskers are so small and so close together that they form a barrier that prevents substances from ever touching the fabric. Nanowhiskers made from silver can even kill bacteria on your feet and stop socks from smelling!

Communicate Write your answer to each question below. Then discuss your answers with a partner.

1. Why are nanowhiskers used to repel stains on fabrics?

_____

_____

_____

_____

_____

_____

2. What uses for nanowhiskers can you imagine?

_____

_____

▶ PLANET DIARY Go to **Planet Diary** to learn more about atomic structure.

Lab zone® Do the Inquiry Warm-Up *What's in the Box?*

Vocabulary
- atom • electron • nucleus • proton • energy level
- neutron • atomic number • isotope • mass number

Skills
- Reading: Compare and Contrast
- Inquiry: Make Models

How Did Atomic Theory Develop?

If you could see a single atom, what would it look like? Studying atoms is difficult because atoms are so small. The smallest visible speck of dust may contain 10 million billion atoms! Scientists have created models to describe atoms because they are so small. Models of the atom have changed many times.

Around 430 B.C., the Greek philosopher Democritus proposed that matter was formed of small pieces that could not be cut into smaller parts. He used the word *atomos*, meaning "uncuttable," for these smallest possible pieces. In modern terms, an **atom** is the smallest particle that still can be considered an element.

The idea of atoms began to develop again in the 1600s. As people did experiments, atomic theory began to take shape. 🔑 **Atomic theory grew as a series of models that developed from experimental evidence. As more evidence was collected, the theory and models were revised.**

Dalton's Atomic Theory Using evidence from many experiments, John Dalton, an English chemist, inferred that atoms had certain characteristics. Dalton thought that atoms were like smooth, hard balls that could not be broken into smaller pieces. The main ideas of Dalton's theory are summarized in **Figure 1**.

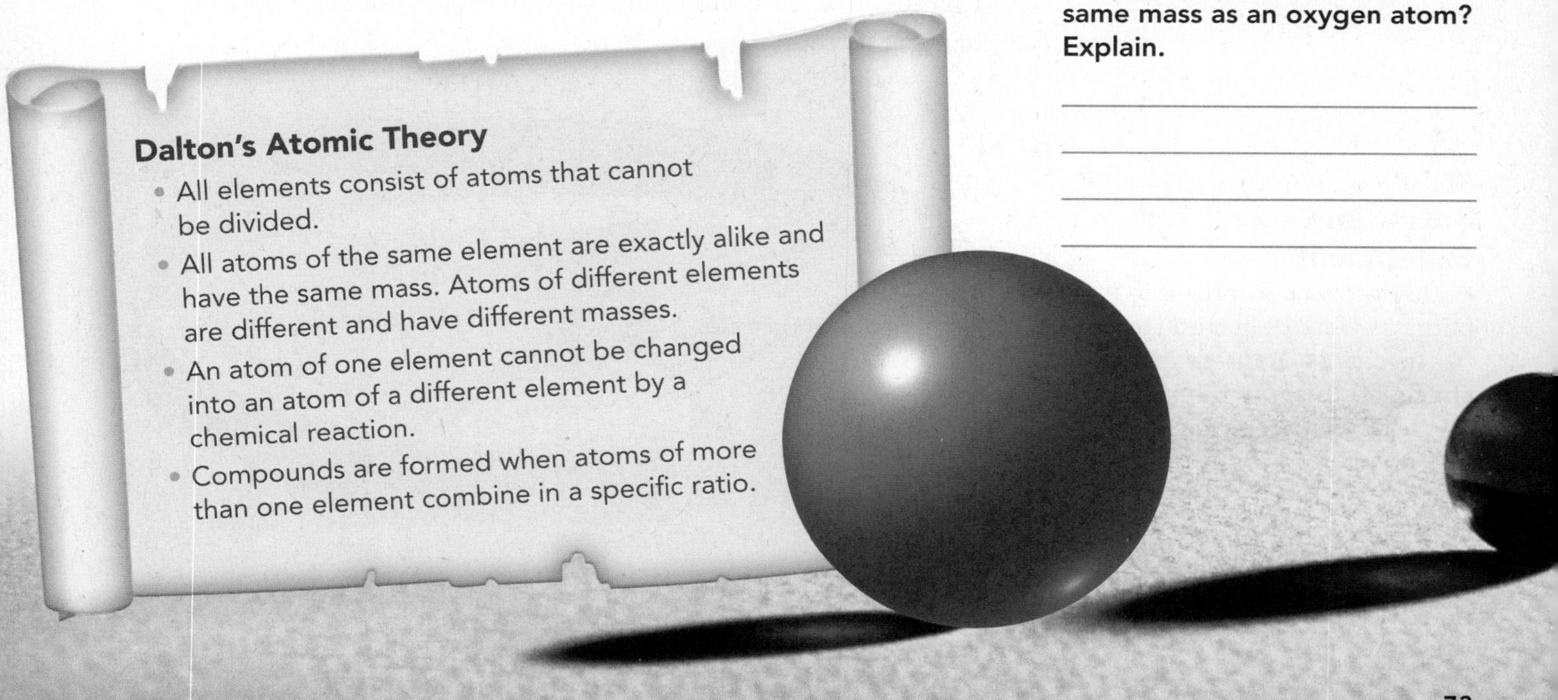

FIGURE 1 ·······························
Dalton's Model
Dalton thought that atoms were smooth, hard balls.

✏️ **Predict Read the summary of Dalton's theory. Based on this theory, would you expect a carbon atom to have the same mass as an oxygen atom? Explain.**

_____

_____

_____

_____

Dalton's Atomic Theory
- All elements consist of atoms that cannot be divided.
- All atoms of the same element are exactly alike and have the same mass. Atoms of different elements are different and have different masses.
- An atom of one element cannot be changed into an atom of a different element by a chemical reaction.
- Compounds are formed when atoms of more than one element combine in a specific ratio.

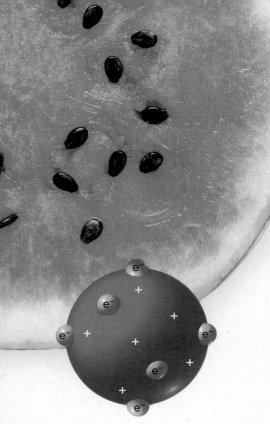

Thomson's Model
Dalton's atomic theory has some similarities to today's models, but there are many differences. One important change is that atoms are now known to be made of even smaller parts. In 1897, J.J. Thomson discovered that atoms contain negatively charged particles called **electrons.** Yet scientists knew that atoms themselves had no electrical charge. So Thomson reasoned that atoms must also contain some sort of positive charge. This positive charge must balance the negative charge of the electrons.

Thomson proposed a model like the one shown in **Figure 2.** He described an atom that had electrons scattered throughout a ball of positive charge—something like seeds in a watermelon.

Rutherford's Model
In 1911, one of Thomson's former students, Ernest Rutherford, found evidence that challenged Thomson's model. Rutherford's research team aimed a beam of positively charged particles at a thin sheet of gold foil. A diagram of the experiment is shown in **Figure 3.** Rutherford and his team predicted that, if Thomson's model were correct, the charged particles would pass straight through the foil. They also predicted that the paths of some particles would bend, or deflect, slightly. The particles would be only slightly deflected because the positive charge was thought to be spread out in the gold atoms.

Rutherford observed that most of the particles passed straight through the foil with little or no deflection. But to everyone's surprise, a few particles were deflected by the gold foil at very large angles. Based on the results of his experiment, Rutherford suggested that the atom is mostly empty space but has a positive charge at its center.

FIGURE 2 ·····················
Thomson's Model
Thomson suggested that atoms had negatively charged electrons set in a positive sphere. Each electron is represented above by the symbol e⁻.

FIGURE 3 ·····················
Rutherford's Gold Foil Experiment
Rutherford was surprised that a few particles were deflected strongly.
✎ **Interpret Diagrams** Place a check (✔) to show the paths of the particles that were not predicted by Thomson's atomic model.

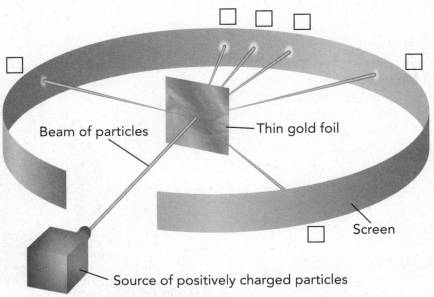

Beam of particles — Thin gold foil

Screen

Source of positively charged particles

Like charges repel each other. So Rutherford inferred that an atom's positive charge must be packed within a small region in its center, called the **nucleus** (NOO klee us). (The plural of *nucleus* is *nuclei*.) Any particle that was deflected strongly had been repelled by a gold atom's nucleus. Rutherford's new model of the atom, which is shown in **Figure 4,** is like a cherry. The pit models the nucleus of the atom. The rest of the fruit is the space taken up by the electrons. Later research suggested that the nucleus was made up of one or more positively charged particles. Rutherford called the positively charged particles in an atom's nucleus **protons.**

FIGURE 4 ······
Rutherford's Model
According to Rutherford's model, an atom was mostly open space. The "6+" in the model means that there are six protons in the nucleus.

apply it!

Use the diagrams below to compare the expected and observed results of Rutherford's gold foil experiment. Part **a** shows the expected paths of the charged particles through the atoms of the gold foil. In part **b**, draw the observed paths of the charged particles. Show at least one particle that is deflected strongly.

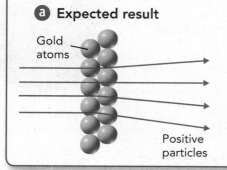

a Expected result

Gold atoms

Positive particles

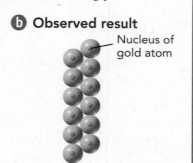

b Observed result

Nucleus of gold atom

Bohr's Model One of Rutherford's students was Niels Bohr, a Danish scientist. In 1913, Bohr revised the atomic model again. Bohr suggested that electrons are found only in specific orbits around the nucleus. The orbits in Bohr's model look like planets orbiting the sun or the rings of a tree, as shown in **Figure 5.** Each possible electron orbit in Bohr's model has a fixed energy.

FIGURE 5 ······
Bohr's Model
Niels Bohr suggested that electrons move in specific orbits around the nucleus of an atom.

75

Cloud Model

Cloud Model In the 1920s, the atomic model changed again. Scientists determined that electrons do not orbit the nucleus like planets, as Bohr suggested. Instead, electrons move rapidly within a cloudlike region around the nucleus. Look at **Figure 6.** The orange "cloud" is a visual model. It represents where electrons are likely to be found. An electron's movement is related to its **energy level,** or the specific amount of energy it has. Electrons at different energy levels are likely to be found in different places.

6+

6e⁻

FIGURE 6 ·····················
Cloud Model
Electrons move rapidly in different directions around the nucleus.

apply it!

Scientists have used models to help them understand atoms. You can too!

❶ **Make Models** Match each object with the atomic model the object most closely represents.

❷ **CHALLENGE** An object is missing for one of the atomic models listed. In the space provided, draw an object that represents this model.

Dalton's Model

Thomson's Model

Bohr's Model

Cloud Model

 Do the Quick Lab
Visualizing an Electron Cloud.

🔑 Assess Your Understanding

1a. Define An atom is _____
_____ .

b. Describe Bohr's model of the atom consisted

of a central _____ surrounded by

electrons moving in specific _____ .

c. 🔄 **Compare and Contrast** How is the cloud model of the atom different from Bohr's model?

_____
_____
_____
_____
_____

got it?···

○ **I get it!** Now I know that atomic theory changed with time because _____
_____

○ **I need extra help with** _____

Go to MY SCIENCE ⓢ COACH *online for help with this subject.*

What Is the Modern Model of the Atom?

In 1932, English scientist James Chadwick showed that another particle exists in the nucleus of atoms. This particle, called a **neutron,** was hard to find because it has no electric charge.

Scientists have learned more about the atom since then. One modern model of the atom is shown in **Figure 7.** 🔑 **At the center of the atom is a tiny, dense nucleus containing protons and neutrons. Surrounding the nucleus is a cloudlike region of moving electrons.**

Most of an atom's volume is the space in which the electrons move. This space is huge compared to the space taken up by the nucleus. Imagine holding a pencil while standing in the middle of a stadium. If the nucleus were the size of the pencil's eraser, the electrons would reach as far away as the top row of seats!

New research supports the modern model of the atom. However, scientists still don't know the details of the smallest scales of matter. Who will develop the next model of the atom? Maybe it will be you!

FIGURE 7 ·····················
Modern Model of an Atom
A carbon atom has a nucleus made up of positively charged protons and neutral neutrons. The nucleus is surrounded by a cloud of negatively charged electrons.
✏️ **Identify How many protons are in the carbon atom?**

_____

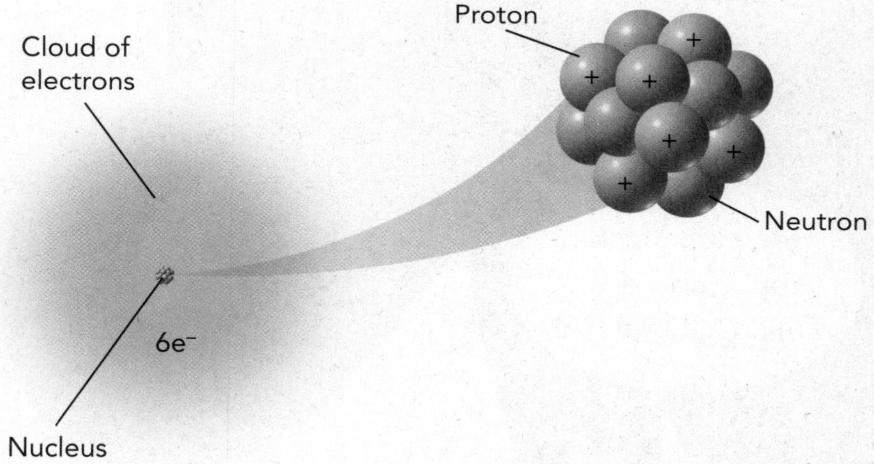

Cloud of electrons

Proton

Neutron

$6e^-$

Nucleus

Particle Charges In **Figure 7,** protons are shown by a plus sign ($+$). Electrons are shown by the symbol e^-. According to the scale used for measuring charge in atoms, protons have a charge of $+1$. Electrons have exactly the opposite charge. So electrons have a charge of -1. If you count the number of protons in **Figure 7,** you'll see there are six. The number of protons equals the number of electrons. As a result, the positive charge from the protons equals the negative charge from the electrons. The charges balance, making the atom neutral. Neutrons don't affect the charge of an atom because they have a charge of zero.

✏️ **Compare and Contrast**
A proton has a charge of _____.
An electron has a charge of _____.
A neutron has a charge of _____.

Comparing Particle Masses Although electrons may balance protons charge for charge, they can't compare when it comes to mass. It takes almost 1,840 electrons to equal the mass of one proton. A proton and a neutron are about equal in mass. Together, the protons and neutrons make up almost all the mass of an atom.

Figure 8 compares the charges and masses of the three atomic particles. Atoms are too small to be described by everyday units of mass, such as grams or kilograms. Sometimes scientists use units known as atomic mass units (amu). A proton or a neutron has a mass equal to about one amu.

Atomic Number Every atom of an element has the same number of protons. For example, every carbon atom has 6 protons and every iron atom has 26 protons. The number of protons in the nucleus of an atom is the **atomic number** of that atom's element. The definition of an element is based on its atomic number. Carbon's atomic number is 6 and iron's is 26.

Hey, pipsqueak... You're only 4 kg. I'm 8,000 kg! HA!

Relative to an elephant, I'm about the same mass as an electron is relative to a proton. Meow!

FIGURE 8 ·······························

> INTERACTIVE ART **Particles in an Atom**
An atom is made up of protons, neutrons, and electrons.

✎ **Review Complete the table by filling in the correct charge for each atomic particle.**

Particles in an Atom

Particle	Symbol	Charge	Mass (amu)	Model
Proton	p⁺	_____	1	●
Neutron	n	_____	1	●
Electron	e⁻	_____	$\frac{1}{1{,}840}$	●

Isotopes All atoms of an element have the same number of protons. The number of neutrons can vary. Atoms with the same number of protons and different numbers of neutrons are called **isotopes** (EYE suh tohps). **Figure 9** shows three isotopes of carbon.

An isotope is identified by its **mass number,** which is the sum of the protons and neutrons in the atom. The most common isotope of carbon has a mass number of 12 (6 protons + 6 neutrons) and may be written as "carbon-12." About 99 percent of naturally occurring carbon is carbon-12. Two other isotopes are carbon-13 and carbon-14. Despite their different mass numbers, all three carbon isotopes react the same way chemically.

FIGURE 9 ⋯⋯⋯⋯⋯⋯⋯⋯⋯⋯
Isotopes of Carbon
All isotopes of carbon contain 6 protons. They differ in the number of neutrons.
✏️ **Relate Text and Visuals** Fill in the missing information for each isotope below.

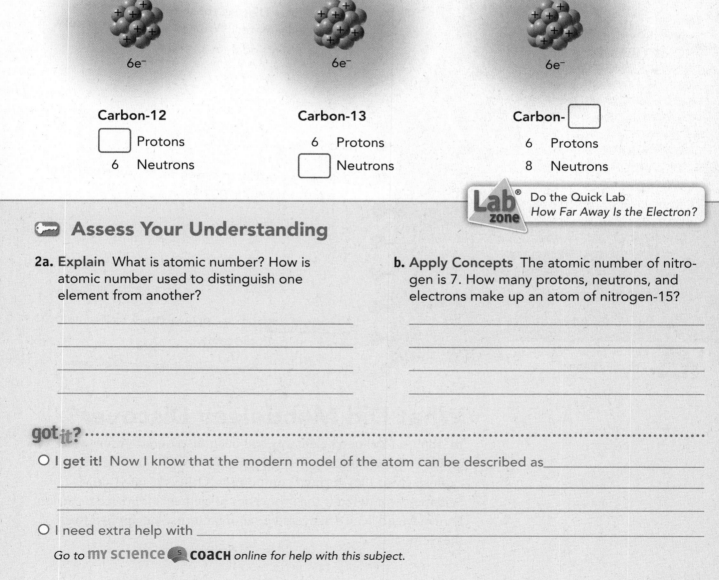

6e⁻

Carbon-12
⬚ Protons
6 Neutrons

6e⁻

Carbon-13
6 Protons
⬚ Neutrons

6e⁻

Carbon-⬚
6 Protons
8 Neutrons

Lab zone® Do the Quick Lab
How Far Away Is the Electron?

🔑 **Assess Your Understanding**

2a. Explain What is atomic number? How is atomic number used to distinguish one element from another?

_____

_____

_____

_____

b. Apply Concepts The atomic number of nitrogen is 7. How many protons, neutrons, and electrons make up an atom of nitrogen-15?

_____

_____

_____

_____

got it? ⋯⋯⋯⋯⋯⋯⋯⋯⋯⋯⋯⋯⋯⋯⋯⋯⋯⋯⋯⋯⋯⋯⋯⋯⋯⋯⋯⋯

○ **I get it!** Now I know that the modern model of the atom can be described as_____

_____

○ **I need extra help with** _____

Go to MY SCIENCE ⓢ COACH online for help with this subject.

2 Organizing the Elements

UNLOCK THE BIG Q?

🔑 **What Did Mendeleev Discover?**

🔑 **What Information Does the Periodic Table Contain?**

🔑 **How Is the Periodic Table Useful?**

MY PLANET DIARY

VOICES FROM HISTORY

Dmitri Mendeleev

The Russian chemist Dmitri Mendeleev (men duh LAY ef) is given credit for creating the first version of the periodic table in 1869. By arranging the elements according to their atomic masses, he predicted that new elements would be discovered:

> We must expect the discovery of many yet unknown elements—for example, elements analogous [similar] to aluminum and silicon—whose atomic weight [mass] would be between 65 and 75.

Within 17 years, chemists had discovered these missing elements.

Communicate Discuss these questions with a group of classmates. Write your answers below.

1. What did Mendeleev predict?

_____

_____

_____

_____

2. Make a prediction based on an observation or a pattern you recognize.

_____

_____

_____

_____

> **PLANET DIARY** Go to **Planet Diary** to learn more about the periodic table.

Lab zone® Do the Inquiry Warm-Up *Which Is Easier?*

What Did Mendeleev Discover?

By 1869, a total of 63 elements had been discovered. A few were gases. Two were liquids. Most were solid metals. Some reacted explosively as they formed compounds. Others reacted slowly. Scientists wondered if the properties of elements followed a pattern. Dmitri Mendeleev discovered a set of patterns that applied to all the elements.

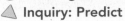
Vocabulary

- atomic mass • periodic table
- chemical symbol • period
- group

Skills

⟳ **Reading:** Relate Text and Visuals

△ **Inquiry:** Predict

Mendeleev's Work Mendeleev knew that some elements had similar chemical and physical properties. For example, silver and copper are both shiny metals. Mendeleev thought these similarities were important clues to a hidden pattern.

To find that pattern, Mendeleev wrote each element's melting point, density, and color on an individual card. He also included the element's atomic mass. The **atomic mass** of an element is the average mass of all the isotopes of that element. Mendeleev tried arranging the cards in different ways.

⬤━ Mendeleev noticed that a pattern of properties appeared when he arranged the elements in order of increasing atomic mass. He found that the properties repeated regularly. For example, lithium, sodium, and potassium showed several common properties. As you can see from **Figure 1,** these elements react with water in a similar way. (The letters *amu* mean "atomic mass units.") Mendeleev lined up the cards for these elements to form their own group. He did the same with other elements that shared similar properties.

FIGURE 1 ·····························

Metals That React With Water

Lithium, sodium, and potassium all react with water.

✎ **Observe** Write down your observations of each reaction.

Lithium
Atomic mass = 7 amu

_____
_____
_____

Sodium
Atomic mass = 23 amu

_____
_____
_____

Potassium
Atomic mass = 39 amu

_____
_____
_____

Relate Text and Visuals

Using **Figure 2**, predict an element that would react with water as lithium (Li), sodium (Na), and potassium (K) did. Explain.

_____

_____

_____

_____

_____

The Periodic Table Mendeleev created the first periodic table in 1869. A **periodic table** is an arrangement of elements showing the repeating pattern of their properties. (The word *periodic* means "in a regular, repeated pattern.") The periodic table shown in **Figure 2** was an improved version published in 1871.

As scientists discovered new elements and learned more about atomic structure, the periodic table changed. It is now known that the number of protons in the nucleus, given by the atomic number, determines the chemical properties of an element. Modern periodic tables are arranged in order of increasing atomic number.

Group I	Group II	Group III	Group IV	Group V	Group VI	Group VII	Group VIII
H = 1							
Li = 7	Be = 9.4	B = 11	C = 12	N = 14	O = 16	F = 19	
Na = 23 K = 39	Mg = 24 Ca = 40	Al = 27.3 — = 44	Si = 28 Ti = 48	P = 31 V = 51	S = 32 Cr = 52	Cl = 35.5 Mn = 55	Fe = 56, Co = 59, Ni = 59, Cu = 63.
(Cu = 63) Rb = 85	Zn = 65 Sr = 87	— = 68 Yt = 88	— = 72 Zr = 90	As = 75 Nb = 94	Se = 78 Mo = 96	Br = 80 — = 100	
(Ag = 108) Cs = 133	Cd = 112 Ba = 137	In = 113 Di = 138	Sn = 118 Ce = 140	Sb = 122 —	Te = 125 —	I = 127 —	Ru = 104, Rh = 104, Pd = 106, Ag = 108.
— (—)	(—) —	— Er = 178	— La = 180	— Ta = 182	— W = 184	— —	— — — — Os = 195, Ir = 197,
(Au = 199) —	Hg = 200 —	Tl = 204 —	Pb = 207 Th = 231	Bi = 208 —	U = 240		Pt = 198, Au = 199.

FIGURE 2
Mendeleev's Periodic Table
In his periodic table, Mendeleev left blank spaces. He predicted that the blank spaces would be filled by elements that had not yet been discovered. He even correctly predicted the properties of those new elements.

Lab zone® Do the Quick Lab
Classifying.

Assess Your Understanding

1a. Review In what order did Mendeleev arrange the elements in his periodic table?

_____

_____

b. Predict How could Mendeleev predict the properties of elements that had not yet been discovered?

_____

_____

got it? ·

O **I get it!** Now I know that when Mendeleev arranged the elements in order of increasing atomic mass, _____

_____

_____

O **I need extra help with** _____

Go to **MY SCIENCE**ⓢ **COACH** *online for help with this subject.*

What Information Does the Periodic Table Contain?

The periodic table contains information about each of the known elements. 🔑 **In this book, the periodic table includes the atomic number, chemical symbol, name, and atomic mass for each element.** The information that the periodic table lists about potassium is shown below in **Figure 3**.

❶ Atomic Number The first piece of information is the number 19, the atomic number of potassium. Every potassium atom has 19 protons in its nucleus.

❷ Chemical Symbol Just below the atomic number is the letter K—the **chemical symbol** for potassium. Chemical symbols contain either one or two letters. Often, an element's symbol is an abbreviation of the element's name in English. Other elements have symbols that are abbreviations of their Latin names.

❸ Atomic Mass The last piece of information is the average atomic mass. For potassium, this value is 39.098 amu (atomic mass units). The atomic mass is an average because most elements consist of a mixture of isotopes.

The modern periodic table is shown in **Figure 4** on the next two pages. Can you find potassium?

FIGURE 3 ·······························

Potassium
Potassium has an atomic number of 19 and an atomic mass of 39.098 amu. Bananas are rich in potassium.

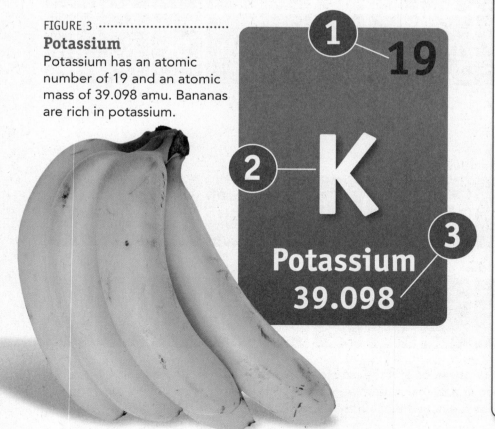

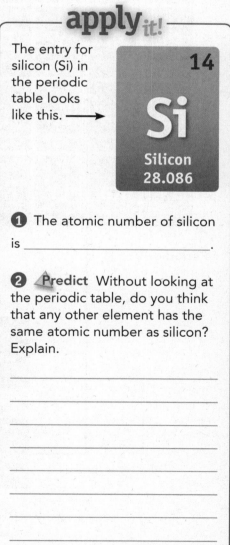

apply it!

The entry for silicon (Si) in the periodic table looks like this. →

❶ The atomic number of silicon is _____.

❷ ⚠ **Predict** Without looking at the periodic table, do you think that any other element has the same atomic number as silicon? Explain.

_____
_____
_____
_____
_____
_____
_____

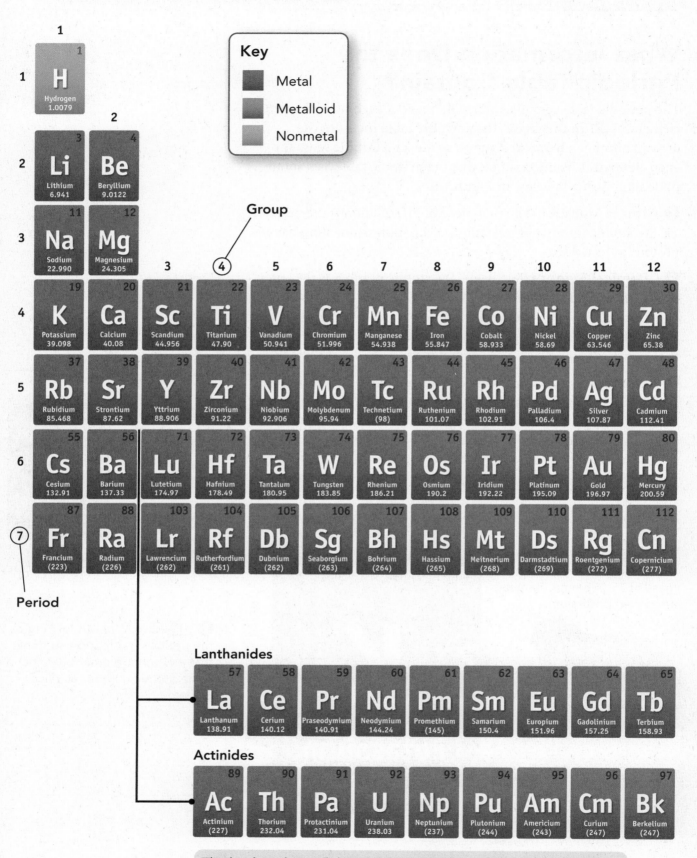

Key
■ Metal
■ Metalloid
■ Nonmetal

Group

Period

The lanthanides and the actinides are placed off the table to save space and to make the rest of the table easier to read. Follow the line to see how they fit in the table.

Many periodic tables include a zigzag line that separates the metals from the nonmetals. Metalloids, found on either side of the line, share properties of both metals and nonmetals.

13	14	15	16	17	18
					2 **He** Helium 4.0026
5 **B** Boron 10.81	6 **C** Carbon 12.011	7 **N** Nitrogen 14.007	8 **O** Oxygen 15.999	9 **F** Fluorine 18.998	10 **Ne** Neon 20.179
13 **Al** Aluminum 26.982	14 **Si** Silicon 28.086	15 **P** Phosphorus 30.974	16 **S** Sulfur 32.06	17 **Cl** Chlorine 35.453	18 **Ar** Argon 39.948
31 **Ga** Gallium 69.72	32 **Ge** Germanium 72.59	33 **As** Arsenic 74.922	34 **Se** Selenium 78.96	35 **Br** Bromine 79.904	36 **Kr** Krypton 83.80
49 **In** Indium 114.82	50 **Sn** Tin 118.69	51 **Sb** Antimony 121.75	52 **Te** Tellurium 127.60	53 **I** Iodine 126.90	54 **Xe** Xenon 131.30
81 **Tl** Thallium 204.37	82 **Pb** Lead 207.2	83 **Bi** Bismuth 208.98	84 **Po** Polonium (209)	85 **At** Astatine (210)	86 **Rn** Radon (222)
113 **Nh** Nihonium (284)	114 **Fl** Flerovium (289)	115 **Mc** Moscovium (288)	116 **Lv** Livermorium (292)	117 **Ts** Tennessine (294)	118 **Og** Oganesson (294)

Atomic masses in parentheses are those of the most stable isotopes.

66 **Dy** Dysprosium 162.50	67 **Ho** Holmium 164.93	68 **Er** Erbium 167.26	69 **Tm** Thulium 168.93	70 **Yb** Ytterbium 173.04
98 **Cf** Californium (251)	99 **Es** Einsteinium (252)	100 **Fm** Fermium (257)	101 **Md** Mendelevium (258)	102 **No** Nobelium (259)

FIGURE 4 ·······························

> INTERACTIVE ART **The Periodic Table**

The periodic table is one of the most valuable tools to a chemist. ✎ **Interpret Tables** Find the element identified by the atomic number 25 on the periodic table. Use the information to fill in the blanks below.

Name of element: _____

Chemical symbol: _____

Atomic mass: _____

Lab zone® Do the Quick Lab
Using the Periodic Table.

🔑 **Assess Your Understanding**

2a. Compare and Contrast Describe two differences between Mendeleev's periodic table and the modern periodic table.

_____
_____
_____
_____
_____
_____

b. Interpret Tables An atom of which element has 47 protons in its nucleus?

_____

got it? ··············

○ **I get it!** Now I know that information found in the periodic table for each element includes _____
_____
_____

○ **I need extra help with** _____

Go to **MY SCIENCE** Ⓢ **COACH** *online for help with this subject.*

How Is the Periodic Table Useful?

Look at the periodic table on the previous two pages. Notice that the atomic numbers increase from left to right. Also notice that each color-coded region corresponds to a different class of elements—metals, nonmetals, and metalloids.

As you look across a row, the elements' properties change in a predictable way. 🔑 **An element's properties can be predicted from its location in the periodic table.** This predictability is the reason that the periodic table is so useful to chemists.

Periods

The periodic table is arranged in rows called **periods.** A period contains a series of different elements. From left to right, the properties of the elements change in a pattern. Metals are shown on the left of the table and nonmetals are located on the right. Metalloids are found between the metals and nonmetals. This pattern is repeated in each period. **Figure 5** shows the elements of Period 3.

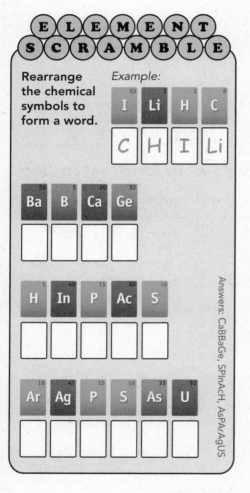

ELEMENT SCRAMBLE

Rearrange the chemical symbols to form a word.

Example:

| ⁵³I | ³Li | ¹H | ⁶C |

| C | H | I | Li |

| ⁵⁶Ba | ⁵B | ²⁰Ca | ³²Ge |

| ¹H | ⁴⁹In | ¹⁵P | ⁸⁹Ac | ¹⁶S |

| ¹⁸Ar | ⁴⁷Ag | ¹⁵P | ¹⁶S | ³³As | ⁹²U |

Answers: CaBBaGe, SPInAcH, AsPArAgUS

FIGURE 5 ·····························

Elements of Period 3

The properties of the Period 3 elements change as you move across the period.

✏️ **Classify** Use three different colors to fill in the key below. Then color in each element in Period 3 according to your key.

11	12	13	14	15	16	17	18
Na	Mg	Al	Si	P	S	Cl	Ar
Sodium 22.990	Magnesium 24.305	Aluminum 26.982	Silicon 28.086	Phosphorus 30.974	Sulfur 32.06	Chlorine 35.453	Argon 39.948

Key

☐ Metal

☐ Metalloid

☐ Nonmetal

Groups

Groups The modern periodic table has 7 periods, which form 18 columns. The elements in a column form a **group.** Groups are also known as families. The groups are numbered from Group 1 on the left of the table to Group 18 on the right.

The pattern of properties repeats in each period, so the elements in each group have similar characteristics. For example, except for hydrogen, the elements in Group 1 are all metals that react violently with water. Group 17 elements are very reactive, but Group 18 elements are generally nonreactive. The elements of Group 10 are shown in **Figure 6.**

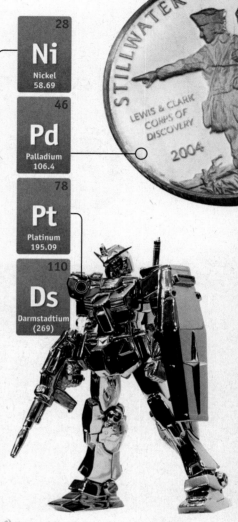

| 28 |
| Ni |
| Nickel |
| 58.69 |

| 46 |
| Pd |
| Palladium |
| 106.4 |

| 78 |
| Pt |
| Platinum |
| 195.09 |

| 110 |
| Ds |
| Darmstadtium |
| (269) |

FIGURE 6 ·····························

Elements of Group 10
The elements of Group 10 include nickel (Ni), palladium (Pd), platinum (Pt), and darmstadtium (Ds). Darmstadtium is not found in nature, but scientists believe it exhibits properties similar to the other Group 10 metals.

✎ CHALLENGE Look at the photos of nickel, palladium, and platinum. What properties would you predict for darmstadtium?

_____

_____

Lab zone® Do the Quick Lab
Expanding the Periodic Table.

🔑 Assess Your Understanding

3a. Name The rows in the periodic table are

called _____. The columns in the

periodic table are called _____.

b. Describe What do elements in the same group in the periodic table have in common?

_____

_____

c. Predict Use the periodic table to name two elements that you would expect to have properties very much like those of calcium (Ca).

_____

_____

_____

_____

got it? ···

○ **I get it!** Now I know that the periodic table is useful because _____

_____

○ **I need extra help with** _____

Go to MY SCIENCE ⑤ COACH *online for help with this subject.*

UNLOCK
THE BIG
?

🔑 **What Are the Properties of Metals?**

🔑 **How Are Metals Classified?**

my PLaneT DiaRY

Recycling Metals

You can find metals in many items that you use every day, including cell phones, computers, appliances, and money. In 2006, the supply of metal in the United States was more than 150 million metric tons. (One metric ton equals 1,000 kilograms.) Many of these metals can be recycled. Recycling helps conserve energy and reduces the amount of waste in landfills.

Metal	Percent of U.S. Supply That Came From Recycling
Aluminum	43
Copper	32.3
Iron and steel	48
Nickel	43
Zinc	24.5

SCIENCE STATS

Communicate Answer the question below. Then discuss your answer with a partner.

Beverage cans contain mostly aluminum. Estimate the percent of beverage cans that you recycle. What other objects that contain metal do you think can be recycled?

_____

_____

_____

_____

> PLANET DIARY   Go to **Planet Diary** to learn more about recycling.

Lab ® Do the Inquiry Warm-Up
zone *Why Use Aluminum?*

Vocabulary

- metal • luster • malleable • ductile • thermal conductivity
- electrical conductivity • reactivity • corrosion • alkali metal
- alkaline earth metal • transition metal

Skills

↻ Reading: Ask Questions
△ Inquiry: Infer

What Are the Properties of Metals?

It's hard to imagine modern life without metals. The cars and buses you ride in are made of steel, which is mostly iron (Fe). Airplanes are covered in aluminum (Al). Copper (Cu) wires carry electric current to lamps, stereos, and computers. Can you identify the objects that contain metals in **Figure 1** below?

Elements can be classified by their properties, including melting temperature, density, hardness, and thermal and electrical conductivity. **Metals** are elements that are good conductors of electric current and heat. They also tend to be shiny and bendable—like copper wire, for instance. The majority of elements in the periodic table are metals. The metals begin on the left side and extend across the periodic table.

FIGURE 1 ·······························

Metals

Many of the objects around you contain metals.

✎ **Communicate** Circle the objects that will set off the metal detector. Then, with a partner, look around your classroom and make a list of the objects you see that contain metals.

_____

_____

_____

This stone, called magnetite, is made out of a compound of iron.

_____

_____

Gold can be pounded into coins.

_____

_____

Copper is often used for electrical wires.

_____

_____

FIGURE 2 ··

Physical Properties of Metals

Metals have certain physical properties.

✎ **Interpret Photos** After reading about the physical properties of metals below, identify the property or properties of metals exhibited by each of the objects above.

Physical Properties **Figure 2** shows some common metal objects. 🔗 **The physical properties of metals include luster, malleability, ductility, and conductivity.** A material that has a high **luster** is shiny and reflective. A **malleable** (MAL ee uh bul) material is one that can be hammered or rolled into flat sheets or other shapes. A **ductile** material is one that can be pulled out, or drawn, into long wires. Copper is both malleable and ductile. It can be made into thin sheets or drawn into wires.

Thermal conductivity is the ability of an object to transfer heat. The ability of an object to carry electric current is called **electrical conductivity.** Most metals are good thermal conductors and electrical conductors. Metals also generally have low specific heats. Recall that specific heat is the amount of energy required to raise the temperature of 1 gram of a material by 1 kelvin. This means that only a small amount of thermal energy is required to raise the temperature of a metal.

Some metals are magnetic. Iron, cobalt (Co), and nickel (Ni) are attracted to magnets and can be made into magnets. Most metals are solids at room temperature. Only mercury (Hg) is a liquid at room temperature.

Chemical Properties

The ease and speed with which an element combines, or reacts, with other substances is called its **reactivity.** Metals usually react by losing electrons to other atoms. Some metals are very reactive. For example, sodium (Na) reacts strongly with water. By comparison, gold (Au) and platinum (Pt) do not react easily with other substances.

The reactivities of other metals fall somewhere between those of sodium and gold. Iron, for example, reacts slowly with oxygen in the air, forming iron oxide, or rust. The iron chain in **Figure 3** is coated with reddish brown rust. The deterioration of a metal due to a chemical reaction in the environment is called **corrosion.**

FIGURE 3 ······················
Reactivity of Metals
This iron chain is coated with rust after being exposed to air and water.

apply it!

The forks shown are made of silver (Ag).

1 Some of the silver forks shown have lost their luster—they have become tarnished. This is an example of _____.

2 Infer What properties of gold and platinum make these metals desirable for jewelry?

_____

_____

_____

Lab zone ® Do the Lab Investigation *Copper or Carbon? That Is the Question.*

🔑 Assess Your Understanding

1a. Explain What does the term *thermal conductivity* mean?

_____

_____

_____

b. Infer What property of metals led to the use of plastic or wooden handles on many metal cooking utensils? Explain.

_____

_____

_____

_____

got it? ···

○ **I get it!** Now I know that the physical properties of metals include _____

_____

○ **I need extra help with** _____

Go to MY SCIENCE ⬤ COACH online for help with this subject.

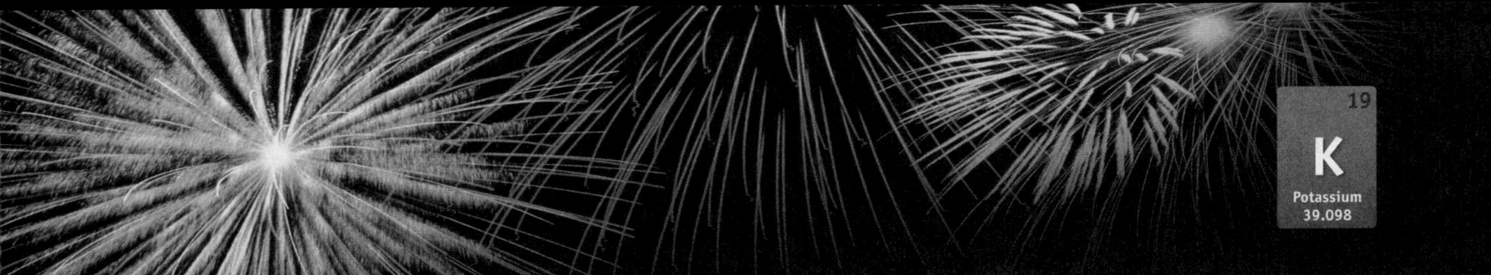

19
K
Potassium
39.098

How Are Metals Classified?

The metals in a group have similar properties. Properties within a group change gradually as you look across the periodic table. For example, the reactivity of metals tends to decrease from left to right across the table. 🔑 **In the periodic table, metals are classified as alkali metals, alkaline earth metals, transition metals, metals in mixed groups, lanthanides, and actinides.**

Alkali Metals The metals of Group 1, from lithium (Li) to francium (Fr), are called the **alkali metals.** These metals are the most reactive metals in the periodic table. Alkali metals are so reactive that they are never found as uncombined elements in nature. They are found only in compounds. Compounds that contain potassium (K) are used in fireworks, such as those shown in **Figure 4.**

> 🖊 Shade in the alkali metals on the periodic table.

In the laboratory, chemists can isolate alkali metals from their compounds. As pure, uncombined elements, some of the alkali metals are shiny and so soft you can cut them with a plastic knife. These elements have low densities and melting points. For example, sodium melts at 98°C and has a density of 0.97 g/cm³—less than water.

Alkaline Earth Metals
The metals of Group 2 are called the **alkaline earth metals.** These metals are harder and denser, and melt at higher temperatures than the alkali metals. For example, magnesium (Mg) is a hard metal that melts at 648.8°C.

> 🖊 Shade in the alkaline earth metals on the periodic table.

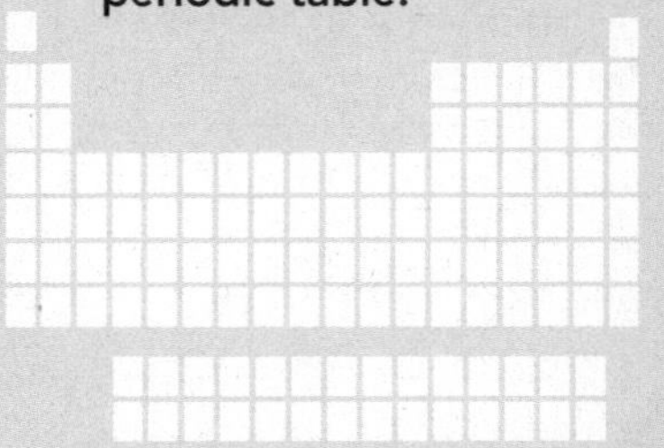

Alkaline earth metals are very reactive, though not as reactive as the alkali metals. These metals are also never found uncombined in nature. Calcium (Ca) is one of the most common alkaline earth metals. Calcium compounds are essential for bone health. **Figure 5** shows an X-ray of healthy bones.

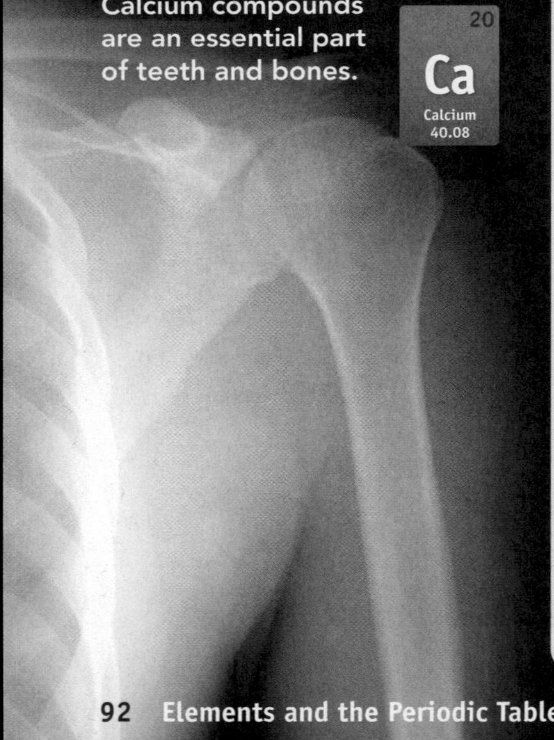

FIGURE 4 ·····································
Fireworks
Compounds containing potassium are used in fireworks.

FIGURE 5 ·····································
X-Ray of Healthy Bones
Calcium compounds are an essential part of teeth and bones.

20
Ca
Calcium
40.08

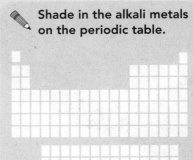

do the math! Analyzing Data

Melting Points in a Group of Elements

Properties of elements in a single group in the periodic table often change according to a certain pattern. The graph shows the melting points of the Group 1 elements, or the alkali metals.

① **Read Graphs** The melting points of the alkali metals (increase/decrease) from lithium to francium.

② **Interpret Data** Which of the alkali metals are liquids at 50°C?

③ CHALLENGE If element 119 were discovered, it would fall below francium in Group 1. Predict the approximate melting point of element 119.

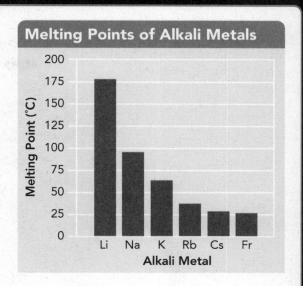

Melting Points of Alkali Metals

Melting Point (°C) vs. Alkali Metal (Li, Na, K, Rb, Cs, Fr)

Transition Metals

The elements in Groups 3 through 12 are called the **transition metals.** The transition metals include iron, copper, nickel, gold, and silver. Most of these metals are hard and shiny solids. However, mercury is a liquid at room temperature. Except for mercury, the transition metals often have high melting points and high densities. They are also good conductors of heat and electric current, and are very malleable. As shown in **Figure 6**, gold is sometimes used to coat an astronaut's visor.

The transition metals are less reactive than the metals in Groups 1 and 2. When iron reacts with air, forming rust, it sometimes takes many years to react completely.

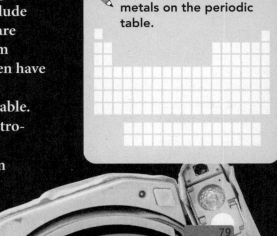

Shade in the transition metals on the periodic table.

79
Au
Gold
196.97

FIGURE 6
Astronaut Visor
The gold film in an astronaut's visor protects the eyes and face from the sun without interfering with vision.

FIGURE 7 ·······

Aluminum Bicycle Frame
Bicycle frames and wheel rims often contain aluminum.

Shade in the metals in mixed groups on the periodic table.

Al
13
Aluminum
26.982

Metals in Mixed Groups

Bicycle frames, such as the one in **Figure 7**, often contain aluminum because it is durable but light. Aluminum is in Group 13 of the periodic table. Only some of the elements in Groups 13 through 16 are metals. Other metals in these groups that you may be familiar with are tin (Sn) and lead (Pb). A thin coating of tin protects steel from corrosion in some cans of food. Lead was once used in paints and water pipes. Lead is no longer used for these purposes because it was found to be poisonous. Now its most common use is in automobile batteries.

Lanthanides and Actinides

Two rows of elements are placed below the main part of the periodic table. The elements in the top row are the lanthanides (LAN thuh nydz). Compounds containing neodymium (Nd), a lanthanide, are used to make laser light. These lasers are used for surgery, for cutting metals, and in laser range finders, such as the one shown in **Figure 8.**

The elements below the lanthanides are called actinides (AK tuh nydz). Many of these elements are not found in nature but are made artificially in laboratories.

Shade in the lanthanides and actinides on the periodic table.

Nd
60
Neodymium
144.24

FIGURE 8 ·······

Laser Range Finder
A compound containing neodymium is used to produce the laser light in a range finder. The range finder uses a laser beam to determine the distance to an object.

Transuranium Elements Elements that follow uranium (U) in the periodic table are transuranium elements. These elements are made, or synthesized, when nuclear particles are forced to crash into one another. They are sometimes called synthetic elements. For example, plutonium (Pu) is synthesized by bombarding nuclei of uranium-238 with neutrons in a nuclear reactor.

To make elements with atomic numbers above 95, scientists use devices called particle accelerators that move atomic nuclei at extremely high speeds. If these nuclei crash into the nuclei of other elements with enough energy, the particles can combine into a single nucleus. An example of a particle accelerator is shown in **Figure 9.**

In general, the difficulty of synthesizing new elements increases with atomic number. So new elements have been synthesized only as more powerful particle accelerators have been built. After elements are synthesized, they have to be confirmed before they are assigned permanent names or symbols.

✎ **Ask Questions** Before reading about transuranium elements, ask a *What* or *How* question. As you read, write the answer to your question.

_____

_____

_____

_____

_____

_____

FIGURE 9 ·······························

Particle Accelerator
The heaviest synthetic elements are synthesized using particle accelerators.

Lab® Do the Quick Lab
zone *Finding Metals.*

🔑 **Assess Your Understanding**

2a. Identify Which family of elements in the periodic table contains the most reactive metals?

_____

b. Infer Period 4 of the periodic table contains the elements potassium, calcium, and copper. Which is the least reactive?

_____

c. Apply Concepts How is plutonium made?

_____

_____

got it? ·······························

○ **I get it!** Now I know that metals are classified in the periodic table as _____

_____

_____

_____

_____

○ **I need extra help with** _____

Go to **my science coach** *online for help with this subject.*

UNLOCK THE BIG
?

🔑 **What Are the Properties of Nonmetals?**

🔑 **What Are the Families Containing Nonmetals?**

my planet DiaRY

MISCONCEPTION

Something in the Air

A common misconception is that the air in the atmosphere is mostly oxygen.

Fact: At sea level, air is actually only about 21 percent oxygen by volume. Nitrogen makes up about 78 percent of the atmosphere. The remaining one percent is made up of several gases, including argon and carbon dioxide.

Evidence: Oxygen is actually toxic at high concentrations. If you breathed in pure oxygen, you would eventually get very sick.

Communicate Write your answer to each question below. Then discuss your answers with a partner.

1. Why don't scuba divers fill their tanks with pure oxygen?

_____

_____

_____

_____

2. Can you think of anything else that is good for you in small amounts but bad for you in large amounts?

_____

_____

_____

_____

> PLANET DIARY Go to **Planet Diary** to learn more about nonmetals.

 Lab zone® Do the Inquiry Warm-Up *What Are the Properties of Charcoal?*

Vocabulary
- nonmetal
- diatomic molecule
- halogen
- noble gas
- metalloid
- semiconductor

Skills
- Reading: Summarize
- Inquiry: Classify

What Are the Properties of Nonmetals?

Life on Earth depends on many nonmetals. For example, carbon (C), nitrogen (N), phosphorus (P), hydrogen (H), and oxygen (O) are all nonmetal elements found in your body's DNA. A model of DNA is shown in **Figure 1.** While many compounds made with nonmetals are essential to life, some nonmetals are poisonous and highly reactive. Still others are nonreactive. Compared to metals, nonmetals have a much wider variety of properties. However, non-metals do have several properties in common.

Physical Properties   A **nonmetal** is an element that lacks most of the properties of a metal. Except for hydrogen, the non-metals are found on the right side of the periodic table. 🗝 **In general, most nonmetals are poor conductors of electric current and heat. Solid nonmetals tend to be dull and brittle.** If you were to hit most solid nonmetals with a hammer, they would break or crumble into a powder. Also, nonmetals usually have lower densi-ties than metals.

Many nonmetals are gases at room temperature. The air you breathe contains mostly nitrogen and oxygen. Some nonmetal elements, such as carbon, sulfur (S), and iodine (I), are solids at room temperature. Bromine (Br) is the only nonmetal that is a liquid at room temperature.

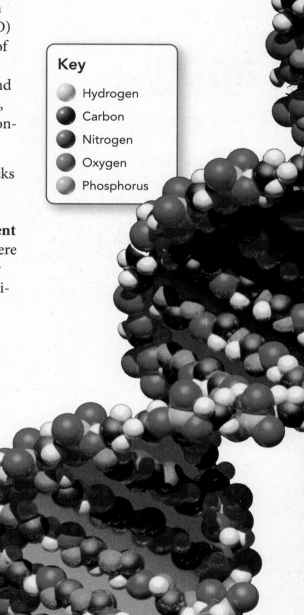

Key
- Hydrogen
- Carbon
- Nitrogen
- Oxygen
- Phosphorus

FIGURE 1 ···

DNA

DNA, which is made up of atoms of nonmetals, is essential to life.

✏️ **Identify** Can you think of other substances essential to life that contain nonmetals?

_____

_____

_____

Chemical Properties Atoms of nonmetals usually gain or share electrons when they react with other atoms. When non-metals and metals react, electrons move from the metal atoms to the nonmetal atoms. For example, when sodium and chlorine react to form table salt (NaCl), an electron moves from the sodium atom to the chlorine atom.

Many nonmetals can form compounds with other nonmetals. In these types of compounds, the atoms share their electrons to form bonds. When two or more atoms bond this way, they form a molecule. A water (H_2O) molecule consists of two hydrogen atoms and one oxygen atom.

apply it!

Most properties of nonmetals are the opposite of the properties of metals.

1 Compare and Contrast Complete the table about the properties of metals and nonmetals.

2 Observe Sulfur, shown at the right, is a nonmetal. What properties can you observe from the photo? What additional properties can you predict?

_____

_____

_____

_____

Properties of Metals	Properties of Nonmetals
Shiny	Dull
Malleable	_____
Good conductors of electric current	_____ _____ _____
_____ _____ _____	Poor conductors of heat

Lab zone Do the Quick Lab *Carbon—A Nonmetal.*

🔑 Assess Your Understanding

1a. Identify What property of nonmetals is the opposite of being *malleable* and *ductile*?

_____

b. Make Generalizations What happens to the atoms of most nonmetals when they react with other elements?

_____

_____

_____

got it?

○ **I get it!** Now I know that the physical proper-

ties of nonmetals are that_____

_____

_____

○ **I need extra help with** _____

_____

Go to **MY SCIENCE** Ⓢ **COACH** *online for help with this subject.*

What Are the Families Containing Nonmetals?

Look back at the periodic table. There are nonmetals in Group 1 and in Groups 14–18. **The families containing nonmetals include the carbon family, the nitrogen family, the oxygen family, the halogen family, the noble gases, and hydrogen.**

Before you read about the families containing nonmetals, refer to the periodic table to complete the table below.

Family	Group	Nonmetals in Family
Carbon family	14	
Nitrogen family	15	
Oxygen family	16	
Halogen family	17	
Noble gases	18	
Hydrogen	1	

The Carbon Family In Group 14, only carbon is a nonmetal. Carbon is especially important in its role in the chemistry of life. Proteins, DNA, and fats all contain carbon.

Most of the fuels that are burned to yield energy contain carbon. Coal contains large amounts of carbon. Gasoline is made from crude oil, a mixture of carbon compounds with one carbon atom to chains of several hundred carbon atoms. A diamond, which is shown in **Figure 2**, is made of pure carbon.

6
C
Carbon
12.011

Shade in the nonmetal in Group 14 on the periodic table.

FIGURE 2

Diamond
Diamonds are made of pure carbon.

99

The Nitrogen Family

Group 15, the nitrogen family, contains two nonmetals, nitrogen and phosphorus. Nitrogen makes up about 78 percent of Earth's atmosphere by volume. In nature, nitrogen exists as two nitrogen atoms bonded together to form a diatomic molecule, N_2. A **diatomic molecule** is made up of two atoms. In this form, nitrogen is not very reactive.

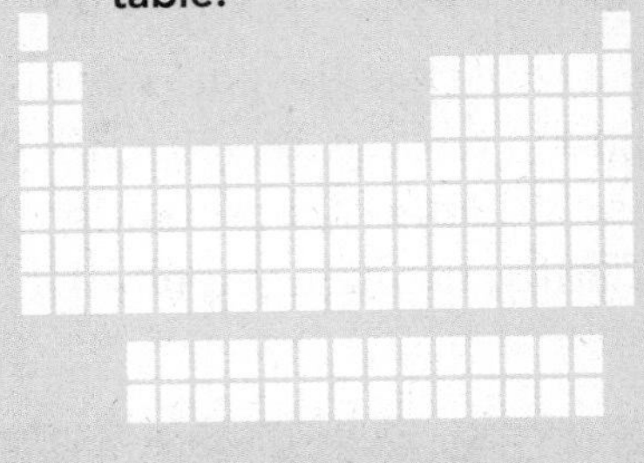

Although living things need nitrogen, most of them are unable to use nitrogen from the air. However, certain kinds of bacteria can use the nitrogen from the air to form compounds. This process is called nitrogen fixation. Plants can then take in these nitrogen compounds formed by the bacteria in the soil. Farmers also add nitrogen compounds to the soil in the form of fertilizers. Lightning, shown in **Figure 3,** also converts nitrogen in the atmosphere into a form that can be used by plants.

Phosphorus is the other nonmetal in the nitrogen family. Much more reactive than nitrogen, phosphorus in nature is always found in compounds.

Shade in the nonmetals in Group 15 on the periodic table.

FIGURE 3 ....

Lightning

The energy released in the atmosphere in the form of lightning is able to break the bonds between nitrogen atoms, causing them to react with oxygen. Plants are able to use the nitrogen in this form.

CHALLENGE How do you get the nitrogen you need?

7

N

Nitrogen
14.007

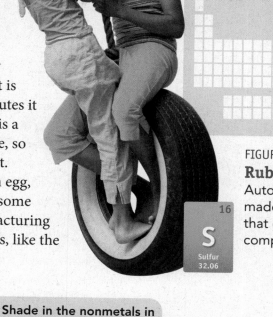

The Oxygen Family

Group 16, the oxygen family, contains three nonmetals—oxygen, sulfur, and selenium (Se). Oxygen is a gas at room temperature, whereas sulfur and selenium are both solids.

You are using oxygen right now. With every breath, oxygen travels into your lungs. There, it is absorbed into your bloodstream, which distributes it all over your body. Like nitrogen, oxygen (O_2) is a diatomic molecule. Oxygen is relatively reactive, so it can combine with almost every other element.

If you have ever smelled the odor of a rotten egg, then you are already familiar with the smell of some sulfur compounds. Sulfur is used in the manufacturing of rubber for rubber bands and automobile tires, like the one shown in **Figure 4.**

Shade in the nonmetals in Group 16 on the periodic table.

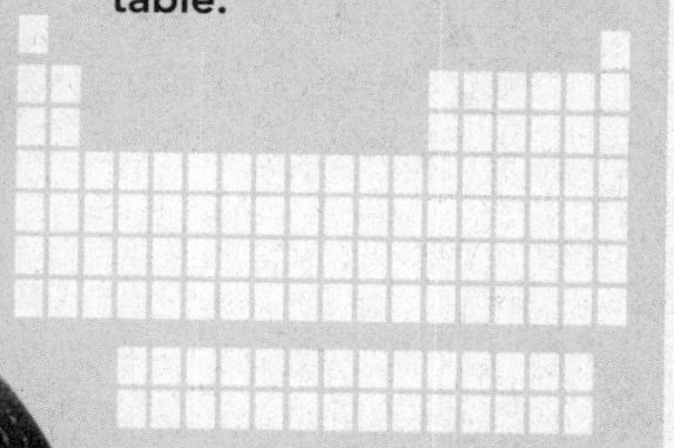

FIGURE 4

Rubber Tires
Automobile tires are made out of rubber that contains sulfur compounds.

16
S
Sulfur
32.06

The Halogen Family

Group 17 contains the nonmetals fluorine (F), chlorine (Cl), bromine, and iodine. These elements are also known as the **halogens,** which means "salt forming." The properties of astatine (At) are unknown because it is extremely rare.

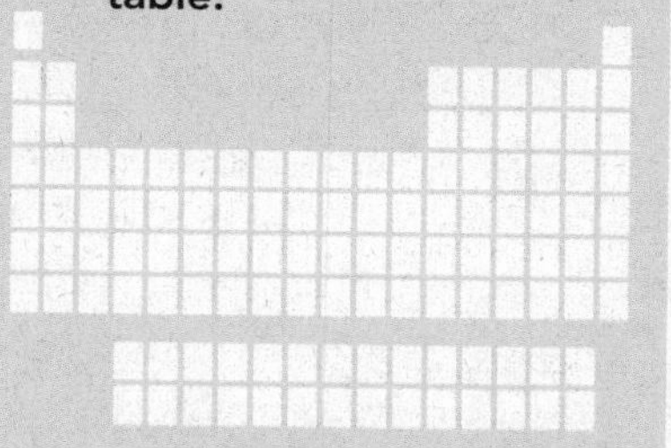

All of the halogens are very reactive. Fluorine is the most reactive of all the elements. It is so reactive that it reacts with almost every known substance, including water. Chlorine gas is extremely dangerous, but it is used in small amounts to kill bacteria in water supplies.

Though the halogen elements are dangerous, many of the compounds that halogens form are quite useful. Compounds of fluorine make up the nonstick coating on cookware. Fluorine compounds are also found in toothpaste, which is shown in **Figure 5,** because they help prevent tooth decay.

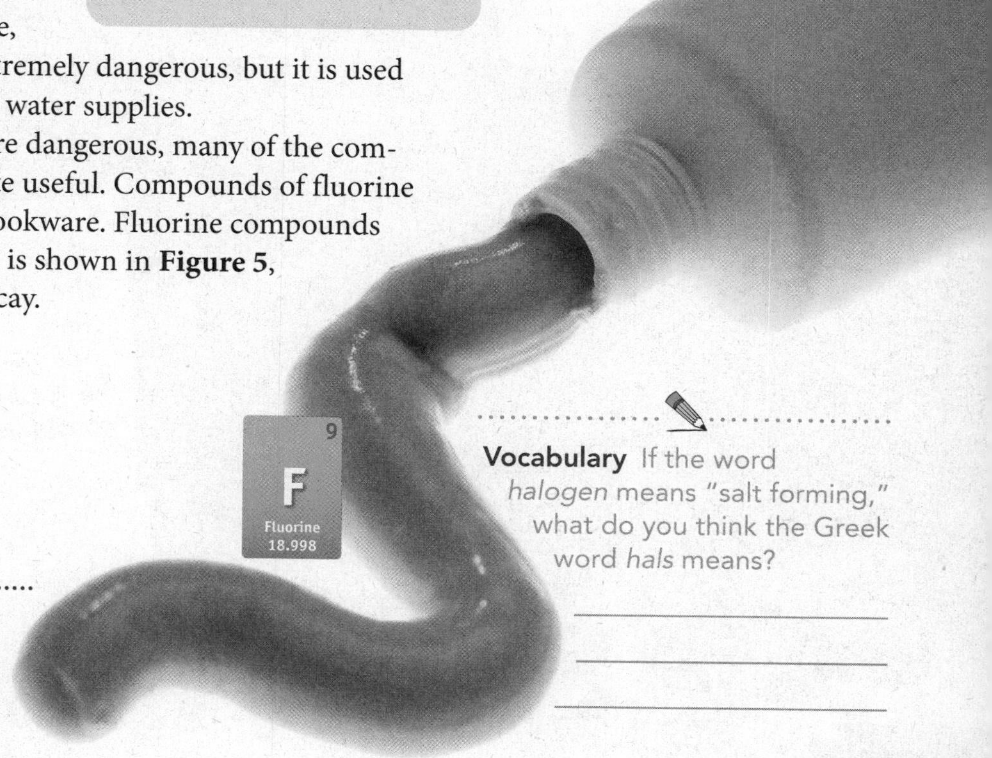

Shade in the nonmetals in Group 17 on the periodic table.

9
F
Fluorine
18.998

Vocabulary If the word *halogen* means "salt forming," what do you think the Greek word *hals* means?

_____

_____

_____

FIGURE 5

Toothpaste
Toothpastes often contain fluorine compounds.

He Ne Ar Kr Xe

FIGURE 6 ....
Neon Lights

Glowing electric lights are often called "neon lights" even though they are usually filled with other noble gases or mixtures of them. The lights above show the symbols for helium (He), neon (Ne), argon (Ar), krypton (Kr), and xenon (Xe).

The Noble Gases The elements in Group 18 are known as the noble gases. They do not ordinarily form compounds because atoms of noble gases do not usually gain, lose, or share electrons. As a result, the noble gases are usually nonreactive. Even so, scientists have been able to synthesize some noble gas compounds in the laboratory.

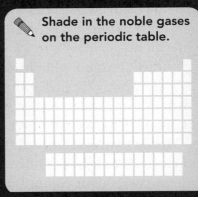

✏ Shade in the noble gases on the periodic table.

You have probably seen a floating balloon filled with helium (He). Noble gases are also used in glowing electric lights, such as the ones shown in **Figure 6.**

Hydrogen Alone in the upper left corner of the periodic table is hydrogen—the element with the simplest atoms. The chemical properties of hydrogen are very different from those of the other elements, so it cannot be grouped in with a family.

Hydrogen makes up more than 90 percent of the atoms in the universe. Stars—like the sun, shown in **Figure 7**—contain massive amounts of hydrogen. But, hydrogen makes up only 1 percent of the mass of Earth's crust, oceans, and atmosphere. Hydrogen is rarely found on Earth as a pure element. Most hydrogen is combined with oxygen in water.

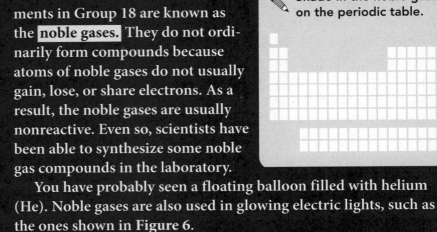

✏ Shade in hydrogen on the periodic table.

FIGURE 7 ....
The Sun
The sun fuses hydrogen atoms together to form helium.

✏ **Explain** Why isn't hydrogen considered an alkali metal?

1
H
Hydrogen
1.0079

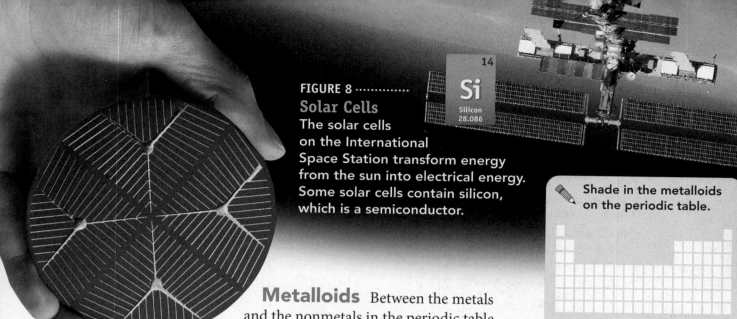

FIGURE 8 ·············
Solar Cells
The solar cells on the International Space Station transform energy from the sun into electrical energy. Some solar cells contain silicon, which is a semiconductor.

Shade in the metalloids on the periodic table.

Metalloids Between the metals and the nonmetals in the periodic table lie the metalloids. The **metalloids** have some properties of metals and some properties of nonmetals. All metalloids are solids at room temperature. The metalloids are brittle, hard, and somewhat reactive.

The most common metalloid is silicon (Si). Ordinary sand, which is mostly silicon dioxide (SiO_2), is the main component of glass. A compound of boron (B) and oxygen is added during the process of glassmaking to make heat-resistant glass.

A metalloid's most useful property is the ability to conduct electric current. The conductivity of a metalloid can depend on temperature, exposure to light, or the presence of impurities. For this reason, metalloids such as silicon and germanium (Ge) are used to make semiconductors. **Semiconductors** are substances that can conduct electric current under some conditions but not under other conditions. Semiconductors are used to make computer chips, transistors, and lasers. Semiconductors are also used in solar cells, such as the ones shown in **Figure 8**.

✎ **Summarize** Summarize the properties of the metalloids.

_____
_____
_____
_____
_____
_____
_____

apply it!

Use this portion of the periodic table to answer the questions.

❶ **Classify** List the chemical symbols of the nonmetals:
_____. The remaining elements are classified as _____

❷ Selenium has properties similar to (sulfur/bromine) because they are in the same (period/group).

Alien Periodic Table

How is the periodic table organized?

FIGURE 9 ·······

> **VIRTUAL LAB** Imagine that inhabitants of another planet send a message to Earth that contains information about 30 elements. However, the message contains different names and symbols for these elements than those used on Earth. ✎ Infer Using the clues provided, fill in the periodic table with these "alien" names.

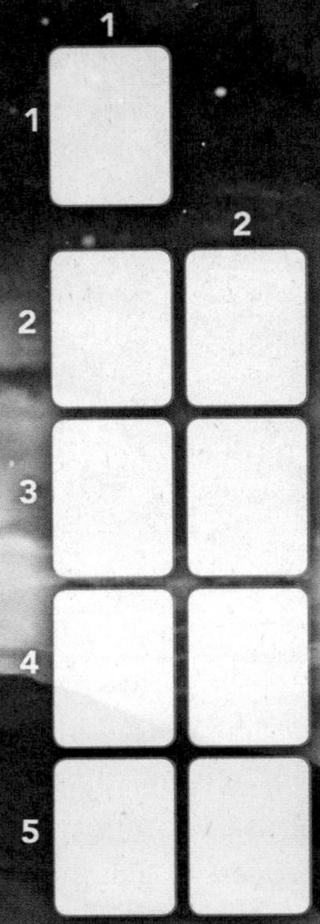

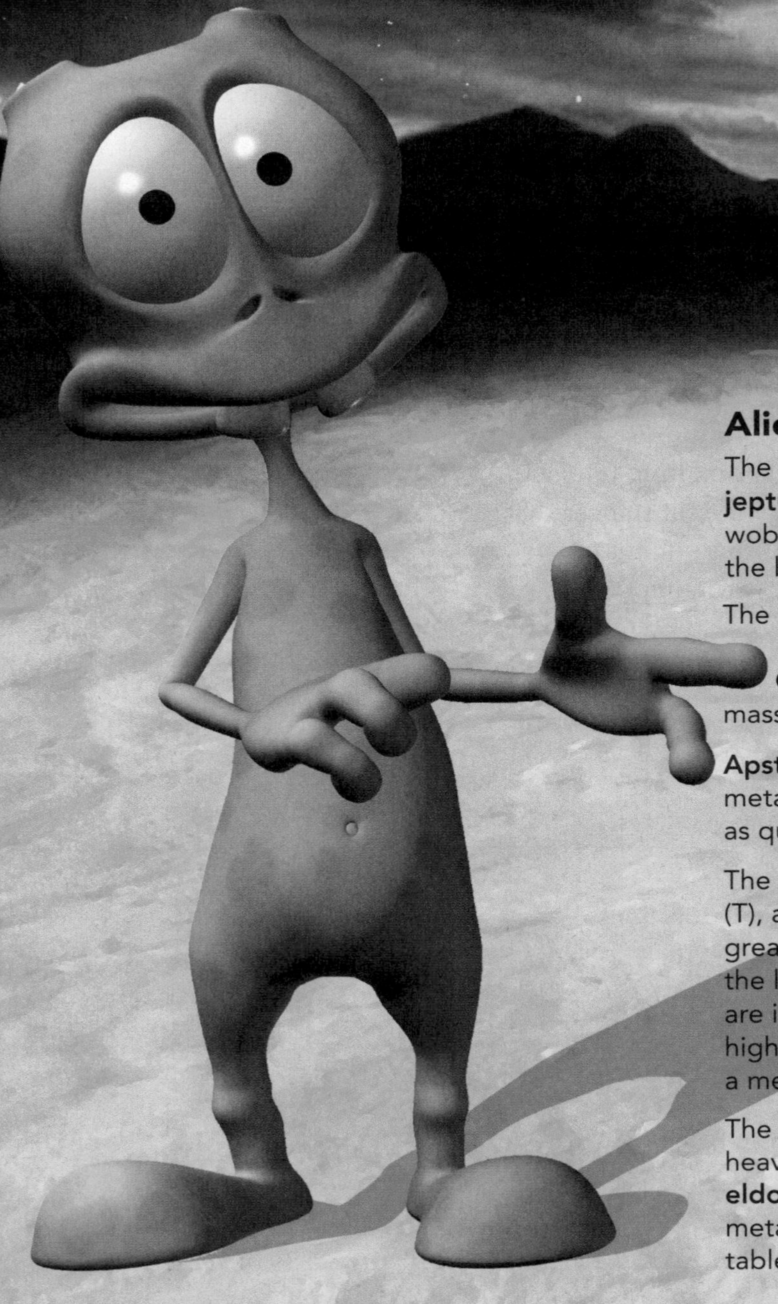

Alien Elements

The noble gases are **bombal** (Bo), **wobble** (Wo), **jeptum** (J), and **logon** (L). Among these gases, wobble has the greatest atomic mass and bombal the least. Logon is lighter than jeptum.

The most reactive group of metals are **xtalt** (X), **byyou** (By), **chow** (Ch), and **quackzil** (Q). Of these metals, chow has the lowest atomic mass. Quackzil is in the same period as wobble.

Apstrom (A), **vulcania** (Vc), and **kratt** (Kt) are nonmetals in Group 17. Vulcania is in the same period as quackzil and wobble.

The metalloids are **ernst** (E), **highho** (Hi), **terriblum** (T), and **sississ** (Ss). Sississ is the metalloid with the greatest atomic mass. Ernst is the metalloid with the lowest atomic mass. Highho and terriblum are in Group 14. Terriblum has more protons than highho. **Yazzer** (Yz) touches the zigzag line, but it's a metal, not a metalloid.

The lightest element of all is called **pfsst** (Pf). The heaviest element in the group of 30 elements is **eldorado** (El). The most chemically active nonmetal is apstrom. Kratt reacts with byyou to form table salt.

| | | | | | 18 |
| 13 | 14 | 15 | 16 | 17 | |

The element **doggone** (D) has only 4 protons in its atoms.

Floxxit (Fx) is important in the chemistry of life. It forms compounds made of long chains of atoms. **Rhaatrap** (R) and **doadeer** (Do) are metals in the fourth period, but rhaatrap is less reactive than doadeer.

Magnificon (M), **goldy** (G), and sississ are all members of Group 15. Goldy has fewer electrons than magnificon.

Urrp (Up), **oz** (Oz), and **nuutye** (Nu) are in Group 16. Nuutye is found as a diatomic molecule and has the same properties as a gas found in Earth's atmosphere. Oz has a lower atomic number than urrp.

The element **anatom** (An) has atoms with a total of 49 electrons. **Zapper** (Z) and **pie** (Pi) are both members of Group 2. Zapper has fewer protons than pie.

 Do the Quick Lab *Finding Nonmetals.*

Assess Your Understanding

2a. List What are the nonmetals in Group 16 of the periodic table?

_____

_____

_____

b. Compare and Contrast How do the chemical properties of the halogens compare to those of the noble gases?

_____

_____

_____

c. ANSWER THE BIG ? How is the periodic table organized?

_____

_____

_____

_____

_____

_____

_____

_____

_____

got it? ....

○ **I get it!** Now I know that the families containing nonmetals include _____

_____

_____

_____

○ **I need extra help with** _____

Go to MY SCIENCE COACH online for help with this subject.

105

Radioactive Elements

🔑 **What Happens to an Atom During Radioactive Decay?**

🔑 **What Does Radioactive Decay Produce?**

🔑 **How Are Radioactive Isotopes Useful?**

my PLaNeT DiaRY

FUN FACTS

Running on Radioactive Isotopes

Did you know that the *Cassini* spacecraft, which is being used to explore Saturn, runs on batteries? The batteries are called radioisotope thermoelectric generators (RTGs).

The batteries you can buy in the store use chemical reactions to generate electrical energy. However, RTGs produce electrical energy by using radioactive decay. RTGs contain unstable isotopes, which are called radioactive isotopes. Heat is released as the radioactive isotopes lose particles from their atoms. The heat is then converted into electrical energy. A single RTG contains several pounds of radioactive material. This is enough fuel to provide power for up to 23 years!

Communicate Write your answer to each question below. Then discuss your answers with a partner.

1. How are RTGs different from the batteries you buy at a store?

_____

_____

_____

_____

2. Imagine being on a spacecraft traveling to distant planets. What are some of the things you might see?

_____

_____

_____

_____

> PLANET DIARY Go to **Planet Diary** to learn more about radioactive decay.

 Lab zone Do the Inquiry Warm-Up *How Much Goes Away?*

Vocabulary
- radioactive decay • nuclear reaction • radioactivity
- alpha particle • beta particle • gamma ray
- half-life • radioactive dating • tracer

Skills
⟳ Reading: Relate Cause and Effect
△ Inquiry: Calculate

What Happens to an Atom During Radioactive Decay?

Suppose you could find a way to turn dull, cheap lead into valuable gold. More than a thousand years ago, many people tried, but nothing worked. As the young scientist in **Figure 1** will soon discover, there is no chemical reaction that converts one element into another. Even so, elements do sometimes change into other elements. For example, atoms of carbon can become atoms of nitrogen. How are these changes possible?

Radioactive Decay Recall that atoms with the same number of protons and different numbers of neutrons are called isotopes. Some isotopes are unstable, so their nuclei do not hold together well. These unstable isotopes are also called radioactive isotopes. In a process called **radioactive decay,** the atomic nuclei of radioactive isotopes release fast-moving particles and energy. ⟤ **During radioactive decay, the identity of an atom changes.**

Radioactive decay is an example of a nuclear reaction. **Nuclear reactions** involve the particles in the nucleus of an atom. Nuclear fission, a process in which an atom's nuclei split apart, and nuclear fusion, the process in which atomic nuclei join together, are both nuclear reactions. These physical processes make it possible for scientists to turn one element into another.

> Goldy, it won't work because
> _____
> _____
> _____
> _____
> _____
> _____

FIGURE 1 ·····························

Trying to Turn Lead Into Gold
Goldy is furiously trying to turn lead into gold in the chemistry lab. Meanwhile, her lab partner Lucy is trying to convince her that it can't be done with a chemical reaction.

✎ **Communicate** Use what you know about nuclear and chemical reactions to complete Lucy's argument.

Discovery of Radioactive Decay In 1896, the French scientist Henri Becquerel accidentally discovered the effects of radioactive decay. He observed that when a mineral containing uranium was exposed to sunlight, it gave off an energy that could fog photographic film plates. Becquerel thought that sunlight was necessary for the energy release. So, on a cloudy day, he put away the mineral in a desk drawer next to a photographic plate wrapped in paper. Later, when Becquerel opened his desk to retrieve his materials, he found an image of the mineral on the photographic plate. Sunlight wasn't necessary after all. Becquerel hypothesized that uranium gives off energy, called radiation, all the time.

Becquerel presented his findings to a young Polish researcher, Marie Curie, and her husband, French chemist Pierre Curie. The Curies showed that a reaction was taking place within the uranium nuclei. The uranium was able to spontaneously emit radiation. Marie Curie called this property **radioactivity.** The Curies, along with Becquerel, won the Nobel Prize in physics for their work on radioactivity. Marie Curie, shown in **Figure 2,** was later awarded the Nobel Prize in chemistry for her research on radioactive elements. She eventually died of cancer, a result of her years of exposure to radium.

FIGURE 2 ·······························

Marie Curie
Marie Curie was the first scientist to win the Nobel Prize in two different subject areas (physics and chemistry). She was also the first woman ever to receive a Nobel Prize.

Do the Quick Lab *What Happens When an Atom Decays?*

🔑 Assess Your Understanding

1a. Define The spontaneous emission of radiation by an unstable atomic nucleus is called

_____

_____

b. Apply Concepts What caused the fogging of the photographic plates that Becquerel observed in 1896?

_____

_____

_____

_____

got it?

○ I get it! Now I know that during radioactive

decay _____

_____

_____

○ I need extra help with _____

_____

Go to MY SCIENCE ⓢ COACH *online for help with this subject.*

What Does Radioactive Decay Produce?

Figure 3 illustrates the three major forms of radiation produced during the decay of an unstable nucleus. 🔑 **Radioactive decay can produce alpha particles, beta particles, and gamma rays.**

FIGURE 3 ···

> ART IN MOTION **Radioactive Decay**

Radioactive elements give off particles and energy during radioactive decay. ✎ **Compare and Contrast Identify the change (if any) that occurs in an unstable nucleus during each form of radioactive decay.**

Alpha Decay

An **alpha particle** consists of two protons and two neutrons. It is positively charged. The release of an alpha particle by an atom during alpha decay decreases the atomic number by 2 and the mass number by 4. For example, a thorium-232 nucleus decays to produce an alpha particle and a radium-228 nucleus.

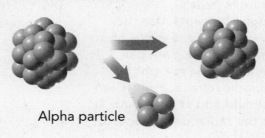

Radioactive nucleus

Alpha particle

2 protons lost
2 neutrons lost

Beta Decay

During beta decay, a neutron in an unstable nucleus changes into a negatively charged beta particle and a proton. A **beta particle** is a fast-moving electron given off by a nucleus during radioactive decay. The new proton remains inside the nucleus. The nucleus is then left with one less neutron and one more proton. Its mass number remains the same but its atomic number increases by one. For example, a carbon-14 nucleus decays to produce a beta particle and a nitrogen-14 nucleus.

Radioactive nucleus

Beta particle

☐ proton(s) (lost/gained)

☐ neutron(s) (lost/gained)

Gamma Radiation

Alpha and beta decay are almost always accompanied by gamma radiation. **Gamma rays** consist of high-energy waves, similar to X-rays. Gamma rays (also called gamma radiation) have no charge and do not cause a change in either the atomic mass or the atomic number.

Radioactive nucleus

Gamma rays

☐ proton(s) (lost/gained)

☐ neutron(s) (lost/gained)

Effects of Nuclear Radiation

Effects of Nuclear Radiation **Figure 4** depicts a radioactive source that emits alpha particles, beta particles, and gamma rays. Alpha particles move very fast, they can be blocked by just a sheet of paper. Alpha radiation can cause an injury to human skin that is much like a bad burn.

Beta particles are much faster and more penetrating than alpha particles. They can pass through paper. But, they are blocked by an aluminum sheet 5 millimeters thick. Beta particles can also travel into the human body and damage its cells.

Gamma radiation is the most penetrating. You would need a piece of lead several centimeters thick or a concrete wall about a meter thick to stop gamma rays. They can pass right through a human body. Gamma rays deliver intense energy to cells and can cause severe damage.

FIGURE 4 ·····················

The Effects of Nuclear Radiation

The three main types of nuclear radiation vary in their ability to penetrate materials.

✏️ **Apply Concepts** Use the key to complete the paths of the alpha particle, beta particle, and gamma ray emitted by the radioactive sample. Each path should end at the point where the radiation is blocked.

Key

—— Alpha particle

----- Beta particle

〰〰 Gamma ray

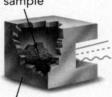

Radioactive sample

Lead box

Paper

Aluminum sheet

Concrete

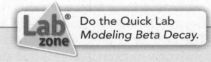

Do the Quick Lab
Modeling Beta Decay.

🔑 Assess Your Understanding

2a. Identify What is the name of the particle produced by radioactive decay that consists of 2 protons and 2 neutrons?

_____

b. Compare and Contrast Rank the three major types of nuclear radiation from 1 (most penetrating) to 3 (least penetrating).

____ Alpha   ____ Beta   ____ Gamma

c. Predict What are the identity and mass number of the nucleus formed during the beta decay of magnesium-28?

_____

got it?

○ **I get it!** Now I know that the three major forms of radiation produced during radioactive

decay are _____

_____

_____

_____

○ **I need extra help with** _____

_____

Go to **MY SCIENCE** 🔵 **COACH** *online for help with this subject.*

How Are Radioactive Isotopes Useful?

Radioactive isotopes have many uses in science and industry. In some cases, the energy released by radioactive isotopes is itself useful. In other cases, radiation is useful because it can be easily detected. 🔑 **Uses of radioactive isotopes include determining the ages of fossils, tracing the steps of chemical reactions and industrial processes, diagnosing and treating disease, and providing sources of energy.**

Radioactive Dating Radioactive isotopes decay at different rates. The **half-life** of a radioactive isotope is the length of time needed for half of the atoms of a sample to decay. The half-life is different for each radioactive isotope. Half-lives can range from less than a second to billions of years!

Fossils are traces or remains of living things that have been preserved. For fossils millions or billions of years old, ages are found from radioactive isotopes with very long half-lives, like uranium. For much younger fossils, carbon-14 is often used. As plants grow, they use carbon dioxide (CO_2) from the air. A fraction of all carbon dioxide contains the radioactive isotope carbon-14. This becomes part of a plant's structures. After the plant dies, it stops taking in carbon dioxide. If the plant's remains are preserved, the amount of carbon-14 present can be measured. Scientists can calculate how many half-lives have passed since the plant died and estimate the age of the fossil. This process is called **radioactive dating.**

do the math!

Data from a fossil of a mammoth tooth shows that carbon-14 has been decaying in the tooth for five half-lives.

❶ **Calculate** Calculate the age of the tooth.

_____ half-lives × _____ years/half-life = _____ years.

❷ **CHALLENGE** What fraction of the amount of carbon-14 that was in the mammoth's tooth when it died is left after five half-lives?

$$\left(\frac{1}{2}\right)^5 = \underline{\quad} \times \underline{\quad} \times \underline{\quad} \times \underline{\quad} \times \underline{\quad} = \underline{\quad}$$

Half-Lives of Some Radioactive Isotopes	
Element	**Half-Life**
Polonium-216	0.16 second
Sodium-24	15 hours
Iodine-131	8.07 days
Phosphorus-32	14.3 days
Cobalt-60	5.26 years
Radium-226	1,600 years
Carbon-14	5,730 years
Chlorine-36	310,000 years
Uranium-235	710 million years
Uranium-238	4.5 billion years

Why are radioactive isotopes useful for following the steps of a chemical reaction?

_____

_____

_____

_____

_____

_____

Uses in Science and Industry
A radioactive isotope, like a lighthouse flashing in the night, "signals" where it is by emitting radiation that can be detected. **Tracers** are radioactive isotopes that can be followed through the steps of a chemical reaction or an industrial process. Tracers behave chemically like nonradioactive forms of an element. For example, phosphorus is used by plants in small amounts for healthy growth. The plant in **Figure 5** will absorb radioactive phosphorus-32 just as it does the nonradioactive form. Radiation will be present in any part of the plant that contains the isotope. In this way, biologists can learn where and how plants use phosphorus.

Tracers are used to find weak spots in metal pipes, especially in oil pipelines. When added to a liquid, tracers can be easily detected if they leak out of the pipes. Gamma rays can pass through metal and be detected by photographic film. The gamma ray images allow structural engineers to detect small cracks in the metal of bridges and building frames before a disaster occurs.

FIGURE 5 ·······

Radioactive Tracers
Phosphorus-32 added to soil is absorbed through a plant's roots. The tracer can be detected in any plant structures in which phosphorus is used. **Explain Write a short caption under each figure to explain what is happening.**

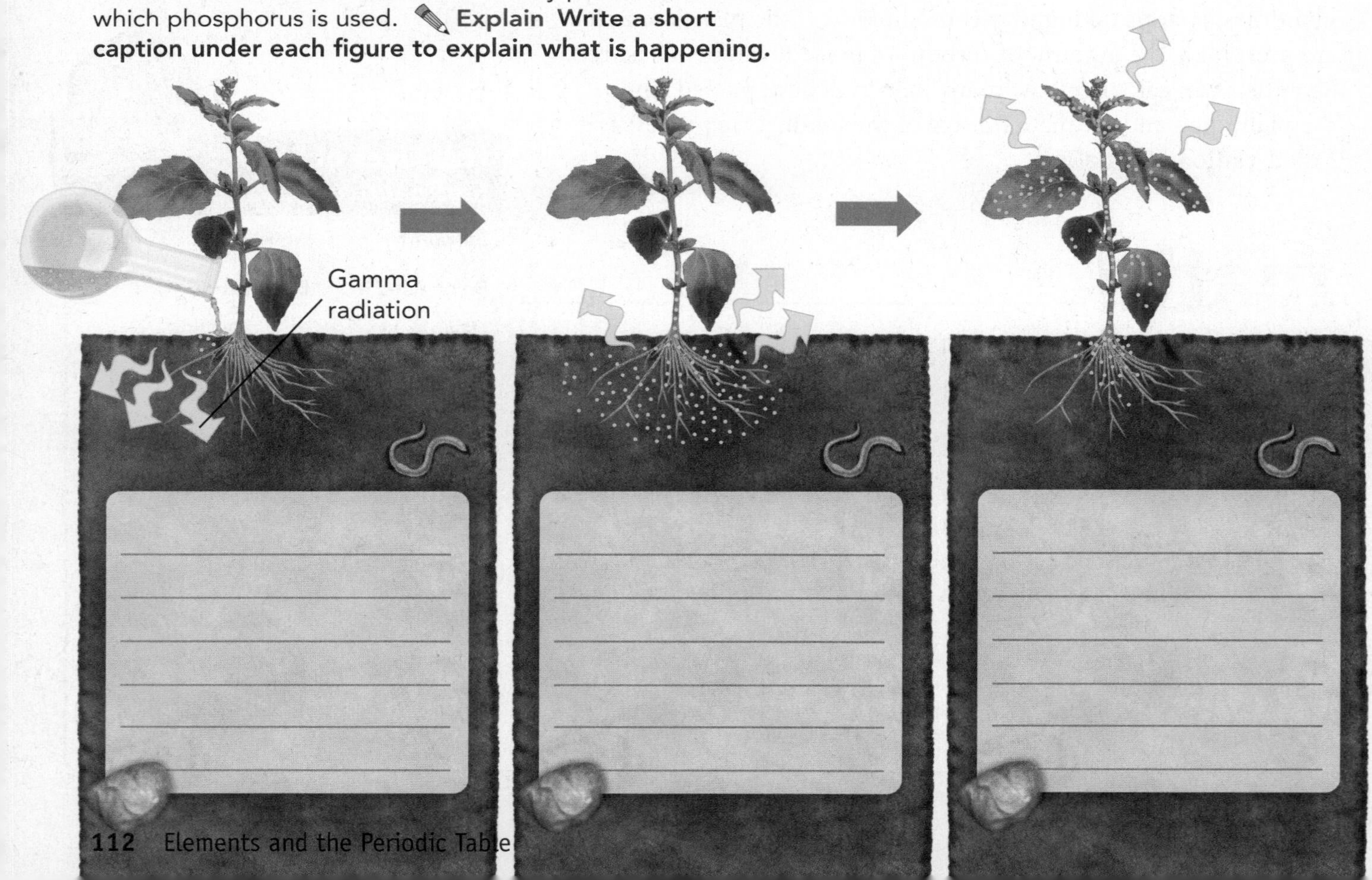

Gamma radiation

Uses in Medicine Doctors use radioactive isotopes to detect medical problems and to treat some diseases. Tracers are injected into the body and travel to organs and other structures in which that chemical is normally used. Technicians make images of the bone, blood vessel, or organ affected using equipment that detects radiation.

Cancer tumors are sometimes treated from outside the body with high-energy gamma rays. Gamma radiation directed toward a cancer tumor damages the cancer cells so that they can no longer function.

Nuclear Energy Many power plants, like the one shown in **Figure 6,** use radioactive isotopes as fuel. Both nuclear fission and nuclear fusion release huge amounts of energy when they react. In a nuclear reactor, atoms of uranium-235 are split under controlled conditions. The energy produced heats water to produce steam. The steam turns a turbine. This generates electricity. Nuclear power plants provide electrical energy in many parts of the world. Nuclear reactions also provide the energy for large submarines and other types of ocean vessels.

FIGURE 6 ···

Nuclear Power Plant
The cooling tower of a nuclear power plant helps control the temperature inside the reactor. The power plant converts thermal energy to electrical energy.

 Do the Quick Lab *Designing Experiments Using Radioactive Tracers.*

🔑 Assess Your Understanding

3a. Explain Why is half-life useful to an archaeologist?

_____
_____
_____
_____

b. 🔄 **Relate Cause and Effect** Why are radioactive isotopes that emit gamma rays useful for treating some forms of cancer?

_____
_____
_____
_____

got it? ···

○ **I get it!** Now I know that four uses of radioactive isotopes are _____

_____
_____
_____

○ **I need extra help with** _____

Go to MY SCIENCE 🔵ˢ COACH online for help with this subject.

113

REVIEW THE BIG ?

In the periodic table, the elements are organized in order of _____ atomic number.
The properties of the elements repeat in each _____.

LESSON 1 Introduction to Atoms

🔑 Atomic theory grew as a series of models that developed from experimental evidence.

🔑 At the center of the atom is a tiny, dense nucleus containing protons and neutrons. Surrounding the nucleus is a cloudlike region of moving electrons.

Vocabulary
- atom • electron • nucleus • proton
- energy level • neutron • atomic number
- isotope • mass number

LESSON 2 Organizing the Elements

🔑 Mendeleev noticed a pattern of properties in elements arranged by increasing atomic mass.

🔑 The periodic table includes each element's atomic number, symbol, name, and atomic mass.

🔑 The properties of an element can be predicted from its location in the periodic table.

Vocabulary
- atomic mass • periodic table
- chemical symbol • period • group

LESSON 3 Metals

🔑 The physical properties of metals include luster, malleability, ductility, and conductivity.

🔑 Metals are classified as alkali metals, alkaline earth metals, transition metals, metals in mixed groups, lanthanides, and actinides.

Vocabulary
- metal • luster • malleable • ductile
- thermal conductivity • electrical conductivity
- reactivity • corrosion • alkali metal
- alkaline earth metal • transition metal

LESSON 4 Nonmetals and Metalloids

🔑 In general, most nonmetals are poor conductors. Solid nonmetals tend to be dull and brittle.

🔑 The families containing nonmetals include the carbon family, the nitrogen family, the oxygen family, the halogen family, the noble gases, and hydrogen.

Vocabulary
- nonmetal • diatomic molecule • halogen
- noble gas • metalloid • semiconductor

LESSON 5 Radioactive Elements

🔑 During radioactive decay, the identity of an atom changes.

🔑 Radioactive decay can produce alpha particles, beta particles, and gamma rays.

🔑 Uses of radioactive isotopes include determining the ages of fossils, tracing the steps of chemical and industrial processes, and providing sources of energy.

Vocabulary
- radioactive decay • nuclear reaction • radioactivity • alpha particle
- beta particle • gamma ray • half-life • radioactive dating • tracer

Review and Assessment

LESSON 1 Introduction to Atoms

1. The atomic number of an element is determined by the number of

   a. protons.   **b.** electrons.

   c. neutrons.   **d.** isotopes.

2. Two isotopes of an element have the same number of _____ but different numbers of _____.

3. **Relate Cause and Effect** How can an atom be electrically neutral when it contains particles that are charged?

_____

_____

_____

_____

4. **Relate Evidence and Explanation** How did Rutherford's experimental evidence lead to the development of a new atomic model?

_____

_____

_____

_____

_____

_____

_____

5. [Write About It] Write a letter that Thomson might have sent to another scientist explaining why an atom must contain positive charges as well as negative charges. The letter should also explain why Thomson proposed the atomic model that he did.

LESSON 2 Organizing the Elements

6. The rows in the periodic table are called

   a. groups.   **b.** periods.

   c. nonmetals.   **d.** metals.

7. Dmitri Mendeleev constructed the first periodic table, which is _____

_____

_____

_____

8. **Apply Concepts** Below is an entry taken from the periodic table. Identify the type of information given by each labeled item.

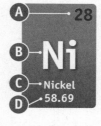

_____

_____

_____

_____

9. **Make Generalizations** Why aren't the atomic masses of most elements whole numbers?

_____

_____

_____

_____

10. [Write About It] Write an advertisement that you could use to sell copies of Mendeleev's periodic table to chemists in 1869. Be sure to emphasize the benefits of the table to the chemical profession. Remember, the chemists have never seen such a table.

LESSON 3 Metals

11. Of the following, the group that contains elements that are the most reactive is the

    a. alkali metals.   **b.** alkaline earth metals.

    c. carbon family.   **d.** noble gases.

12. A property of metals is high thermal conductivity, which is _____ _____ .

13. Predict Using the periodic table, predict which element—potassium, aluminum, or iron—is most reactive. Explain your answer.

_____

_____

_____

_____

LESSON 4 Nonmetals and Metalloids

14. Unlike metals, solid nonmetals are

    a. good conductors of heat and electric current.

    b. malleable.

    c. dull and brittle.

    d. ductile.

15. Two elements that have properties similar to those of chlorine are _____ _____ .

16. Infer What property of the materials used in computer chips makes them useful as switches that turn electricity on and off?

_____

_____

_____

_____

LESSON 5 Radioactive Elements

17. Unstable atomic nuclei that release fast-moving particles and energy are

    a. radioactive.   **b.** alloys.

    c. isotopes.   **d.** alpha particles.

18. A radioactive isotope that can be followed through a chemical reaction or industrial process is called a(n) _____ .

19. Classify What type of radioactive decay results in uranium-238 becoming thorium-234?

_____

20. Write About It Suppose you could go back in time to interview Henri Becquerel on the day he discovered radioactivity. From his perspective, write an account of the discovery.

APPLY THE BIG ? **How is the periodic table organized?**

5	6	7	8
B Boron 10.81	**C** Carbon 12.011	**N** Nitrogen 14.007	**O** Oxygen 15.999
13	14	15	16
Al Aluminum 26.982	**Si** Silicon 28.086	**P** Phosphorus 30.974	**S** Sulfur 32.06

21. A portion of the periodic table is shown above. Which element on the periodic table has properties that are most similar to those of nitrogen (N)? Explain.

_____

_____

_____

_____

_____

Standardized Test Prep

Multiple Choice

Circle the letter of the best answer.

1. A portion of the periodic table is shown below.

Which elements are noble gases?

A   oxygen, fluorine, and neon

B   sulfur, chlorine, and argon

C   fluorine and chlorine

D   neon and argon

2. Why is the mass of a carbon atom greater than the total mass of its protons and electrons?

A   The mass of a proton is greater than the mass of an electron.

B   A proton is positively charged and an electron is negatively charged.

C   Most of the atom's volume is the sphere-shaped cloud of electrons.

D   The neutrons in the nucleus add mass to the atom.

3. Elements that are gases at room temperature are likely to be classified as which of the following?

A   metals

B   nonmetals

C   metalloids

D   semiconductors

4. Which property of aluminum makes it a suitable metal for soft-drink cans?

A   It has good electrical conductivity.

B   It can be hammered into a thin sheet (malleability).

C   It can be drawn into long wires (ductility).

D   It can reflect light (luster).

5. Radioactive isotopes give off radiation that can be detected. This property makes them useful in which of the following ways?

A   as tracers in chemical reactions

B   in detecting leaks in oil pipelines

C   in diagnosing certain medical problems

D   all of the above

Constructed Response

Use the table below to help you answer Question 6. Write your answer on a separate sheet of paper.

Element	Appearance	Reactivity	Conducts Electricity
A	Greenish-yellow gas	High	No
B	Shiny red solid	Moderate	Yes
C	Colorless gas	None	No
D	Silver-white solid	High	Yes

6. Identify each element as an alkali metal, transition metal, halogen, or noble gas. Explain your answers.

Discovery of the Elements

More than 100 chemical elements have been discovered or created on Earth. The following stories describe some of the spectacular ways in which elements have been discovered:

1669 Phosphorus

In 1669, alchemist Hennig Brand was searching for a way to turn lead into gold. He hypothesized that animal urine might contain a substance that could cause the transformation. In the process of heating the urine to obtain a pure substance, he discovered a material that glowed in the dark. That material is phosphorus, which is important in maintaining a healthy body.

1811 Iodine

As French chemist Barnard Courtois isolated sodium and potassium compounds from seaweed ashes, he accidentally added too much sulfuric acid. The mess he created sent out a cloud of violet-colored gas that condensed on metal surfaces in the room. That gas was iodine. Even today, some iodine is isolated from seaweed. Having enough iodine in your diet can prevent illness and allow for healthy development.

1936 Technetium

Italian chemists Emilio Segrè and Carlo Perrier made technetium in a cyclotron in 1936. This was the first element to be produced artificially. Technetium is similar in appearance to platinum, but is very radioactive. Because it breaks down quickly, technetium is not found in nature.

Flame tests historically helped chemists to identify elements. ▶

Research It Find out more about the discovery of the following elements: helium, copper, americium, aluminum, and silicon. Then, create a timeline that shows when each element was discovered and how that discovery affected human life.

Elements
of the Human Body

It's elemental! Atoms of only five different elements make up 98 percent of the mass of the human body.

Oxygen and Hydrogen About two thirds of the body consists of water. So, in terms of mass, more than half of the body is oxygen atoms, and another 10 percent is hydrogen atoms. Both oxygen and hydrogen are also present in other body parts.

Carbon The key element in organic molecules is carbon. Organic molecules make up all body tissues, including muscles.

Calcium and Phosphorus The hard, strong parts of bones are built mostly of calcium phosphate crystals, which contain calcium, phosphorus, and oxygen.

Trace Elements Some elements exist in the body in small amounts, but play important roles. For example, chemical reactions inside body organs require enzymes that contain magnesium. The thyroid gland needs iodine to control growth. The element iron makes up less than one twentieth of 1 percent of the body, yet is an extremely important part of the hemoglobin molecule. Red blood cells use hemoglobin to carry oxygen throughout the body.

Graph It Research how the human body acquires these elements. Then use the data from the table of Elements in the Human Body to create a circle graph that shows the relative percentages of each element in the body.

Elements in the Human Body	
Element	Approximate mass (%)
Oxygen	65
Carbon	18
Hydrogen	10
Nitrogen	3
Calcium	1
Phosphorus	1
Potassium, Sulfur, Sodium, Chlorine	0.1–0.3 percent each
Copper, Magnesium, Zinc, Iron, Selenium, Molybdenum, Fluorine, Iodine, Manganese, Cobalt	less than 0.1 percent each

WHAT IS GROWING IN THIS CAVE?

How can bonding determine the properties of a substance?

Mexico's Cave of Crystals contains the world's largest natural crystals. These rocks are made of the mineral gypsum. They grew under water for as many as 500,000 years. The water was pumped out to reveal thousands of giant crystals up to 11 meters in length and 50,000 kilograms in mass. The cave might appear to be a fun place to climb around, but temperatures inside can reach 65°C (hotter than a desert afternoon). This makes it deadly for human exploration without specialized equipment.

Form Operational Definitions Based on the photograph of the Cave of Crystals, how would you define a crystal?

_____

_____

_____

> **UNTAMED SCIENCE** Watch the **Untamed Science** video to learn more about chemical bonding.

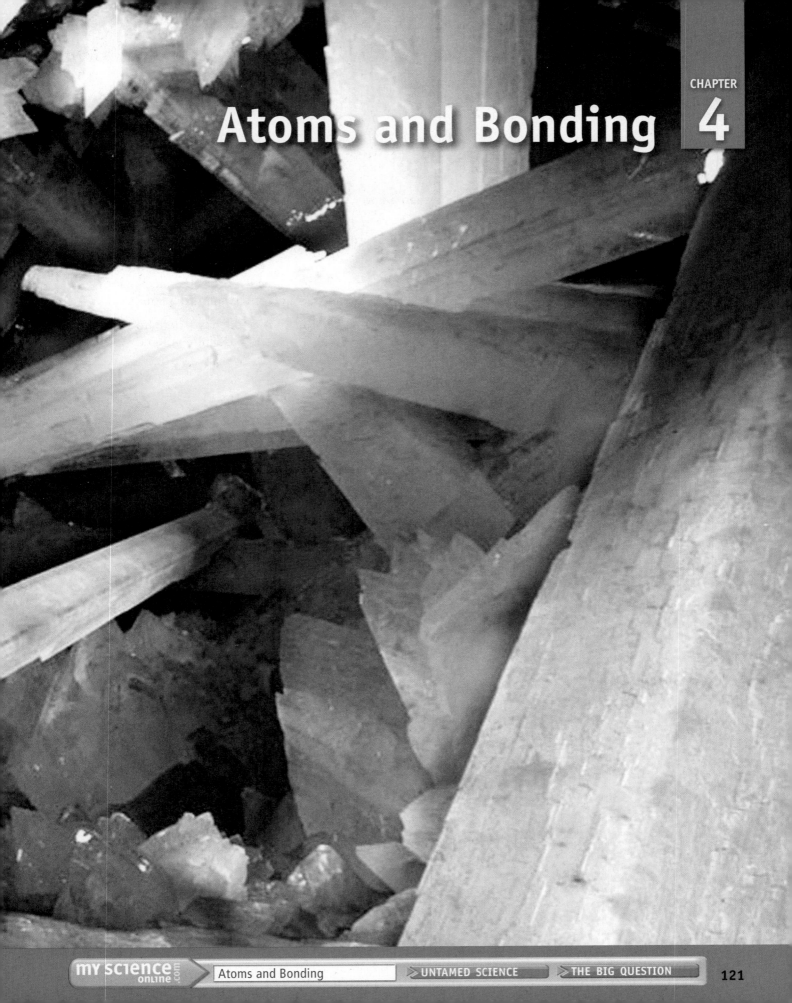

Atoms and Bonding

4 Getting Started

Check Your Understanding

1. Background Read the paragraph below and then answer the question.

Marcy fills an ice cube tray with water and places it in a freezer. The temperature in the freezer is −18°C, which is lower than the **melting point** of water (0°C). When Marcy opens the freezer a few hours later, she finds that the water has frozen into **solid** ice cubes.

> The **melting point** of a substance is the temperature at which the substance changes from a solid to a liquid.
>
> A **solid** has a definite shape and a definite volume.

- What will happen to an ice cube if it is left outside on a warm, sunny day? Explain.

_____

_____

_____

> **MY READING WEB** If you had trouble answering the question above, visit **My Reading Web** and type in *Atoms and Bonding*.

Vocabulary Skill

High-Use Academic Words High-use academic words are words you are likely to encounter while reading textbooks. Look for the following words in context as you read this chapter.

Word	Definition	Example Sentence
stable	*adj.* not easily or quickly changed from one state to another	Gold is a *stable* metal that does not rust or tarnish.
symbol	*n.* a written sign that stands for something else	The *symbol* for the element oxygen is O.

2. Quick Check Choose the word that best completes the sentence.

- The letter H is the _____ for hydrogen.
- Platinum jewelry lasts a long time because the metal is very

_____

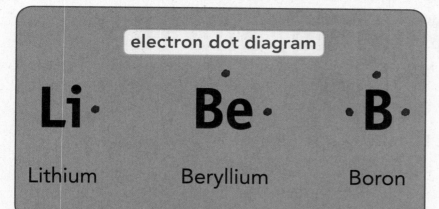

electron dot diagram

Li· · Be· ·B·

Lithium   Beryllium   Boron

ionic compound

CaCO₃

crystal

I want it!

I want it more!

polar bond

Chapter Preview

LESSON 1
- valence electron
- electron dot diagram
- chemical bond
- ↻ Relate Cause and Effect
- △ Predict

LESSON 2
- ion
- polyatomic ion
- ionic bond
- ionic compound
- chemical formula
- subscript
- crystal
- ↻ Relate Text and Visuals
- △ Interpret Data

LESSON 3
- covalent bond
- molecule
- double bond
- triple bond
- molecular compound
- nonpolar bond
- polar bond
- ↻ Compare and Contrast
- △ Graph

LESSON 4
- metallic bond
- alloy
- ↻ Identify the Main Idea
- △ Classify

> VOCAB FLASH CARDS For extra help with vocabulary, visit **Vocab Flash Cards** and type in *Atoms and Bonding.*

Atoms, Bonding, and the Periodic Table

UNLOCK THE BIG ?

🔑 **What Determines an Element's Chemistry?**

my planeT DiARY

FUN FACTS

Elemental Effects

Many people enjoy fireworks displays. Did you know that chemistry plays a big part in the beauty and the noise? The different colors and effects produced depend on the properties of the elements in the chemical compounds used in each firework rocket. These compounds produce smoke, color bursts, loud noises, or a combination of these effects when they are detonated.

The table below lists some elements found in the compounds used in rockets. It shows the effects these elements produce.

Using what you know about the periodic table, answer the questions below. After you finish the lesson, check your answers.

What elements do you think were used to produce the fireworks display in the photo? What groups of the periodic table do these elements belong to?

_____

_____

_____

Element	Effect
Strontium	Red color
Barium	Green color
Copper	Blue color
Sodium	Yellow color
Magnesium or aluminum	White color
Potassium or sodium	Whistling sound
Potassium and sulfur	White smoke

> PLANET DIARY Go to **Planet Diary** to learn more about elements.

Lab zone® Do the Inquiry Warm-Up *What Are the Trends in the Periodic Table?*

Vocabulary
- valence electron
- electron dot diagram
- chemical bond

Skills
- ↻ Reading: Relate Cause and Effect
- △ Inquiry: Predict

What Determines an Element's Chemistry?

How do atoms combine to form compounds? The answer has to do with electrons and their energy levels.

Valence Electrons The number of protons in a neutral atom equals the number of electrons. The electrons of an atom are found in different energy levels. Electrons at higher energy levels have higher amounts of energy. The **valence electrons** (VAY luns) of an atom are those electrons that have the highest energy. Valence electrons are involved in chemical bonding. 🗝 **The number of valence electrons in each atom helps determine the chemical properties of that element.**

Electron Dot Diagrams Each atom of an element has a certain number of valence electrons. The number of valence electrons is specific to that element. Different elements can have from 1 to 8 valence electrons. **Figure 1** demonstrates one way to show the number of valence electrons in an element. An **electron dot diagram** includes the symbol for the element surrounded by dots. Each dot stands for one valence electron.

Bonding Atoms tend to be more stable if they have 8 valence electrons. Atoms of neon (Ne), argon (Ar), krypton (Kr), and xenon (Xe) have 8 valence electrons. These elements are nonreactive, or stable. Helium (He) is stable with 2 electrons.

Atoms tend to form bonds so that they have 8 valence electrons and become more stable. Hydrogen needs only 2 to be stable. When atoms bond, valence electrons may be transferred from one atom to another. Or they may be shared between the atoms. A **chemical bond** is the force of attraction that holds atoms together as a result of the rearrangement of electrons between them.

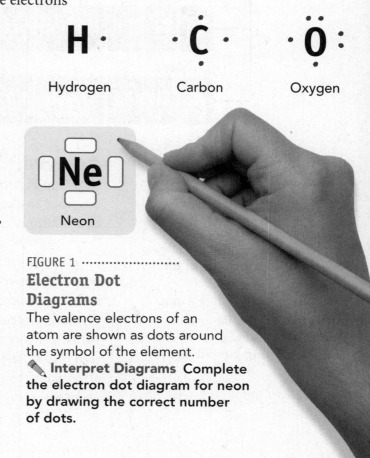

H·   ·Ċ·   ·Ö:

Hydrogen   Carbon   Oxygen

Ne
Neon

FIGURE 1 ·····················
Electron Dot Diagrams
The valence electrons of an atom are shown as dots around the symbol of the element.

✎ **Interpret Diagrams** Complete the electron dot diagram for neon by drawing the correct number of dots.

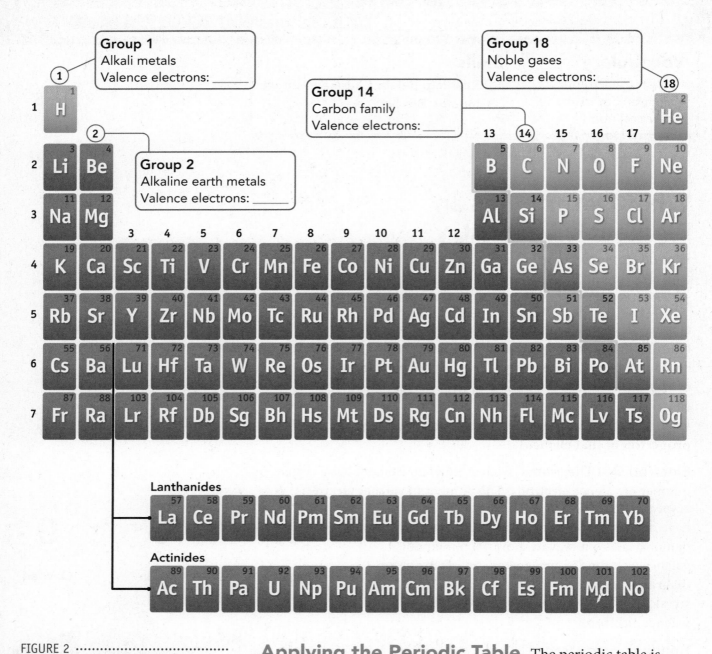

Group 1
Alkali metals
Valence electrons: _____

Group 18
Noble gases
Valence electrons: _____

Group 14
Carbon family
Valence electrons: _____

Group 2
Alkaline earth metals
Valence electrons: _____

Lanthanides

| 57 | 58 | 59 | 60 | 61 | 62 | 63 | 64 | 65 | 66 | 67 | 68 | 69 | 70 |
| La | Ce | Pr | Nd | Pm | Sm | Eu | Gd | Tb | Dy | Ho | Er | Tm | Yb |

Actinides

| 89 | 90 | 91 | 92 | 93 | 94 | 95 | 96 | 97 | 98 | 99 | 100 | 101 | 102 |
| Ac | Th | Pa | U | Np | Pu | Am | Cm | Bk | Cf | Es | Fm | Md | No |

FIGURE 2 ·······························

INTERACTIVE ART Periodic
Table of the Elements
The periodic table is arranged
in order of increasing atomic
number. The number of valence
electrons also increases from left
to right across a period.

✏ **Interpret Tables** As you
read the lesson, fill in the
number of valence electrons
for each group circled above.

Applying the Periodic Table The periodic table is
shown in **Figure 2.** It gives you information about the valence
electrons in atoms. The table is organized into rows, called periods,
and columns, called groups. The atomic number of an element is
the number of protons in each atom of that element.

The elements in the periodic table are in order by increasing
atomic number. The number of valence electrons increases from
left to right across each period. Each period begins with an element
that has 1 valence electron. Except for Period 1, a given period ends
with an element that has 8 valence electrons. This repeating pattern means that the elements within a group (except for Period 1)
always have the same number of valence electrons. As a result, the
elements in each group have similar properties.

Each element in Periods 2 and 3 has one more valence electron than the element to its left. Group 1 elements have 1. Group 2 elements have 2. Group 13 elements have 3 valence electrons. Group 14 elements have 4, and so on. (Elements in Groups 3 to 12 follow a slightly different pattern.)

apply it!

The symbols for the elements in Periods 2 and 3 are shown below. The correct electron dot diagrams are shown for only half of the elements.

1 Complete the electron dot diagrams for nitrogen, oxygen, fluorine, sodium, magnesium, aluminum, silicon, and argon.

2 Fluorine (F) and Chlorine (Cl) are in Group ____. A fluorine atom has _____ valence electrons. A chlorine atom has _____ valence electrons.

3 Predict How many valence electrons does a bromine (Br) atom have? _____

Li·	Be·	·B·	·C̤·	N	O	F	:Ne:
Lithium	Beryllium	Boron	Carbon	Nitrogen	Oxygen	Fluorine	Neon

Na	Mg	Al	Si	·P:	·S̤:	·C̤l:	Ar
Sodium	Magnesium	Aluminum	Silicon	Phosphorus	Sulfur	Chlorine	Argon

Noble Gases The Group 18 elements are the noble gases. Atoms of the noble gases have 8 valence electrons, except for helium, which has 2. Atoms with 8 valence electrons (or 2, in the case of helium) are stable. They are unlikely to gain or lose electrons or to share electrons with other atoms. Noble gases do not react easily with other elements. Some don't react at all. But, chemists have been able to make some noble gases form compounds with a few other elements.

FIGURE 3 ·····························

Camera Flashes
Argon, a noble gas, is used to produce camera flashes.

127

Vocabulary Use the word *stable* to explain why the alkali metals tend to lose 1 valence electron.

_____

_____

_____

_____

_____

_____

Relate Cause and Effect
Underline the cause and circle the effect in the paragraph at the right.

Metals The metals are the elements in the blue section of the periodic table in **Figure 2.** Metal atoms react by losing their valence electrons. In general, the reactivity of a metal depends on how easily its atoms lose valence electrons. The reactivity of metals decreases from left to right across the periodic table.

At the far left side of the periodic table is Group 1, the alkali metals. Each alkali metal is the most reactive element in its period. Atoms of the alkali metals have 1 valence electron. Except for lithium (Li), when a Group 1 atom loses an electron, it is left with a stable arrangement of 8 electrons in the highest energy level. These electrons are in a lower energy level than the 1 valence electron that was lost. (Lithium atoms are left with a stable arrangement of 2 electrons.) The alkali metals are so reactive that they can cause an explosion when added to water!

Nonmetals The elements in the orange section of the periodic table in **Figure 2** are the nonmetals. Nonmetal atoms become stable when they gain or share enough electrons to have 8 valence electrons. (Hydrogen atoms are left with a stable arrangement of 2 electrons.)

The nonmetals usually combine with metals by gaining electrons. Nonmetals can also combine with other nonmetals and metalloids by sharing electrons.

Atoms of Group 17, the halogens, have 7 valence electrons. A gain of one more electron gives these atoms a stable 8 electrons. The halogens react easily with other elements. **Figure 4** shows the reaction of bromine (Br), a halogen, with aluminum (Al).

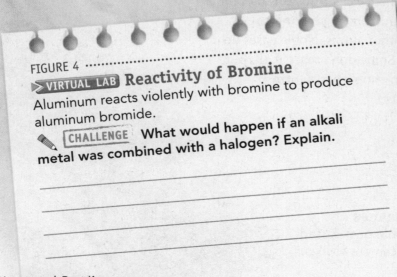

FIGURE 4
VIRTUAL LAB **Reactivity of Bromine**
Aluminum reacts violently with bromine to produce aluminum bromide.

CHALLENGE What would happen if an alkali metal was combined with a halogen? Explain.

_____

_____

_____

_____

Complete the table about groups of elements in the periodic table.

Group Number	Group Name	Number of Valence Electrons	Reactivity (High/Low)
1	Alkali metals	_____	_____
17	Halogens	_____	_____
18	Noble gases	_____	_____

Metalloids The metalloids lie along the zigzag line in the periodic table, between the metals and the nonmetals. Atoms of the metalloids can either lose or share electrons when they combine with other elements. Each metalloid has some of the properties of metals and some of the properties of nonmetals.

Hydrogen Hydrogen (H) is placed in Group 1 in the periodic table because it has 1 valence electron, but hydrogen is considered to be a nonmetal. The properties of hydrogen are very different from the properties of the alkali metals. Hydrogen shares its electron when forming compounds with other nonmetals to obtain a stable arrangement of 2 electrons.

FIGURE 5 ·······································
Computer Chip
Silicon, a metalloid, is one of the most abundant elements on Earth. It is used to make computer processor chips.

Lab zone® Do the Quick Lab Element Chemistry.

🗝 Assess Your Understanding

1a. Define What are valence electrons?

_____

_____

b. Explain Why do the properties of elements change in a regular way across a period?

_____

_____

_____

c. 🔄 **Relate Cause and Effect** Explain the reactivity of the noble gases in terms of valence electrons.

_____

_____

_____

_____

_____

got it? ···

O **I get it!** Now I know that the chemical properties of an element are determined by _____

_____

O I need extra help with _____

Go to MY SCIENCE 🔵ˢ COACH *online for help with this subject.*

Ionic Bonds

UNLOCK THE BIG

🔑 **How Do Ions Form?**

🔑 **How Are the Formulas and Names of Ionic Compounds Written?**

🔑 **What Are Properties of Ionic Compounds?**

my pLaneT DiaRY

FUN FACTS

The Periodic Palette

Imagine calling the colors of the rainbow cadmium, chromium, cobalt, and manganese. These may not sound like the typical colors of the rainbow to you, but they do to many artists and painters!

The "colors" listed above are transition metal elements. These metals can form compounds known as ionic compounds. Many transition metal compounds are brightly colored. They can be used to make the pigments found in oil, acrylic, and watercolor paints. For example, cadmium and chromium compounds are used for red, orange, yellow, or green paints. Cobalt and manganese compounds are used for blue and violet paints.

Communicate Write your answer to each question below. Then discuss your answers with a partner.

1. Why are transition metal compounds often used in paint pigments?

_____

_____

_____

2. Some of the compounds used in paint pigments may cause serious health problems. Do you think that using these types of paints is worth the possible health risks? Why or why not?

_____

_____

_____

▷ PLANET DIARY Go to **Planet Diary** to learn more about ionic compounds.

Lab zone® Do the Inquiry Warm-Up *How Do Ions Form?*

Vocabulary
- ion • polyatomic ion • ionic bond • ionic compound
- chemical formula • subscript • crystal

Skills
- Reading: Relate Text and Visuals
- Inquiry: Interpret Data

How Do Ions Form?

You and a friend walk past a market that sells apples for 40 cents each and pears for 50 cents each. You have 45 cents and want an apple. Your friend also has 45 cents but wants a pear. If you give your friend a nickel, she will have 50 cents and can buy a pear. You will have 40 cents left to buy an apple. Transferring the nickel gets both of you what you want. In a simple way, your actions model what can happen between atoms.

FIGURE 1 ·····················

How Ions Form
An atom that loses one of its electrons becomes a positively charged ion. The atom that gains the electron becomes a negatively charged ion.

Interpret Diagrams
Complete the electron dot diagrams for potassium (K) and fluorine (F) before and after the electron is transferred.

·····················

Relate Text and Visuals
Using the cartoon in **Figure 1**, explain why the potassium atom becomes positively charged and the fluorine atom becomes negatively charged.

_____

_____

_____

_____

_____

_____

Ions An **ion** (EYE ahn) is an atom or group of atoms that has an electric charge. **When a neutral atom loses a valence electron, it loses a negative charge. It becomes a positive ion. When a neutral atom gains an electron, it gains a negative charge. It becomes a negative ion.** This is shown in **Figure 1.**

Metal atoms are likely to lose electrons. These atoms lose enough electrons to have a stable arrangement of 8 valence electrons at a lower energy level. A potassium (K) atom easily loses its 1 valence electron to become more stable. Nonmetal atoms are likely to gain electrons. These atoms gain enough electrons so that they have 8 valence electrons. A fluorine (F) atom gains 1 electron to have a stable arrangement of 8 valence electrons.

FIGURE 2 ·····················

▶ INTERACTIVE ART **Ions**

Ions have electric charges.

Common Ions and Their Charges		
Name	Charge	Symbol or Formula
Lithium	1+	Li^+
Sodium	1+	Na^+
Potassium	1+	K^+
Ammonium	1+	NH_4^+
Calcium	2+	Ca^{2+}
Magnesium	2+	Mg^{2+}
Aluminum	3+	Al^{3+}
Fluoride	1–	F^-
Chloride	1–	Cl^-
Iodide	1–	I^-
Bicarbonate	1–	HCO_3^-
Nitrate	1–	NO_3^-
Oxide	2–	O^{2-}
Sulfide	2–	S^{2-}
Carbonate	2–	CO_3^{2-}
Sulfate	2–	SO_4^{2-}

Common Ions **Figure 2** lists the names of some common ions. Notice that some ions are made of several atoms. The ammonium ion is made of 1 nitrogen atom and 4 hydrogen atoms. Ions that are made of more than 1 atom are called **polyatomic ions** (pahl ee uh TAHM ik). The prefix *poly-* means "many," so *polyatomic* means "many atoms." Like other ions, polyatomic ions have an overall positive or negative charge.

Ionic Bonds When atoms that easily lose electrons react with atoms that easily gain electrons, valence electrons are transferred from one type of atom to another. The transfer gives each type of atom a more stable arrangement of electrons. Look at **Figure 3** to see how sodium atoms and chlorine atoms react to form sodium chloride (table salt).

❶ The sodium atom has 1 valence electron. The chlorine atom has 7 valence electrons.

❷ The valence electron of the sodium atom is transferred to the chlorine atom. Both atoms become ions. The sodium atom becomes a positive ion (Na^+). The chlorine atom becomes a negative ion (Cl^-).

❸ Oppositely charged particles attract, so the positive Na^+ ion and the negative Cl^- ion attract. An **ionic bond** is the attraction between two oppositely charged ions. The resulting compound is called an **ionic compound.** It is made up of positive and negative ions. In an ionic compound, the total positive charge of all the positive ions equals the total negative charge of all the negative ions.

FIGURE 3 ·····························

Formation of an Ionic Bond

Follow the steps to see how an ionic bond forms between a sodium atom and a chlorine atom.

✏️ **Infer** Complete the electron dot diagrams for the sodium and chlorine atoms and their ions.

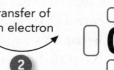
▲ Sodium metal

1 **Na**

Transfer of an electron
2

Cl
▲ Chlorine gas

3 **Na⁺** **Cl⁻**
Sodium ion   Chloride ion

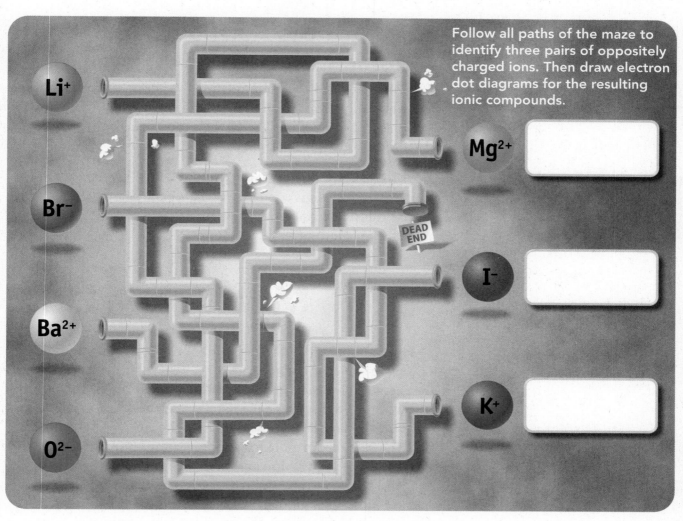

Follow all paths of the maze to identify three pairs of oppositely charged ions. Then draw electron dot diagrams for the resulting ionic compounds.

Li⁺

Br⁻

Ba²⁺

O²⁻

DEAD END

Mg²⁺

I⁻

K⁺

Lab zone® Do the Quick Lab *Ion Formation.*

🔑 Assess Your Understanding

1a. Review An atom that loses a valence electron becomes a (positive/negative) ion. An atom that gains a valence electron becomes a (positive/negative) ion.

b. Apply Concepts Write the symbols for the ions that form when potassium and iodine react to form the ionic compound potassium iodide.

_____

c. Relate Cause and Effect Why is potassium iodide electrically neutral?

_____
_____
_____
_____
_____

got it? ....

○ **I get it!** Now I know ions form when _____
_____

○ **I need extra help with** _____

Go to **my science** 🔊 **coach** online for help with this subject.

How Are the Formulas and Names of Ionic Compounds Written?

You will often see a compound represented by its chemical formula. A **chemical formula** is a group of symbols that shows the ratio of elements in a compound. The formula for magnesium chloride is $MgCl_2$. What does this formula tell you?

Formulas of Ionic Compounds When ionic compounds form, the ions combine to balance the charges on the ions. The chemical formula for the compound reflects this balance. Look at the formula for magnesium chloride.

Chemical symbols ——→

$MgCl_2$ ←—— Subscript

Figure 2 shows that the charge on the magnesium ion is 2+. The charge on each chloride ion is 1−. Two chloride ions balance the charge on the magnesium ion. The number "2" in the formula is a subscript. **Subscripts** tell the ratio of elements in a compound. The ratio of magnesium ions to chloride ions in $MgCl_2$ is 1 to 2. **To write the formula for an ionic compound, write the symbol of the positive ion and then the symbol of the negative ion. Add the subscripts that are needed to balance the charges.**

If no subscript is written, it is understood that the subscript is 1. The formula NaCl tells you that there is a 1-to-1 ratio of sodium ions to chloride ions. Formulas for compounds of polyatomic ions are written in a similar way. Calcium carbonate has the formula $CaCO_3$. There is one calcium ion (Ca^{2+}) for each carbonate ion (CO_3^{2-}).

Vocabulary Choose the word that best completes the following sentence.

Mg is the _____ for magnesium.

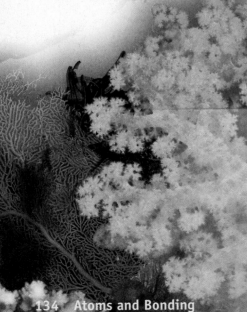

FIGURE 4 ·······················
Coral Reefs
Corals make calcium carbonate, which helps protect them. When coral dies, its calcium carbonate shell remains and adds structure to the reef.

✎ **Identify** Circle the part of the formula representing the carbonate ion. Then identify the charge of each ion in the compound.

$CaCO_3$

Naming Ionic Compounds

Magnesium chloride, sodium bicarbonate, sodium oxide—where do these names come from? **For an ionic compound, the name of the positive ion comes first, followed by the name of the negative ion.** The name of the positive ion is usually the name of a metal. But, a few positive polyatomic ions exist, such as the ammonium ion (NH_4^+). If the negative ion is a single element, the end of its name changes to -ide. For example, MgO is named magnesium oxide. If the negative ion is polyatomic, its name usually ends in -ate or -ite. Ammonium nitrate (NH_4NO_3) is a common fertilizer for plants.

did you know?

Calcium oxide (CaO), also known as lime, gives off a white light when heated. Theaters once used special lamps to focus this bright light on a single actor. So, the expression *in the limelight* describes a person who receives favorable attention.

apply it!

Chemists refer to compounds by either their names or their chemical formulas.

Interpret Data Use the periodic table and **Figure 2** to fill in the table.

Name	Positive Ion	Negative Ion	Formula
Magnesium chloride	Mg^{2+}	Cl^-	$MgCl_2$
Sodium bromide			
			Li_2O
	Mg^{2+}	S^{2-}	
Aluminum fluoride			
			KNO_3
	NH_4^+	Cl^-	

Lab zone Do the Quick Lab *How Do You Write Ionic Names and Formulas?*

Assess Your Understanding

2a. Explain The formula for sodium sulfide is Na_2S. Explain what this formula means.

_____

_____

_____

b. Apply Concepts Write the formula for calcium chloride. Explain how you determined this formula.

_____

_____

_____

got it?

○ **I get it!** Now I know that to write the formula for an ionic compound, _____

_____

○ **I need extra help with** _____

Go to MY SCIENCE COACH *online for help with this subject.*

What Are Properties of Ionic Compounds?

Compounds have properties that are different from their component elements. You have already read about the properties of metals and nonmetals, but what are the properties of the ionic compounds that form when metals and nonmetals react? 🔑 **In general, ionic compounds form hard, brittle crystals that have high melting points. They conduct electric current when dissolved in water or melted.**

Ionic Crystals Ionic compounds form solids by building up repeating patterns of ions. **Figure 5** shows a chunk of halite, which is how sodium chloride occurs naturally. Pieces of halite have a cubic shape. Equal numbers of Na^+ and Cl^- ions in halite are attracted in an alternating pattern, as shown in the diagram. The ions form an orderly, three-dimensional arrangement called a **crystal.**

Every ion in an ionic compound is attracted to ions of an opposite charge that surround it. The pattern formed by the ions is the same no matter what the size of the crystal. In a single grain of salt, the crystal pattern extends for millions of ions in every direction. Many crystals of ionic compounds are hard and brittle. This is due to the strength of their ionic bonds and the attractions among all the ions.

High Melting Points The ions in the crystal have to break apart for an ionic compound to melt. It takes a huge amount of energy to separate the ions in a crystal, because the attraction between the positive and negative ions is so great. As a result, ionic compounds have very high melting points. The melting point of sodium chloride is 801°C.

FIGURE 5 ·····································
Halite
The ions in ionic compounds are arranged in specific three-dimensional shapes called crystals. Some crystals have a cubic shape, like these crystals of halite, or sodium chloride.

Na⁺

Cl⁻

apply it!

Galena, or lead sulfide (PbS), has a structure similar to that of table salt.

S²⁻

Pb²⁺

1 Infer The chemical formula of lead sulfide tells you that it contains _____ S^{2-} ion(s) for every Pb^{2+} ion.

2 What holds the ions together in galena?

_____

_____

3 CHALLENGE If the pattern of ions shown here for galena is expanded in every direction, how many sulfide ions would surround each lead ion? _____ How many lead ions would surround each sulfide ion? _____

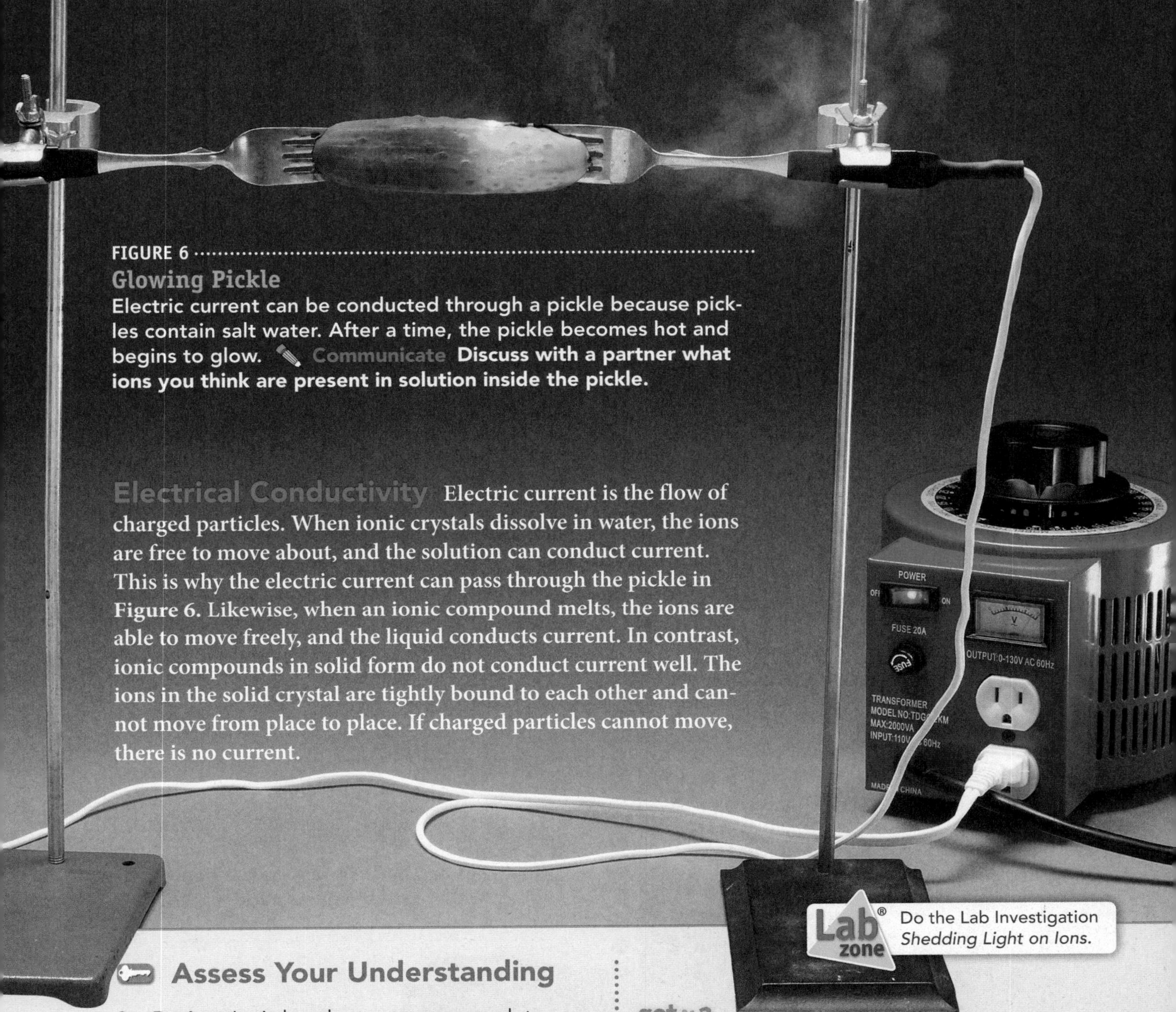

FIGURE 6 ....

Glowing Pickle

Electric current can be conducted through a pickle because pickles contain salt water. After a time, the pickle becomes hot and begins to glow. ✎ Communicate **Discuss with a partner what ions you think are present in solution inside the pickle.**

Electrical Conductivity Electric current is the flow of charged particles. When ionic crystals dissolve in water, the ions are free to move about, and the solution can conduct current. This is why the electric current can pass through the pickle in **Figure 6.** Likewise, when an ionic compound melts, the ions are able to move freely, and the liquid conducts current. In contrast, ionic compounds in solid form do not conduct current well. The ions in the solid crystal are tightly bound to each other and cannot move from place to place. If charged particles cannot move, there is no current.

Lab zone® Do the Lab Investigation *Shedding Light on Ions.*

🔑 Assess Your Understanding

3a. Review Ionic bonds are strong enough to cause almost all ionic compounds to be

_____ at room temperature.

b. Relate Cause and Effect Solid table salt does not conduct electric current. How does dissolving salt in water allow electric current to flow?

_____

_____

_____

got it? ....

○ **I get it!** Now I know that properties of ionic

compounds include _____

_____

_____

○ **I need extra help with** _____

_____

Go to **my science** 🅢 **coach** *online for help with this subject.*

Covalent Bonds

UNLOCK THE BIG ?

🔑 **How Are Atoms Held Together in a Covalent Bond?**

🔑 **What Are Properties of Molecular Compounds?**

🔑 **How Do Bonded Atoms Become Partially Charged?**

my planet Diary

Sticky Feet

Have you ever seen a gecko climbing up a wall or running across a ceiling? Geckos seem to defy gravity. They have tiny hairs that cover the pads of their feet. These hairs branch out into hundreds of smaller structures, called *spatulae.* When a gecko climbs a wall, billions of spatulae on its feet come into contact with the surface. Scientists believe that geckos can stick to surfaces because of the billions of small attractive forces, called van der Waals forces, between the molecules of the spatulae and the molecules on the surface. Now, scientists are developing adhesives that can copy the characteristics of the spatulae.

FUN FACTS

Communicate Answer the following questions. Then discuss your answers with a partner.

1. Why is it important that billions of spatulae come into contact with the surface the gecko is climbing?

_____

_____

_____

_____

_____

2. What uses do you think you could find for an adhesive that works like the gecko's foot?

_____

_____

_____

_____

> **PLANET DIARY** Go to **Planet Diary** to learn more about attractions between molecules.

 Do the Inquiry Warm-Up *Covalent Bonds.*

Vocabulary

- covalent bond • molecule • double bond • triple bond
- molecular compound • nonpolar bond • polar bond

Skills

Reading: Compare and Contrast

Inquiry: Graph

How Are Atoms Held Together in a Covalent Bond?

You and a friend walk past a bakery that sells giant chocolate chip cookies for one dollar each. But each of you has only 50 cents. If you combine your money, you can buy a cookie and split it. So, you can afford a cookie by sharing your money. Similarly, 2 atoms can form a bond by sharing electrons. The chemical bond formed when 2 atoms share electrons is called a **covalent bond.** Covalent bonds usually form between nonmetal atoms. Ionic bonds usually form when a metal combines with a nonmetal.

Electron Sharing Nonmetals can bond to other nonmetals by sharing electrons. Atoms of some nonmetals can bond with each other. **Figure 1** shows how 2 fluorine atoms can react by sharing a pair of electrons. By sharing electrons, each fluorine atom is surrounded by 8 valence electrons. ☞ **The attractions between the shared electrons and the protons in the nucleus of each atom hold the atoms together in a covalent bond.** The 2 bonded fluorine atoms form a **molecule.** A molecule is a neutral group of atoms joined by covalent bonds.

FIGURE 1 ·····································

Sharing Electrons

By sharing 2 electrons in a covalent bond, each fluorine atom gains a stable set of 8 valence electrons.

✎ **Interpret Diagrams** Circle the shared electrons that form a covalent bond between the 2 fluorine atoms.

Fluorine atom   Fluorine atom

Fluorine molecule

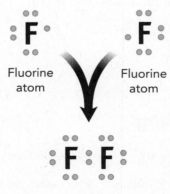

apply it!

Apply Concepts Draw electron dot diagrams to show how 2 iodine atoms bond together to form a molecule.

Single Bonds	Double Bond	Triple Bond

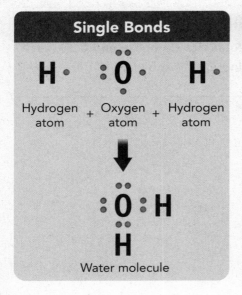

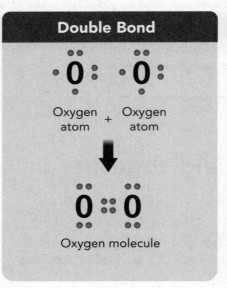

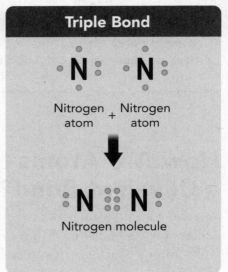

FIGURE 2 ·······················

Covalent Bonds

Atoms can form single, double, and triple covalent bonds by sharing one or more pairs of electrons.

How Many Bonds? Look at the electron dot diagrams in **Figure 2.** Count the valence electrons around each hydrogen and oxygen atom. Hydrogen has 1 valence electron. Oxygen has 6 valence electrons. In a water molecule, oxygen forms one covalent bond with each of 2 hydrogen atoms. As a result, the oxygen atom has a stable arrangement of 8 valence electrons. Each hydrogen atom forms one bond because it needs only 2 electrons to be stable.

Look at the electron dot diagram of the oxygen molecule (O_2) in **Figure 2.** This time the 2 atoms share 2 pairs of electrons, forming a **double bond.** Atoms of some elements, such as nitrogen, can share 3 pairs of electrons, forming a **triple bond.** The electron dot diagram for the nitrogen molecule (N_2) is also shown in **Figure 2.**

✎ [CHALLENGE] **In a carbon dioxide (CO_2) molecule, the carbon atom forms a double bond with each of the 2 oxygen atoms. Draw the electron dot diagram for carbon dioxide below.**

 Do the Quick Lab *Sharing Electrons.*

🔑 Assess Your Understanding

got it? ···

○ **I get it!** Now I know that the atoms in a covalent bond are held together by _____

_____

_____

○ I need extra help with _____

Go to MY SCIENCE ⓢ COACH online for help with this subject.

What Are Properties of Molecular Compounds?

Water, oxygen, and sucrose (table sugar, $C_{12}H_{22}O_{11}$) are all examples of molecular compounds. A **molecular compound** is a compound that is made up of molecules. The molecules of a molecular compound contain atoms that are covalently bonded. Ionic compounds are made up of ions and do not form molecules. ⚷ **Unlike ionic compounds, molecular compounds usually do not conduct electric current when melted or dissolved in water. Also, compared to ionic compounds, molecular compounds generally have lower melting points and boiling points.**

Poor Conductivity Most molecular compounds do not conduct electric current. Molecular compounds do not contain charged particles that are available to move, so there is no current. Have you ever noticed that some wires are insulated with plastic or rubber? These materials are made up of molecular compounds. Even as liquids, molecular compounds are poor conductors. Pure water does not conduct electric current. Neither does table sugar when it is melted or dissolved in pure water.

Low Melting Points and Boiling Points
Forces hold the molecules close to one another in a molecular solid. But the forces between molecules are much weaker than the forces between ions. Compared with an ionic solid, less heat must be added to a molecular solid to separate the molecules and change it from a solid to a liquid. For example, table salt melts at 801°C, but table sugar melts at about 190°C.

FIGURE 3 ·········

Headphones
Wires, such as the ones found on your headphones, are insulated with plastic or rubber to prevent electric current from flowing between the wires. The insulation also allows you to touch the wires without being shocked or electrocuted.

✎ **Observe** What are some other objects that have insulated wires?

_____

_____

_____

_____

141

do the math! Analyzing Data

Molecular and Ionic Compounds

The table shows the melting points and boiling points of a few molecular compounds and ionic compounds.

1 **Graph** In the space below, draw a bar graph of the melting points of these compounds. Arrange the bars in order of increasing melting point. Label each bar with the chemical formula of the compound.

2 The melting points of molecular compounds are (lower/higher) than those of ionic compounds.

3 The boiling points of molecular compounds are (lower/higher) than those of ionic compounds.

Substance	Formula	Melting Point (°C)	Boiling Point (°C)
Calcium chloride	$CaCl_2$	775	1,935
Isopropyl alcohol	C_3H_8O	−87.9	82.3
Octane	C_8H_{18}	−56.8	125.6
Sodium chloride	NaCl	800.7	1,465
Water	H_2O	0	100

◻ Molecular compound   ◻ Ionic compound

4 **Predict** Ammonia (NH_3) has a melting point of −78°C and a boiling point of −34°C. These data suggest that ammonia is a(n) (molecular/ionic) compound.

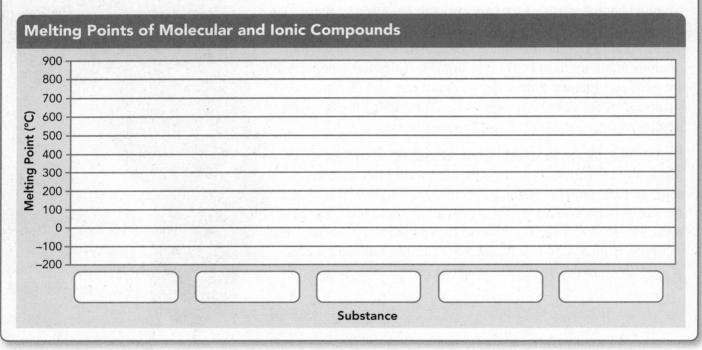

Melting Points of Molecular and Ionic Compounds

Melting Point (°C): 900, 800, 700, 600, 500, 400, 300, 200, 100, 0, −100, −200

Substance

Lab zone® Do the Quick Lab *Properties of Molecular Compounds.*

🔑 Assess Your Understanding

got it? ....

○ **I get it!** Now I know that properties of molecular compounds include _____

_____

○ **I need extra help with** _____

Go to **MY SCIENCE COACH** online for help with this subject.

How Do Bonded Atoms Become Partially Charged?

Have you ever played tug-of-war? If you have, you know that when one team pulls the rope with more force than the other team, the rope moves toward the side of the stronger team. The same is true of electrons in a covalent bond. Atoms of some elements pull more strongly on the shared electrons of a covalent bond than do atoms of other elements. As a result, the electrons are shared unequally. ⚷ **Unequal sharing of electrons causes covalently bonded atoms to have slight electric charges.**

Nonpolar Bonds and Polar Bonds If 2 atoms pull equally on the electrons, neither atom becomes charged. This happens when identical atoms are bonded. A covalent bond in which electrons are shared equally is a **nonpolar bond.** The hydrogen molecule (H_2) shown in **Figure 4** has a nonpolar bond.

When electrons in a covalent bond are shared unequally, the atom with the stronger pull gains a slightly negative charge. The atom with the weaker pull gains a slightly positive charge. A covalent bond in which electrons are shared unequally is a **polar bond.** Hydrogen fluoride (HF), also shown in **Figure 4,** has a polar bond.

✎ **Compare and Contrast**
In a nonpolar bond electrons are shared (equally/unequally).
In a polar bond electrons are shared (equally/unequally).

FIGURE 4 ·················

> ART IN MOTION **Nonpolar and Polar Bonds**
Hydrogen forms a nonpolar bond with another hydrogen atom. In hydrogen fluoride, fluorine attracts electrons more strongly than hydrogen does. The bond formed is polar.

Round 1: H₂

Round 2: HF

I want it!
I want it more!

✎ **Communicate** Imagine you're a sportscaster. Write a commentary describing each of the "tug-of-war" matchups below.

Round 1: Hydrogen (H₂)

_____

_____

_____

_____

Round 2: Hydrogen Fluoride (HF)

_____

_____

_____

_____

143

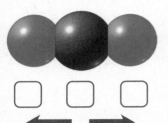

Nonpolar Molecule
Carbon dioxide

Opposite pulling cancels.

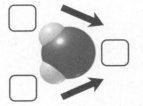

Polar Molecule
Water

Electrons pulled toward oxygen

FIGURE 5 ....

Nonpolar and Polar Molecules

Both carbon dioxide and water molecules contain polar bonds. However, only water is a polar molecule.

✎ **Interpret Diagrams** Draw a positive (+) sign next to the atoms that gain a slight positive charge. Draw a negative (–) sign next to the atoms that gain a slight negative charge.

Polar Bonds in Molecules

A molecule is polar if it has a positively charged end and a negatively charged end. However, not all molecules containing polar bonds are polar overall. In a carbon dioxide molecule, the oxygen atoms attract electrons more strongly than the carbon atom does. The bonds between the oxygen and carbon atoms are polar. But, as you can see in **Figure 5,** a carbon dioxide molecule has a straight-line shape. The two oxygen atoms pull with equal strength in opposite directions. The attractions cancel out, so the molecule is nonpolar.

A water molecule, with its two polar bonds, is itself polar. As you can see in **Figure 5,** a water molecule has a bent shape. The two hydrogen atoms are at one end of the molecule. The oxygen atom is at the other end of the molecule. The oxygen atom attracts electrons more strongly than do the hydrogen atoms. As a result, the end of the molecule with the oxygen atom has a slight negative charge. The end of the molecule with the hydrogen atoms has a slight positive charge.

EXPLORE
THE BIG
?

A Sea of Bonding

How can bonding determine the properties of a substance?

FIGURE 6 ....
▶ **INTERACTIVE ART** The Dead Sea is a saltwater lake in the Middle East. It is so salty that neither fish nor plants can survive in it. The water contains many dissolved compounds, including sodium chloride, magnesium chloride, and potassium chloride.

✎ **Review** Answer the questions about water and sodium chloride.

Water (H_2O)

Water is an example of a(n) (ionic/molecular) compound.

This type of bond forms when _____
_____
_____

Properties of these compounds

include _____
_____
_____
_____

Close-up of salt

Attractions Between Molecules

Opposite charges attract. Polar molecules are connected to each other by weak attractions between their slight negative and positive charges. These attractions are called van der Waals forces. The negatively charged oxygen ends of the polar water molecules attract the positively charged hydrogen ends of nearby water molecules. Van der Waals forces pull water molecules toward each other. They are also the reason a gecko's feet can grip onto smooth surfaces, such as glass.

The properties of polar and nonpolar compounds are different because of differences in attractions between their molecules. The melting point and boiling point of water are much higher than the melting point and boiling point of oxygen. The attractions between the polar water molecules require more energy to overcome than the attractions between the nonpolar oxygen molecules.

Sodium Chloride (NaCl)

Sodium chloride is an example of a(n) (ionic/molecular) compound.

This type of bond forms when _____

_____

_____

Properties of these compounds include _____

_____

_____

_____

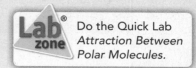
Do the Quick Lab
Attraction Between Polar Molecules.

🗝 Assess Your Understanding

1a. Review What type of bonds are formed when atoms share electrons unequally?

_____

b. Predict Would carbon dioxide or water have a higher boiling point? Explain.

_____

_____

_____

_____

_____

_____

c. ANSWER THE BIG **?** How can bonding determine the properties of a substance?

_____

_____

_____

_____

_____

_____

_____

_____

got it? ·······················

○ **I get it!** Now I know that some atoms in covalent bonds become slightly negative or slightly positive when _____

_____

○ **I need extra help with** _____

_____

Go to MY SCIENCE ⓢ COACH *online for help with this subject.*

Bonding in Metals

UNLOCK
THE BIG
?

🔑 **What Is the Structure of a Metal Crystal?**

🔑 **What Are Properties of Metals?**

my planet diary

Superconductors

In 1911, physicist Heike Kamerlingh Onnes made a remarkable discovery. When he cooled mercury to −269°C (4 kelvins), the mercury no longer resisted the flow of electric current! The cooled mercury became the world's first superconductor. A superconductor is a material that has no resistance to the flow of electric current.

Certain metals and alloys become superconductors as they are cooled to very low temperatures. This means they can carry electric currents for long periods of time without losing energy as heat. Superconductors can also be used to produce very powerful magnetic fields. These magnetic fields can be used to levitate and move high-speed trains.

Communicate Write your answers to each question below. Then discuss your answers with a partner.

1. How is a superconductor different from a regular conductor?

_____

_____

_____

_____

2. Power lines lose 10 to 15 percent of the electric current they carry to heat. Why might scientists want to create superconducting power lines?

_____

_____

_____

_____

> PLANET DIARY Go to **Planet Diary** to learn more about metals.

Lab® zone

Do the Inquiry Warm-Up
Are They "Steel" the Same?

Vocabulary
• metallic bond
• alloy

Skills
↻ Reading: Identify the Main Idea
△ Inquiry: Classify

What Is the Structure of a Metal Crystal?

The properties of solid metals can be explained by the structure of metal atoms and the bonding among those atoms. When metal atoms combine chemically with atoms of other elements, they usually lose valence electrons. They then become positively charged metal ions. Metal atoms lose electrons easily because they do not hold onto their valence electrons very strongly.

The loosely held valence electrons in metal atoms result in a type of bonding that happens in metals. Most metals are crystalline solids. ⚷ **A metal crystal is composed of closely packed, positively charged metal ions. The valence electrons drift among the ions.** Each metal ion is held in the crystal by a **metallic bond**—an attraction between a positive metal ion and the electrons surrounding it. **Figure 1** illustrates the metallic bonds that hold together aluminum foil.

FIGURE 1 ···

Metallic Bonding
The positively charged metal ions are embedded in a "sea" of valence electrons.

✎ **Infer** Why would nonmetals be unlikely to have the type of bonding shown here?

_____

_____

_____

Lab® zone Do the Quick Lab
Metal Crystals.

⚷ **Assess Your Understanding**

got it? ···

○ **I get it!** Now I know that a metal crystal consists of _____

_____

○ **I need extra help with** _____

Go to **MY SCIENCE** ⬤ᵉ **COACH** online for help with this subject.

What Are Properties of Metals?

You know a piece of metal when you see it. It's usually hard, dense, and shiny. Almost all metals are solids at room temperature. They can be hammered into sheets or drawn out into thin wires. Electronics such as stereos, computers, and MP3 players have metal parts because metals conduct electric current. Metallic bonding explains many of the common physical properties of metals.

🔑 **Properties of metals include a shiny luster, and high levels of malleability, ductility, electrical conductivity, and thermal conductivity.** Each of these properties is related to the behavior of valence electrons in metal atoms.

Luster Some of the parts of the motorcycle shown in **Figure 2** are covered in chromium, which is shiny. Polished metals have a shiny and reflective luster, called metallic luster. The luster of a metal is due to its valence electrons. When light strikes these electrons, they absorb the light and then re-emit the light.

✏️ **Identify the Main Idea**
Underline the main idea of this section on the properties of metals. As you read, circle the supporting details.

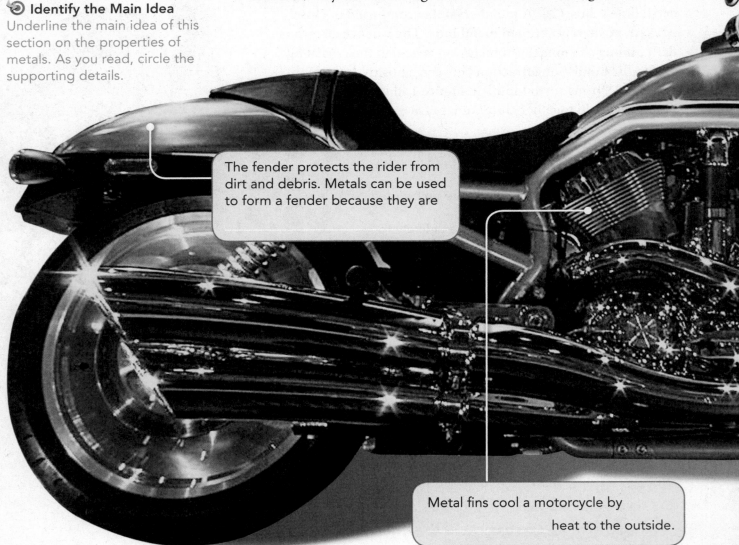

The fender protects the rider from dirt and debris. Metals can be used to form a fender because they are

Metal fins cool a motorcycle by _____ heat to the outside.

Malleability and Ductility

Metals are ductile. They can be bent easily and pulled into thin strands or wires. Metals are also malleable. They can be rolled into thin sheets, as with aluminum foil, or beaten into complex shapes. Metals act this way because the positive metal ions are attracted to the loose electrons all around them rather than to other metal ions. These ions can be made to change position. However, the metallic bonds between the ion and the surrounding electrons keep the metal ions from breaking apart from one another.

Thermal Conductivity

Thermal energy is the total energy of motion of all the particles in an object. Thermal energy flows from warmer matter to cooler matter. The greater energy of the particles in the warmer parts of the material is transferred to the particles in the cooler parts. This transfer of thermal energy is known as heat. Metals conduct heat easily because the valence electrons within a metal are free to move. Electrons in the warmer part of the metal can transfer energy to electrons in the cooler part of the metal.

FIGURE 2 ....

Properties of Metals

The unique properties of metals result from the ability of their valence electrons to move about freely.

✎ **Interpret Photos** Complete each sentence with the correct term.

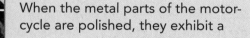

When the metal parts of the motorcycle are polished, they exhibit a

_____

Electrical Conductivity Charged particles that are free to move can conduct an electric current. Metals conduct electric current easily because the valence electrons in a metal can move freely among the atoms. Electrical wires are made out of metal. Circuit boards, such as the one shown in **Figure 3,** contain metal strips that conduct electric current throughout the circuit.

FIGURE 3 ·······················
Electrical Conductivity
Metal strips on a circuit board inside this MP3 player conduct electric current throughout the circuit.

apply it!

Many objects that are made out of metal take advantage of one or more properties of metals.

❶ **Classify** Draw arrows from each physical property listed below to the object or objects you think best exhibit that particular property.

Luster

Malleability

Ductility

Thermal Conductivity

Electrical Conductivity

❷ **Communicate** Compare your answers with a classmate's. Did your answers match? If not, discuss the differences in your answers.

❸ CHALLENGE Name an example of a metal object that shows both luster and malleability.

_____

_____

_____

Alloys

Very few of the "metals" you use every day are made up of just one element. Most of the metallic objects you see and use are made of alloys. An **alloy** is a mixture made of two or more elements, at least one of which is a metal. Alloys are generally stronger and less reactive than the pure metals from which they are made.

Pure gold is shiny, but it is soft and easily bent. For that reason, gold jewelry is made of an alloy of gold mixed with a harder element, such as copper or silver. Gold alloys are much harder than pure gold but still retain its beauty and shine.

Iron is a strong metal, but iron objects rust when they are exposed to air and water. For this reason, iron is often alloyed with one or more other elements to make steel. Objects made of iron alloys, such as the shark suit worn by the diver in Figure 4, are much stronger than iron and resist rust much better. Forks and spoons made of stainless steel can be washed over and over again without rusting. That's because stainless steel—an alloy of iron, carbon, nickel, and chromium—does not react with air and water as iron does.

FIGURE 4 ·····

Alloys
A steel suit prevents the diver from being injured by a shark.

✎ **List** What other objects do you think contain steel?

_____

_____

Lab® zone
Do the Quick Lab
What Do Metals Do?

🔑 Assess Your Understanding

1a. Identify What accounts for the properties of metals?

_____

_____

b. Explain Explain why metals are good conductors of electric current.

_____

_____

c. Apply Concepts Why is it safer to use a non-metal mixing spoon when cooking something on the stove?

_____

_____

_____

_____

_____

got it? ·····························

○ **I get it!** Now I know that properties of metals include _____

_____

○ **I need extra help with** _____

Go to **MY SCIENCE COACH** online for help with this subject.

151

Compared to molecular compounds, ionic compounds have _____ melting points.

Ionic compounds conduct electric current when _____

LESSON 1 Atoms, Bonding, and the Periodic Table

🔑 The number of valence electrons in each atom of an element helps determine the chemical properties of that element.

Vocabulary
- valence electron
- electron dot diagram
- chemical bond

Carbon

LESSON 2 Ionic Bonds

🔑 When a neutral atom loses or gains a valence electron, it becomes an ion.

🔑 For an ionic compound, the name of the negative ion follows the name of the positive ion.

🔑 Ionic compounds have high melting points.

Vocabulary
- ion • polyatomic ion • ionic bond
- ionic compound • chemical formula
- subscript • crystal

LESSON 3 Covalent Bonds

🔑 Attractions between the shared electrons and the protons in the nucleus of each atom hold the atoms together in a covalent bond.

🔑 Molecular compounds have low melting points and do not conduct electric current.

🔑 Unequal sharing of electrons causes bonded atoms to have slight electric charges.

Vocabulary
- covalent bond • molecule • double bond • triple bond
- molecular compound • nonpolar bond • polar bond

LESSON 4 Bonding in Metals

🔑 A metal crystal is composed of closely packed, positively charged metal ions. The valence electrons drift among the ions.

🔑 Properties of metals include a shiny luster, and high levels of malleability, ductility, electrical conductivity, and thermal conductivity.

Vocabulary
- metallic bond
- alloy

Review and Assessment

LESSON 1 Atoms, Bonding, and the Periodic Table

1. An electron dot diagram shows an atom's number of
   a. protons.
   b. electrons.
   c. valence electrons.
   d. chemical bonds.

2. When atoms react, they form a chemical bond, which is defined as _____ _____ _____

Use the diagrams to answer Questions 3 and 4.

Ca   :Ar: Na

Calcium   Argon   Sodium

:N   :O: :Cl:

Nitrogen   Oxygen   Chlorine

3. **Infer** Which of these elements can become stable by losing 1 electron? Explain.
   _____
   _____
   _____

4. **Draw Conclusions** Which of these elements is least likely to react with other elements? Explain.
   _____
   _____

5. **Write About It** Go to your local grocery store and observe how the products on the shelves are organized. Write a paragraph comparing how food products are organized in a grocery store and how elements are organized in the periodic table.

LESSON 2 Ionic Bonds

6. When an atom loses or gains electrons, it becomes a(n)
   a. ion.
   b. formula.
   c. crystal.
   d. subscript.

7. Magnesium chloride is an example of an ionic compound, which is a compound composed of
   _____

8. **Classify** Based on their chemical formulas, which of these compounds is not likely to be an ionic compound: KBr, SO_2, or $AlCl_3$? Explain your answer.
   _____
   _____
   _____

9. **Interpret Tables** Use the periodic table to find the number of valence electrons for calcium (Ca), aluminum (Al), rubidium (Rb), oxygen (O), sulfur (S), and iodine (I). Then use that information to predict the formula for each of the following compounds: calcium oxide, aluminum iodide, rubidium sulfide, and aluminum oxide.
   _____
   _____
   _____
   _____

10. **Write About It** Pretend that you are the size of an atom and you are observing a reaction between a potassium ion and a fluorine atom. Describe how an ionic bond forms as the atoms react. Tell what happens to the valence electrons in each atom and how each atom is changed by losing or gaining electrons.

LESSON 3 Covalent Bonds

11. A covalent bond in which electrons are shared equally is called a

   a. double bond.   **b.** triple bond.

   c. polar bond.   **d.** nonpolar bond.

12. The formulas N_2, H_2O, and CO_2 all represent molecules, which are defined as _____

_____

_____

13. Infer A carbon atom can form four covalent bonds. How many valence electrons does a carbon atom have?

_____

14. Classify Identify each molecule below as either a polar molecule or a nonpolar molecule. Explain your reasoning.

   Oxygen   Carbon dioxide

_____

_____

_____

_____

_____

_____

_____

_____

_____

LESSON 4 Bonding in Metals

15. The metal atoms in iron are held together by

   a. ionic bonds.   **b.** polar bonds.

   c. covalent bonds.   **d.** metallic bonds.

16. Polished metals have a metallic luster, which means that _____

_____

17. Apply Concepts Why does an aluminum horseshoe bend but not break when a blacksmith pounds it into shape with a hammer?

_____

_____

_____

_____

_____

APPLY THE BIG Q? **How can bonding determine the properties of a substance?**

18. An ice cube and a scoop of table salt are left outside on a warm, sunny day. Explain why the ice cube melts and the salt does not.

_____

_____

_____

_____

Standardized Test Prep

Multiple Choice

Circle the letter of the best answer.

1. The table below lists some ions and their charges.

Ions and Their Charges

Name	Charge	Symbol/Formula
Sodium	1+	Na^+
Calcium	2+	Ca^{2+}
Chloride	1–	Cl^-
Phosphate	3–	PO_4^{3-}

How many sodium ions are needed to balance the charge of one phosphate ion?

A 1
B 2
C 3
D 4

2. The chemical formula for a glucose molecule is $C_6H_{12}O_6$. The subscripts represent the

A mass of each element.
B number of atoms of each element in a glucose molecule.
C total number of bonds made by each atom.
D number of valence electrons in each atom.

3. Elements that have the same number of valence electrons are

A within the same group of the periodic table.
B within the same period of the periodic table.
C called noble gases.
D called metalloids.

4. When an atom loses an electron, it

A becomes a negative ion.
B becomes a positive ion.
C forms a covalent bond.
D gains a proton.

5. All of the following are characteristics that result from metallic bonding except

A the tendency to form hard, brittle crystals.
B the ability to conduct electric current.
C the ability to be hammered into sheets.
D luster.

Constructed Response

Use the electron dot diagrams to help you answer Question 6. Write your answer on a separate sheet of paper.

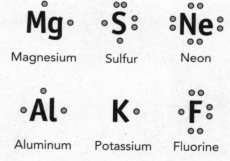

Magnesium   Sulfur   Neon

Aluminum   Potassium   Fluorine

6. Predict the formula for the compounds, if any, that would form from each of the following combinations of elements: magnesium and fluorine, aluminum and sulfur, and potassium and neon. If a compound is unlikely to form, explain the reason why.

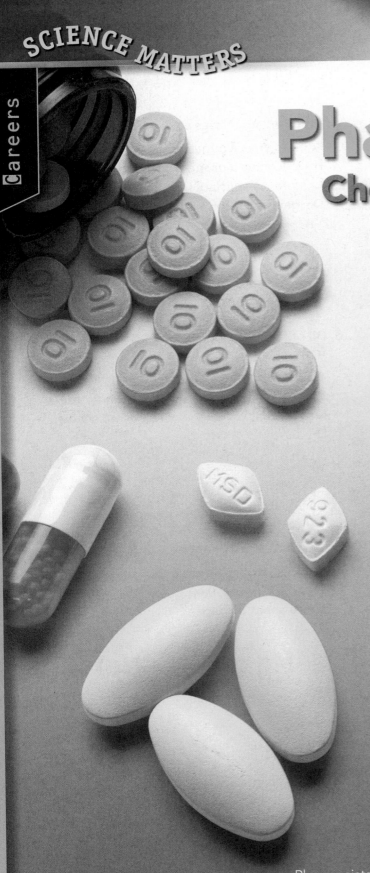

Pharmacists
Chemists at Work

Interested in science—specifically in chemistry? Your local drugstore pharmacist is a highly trained chemist.

Pharmacists work with medications. All pharmacists earn an advanced degree in pharmacy. They must also take an exam in their state before they can receive their license.

Retail pharmacists dispense medications from behind a pharmacy counter at a drugstore. They work with customers to make sure the customers' medications are safe for them to take. This means knowing how medications interact with each other, and which are safe to take at the same time.

But drugstore pharmacies aren't the only places you'll find pharmacists. Research pharmacists develop and test new medications in labs. These medicines may improve and save lives, lives of people you know.

Research It Find out more about what a research pharmacist or a retail pharmacist does, and create an informational poster about this person's work.

Pharmacists are trained to be experts in handling medications. ▶

THE SUPERHERO OF GLUES

It bonds instantly to put together a broken dish, close a hole in a fish's skin, or stick a ton of concrete to a metal beam! Magic? No, it's cyanoacrylate, a special glue. Just three square centimeters of cyanoacrylate can hold more than one ton of just about anything to any surface.

Cyanoacrylate ($C_5H_5NO_2(l)$) forms strong bonds when it comes into contact with hydroxide ions ($OH^-(g)$), found in water. Almost the moment you squeeze it out of the tube, the adhesive comes into contact with water vapor in the air and hardens, changing from liquid to solid.

Cyanoacrylate's powerful electron-attracting groups form chains of molecules, linked together. These chains form a rigid, plastic net that holds any molecules it comes into contact with! You have one super sticky situation.

Design It Design a cartoon strip explaining how the cyanoacrylate molecule forms chains to produce super bonds.

◀ Cyanoacrylate glue is used to attach a researcher's tag to a loggerhead sea turtle.

Sci-Fi Metal

Scientists in California have produced an amorphous, or glassy, metal that acts like plastic but is stronger than titanium. To produce the metal, elements are mixed and melted together, and then cooled very quickly.

A glassy metal is stronger than other metals because its atoms do not cool into a crystalline pattern. Instead, it has a random arrangement of atoms, which makes it able to transfer energy faster and last longer than other metals.

Research It Research the advantages and disadvantages of using glassy metals. What impact might glassy metals have on industry and society?

▲ NASA has used amorphous metal, which has a mirrored surface, to make solar wind collector tiles.

HOW DO BEES MAKE HONEY?

How is matter conserved in a chemical reaction?

Honeybees drink nectar from flowers. They store the nectar in a honey sac found inside their bodies. Nectar begins changing into honey in the honey sac. Nectar is mostly water, which evaporates during the honey-making process.

After collecting nectar, the honeybees return to the hive where they spit the nectar into the mouths of house bees. Chemicals in the mouths of the house bees continue changing the nectar into honey until it is ready to be stored in the honeycomb.

Draw Conclusions Explain why the amount of nectar that bees collect is larger than the amount of honey they produce.

_____

_____

_____

▶ **UNTAMED SCIENCE** Watch the **Untamed Science** video to learn more about chemical reactions.

Chemical Reactions

5 Getting Started

Check Your Understanding

1. **Background** Read the paragraph below and then answer the question.

> Alex is doing an experiment to see how vinegar reacts with **ionic compounds.** He measures the **mass** of a sample of baking soda. Alex records the measurement in his lab book next to the **chemical formula** for baking soda, $NaHCO_3$.

> An **ionic compound** consists of positive and negative ions.
>
> **Mass** is the amount of material in an object.
>
> A **chemical formula** shows the ratio of elements in a compound.

- Which substance is an ionic compound in the experiment that Alex is conducting?

_____

> MY READING WEB If you had trouble completing the question above, visit **My Reading Web** and type in *Chemical Reactions*.

Vocabulary Skill

Identify Multiple Meanings Some familiar words have more than one meaning. Words you use every day may have different meanings in science.

Word	Everyday Meaning	Scientific Meaning
matter	*n.* a subject of discussion, concern, or action **Example:** We had an important *matter* to discuss in the meeting.	*n.* anything that has mass and takes up space **Example:** Solids, liquids, and gases are states of *matter*.
product	*n.* anything that is made or created **Example:** Milk and cheese are dairy *products*.	*n.* a substance formed as a result of a chemical reaction **Example:** In a chemical reaction, substances can combine or split up to form *products*.

2. **Quick Check** Circle the sentence below that uses the scientific meaning of the word *product*.

- She brought napkins and other paper **products** to the picnic.
- Table salt is the **product** of the reaction of sodium and chlorine.

chemical change

precipitate

open system

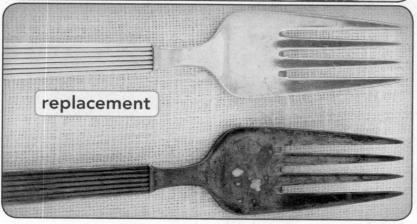

replacement

Chapter Preview

LESSON 1
- physical change
- chemical change
- reactant
- product
- precipitate
- exothermic reaction
- endothermic reaction

↻ **Relate Cause and Effect**
△ **Graph**

LESSON 2
- chemical equation
- law of conservation of mass
- open system
- closed system
- coefficient
- synthesis
- decomposition
- replacement

↻ **Summarize**
△ **Make Models**

LESSON 3
- activation energy
- concentration
- catalyst
- enzyme
- inhibitor

↻ **Ask Questions**
△ **Predict**

> **VOCAB FLASH CARDS** For extra help with vocabulary, visit **Vocab Flash Cards** and type in *Chemical Reactions.*

Observing Chemical Change

UNLOCK
THE BIG
?

🔑 **How Can Changes in Matter Be Described?**

🔑 **How Do You Identify a Chemical Reaction?**

my PLANET DiARY

Chemistry in the Kitchen

Teen chef Fatoumata Dembele knows that chemical reactions are an important part of cooking great food. In fact, Fatoumata is so skilled at using chemistry in the kitchen that she won an award for her recipes.

Fatoumata knows that to prepare some foods, such as eggs, adding heat is required. Other foods, such as gelatin, need to have heat removed to taste best. Fatoumata says you have to keep a close eye on food while it's cooking. A good chef always pays attention to signs of change. For example, when you cook meat, the color is what tells you when it's ready. A raw steak is red, but a medium steak should be dark brown on the outside and pink in the center. Fatoumata prefers her steak well done. She knows it's ready when the meat is brown all the way through. For chefs like Fatoumata, there is one particular property that matters the most. It's the taste!

Write your answers to the questions below.

1. Energy is required for chemical reactions to take place. What form of energy is used in cooking?

_____

2. Think of something you've cooked before. What changes did you observe in the food?

_____

_____

_____

▶ PLANET DIARY Go to **Planet Diary** to learn more about chemical changes.

Lab
zone®
Do the Inquiry Warm-Up
*What Happens When
Chemicals React?*

Vocabulary
- physical change • chemical change
- reactant • product • precipitate
- exothermic reaction • endothermic reaction

Skills
↻ **Reading: Relate Cause and Effect**
△ **Inquiry: Graph**

How Can Changes in Matter Be Described?

Picture yourself frying an egg. You crack open the shell, and the yolk and egg white spill into the pan. As the egg heats up, the white changes from a clear liquid to a white solid. The egg, the pan, and the stove are all examples of matter. Recall that matter is anything that has mass and takes up space. An important part of chemistry is describing matter.

Properties of Matter Matter is often described by its characteristics, or properties, and how it changes. There are two kinds of properties of matter—physical properties and chemical properties.

How would you describe the penny in **Figure 1A**? It is solid, shiny, and hard. A physical property is a characteristic of a substance that can be observed without changing the substance into another substance. The temperature at which a solid melts is a physical property. Color, texture, density, and conductivity are other physical properties of matter.

A chemical property is a characteristic of a substance that describes its ability to change into other substances. To observe the chemical properties of a substance, you must try to change it into another substance. For example, **Figure 1B** shows a penny that has turned green. This color change demonstrates a chemical property of the penny's copper coating. When copper is exposed to air, it reacts over time to form a dull, crusty solid. Another chemical property is a material's ability to burn in the presence of oxygen. This property is called flammability.

FIGURE 1 ·····················
Properties of Copper
Pennies are coated with copper.

✎ **Complete the following tasks.**

1. **Classify** Check off which properties of copper are physical properties and which are chemical properties.

2. **Communicate** Add two properties to the list and ask a classmate to classify them as physical or chemical.

Copper

Property	Physical	Chemical
• Reddish color	☐	☐
• Reacts with oxygen	☐	☐
• Smooth texture	☐	☐
• Conducts heat	☐	☐
• Not flammable	☐	☐
• _____	☐	☐
• _____	☐	☐

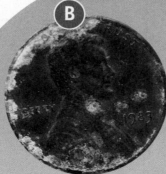

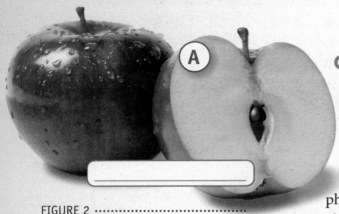

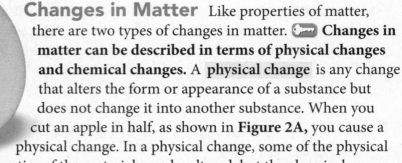

Changes in Matter

Like properties of matter, there are two types of changes in matter. ◄━━► **Changes in matter can be described in terms of physical changes and chemical changes.** A **physical change** is any change that alters the form or appearance of a substance but does not change it into another substance. When you cut an apple in half, as shown in **Figure 2A,** you cause a physical change. In a physical change, some of the physical properties of the material may be altered, but the chemical composition remains the same. Bending, crushing, and cutting are all physical changes. Changes in the state of matter, such as melting, freezing, and boiling, are also physical changes.

Sometimes when matter changes, its chemical composition is changed. For example, when a cut apple is left out in the air, it turns brown, as shown in **Figure 2B.** Compounds in the apple react with the oxygen in the air to form new compounds. A change in matter that produces one or more new substances is a **chemical change,** or chemical reaction. In a chemical change, the atoms rearrange to form new substances. When a substance undergoes a chemical change, it results in different physical properties as well. Burning and rusting are both chemical changes. Substances that undergo the chemical changes are called **reactants.** The new substances that form are the **products.**

FIGURE 2 ·····················
▶ INTERACTIVE ART **Changes in Matter**
Matter can undergo both physical and chemical changes.

✎ **Identify** Label each apple with the type of change it has undergone.

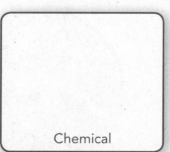

apply it!

Changes in matter occur everywhere in your daily life.

❶ Apply Concepts Paper that has been (torn/burned) has undergone a chemical change.

❷ Interpret Photos Label the change in each set of pictures as a physical or chemical change.

❸ CHALLENGE In the correct box, draw or explain how the leaf will look if it undergoes a physical change and if it undergoes a chemical change.

Physical

Chemical

Bonding and Chemical Change

Chemical changes occur when existing bonds break and new bonds form. As a result, new substances are produced. Atoms form bonds when they share or transfer electrons. The reaction pictured in **Figure 3** involves both the breaking of shared bonds and the transfer of electrons.

Oxygen gas (O_2) in the air consists of molecules made up of two oxygen atoms bonded together. These bonds break when oxygen reacts with magnesium (Mg) and a new ionic bond forms. The compound magnesium oxide (MgO) is produced. Magnesium oxide, a white powder, has properties that differ from those of either shiny magnesium or invisible oxygen gas. For example, while magnesium melts at 650°C, magnesium oxide melts at 2,800°C.

✎
🔁 **Relate Cause and Effect**
Find and underline the effect caused by breaking and forming bonds.

FIGURE 3 ····················

Breaking and Making Bonds

✎ **Summarize** On the lines below the diagrams, describe what happens to the bonds in each of the steps as oxygen reacts with magnesium.

① O⋮⋮O → O⋮ + ⋮O

② Mg⋮ + ⋮O⋮ → Mg^{2+}⋮O^{2-}

Lab zone® Do the Quick Lab *Observing Change.*

🔑 Assess Your Understanding

1a. Review The freezing point of water is a (physical/chemical) property. The ability of oxygen to react with iron to cause rust is a (physical/chemical) property.

b. Pose Questions When silver coins are found in ancient shipwrecks, they are coated with a black crust. Ask a question that could help you determine whether the silver underwent a chemical change or physical change. Explain.

_____

_____

_____

_____

got it?

○ **I get it!** Now I know that two ways changes in matter can be described are _____

_____

_____

_____

_____

○ **I need extra help with** _____

Go to **MY SCIENCE** ⑤ **COACH** online for help with this subject.

How Do You Identify a Chemical Reaction?

Look at the images in **Figure 4**. Even without reading the caption, you probably can tell that each image shows a chemical reaction. How can you tell when a chemical reaction occurs? **Chemical reactions involve changes in properties and changes in energy that you can often observe.**

Changes in Properties One way to detect chemical reactions is to observe changes in the physical properties of the materials. Changes in properties result when new substances form. For instance, formation of a precipitate, gas production, and a color change are all possible evidence that a chemical reaction has taken place. Many times, physical properties such as texture and hardness may also change in a chemical reaction.

Changes in physical properties can be easy to recognize in a chemical reaction, but what about the chemical properties? During a chemical reaction, reactants interact to form products with different chemical properties. For example, sodium (Na) and chlorine (Cl_2) react to form an ionic compound, sodium chloride (NaCl). Both reactants are very reactive elements. However, the product, sodium chloride, is a very stable compound.

Vocabulary Identify Multiple Meanings Precipitation can mean rain, snow, or hail. In chemistry, precipitation is the formation of a solid from

_____

_____

❶ Formation of a Precipitate
The mixing of two liquids may form a precipitate. A **precipitate** (pree SIP uh tayt) is a solid that forms from liquids during a chemical reaction. For example, the precipitate seen in this curdled milk has formed from the liquids milk and lemon juice.

FIGURE 4 ••••••••••••••••••••••••••••••••••
Evidence of Chemical Reactions
Many kinds of change provide evidence that a chemical reaction has occurred.

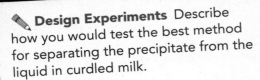

Design Experiments Describe how you would test the best method for separating the precipitate from the liquid in curdled milk.

_____

_____

_____

_____

_____

_____

_____

_____

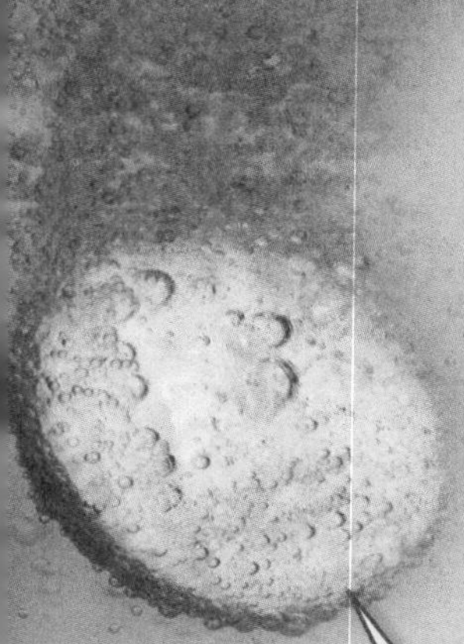

Although you may observe a change in matter, the change does not always indicate that a chemical reaction has taken place. Sometimes physical changes give similar results. For example, when water boils, the gas bubbles you see are made of molecules of water, just as the liquid was. Boiling is a physical change. The only sure evidence of a chemical reaction is that one or more new substances are produced.

❷ Gas Production

Another observable change is the formation of a gas from solid or liquid reactants. Often, the gas formed can be seen as bubbles.

✎ **Observe** Bread dough rises from gas bubbles produced when yeast reacts with sugar. What evidence in a slice of bread shows the presence of gas?

_____

_____

_____

_____

_____

❸ Color Change

A color change can signal that a new substance has formed. For example, avocados turn brown when they react with oxygen in the air.

✎ **Apply Concepts** Draw or describe evidence of a chemical reaction you have observed in food or in other types of matter. Label the evidence as a color change, formation of a precipitate, or gas production.

✎ **Relate Evidence and Explanation** Adding food coloring to water causes a color change. Is this evidence of a chemical reaction? Explain.

_____

_____

_____

_____

_____

_____

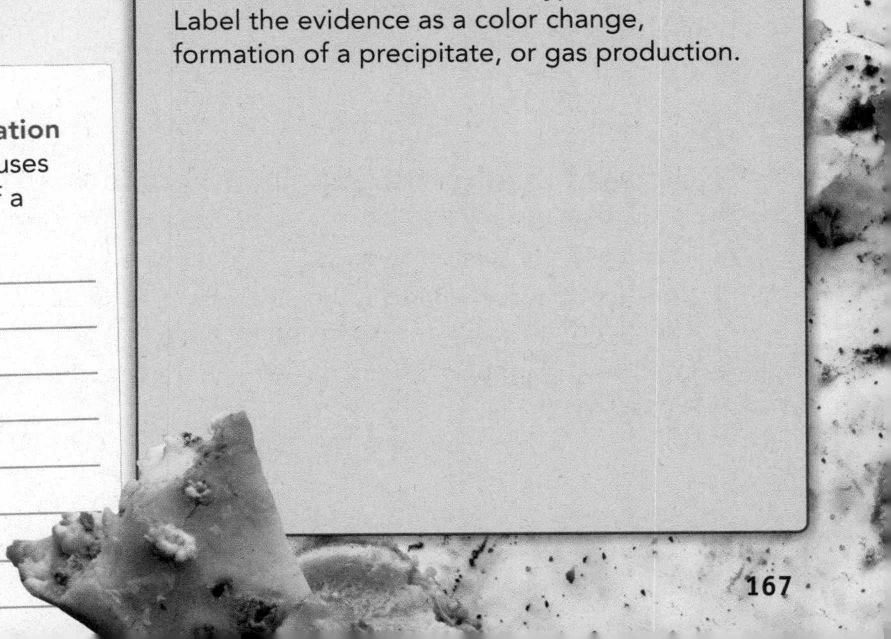

167

Exothermic

Energy

Energy

Changes in Energy Recall that a chemical reaction occurs when bonds break and new bonds form. Breaking bonds between atoms or ions requires energy, while forming bonds releases energy.

In an **exothermic reaction** (ek soh THUR mik), the energy released as the products form is greater than the energy required to break the bonds of the reactants. The energy is usually released as heat. For example, some stoves use natural gas. When natural gas burns, it releases heat. This heat is used to cook your food. Similarly, the reaction between oxygen and other fuels that produce fire, such as wood, coal, oil, or the wax of the candle shown in **Figure 5,** release energy in the form of light and heat.

In an **endothermic reaction** (en doh THUR mik), more energy is required to break the bonds of the reactants than is released by the formation of the products. The energy can be absorbed from nearby matter. When energy is absorbed, it causes the surroundings to become cooler. In **Figure 5,** baking soda undergoes an endothermic reaction when it is mixed with vinegar. The reaction absorbs heat from its surroundings, so the reaction feels cold. Not all endothermic reactions result in a temperature decrease. Many endothermic reactions occur only when heat is constantly added, as when you fry an egg. Heat must be applied throughout the entire process in order for the reactions that cook the egg to continue.

Energy

Energy

Endothermic

FIGURE 5 ···

▷ VIRTUAL LAB **Exothermic and Endothermic Reactions**
Chemical reactions either absorb energy or release energy.

✎ **Complete the following tasks.**

1. **Interpret Photos** Shade in the arrow that indicates the direction the net energy is moving for each reaction.

2. **Infer** How might each reaction feel if you were to put your hands near it?

do the math! Analyzing Data

A student adds magnesium oxide to hydrochloric acid. She measures the temperature of the reaction every minute. Her data are recorded in the table.

1 Graph Plot the data from the table onto the graph. Then name the graph.

Time (min)	Temperature (°C)
0	20
1	24
2	27
3	29
4	29

2 Interpret Data Is the reaction endothermic or exothermic? Explain.

____

____

____

____

____

____

____

3 Read Graphs In which time interval did the temperature increase the most?

____

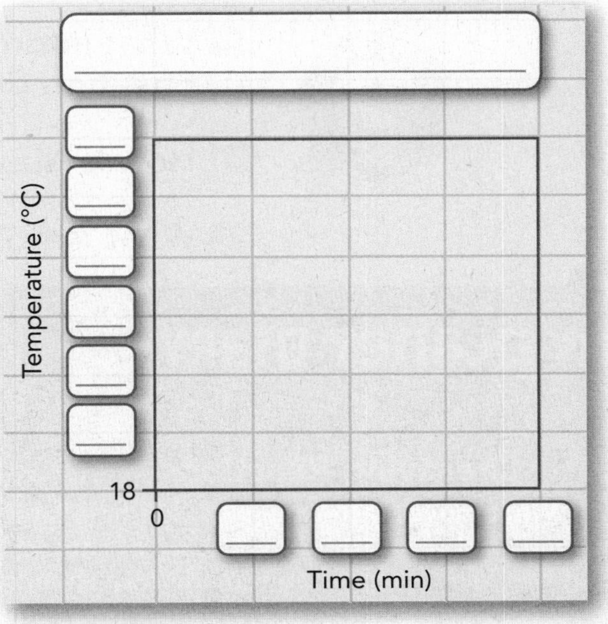

Lab zone® Do the Lab Investigation *Where's the Evidence?*

Assess Your Understanding

2a. List What changes in physical properties can be used as evidence that a chemical reaction has occurred?

____

____

____

b. Apply Concepts What evidence of a chemical change is observed when rust forms on iron?

____

____

c. Compare and Contrast How are endothermic and exothermic reactions the same? How are they different?

____

____

____

____

____

____

____

got it?

O **I get it!** Now I know that two kinds of changes you can observe when chemical reactions occur are ______________________________________

O I need extra help with ______________________________________

Go to MY SCIENCE COACH *online for help with this subject.*

Describing Chemical Reactions

🔑 **What Information Does a Chemical Equation Contain?**

🔑 **How Is Mass Conserved During a Chemical Reaction?**

🔑 **What Are Three Types of Chemical Reactions?**

MY PLANET DiARY

Lifesaving Reactions

What moves faster than 300 km/h, inflates in less than a second, and saves lives? An airbag, of course! Did you know that the "air" in an airbag is made by a chemical reaction? A

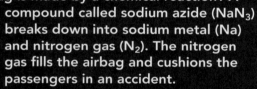

compound called sodium azide (NaN_3) breaks down into sodium metal (Na) and nitrogen gas (N_2). The nitrogen gas fills the airbag and cushions the passengers in an accident.

It's important that the correct amount of sodium azide is used. The mass of sodium azide in the airbag before the collision will equal the mass of sodium and nitrogen that is made by the reaction. If too little or too much nitrogen gas is made, the airbag will not inflate properly.

FUN FACTS

Write your answer to the question below.

What might happen if an airbag doesn't contain the correct amount of sodium azide?

_____

_____

_____

_____

_____

▷ **PLANET DIARY** Go to **Planet Diary** to learn more about the law of conservation of mass.

 Lab zone® Do the Inquiry Warm-Up *Did You Lose Anything?*

What Information Does a Chemical Equation Contain?

Cell phone text messages, like the one shown in **Figure 1**, use symbols and abbreviations to express ideas in shorter form. A type of shorthand is used in chemistry, too. A **chemical equation** is a way to show a chemical reaction, using symbols instead of words. Chemical equations are shorter than sentences, but they contain plenty of information. In chemical equations, chemical formulas and other symbols are used to summarize a reaction.

Vocabulary
- chemical equation • law of conservation of mass
- open system • closed system • coefficient
- synthesis • decomposition • replacement

Skills
↻ Reading: Summarize
△ Inquiry: Make Models

FIGURE 1 ·····························

Symbols and Abbreviations
Text messages, like chemical equations, let you express ideas in shorter form.

🖊 **Interpret Photos** Translate the text message using complete words and sentences.

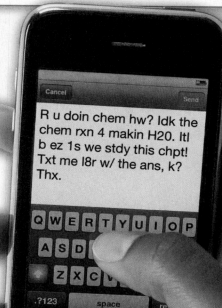

Formulas in an Equation
You may recall that a chemical formula is a combination of symbols that represents the elements in a compound. For example, CO_2 is the formula for carbon dioxide. The formula tells you that the ratio of carbon atoms to oxygen atoms in this compound is 1 to 2. Carbon dioxide is a molecular compound. Each carbon dioxide molecule has 1 carbon atom and 2 oxygen atoms. **Figure 2** lists the formulas of other familiar compounds.

FIGURE 2 ··

Chemical Formulas
The formula of a compound identifies the elements in the compound and the ratio in which their atoms or ions are present.

🖊 **Interpret Tables** Complete the table by filling in the missing chemical formulas.

Formulas of Familiar Compounds	
Compound	Formula
Propane	C_3H_8
Sugar (sucrose)	$C_{12}H_{22}O_{11}$
Rubbing alcohol	C_3H_8O
Ammonia	NH_3
Baking soda	$NaHCO_3$
Water	
Carbon dioxide	
Sodium chloride	

FIGURE 3 ···

Modeling a Chemical Equation

Like a skateboard, a chemical equation has a basic structure.

Make Models Complete the equation by filling in the number of the skateboard parts shown. Determine the number of complete skateboards that can be made and draw them as the product.

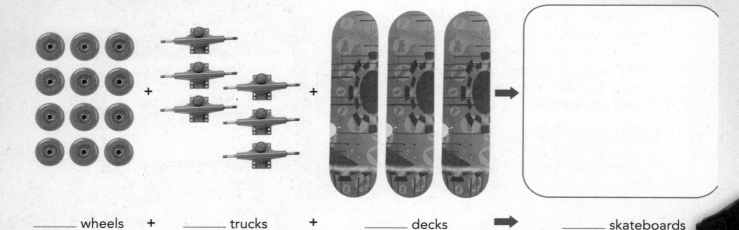

_____ wheels   +   _____ trucks   +   _____ decks   ➡   _____ skateboards

Structure of an Equation

Suppose you are building a skateboard. What parts do you need? How many of each part are necessary to build a complete skateboard? **Figure 3** summarizes everything you need to build several skateboards. Similarly, a chemical equation summarizes everything needed to carry out a chemical reaction.

All chemical equations have a basic structure that is followed. **A chemical equation tells you the substances you start with in a reaction and the substances that are formed at the end.** The substances you have at the beginning are the reactants. When the reaction is complete, you have new substances, called the products.

The formulas for the reactants are written on the left, followed by an arrow. You read the arrow as "yields," or "reacts to form." The formulas for the products are written to the right of the arrow. When there are two or more reactants, they are separated by plus signs. In a similar way, plus signs are used to separate two or more products. Below is the general structure of a chemical equation.

Reactant + Reactant → Product + Product

The number of reactants and products can vary. Some reactions have only one reactant or product. Other reactions have two, three, or more reactants or products. For example, the reaction that occurs when limestone, or calcium carbonate ($CaCO_3$), is heated has one reactant and two products (CaO and CO_2).

$$CaCO_3 \rightarrow CaO + CO_2$$

apply it!

Molecules of nitrogen (N_2) and hydrogen (H_2) react to form ammonia (NH_3).

1 Identify Indicate the number of H_2 and N_2 molecules needed to yield two molecules of NH_3.

2 Make Models Draw the correct number of reactant molecules in the boxes on the left side of the equation.

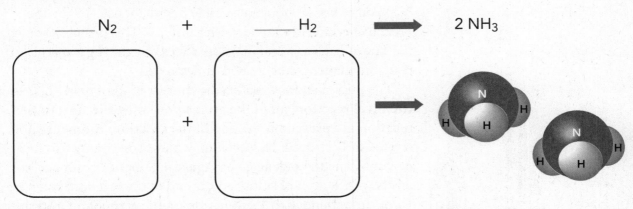

_____ N_2 +   _____ H_2 ⟶   2 NH_3

+

3 Describe What bonds of the reactants are broken in this reaction? What bonds are formed in the product?

_____

_____

_____

_____

Do the Quick Lab *Information in a Chemical Equation.*

🔑 Assess Your Understanding

1a. Explain What do the formulas, arrows, and plus signs tell you in a chemical equation?

_____

_____

_____

_____

_____

_____

b. Interpret Data Write the chemical equation for the following reaction: The elements carbon and oxygen combine to yield the compound carbon dioxide.

_____

got it? ....

○ **I get it!** Now I know that a chemical equation tells you _____

○ **I need extra help with** _____

Go to **MY SCIENCE COACH** online for help with this subject.

How Is Mass Conserved During a Chemical Reaction?

Look at the reaction below in **Figure 4.** Iron and sulfur can react to form iron sulfide (FeS). Can you predict the mass of iron sulfide, knowing the mass of the reactants? It might help you to know about a principle first demonstrated by the French chemist Antoine Lavoisier in 1774. This principle, called the **law of conservation of mass,** states that during a chemical reaction, matter is not created or destroyed.

The idea of atoms explains the conservation of mass. 🔑 **In a chemical reaction, all of the atoms present at the start of the reaction are present at the end of the reaction.** Atoms are not created or destroyed. However, they may be rearranged to form new substances. Look again at **Figure 4.** Suppose 1 atom of iron reacts with 1 atom of sulfur. At the end of the reaction, you have 1 iron atom bonded to 1 sulfur atom in the compound iron sulfide (FeS). All the atoms in the reactants are present in the products. The amount of matter does not change. According to the law of conservation of mass, the total mass stays the same before and after the reaction.

FIGURE 4

▶ **INTERACTIVE ART** **Conservation of Mass**

In a chemical reaction, matter is not created or destroyed.

✏️ **Calculate** On the balance, write the mass of iron sulfide produced by this reaction.

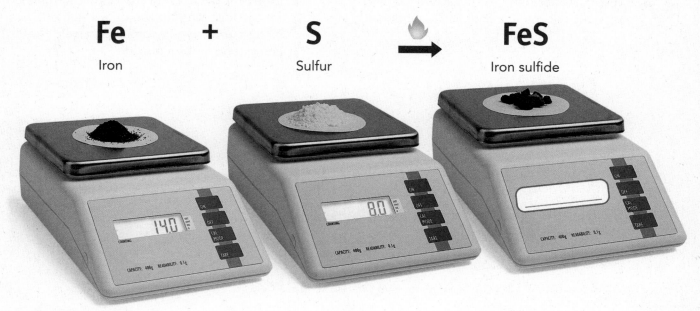

Fe + S 🔥 → FeS

Iron   Sulfur   Iron sulfide

14.0   **8.0**

Open and Closed Systems

At first glance, some reactions may seem to violate the principle of conservation of mass. It's not always easy to measure all the matter involved in a reaction. For example, if you burn a match, oxygen comes into the reaction from the surrounding air, but how much? Likewise, the products escape into the air. Again, how much?

A fish bowl is an example of an open system. It contains different types of matter that are interacting with each other. In an **open system,** matter can enter from or escape to the surroundings. If you want to measure all the matter before and after a reaction, you have to be able to contain it. In a **closed system,** matter does not enter or leave. A chemical reaction that occurs inside a sealed, airtight container is a closed system. The enclosed ecosphere shown in **Figure 5** doesn't allow any mass to enter or escape.

FIGURE 5 ·······

Open and Closed Systems

Matter cannot enter or leave a closed system, as it can in an open system.

✎ **Complete the following tasks.**

1. **Identify** Label each system as open or closed.

2. **Design Experiments** Which system would you use to demonstrate conservation of mass? Why?

_____

_____

_____

_____

3. [CHALLENGE] Why do you think the fish bowl above is considered a system, but an empty fish bowl is not?

_____

_____

_____

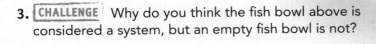

Balancing Chemical Equations

The principle of conservation of mass means that the total number of atoms of each element in the reactants must equal the total number of atoms of each element in the products. To be accurate, a chemical equation must show the same number of atoms of each element on both sides of the equation. Chemists say an equation is balanced when conservation of mass is correctly shown. How can you write a balanced chemical equation?

STEP ① Write the Equation Suppose you want to write a balanced chemical equation for the reaction between hydrogen and oxygen that forms water. To begin, write the correct chemical formulas for both reactants and the product. Place the reactants, H_2 and O_2, on the left side of the arrow, separated by a plus sign. Then write the product, H_2O, on the right side of the arrow.

Hydrogen   +   Oxygen   →   Water

STEP ② Count the Atoms Count the number of atoms of each element on each side of the equation. Recall that a subscript tells you the ratio of elements in a compound.

☐ Hydrogen + ☐ Oxygen → ☐ Hydrogen atom(s)
  atom(s)   atom(s)   ☐ Oxygen atom(s)

After counting, you find 2 atoms of oxygen in the reactants but only 1 atom of oxygen in the product. How can the number of oxygen atoms on both sides of the equation be made equal? You cannot change the formula for water to H_2O_2 because H_2O_2 is the formula for hydrogen peroxide, a completely different compound. So how can you show that mass is conserved?

STEP 3 Use Coefficients to Balance Atoms To balance the equation, use coefficients. A **coefficient** (koh uh FISH unt) is a number placed in front of a chemical formula in an equation. It tells you the amount of a reactant or a product that takes part in a reaction. The coefficient applies to every atom of the formula it is in front of. If the coefficient is 1, you don't need to write it.

Balance the number of oxygen atoms by changing the coefficient of H_2O to 2. Again, count the number of atoms on each side of the equation.

✎

Summarize Describe the steps to balancing a chemical equation.

_____
_____
_____
_____
_____
_____
_____
_____

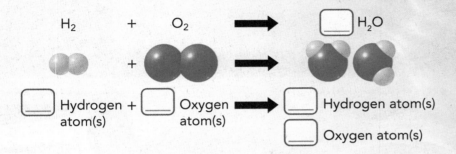

H_2 + O_2 ⟶ ☐ H_2O

☐ Hydrogen + ☐ Oxygen ⟶ ☐ Hydrogen atom(s)
atom(s)   atom(s)

☐ Oxygen atom(s)

Balancing the oxygen atoms "unbalances" the number of hydrogen atoms. There are now 2 hydrogen atoms in the reactants and 4 in the product. How can you balance the hydrogen? Try changing the coefficient of H_2 to 2. Then, count the atoms again.

☐ H_2 + O_2 ⟶ 2 H_2O

☐ Hydrogen + ☐ Oxygen ⟶ ☐ Hydrogen atom(s)
atom(s)   atom(s)

☐ Oxygen atom(s)

STEP 4 Look Back and Check Is the number of atoms of each element in the reactants equal to the number of atoms of each element in the products? If so, mass is conserved and the equation is balanced. The balanced equation tells you 2 hydrogen molecules react with 1 oxygen molecule to yield 2 water molecules.

do the math! Sample Problem
....

Apply Concepts Use the sample problem in the blue box below to help you balance the following equations.

❶ $KClO_3 \rightarrow KCl + O_2$

_____

❷ $NaBr + Cl_2 \rightarrow NaCl + Br_2$

_____
_____

❸ $Na + Cl_2 \rightarrow NaCl$

_____

❶ Write the equation.
$Mg + O_2 \rightarrow MgO$

❷ Count the atoms.
$Mg + O_2 \rightarrow MgO$
 1   2   1 1

❸ Use coefficients to balance.
$2 Mg + O_2 \rightarrow 2 MgO$
 2   2   2 2

❹ Look back and check.

How Can Chemical Reactions Generate *SPEED*?

How is matter conserved in a chemical reaction?

FIGURE 6 ···

> **INTERACTIVE ART** One day, you might be able to drink the exhaust from your car! Sounds gross, right? Well, it could be possible with hydrogen fuel cells. Hydrogen fuel cells use a chemical reaction between hydrogen and oxygen to generate energy for running a car. In the process, water is produced.

✎ **Review** Use what you've learned about chemical reactions to answer questions about fuel cells.

1 Endothermic or Exothermic?

The reaction in a fuel cell is used to power cars and other devices. Is it an endothermic or exothermic reaction? Explain.

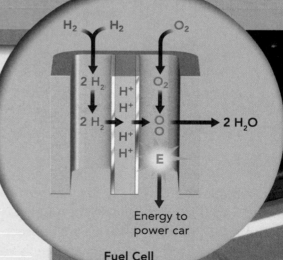

2 Conservation of Mass

Inside a fuel cell, hydrogen is converted into H^+ ions. These ions combine with oxygen to produce energy for the car and water as exhaust. Describe how the fuel cell obeys the law of conservation of mass.

H_2 H_2 O_2

$2 H_2$ H^+ O_2
H^+
$2 H_2 \rightarrow$ O O $\rightarrow 2 H_2O$
H^+
H^+ E

Energy to power car

Fuel Cell

An astronaut gathers packets for drinking.

 Do the Quick Lab
Is Matter Conserved?

🔑 Assess Your Understanding

2a. Infer If the total mass of the products in a reaction is 90 grams, what was the total mass of the reactants?

_____

b. Apply Concepts Balance the equations.

• $Al + CuO \rightarrow Al_2O_3 + Cu$

• $Fe_2O_3 + C \rightarrow Fe + CO_2$

• $SO_2 + O_2 \rightarrow SO_3$

_____

_____

_____

_____

c. ANSWER THE BIG ? How is matter conserved in a chemical reaction?

_____

_____

_____

_____

_____

_____

_____

_____

_____

3 Properties of Matter

Hydrogen fuel cells power missions in space. Describe why the product of fuel cells would be more beneficial to space missions than that of other fuels.

_____

_____

_____

_____

_____

_____

4 Balance the Chemical Equation

Hydrogen must be obtained from decomposing fuels like methane (CH_4). Balance the equation for generating hydrogen for fuel cells.

$$CH_4 + H_2O \rightarrow CO + H_2$$

got it? ●

○ **I get it!** Now I know that the masses of reactants and products must be _____

_____

○ **I need extra help with** _____

Go to **MY SCIENCE** 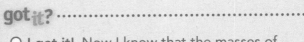 **COACH** *online for help with this subject.*

What Are Three Types of Chemical Reactions?

In a chemical reaction, substances may combine to make a more complex substance. They may break apart to make simpler substances. They may even exchange parts. In each case, new substances are formed. 🔑 **Three types of chemical reactions are synthesis, decomposition, and replacement.**

Synthesis Some musicians use a machine called a synthesizer. A synthesizer combines different electronic sounds to make music. To synthesize is to put things together. In chemistry, when two or more elements or compounds combine to make a more complex substance, the reaction is classified as **synthesis** (SIN thuh sis). The reaction of phosphorus with oxygen is a synthesis reaction.

$$P_4 + 3\ O_2 \rightarrow P_4O_6$$

Decomposition In contrast to a synthesis reaction, a **decomposition** reaction occurs when compounds break down into simpler products. You probably have a bottle of hydrogen peroxide (H_2O_2) in your house to clean cuts. If you keep such a bottle for a very long time, you'll have water instead. Hydrogen peroxide decomposes into water and oxygen gas.

$$2\ H_2O_2 \rightarrow 2\ H_2O + O_2$$

Replacement When one element replaces another element in a compound, or if two elements in different compounds trade places, the reaction is called a **replacement.** Look at this example.

$$2\ Cu_2O + C \rightarrow 4\ Cu + CO_2$$

Copper metal is obtained by heating copper oxide with carbon. The carbon replaces the copper in the compound with oxygen.

The reaction between copper oxide and carbon is called a *single* replacement reaction because one element, carbon, replaces another element, copper, in the compound. In a *double* replacement reaction, elements in a compound appear to trade places with the elements in another compound. The following reaction is an example of a double replacement.

$$FeS + 2\ HCl \rightarrow FeCl_2 + H_2S$$

FIGURE 7 ···

Types of Reactions

✎ Complete the following tasks.

1. Interpret Diagrams Label each type of reaction represented.

2. Explain How are synthesis and decomposition reactions related to each other?

_____

_____

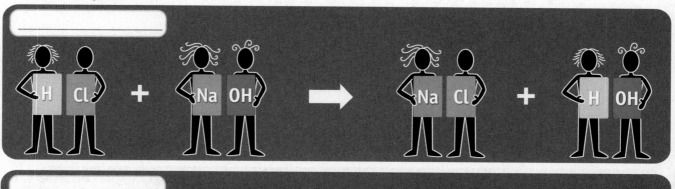

 Do the Quick Lab *Categories of Chemical Reactions.*

🔑 Assess Your Understanding

3a. Classify What type of chemical reaction is shown in the chemical equation below?

$$Zn + 2\ HCl \rightarrow H_2 + ZnCl_2$$

_____

_____

b. Draw Conclusions The elements iron and oxygen can react to form the compound iron oxide. What type of reaction is this? Explain.

_____

_____

_____

got it? ···

○ **I get it!** Now I know that three types of chemical reactions are _____

_____

○ **I need extra help with** _____

Go to **my science ⒮ coach** online for help with this subject.

Controlling Chemical Reactions

How Do Reactions Get Started?

What Affects the Rate of a Chemical Reaction?

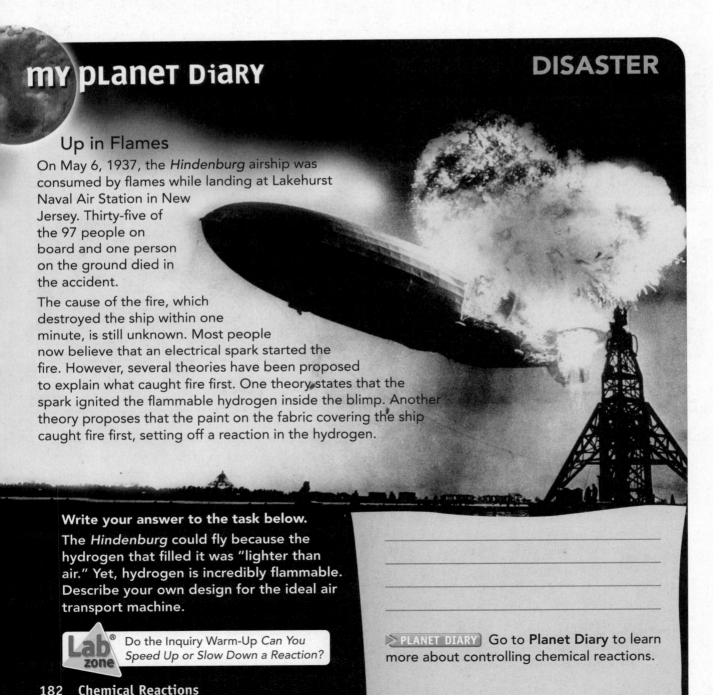

my planet Diary

DISASTER

Up in Flames

On May 6, 1937, the *Hindenburg* airship was consumed by flames while landing at Lakehurst Naval Air Station in New Jersey. Thirty-five of the 97 people on board and one person on the ground died in the accident.

The cause of the fire, which destroyed the ship within one minute, is still unknown. Most people now believe that an electrical spark started the fire. However, several theories have been proposed to explain what caught fire first. One theory states that the spark ignited the flammable hydrogen inside the blimp. Another theory proposes that the paint on the fabric covering the ship caught fire first, setting off a reaction in the hydrogen.

Write your answer to the task below.

The *Hindenburg* could fly because the hydrogen that filled it was "lighter than air." Yet, hydrogen is incredibly flammable. Describe your own design for the ideal air transport machine.

_____

_____

_____

_____

Lab zone Do the Inquiry Warm-Up *Can You Speed Up or Slow Down a Reaction?*

> **PLANET DIARY** Go to **Planet Diary** to learn more about controlling chemical reactions.

Vocabulary
- activation energy
- concentration • catalyst
- enzyme • inhibitor

Skills
- Reading: Ask Questions
- Inquiry: Predict

How Do Reactions Get Started?

Suppose you're a snowboarder, like the one shown in **Figure 1.** You know that the only way to ride down the mountain is to first get to the top. One way to get there is by riding the chairlift. Once you reach the top of the mountain, you can get off the lift and enjoy the ride down. If you never get to the top, you will never be able to go down the mountain.

Activation Energy Chemical reactions can be like snow-boarding. A reaction won't begin until the reactants have enough energy to push them to the "top of the mountain." The energy is used to break the chemical bonds of the reactants. Then the atoms form the new bonds of the products. **Activation energy** is the minimum amount of energy needed to start a chemical reaction. **All chemical reactions need a certain amount of activation energy to get started.** Usually, once a few molecules react, the rest will quickly follow. The first few reactions provide the activation energy for more molecules to react.

Hydrogen and oxygen can react to form water. However, if you just mix the two gases together, nothing happens. For the reaction to start, activation energy must be added. An electric spark or adding heat can provide that energy. A few of the hydrogen and oxygen molecules will react, producing energy. That energy will provide the activation energy needed for even more molecules to react.

Ask Questions Is it clear where chemical reactions get activation energy from? Write a question about this topic that you want answered.

_____

_____

_____

_____

_____

_____

FIGURE 1 ·····················
Activation Energy
✎ A chemical reaction needs a push to the "top of the mountain" to get started.

1. **Infer** Place an arrow at the point where enough activation energy has been added to start the reaction.

2. **Interpret Diagrams** Where does the snowboarder get the activation energy needed to reach the top of the mountain?

_____

Graphing Changes in Energy Every chemical reaction needs activation energy to start. Whether or not a reaction still needs more energy from the environment to keep going depends on whether it is exothermic or endothermic.

Exothermic reactions follow the pattern you can see in **Figure 2A.** The dotted line marks the energy of the reactants before the reaction begins. The peak on the graph shows the activation energy. Notice that at the end of the reaction, the products have less energy than the reactants. This type of reaction results in a release of energy. The burning of fuels, such as wood, natural gas, or oil, is an example of an exothermic reaction.

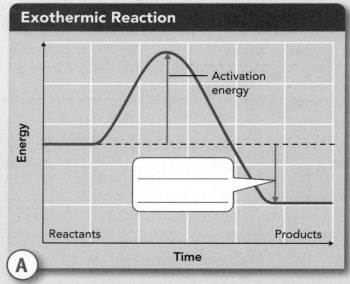

Exothermic Reaction

A

FIGURE 2 ···

▶ **ART IN MOTION** **Graphs of Exothermic and Endothermic Reactions**
Each of the graphs shows the amount of energy before and after the reaction.

✎ **Read Graphs** On each graph, label whether energy is absorbed or released.

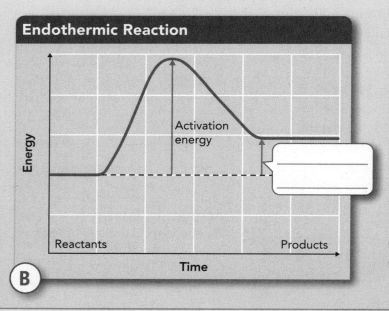

Endothermic Reaction

B

Now look at the graph of an endothermic reaction in **Figure 2B.** Endothermic reactions also need activation energy to get started. In addition, they need energy to continue. Notice that the energy of the products is greater than the energy of the reactants. This means that the reaction must continually absorb energy to keep going. Some endothermic reactions draw energy from the surroundings, leaving the area feeling cold. However, most endothermic reactions require continuous energy. For example, cooking a hamburger requires adding energy constantly until the meat is done.

Lab zone ® Do the Quick Lab *Modeling Activation Energy.*

⚷ **Assess Your Understanding**

got it? ···

O **I get it!** Now I know that in order for reactions to get started _____

_____

O **I need extra help with** _____

Go to **MY SCIENCE COACH** online for help with this subject.

What Affects the Rate of a Chemical Reaction?

Chemical reactions don't all occur at the same rate. Some, like explosions, are very fast. Others, like the rusting of iron in air, are slow. A particular reaction can occur at different rates depending on the conditions.

If you want to make a chemical reaction happen faster, the particles of the reactants need to collide either more quickly or with more energy. Also, if more particles are available to react, the reaction will happen faster. To slow down a reaction, you need to do the opposite. **Factors that can affect rates of reactions include surface area, temperature, concentration, and the presence of catalysts and inhibitors.**

Surface Area Look at the burning building in **Figure 3.** It used to be a sugar factory. The factory exploded when sugar dust ignited in the air above the stored piles of sugar. Although the sugar itself doesn't react violently in air, the dust can. This difference is related to surface area. When a piece of solid substance reacts with a liquid or gas, only the particles on the surface of the solid come into contact with the other reactant. If you break the solid into smaller pieces, more particles are exposed to the surface and the reaction happens faster. Speeding up a reaction by increasing surface area can be dangerous, but it can also be useful. For example, chewing your food breaks it into smaller pieces that your body can digest more easily and quickly.

do the math!

To find the surface area of a cube with 2-cm-long sides, find the area of each face of the cube.

$$\text{Area} = \text{Length} \times \text{Width}$$

$$4\ cm^2 = 2\ cm \times 2\ cm$$

Then add them together.

$$4\ cm^2 + 4\ cm^2 + 4\ cm^2 + 4\ cm^2 + 4\ cm^2 + 4\ cm^2 = 24\ cm^2$$

Imagine cutting the cube in half. Find the surface area of each half. Add the values together to get the total surface area.

FIGURE 3

Surface Area and Reaction Rate

Sugar dust can react quickly because it has a greater surface area than a pile of sugar. A chemical reaction that moves quickly can cause an explosion.

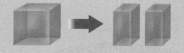

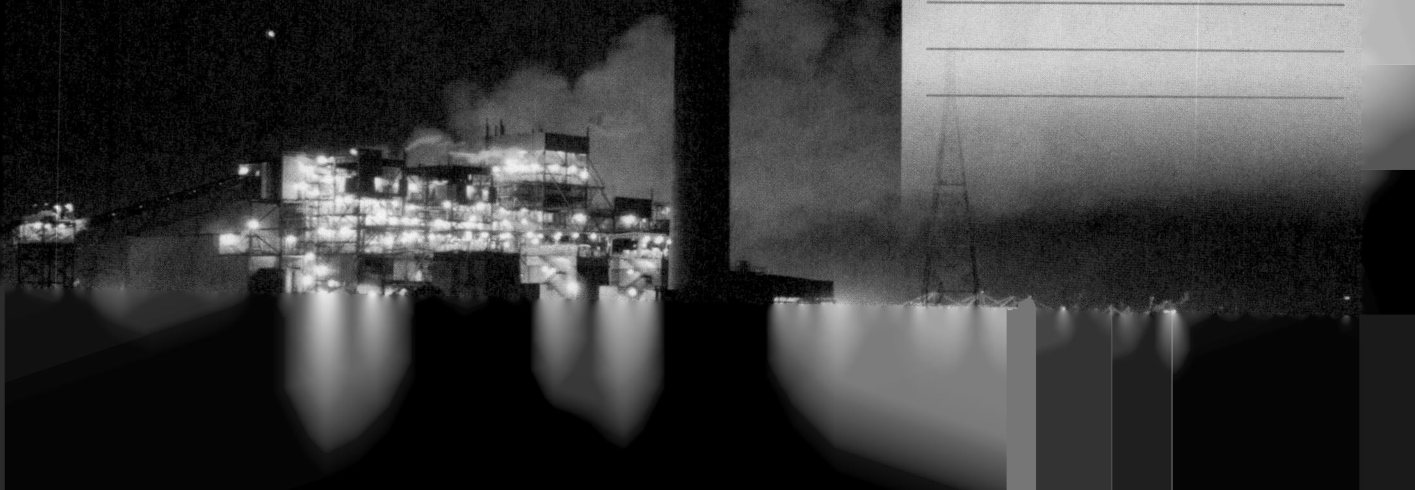

apply it!

A chemical reaction takes place in glow sticks. Changing the temperature affects the rate of the reaction.

1 Relate Cause and Effect When the temperature increases, the rate of a chemical reaction (increases/decreases).

2 Predict The brightness of a glow stick's light is affected by temperature. What would happen if the glow stick were placed in boiling water?

_____

_____

_____

3 CHALLENGE The military uses glow sticks for lighting at night. Suggest a method for storing them during the day to maximize their use at night.

_____

_____

_____

_____

_____

Temperature Changing the temperature of a chemical reaction also affects the reaction rate. When you heat a substance, its particles move faster. Faster-moving particles have more energy, which helps reactants get over the activation energy barrier more quickly. Also, faster-moving particles come in contact more often, giving more chances for a reaction to happen.

In contrast, reducing temperature slows down reaction rates. For example, milk contains bacteria, which carry out thousands of chemical reactions as they live and reproduce. You store milk and other foods in the refrigerator because keeping foods cold slows down those reactions, so your foods stay fresh longer.

Concentration Another way to increase the rate of a chemical reaction is to increase the concentration of the reactants. **Concentration** is the amount of a substance in a given volume. For example, adding a small spoonful of sugar to a cup of tea will make it sweet. Adding a large spoonful of sugar makes the tea even sweeter. The cup of tea with more sugar has a greater concentration of sugar molecules.

Increasing the concentration of reactants supplies more particles to react. Look at the tower of bubbles in **Figure 4.** This is the product of the decomposition reaction of a 35 percent hydrogen peroxide solution in water. Hydrogen peroxide that you buy at your local drug store is usually between 3 percent and 12 percent. The high concentration of hydrogen peroxide solution used in this reaction will release huge amounts of oxygen gas more quickly than a lower concentration would.

FIGURE 4 ....

Elephant Toothpaste

This reaction is nicknamed "elephant toothpaste" because of the enormous amount of bubbles it produces.

Predict How would using a lower concentration of hydrogen peroxide affect the rate of reaction?

_____

_____

_____

_____

Catalysts and Inhibitors Another way to control the rate of a reaction is to change the activation energy needed. A **catalyst** (KAT uh list) increases the reaction rate by lowering the activation energy needed. Although catalysts affect a reaction's rate, they are not permanently changed by a reaction and are not considered reactants.

Many chemical reactions can normally only happen at temperatures that would kill living things. Yet, some of these reactions are necessary for life. The cells in your body contain thousands of biological catalysts called **enzymes** (EN zymz) that help these reactions occur at body temperature. Each one is specific to only one chemical reaction. Enzymes provide a surface on which reactions can take place. Since enzymes bring reactant molecules close together, chemical reactions using enzymes require less activation energy and can happen at lower temperatures.

Sometimes it is more useful to slow down a reaction rather than speed it up. A material used to decrease the rate of a chemical reaction is an **inhibitor.** Inhibitors called preservatives are added to food to prevent spoiling.

FIGURE 5 ··

Catalysts

Adding a catalyst speeds up a chemical reaction.

✎ **Graph Draw and label the energy graph for the same chemical reaction when using a catalyst.**

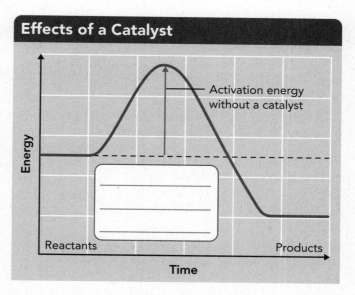

Effects of a Catalyst

Energy — Activation energy without a catalyst

Reactants — Products

Time

Do the Quick Lab *Effect of Temperature on Chemical Reactions.*

Assess Your Understanding

1a. Describe To slow down a reaction, you can (increase/decrease) the concentration of the reactants.

b. Compare and Contrast What would react more quickly in the air, a pile of grain or a cloud of grain dust? Explain.

_____

_____

c. Explain How do enzymes speed up chemical reactions in your body?

_____

_____

_____

_____

_____

_____

got it? ···

○ **I get it!** Now I know that the rate of a chemical reaction can be affected by_____

_____

_____

○ **I need extra help with** _____

Go to **MY SCIENCE COACH** online for help with this subject.

REVIEW
THE BIG
?

The total mass before a chemical reaction equals _____

_____.

LESSON 1 **Observing Chemical Change**

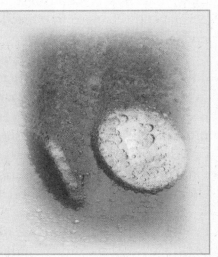

🔑 Changes in matter can be described in terms of physical changes and chemical changes.

🔑 Chemical reactions involve changes in properties and changes in energy that you can often observe.

Vocabulary
- physical change • chemical change
- reactant • product • precipitate
- exothermic reaction • endothermic reaction

LESSON 2 **Describing Chemical Reactions**

🔑 A chemical equation tells you the substances you start with in a reaction and the substances that are formed at the end.

🔑 In a chemical reaction, all of the atoms present at the start of the reaction are present at the end of the reaction.

🔑 Three types of chemical reactions are synthesis, decomposition, and replacement.

Vocabulary
- chemical equation • law of conservation of mass
- open system • closed system • coefficient
- synthesis • decomposition • replacement

$$2\,H_2 \quad + \quad O_2 \quad \longrightarrow \quad 2\,H_2O$$

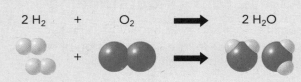

LESSON 3 **Controlling Chemical Reactions**

🔑 All chemical reactions need a certain amount of activation energy to get started.

🔑 Factors that can affect rates of reactions include surface area, temperature, concentration, and the presence of catalysts and inhibitors.

Vocabulary
- activation energy
- concentration
- catalyst
- enzyme
- inhibitor

Review and Assessment

LESSON 1 Observing Chemical Change

1. Which of the following results in a chemical change in matter?

   a. bending a straw   b. boiling water

   c. braiding hair   d. burning wood

2. A solid that forms from liquids in a chemical reaction is called a(n)_____

3. **Interpret Photos** What evidence in the photo below tells you that a chemical reaction may have occurred?

_____

_____

4. **Solve Problems** Steel that is exposed to water and salt rusts quickly. If you were a shipbuilder, how would you protect a new ship? Explain.

_____

_____

_____

_____

_____

5. Write About It Suppose you have an Internet friend who is studying chemistry just like you are. Your friend claims the change from liquid water to water vapor is a chemical change. Write a brief e-mail that might convince your friend otherwise.

LESSON 2 Describing Chemical Reactions

6. How can you balance a chemical equation?

   a. Change the coefficients.

   b. Change the products.

   c. Change the reactants.

   d. Change the subscripts.

7. In an open system, such as a campfire, matter can _____

_____

8. **Classify** Identify each of the balanced equations below as synthesis, decomposition, or replacement.

   $2 Al + Fe_2O_3 \rightarrow 2 Fe + Al_2O_3$

   _____

   $2 Ag + S \rightarrow Ag_2S$

   _____

   $CaCO_3 \rightarrow CaO + CO_2$

   _____

9. **Calculate** Water decomposes into hydrogen (H_2) and oxygen (O_2) when an electric current is applied. How many grams of water must decompose to produce 2 grams of hydrogen and 16 grams of oxygen?

   _____

   _____

10. **math!** Balance the equations.

   $MgO + HBr \rightarrow MgBr_2 + H_2O$

   $N_2 + O_2 \rightarrow N_2O_5$

   $C_2H_4 + O_2 \rightarrow CO_2 + H_2O$

   $Fe + HCl \rightarrow FeCl_2 + H_2$

LESSON 3 Controlling Chemical Reactions

11. In general, what happens when you increase the temperature of a reaction?

a. The heat destroys the reactants.

b. The rate of the reaction decreases.

c. The rate of the reaction increases.

d. The rate of the reaction stays the same.

Graphs A and B represent the same chemical reaction under different conditions. Use the graphs to answer Questions 12 and 13.

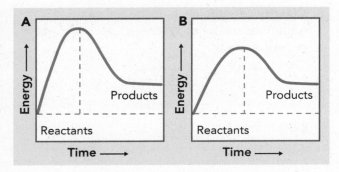

12. Interpret Data How does the energy of the products compare with the energy of the reactants?

_____

_____

_____

_____

13. Apply Concepts What change in condition might account for the lower activation energy barrier in the second graph? Explain.

_____

_____

_____

_____

APPLY THE BIG ? **How is matter conserved in a chemical reaction?**

14. Rust forms when iron metal (Fe) reacts with oxygen (O_2) to produce iron oxide (Fe_2O_3). Write a balanced equation for this reaction. Suppose you find the mass of an iron object, let it rust, and measure the mass again. Predict whether the mass will increase, decrease, or stay the same. Explain your answer in terms of the law of conservation of mass.

_____

_____

_____

_____

_____

_____

_____

_____

_____

_____

_____

_____

_____

_____

_____

_____

Standardized Test Prep

Multiple Choice

Circle the letter of the best answer.

1. The diagram below represents molecules of two different elements. The elements react chemically to produce a compound.

The diagram represents an

  A endothermic reaction in which energy is absorbed.

  B endothermic reaction in which energy is released.

  C exothermic reaction in which energy is absorbed.

  D exothermic reaction in which energy is released.

2. Which of the following is the **best** evidence for a chemical reaction?

  A change in temperature

  B change of state

  C formation of a new substance

  D gas bubbles

3. Which shows a balanced chemical equation for the decomposition of aluminum oxide (Al_2O_3)?

  A $Al_2O_3 \rightarrow 2\ Al + O_2$

  B $Al_2O_3 \rightarrow 2\ Al + 3\ O_2$

  C $2\ Al_2O_3 \rightarrow 4\ Al + O_2$

  D $2\ Al_2O_3 \rightarrow 4\ Al + 3\ O_2$

4. Which of the following would increase the rate of reaction?

  A maintain a constant temperature

  B increase the concentration of the reactants

  C increase the activation energy

  D add an inhibitor

5. Which equation describes a synthesis reaction?

  A $2\ Na + Cl_2 \rightarrow 2\ NaCl$

  B $Mg + CuSO_4 \rightarrow MgSO_4 + Cu$

  C $2\ KI \rightarrow 2\ K + I_2$

  D $CH_4 + 2\ O_2 \rightarrow CO_2 + 2\ H_2O$

Constructed Response

Use the table below and your knowledge of science to help you answer Question 6. Write your answer on a separate sheet of paper.

Compound	Formula
Carbon dioxide	CO_2
Methane	CH_4
Oxygen	O_2
Water	H_2O

6. The main compound of natural gas is methane. When methane reacts with oxygen gas, carbon dioxide and water vapor are produced. Write a balanced equation for this reaction. Explain why the burning of methane is a chemical change, not a physical change. Does this change absorb heat or release heat?

A Shrinking Storehouse

Carbon is present in the atmosphere in carbon dioxide. Plants are natural storehouses of carbon, too. The carbon is stored in the tissues of plants during the process of photosynthesis. In this reaction, energy from the sun transforms the reactants carbon dioxide and water into the products of glucose— a type of sugar—and oxygen. The overall chemical reaction in this process follows:

$$6\,CO_2 + 6\,H_2O \xrightarrow{\text{light}} C_6H_{12}O_6 + 6\,O_2$$

But this process can only be carried out if carbon dioxide, energy from the sun, and water all are present. In 2010, researchers reported that in some parts of the world, one of these essential ingredients had been in short supply from 2000 to 2009. Which ingredient? Water!

Images from Earth-orbiting satellites showed that during the first decade of the 21st century, a lack of precipitation caused drought in many areas, including parts of South America, Africa, Australia, and Southeast Asia. The red areas on the images of Earth show where drought caused plant life to die. In these areas, fewer plants were available to remove carbon dioxide from the air during photosynthesis. This contributed to increasing levels of carbon dioxide in the atmosphere.

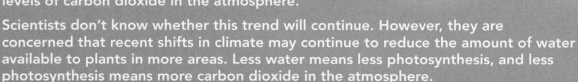

Scientists don't know whether this trend will continue. However, they are concerned that recent shifts in climate may continue to reduce the amount of water available to plants in more areas. Less water means less photosynthesis, and less photosynthesis means more carbon dioxide in the atmosphere.

Design It Find out more about carbon dioxide's role in the atmosphere. Use what you learn to write a short essay on how the events presented in this feature might affect worldwide temperatures.

A Race to the Finish!

BEEEEP! The starter signal goes off. You run around the track—faster, faster. Your heart is racing—faster, faster. Your breathing increases—faster, faster. After the race ends, you are exhausted. You walk around slowly and breathe deeply to catch your breath. What process allows your body to get energy quickly for such a race? Cellular respiration.

During cellular respiration, oxygen in your body's cells reacts with glucose to produce the energy you need to power your body and stay alive. At the same time, the waste products of respiration—carbon dioxide and water—are delivered to your bloodstream. The circulatory system returns most of these waste products to your lungs where they are exhaled. Your cells carry out this process 24 hours a day, seven days a week. However, some activities, like running, demand a lot of energy. Waste products build up. Your breathing increases to take in oxygen and to remove carbon dioxide more quickly. At the same time, your heart rate increases, and blood circulates more quickly to move oxygen and glucose to cells and carbon dioxide and water away from cells. At the end of the race, you slow down and "catch your breath." Your heart rate and breathing rate return to normal. You are ready to accept the prize for winning the race!

Research It Find out more about cellular respiration. Identify the cell part where this process takes place, and how the amount of energy produced changes as more energy demands are made on muscle cells during a race. Try to answer this question: When runners race for 20 minutes, how do their bodies obtain energy?

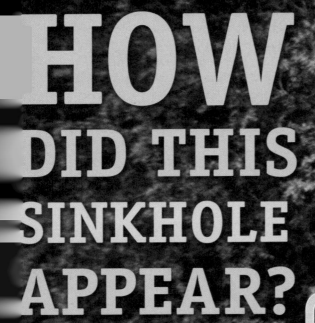

HOW DID THIS SINKHOLE APPEAR?

What determines the properties of a solution?

You might be wondering, "What is a sinkhole?" A sinkhole forms when the ground suddenly collapses. Sometimes sinkholes are caused by human activities like mining or by broken water pipes. In this photograph, divers are exploring a sinkhole that happened naturally when the underground rock, called limestone, mixed with slightly acidic water. The water actually dissolved the rock!

> UNTAMED SCIENCE Watch the **Untamed Science** video to learn more about solutions.

△Infer Do you think this sinkhole appeared suddenly or gradually over time? Explain your reasoning.

_____

_____

_____

_____

Acids, Bases, and Solutions

6 Getting Started

Check Your Understanding

1. **Background** Read the paragraph below and then answer the question.

When we breathe, we take in oxygen (O_2) and exhale carbon dioxide (CO_2). The bonds between the oxygen atoms in O_2 are **nonpolar bonds.** The bonds between the carbon and oxygen atoms in CO_2 are **polar bonds.** However, carbon dioxide is a nonpolar molecule.

A covalent bond in which electrons are shared equally is a **nonpolar bond.**

A covalent bond in which electrons are shared unequally is a **polar bond.**

• Carbon monoxide (CO) is an air pollutant. What type of bonds are in carbon monoxide?

_____

> **MY READING WEB** If you had trouble completing the question above, visit **My Reading Web** and type in *Acids, Bases, and Solutions.*

Vocabulary Skill

Identify Related Word Forms You can expand your vocabulary by learning the related forms of a word. For example, the common verb *to bake* is related to the noun *baker* and the adjective *baked.*

Verb	Noun	Adjective
indicate to show; to point	**indicator** something that shows or points to	**indicative** serving as a sign; showing
saturate to fill up as much as possible	**saturation** the condition of holding as much as possible	**saturated** to be full; to hold as much as is possible

2. **Quick Check** Review the words related to *saturate.* Complete the following sentences with the correct form of the word.

• The _____ sponge could hold no more water.

• He continued to add water to the point of _____

solution

solute

colloid

saturated solution

Chapter Preview

LESSON 1
- solution
- solvent
- solute
- colloid
- suspension
- 🔄 Identify Supporting Evidence
- 🔺 Interpret Data

LESSON 2
- dilute solution
- concentrated solution
- solubility
- saturated solution
- 🔄 Identify the Main Idea
- 🔺 Calculate

LESSON 3
- acid
- corrosive
- indicator
- base
- 🔄 Summarize
- 🔺 Predict

LESSON 4
- hydrogen ion (H^+)
- hydroxide ion (OH^-)
- pH scale
- neutralization
- salt
- 🔄 Relate Cause and Effect
- 🔺 Measure

> **VOCAB FLASH CARDS** For extra help with vocabulary, visit **Vocab Flash Cards** and type in *Acids, Bases, and Solutions.*

Understanding Solutions

🔑 **How Are Mixtures Classified?**

🔑 **How Does a Solution Form?**

my pLaneT DiaRY

MISCONCEPTION

Killer Quicksand?

Misconception: You may have watched scenes in a movie like the one below. It's a common misconception that if you fall into a pit of quicksand, it is nearly impossible to escape its muddy clutches.

Fact: Although it is real, quicksand is not as deadly as it's often made out to be. Quicksand is a mixture of sand and water and is rarely more than a few feet deep. It forms when too much water mixes with loose sand. Water molecules surround the individual grains of sand, reducing the friction between them. The sand grains easily slide past each other and can no longer support any weight.

Fortunately, a human body is less dense than quicksand, which means you can float on it. By relaxing and lying on your back, you'll eventually float to the top.

Write your answer to the question below.

Quicksand can be frightening until you understand how it works. Describe something that seemed scary to you until you learned more about it.

_____

_____

_____

_____

_____

_____

_____

> **PLANET DIARY** Go to **Planet Diary** to learn more about solutions.

Lab zone® Do the Inquiry Warm-Up *What Makes a Mixture a Solution?*

Vocabulary
- solution • solvent
- solute • colloid
- suspension

Skills
- ⤸ Reading: Identify Supporting Evidence
- △ Inquiry: Interpret Data

How Are Mixtures Classified?

What do peanut butter, lemonade, and salad dressing have in common? All of these are examples of different types of mixtures. ⬡ **A mixture is classified as a solution, colloid, or suspension based on the size of its largest particles.**

Solutions Grape juice is one example of a mixture called a solution. A **solution** is a mixture containing a solvent and at least one solute and has the same properties throughout. The **solvent** is the part of a solution usually present in the largest amount. It dissolves the other substances. The **solute** is the substance that is dissolved by the solvent. Solutes can be gases, liquids, or solids. Water is the solvent in grape juice. Sugar and other ingredients are the solutes. A solution has the same properties throughout. It contains solute, molecules or ions that are too small to see.

Water as a Solvent In many common solutions, the solvent is water. Water dissolves so many substances that it is often called the "universal solvent." Life depends on water solutions. Nutrients used by plants are dissolved in water in the soil. Water is the solvent in blood, saliva, sweat, urine, and tears.

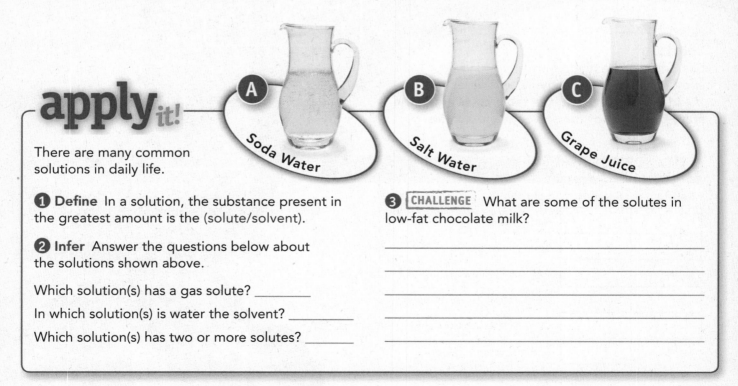

apply it!

There are many common solutions in daily life.

A Soda Water **B** Salt Water **C** Grape Juice

❶ **Define** In a solution, the substance present in the greatest amount is the (solute/solvent).

❷ **Infer** Answer the questions below about the solutions shown above.

Which solution(s) has a gas solute? _____

In which solution(s) is water the solvent? _____

Which solution(s) has two or more solutes? _____

❸ **CHALLENGE** What are some of the solutes in low-fat chocolate milk?

_____

_____

_____

_____

Other Solvents Although water is the most common solvent, it is certainly not the only one. Many solutions are made with solvents other than water, as shown in the table in **Figure 1.** For example, gasoline is a solution of several different liquid fuels. Solvents don't even have to be liquids. A solution may be a combination of gases, liquids, or solids. Air is an example of a solution that is made up of nitrogen, oxygen, and other gases. Solutions can even be made up of solids. Metal alloys like bronze, brass, and steel are solutions of different solid elements.

Sea water is a solution of sodium chloride and other compounds in water.

The air in these gas bubbles is a solution of oxygen and other gases in nitrogen.

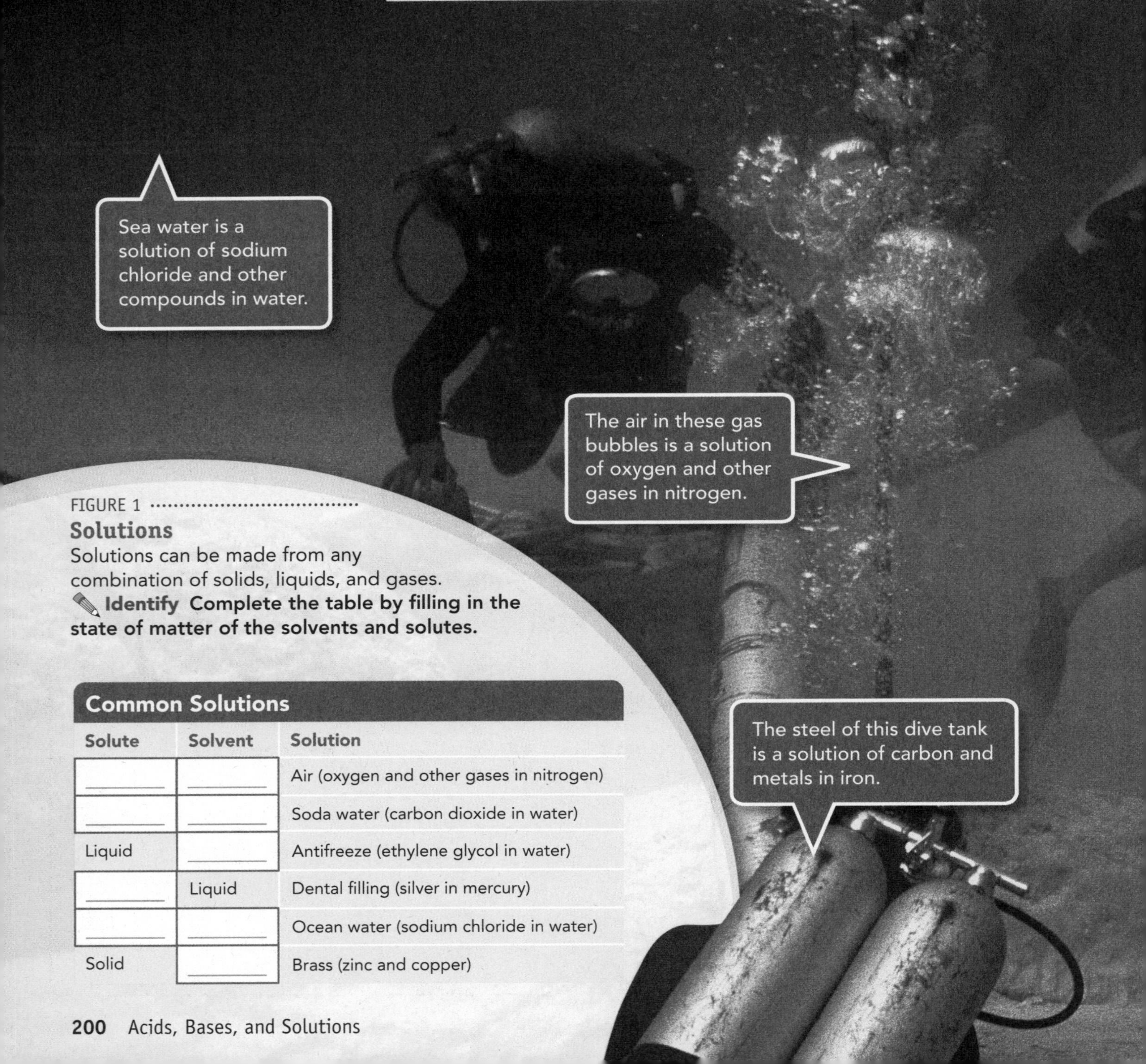

FIGURE 1 ·····················

Solutions

Solutions can be made from any combination of solids, liquids, and gases.

✎ **Identify Complete the table by filling in the state of matter of the solvents and solutes.**

The steel of this dive tank is a solution of carbon and metals in iron.

Common Solutions		
Solute	Solvent	Solution
_____	_____	Air (oxygen and other gases in nitrogen)
_____	_____	Soda water (carbon dioxide in water)
Liquid	_____	Antifreeze (ethylene glycol in water)
_____	Liquid	Dental filling (silver in mercury)
_____	_____	Ocean water (sodium chloride in water)
Solid	_____	Brass (zinc and copper)

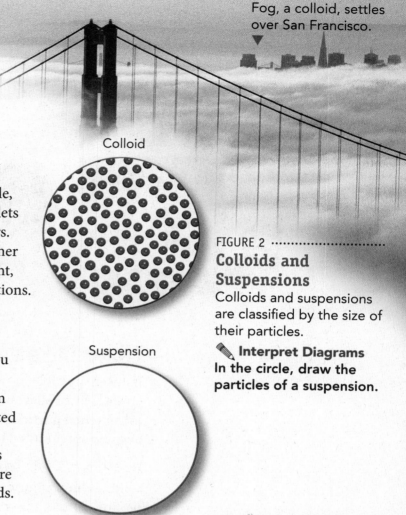

Fog, a colloid, settles over San Francisco.

Colloids Not all mixtures are solutions. As shown in **Figure 2,** a **colloid** (KAHL oyd) is a mixture containing small, undissolved particles that do not settle out. The particles in a colloid are too small to be seen without a microscope, yet they are large enough to scatter a beam of light. For example, fog is a colloid that is made up of water droplets in air. Fog scatters the headlight beams of cars. Milk, shaving cream, and smoke are some other examples of colloids. Because they scatter light, most colloids are not clear, unlike many solutions.

Suspensions If you tried to mix sand in water, you would find that the sand never dissolves completely, no matter how much you stir it. Sand and water make up a suspension. A **suspension** (suh SPEN shun) is a mixture in which particles can be seen and easily separated by settling or filtration. Unlike a solution, a suspension does not have the same properties throughout. It contains visible particles that are larger than the particles in solutions or colloids.

Colloid

Suspension

FIGURE 2 ·······························
Colloids and Suspensions
Colloids and suspensions are classified by the size of their particles.

✎ **Interpret Diagrams** In the circle, draw the particles of a suspension.

Do the Quick Lab
Scattered Light.

Assess Your Understanding

1a. Review What is a solution?

_____

_____

_____

b. Compare and Contrast How are colloids and suspensions different from solutions?

_____

_____

c. Infer Suppose you mix food coloring in water to make it blue. Have you made a solution or a suspension? Explain.

_____

_____

_____

_____

_____

_____

_____

got it? ···

○ **I get it!** Now I know that classifying mixtures as solutions, colloids, and suspensions is based on _____

_____

○ **I need extra help with** _____

Go to **MY SCIENCE** Ⓢ **COACH** online for help with this subject.

How Does a Solution Form?

If it were possible to see the particles of a solution, you could see how a solute behaves when it's mixed in a solution. 🔑 **A solution forms when particles of the solute separate from each other and become surrounded by particles of the solvent.**

Ionic and Molecular Solutes **Figure 3** shows an ionic solid, sodium chloride (NaCl), mixed with water. The positive and negative ions of the solute are attracted to the partially charged polar water molecules. Eventually, water molecules will surround all of the ions and the solid crystal will be completely dissolved.

Molecular compounds, such as table sugar, break up into individual neutral molecules in water. The polar water molecules attract the polar sugar molecules. This causes the sugar molecules to move away from each other. The covalent bonds within the molecules remain unbroken.

FIGURE 3 ·····························

> INTERACTIVE ART

Forming a Solution

✎ **Sequence** Explain what occurs as sodium chloride, an ionic solid, dissolves in water.

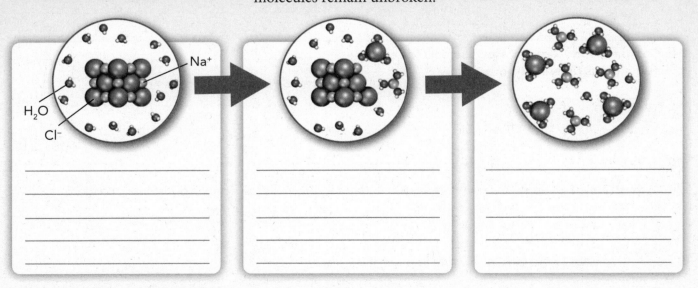

do the math! Analyzing Data

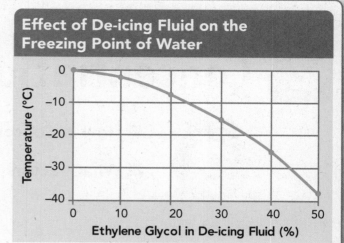

Effect of De-icing Fluid on the Freezing Point of Water

Airplane de-icing fluids are typically solutions of ethylene glycol in water. The freezing point of pure water is 0°C.

1 **Explain** How is the percent of ethylene glycol in de-icing fluid related to water's freezing point?

_____

_____

_____

2 **Read Graphs** How much does a 45% solution of de-icing fluid lower the freezing point of water?

_____

3 **Interpret Data** Would you allow a plane to take off in −20°C weather if it were de-iced with a solution of 30% ethylene glycol? Explain.

_____

_____

Solutes and Conductivity

How could you find out if the solute of a water solution was salt or sugar? Ionic compounds in water conduct electric current, but a solution of molecular compounds may not. If ions are present, electric current will flow and you'll know the solute is salt.

Effects of Solutes

Solutes raise the boiling point of a solution above that of the solvent. As the temperature of a liquid rises, the molecules gain energy and escape as gas. In a liquid solution, the solute particles prevent the solvent molecules' escape. The temperature must go above the boiling point of the solvent in order for the solution to boil. However, the temperature increases only slightly and is not enough to cook food faster.

Solutes lower the freezing point of a solution below that of the solvent alone. When pure liquid water freezes at 0°C, the molecules pack together to form crystals of ice. In a solution, the solute particles get in the way of the water molecules forming ice crystals. The temperature must drop below 0°C in order for the solution to freeze.

Lab zone ® Do the Lab Investigation *Speedy Solutions.*

🔑 Assess Your Understanding

2. Apply Concepts Why is salt sprinkled on icy roads and sidewalks?

_____

_____

_____

_____

_____

got it? ···

○ **I get it!** Now I know that in a solution the particles of solute _____

_____

○ **I need extra help with** _____

Go to **my science** ⓢ **coach** *online for help with this subject.*

Concentration and Solubility

🔑 How Is Concentration Changed?

🔑 What Factors Affect Solubility?

MY PLANET DiARY

DISCOVERY

Even Whales Get the Bends

Decompression sickness, or "the bends" as it's commonly known, is a fear for many scuba divers. Under the extreme pressure of the deep ocean, nitrogen and other gases from the air dissolve in a diver's body tissues. If the diver rises too quickly, the sudden decrease in pressure causes the dissolved gas to bubble out of the tissue. The bubbles can enter a blood vessel and cause intense pain, and sometimes more severe injury.

But what if the diver is a whale? Previously, it was thought that whales did not suffer from the bends. Scientists have discovered evidence in beached whales of nitrogen bubbles expanding and damaging vital organs. It is believed that sonar waves from nearby ships may have frightened the whales, causing them to surface too quickly. This can result in the bends.

Write your answers to the questions below.

1. Scientists have found small gashes in the bones of whale fossils, which are a sign of the bends. What conclusions can you draw from these fossils?

_____

_____

_____

_____

_____

2. Scuba diving is a popular activity. Would you scuba dive knowing the risks of getting the bends?

_____

_____

_____

_____

▷ PLANET DIARY Go to **Planet Diary** to learn more about solubility.

Lab® zone Do the Inquiry Warm-Up *Does It Dissolve?*

Vocabulary
- dilute solution
- concentrated solution
- solubility
- saturated solution

Skills
- Reading: Identify the Main Idea
- Inquiry: Calculate

How Is Concentration Changed?

Have you ever had maple syrup on your pancakes? You probably know that it's made from the sap of maple trees. Is something that sweet really made in a tree? Well, not exactly.

The sap of a maple tree and maple syrup differ in their concentrations. That is, they differ in the amount of solute (sugar and other compounds) dissolved in a certain amount of solvent (water). A **dilute solution** is a mixture that has only a little solute dissolved in a certain amount of solvent. A **concentrated solution** is a mixture that has a lot of solute dissolved in the solvent. The sap is a dilute solution and the syrup is a concentrated solution.

Changing Concentration How is sap turned into syrup? **You can change the concentration of a solution by adding solute. You can also change it by adding or removing solvent.** For example, water is removed from the dilute sap to make the more concentrated syrup.

Vocabulary Identify Related Word Forms To *concentrate* is the verb form of the adjective *concentrated*. Write a sentence about solutions using the verb *concentrate*.

_____

_____

_____

_____

FIGURE 1 ·······································
Changing the Concentration of a Solution

✎ The solution above is made with two droppers of coloring.

1. **Apply Concepts** Show two ways you can make a more concentrated solution by shading in the droppers and water level you would use.

2. **Explain** Describe your methods on the lines.

Ⓐ

_____

_____

_____

_____

Ⓑ

_____

_____

_____

_____

Calculating Concentration You know that maple syrup is more concentrated than maple sap. What is the actual concentration of either solution? To determine the concentration of a solution, compare the amount of solute to the total amount of solution. You can report concentration as the percent of solute in solution by volume or mass.

do the math! Sample Problem

To calculate concentration, compare the amount of solute to the amount of solution. For example, if a 100-gram solution contains 10 grams of solute, its concentration is 10% by weight.

$$\frac{10 \text{ g}}{100 \text{ g}} \times 100\% = 10\%$$

Calculate Determine the concentration of the contact solution.

_____

_____

_____

10.7 grams hydrogen peroxide
355 grams solution

Contact Solution

10.7 grams hydrogen peroxide
355 grams solution

Lab zone® Do the Quick Lab
Measuring Concentration.

⚐ Assess Your Understanding

1a. Describe What is a concentrated solution?

_____

_____

_____

b. Calculate Find the concentration of a solution with 30 grams of solute in 250 grams of solution.

_____

c. CHALLENGE Solution A has twice as much solute as Solution B. Is it possible for the solutions to have the same concentration? Explain.

_____

_____

_____

_____

_____

_____

got it? ∙∙

○ **I get it!** Now I know that the concentration of a solution can be changed by _____

_____

○ **I need extra help with** _____

Go to MY SCIENCE ⓢ COACH online for help with this subject.

What Factors Affect Solubility?

Suppose you add sugar to a cup of hot tea. Is there a limit to how sweet you can make the tea? Yes, at some point, no more sugar will dissolve. **Solubility** is a measure of how much solute can dissolve in a solvent at a given temperature. 🗝 **Factors that can affect the solubility of a substance include pressure, the type of solvent, and temperature.**

When you've added so much solute that no more dissolves, you have a **saturated solution.** If you can continue to dissolve more solute in a solution, then the solution is unsaturated.

Certain factors also affect the rate at which a solution forms. Smaller particles of solute dissolve more quickly than larger particles. Stirring and warmer temperatures can speed up the dissolving of the solute, too. Also, the more saturated a solution, the slower it will dissolve additional solute.

Working With Solubility
Look at the table in **Figure 2**. It compares the solubilities of familiar compounds in 100 grams of water at 20°C. You can see that only 9.6 grams of baking soda will dissolve in these conditions. However, 204 grams of table sugar will dissolve in the same amount of water at the same temperature.

Solubility can be used to help identify a substance. It is a characteristic property of matter. Suppose you had a white powder that looked like table salt or sugar. Since you never taste unknown substances, how could you identify the powder? You could measure its solubility in 100 grams of water at 20°C. Then compare the results to the data in **Figure 2** to identify the substance.

FIGURE 2 ··

Solubility
Pickling requires saturated solutions of salt in water.

✎ **Calculate Using the table below, determine the amount of sodium chloride you would need to make pickles using 500 grams of water.**

Solubility in 100 g of Water at 20°C	
Compound	Solubility (g)
Baking soda (sodium bicarbonate, NaHCO$_3$)	9.6
Table salt (sodium chloride, NaCl)	35.9
Table sugar (sucrose, C$_{12}$H$_{22}$O$_{11}$)	204

Factors Affecting Solubility

You have already read that there is a limit to solubility. By changing certain conditions, you can change a substance's solubility.

Pressure The solubility of a gas solute in a liquid solvent increases as the pressure of the gas over the solution increases. To increase the carbon dioxide concentration in soda water, the gas is added to the liquid under high pressure. Opening the bottle or can reduces the pressure. The escaping gas makes the fizzing sound you hear.

Scuba divers must be aware of the effects of pressure on gases if they want to avoid decompression sickness. Under water, divers breathe from tanks of compressed air. The air dissolves in their blood in greater amounts as they dive deeper. If divers return to the surface too quickly, the gases can bubble out of solution. The bubbles can block blood flow. Divers double over in pain, which is why you may have heard this condition called "the bends."

Solvents Sometimes you just can't make a solution because the solute and solvent are not compatible, as shown in **Figure 3.** This happens with motor oil and water. Have you ever tried to mix oil and water? If so, you've seen how quickly they separate into layers after you stop mixing them. Oil and water separate because water is a polar compound and oil is nonpolar. Some polar and nonpolar compounds do not mix very well.

For liquid solutions, ionic and polar compounds usually dissolve in polar solvents. Nonpolar compounds do not usually dissolve in very polar solvents, but they will dissolve in nonpolar solvents.

did you know?

The popping sound you hear when you crack your knuckles is dissolved gas coming out of the fluid between the joints because of a decrease in pressure. That's why you can't crack the same knuckle twice in a row. You have to wait a few minutes for the gas to dissolve back into the fluid.

◀ Polar water mixed with nonpolar motor oil

FIGURE 3 ···

Solvents and Solubility

Some polar and nonpolar compounds form layers when they are mixed together.

✏ [CHALLENGE] **Determine which of these liquids are polar and which are nonpolar by the way they form layers or mix together. The first answer is given.**

A. Polar

B. _____

C. _____

D. _____

E. _____

F. _____

208 Acids, Bases, and Solutions

Temperature For most solid solutes, solubility increases as temperature increases. For example, the solubility of table sugar in 100 grams of water at 0°C is 180 grams. However, the solubility increases to 231 grams at 25°C and 487 grams at 100°C.

Cooks use this increased solubility of sugar to make candy. At room temperature, not enough sugar for candy can dissolve in the water. Solutions must be heated for all the sugar to dissolve.

When heated, a solution can dissolve more solute than it can at cooler temperatures. If a heated, saturated solution cools slowly, the extra solute may remain dissolved to become a supersaturated solution. It has more dissolved solute than is predicted by its solubility at the given temperature. If you disturb a supersaturated solution, the extra solute will quickly come out of solution. You can see an example of a supersaturated solution in **Figure 4.**

Unlike most solids, gases become less soluble when the temperature goes up. For example, more carbon dioxide can dissolve in cold water than in hot water. If you open a warm bottle of soda water, carbon dioxide escapes the liquid in greater amounts than if the soda water had been chilled. Why does a warm soda taste "flat" when it's opened? It contains less gas. If you like soda water that's very fizzy, open it when it's cold!

FIGURE 4 ·······························
Supersaturated Solution
Dropping a crystal of solute into a supersaturated solution causes the extra solute to rapidly come out of solution.

··· ✏️
⟳ **Identify the Main Idea**
Underline the sentences on this page that explain how increasing temperature affects the solubility of both solid and gas solutes.

apply _it!_

Crystallized honey, a supersaturated solution, can be more than 70 percent sugar.

❶ Calculate How many grams of sugar could be in 50 grams of crystallized honey?

_____

_____

❷ Develop Hypotheses How would you explain why certain types of honey rarely crystallize?

_____

_____

❸ CHALLENGE Is there a way to turn crystallized honey back into liquid honey? Explain.

_____

_____

_____

_____

_____

_____

EXPLORE THE BIG Q

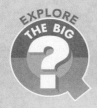

Cooking With Chemistry

What determines the properties of a solution?

FIGURE 5

INTERACTIVE ART At the Solutions Shack Diner, solutions are found everywhere on the menu. In order to serve his customers, the chef must know about the properties of solutions.

Solve Problems Use what you know about the properties of solutions to help the chef in the kitchen.

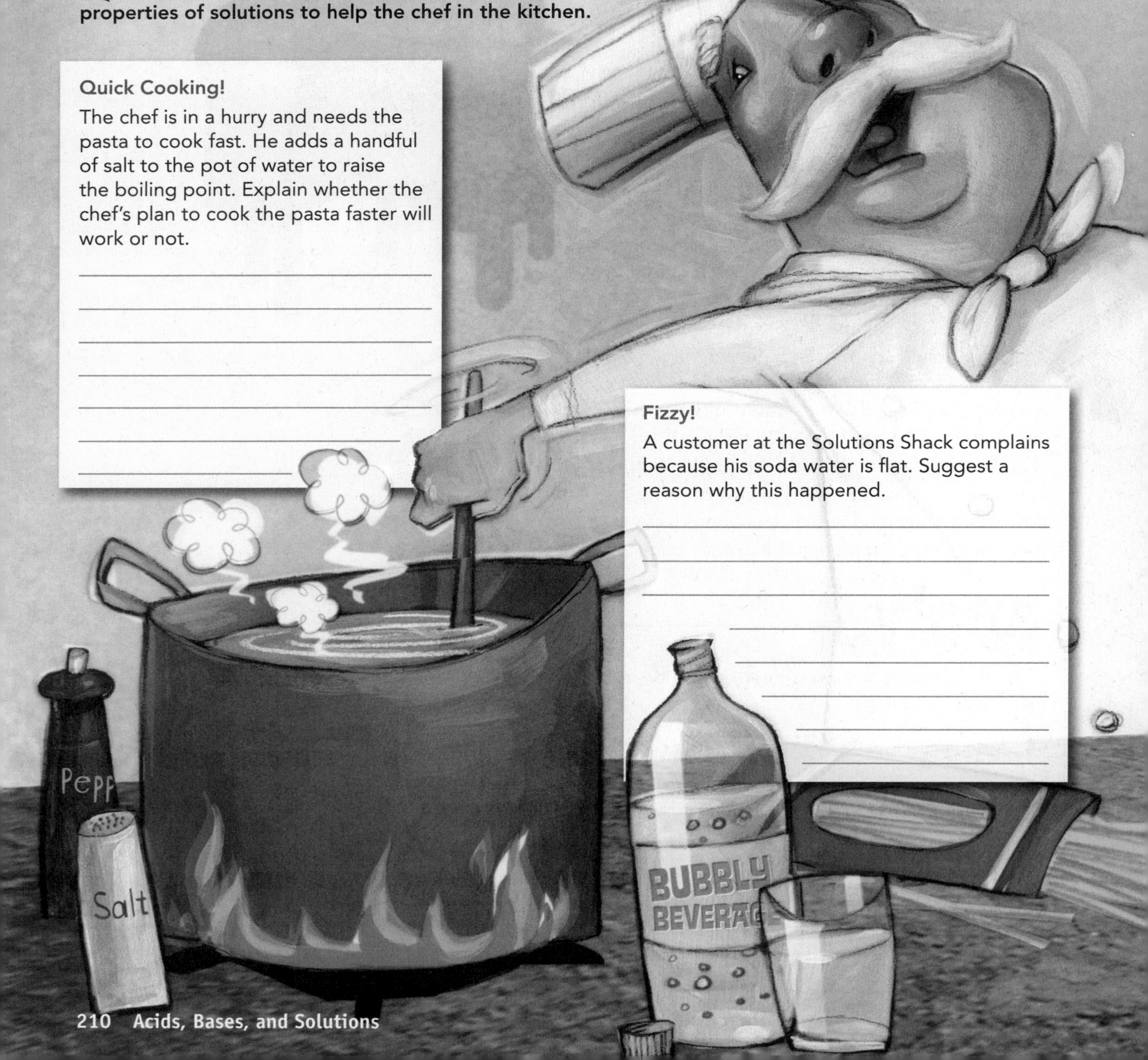

Quick Cooking!

The chef is in a hurry and needs the pasta to cook fast. He adds a handful of salt to the pot of water to raise the boiling point. Explain whether the chef's plan to cook the pasta faster will work or not.

____

____

____

____

____

____

____

Fizzy!

A customer at the Solutions Shack complains because his soda water is flat. Suggest a reason why this happened.

____

____

____

____

____

____

____

____

Mix It Up!
The chef is making salad dressing with vinegar, olive oil, and pepper, but the ingredients are not mixing together. Why?

_____

_____

_____

_____

_____

Yum!
The chef makes the best iced tea. His secret is to make it exactly 15 percent sugar by mass. If he wants to make 3,000 grams of iced tea, how many grams of sugar should he use?

- ◯ 200 grams
- ◯ 20,000 grams
- ◯ 450 grams
- ◯ 45,000 grams

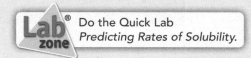

Do the Quick Lab
Predicting Rates of Solubility.

🔑 Assess Your Understanding

2a. Review How can you tell when a solution is saturated?

_____

_____

b. Control Variables You are given two white powdery substances. How would you use solubility to identify them?

_____

_____

_____

_____

_____

_____

_____

_____

c. ANSWER THE BIG ? What determines the properties of a solution?

_____

_____

_____

_____

_____

_____

_____

_____

got it? ·····················

◯ **I get it!** Now I know that the solubility of a substance can be affected by _____

_____

_____

◯ **I need extra help with** _____

Go to MY SCIENCE Ⓢ COACH *online for help with this subject.*

211

Describing Acids and Bases

🔑 **What Are the Properties of Acids?**

🔑 **What Are the Properties of Bases?**

MY PLANET DIARY

VOICES FROM HISTORY

Bog Bodies

Even in Shakespeare's time it was known that tanning, the process of making leather, helps preserve body tissues. Hundreds of years later, the body of a 2,300-year-old man was found in the peat bogs of Europe. The man is a bog body. Bog bodies are the remains of human bodies that have been preserved in the highly acidic conditions of peat bogs.

The bog acids are similar in strength to vinegar. They naturally pickle the human bodies. The lack of oxygen and cold temperatures of Northern Europe cause the acids to saturate body tissues before they decay. As a result, the organs, hair, and skin are all preserved. The acids dissolve the bones of the bog bodies, but details like tattoos and fingerprints can still be seen on some of the bodies.

> **GRAVE DIGGER.** . . . A tanner will last you nine year.
>
> **HAMLET.** Why he, more than another?
>
> **GRAVE DIGGER.** Why, sir, his hide is so tanned with his trade that he will keep out water a great while, and your water is a sore decayer of your . . . dead body.
>
> —Shakespeare, *Hamlet*

Write your answers to the questions below.

1. Hypothesize why bog acids react differently with the bones of the bodies than they do with the organs, hair, and skin.

_____

_____

_____

_____

_____

2. How are pickles similar to bog bodies?

_____

_____

> **PLANET DIARY** Go to **Planet Diary** to learn more about acids.

 Do the Inquiry Warm-Up *What Color Does Litmus Paper Turn?*

Vocabulary
• acid • corrosive
• indicator • base

Skills
Reading: Summarize
Inquiry: Predict

What Are the Properties of Acids?

Have you had any fruit to eat recently? If so, an acid was probably part of your meal. Many common items contain acids. **Acids** are compounds with specific characteristic properties. **An acid reacts with metals and carbonates, tastes sour, and turns blue litmus paper red.**

Acids are an important part of our lives. Folic acid, found in green, leafy vegetables, is important for cell growth. Hydrochloric acid in your stomach helps with digestion. Phosphoric acid is used to make plant fertilizers. Sulfuric acid drives many types of batteries, giving it the nickname "battery acid."

Reactions With Metals Acids react with certain metals to produce hydrogen gas. Platinum and gold don't react with most acids, but copper, zinc, and iron do. When they react, the metals seem to disappear in the solution. This is one reason acids are described as **corrosive,** meaning they "wear away" other materials.

The purity of precious metals can be determined using acids. **Figure 1** shows a touchstone, which is used to test the purity of gold. The gold object is scraped on the touchstone. Then, acid is poured onto the streak. The more gas bubbles the streak produces, the lower the purity of the gold.

FIGURE 1 ....
Reaction With Metals
Acids are used to test the purity of precious metals.

✎ **Infer** What could you determine about a gold necklace that bubbles when it is exposed to an acid?

_____

_____

_____

_____

_____

Reactions With Carbonates
Acids also react with carbonate ions. Carbonate ions contain carbon and oxygen atoms bonded together with an overall negative charge (CO_3^{2-}). One product of the reaction of an acid with a carbonate is the gas carbon dioxide.

Objects that contain carbonate ions include seashells, eggshells, chalk, and limestone. The sculpture shown in **Figure 2** is carved from limestone. Geologists use this property of acids to identify rocks. If carbon dioxide gas is produced when dilute acid is poured on a rock's surface, then the rock could be made of limestone.

Sour Taste
If you've ever tasted a lemon, you've had firsthand experience with the sour taste of acids. Citrus fruits, such as lemons, grapefruit, and oranges, all contain citric acid. Other foods such as vinegar and tomatoes also contain acids.

Although sour taste is a characteristic of many acids, it is not one you should use to identify a compound as an acid. Scientists don't taste chemicals. It is never safe to taste unknown chemicals.

Reactions With Indicators
Chemists use indicators to test for acids. Litmus paper is an example of an **indicator,** a compound that changes color when it comes in contact with an acid. Acids turn blue litmus paper red.

FIGURE 2 ·······························
Reactions With Carbonates
Acids react with the carbonates in limestone.

✎ Predict **Describe what a geologist would observe if she poured acid on the sculpture.**

_____
_____
_____
_____
_____

▲
Blue litmus paper turns red in the presence of acid.

 Do the Quick Lab
Properties of Acids.

🔑 Assess Your Understanding

1a. Define What is a compound that changes color in an acid called?

○ metal ○ indicator ○ carbonate

b. Explain Why are acids described as corrosive?

_____
_____

c. Draw Conclusions How might you tell if a food contains an acid?

_____
_____
_____
_____
_____

got it? ···

○ **I get it!** Now I know that the properties of acids include _____

_____

○ **I need extra help with** _____

Go to MY SCIENCE ⬤ COACH online for help with this subject.

What Are the Properties of Bases?

Bases are another group of compounds that can be identified by their common properties. 🔑 **A base tastes bitter, feels slippery, and turns red litmus paper blue.** The properties of bases are often described as the "opposite" of acids. Bases have many uses. Ammonia is used in fertilizers and household cleaners. Baking soda is a base called sodium bicarbonate, which causes baked goods to rise.

▲ Cocoa beans

Bitter Taste Have you ever tasted tonic water? The base, quinine, causes the slightly bitter taste. Bases taste bitter. Other foods that contain bases include bitter melon, almonds, and cocoa beans, like those shown above.

Slippery Feel Bases have a slippery feel. Many soaps and detergents contain bases. The slippery feeling of your shampoo is a property of the bases it contains.

Just as you avoid tasting an unknown substance, you wouldn't want to touch one either. Strong bases can irritate your skin. A safer way to identify bases is by their other properties.

↰ **Summarize** What are some uses of bases?

_____

_____

_____

FIGURE 3 ···

Acid and Base Properties

✎ **Classify** Draw an arrow from each item to the word "acid" or "base" that describes its properties.

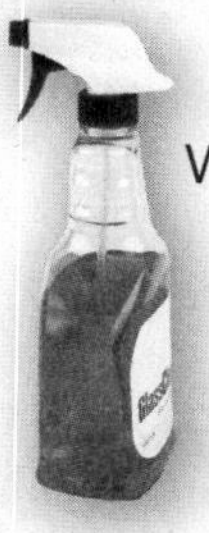

Window cleaner

Limes

(ACID)   (BASE)

Vinegar

Dish soap

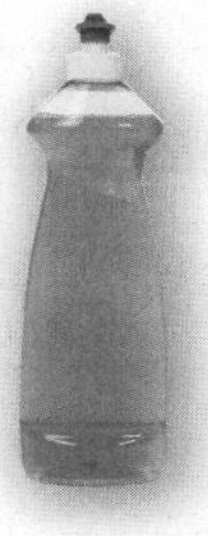

Reactions of Bases

Unlike acids, bases don't react with metals. They also don't react with carbonates to form carbon dioxide gas. The lack of a reaction can be a useful property in identifying bases. If you know that a compound doesn't react with metals, you know something about it. For example, you know the compound is probably not an acid. Another important property of bases is how they react with acids in a type of chemical reaction called neutralization, in which acids and bases deactivate one another.

Reactions With Indicators

Since litmus paper can be used to test acids, it can be used to test bases, too, as shown in **Figure 4.** Unlike acids, however, bases turn red litmus paper blue. An easy way to remember this is to think of the letter *b*. **B**ases turn litmus paper **b**lue.

FIGURE 4 ·······································

Litmus Paper

Litmus paper is used to test if a substance is an acid or a base.

✎ **Look at the apple and soap photos to complete the following tasks.**

1. **Predict** Color or label each strip of litmus paper with the color you would expect to see from the substance.

2. **Infer** What would you infer about a substance that did not change the color of red or blue litmus paper?

_____

_____

FIGURE 5 ···

Properties of Acids and Bases

✎ **Compare and Contrast Complete the table of properties of acids and bases.**

Properties	Acids	Bases
Reaction with metals		
Reaction with carbonates		
Taste		
Reaction with litmus paper		
Uses		

apply it!

Bee venom is slightly acidic, but wasp venom is closer to neutral, meaning it's not an acid or a base. Pure water is another neutral substance.

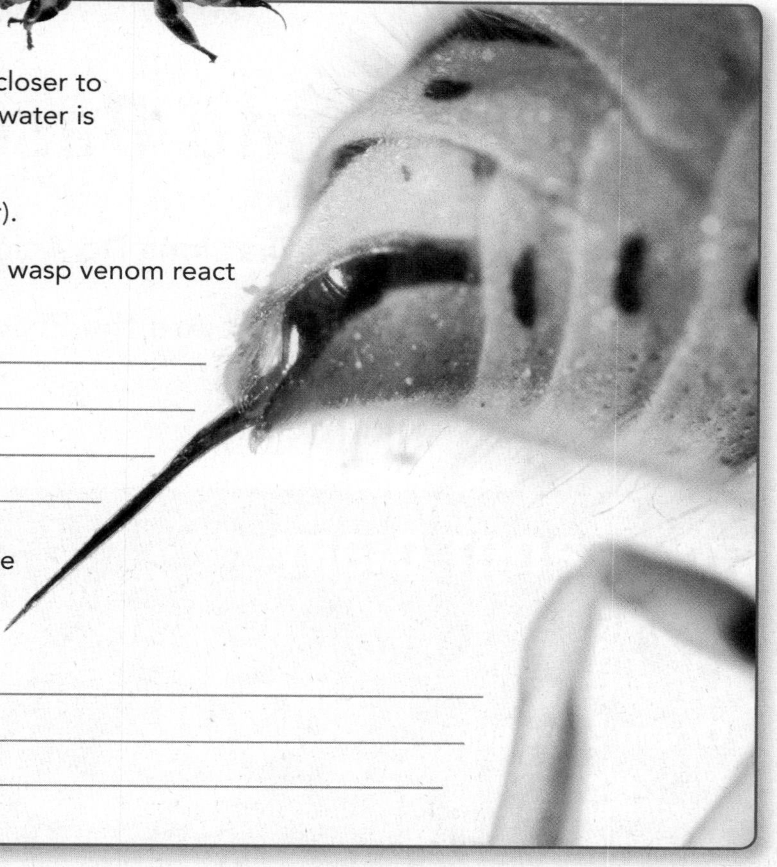

1 **Predict** Bee venom would taste (bitter/sour).

2 **Apply Concepts** How would bee venom and wasp venom react with litmus paper?

_____

_____

_____

_____

3 [CHALLENGE] One suggestion for treating a bee sting is cleaning it with vinegar. Is this a cure that you would try? Explain.

_____

_____

_____

Lab zone® Do the Quick Lab *Properties of Bases.*

🔑 Assess Your Understanding

2a. Review The properties of bases are often considered (identical/opposite) to acids.

b. Apply Concepts In what products are you most likely to find bases in your home?

_____

_____

_____

_____

c. Pose Questions The color of hydrangea flowers depends on the amount of acid or base in the soil. Write a question that helps you determine the cause of a pink hydrangea.

_____

_____

_____

_____

_____

got it?

○ **I get it!** Now I know that the properties of bases include _____

_____

○ **I need extra help with** _____

Go to MY SCIENCE ⓢ COACH *online for help with this subject.*

UNLOCK THE BIG Q?

🔑 **What Ions Do Acids and Bases Form in Water?**

🔑 **What Are the Products of Neutralization?**

MY PLANET DIARY

FUN FACT

Ocean Stingers

You've probably heard of venomous animals like rattlesnakes and black widow spiders. Did you know that some of the most venomous creatures in the world are jellyfish? Some jellyfish stings can permanently scar and even kill their victims. Jellyfish use their venom to stun and paralyze both prey and predators, including humans. A jellyfish sting can quickly turn a day at the beach into a dash to the hospital. Luckily, most jellyfish stings can be easily treated. The venom of some jellyfish contains bases. Bases can be neutralized, or deactivated, by an acid. The best way to treat some jellyfish stings is to rinse the affected area with vinegar. Vinegar is a solution containing acetic acid, which is a weak acid that is safe for your skin.

Write your answers to the questions below.

1. Stings from other kinds of animals can be acidic. How might you treat a sting that contains an acid?

_____

_____

_____

_____

2. Since jellyfish are nearly invisible, most people never know they're in danger. What advice would you give to a person planning on spending a day at the beach?

_____

_____

_____

> PLANET DIARY Go to **Planet Diary** to learn more about neutralization.

Lab zone® Do the Inquiry Warm-Up *What Can Cabbage Juice Tell You?*

Vocabulary
- hydrogen ion (H⁺) • hydroxide ion (OH⁻)
- pH scale • neutralization • salt

Skills
↺ Reading: Relate Cause and Effect
△ Inquiry: Measure

What Ions Do Acids and Bases Form in Water?

A chemist pours hydrochloric acid into a beaker. Then she slowly adds a base, sodium hydroxide, to the acid. What happens when these two chemicals mix? To answer this question, you must know what happens to acids and bases in solution.

Acids in Solution **Figure 1** lists some common acids. Notice that each formula begins with the letter H, the symbol for hydrogen. In a solution with water, most acids separate into hydrogen ions and negative ions. A **hydrogen ion (H⁺)** is an atom of hydrogen that has lost its electron. In the case of hydrochloric acid, for example, hydrogen ions and chloride ions form.

$$HCl \rightarrow H^+ + Cl^-$$

The production of hydrogen ions helps define an acid. 🔑 **An acid produces hydrogen ions (H⁺) in water.** These hydrogen ions are responsible for corroding metals and turning blue litmus paper red. Acids may be strong or weak. Strength refers to how well the acid dissociates, or separates, into ions in water. As shown in **Figure 2,** molecules of a strong acid, such as nitric acid, dissociate to form hydrogen ions in solution. With a weak acid, like acetic acid, very few particles separate to form ions in solution.

FIGURE 1 ······················
Common Acids
The table lists some common acids.

Acid	Formula
Hydrochloric acid	HCl
Nitric acid	HNO_3
Sulfuric acid	H_2SO_4
Acetic acid	$HC_2H_3O_2$

FIGURE 2 ··
Strength of Acids
In solution, strong acids act differently than weak acids do.

✎ **Compare and Contrast** In the empty beaker, use the key to draw how ions of acetic acid would act in solution.

Key
- ◼ Nitrate ion (NO₃⁻)
- • Hydrogen ion (H⁺)
- ▷ Acetate ion (C₂H₃O₂⁻)

Strong Acid

Weak Acid

Bases in Solution

Look at the table in **Figure 3**. Many of the bases shown are made of positive ions combined with hydroxide ions. The **hydroxide ion (OH⁻)** is a negative ion made of oxygen and hydrogen. When some bases dissolve in water, they separate into positive ions and hydroxide ions. Look, for example, at what happens to sodium hydroxide in water.

$$NaOH \rightarrow Na^+ + OH^-$$

Not every base contains hydroxide ions. For example, ammonia (NH_3) does not. In solution, ammonia reacts with water to form hydroxide ions.

$$NH_3 + H_2O \rightarrow NH_4^+ + OH^-$$

Notice that both reactions produce negative hydroxide ions.
🔑 **A base produces hydroxide ions (OH⁻) in water.** Hydroxide ions are responsible for the bitter taste and slippery feel of bases, and for turning red litmus paper blue. Strong bases, like sodium hydroxide, readily produce hydroxide ions in water. Weak bases, such as ammonia, do not.

Base	Formula
Sodium hydroxide	NaOH
Potassium hydroxide	KOH
Calcium hydroxide	Ca(OH)₂
Aluminum hydroxide	Al(OH)₃
Ammonia	NH₃
Calcium oxide	CaO

FIGURE 3 ⋯⋯⋯⋯⋯⋯⋯⋯
Common Bases

Measuring pH

To determine the strength of an acid or base, chemists use a scale called pH. As shown in **Figure 4,** the **pH scale** ranges from 0 to 14. It expresses the concentration of hydrogen ions in a solution.

The most acidic substances are found at the low end of the scale, while basic substances are found at the high end. A low pH tells you that the concentration of hydrogen ions is high and the concentration of hydroxide ions is low. A high pH tells you that the opposite is true.

You can find the pH of a solution using indicator paper, which changes a different color for each pH value. Matching the color of the paper with the colors on the scale tells you the solution's pH. A pH lower than 7 is acidic. A pH higher than 7 is basic. If the pH is 7, the solution is neutral, meaning it's neither an acid nor a base.

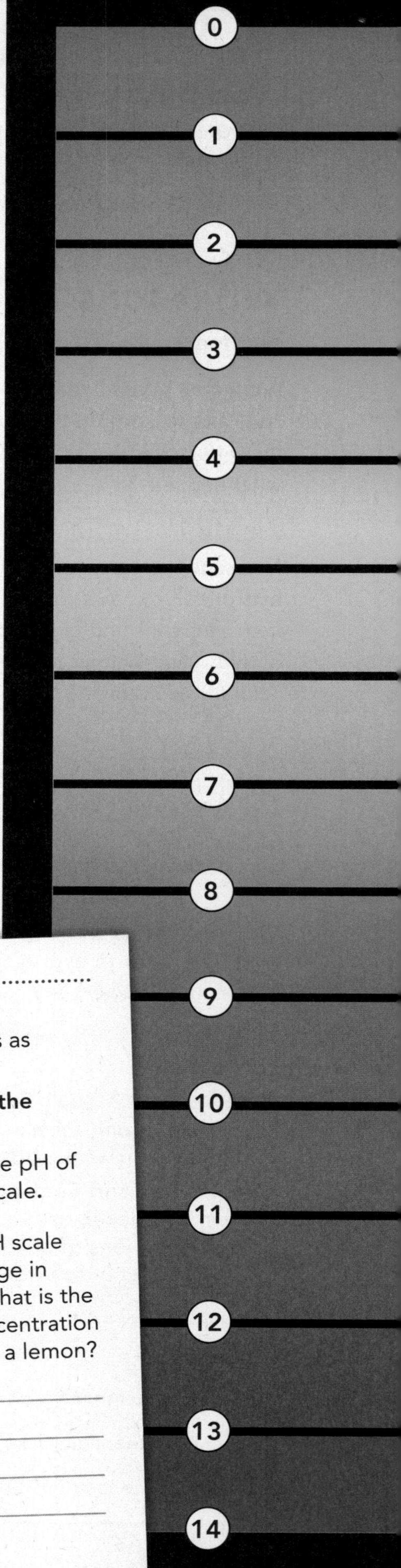

FIGURE 4 ⋯⋯⋯⋯⋯⋯⋯⋯⋯⋯⋯⋯
▷ INTERACTIVE ART **The pH Scale**
The pH scale helps classify solutions as acidic or basic.

✎ **Use the pH scale to complete the following tasks.**

1. ⚠ **Measure** Find the approximate pH of each substance shown on the scale.

2. CHALLENGE Each unit of the pH scale represents a tenfold (10x) change in hydrogen ion concentration. What is the difference in hydrogen ion concentration between hydrochloric acid and a lemon?

_____

_____

_____

_____

0
1
2
3
4
5
6
7
8
9
10
11
12
13
14

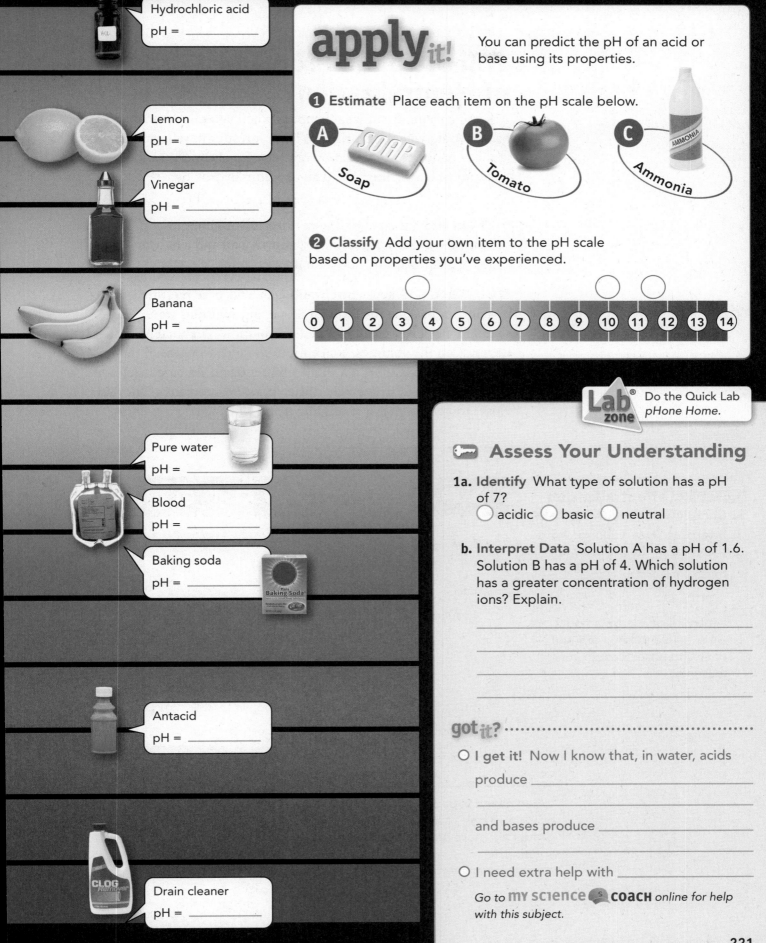

Hydrochloric acid
pH = _____

Lemon
pH = _____

Vinegar
pH = _____

Banana
pH = _____

Pure water
pH = _____

Blood
pH = _____

Baking soda
pH = _____

Antacid
pH = _____

Drain cleaner
pH = _____

apply it!

You can predict the pH of an acid or base using its properties.

1 Estimate Place each item on the pH scale below.

A Soap
B Tomato
C Ammonia

2 Classify Add your own item to the pH scale based on properties you've experienced.

0 1 2 3 4 5 6 7 8 9 10 11 12 13 14

Lab zone® Do the Quick Lab *pHone Home.*

Assess Your Understanding

1a. Identify What type of solution has a pH of 7?
○ acidic ○ basic ○ neutral

b. Interpret Data Solution A has a pH of 1.6. Solution B has a pH of 4. Which solution has a greater concentration of hydrogen ions? Explain.

_____
_____
_____
_____

got it? ....

○ **I get it!** Now I know that, in water, acids

produce _____

_____

and bases produce _____

○ **I need extra help with** _____

Go to **MY SCIENCE** Ⓢ **COACH** *online for help with this subject.*

221

What Are the Products of Neutralization?

Are you curious about what happens when you mix an acid and a base? Would you be surprised to learn it results in salt water? Look at the equation for the reaction between equal concentrations and amounts of hydrochloric acid and sodium hydroxide.

$$HCl + NaOH \rightarrow H_2O + Na^+ + Cl^-$$

If you tested the pH of the mixture, it would be close to 7, or neutral. In fact, a reaction between an acid and a base is called **neutralization** (noo truh lih ZAY shun).

Reactants After neutralization, an acid-base mixture is not as acidic or basic as the individual starting solutions were. The reaction may even result in a neutral solution. The final pH depends on the volumes, concentrations, and strengths of the reactants. For example, if a small amount of strong base reacts with a large amount of strong acid, the solution will remain acidic, but closer to neutral than the original pH.

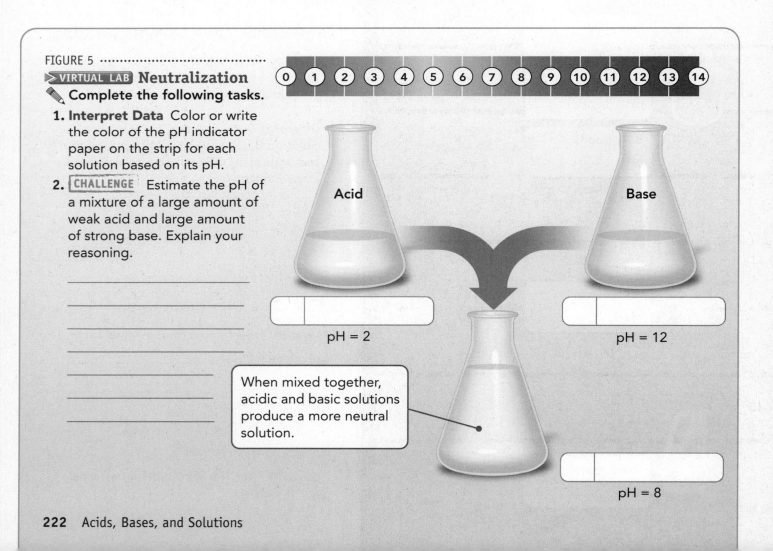

FIGURE 5 ·····················

> VIRTUAL LAB **Neutralization**

✎ **Complete the following tasks.**

1. **Interpret Data** Color or write the color of the pH indicator paper on the strip for each solution based on its pH.

2. CHALLENGE Estimate the pH of a mixture of a large amount of weak acid and large amount of strong base. Explain your reasoning.

_____

_____

_____

_____

_____

_____

0 1 2 3 4 5 6 7 8 9 10 11 12 13 14

Acid

pH = 2

Base

pH = 12

When mixed together, acidic and basic solutions produce a more neutral solution.

pH = 8

Products

"Salt" may be the familiar name of the stuff you sprinkle on food, but to a chemist, the word refers to a specific group of compounds. A **salt** is any ionic compound that can be made from a neutralization reaction. A salt is made from the positive ion of a base and the negative ion of an acid. The reaction of a metal with a nonmetal is a neutralization reaction and produces a salt.

Look at the equation for the neutralization reaction of nitric acid with potassium hydroxide that forms potassium nitrate salt.

$$HNO_3 + KOH \rightarrow H_2O + K^+ + NO_3^-$$
$$\text{(acid)} \quad \text{(base)} \quad \text{(water)} \quad \text{(salt)}$$

🔑 **In a neutralization reaction, an acid reacts with a base to produce a salt and water.** Some common salts are shown in the table in **Figure 6.**

FIGURE 6

Common Salts

The table lists common salts produced from neutralization reactions.

✏️ **Interpret Tables** Complete the table with the formula for each salt.

Common Salts			
Salt	**Neutralization reaction**	**Salt formula**	**Use**
Sodium chloride	$NaOH + HCl \longrightarrow H_2O + Na^+ + Cl^-$	_____	Table salt
Potassium iodide	$KOH + HI \longrightarrow H_2O + K^+ + I^-$	_____	Disinfectants
Potassium chloride	$KOH + HCl \longrightarrow H_2O + K^+ + Cl^-$	_____	Salt substitute
Calcium carbonate	$Ca(OH)_2 + H_2CO_3 \longrightarrow 2 H_2O + Ca^{2+} + CO_3^{2-}$	_____	Limestone

✏️ **Relate Cause and Effect**
Choose all of the following that result from neutralization.

○ Water is produced.

○ pH of the product is closer to 7 than the reactants' pH.

○ Acids turn into bases.

Do the Quick Lab
The Antacid Test.

🔑 Assess Your Understanding

2a. Define How is the scientific meaning of salt different from the common meaning of salt?

_____

_____

_____

_____

b. Make Generalizations Is the pH of an acid-base neutralization always 7? Why or why not?

_____

_____

_____

_____

got it?

○ **I get it!** Now I know that a neutralization reaction produces _____

_____

○ **I need extra help with** _____

Go to **my science** **COACH** online for help with this subject.

6 Study Guide

Solutions contain a _____ and at least one _____ . The solubility of a substance depends on _____ .

LESSON 1 Understanding Solutions

🔑 A mixture is classified as a solution, colloid, or suspension based on the size of its largest particles.

🔑 A solution forms when particles of the solute separate from each other and become surrounded by particles of the solvent.

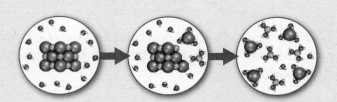

Vocabulary
• solution • solvent • solute
• colloid • suspension

LESSON 2 Concentration and Solubility

🔑 You can change the concentration of a solution by adding solute. You can also change it by adding or removing solvent.

🔑 Factors that can affect the solubility of a substance include pressure, the type of solvent, and temperature.

Vocabulary
• dilute solution • concentrated solution
• solubility • saturated solution

LESSON 3 Describing Acids and Bases

🔑 An acid reacts with metals and carbonates, tastes sour, and turns blue litmus paper red.

🔑 A base tastes bitter, feels slippery, and turns red litmus paper blue.

Vocabulary
• acid • corrosive • indicator • base

LESSON 4 Acids and Bases in Solution

🔑 An acid produces hydrogen ions (H^+) in water.

🔑 A base produces hydroxide ions (OH^-) in water.

🔑 In a neutralization reaction, an acid reacts with a base to produce a salt and water.

Vocabulary
• hydrogen ion (H^+) • hydroxide ion (OH^-)
• pH scale • neutralization • salt

Review and Assessment

LESSON 1 Understanding Solutions

1. Which of the following is an example of a solution?

a. fog   **b.** soda water

c. milk   **d.** mud

2. A mixture of pepper and water is a suspension

because _____

_____

_____

3. Apply Concepts The table below shows the main components of Earth's atmosphere. What is the solvent in air? What are the solutes?

Composition of Earth's Atmosphere	
Compound	**Percent Volume**
Argon (Ar)	0.93
Carbon dioxide (CO_2)	0.03
Nitrogen (N_2)	78.08
Oxygen (O_2)	20.95
Water vapor (H_2O)	0 to 3

_____

_____

_____

_____

4. Predict Suppose you put equal amounts of pure water and salt water into separate ice cube trays of the same size and shape. What would you expect to happen when you put both trays in the freezer? Explain.

_____

_____

_____

_____

_____

LESSON 2 Concentration and Solubility

5. How can you increase the concentration of a solution?

a. add solute   **b.** increase temperature

c. add solvent   **d.** decrease pressure

6. Most gases become more soluble in liquid as

the temperature _____

7. Interpret Diagrams Which of the diagrams below shows a dilute solution? Which one shows a concentrated solution? Explain.

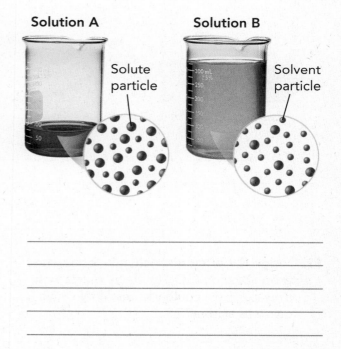

Solution A   Solution B

Solute particle   Solvent particle

_____

_____

_____

_____

_____

_____

_____

8. math! The concentration of a water and alcohol solution is 25 percent alcohol by volume. Calculate what the volume of alcohol would be in 200 mL of the solution.

LESSON 3 Describing Acids and Bases

9. Which of the following is a property of bases?

   a. sour taste

   b. slippery feel

   c. turns blue litmus paper red

   d. reacts with some metals

10. Litmus paper is an example of an indicator

    because _____

    _____

11. **Classify** Which of the following substances contain bases? Explain your reasoning.

   Lemon   Tonic Water   Soap

   _____

   _____

   _____

   _____

12. **Design Experiments** Acid rain forms when carbon dioxide (CO_2) in the air reacts with rainwater. How could you test if rain in your town was acid rain?

    _____

    _____

    _____

    _____

13. 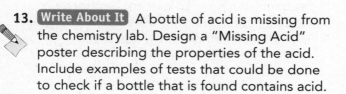 **Write About It** A bottle of acid is missing from the chemistry lab. Design a "Missing Acid" poster describing the properties of the acid. Include examples of tests that could be done to check if a bottle that is found contains acid.

LESSON 4 Acids and Bases in Solution

14. What is an ion called that is made of hydrogen and oxygen?

   a. an acid   b. a base

   c. a hydrogen ion   d. a hydroxide ion

15. In water, acids separate into _____

    _____

    _____

    _____

16. **Apply Concepts** Suppose you have a solution that is either an acid or a base. It doesn't react with any metals. Is the pH of the solution more likely to be 4 or 9? Explain.

    _____

    _____

    _____

    _____

What determines the properties of a solution?

17. You are given three beakers of unknown liquids. One beaker contains pure water. One contains salt water. One contains sugar water. Without tasting the liquids, how could you identify the liquid in each beaker?

    _____

    _____

    _____

    _____

    _____

    _____

    _____

    _____

Standardized Test Prep

Multiple Choice

Circle the letter of the best answer.

1. The graph below shows how the solubility of potassium chloride (KCl) in water changes with temperature.

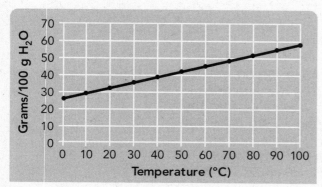

Thirty grams of potassium chloride are dissolved in 100 grams of water at 60°C. Which **best** describes the solution?

A saturated   B supersaturated

C unsaturated   D acidic

2. Which of the following pH values indicates a solution with the highest concentration of hydrogen ions?

A pH = 1
B pH = 2
C pH = 7
D pH = 14

3. Three sugar cubes are placed in a beaker containing 50 milliliters of water at 20°C. Which action would speed up the rate at which the sugar cubes dissolve in the water?

A Use less water.
B Transfer the contents to a larger beaker.
C Cool the water and sugar cubes to 5°C.
D Heat and stir the contents of the beaker.

4. A scientist observes that an unknown solution turns blue litmus paper red and reacts with zinc to produce hydrogen gas. Which of the following **best** describes the unknown solution?

A a colloid
B an acid
C a base
D a suspension

5. Why is dissolving table salt in water an example of a physical change?

A Neither of the substances changes into a new substance.
B The salt cannot be separated from the water.
C The water cannot become saturated with salt.
D A physical change occurs whenever a substance is mixed with water.

Constructed Response

Use the diagram below and your knowledge of science to help you answer Question 6. Write your answer on a separate sheet of paper.

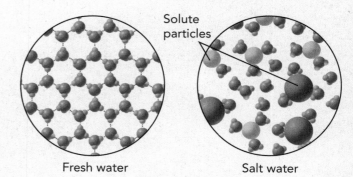

Fresh water   Salt water

6. At temperatures below 0°C, fresh water on the surface of a lake is frozen while a nearby body of salt water is not frozen. Explain this observation in terms of what happens to water molecules when water freezes.

LIMESTONE AND ACID DRAINAGE

Sport Meets Science

Fifteen-year-old Luke Andraka likes to go kayaking on the Cheat River in West Virginia. On a trip during the summer of 2007, he did more than paddle around. Observing that the water in some areas was orange, Luke began asking questions. He learned that acid runoff from a nearby mine flowed into the stream. The acid changed the chemistry of the stream, causing dead zones, where plants and shellfish could not live and the color of the water changed.

This gave Luke an idea for his science fair project. Luke knew that limestone can neutralize acid rain. He hypothesized that adding limestone to the water could reverse the effects of the runoff from the mine. He experimented to see whether adding small pieces of limestone would work better than adding large pieces of limestone. He proved that limestone could raise the pH level in the stream and clear the stream's pollution without harming the organisms living in the river habitat. Luke also found that limestone sand would work more quickly than an equal mass of limestone rocks.

Write About It Be a keen observer. Research one environmental issue in your community. Identify a possible cause, and present one possible solution. Explain in a letter to your local newspaper how you would research the effectiveness of that solution.

◀ Acid runoff from mines caused dead zones, where the water in the Cheat River changed color.

vinegar

Pucker Up!

From West Africa, we have chicken yassa—seasoned with malt or cider vinegar. From Japan, we have sushi rice—seasoned with rice vinegar. From Italy we have grilled sea bass with anchovy dressing—seasoned with balsamic vinegar. All the world loves vinegar!

This sour-tasting ingredient is made from the oxidation of ethanol in a liquid. Most vinegar is 3 to 5 percent acetic acid by volume, which is why it curdles with basic ingredients that have a basic pH, such as milk.

Why does vinegar taste so sour? For a long time, scientists weren't sure. Then a team led by scientists at Duke University Medical Center identified two proteins on the surface of our tongues—PKD1L3 and PKD2L1. They also tracked the process that sends an electrical signal to your brain to pucker up. Another study showed that your genes may play a role in how sour something tastes to you.

Design It Work with a partner to design an experiment to find out more about people's taste for sour flavors. How do different people respond to the same sour food and drink? Consider how you can test their reactions. How many people would you need to test? Will repeated trials help you to draw a conclusion?

◀ PKD1L3 and PKD2L1 are two proteins on the surface of the tongue. They cause vinegar to taste sour.

HOW CAN YOU DESCRIBE THIS COASTER'S MOTION?

 THE BIG ?

How do you describe the motion of an object?

First there is the long, slow climb up the hill. Then the big plunge down. Your body momentarily leaves the seat. The coaster enters a loop the loop and you are upside down! Up and down faster, slower until you finally stop—PHEW!

Classify What kinds of motion happen during a roller coaster ride?

_____

_____

_____

_____

_____

_____

_____

UNTAMED SCIENCE Watch the **Untamed Science** video to learn more about motion.

Getting Started

Check Your Understanding

1. **Background** Read the paragraph below and then answer the question.

Jenny is watching television. Suddenly, a warning from the National Weather Service appears on the screen. A thunderstorm is heading in her **direction**. At that **instant,** Jenny sees a bolt of lightning in the distant sky. Jenny hopes the storm will be over in **time** for her soccer game.

Direction is the line along which something moves.

Instant is a point or very short space in time.

Time is the period of duration between two events.

- What might happen if the storm were to change direction?

_____

_____

▶ MY READING WEB If you had trouble completing the question above, visit **My Reading Web** and type in *Motion.*

Vocabulary Skill

High-Use Academic Words Knowing these academic words will help you become a better reader in all subject areas. Look for these words as you read this chapter.

Word	Definition	Example
system	*n.* an established way of doing something	People have different *systems* for keeping their music collections organized.
equation	*n.* a statement of equality between two quantities, as shown by the equal sign (=).	The *equation* for the area of a circle is $A = \pi \times r^2$.
conclude	*v.* to decide by reasoning	After investigating the evidence, they *concluded* that everyone should wear a bicycle helmet.

2. **Quick Check** Choose the word from the table that best completes the sentence.

- After waiting for 20 minutes, he _____ that his friend was not coming.

motion

speed

velocity

acceleration

Chapter Preview

LESSON 1

- motion
- reference point
- International System of Units
- distance

🔄 **Compare and Contrast**
🔺 **Measure**

LESSON 2

- speed
- average speed
- instantaneous speed
- velocity
- slope

🔄 **Identify Supporting Evidence**
🔺 **Calculate**

LESSON 3

- acceleration

🔄 **Identify the Main Idea**
🔺 **Graph**

> VOCAB FLASH CARDS For extra help with vocabulary, visit **Vocab Flash Cards** and type in *Motion.*

Describing Motion

UNLOCK THE BIG ? 🔑 **When Is an Object in Motion?**

my planet Diary — VOICES FROM HISTORY

Nicolaus Copernicus

Why would anyone think that Earth moves around the sun? After all, on a clear day you can see the sun move across the sky. But Polish astronomer Nicolaus Copernicus realized that an object revolving around you from left to right looks the same as an object standing still while you rotate from right to left. In *On the Revolution of the Heavenly Spheres,* he wrote

Every apparent change in respect of position is due to motion of the object observed, or of the observer, or indeed to an unequal change of both.

This book was published in 1543. It was a summary of more than 30 years of Copernicus's studies on the solar system.

Write your answer to the question below.

For thousands of years, many people thought Earth was the center of the universe. Name one possible reason why they thought this.

_____

_____

_____

_____

_____

_____

> PLANET DIARY Go to **Planet Diary** to learn more about motion.

 Do the Inquiry Warm-Up *What Is Motion?*

When Is an Object in Motion?

Deciding if an object is in motion isn't as easy as you might think. For example, you are probably sitting in a chair as you read this book. Are you moving? Parts of you are. Your eyes blink and your chest moves up and down. But you would probably say that you are not moving. An object is in **motion** if its position changes relative to another object. Because your position relative to your chair does not change, you could say that you are not in motion.

Vocabulary
- motion • reference point
- International System of Units • distance

Skills
- Reading: Compare and Contrast
- Inquiry: Measure

Reference Points To decide if you are moving, you use your chair as a reference point. A **reference point** is a place or object used for comparison to determine if something is in motion. 🔑 **An object is in motion if it changes position relative to a reference point.** Objects that are fixed relative to Earth—such as a building, a tree, or a sign—make good reference points.

You may already know what happens if your reference point is moving relative to Earth. Have you ever been in a school bus parked next to another bus? Suddenly, you think that your bus is moving backward. When you look out the window again for a fixed point, you find that your bus isn't moving at all—the other bus is moving forward! Your bus seemed to be moving backward because you had used the other bus as a reference point.

did you know?

Because of Earth's spin, the stars appear to move in circular arcs across the night sky. Only the North Star remains in a fixed position. Historically, sailors have used the North Star to help them navigate.

FIGURE 1 ....

> ART IN MOTION **Reference Point**
The top photo was taken shortly before the bottom photo.

✎ **Answer the following questions.**

1. **Interpret Photos** Did the car that the boy is in move, or did the car in the background move? Explain your answer.

_____

_____

_____

_____

2. **Identify** What objects in this photo make good reference points?

_____

_____

_____

Relative Motion If you use your chair as your reference point as you sit and read, you are not moving. If you choose another object as a reference point, you may be moving.

Suppose you use the sun as a reference point instead of your chair. If you compare your position to the sun, you are moving quite rapidly because you and your chair are on Earth, which revolves around the sun. Earth moves around the sun at a speed of about 30 kilometers every second. So you and everything else on Earth are moving that quickly as well. Going that fast, you could travel from New York City to Los Angeles in about two minutes! Relative to the sun, both you and your chair are in motion. But because you are moving with Earth, you do not seem to be moving.

Compare and Contrast
A tree is (stationary/in motion) relative to Earth. A tree is (stationary/in motion) relative to the sun.

apply it!

The people in the photo are riding on a spinning carousel.

1 Interpret Photos Are the people moving relative to each other? Are they moving relative to objects on the ground? Explain.

_____

_____

_____

_____

_____

_____

_____

_____

2 Explain How is your choice of reference point important when describing the motion of the people?

_____

_____

_____

_____

_____

_____

_____

_____

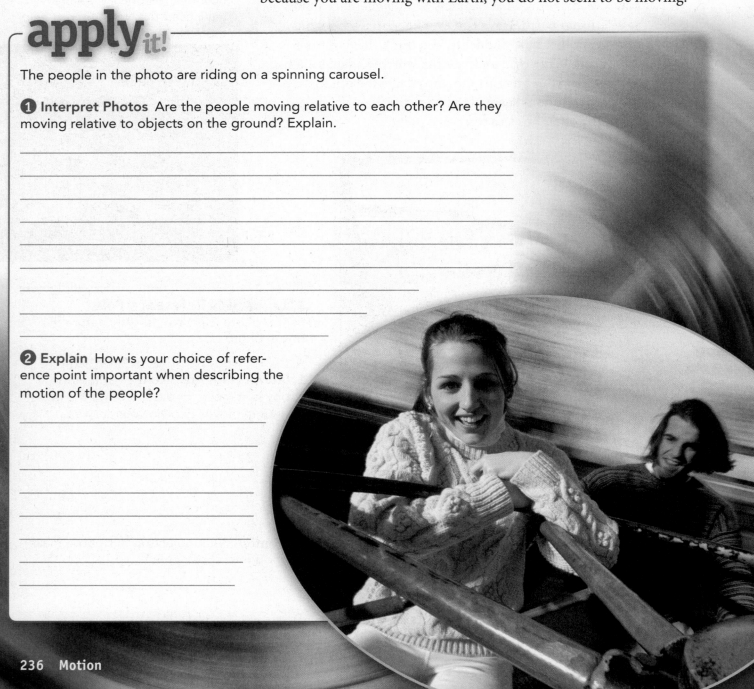

Measuring Distance

To describe motion completely, you need to use units of measurement. Scientists use a system of measurement called the **International System of Units** or, in French, *Système International* (SI). **Distance** is the length of the path between two points. The SI unit for length is the meter (m). The distance from the floor to a doorknob is about 1 meter.

Scientists use other units to measure distances much smaller or much larger than a meter. For example, the width of the spider shown in **Figure 2** can be measured in centimeters (cm). The prefix *centi-* means "one hundredth." A centimeter is one hundredth of a meter, so there are 100 centimeters in a meter. For lengths smaller than a centimeter, the millimeter (mm) is used. The prefix *milli-* means "one thousandth," so there are 1,000 millimeters in a meter. Distances much longer than a meter can be measured in kilometers (km). The prefix *kilo-* means "one thousand," so there are 1,000 meters in a kilometer. A straight line between San Francisco and Boston would measure about 4,300 kilometers.

FIGURE 2

Measuring Distance

The unit of length that you use to measure distance depends on the size of the distance.

✏️ **Answer the following questions.**

1. **Review** Fill in the following common conversions for length.

   1 m = _____ mm

   1 m = _____ cm

   1 km = _____ m

2. **Measure** What is the distance in centimeters from points A to B on the spider? _____

3. [CHALLENGE] How many of these spiders would fit side by side in the length of 1 meter?

   _____

   _____

A   B

Lab zone® Do the Quick Lab
Identifying Motion.

🔑 Assess Your Understanding

1a. Review A _____ is a place or object used for comparison to determine if something is in motion.

b. Explain Why is it important to know if your reference point is moving?

_____

_____

_____

_____

got it?

○ **I get it!** Now I know that an object is in motion if _____

_____

_____

_____

○ **I need extra help with** _____

Go to MY SCIENCE ⓢ COACH *online for help with this subject.*

Speed and Velocity

UNLOCK THE BIG ?

🔑 **How Do You Calculate Speed?**

🔑 **How Do You Describe Velocity?**

🔑 **How Do You Graph Motion?**

my planet diary

BLOG

Posted by: Mallory

Location: Fountain Valley, California

Once my sister talked me into going to the roller-skating rink with her. I hate skating, but against my better judgment, I agreed to go. I can skate, but I don't go very fast. At the rink, there were these speed skaters, or, as I like to call them, "assassin skaters." The assassin skaters went ridiculously fast. They were probably going approximately 20 miles per hour in the same direction as me. They zipped past me, just barely missing me.

The worst part about going skating was getting stuck behind a group of skaters or a couple. They went so slowly that you had to speed up to get around them.

Communicate Answer the questions. Discuss your answers with a partner.

1. Do all the skaters in the rink move at the same speed? Explain.

_____

_____

_____

2. Describe a sport or activity in which speed is important.

_____

_____

_____

_____

> **PLANET DIARY** Go to **Planet Diary** to learn more about speed and velocity.

Lab zone® Do the Inquiry Warm-Up *How Fast and How Far?*

Vocabulary
- speed - average speed
- instantaneous speed
- velocity - slope

Skills
↻ Reading: Identify Supporting Evidence
△ Inquiry: Calculate

How Do You Calculate Speed?

You might describe the motion of an airplane as fast or the motion of a snail as slow. By using these words, you are describing the object's speed. The **speed** of an object is the distance the object moves per unit of time. Speed is a type of rate. A rate tells you the amount of something that occurs or changes in one unit of time.

The Speed Equation **To calculate the speed of an object, divide the distance the object travels by the amount of time it takes to travel that distance.** This relationship can be written as an equation.

$$\text{Speed} = \frac{\text{Distance}}{\text{Time}}$$

The speed equation contains a unit of distance divided by a unit of time. If you measure distance in meters and time in seconds, the SI unit for speed is meters per second, or m/s. (The slash is read as "per.") For example, at its cruising altitude, an airplane might travel at a constant speed of 260 m/s. This means that the airplane will travel a distance of 260 meters in 1 second. The speed of a snail is about 1 mm/s. This means that the snail will travel a distance of 1 millimeter in 1 second. The speed of the airplane is much greater than the speed of the snail because the airplane travels much farther than the snail in the same amount of time.

Vocabulary High-Use Academic Words Complete the following sentence. The relationship between speed, distance, and time can be written as a(n)

_____

apply it!

The cyclist shown in the diagram is moving at a constant speed of 10 m/s during her ride.

❶ **Identify** Draw arrows on the scale to mark how far the cyclist travels after 1, 2, 3, 3.5, and 4 seconds.

❷ **CHALLENGE** How long will it take the cyclist to travel 400 meters?

FIGURE 1 ·······························

Average Speed

Triathletes A and B are competing in a triathlon. The first two legs of the race are swimming and biking.

✎ Calculate Use the data in the boxes below to calculate each triathlete's average speed during the swimming and biking legs of the race.

Average Speed

When a plane is at its cruising altitude, it can travel at a constant speed for many hours. But the speed of most moving objects is not constant. In a race known as the triathlon, the competitors (or triathletes) first swim, then bike, and finally run. The speeds of the triathletes change throughout the race. They travel slowest when they swim, a little faster when they run, and fastest when they bike.

Although the triathletes do not travel at a constant speed, they do have an average speed throughout the race. To calculate **average speed,** divide the total distance traveled by the total time. For example, suppose a triathlete swims a distance of 3 kilometers in 1 hour. Then the triathlete bikes a distance of 50 kilometers in 3 hours. Finally, the triathlete runs a distance of 12 kilometers in 1 hour. The average speed of the triathlete is the total distance divided by the total time.

Total distance = 3 km + 50 km + 12 km = 65 km

Total time = 1 h + 3 h + 1 h = 5 h

$$\text{Average speed} = \frac{65 \text{ km}}{5 \text{ h}} = 13 \text{ km/h}$$

The triathlete's average speed is 13 kilometers per hour.

Leg 1 *Swimming*

Total distance: 3.0 km
Triathlete A's total time: 0.8 h
Triathlete B's total time: 1.0 h

Triathlete A's average speed =

Triathlete B's average speed =

Leg 2 *Biking*

Total distance: 50.0 km
Triathlete A's total time: 3.0 h
Triathlete B's total time: 2.5 h

Triathlete A's average speed =

Triathlete B's average speed =

Instantaneous Speed Suppose Triathlete B passes Tri-athlete A during the biking leg. At that moment, Triathlete B has a greater instantaneous speed than Triathlete A. **Instantaneous speed** is the speed at which an object is moving at a given instant in time. It is important not to confuse instantaneous speed with average speed. The triathlete with the greatest average speed, not the greatest instantaneous speed, wins the race.

apply it!

The triathletes run in the third and final leg of the triathlon.

1 ⚠ **Calculate** Use the data from all three legs to solve for each triathlete's average speed.

Leg 3 Running
Total distance: 12.0 km
Triathlete A's total time: 1.2 h
Triathlete B's total time: 1.0 h

Total distance =	
Triathlete A's total time =	
Triathlete A's average speed =	
Triathlete B's total time =	
Triathlete B's average speed =	

2 **Identify** Which triathlete finishes first? _____

🔑 **Assess Your Understanding**

1a. **Identify** The (instantaneous/average) speed is the speed of the object at a given instant in time. The (instantaneous/average) speed is the speed of the object over a longer period of time.

b. **Apply Concepts** The speedometer in a car gives the car's _____ speed.

Lab ® **zone** Do the Lab Investigation *Stopping on a Dime.*

got it?

○ **I get it!** Now I know to calculate the speed of an object, I need to _____

_____

○ **I need extra help with** _____

Go to **MY SCIENCE** ⬤ⁱ **COACH** *online for help with this subject.*

How Do You Describe Velocity?

Knowing the speed at which something travels does not tell you everything about its motion. To describe an object's motion, you also need to know its direction. For example, suppose you hear that a thunderstorm is traveling at a speed of 25 km/h. Should you prepare for the storm? That depends on the direction of the storm's motion. Because storms usually travel from west to east in the United States, you probably need not worry if you live west of the storm. You probably should take cover if you live east of the storm.

When you know both the speed and direction of an object's motion, you know the velocity of the object. Speed in a given direction is called **velocity**. You know the velocity of the storm when you know that it is moving 25 km/h eastward.

At times, describing the velocity of moving objects can be very important. For example, air traffic controllers must keep close track of the velocities of the aircraft under their control. These velocities change as airplanes move overhead and on the runways. An error in determining a velocity, either in speed or in direction, could lead to a collision.

Velocity is also important to airplane pilots. For example, the stunt pilots in **Figure 2** make spectacular use of their control over the velocity of their aircraft. Stunt pilots use this control to stay in close formation while flying graceful maneuvers at high speeds.

Identify Supporting Evidence Underline the reason why velocity is important to air traffic controllers.

FIGURE 2 ⋯⋯⋯⋯⋯⋯⋯⋯
Velocity
These stunt pilots are performing at an air show.

Explain Why is velocity and not just speed important to these pilots?

_____

_____

_____

_____

_____

_____

_____

_____

Going Somewhere?

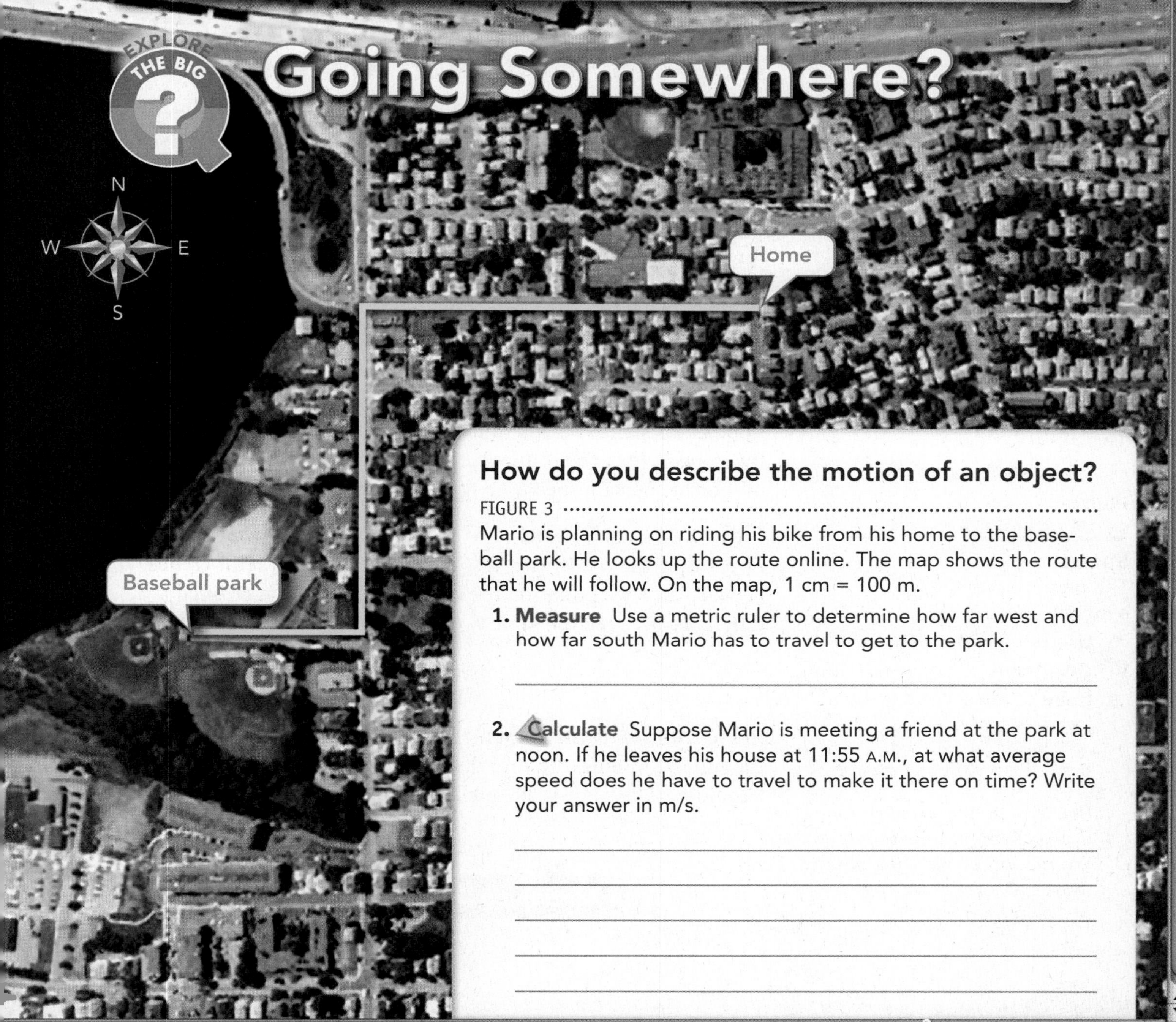

Home

Baseball park

How do you describe the motion of an object?

FIGURE 3 ···

Mario is planning on riding his bike from his home to the base-ball park. He looks up the route online. The map shows the route that he will follow. On the map, 1 cm = 100 m.

1. **Measure** Use a metric ruler to determine how far west and how far south Mario has to travel to get to the park.

_____

2. **Calculate** Suppose Mario is meeting a friend at the park at noon. If he leaves his house at 11:55 A.M., at what average speed does he have to travel to make it there on time? Write your answer in m/s.

_____

_____

_____

_____

_____

 Lab zone® Do the Quick Lab *Velocity.*

Assess Your Understanding

2. **ANSWER THE BIG ?** How do you describe the motion of an object?

_____

_____

_____

_____

got it?

○ **I get it!** Now I know that the velocity of an object is the _____

_____

○ **I need extra help with** _____

Go to **MY SCIENCE** ⑤ **COACH** *online for help with this subject.*

How Do You Graph Motion?

The graphs you see in **Figure 4** and **Figure 5** are distance-versus-time motion graphs. 🔑 **You can show the motion of an object on a line graph in which you plot distance versus time.** By tradition, time is shown on the horizontal axis, or *x*-axis. Distance is shown on the vertical axis, or *y*-axis. A point on the line represents the distance an object has traveled during a particular time. The *x* value of the point is time, and the *y* value is distance.

The steepness of a line on a graph is called **slope.** The slope tells you how fast one variable changes in relation to the other variable in the graph. In other words, slope tells you the rate of change. Since speed is the rate that distance changes in relation to time, the slope of a distance-versus-time graph represents speed. The steeper the slope is, the greater the speed. A constant slope represents motion at constant speed.

Calculating Slope

You can calculate the slope of a line by dividing the rise by the run. The rise is the vertical difference between any two points on the line. The run is the horizontal difference between the same two points.

$$\text{Slope} = \frac{\text{Rise}}{\text{Run}}$$

In **Figure 4,** using the points shown, the rise is 400 meters and the run is 2 minutes. To find the slope, you divide 400 meters by 2 minutes. The slope is 200 meters per minute.

FIGURE 4 ······························

> **INTERACTIVE ART** **Constant Speed**
The graph shows the motion of a jogger.

✎ **Use the graph to answer the questions.**

1. **Read Graphs** What is the jogger's speed?

_____

2. **Predict** On the same graph, draw a line that represents the motion of a jogger who moves at a constant speed of 100 m/min.

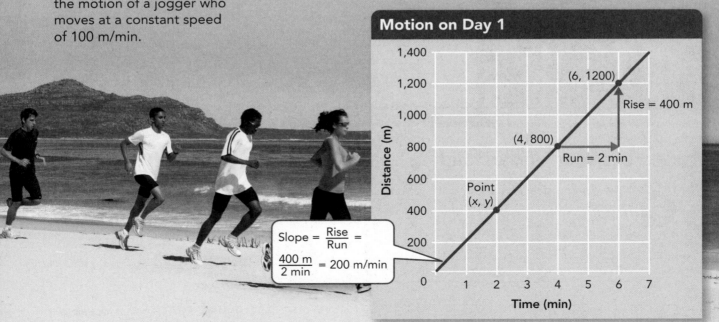

Motion on Day 1

Slope = $\dfrac{\text{Rise}}{\text{Run}}$ = $\dfrac{400 \text{ m}}{2 \text{ min}}$ = 200 m/min

(6, 1200)

Rise = 400 m

(4, 800)

Run = 2 min

Point (x, y)

Distance (m)

Time (min)

Different Slopes

Different Slopes Most moving objects do not travel at a constant speed. For example, the graph in **Figure 5** shows a jogger's motion on the second day of training. The line is divided into three segments. The slope of each segment is different. From the steepness of the slopes you can tell that the jogger ran fastest during the third segment. The horizontal line in the second segment shows that the jogger's distance did not change at all. The jogger was resting during the second segment.

FIGURE 5 ···
Changing Speed
The graph shows how the speed of a jogger varies during her second day of training.

✎ **Read Graphs** Find the rise, the run, and the slope for each segment of the graph. Write the answers in the boxes below.

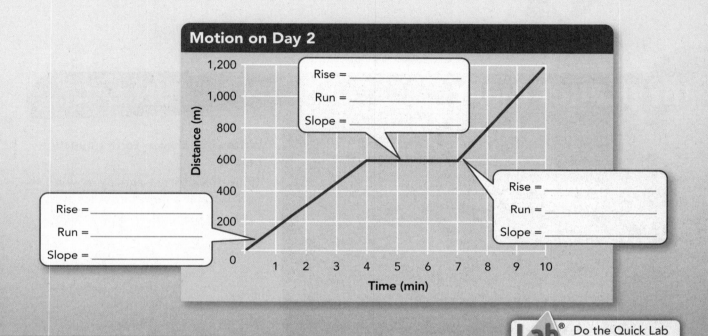

Motion on Day 2

Rise = _____
Run = _____
Slope = _____

Rise = _____
Run = _____
Slope = _____

Rise = _____
Run = _____
Slope = _____

Distance (m) — 0, 200, 400, 600, 800, 1,000, 1,200

Time (min) — 1, 2, 3, 4, 5, 6, 7, 8, 9, 10

Lab ® Do the Quick Lab
zone *Motion Graphs.*

🔑 Assess Your Understanding

3a. Identify The _____ of a distance-versus-time graph shows you the speed of a moving object.

b. Calculate The rise of a line on a distance-versus-time graph is 900 m and the run is 3 min. What is the slope of the line?

_____

_____

c. Apply Concepts Is it possible for a distance-versus-time graph to be a vertical line? Explain.

_____

_____

_____

_____

_____

got it? ···

○ **I get it!** Now I know to show the motion of an object on a line graph, you _____

_____

○ **I need extra help with** _____

Go to **my science** ⑤ **coach** *online for help with this subject.*

🔑 **What Is Acceleration?**

🔑 **How Do You Graph Acceleration?**

MY PLANET DIARY

Jumping Spider

A small spider, less than 2 centimeters long, spots an insect. The spider crouches and crawls slowly forward. Then it lifts its front legs and leaps, landing right on its victim!

Amazingly, a jumping spider can jump 10 to 40 times its body length. To capture prey from that far away, it must accurately estimate its initial velocity. Once the spider jumps, the force of gravity controls its motion, causing it to follow a curved path. Its velocity changes at every point along the path until it lands on its prey.

FUN FACT

Write your answer to the question below.

Think of a sport or activity in which the goal is to hit a target from far away. What are some of the challenges?

_____

_____

_____

_____

_____

▶ **PLANET DIARY** Go to **Planet Diary** to learn more about acceleration.

Lab zone® Do the Inquiry Warm-Up *Will You Hurry Up?*

What Is Acceleration?

Suppose you are a passenger in a car stopped at a red light. When the light changes to green, the driver steps on the accelerator. As a result, the car speeds up, or accelerates. In everyday language, acceleration means "the process of speeding up."

Acceleration has a more precise definition in science. Scientists define **acceleration** as the rate at which velocity changes. Recall that velocity describes both the speed and direction of an object. A change in velocity can involve a change in either speed or direction—or both. 🔑 **In science, acceleration refers to increasing speed, decreasing speed, or changing direction.**

Vocabulary
• acceleration

Skills
🔄 Reading: Identify the Main Idea
🔺 Inquiry: Graph

Changing Speed Whenever an object's speed changes, the object accelerates. A car that begins to move from a stopped position or speeds up to pass another car is accelerating. People can accelerate too. For example, you accelerate when you coast down a hill on your bike.

Just as objects can speed up, they can also slow down. This change in speed is sometimes called deceleration, or negative acceleration. A car decelerates as it comes to a stop at a red light. A water skier decelerates as the boat slows down.

Changing Direction Even an object that is traveling at a constant speed can be accelerating. Recall that acceleration can be a change in direction as well as a change in speed. Therefore, a car accelerates as it follows a gentle curve in the road or changes lanes. Runners accelerate as they round the curve in a track. A softball accelerates when it changes direction as it is hit.

Many objects continuously change direction without changing speed. The simplest example of this type of motion is circular motion, or motion along a circular path. For example, the seats on a Ferris wheel accelerate because they move in a circle.

🔄 **Identify the Main Idea**
Underline the main idea in the section called Changing Speed.

FIGURE 1 ·······························

Acceleration
During the game of soccer, a soccer ball can show three types of acceleration—increasing speed, decreasing speed, and changing direction.

✏️ **Interpret Photos** Label the type of acceleration that is occurring in each of the photos.

FIGURE 2 ·······································

Acceleration
The airplane is accelerating at a rate of 8 m/s².

✎ **Predict** Determine the speed of the airplane at 4.0 s and 5.0 s. Write your answers in the boxes next to each airplane.

Calculating Acceleration
Acceleration describes the rate at which velocity changes. If an object is not changing direction, you can describe its acceleration as the rate at which its speed changes. To determine the acceleration of an object moving in a straight line, you calculate the change in speed per unit of time. This is summarized by the following equation.

$$\text{Acceleration} = \frac{\text{Final Speed} - \text{Initial Speed}}{\text{Time}}$$

If speed is measured in meters per second (m/s) and time is measured in seconds, the SI unit of acceleration is meters per second per second, or m/s². Suppose speed is measured in kilometers per hour and time is measured in hours. Then the unit for acceleration is kilometers per hour per hour, or km/h².

To understand acceleration, imagine a small airplane moving down a runway. **Figure 2** shows the airplane's speed after each second of the first three seconds of its acceleration. To calculate the acceleration of the airplane, you must first subtract the initial speed of 0 m/s from its final speed of 24 m/s. Then divide the change in speed by the time, 3 seconds.

$$\text{Acceleration} = \frac{24 \text{ m/s} - 0 \text{ m/s}}{3 \text{ s}}$$

$$\text{Acceleration} = 8 \text{ m/s}^2$$

The airplane accelerates at a rate of 8 m/s². This means that the airplane's speed increases by 8 m/s every second. Notice in **Figure 2** that after each second of travel, the airplane's speed is 8 m/s greater than its speed in the previous second.

FIGURE 3 ·······································

Deceleration
An airplane touches down on the runway with a speed of 70 m/s. It decelerates at a rate of –5 m/s².

✎ **Predict** Determine the speed of the airplane after each second of its deceleration. Write your answers in the table to the right.

Time (s)	1	2	3	4
Speed (m/s)				

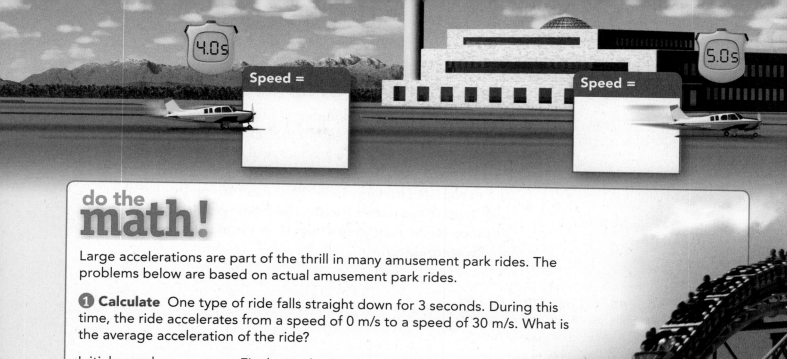

Speed = _____

Speed = _____

do the math!

Large accelerations are part of the thrill in many amusement park rides. The problems below are based on actual amusement park rides.

1 Calculate One type of ride falls straight down for 3 seconds. During this time, the ride accelerates from a speed of 0 m/s to a speed of 30 m/s. What is the average acceleration of the ride?

Initial speed = _____ Final speed = _____ Time = _____
Average acceleration =

2 Calculate A roller coaster accelerates from a speed of 4 m/s to 22 m/s in 3 seconds. What is the average acceleration of the ride?

Initial speed = _____ Final speed = _____ Time = _____
Average acceleration =

Lab ® Do the Quick Lab
zone *Describing Acceleration.*

🔑 Assess Your Understanding

1a. Define The rate at which velocity changes is

called _____

b. Infer A softball has a (positive/negative) acceleration when it is thrown. A softball has a (positive/negative) acceleration when it is caught.

c. Explain A girl skates around the perimeter of a circular ice rink at a constant speed of 2 m/s. Is the girl accelerating? Explain.

_____

_____

got it?

○ **I get it!** Now I know that in science

acceleration refers to _____

_____

_____

_____

_____

○ **I need extra help with** _____

Go to **MY SCIENCE** ⓢ **COACH** *online for help with this subject.*

249

How Do You Graph Acceleration?

Suppose you bike down a long, steep hill. At the top of the hill, your speed is 0 m/s. As you start down the hill, your speed increases. Each second, you move at a greater speed and travel a greater distance than the second before. During the five seconds it takes you to reach the bottom of the hill, you are an accelerating object.

🔑 **You can use both a speed-versus-time graph and a distance-versus-time graph to analyze the motion of an accelerating object.**

FIGURE 4 ⋯⋯⋯⋯⋯⋯⋯⋯⋯⋯⋯⋯⋯⋯⋯⋯

> VIRTUAL LAB **Speed-Versus-Time Graph**
The data in the table show how your speed changes during each second of your bike ride.

✎ **Use the data to answer the questions.**

Time (s)	Speed (m/s)
0	0
1	2
2	4
3	6
4	8
5	10

1. **Graph** Use this data to plot a line graph. Plot time on the horizontal axis. Plot speed on the vertical axis. Give the graph a title.

2. **Calculate** What is the slope of the graph?

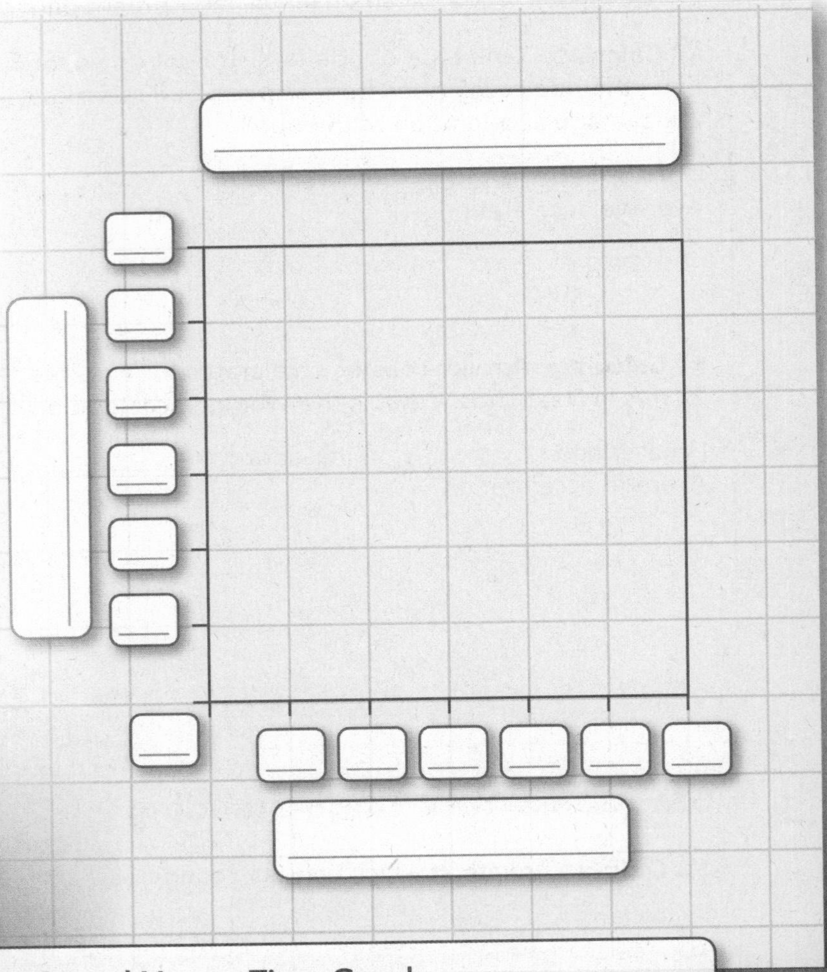

Analyzing a Speed-Versus-Time Graph

Look at the speed-versus-time graph that you made in **Figure 4.** What can you learn about your motion by analyzing this graph? First, since the line slants upward, the graph shows that your speed was increasing. Next, since the line is straight, you can tell that your acceleration was constant. A slanted, straight line on a speed-versus-time graph means that the object is accelerating at a constant rate. Your acceleration is the slope of the line.

FIGURE 5 ··

> INTERACTIVE ART **Distance-Versus-Time Graph**
The data in the table show how your distance changes during each second of your bike ride.

✎ **Use the data to answer the questions.**

Time (s)	Distance (m)
0	0
1	1
2	4
3	9
4	16
5	25

1. **Graph** Use this data to create a line graph. Plot time on the horizontal axis. Plot distance on the vertical axis. Give the graph a title.

2. **CHALLENGE** How does the distance change with time?

_____
_____
_____
_____

Analyzing a Distance-Versus-Time Graph

Look at the distance-versus-time graph that you made in **Figure 5.** The curved line tells you that during each second, you traveled a greater distance than the second before. For example, you traveled a greater distance during the third second than you did during the first second.

The curved line in **Figure 5** also tells you that during each second your speed was greater than the second before. Recall that the slope of a distance-versus-time graph is the speed of an object. From second to second, the slope of the line in **Figure 5** gets steeper. Since the slope is increasing, you can conclude that your speed was also increasing. You were accelerating.

Lab zone Do the Quick Lab *Graphing Acceleration.*

🔑 Assess Your Understanding

got it? ···

○ **I get it!** Now I know that the two types of graphs that you can use to analyze the motion of an accelerating object are _____
_____

○ **I need extra help with** _____

Go to **my science** COACH online for help with this subject.

Study Guide

Which term, speed or velocity, gives you more information about an object's motion? Why?

___

LESSON 1 Describing Motion

🔑 An object is in motion if it changes position relative to a reference point.

Vocabulary
- motion
- reference point
- International System of Units
- distance

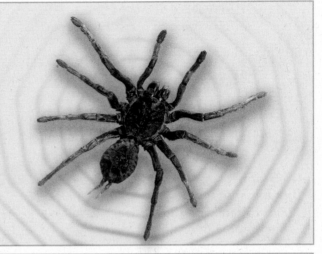

LESSON 2 Speed and Velocity

🔑 To calculate the speed of an object, divide the distance the object travels by the amount of time it takes to travel the distance.

🔑 When you know both the speed and direction of an object's motion, you know the velocity of the object.

🔑 You can show the motion of an object on a line graph in which you plot distance versus time.

Vocabulary
- speed • average speed
- instantaneous speed • velocity • slope

LESSON 3 Acceleration

🔑 In science, acceleration refers to increasing speed, decreasing speed, or changing direction.

🔑 You can use both a speed-versus-time graph and a distance-versus-time graph to analyze the motion of an accelerating object.

Vocabulary
- acceleration

Review and Assessment

LESSON 1 Describing Motion

1. What is the SI unit of distance?

   a. foot   **b.** meter

   c. mile   **d.** kilometer

2. A change in position with respect to a reference point is _____

3. **Classify** Suppose you are in a train. List some objects that make good reference points to determine whether or not the train is moving.

_____

Use the illustration to answer Questions 4 and 5.

4. **Compare and Contrast** Suppose you are standing on the sidewalk. Describe the direction of your motion relative to the car and the plane.

_____

_____

_____

5. **Compare and Contrast** Suppose you are riding in the plane. Describe the direction of your motion relative to the person standing on the sidewalk and the car.

_____

_____

_____

_____

LESSON 2 Speed and Velocity

6. What quantity can you calculate if you know that a car travels 30 kilometers in 20 minutes?

   a. average speed   **b.** direction

   c. velocity   **d.** instantaneous speed

7. On a graph of distance versus time, the slope of the line indicates the _____ of an object.

The graph shows the motion of a remote-control car. Use the graph to answer Questions 8 and 9.

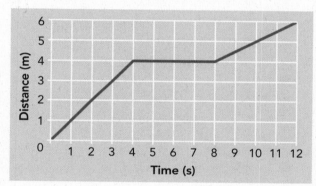

8. **Read Graphs** During which time period was the car moving the fastest?

_____

9. **Calculate** What was the speed of the car during the first four seconds?

_____

_____

10. **Apply Concepts** A family takes a car trip. They travel for an hour at 80 km/h and then 2 hours at 40 km/h. Find their average speed during the trip.

_____

_____

_____

_____

LESSON 3 Acceleration

11. The rate at which velocity changes is

    a. acceleration.   **b.** direction.

    c. speed.   **d.** velocity.

12. You can calculate the acceleration of an object moving in a straight line by dividing the _____ by the time.

The graph below shows the speed of a downhill skier during a period of several seconds. Use the graph to answer Question 13.

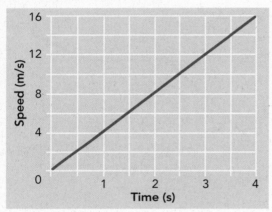

13. Read Graphs What is the skier's acceleration?

_____

_____

_____

14. math! A ball is dropped from a window and takes 2 seconds to reach the ground. It starts from rest and reaches a final speed of 20 m/s. What is the ball's acceleration?

_____

_____

_____

_____

15. Write About It Describe how a baseball player accelerates as he runs around the bases after hitting a home run.

 APPLY THE BIG **How do you describe the motion of an object?**

16. The distance-versus-time graph is for two runners in a 50-meter race. Describe the motion of the runners in as much detail as you can. Which runner won the race? How do you know? Suppose the graph showed the runners' motion until they came to a stop. Describe how the graph would change.

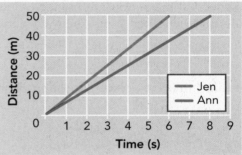

_____

_____

_____

_____

_____

_____

_____

_____

_____

_____

_____

_____

_____

_____

_____

_____

_____

_____

_____

Standardized Test Prep

Multiple Choice

Circle the letter of the best answer.

1. The graph below shows the motion of a runner.

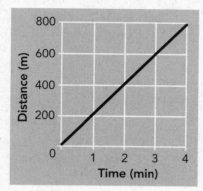

What could the runner do to make the slope of the line rise?

A stop running

B decrease speed

C maintain the same speed

D increase speed

2. Members of the Fairview Track Running Club are running a 5-kilometer race. What is the distance of the race in meters?

A 0.5 m

B 50 m

C 500 m

D 5000 m

3. What condition is necessary for an object to make a good reference point?

A The object is moving at a constant speed.

B The object is accelerating.

C The object is fixed relative to the motion you are trying to describe.

D The object is large.

4. Two objects traveling at the same speed have different velocities if they

A start at different times.

B travel different distances.

C have different masses.

D move in different directions.

5. Your family is driving to the beach. You travel 200 kilometers in the first two hours. During the next hour, you stop for lunch and only travel 25 kilometers. What was your average speed?

A 60 km/h

B 75 km/h

C 100 km/h

D 225 km/h

Constructed Response

Use the graph to answer Question 6. Write your answer on a separate sheet of paper.

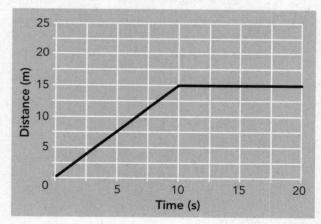

6. The graph above shows the motion of a person. Describe the motion.

THE RACE FOR SPEED

As soon as people started driving automobiles, someone started racing them. We've been trying to go faster ever since.

So how fast can we go? The official top land speed record was set by a man named Andy Green in Blackrock, Nevada, in 1997. Green and his vehicle, named the *Thrust SSC*, reached a speed of 1,288 km/h. That's faster than the speed of sound! In fact, the *Thrust SSC* produced a sonic boom. A sonic boom sounds a lot like an explosion. Thunder is a natural sonic boom.

How did the *Thrust SSC* go so fast? It used two turbo jet engines. So Green's previous experience as a fighter pilot came in handy when he was learning to drive this car.

▲ Andy Green and the jet-propelled *Thrust SSC*.

Graph It There are lots of other speed records. Research the wheel-driven land speed record and the rail speed record, to start. Make a graph or chart that compares all of the speed records you can find. Share your results with your class.

STOP SIGN

If you've ever watched a movie about jet pilots or race car drivers, you've probably heard someone talk about "pulling Gs." But what does that mean? A G-force is an informal unit of measurement used in aeronautics and space engineering. One G-force is the average acceleration due to gravity at Earth's surface. You experience one G-force all the time.

In the 1940s and 1950s, Colonel John Paul Stapp experienced a lot more than one G-force. At what is now Edwards Air Force Base, Colonel Stapp strapped himself into a device that scientists called the Gee Whiz. This was a rocket sled that hurled volunteers forward before bringing them to a sudden stop along the track. In one of his runs, Colonel Stapp was subjected to 46 Gs! His work had an impact on everything from seat belts to the restraints worn by astronauts.

Share It Research what happens when people experience extreme G-forces. Find out what physical symptoms they are likely to experience and how those symptoms can be prevented. Design a safety pamphlet describing your findings.

WHY WON'T THIS ACROBAT LAND ON HER HEAD?

How do objects react to forces?

This teen is part of a traveling youth circus that performs in New England. As a circus trouper, she may do stunts such as tumbling and swinging on a trapeze. These stunts often appear to be gravity-defying and dangerous, but the troupers know how to perform in a way that lets them land safely.

Develop Hypotheses **How does this athlete land on her feet?**

_____

_____

_____

_____

_____

_____

▷ **UNTAMED SCIENCE** Watch the **Untamed Science** video to learn more about forces.

Forces

Getting Started

Check Your Understanding

1. **Background** Read the paragraph below and then answer the question.

The dashboard of a car displays your **speed** so that you know how fast you're going. Since this reading doesn't change when you turn, you don't know the car's **velocity.** If the car did show you your change in velocity, you could calculate the car's **acceleration.**

> **Speed** is the distance an object travels per unit of time.
>
> **Velocity** is speed in a given direction.
>
> **Acceleration** is the rate at which velocity changes with time.

- What are three ways to accelerate (change velocity)?

_____

_____

> **MY READING WEB** If you had trouble completing the question above, visit **My Reading Web** and type in *Forces*.

Vocabulary Skill

Latin Word Origins Many science words in English come from Latin. For example, the word *solar*, which means "of the sun," comes from the Latin *sol*, which means "sun."

Latin Word	Meaning of Latin Word	Example
fortis	strong	force, *n.* a push or pull exerted on an object
iners	inactivity	inertia, *n.* the tendency of an object to resist any change in its motion
centrum	center	centripetal force, *n.* a force that causes an object to move in a circle

2. **Quick Check** Choose the word that best completes the sentence.

- A _____ always points toward the center of a circle.

force

friction

gravity

inertia

Chapter Preview

LESSON 1
- force
- newton
- net force
- ↻ **Relate Text and Visuals**
- △ **Make Models**

LESSON 2
- friction
- sliding friction
- static friction
- fluid friction
- rolling friction
- gravity
- mass
- weight
- ↻ **Identify Supporting Evidence**
- △ **Design Experiments**

LESSON 3
- inertia
- ↻ **Ask Questions**
- △ **Infer**

LESSON 4
- momentum
- law of conservation of momentum
- ↻ **Identify the Main Idea**
- △ **Calculate**

LESSON 5
- free fall
- satellite
- centripetal force
- ↻ **Relate Cause and Effect**
- △ **Create Data Tables**

LESSON 6
- buoyant force
- ↻ **Relate Cause and Effect**
- △ **Control Variables**

▷ **VOCAB FLASH CARDS** For extra help with vocabulary, visit **Vocab Flash Cards** and type in *Forces*.

The Nature of Force

UNLOCK THE BIG ?

🔑 **How Are Forces Described?**

🔑 **How Do Forces Affect Motion?**

my planet Diary

MISCONCEPTIONS

Forced to Change

Misconception: Any object that is set in motion will slow down on its own.

Fact: A force is needed to change an object's state of motion.

A soccer ball sits at rest. You come along and kick it, sending it flying across the field. It eventually slows to a stop. You applied a force to start it moving, and then it stopped all on its own, right?

No! Forces cause *all* changes in motion. Just as you applied a force to the ball to speed it up from rest, the ground applied a force to slow it down to a stop. If the ground didn't apply a force to the ball, it would keep rolling forever without slowing down or stopping.

Answer the questions below.

1. Give an example of a force you apply to slow something down.

_____

_____

2. Where might it be possible to kick a soccer ball and have it never slow down?

_____

_____

_____

▶ **PLANET DIARY** Go to **Planet Diary** to learn more about forces.

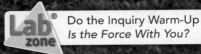

Lab zone® Do the Inquiry Warm-Up *Is the Force With You?*

Vocabulary
- force - newton
- net force

Skills
- Reading: Relate Text and Visuals
- Inquiry: Make Models

How Are Forces Described?

In science, the word *force* has a simple and specific meaning. A **force** is a push or a pull. When one object pushes or pulls another object, the first object exerts a force on the second object. You exert a force on a computer key when you push it. You exert a force on a chair when you pull it away from a table.

🔑 **Like velocity and acceleration, a force is described by its strength and by the direction in which it acts.** Pushing to the left is a different force from pushing to the right. The direction and strength of a force can be represented by an arrow. The arrow points in the direction of the force, as shown in **Figure 1.** The length of the arrow tells you the strength of the force—the longer the arrow, the greater the force. The strength of a force is measured in the SI unit called the **newton** (N), after scientist Sir Isaac Newton.

FIGURE 1 ··

Describing Forces

Forces act on you whenever your motion changes. In the photos at the right, two men are celebrating an Olympic victory. Forces cause them to pull each other in for a hug, lean over, and fall into the pool.

✏️ **Identify** In the box within each photo, draw an arrow that represents the force acting on the person on the right. The first one is done as an example.

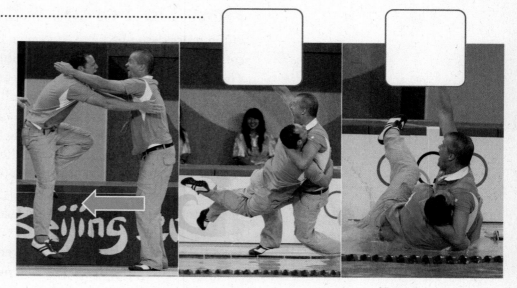

Do the Quick Lab
What Is Force?

🔑 **Assess Your Understanding**

got it? ···

○ I get it! Now I know that forces are described by _____

_____

○ I need extra help with _____

Go to MY SCIENCE ⑤ COACH online for help with this subject.

FIGURE 2 ···

> INTERACTIVE ART **Net Force**

The change in motion of an object is determined by
the net force acting on the object.

✎ **Make Models** **Calculate and draw an arrow for the
net force for each situation in the boxes below.**

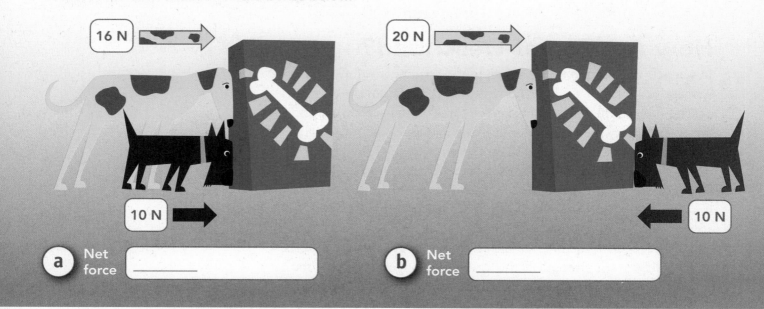

a Net force _____

b Net force _____

How Do Forces Affect Motion?

Often more than one force acts on an object at the same time. The
combination of all the forces on an object is called the **net force.**
The net force determines if and how an object will accelerate.

You can find the net force on an object by adding together the
strengths of all the individual forces acting on the object. Look at
Figure 2a. The big dog pushes on the box with a force of 16 N to
the right. The small dog pushes on the box with a force of 10 N to
the right. The net force on the box is the sum of these forces. The
box will accelerate to the right. In this situation, there is a nonzero
net force. ⚷ **A nonzero net force causes a change in the object's
motion.**

What if the forces on an object aren't acting in the same
direction? In **Figure 2b,** the big dog pushes with a force of 20 N.
The small dog still pushes with a force of 10 N, but now they're
pushing against each other. When forces on an object act in
opposite directions, the strength of the net force is found by
subtracting the strength of the smaller force from the strength
of the larger force. You can still think of this as *adding* the forces
together if you think of all forces that act to the right as positive
forces and all forces that act to the left as negative forces. The box
will accelerate to the right. When forces act in opposite directions,
the net force is in the same direction as the larger force.

·································· ✎ ··················

↺ **Relate Text and Visuals** Use
the information in the text to
determine the net force of these
two force arrows.

3 N **5 N**

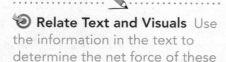

Circle the net force below.

→ **8 N**

← **2 N**

⟵ **8 N**

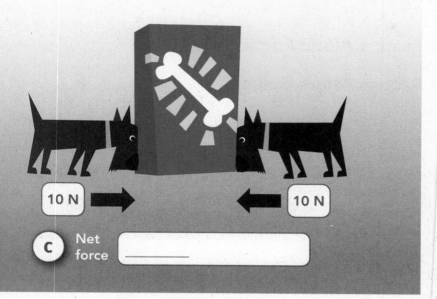

10 N ➡️   ⬅️ 10 N

C Net force _____

1 You pull on your dog's leash to the right with a 12 N force. Your dog pulls to the left with a 6 N force. Sketch this situation, including labeled force arrows, below.

Use what you know about net force to describe the motion of the box in **Figure 2c.** Assume that the box starts at rest.

_____

_____

_____

_____

2 What is the net force on the leash? Calculate it. Draw and label it in the space above.

_____

Lab zone ® Do the Quick Lab *Modeling Unbalanced Forces.*

Assess Your Understanding

1a. Calculate You push on a desk with a force of 120 N to the right. Your friend pushes on the same desk with a force of 90 N to the left. What is the net force on the desk?

_____

_____

b. Predict Your friend increases her force on the desk by 30 N. She doesn't change the direction of her push. What happens to the net force on the desk? Will the desk accelerate?

_____

_____

got it? ....

○ **I get it!** Now I know that changes in motion are caused by _____

_____

○ **I need extra help with** _____

Go to **my science** ⓢ **coach** *online for help with this subject.*

Friction and Gravity

UNLOCK THE BIG **?**

🗝 **What Factors Affect Friction?**

🗝 **What Factors Affect Gravity?**

my planet Diary

CAREERS

Space Athletes

Have you ever seen pictures of astronauts playing golf on the moon or playing catch in a space station? Golf balls and baseballs can float or fly farther in space, where gravitational forces are weaker than they are on Earth. Imagine what professional sports would be like in reduced gravity!

You may not have to imagine much longer. At least one company specializes in airplane flights that simulate a reduced gravity environment. Similar to NASA training flights that astronauts use when preparing to go into space, these flights allow passengers to fly around the cabin. In environments with reduced gravity, athletes can perform jumps and stunts that would be impossible on Earth. As technology improves, permanent stadiums could be built in space for a whole new generation of athletes.

Communicate Discuss these questions with a partner and then answer them below.

1. Sports can be more fun in reduced gravity. What jobs could be harder or less fun to do in space? Why?

_____

_____

_____

2. What kinds of sports do you think could be more fun in space? Why?

_____

_____

_____

> PLANET DIARY Go to **Planet Diary** to learn more about everyday forces.

Lab® zone   Do the Inquiry Warm-Up *Observing Friction.*

Vocabulary
- friction • sliding friction • static friction
- fluid friction • rolling friction • gravity
- mass • weight

Skills
- Reading: Identify Supporting Evidence
- Inquiry: Design Experiments

What Factors Affect Friction?

If you slide a book across a table, the surface of the book rubs against the surface of the table. The force that two surfaces exert on each other when they rub against each other is called **friction.**

Two factors that affect the force of friction are the types of surfaces involved and how hard the surfaces are pushed together. The football player in **Figure 1** is pushing on a blocking sled. If his coach wanted to make it harder to move the sled, the coach could change the surface of the sled. Covering the bottom of the sled with rubber would increase friction and make the sled harder to move. In general, smooth surfaces produce less friction than rough surfaces.

What would happen if the football player switched to a much heavier sled? He would find the heavier sled harder to push because it pushes down harder against the ground. Similarly, if you rubbed your hands together forcefully, there would be more friction than if you rubbed your hands together lightly. Friction increases when surfaces push harder against each other.

Friction acts in a direction opposite to the direction of the object's motion. Without friction, a moving object will not stop until it strikes another object.

Vocabulary Latin Word Origins *Friction* comes from the Latin word *fricare*. Based on the definition of *friction*, what do you think *fricare* means?
- ○ to burn
- ○ to rub
- ○ to melt

FIGURE 1 ······························

> ART IN MOTION **Friction and Different Surfaces**
The strength of friction depends on the types of surfaces involved. **Sequence** Rank the surfaces above by how hard it would be to push a sled over them, from easiest (1) to hardest (3). (Each surface is flat.) What does this ranking tell you about the amount of friction over these surfaces?

_____

_____

Sliding Friction

Sliding friction occurs when two solid surfaces slide over each other. Sliding friction is what makes moving objects slow down and stop. Without sliding friction, a penguin that slid down a hill wouldn't stop until he hit a wall!

✏️ **Classify** Label five examples of sliding friction and compare with a classmate.

Friction acts opposite the direction of motion.

Direction of motion →

← Friction

Static Friction

Static friction acts between objects that aren't moving. Think about trying to push a couch across the room. If you don't push hard enough, it won't move. The force that's keeping you from moving it is static friction. Once you push hard enough to overcome static friction, the couch starts moving and there is no more static friction. However, there is sliding friction.

✏️ **Classify** Label five examples of static friction and compare with a classmate.

Draw an arrow representing the frictional force at work.

Fluid Friction

Fluids, such as water and air, are materials that flow easily. **Fluid friction** occurs when a solid object moves through a fluid. Fluid friction is easier to overcome than sliding friction. This is why sidewalks become slippery when they get wet.

✏️ **Classify** **Label five examples of fluid friction and compare with a classmate.**

Draw an arrow representing the frictional force at work.

Rolling Friction

When an object rolls across a surface, **rolling friction** occurs. Rolling friction is much easier to overcome than sliding friction for similar materials. That's why it's easy to push a bike along the sidewalk when the wheels can turn, but much harder to push the bike if you're applying the brakes and the tires slide, not roll.

✏️ **Classify** **Label five examples of rolling friction and compare with a classmate.**

Draw an arrow representing the frictional force at work.

269

it!

Your family is moving and isn't sure how to best overcome friction while moving furniture. You have a spring scale, wood blocks to represent your furniture, and sandpaper, aluminum foil, marbles, and olive oil as possible surfaces to slide your furniture over.

⬆ **Design Experiments** **Design an experiment that will help you determine which material will reduce friction the most.**

You know that friction occurs between surfaces when they slide against each other. If you measure the applied force required to push something across a surface, you know that your applied force would (increase/decrease) as friction increased.

STEP ① Measure How would you determine your applied force in this experiment?

_____
_____
_____

STEP ② Control Variables What variables would you have to control to keep your results accurate?

_____
_____
_____

STEP ③ Create Data Tables Draw the data table you would use when performing this experiment.

 Do the Lab Investigation
Sticky Sneakers.

🗝 Assess Your Understanding

1a. List Name four types of friction and give an example of each.

_____
_____
_____
_____

b. Classify What types of friction occur between your bike tires and the ground when you ride over cement, ride through a puddle, and apply your brakes?

_____

got it?

○ I get it! Now I know that friction is affected by

_____
_____
_____

○ I need extra help with _____

_____

Go to **my science coach** *online for help with this subject.*

What Factors Affect Gravity?

A skydiver would be surprised if she jumped out of a plane and did not fall. We are so used to objects falling that we may not have thought about why they fall. One person who thought about it was Sir Isaac Newton. He concluded that a force acts to pull objects straight down toward the center of Earth. **Gravity** is a force that pulls objects toward each other.

Universal Gravitation Newton realized that gravity acts everywhere in the universe, not just on Earth. It is the force that makes the skydivers in **Figure 2** fall to the ground. It is the force that keeps the moon orbiting around Earth. It is the force that keeps all the planets in our solar system orbiting around the sun.

What Newton realized is now called the law of universal gravitation. The law of universal gravitation states that the force of gravity acts between all objects in the universe that have mass. This means that any two objects in the universe that have mass attract each other. You are attracted not only to Earth but also to the moon, the other planets in the solar system, and all the objects around you. Earth and the objects around you are attracted to you as well. However, you do not notice the attraction among small objects because these forces are extremely small compared to the force of Earth's attraction.

FIGURE 2 ....

Observing Gravity
Newton published his work on gravity in 1687.

✎ **Observe** What observations might you make today that would lead you to the same conclusions about gravity? Write down your ideas below.

_____

_____

_____

_____

_____

_____

_____

Factors Affecting Gravity A gravitational force exists between any two objects in the universe. However, you don't see your pencil fly toward the wall the way you see it fall toward Earth. That's because the gravitational force between some objects is stronger than the force between others. You observe only the effects of the strongest gravitational forces. 🔑 **Two factors affect the gravitational attraction between objects: mass and distance.** **Mass** is a measure of the amount of matter in an object. The SI unit of mass is the kilogram.

The more mass an object has, the greater the gravitational force between it and other objects. Earth's gravitational force on nearby objects is strong because the mass of Earth is so large. The more massive planets in **Figure 3** interact with a greater gravitational force than the less massive planets. Gravitational force also depends on the distance between the objects' centers. As distance increases, gravitational force decreases. That's why Earth can exert a visible gravitational force on a pencil in your room and not on a pencil on the moon.

🔄 **Identify Supporting Evidence** Underline the factors that determine how strong the gravitational force is between two objects.

FIGURE 3 ·····

Gravitational Attraction
Gravitational attraction depends on two factors: mass and distance. Suppose there was a solar system that looked like this.
✏️ **Interpret Diagrams** Use the diagram below to compare the gravitational force between different planets and their sun. Assume all planets are made of the same material, so bigger planets have more mass.

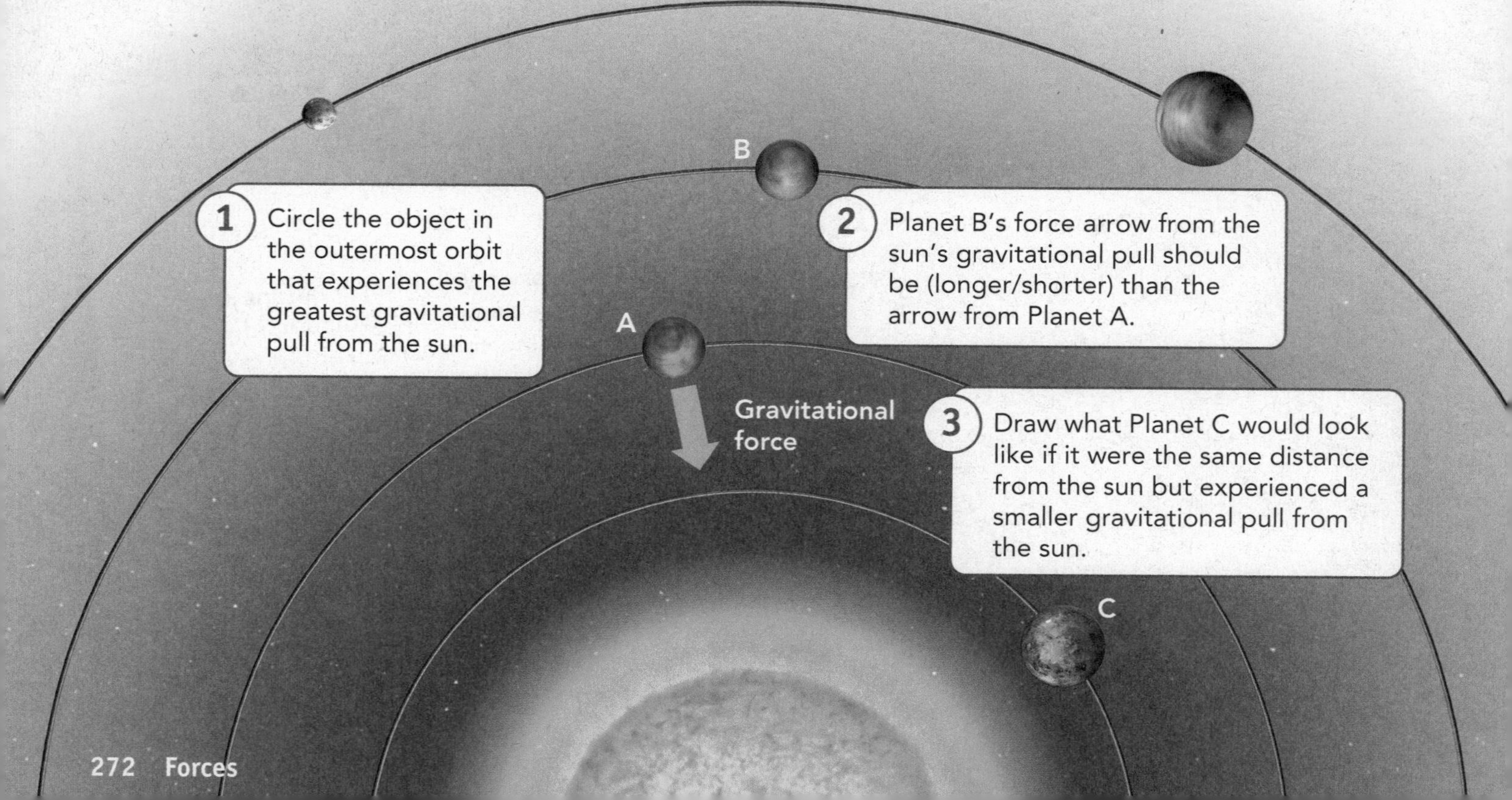

B

1 Circle the object in the outermost orbit that experiences the greatest gravitational pull from the sun.

2 Planet B's force arrow from the sun's gravitational pull should be (longer/shorter) than the arrow from Planet A.

A

Gravitational force

3 Draw what Planet C would look like if it were the same distance from the sun but experienced a smaller gravitational pull from the sun.

C

Earth
60 N

Moon
____N

Mars
____N

Weight and Mass

Mass is sometimes confused with weight. Mass is a measure of the amount of matter in an object. **Weight** is a measure of the force of gravity on an object. When you stand on a bathroom scale, it displays the gravitational force Earth is exerting on you.

At any given time, your mass is the same on Earth as it would be on any other planet. But weight varies with the strength of the gravitational force. The dog in **Figure 4** has a different weight at different places in the solar system. On the moon, he would weigh about one sixth of what he does on Earth. On Mars, he would weigh just over a third of what he does on Earth.

FIGURE 4 ·······································
Weight and Mass

The Mars Phoenix Lander weighs about 3,400 N on Earth. It weighs about 1,300 N on Mars. ✎ **Predict** **The first scale shows the dog's weight on Earth. Predict its weight on the moon and on Mars. Enter those weights in the boxes on the other two scales.**

Lab zone® Do the Quick Lab Calculating.

🔑 Assess Your Understanding

2a. Describe What happens to the gravitational force between two objects when their masses are increased? What happens when the distance between the objects increases?

_____

_____

_____

b. Relate Cause and Effect If the mass of Earth increased, what would happen to your weight? What about your mass?

_____

_____

_____

got it? ·······································

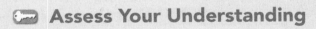

○ **I get it!** Now I know that the factors that affect the gravitational force between objects are _____

_____

○ **I need extra help with** _____

Go to MY SCIENCE 🔵ˢ COACH *online for help with this subject.*

Newton's Laws of Motion

🔑 **What Is Newton's First Law of Motion?**

🔑 **What Is Newton's Second Law of Motion?**

🔑 **What Is Newton's Third Law of Motion?**

my planet diary

VOICES FROM HISTORY

Horse Force

"If a horse draws a stone tied to a rope, the horse (if I may so say) will be equally drawn back towards the stone...."

—Sir Isaac Newton

Scientists have used everyday examples to explain their ideas for hundreds of years. The quotation is from Newton's *Mathematical Principles of Natural Philosophy*, which was first published in the 1680s. Newton used this book to set down his laws of motion. These three simple laws describe much of the motion around you, and they continue to be studied today.

Answer the question below.

What current scientific discoveries might be taught in schools hundreds of years from now?

_____

_____

_____

_____

▶ PLANET DIARY Go to **Planet Diary** to learn more about Newton.

Lab zone ® Do the Inquiry Warm-Up *What Changes Motion?*

What Is Newton's First Law of Motion?

You would be surprised if a rock started rolling on its own or a raindrop paused in midair. If an object is not moving, it will not start moving until a force acts on it. If an object is moving, it will continue at a constant velocity until a force acts to change its speed or its direction. 🔑 **Newton's first law of motion states that an object at rest will remain at rest unless acted upon by a nonzero net force. An object moving at a constant velocity will continue moving at a constant velocity unless acted upon by a nonzero net force.**

Vocabulary
- inertia

Skills
- ⟳ Reading: Ask Questions
- △ Inquiry: Infer

Inertia All objects, moving or not, resist changes in motion. Resistance to change in motion is called **inertia** (in UR shuh). Newton's first law of motion is also called the law of inertia. Inertia explains many common events, including why you move forward in your seat when the car you are in stops suddenly. You keep moving forward because of inertia. A force, such as the pull of a seat belt, is needed to pull you back. Roller coasters like the one in **Figure 1** have safety bars for the same reason.

Inertia Depends on Mass Some objects have more inertia than others. Suppose you need to move an empty backpack and a full backpack. The greater the mass of an object, the greater its inertia, and the greater the force required to change its motion. The full backpack is harder to move than the empty one because it has more mass and therefore more inertia.

FIGURE 1 ....
Inertia
A roller coaster is hard to stop because it has a lot of inertia. ✏ △ Infer **Use Newton's first law of motion to explain why you feel tossed around whenever a roller coaster goes over a hill or through a loop.**

_____
_____
_____
_____
_____

Lab ® Do the Quick Lab
zone *Around and Around.*

☞ Assess Your Understanding

got it? ....

○ I get it! Now I know that Newton's first law of motion states that _____
_____

○ I need extra help with _____

Go to MY SCIENCE ⓢ COACH online for help with this subject.

What Is Newton's Second Law of Motion?

Which is harder to push, a full shopping cart or an empty one? Who can cause a greater acceleration on a shopping cart, a small child or a grown adult?

Changes in Force and Mass Suppose you increase the force on a cart without changing its mass. The acceleration of the cart will also increase. Your cart will also accelerate faster if something falls out. This reduces the mass of the cart, and you keep pushing just as hard. The acceleration of the sled in **Figure 2** will change depending on the mass of the people on it and the force the sled dogs apply. Newton realized these relationships and found a way to represent them mathematically.

Determining Acceleration 🔑 Newton's second law **of motion states that an object's acceleration depends on its mass and on the net force acting on it.** This relationship can be written as follows.

$$\text{Acceleration} = \frac{\text{Net force}}{\text{Mass}}$$

This formula can be rearranged to show how much force must be applied to an object to get it to accelerate at a certain rate.

$$\text{Net force} = \text{Mass} \times \text{Acceleration}$$

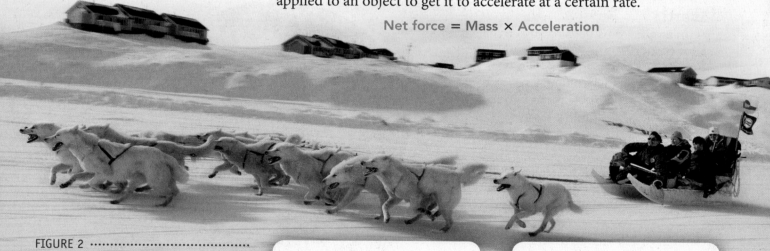

FIGURE 2 ·······························
Newton's Second Law
Suppose that four dogs pull a sled carrying two people.
✎ **Explain** Use words and fill in the pictures to show how you can change the dog/person arrangement to change the sled's acceleration.

How could you increase the sled's acceleration?
_____
_____
_____
_____

How could you decrease the sled's acceleration?
_____
_____
_____
_____

Acceleration is measured in meters per second per second (m/s^2). Mass is measured in kilograms (kg). Newton's second law shows that force is measured in kilograms times meters per second per second ($kg \cdot m/s^2$). This unit is also called the newton (N), which is the SI unit of force. One newton is the force required to give a 1-kg mass an acceleration of 1 m/s^2.

do the math!

Every year in cities around the world, teams create cars, push them across platforms, and hope they will fly. Unfortunately, the cars always end up accelerating down into the water.

1 **Calculate** If a 100-N net force acts on a 50-kg car, what will the acceleration of the car be?

_____

2 After that same car leaves the platform, gravity causes it to accelerate downward at a rate of 9.8 m/s^2. What is the gravitational force on the car?

_____

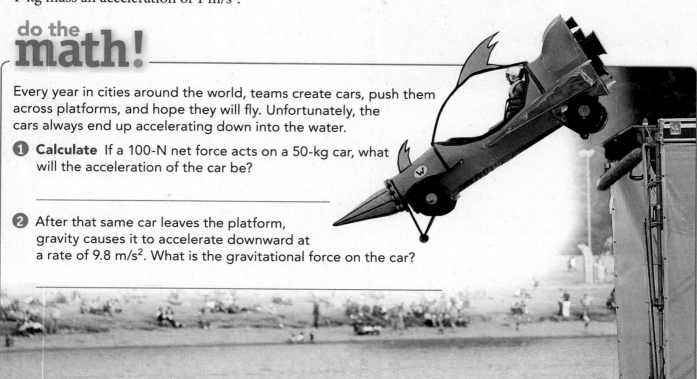

Lab zone® Do the Quick Lab
Newton's Second Law.

🔑 Assess Your Understanding

1a. **Review** What equation allows you to calculate the force acting on an object?

_____

_____

b. **Calculate** What is the net force on a 2-kg skateboard accelerating at a rate of 2 m/s^2?

_____

c. **Predict** If the mass of the skateboard doubled but the net force on it remained constant, what would happen to the acceleration of the skateboard?

_____

_____

_____

got it? ....

○ **I get it!** Now I know that Newton's second law of motion describes the relationship _____

_____

○ **I need extra help with** _____

   Go to **MY SCIENCE** ⓢ **COACH** online for help with this subject.

FIGURE 3 ···

Action-Reaction Pairs
A swimmer moves because the water pushes her forward when she pushes back on it.

✎ **Interpret Diagrams** Draw arrows to show the action and reaction forces between the gymnast and the balance beam. Draw your own example in the space provided.

Reaction force   Action force

What Is Newton's Third Law of Motion?

If you leaned against a wall and it didn't push back on you, you'd fall through. The force exerted by the wall is equal in strength and opposite in direction to the force you exert on the wall. 🔑 **Newton's third law of motion states that if one object exerts a force on another object, then the second object exerts a force of equal strength in the opposite direction on the first object.** Another way to state Newton's third law is that for every action there is an equal but opposite reaction.

Action-Reaction Pairs Pairs of action and reaction forces are all around you. When you walk, you push backward on the ground with your feet. Think of this as an action force. (It doesn't matter which force is called the "action" force and which is called the "reaction" force.) The ground pushes forward on your feet with an equal and opposite force. This is the reaction force. You can only walk because the ground pushes you forward! In a similar way, the swimmer in **Figure 3** moves forward by exerting an action force on the water with her hands. The water pushes on her hands with an equal reaction force that propels her body forward.

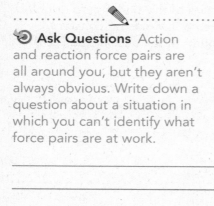

🔄 **Ask Questions** Action and reaction force pairs are all around you, but they aren't always obvious. Write down a question about a situation in which you can't identify what force pairs are at work.

_____

_____

_____

_____

_____

_____

Detecting Motion If you drop your pen, gravity pulls the pen downward. According to Newton's third law, the pen pulls Earth upward with an equal and opposite reaction force. You see the pen fall. You *don't* see Earth accelerate toward the pen. Remember Newton's second law. If mass increases and force stays the same, acceleration decreases. The same force acts on both Earth and your pen. Since Earth has such a large mass, its acceleration is so small that you don't notice it.

Do Action-Reaction Forces Cancel? You have learned that two equal forces acting in opposite directions on an object cancel each other out and produce no change in motion. So why don't the action and reaction forces in Newton's third law of motion cancel out as well?

Action and reaction forces do not cancel out because they act on different objects. The swimmer in **Figure 3** exerts a backward action force on the water. The water exerts an equal but opposite forward reaction force on her hands. The action and reaction forces act on different objects—the action force acts on the water and the reaction force acts on her hands.

Unlike the swimmer and the water, the volleyball players in **Figure 4** both exert a force on the *same* object—the volleyball. Each player exerts a force on the ball equal in strength but opposite in direction. The forces on the volleyball are balanced. The ball does not move toward one player or the other.

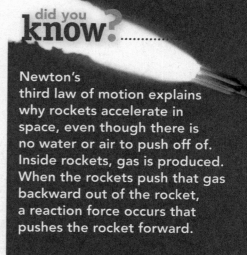

did you **know?**

Newton's third law of motion explains why rockets accelerate in space, even though there is no water or air to push off of. Inside rockets, gas is produced. When the rockets push that gas backward out of the rocket, a reaction force occurs that pushes the rocket forward.

Forces on hands

Force on ball

Force on ball

FIGURE 4 ·······················

Action-Reaction Forces
All the horizontal forces on the volleyball cancel out.

✎ **Apply Concepts** In the dog illustration above, use Newton's third law of motion to draw and label any missing force arrows for all the objects.

What Makes a Bug Go *Splat*?

How do objects react to forces?

FIGURE 5 ···

> **VIRTUAL LAB** Splat! A bug has just flown into the windshield of an oncoming car. The car must have hit the bug much harder than the bug hit the car, right? ✎ **Apply Concepts** Use Newton's laws of motion to make sense of the situation and answer the questions.

A

Buzz!

In order for the bug to fly through the air, a force has to push the bug forward. Identify this force. How does the bug produce it? (*Hint:* Think back to how a swimmer moves through the water.)

_____

_____

_____

_____

_____

The bug was at rest on a tree when it saw the car and decided to fly toward it. If the bug has a mass of 0.05 kg and accelerates at 2 m/s², what's the net force on the bug?

_____

10 - LG - SP

B

Vroom!

The driver hates killing bugs. When she saw one coming toward the windshield, she braked suddenly and hoped it would get out of the way. (Sadly, it did not.) When she hit the brakes, she felt that she was thrown forward. Use one of Newton's laws to explain why.

_____
_____
_____
_____
_____

C

Splat!

The unfortunate bug hits the windshield with a force of 1 N. If you call this the action force, what is the reaction force? Does the car hit the bug any harder than the bug hits the car? Use one of Newton's laws to explain why or why not.

_____
_____
_____
_____
_____

Compare the forces on the bug and the car again. Use another one of Newton's laws to explain why the bug goes *splat* and the car keeps going, without noticeably slowing down.

_____
_____
_____
_____

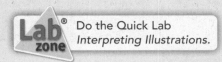

Lab zone® Do the Quick Lab
Interpreting Illustrations.

🔑 Assess Your Understanding

2a. Identify A dog pulls on his leash with a 10-N force to the left, but doesn't move. Identify the reaction force.

_____
_____
_____
_____

b. **ANSWER THE BIG ?** Using all three of Newton's laws, explain how objects react to forces.

_____
_____
_____
_____
_____
_____
_____
_____
_____
_____
_____
_____
_____
_____
_____

got it? ....

○ **I get it!** Now I know that Newton's third law of motion states that _____

_____
_____
_____

○ **I need extra help with** _____

_____
_____

✏ Go to **MY SCIENCE ⓢ COACH** *online for help with this subject.*

4 Momentum

🔑 **What Is an Object's Momentum?**

MY PLANET DIARY

Air Hockey Science

Whoosh—you've just scored a goal! The puck is about to go back into play. How can you keep the puck out of your goal and get it back into your opponent's? One of the factors you have to consider is momentum. Momentum is a physical quantity that all moving objects have. If you know about momentum, you can predict how an object will act when it collides with other objects. With some quick scientific thinking, you can get the puck to bounce all over the table and back into your opponent's goal!

FUN FACTS

Answer the questions below.

1. Why might it be better to try to bounce a puck off the wall rather than shoot it straight into your opponent's goal?

_____

_____

_____

_____

2. Where else could it be helpful to know how objects act after colliding?

_____

_____

_____

_____

> **PLANET DIARY** Go to **Planet Diary** to learn more about momentum.

 Lab zone Do the Inquiry Warm-Up *How Pushy Is a Straw?*

Vocabulary
- momentum
- law of conservation of momentum

Skills
- Reading: Identify the Main Idea
- Inquiry: Calculate

What Is an Object's Momentum?

Is it harder to stop a rolling bowling ball or a rolling marble? Does your answer depend on the velocities of the objects? All moving objects have what Newton called a "quantity of motion." Today it's called momentum. **Momentum** (moh MEN tum) is a characteristic of a moving object that is related to the mass and the velocity of the object. ➤ **The momentum of a moving object can be determined by multiplying the object's mass by its velocity.**

Momentum = Mass × Velocity

Since mass is measured in kilograms and velocity is measured in meters per second, the unit for momentum is kilograms times meters per second (kg·m/s). Like velocity, acceleration, and force, momentum is described by both a direction and a strength. The momentum of an object is in the same direction as its velocity.

The more momentum a moving object has, the harder it is to stop. For example, a 0.1-kg baseball moving at 40 m/s has a momentum of 4 kg·m/s in the direction it's moving.

Momentum = 0.1 kg × 40 m/s

Momentum = 4 kg·m/s

But a 1,200-kg car moving at the same speed as the baseball has a much greater momentum: 48,000 kg·m/s. The velocity of an object also affects the amount of momentum it has. For example, a tennis ball served by a professional tennis player has a large momentum. Although the ball has a small mass, it travels at a high velocity.

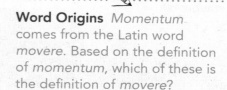

Word Origins *Momentum* comes from the Latin word *movere.* Based on the definition of *momentum,* which of these is the definition of *movere?*

- ○ to spin
- ○ to move
- ○ to sit

apply it!

△ Calculate In each question below, calculate the desired quantity.

1 The lioness has a mass of 180 kg and a velocity of 16 m/s to the right. What is her momentum?

_____

_____

_____

2 The warthog has a mass of 100 kg. What does the warthog's speed have to be for it to have the same momentum as the lioness?

_____

Identify the Main Idea
Circle a sentence that relates the main idea of this section to two colliding cars. Then underline two supporting examples.

FIGURE 1 ....

▶ INTERACTIVE ART **Conservation of Momentum**

Calculate **Complete the equations describing the momentum of each collision. Identify the direction in each case.**

Conservation of Momentum Imagine you're driving a go-cart. If you ran into another go-cart that was at rest and got stuck to it, what do you think would happen to your momentum? Before you hit the other go-cart, your momentum was just your mass times your velocity. How has the additional mass changed that momentum? It actually hasn't changed it at all!

A quantity that is conserved is the same after an event as it was before. The **law of conservation of momentum** states that, in the absence of outside forces like friction, the total momentum of objects that interact does not change. The amount of momentum two cars have is the same before and after they interact.

🔑 **The total momentum of any group of objects remains the same, or is conserved, unless outside forces act on the objects.**

Before   → 4 m/s   → 2 m/s

100 kg   100 kg

Momentum = 400 kg·m/s to the right

Momentum = 200 kg·m/s to the right

Total momentum = _____ kg·m/s _____

After   → 2 m/s   → 4 m/s

Momentum = _____ kg·m/s to the right   Momentum = _____ kg·m/s to the right

Total momentum = _____ kg·m/s _____

"Non-Sticky" Collisions
Look at this example of a collision. When two objects of the same mass don't stick together and outside forces (such as friction) are negligible, the objects just trade velocities. The car that is going faster before the collision will end up slowing down, and the car that is going slower before the collision will end up speeding up.

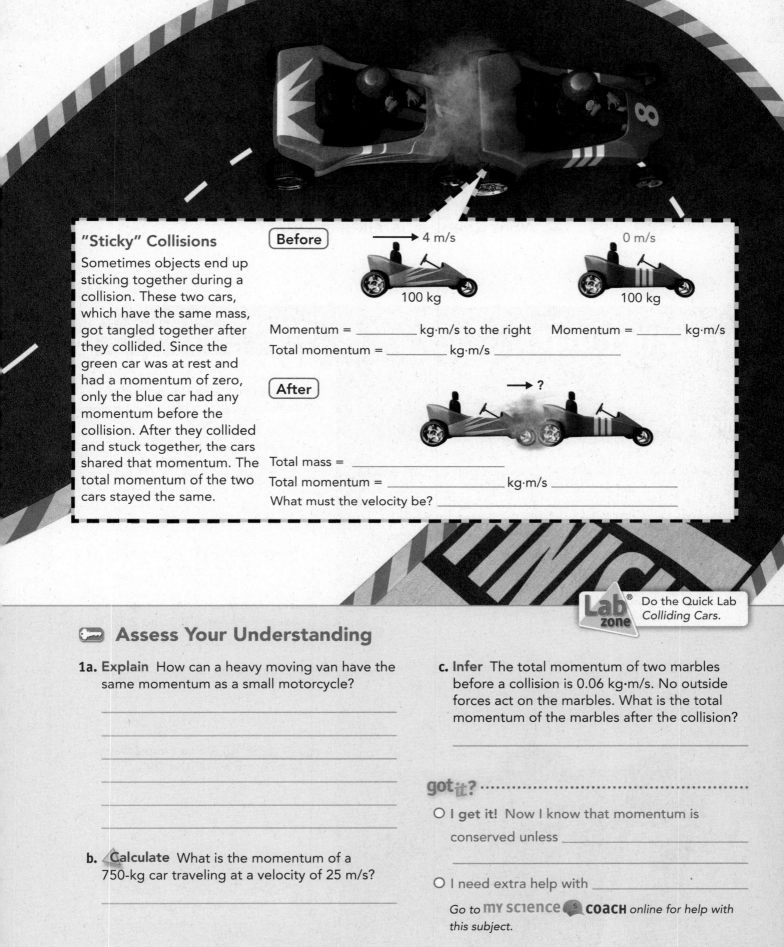

"Sticky" Collisions

Sometimes objects end up sticking together during a collision. These two cars, which have the same mass, got tangled together after they collided. Since the green car was at rest and had a momentum of zero, only the blue car had any momentum before the collision. After they collided and stuck together, the cars shared that momentum. The total momentum of the two cars stayed the same.

Before

4 m/s   0 m/s

100 kg   100 kg

Momentum = _____ kg·m/s to the right   Momentum = _____ kg·m/s

Total momentum = _____ kg·m/s _____

After

→ ?

Total mass = _____

Total momentum = _____ kg·m/s _____

What must the velocity be? _____

Lab zone Do the Quick Lab *Colliding Cars.*

🔑 Assess Your Understanding

1a. Explain How can a heavy moving van have the same momentum as a small motorcycle?

_____

_____

_____

_____

_____

_____

b. Calculate What is the momentum of a 750-kg car traveling at a velocity of 25 m/s?

_____

c. Infer The total momentum of two marbles before a collision is 0.06 kg·m/s. No outside forces act on the marbles. What is the total momentum of the marbles after the collision?

_____

got it? ••

○ **I get it!** Now I know that momentum is

conserved unless _____

_____

○ **I need extra help with** _____

Go to MY SCIENCE ⓢ COACH *online for help with this subject.*

285

Free Fall and Circular Motion

🔑 **What Is Free Fall?**

🔑 **What Keeps a Satellite in Orbit?**

my PLaneT DiaRY

Finding Yourself

The GPS (Global Positioning System) is a "constellation" of satellites that orbit 10,600 miles above Earth. The GPS makes it possible for people with ground receivers to pinpoint their geographic location. The first GPS satellites were placed in orbit in 1978. These early satellites were expected to operate for approximately five years. Newer satellites have an expected lifespan of seven to eight years.

GPS Satellites in Orbit

Years	Number of GPS Satellites Launched	Number of Operating GPS Satellites
1978–1982	6	6
1983–1987	4	8
1988–1992	17	21
1993–1997	12	27
1998–2002	5	28
2003–2007	11	31

SCIENCE STATS

Interpret Data Use the data in the table to answer the questions below.

1. What is the total number of satellites launched from 1978 to 2007? How many were still operating as of 2007?

_____

_____

_____

_____

2. How many satellites stopped operating between 2003 and 2007?

_____

_____

_____

_____

▶ **PLANET DIARY** Go to **Planet Diary** to learn more about the GPS.

Lab zone® Do the Inquiry Warm-Up *What Makes an Object Move in a Circle?*

Vocabulary
- free fall   • satellite
- centripetal force

Skills
↪ **Reading: Relate Cause and Effect**
△ **Inquiry: Create Data Tables**

What Is Free Fall?

When the only force acting on an object is gravity, the object is said to be in **free fall.** The force of gravity causes the object to accelerate. ▱ **Free fall is motion where the acceleration is caused by gravity.** When something falls on Earth, there is fluid friction from the air around it. This friction acts against gravity, reducing the acceleration of falling objects. Air friction increases as an object falls. If an object falls for long enough, increased air friction will reduce its acceleration to zero. The object will continue to fall, but it will fall at a constant velocity.

Near the surface of Earth, the acceleration due to gravity is 9.8 m/s². If there were no air friction, a falling object would have a velocity of 9.8 m/s after one second and 19.6 m/s after two seconds. Since air friction reduces acceleration, an object falling on Earth for one second will actually have a velocity that is less than 9.8 m/s.

FIGURE 1 ···

Free Fall

The photo shows a tennis ball and a crumpled piece of paper of different masses as they fall during a fraction of a second. If the only force acting on them were gravity, they would fall at exactly the same rate and line up perfectly. However, air friction is also present. Air friction has a greater effect on the paper's acceleration than on the tennis ball's acceleration. This causes the tennis ball to fall faster.

do the math! ·····························

✏ ◿ Create Data Tables
Suppose you had a chamber with no air, eliminating the force of air friction. Complete the table below for an object that is dropped from rest. Remember the formula **Velocity = Acceleration × Time.** The acceleration due to gravity is 9.8 m/s².

Time (s)	Velocity (m/s)
0	_____
1	_____
2	_____
3	_____
4	_____

Lab zone Do the Quick Lab
Which Lands First?

▱ **Assess Your Understanding**

got it? ···

○ **I get it!** Now I know that free fall is _____

_____

○ **I need extra help with** _____

Go to **my science COACH** online for help with this subject.

What Keeps a Satellite in Orbit?

Objects don't always fall down in straight lines. If you throw a ball horizontally, the ball will move away from you while gravity pulls the ball to the ground. The horizontal and vertical motions act independently, and the ball follows a curved path toward the ground. If you throw the ball faster, it will land even farther in front of you. The faster you throw an object, the farther it travels before it lands.

Satellite Motion This explains how satellites, which are objects that orbit around other objects in space, follow a curved path around Earth. What would happen if you were on a high mountain and could throw a ball as fast as you wanted? The faster you threw it, the farther away it would land. But, at a certain speed, the curved path of the ball would match the curved surface of Earth. Although the ball would keep falling due to gravity, Earth's surface would curve away from the ball at the same rate. The ball would fall around Earth in a circle, as shown in Figure 2.

↻ **Relate Cause and Effect**
On the next page, underline the effect a centripetal force has on an object's motion. Circle the effect of turning off a centripetal force.

FIGURE 2 ···

Satellite Motion
A satellite launched from Earth enters orbit because the curve of its path matches the curved surface of Earth.

✎ **Make Models** On the picture at the right, draw arrows representing the gravitational force on the ball at each point.

[CHALLENGE] Explain why Earth's atmosphere would prevent this baseball from ever actually being thrown into orbit. Why is this not a problem for satellites?

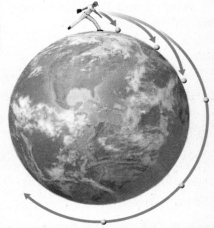

_____

_____

_____

Satellites in orbit around Earth continuously fall toward Earth, but because Earth is curved they travel around it. In other words, a satellite is a falling object that keeps missing the ground! It falls around Earth rather than onto it. Once it has entered a stable orbit, a satellite does not need fuel. It continues to move ahead due to its inertia. At the same time, gravity continuously changes the satellite's direction. Most satellites are launched at a speed of about 7,900 m/s. That's more than 17,000 miles per hour!

Centripetal Force

Many manufactured satellites orbit Earth in an almost circular path. Recall that an object traveling in a circle is accelerating because it constantly changes direction. If an object is accelerating, a force must be acting on it. A force that causes an object to move in a circular path is a **centripetal force** (sen TRIP ih tul). The word *centripetal* means "center-seeking." Centripetal forces always point toward the center of the circle an object is moving in. If you could turn off a centripetal force, inertia would cause the object to fly off in a straight line. For example, the string of a yo-yo being swung in a circle provides a centripetal force. Cutting the string would cut off the centripetal force, and the yo-yo would fly off in a straight line.

apply it!

Identify What is creating the centripetal force in each situation below?

1 A tetherball swinging around a pole

_____

2 Mars orbiting around the sun

_____

3 A child standing on a merry-go-round

_____

Lab zone Do the Quick Lab *Orbiting Earth.*

Assess Your Understanding

1a. Identify What is the force that causes objects to move in circles?

_____

b. Predict If Earth's gravity could be turned off, what would happen to satellites that are currently in orbit? Explain your reasoning.

_____

_____

_____

_____

got it?

○ **I get it!** Now I know that satellites stay in orbit because _____

_____

_____

○ **I need extra help with** _____

_____

Go to **my science** **COACH** *online for help with this subject.*

Sinking and Floating

🔑 **What Makes Things Float?**

🔑 **What Will Float?**

MY PLANET DiaRY

BLOG

Posted by Katie

Location Queens, NY

For several decades in the nineteenth and twentieth centuries, the Greenpoint oil spill polluted the Newtown Creek between Brooklyn and Queens in New York City. I happen to live in Queens and love animals and the water. The spill caused oil and other chemicals to float on top of the water. It threatened all the sea life that lived in the New York Harbor.

I am happy that our government declared Newtown Creek a Superfund site in 2010. The Superfund program is responsible for cleaning up the most dangerous and harmful waste sites in the United States. I hope that in a few years the oil and chemicals will be gone and the sea life will swim in Newtown Creek once again.

Discuss these questions with a group of classmates. Write your answers below.

1. How do you think the fact that oil floats affects the clean-up process?

_____

_____

_____

2. What would you do to help clean up or prevent an environmental disaster near where you live?

_____

_____

_____

▶ **PLANET DIARY** Go to **Planet Diary** to learn more about oil spills.

CAUTION

Lab zone® Do the Inquiry Warm-Up *Why Redesign?*

Vocabulary
• buoyant force

Skills
🔁 Reading: Cause & Effect
🔺 Inquiry: Controlling Variables

What Makes Things Float?

The ability to float is called buoyancy. You know that ships float. However, things can happen that make a ship sink. Small craft on a pond or huge oil tankers that cross the ocean can become sunken wrecks within a few hours. How could this happen? To understand buoyancy, you need to understand the buoyant force.

Buoyant Force If you have ever picked up an object under water, you know that it seems much lighter in water than in air. Water and other fluids exert an upward force, called **buoyant force,** on a submerged object.

Fluid pressure is exerted in all directions. Because fluid pressure increases with depth, there is greater force exerted on the bottom of a submerged object than on top. As you can see in **Figure 1**, this difference in pressure results in a net force in the upward direction, called buoyant force. 🔑 **Buoyant force acts in the opposite direction to the force of gravity, so it makes an object feel lighter.**

Measuring Buoyant Force You know that all objects take up space. A submerged object displaces, or takes the place of, a volume of fluid equal to its own volume. A partly submerged object, however, displaces a volume of fluid equal to the volume of its submerged portion only.

Word Origins Buoyant is thought to come from the Spanish word boyar. Based on the definition of buoyant force, what do you think boyar means?
◯ to sink
◯ to float
◯ to push

FIGURE 1 ....
Buoyant Force
Fluid pressure is shown by the green force arrows surrounding the balls.

Unequal Forces
Fluid pressure exerts force all over the ball's surface. The total force pushing upward is greater than the total force pushing down.

Net Buoyant Force
The result of the forces pushing on the ball is a net upward force, called buoyant force. The blue arrow shows the buoyant force on the ball.

✎ **Answer the following questions.**

1. Observe Where on the ball does fluid pressure exert a greater force?

_____

2. Identify In which direction does the net force act?

_____

291

apply it!

All fluids, including milk, shampoo, and air, exert buoyant force. Some fluids exert a stronger buoyant force than others.

1 Observe The brick weighs the most in (air/water/syrup).

2 (Water/Syrup) exerts greater buoyant force on the brick.

3 Water's buoyant force makes the brick feel _____

_____. Syrup's buoyant

force makes the brick feel

_____.

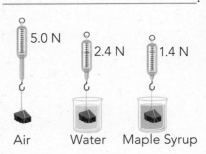

5.0 N   2.4 N   1.4 N

Air   Water   Maple Syrup

4 Control Variables What variables are controlled in the experiment?

_____

_____

A ship floats as long as the buoyant force acting on it is equal to its total weight. If the empty spaces in a ship fill with water, then the buoyant force will no longer be able to keep the ship afloat. The ship will sink.

The floating personal watercraft in **Figure 2** displaces a certain volume of water. The weight of the displaced water equals the buoyant force acting on the watercraft.

FIGURE 2 ··············

Displacement

The personal watercraft is only partly submerged, so it displaces a volume of water equal to just the part that is submerged. **Use a pencil to fill in the space taken up by the watercraft.**

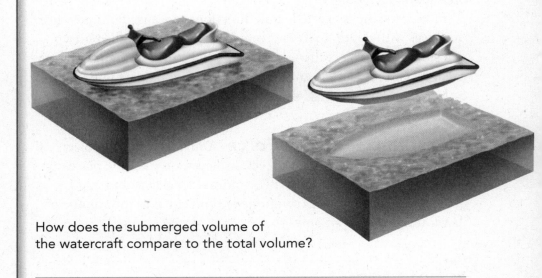

How does the submerged volume of the watercraft compare to the total volume?

_____

_____

_____

🔑 Assess Your Understanding

1a. Explain Buoyant force results from fluid pressure (increasing/decreasing) with depth.

b. Apply Concepts Dense fluids exert

_____ buoyant force than less dense fluids because they have more mass within a certain volume than a less dense fluid.

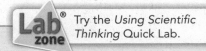 Try the *Using Scientific Thinking* Quick Lab.

got it?

○ **I get it!** Now I know that buoyancy _____

_____

○ **I need extra help with** _____

Go to **MY SCIENCE** 🔊 **COACH** *online for help with this subject.*

What Will Float?

There are two ways to determine whether an object will sink or float in a fluid. 🔑 **To predict whether an object will sink or float, you can compare the densities of the object and the fluid it is in, or you can find the net force acting on the object.**

Density and Floating Think about a bottle of oil-and-vinegar salad dressing. Recall how the dressing separates into layers as it sits undisturbed on a counter. Even though the oil appears thick and sticky, its density is less than the density of the vinegar in the dressing. The oil rises to the surface of the vinegar and floats.

Changing Density A pure substance has a characteristic density. However, density can be affected by phase changes and variables such as temperature. For example, when liquid water freezes, its particles move farther apart. As a result, an ice cube occupies slightly more space than the same mass of liquid water. That's why ice is less dense than water, and why ice floats in water.

You can make an object sink or float in a fluid by changing its density. Some submarines work this way. To make the submarine rise, water is pumped out of special tanks, reducing the submarine's mass while its volume remains the same. To make the submarine sink, water is let into the tanks.

do the math!

Calculate Complete the table below by determining the density of each substance. Then mark and label in the graduated cylinder where each material would float.

Recall the formula for density:
$$\text{Density} = \frac{\text{Mass}}{\text{Volume}}$$

Substance	Mass	Volume	Density
Plexiglass	1.53 g	1.3 cm^3	a. _____
Butter	2.6 g	3 cm^3	b. _____
Chicken bone	4.25 g	2.47 cm^3	c. _____
Sea water	6.15 g	6 cm^3	d. _____

Wood
0.7 g/cm^3

Corn oil
0.925 g/cm^3

Plastic
0.93 g/cm^3

Water
1.0 g/cm^3

Tar ball
1.02 g/cm^3

Glycerin
1.26 g/cm^3

Rubber washer
1.34 g/cm^3

Corn syrup
1.38 g/cm^3

Copper wire
8.8 g/cm^3

Mercury
13.6 g/cm^3

Buoyant Force and Floating

Remember that the weight of an object is a downward force determined by its mass and the force of gravity. The combination of an object's weight and the buoyant force is the net force acting on the object. The net force determines whether the object sinks or floats:

- If the weight of an object is greater than the buoyant force, the net force will be downward and the object will sink.
- If the weight of an object is less than the buoyant force, the net force will be upward and the object will rise.
- If the weight and buoyant force are equal and not in motion, or balanced, there is no net force and the object will neither rise nor sink.

Figure 3 shows how the net force is different for three objects with about the same volume. You can also think about how buoyant force can change for a certain amount of mass. A solid clay ball will sink in water. However, if you shape the clay into a bowl, it takes up more volume. If big enough, the bowl will generate a buoyant force big enough to counteract the weight of clay.

Relate Cause and Effect
Underline the cause and circle the effect in each of the three bulleted sentences at the right.

FIGURE 3 ·······························

> INTERACTIVE ART **Rising or Sinking**

Infer You release a basketball, a full water balloon, and a rock underwater. Use the force arrows shown to indicate whether each object will rise, sink, or stay in place. Write your answers in the boxes.

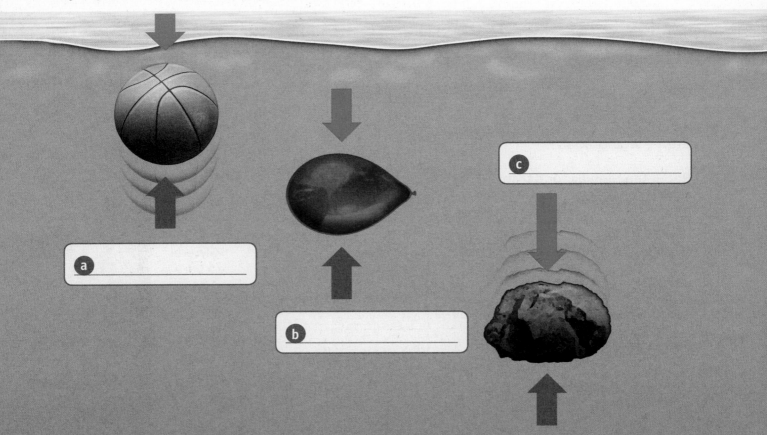

a _____

b _____

c _____

Think again about a ship floating in the water. The weight of the water displaced by the ship equals the weight of the ship, so the ship floats. If the ship is damaged, it begins to fill with water. The water increases the ship's weight by replacing air, which is lighter. The buoyant force also increases as more of the ship sinks into the water. But once the entire ship sinks into the water, the buoyant force can no longer increase. The ship continues to fill with water. The weight of the ship becomes greater than the buoyant force, so the ship sinks.

The larger an object, the more buoyant force it will generate. But as you have learned, the buoyant force must equal the object's weight for it to float. One way to make an object bigger while keeping its weight the same is to decrease its density. For example, a solid block of steel sinks. But if the steel were shaped into a ship, which is bigger and less dense than the block, the ship would float. The ship displaces more water than the steel block and thus generates enough buoyant force to balance the steel's weight.

apply it!

The personal watercraft shown here floats because the buoyant force acting on it balances its weight. What happens when two people sit on the watercraft?

1 The weight (increases/decreases/is the same).

2 Does the watercraft displace more water, less water, or the same amount of water? Explain.

_____

_____

3 How does the buoyant force change? Explain.

_____

_____

4 **CHALLENGE** Use your answers to complete the second drawing by coloring in the water to the correct height.

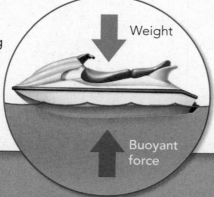

Weight

Buoyant force

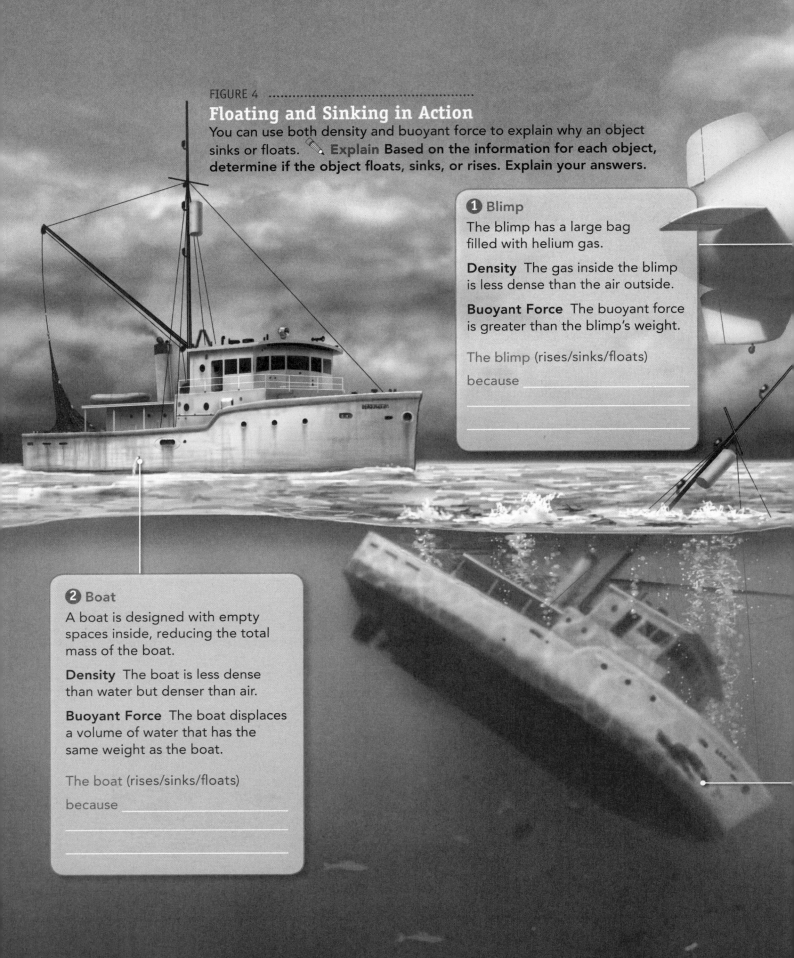

FIGURE 4 ·······························

Floating and Sinking in Action

You can use both density and buoyant force to explain why an object sinks or floats. ✎ **Explain** Based on the information for each object, determine if the object floats, sinks, or rises. Explain your answers.

❶ Blimp

The blimp has a large bag filled with helium gas.

Density The gas inside the blimp is less dense than the air outside.

Buoyant Force The buoyant force is greater than the blimp's weight.

The blimp (rises/sinks/floats)

because _____

_____

_____

❷ Boat

A boat is designed with empty spaces inside, reducing the total mass of the boat.

Density The boat is less dense than water but denser than air.

Buoyant Force The boat displaces a volume of water that has the same weight as the boat.

The boat (rises/sinks/floats)

because _____

_____

_____

3 **Damaged boat**

When a boat is damaged, its air-filled spaces fill with water.

Density The boat's mass increases while its volume remains the same.

Buoyant Force The boat's weight increases while the volume of the water it displaces stays the same.

The boat (rises/sinks/floats)

because _____

_____

_____

 Try the *How Close Is It?* Quick Lab.

Assess Your Understanding

2. Review Underline the sentence that uses the scientific meaning of force. Then write the scientific definition.

> •I had to force my sister to give me the balloon.
>
> •The net force on the balloon was in an upward direction.

_____

_____

_____

_____

3a. Describe An object that is (less/more) dense than the fluid it is in will sink. An object that is (less/more) dense than the fluid it is in will float.

b. Infer The net force acting on an object that is sinking is

_____

_____

_____

_____

got it? ....

○ **I get it!** Now I know that an object will

neither sink nor float if _____

_____

_____

○ I need extra help with _____

_____

_____

Go to **MY SCIENCE COACH** *online for help with this subject.*

297

Study Guide

Changes in motion are caused by _____. _____ laws describe these changes in motion.

LESSON 1 The Nature of Force

🔑 Like velocity and acceleration, a force is described by its strength and by the direction in which it acts.

🔑 A nonzero net force causes a change in the object's motion.

Vocabulary
- force • newton
- net force

LESSON 2 Friction and Gravity

🔑 Two factors that affect the force of friction are the types of surfaces involved and how hard the surfaces are pushed together.

🔑 Two factors affect the gravitational attraction between objects: their masses and distance.

Vocabulary
- friction • sliding friction
- static friction • fluid friction
- rolling friction • gravity
- mass • weight

LESSON 3 Newton's Laws of Motion

🔑 Objects at rest will remain at rest and objects moving at a constant velocity will continue moving at a constant velocity unless they are acted upon by nonzero net forces.

🔑 The acceleration of an object depends on its mass and on the net force acting on it.

🔑 If one object exerts a force on another object, then the second object exerts a force of equal strength in the opposite direction on the first object.

Vocabulary
- inertia

LESSON 4 Momentum

🔑 The momentum of a moving object can be determined by multiplying the object's mass by its velocity.

🔑 The total momentum of any group of objects remains the same, or is conserved, unless outside forces act on the objects.

Vocabulary
- momentum
- law of conservation of momentum

LESSON 5 Free Fall and Circular Motion

🔑 Free fall is motion where the acceleration is caused by gravity.

🔑 Satellites in orbit around Earth continuously fall toward Earth, but because Earth is curved they travel around it.

Vocabulary
- free fall • satellite • centripetal force

LESSON 6 Sinking and Floating

🔑 Buoyant force acts in the opposite direction to the force of gravity, so it makes an object feel lighter.

🔑 To predict whether an object will sink or float, you can compare the densities of the object and the fluid it is in, or you can find the net force acting on the object.

Vocabulary
- buoyant force

Review and Assessment

LESSON 1 The Nature of Force

1. When a nonzero net force acts on an object, the force

    a. changes the motion of the object.

    b. must be greater than the reaction force.

    c. does not change the motion of the object.

    d. is equal to the weight of the object.

2. The SI unit of force is the _____

3. Calculate What is the net force on the box? Be sure to specify direction.

15 N ➡️

⬅️ 10 N

_____

LESSON 2 Friction and Gravity

4. Friction always acts

    a. in the same direction as motion.

    b. opposite the direction of motion.

    c. perpendicular to the direction of motion.

    d. at a 30° angle to the direction of motion.

5. The factors that affect the gravitational force between two objects are _____

_____

6. List What are two ways you can increase the frictional force between two objects?

_____

_____

7. 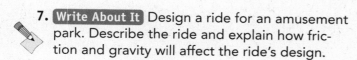 **Write About It** Design a ride for an amusement park. Describe the ride and explain how friction and gravity will affect the ride's design.

LESSON 3 Newton's Laws of Motion

8. Which of Newton's laws of motion is also called the law of inertia?

    a. First   **b.** Second

    c. Third   **d.** Fourth

9. Newton's second law states that force is equal to _____

10. Interpret Diagrams Look at the diagram below of two students pulling a bag of volleyball equipment. The friction force between the bag and the floor is 4 N. What is the net force acting on the bag? What is the acceleration of the bag?

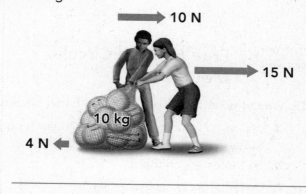

10 N

15 N

10 kg

4 N ⬅️

_____

_____

_____

_____

_____

11. Apply Concepts Suppose you are an astronaut making a space walk outside your space station and your jet pack runs out of fuel. How can you use your empty jet pack to get you back to the station?

_____

_____

_____

_____

_____

_____

Momentum

12. Momentum is calculated by multiplying

    a. mass times velocity. **b.** weight times mass.

    c. force times speed.   **d.** inertia times force.

13. The SI unit of momentum is _____

14. **Explain** How can two objects of different masses have the same momentum?

_____

_____

_____

_____

_____

Free Fall and Circular Motion

15. Satellites remain in orbit around Earth because

    a. the moon's gravitational pull on them is equal to Earth's pull.

    b. no forces act on them.

    c. their motors keep them moving in circles.

    d. the curve of their paths as they fall matches the curve of Earth.

16. Centripetal forces always point _____

_____

17. **Calculate** Determine the velocity of an object that started from rest and has been in free fall for 10 seconds. Assume there is no air resistance.

_____

Sinking and Floating

18. A helium-filled balloon will float in air because

    a. there is more air than helium.

    b. helium is less dense than air.

    c. helium is more dense than air.

    d. helium and air have equal densities.

19. **Apply Concepts** Iron has a density of 7.9 g/cm^3. Mercury has a density of 13.6 g/cm^3. Determine whether iron will float or sink in mercury, and tell why.

_____

_____

_____

APPLY THE BIG Q **How do objects react to forces?**

20. Forces are all around you. Describe an example of each of Newton's laws of motion that you experience before you get to school in the morning.

_____

_____

_____

_____

_____

_____

_____

_____

_____

_____

_____

Standardized Test Prep

Multiple Choice

Circle the letter of the best answer.

Force Force   Motion

1. In the balloon diagram above, why don't the two forces cancel each other out?

   A They are not equal.
   B They both act on the air.
   C They both act on the balloon.
   D They act on different objects.

2. An object is floating in a container of water. Which force opposes gravity?

   A inertia
   B friction
   C buoyant force
   D centripetal force

3. What force makes it less likely for a person to slip on a dry sidewalk than on an icy sidewalk?

   A gravity
   B friction
   C inertia
   D momentum

4. A satellite orbits Earth at a constant speed. What part of the satellite's motion is changing?

   A speed
   B friction
   C inertia
   D acceleration

5. Where would a 5-kg object experience the greatest gravitational force?

   A on the moon
   B at sea level
   C at the top of a tall mountain
   D at the bottom of the ocean

6. In a game of tug-of-war, you pull on the rope with a force of 100 N to the right and your friend pulls on the rope with a force of 100 N to the left. What is the net force on the rope?

   A 200 N to the right
   B 200 N to the left
   C 0 N
   D 100 N to the right

Constructed Response

Use your knowledge of science to help you answer Question 7. Write your answer on a separate sheet of paper.

7. Use all three of Newton's laws of motion to describe what happens when a car starts off at rest, is pushed across a platform, and then accelerates downward.

safety restraints

Did you wear your seat belt the last time you rode in a car? Seat belts are safety restraints designed to protect you from injury while you travel in a moving vehicle, whether you stop suddenly to avoid a crash or are stopped suddenly by a crash.

Without a seat belt, inertia would cause the driver and passengers in a car that suddenly stopped to continue traveling forward. Without a restraint, a 75-kilogram driver driving at 50 km/h would experience 12,000 newtons of force in a crash! A safety restraint prevents that forward motion and keeps the driver and passengers safe.

Safety harnesses and seat belts are available in many different designs. Most seat belts are three-point harnesses. Five- and seven-point harnesses are used in vehicles like race cars and fighter jets.

Debate It Most states have laws that require drivers and passengers to wear seat belts. Research the seat belt laws in your state, and participate in a class debate about whether the seat belt laws are strong enough.

Race car drivers travel at higher speeds than most drivers experience. A five-point harness provides extra security at these high speeds. ▼

Forceful Fluids

Could you lift an elephant with water? It depends on the container the water is in! Suppose you have a sealed container completely full of water. If you apply pressure to one area of the container, that pressure is exerted equally in all parts of the fluid and on the inner surfaces of the container. This is Pascal's principle, named for Blaise Pascal, a French scientist who lived in the 1600s.

Hydraulic systems are based on Pascal's principle. In these systems, a force presses a piston against an enclosed fluid. The force transfers with the same pressure throughout the fluid and presses a second piston outward. If the two pistons are the same size, the inward force and the outward force are the same.

What if the surface areas of the two pistons differ? Suppose the output piston's surface area is four times greater than that of the input piston. Four times more fluid presses against the output piston, which applies four times the force. With a system like that, you could lift an elephant with water!

Design It Hydraulic car lifts and hydraulic brakes are two technologies that work because of Pascal's principle. Research another hydraulic device and diagram how it works. Share your diagram with your class.

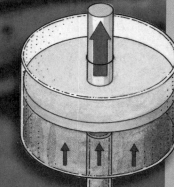

HOW CAN A MECHANIC LIFT A RACE CAR?

THE BIG ?

How do machines make it easier to do work?

This Formula 1 race car is waved into the pit, where a group of mechanics is ready to replace the tires. Formula 1 race cars are heavy—they must have a mass of at least 605 kg, including the driver. The pit crew can't lift the car or replace the tires by hand, so they use many tools to help get the job done. With the right tools, the pit crew can quickly get their car back into the race. **Develop Hypotheses** **How does a mechanic lift up a heavy race car?**

> **UNTAMED SCIENCE** Watch the **Untamed Science** video to learn more about work and machines.

Work and Machines

Getting Started

Check Your Understanding

1. **Background** Read the paragraph below and then answer the question.

> Charles wants to move his bed across the room, but the **weight** of the bed is too great for him to lift it. However, he can generate enough **force** to push the bed.

> A **force** is a push or pull exerted on an object.
>
> **Weight** is a measure of the force of gravity on an object.

- What forces are acting on the bed as Charles pushes it across the floor?

_____

_____

> **MY READING WEB** If you had trouble completing the question above, visit **My Reading Web** and type in *Work and Machines.*

Vocabulary Skill

Identify Multiple Meanings Some familiar words have more than one meaning. Words you use every day may have different meanings in science. Look at the different meanings of the words below.

Word	Everyday Meaning	Scientific Meaning
work	*n.* A job or responsibility Example: She carried her backpack to work every day.	*n.* The product of a force and the distance over which that force is exerted Example: It takes twice as much work to lift a suitcase 2 meters as it does to lift it 1 meter.
machine	*n.* A motorized device Example: A washing machine contains a large rotating basin.	*n.* Any device that makes work easier Example: A wheelbarrow is a machine that lets you lift more weight than you normally could.

2. **Quick Check** Circle the sentence below that uses the scientific meaning of the word *work*.

- Jim did **work** on the bed to move it out of his room.
- Tina had a lot of **work** to do at the end of the semester.

work

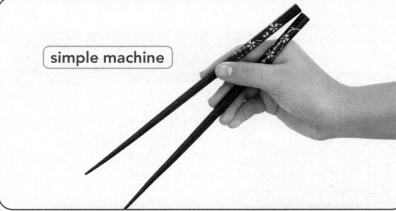

simple machine

inclined plane

pulley

Chapter Preview

LESSON 1
- work
- joule
- power
- watt

↻ **Identify Supporting Evidence**
△ **Calculate**

LESSON 2
- machine
- input force
- output force
- mechanical advantage
- efficiency

↻ **Compare and Contrast**
△ **Predict**

LESSON 3
- simple machine
- inclined plane
- wedge
- screw
- lever
- fulcrum

↻ **Relate Cause and Effect**
△ **Infer**

LESSON 4
- pulley
- wheel and axle
- compound machine

↻ **Summarize**
△ **Classify**

> **VOCAB FLASH CARDS** For extra help with vocabulary, visit **Vocab Flash Cards** and type in *Work and Machines.*

Work and Power

UNLOCK THE BIG ?

🔑 **How Is Work Defined?**

🔑 **What Is Power?**

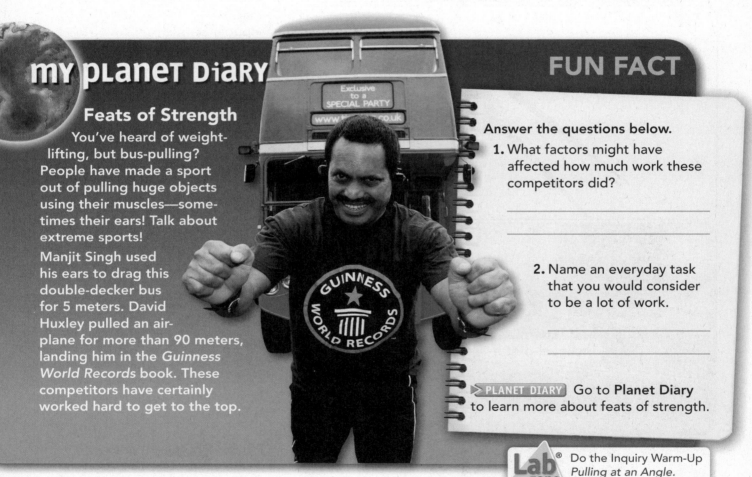

MY PLANET DiARY

Feats of Strength

You've heard of weight-lifting, but bus-pulling? People have made a sport out of pulling huge objects using their muscles—sometimes their ears! Talk about extreme sports!

Manjit Singh used his ears to drag this double-decker bus for 5 meters. David Huxley pulled an airplane for more than 90 meters, landing him in the *Guinness World Records* book. These competitors have certainly worked hard to get to the top.

FUN FACT

Answer the questions below.

1. What factors might have affected how much work these competitors did?

_____

_____

2. Name an everyday task that you would consider to be a lot of work.

_____

_____

▷ PLANET DIARY Go to **Planet Diary** to learn more about feats of strength.

Lab zone® Do the Inquiry Warm-Up *Pulling at an Angle.*

How Is Work Defined?

If you push a child on a swing, you are doing work on the child. If you pull your books out of your backpack, you do work on your books. In scientific terms, you do **work** any time you exert a force on an object that causes the object to move some distance.

🔑 **Work is done on an object when the object moves in the same direction in which the force is exerted.**

Vocabulary
- work • joule
- power • watt

Skills
↻ Reading: Identify Supporting Evidence
△ Inquiry: Calculate

No Work Without Motion

Suppose you push on a car that is stuck in the mud. You certainly exert a force on the car, so it might seem as if you do work. But if the force you exert does not make the car move, you are not doing any work on it. To do work on an object, the object must move some distance as a result of your force. If the object does not move, no work is done, no matter how much force is exerted.

Force in the Same Direction

Think about carrying your backpack to school in the morning. You know that you exert a force on your backpack when you carry it, but you do not do any work on it. To do work on an object, the force you exert must be in the same direction as the object's motion. When you carry an object while walking at constant velocity, you exert an upward force on the object. The motion of the object is in the horizontal direction. Since the force is vertical and the motion is horizontal, you don't do any work.

Figure 1 shows three different ways to move a cello. You can lift it off the ground and carry it, you can push it parallel to the ground, or you can pull it at an angle to the ground. The weight of the cello is the same in each situation, but the amount of work varies.

FIGURE 1 ···

Force, Motion, and Work
The amount of work that you do on something depends on the direction of your force and the object's motion. ✎ **Describe** Suppose you are moving a rolling suitcase. Describe three ways of moving it that require different amounts of work.

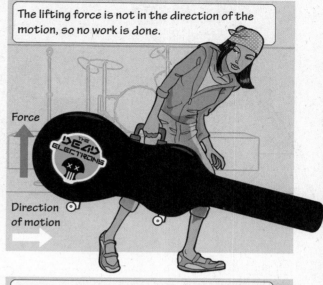
The lifting force is not in the direction of the motion, so no work is done.

Force

Direction of motion

The force acts in the same direction as the motion, so the maximum work is done.

Direction of motion

Force

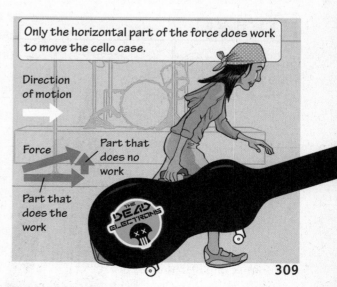
Only the horizontal part of the force does work to move the cello case.

Direction of motion

Force

Part that does no work

Part that does the work

Two factors affect the amount of work April does to hand her friend an instrument: the force she must apply and the distance she must apply the force through.

FIGURE 2 ···

> **INTERACTIVE ART** **Amount of Work**

When April lifts a trumpet or a tuba up the stairs, she does work.

✎ **Draw Conclusions** If April's friend wanted to reduce the amount of work April needed to do to hand the trumpet to him, where could he stand? Circle the step(s). If the stage were higher, what would happen to the total amount of work required to lift the trumpet from the floor to the stage?

Participants in the Empire State Building Run-Up race up the skyscraper's stairs. For a 500 N person to climb 1,576 steps (320 m) it takes 160,000 J of work. That's enough work to lift an elephant over 3 m!

Calculating Work

Look at **Figure 2**. Which do you think involves more work: lifting a 40-newton tuba up three steps (about 0.5 meters), or lifting a 5-newton trumpet up the same three steps? Your common sense may suggest that lifting a heavier object requires more work than lifting a lighter object. This is true. But is it more work to lift an instrument up three steps or up to the top story of a building? As you might guess, moving an object a greater distance requires more work than moving the same object a shorter distance.

The amount of work you do depends on both the amount of force you exert and the distance the object moves. 🔑 **The amount of work done on an object can be determined by multiplying force times distance.**

$$\text{Work} = \text{Force} \times \text{Distance}$$

When you lift an object, the upward force you exert must be at least equal to the object's weight. So, to lift the trumpet, you would have to exert a force of 5 newtons. The distance you lift the trumpet is 0.5 meters. The amount of work you do on the trumpet can be calculated using the work formula.

$$\text{Work} = \text{Force} \times \text{Distance}$$

$$\text{Work} = 5 \text{ N} \times 0.5 \text{ m}$$

$$\text{Work} = 2.5 \text{ N·m}$$

To lift the tuba, you would have to exert a force of 40 newtons. So the amount of work you do would be 40 newtons × 0.5 meters, or 20 N·m. You do more work to lift the heavier object.

When force is measured in newtons and distance in meters, the SI unit of work is the newton-meter (N•m). This unit is also called a **joule** (JOOL) in honor of James Prescott Joule, a physicist who studied work in the mid-1800s. One joule (J) is the amount of work you do when you exert a force of 1 newton to move an object a distance of 1 meter. It takes 2.5 joules of work to lift the trumpet up three steps. Lifting the tuba the same distance requires 20 joules of work.

apply it!

The climber on the right does work on his equipment as he carries it up the mountain.

1 On a warm day, the climber does 3,000 J of work to get his pack up the mountain. On a snowy day, he adds equipment to his pack. If he climbs to the same height, he would do (more/less/the same amount of) work.

2 If the climber's pack stayed the same weight and the climber only climbed halfway up, he would do (more/less/the same amount of) work.

3 Calculate How much work does the climber do on his pack if his pack weighs 90 N and he climbs to a height of 30 m?

_____

4 [CHALLENGE] On a different trip, the climber's pack weighs twice as much and he climbs twice as high. How many times more work does he do on this pack than the one in question 3?

_____

Do the Quick Lab
What is Work?

🔑 Assess Your Understanding

1a. Describe A waiter carries a 5-newton tray of food while he walks a distance of 10 meters. Is work done on the tray? Why or why not?

_____

_____

_____

b. Explain You're holding your dog's leash and trying to stand still as he pulls on the leash at an angle. You move forward. (All of/Some of/ None of) his force does work on you.

c. Calculate How much work do you do when you push a shopping cart with a force of 50 N for a distance of 5 m?

_____

got it? . . . .

○ **I get it!** Now I know that work is _____

○ **I need extra help with** _____

Go to **MY SCIENCE ⓢ COACH** *online for help with this subject.*

What Is Power?

If you carry a backpack up a flight of stairs, the work you do is the same whether you walk or run. The amount of work you do on an object is not affected by the time it takes to do the work. But scientists keep track of how fast work is done with a rate called power.

Power is the rate at which work is done. 🔑 **Power equals the amount of work done on an object in a unit of time.** You need more power to run up the stairs with your backpack than to walk because it takes you less time to do the same work.

You can think of power in another way. An object that has more power than another object does more work in the same time. It can also mean doing the same amount of work in less time.

Calculating Power Whenever you know how fast work is done, you can calculate power. Power is calculated by dividing the amount of work done by the amount of time it takes to do the work. This can be written as the following formula.

$$\text{Power} = \frac{\text{Work}}{\text{Time}}$$

Since work is equal to force times distance, you can rewrite the equation for power as follows.

$$\text{Power} = \frac{\text{Force} \times \text{Distance}}{\text{Time}}$$

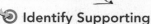

🔍 Identify Supporting Evidence Underline details and examples that support the main idea of this section.

FIGURE 3 ·

Work and Power
April carried her moving boxes up a flight of stairs. Notice how much time it took her.

✏️ **Estimate** Suppose April ran instead. Fill in the second panel to show how much time it would take her.

Power Units

You may have heard car advertisements mention horsepower. The term isn't misleading. It's the same kind of power you just learned how to calculate. When work is measured in joules and time in seconds, the SI unit of power is the joule per second (J/s). This unit is also known as the watt (W). One joule of work done in one second is one **watt** of power. In other words, 1 J/s = 1 W. A watt is very small, so power is often measured in larger units such as kilowatts or horsepower. One kilowatt (kW) equals 1,000 watts. One horsepower equals 746 watts.

Vocabulary Identify Multiple Meanings What is the scientific meaning of *power*?

_____

_____

_____

do the math!

When a tow truck pulls a car, it applies a force over a distance. Work is done in a horizontal direction. **Calculate** Complete the table by calculating the power of the tow truck in each case.

Recall the formula for power is

$$\text{Power} = \frac{\text{Work}}{\text{Time}}$$

If a tow truck does 10,000 J of work in 5 seconds, then the power of the truck is calculated as follows.

$$\text{Power} = \frac{10,000 \text{ J}}{5 \text{ s}} = 2,000 \text{ W}$$

Tow Truck Power

Work (J)	Time (s)	Power (W)
120,000	60	_____
69,000	30	_____
67,500	45	_____

Lab zone
Do the Quick Lab
Investigating Power.

Assess Your Understanding

got it?

○ **I get it!** Now I know that power _____

_____

○ **I need extra help with** _____

Go to **my science coach** *online for help with this subject.*

Understanding Machines

🔑 **What Does a Machine Do?**

🔑 **What Is Mechanical Advantage?**

🔑 **What Is Efficiency?**

my PLANET DiARY

FUN FACT

Sticks and Stones

When you need to peel an apple or open a can of soup, you reach for the right tool to do the job.

Some animals use items such as sticks and rocks to make finding or eating their food easier. For example, woodpecker finches and capuchin monkeys use sticks to get food out of places they can't reach. Sea otters and Egyptian vultures both use rocks as tools. Otters use rocks to pry shellfish away from other rocks. Egyptian vultures use their beaks to pick up rocks and break open eggs to eat.

Communicate Discuss these questions with a partner. Write your answers below.

1. How does the rock make it easier for the chimpanzee in the photo to crack open nuts?

_____

_____

_____

_____

_____

2. What human tools would you use to do the same job?

_____

_____

_____

_____

> PLANET DIARY Go to **Planet Diary** to learn more about tools.

 Do the Inquiry Warm-Up *Is It a Machine?*

Vocabulary
- machine   • input force   • output force
- mechanical advantage   • efficiency

Skills
↻ Reading: Compare and Contrast
△ Inquiry: Predict

What Does a Machine Do?

What do you picture when you hear the word *machine*? You may think of machines as complex gadgets with motors, but a machine can be as simple as a ramp. **Machines** are devices that allow you to do work in an easier way. Machines do not reduce the amount of work you do. Instead, they just change the way you do work. In **Figure 1**, April does the same amount of work to move her speaker onto the stage whether or not she uses a ramp. The ramp makes that work easier. **🔧 A machine makes work easier by changing at least one of three factors: the amount of force you exert, the distance over which you exert your force, or the direction in which you exert your force.**

Input Versus Output When you do work, the force you exert is called the **input force.** You exert your input force over the input distance. In **Figure 1B,** April's input force is the force she uses to pull the speaker up the ramp. The input distance is the length of the ramp. The machine exerts the **output force** over the output distance. The weight of the speaker is the output force. The height of the ramp is the output distance. Input force times input distance equals input work. Output force times output distance equals output work. Since machines do not reduce the work you do, your output work can never be greater than your input work.

FIGURE 1 ·······························
Using Machines
Using a ramp makes it easier for April to move the speaker onto the stage.

✎ **Interpret Diagrams** In Figure 1B, draw a line that represents April's output distance and an arrow that represents her output force.

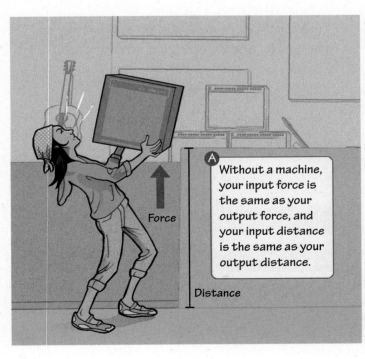

A Without a machine, your input force is the same as your output force, and your input distance is the same as your output distance.

Force

Distance

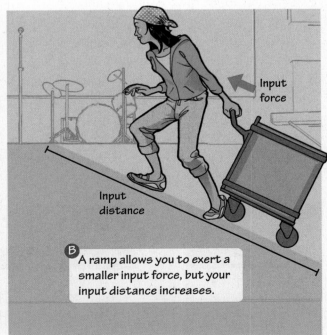

Input force

Input distance

B A ramp allows you to exert a smaller input force, but your input distance increases.

315

FIGURE 2

Making Work Easier

The devices shown all make work easier in different ways. The arrows on the photos show how the machines change input work.

Input force

Output force

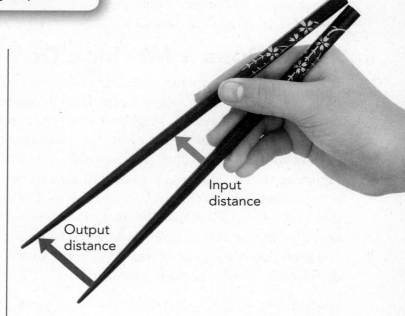

Input distance

Output distance

Changing Force

In some machines, the output force is *greater* than the input force. How can this happen? Recall the formula for work: **Work** = Force × Distance. If the amount of work stays the same, a decrease in force means an increase in distance. So if a machine allows you to use less input force to do the same amount of work, you must apply that smaller input force over a greater distance.

You see machines that work like this every day. How hard would it be to turn on a faucet that didn't have a handle? Since the handle is wider than the shaft of the faucet, your hand turns a greater distance than it would if you turned the shaft directly. Turning the handle a greater distance allows you to use less force.

Changing Distance

In some machines, the output force is less than the input force. This kind of machine allows you to exert your input force over a shorter distance. In order to apply a force over a shorter distance, you need to apply a greater input force. When do you use this kind of machine? Think of a pair of chopsticks. When you use chopsticks to eat, you move the hand holding the chopsticks a short distance. The other end of the chopsticks moves a greater distance, allowing you to pick up and eat a large piece of food with a small movement.

Complete the equation below. Be sure to describe each quantity as *large* or *small*.

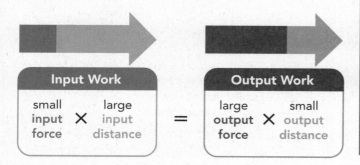

Input Work		Output Work	
small **input force** × large input distance	=	large **output force** × small output distance	

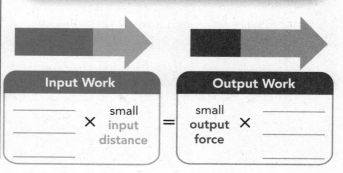

Input Work		Output Work	
_____ × small input distance	=	small **output force** × _____	

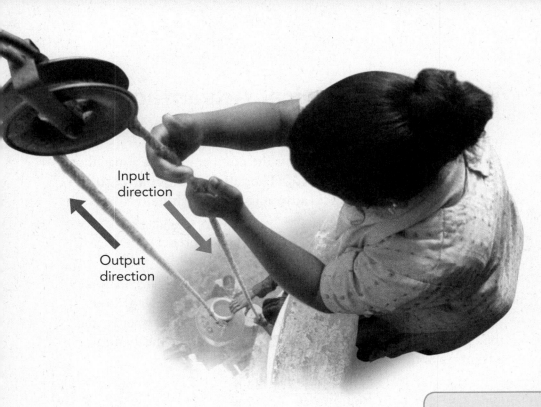

Input direction

Output direction

Changing Direction Some machines don't change either force or distance. The photo above shows a machine called a *pulley* attached to a bucket. (You'll learn more about pulleys soon.) The pulley doesn't increase input force or distance. However, by changing the direction of the input force, the pulley makes it much easier to move the bucket to the top of a building—you can just pull down on the rope. Without a pulley, you would have to carry the bucket up a ladder or staircase. A flagpole rigging is also a pulley.

Complete the equation below. Be sure to describe each quantity as *large* or *small*.

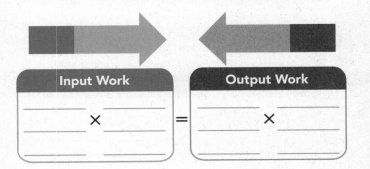

Input Work		Output Work	
_____ × _____	=	_____ × _____

Lab zone® Do the Quick Lab *Going Up.*

🔑 Assess Your Understanding

1a. List Name two examples of machines for which the output force is greater than the input force.

_____

_____

b. Apply Concepts Suppose that you use a pair of chopsticks and apply a force of 1 N over a distance of 0.01 m. How much work do you do? If the output force of the chopsticks is only 0.5 N, how far do the tips of the chopsticks move?

_____

_____

got it? ....

○ **I get it!** Now I know that machines make work easier by _____

_____

○ **I need extra help with** _____

Go to **MY SCIENCE** Ⓢ **COACH** *online for help with this subject.*

317

What Is Mechanical Advantage?

You've just learned how to describe machines using words, but you can also describe machines with numbers. A machine's **mechanical advantage** is the number of times a machine increases a force exerted on it. 🔑 **The ratio of output force to input force is the mechanical advantage of a machine.**

$$\text{Mechanical advantage} = \frac{\text{Output force}}{\text{Input force}}$$

Increasing Force When the output force is greater than the input force, the mechanical advantage of a machine is greater than 1. You exert an input force of 10 newtons on a can opener, and the opener exerts an output force of 30 newtons. The mechanical advantage of the can opener is calculated below.

$$\frac{\text{Output force}}{\text{Input force}} = \frac{30\ \text{N}}{10\ \text{N}} = 3$$

The can opener triples your input force!

Increasing Distance When a machine increases distance, the output force is less than the input force. The mechanical advantage is less than 1. If input force is 20 newtons and the output force is 10 newtons, the mechanical advantage is shown below.

$$\frac{\text{Output force}}{\text{Input force}} = \frac{10\ \text{N}}{20\ \text{N}} = 0.5$$

Your input force is cut in half, but your input distance is doubled.

✏️ **Compare and Contrast** On these two pages, underline the sentences that explain how to distinguish among machines based on their mechanical advantages.

FIGURE 3

Mechanical Advantage
Drums are tuned by tightening and loosening bolts. Drum keys make the bolts easier to turn.
✏️ **Identify** Draw an arrow for the key's output force.

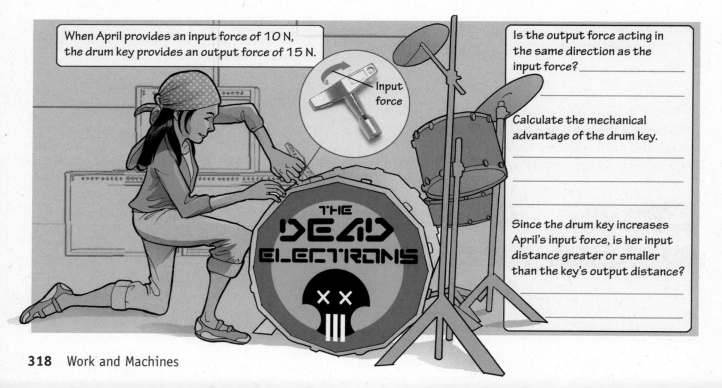

When April provides an input force of 10 N, the drum key provides an output force of 15 N.

Input force

Is the output force acting in the same direction as the input force? _____

Calculate the mechanical advantage of the drum key.

Since the drum key increases April's input force, is her input distance greater or smaller than the key's output distance?

Changing Direction What can you predict about the mechanical advantage of a machine that changes the direction of the force? If only the direction changes, input force will be the same as the output force. The mechanical advantage will always be 1.

do the math!

The graph shows input and output force data for three different ramps. Use the graph to answer the questions below. (The actual ramps are not pictured. Do not confuse the lines in the graph with the ramps themselves!)

① Read Graphs If an 80 N input force is exerted on Ramp 2, what is the output force?

_____

② Interpret Data Find the slope of the line for each ramp.

_____

_____

_____

③ Draw Conclusions Why does the slope represent each ramp's mechanical advantage?

_____

_____

_____

_____

_____

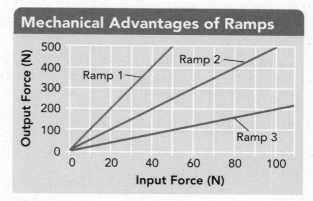

Mechanical Advantages of Ramps

④ Graph On the graph above, plot a line for a ramp that has a mechanical advantage of 3.

⑤ CHALLENGE Predict Which ramp is the steepest? How do you know?

_____

_____

_____

_____

_____

Lab zone® Do the Quick Lab *Mechanical Advantage.*

🔑 Assess Your Understanding

got it? ···

O **I get it!** Now I know that mechanical advantage _____

_____

O **I need extra help with** _____

Go to **MY SCIENCE** s **COACH** *online for help with this subject.*

What Is Efficiency?

So far you have assumed that the work you put into a machine is exactly equal to the work done by the machine. In an ideal situation, this would be true. In real situations, however, the output work is always less than the input work.

Overcoming Friction If you have ever tried to cut something with rusty scissors, you know that a large part of your work is wasted overcoming the friction between the parts of the scissors.

All machines waste some work overcoming the force of friction. A common way to reduce friction is to lubricate or wax surfaces. The less friction there is, the closer the output work is to the input work. The **efficiency** of a machine compares output work to input work. Efficiency is expressed as a percentage. The higher the percentage, the more efficient the machine is. If you know the input work and output work for a machine, you can calculate a machine's efficiency.

Calculating Efficiency **To calculate the efficiency of a machine, divide the output work by the input work and multiply the result by 100 percent.** This is summarized by the following formula.

$$\text{Efficiency} = \frac{\text{Output work}}{\text{Input work}} \times 100\%$$

Vocabulary Identify Multiple Meanings Underline the scientific definition of *efficiency* in the text. Then write a sentence that uses the everyday meaning of *efficient*.

_____

_____

_____

_____

apply it!

❶ Calculate the efficiency of this bicycle if the input work to turn the pedals is 45 J and the output work is 30 J. Show your calculations.

_____

_____

_____

_____

_____

❷ Predict What will happen to the efficiency of the bike after the gears have been cleaned and the chain has been oiled?

_____

_____

_____

Real and Ideal Machines

A machine with an efficiency of 100 percent would be an ideal machine. Since all machines lose work to friction, ideal machines do not exist. All machines have an efficiency of less than 100 percent.

How does this affect mechanical advantage? *Ideal* mechanical advantage is your input distance divided by the machine's output distance. It is often related to the measurements of a machine. What you have calculated so far (output force divided by input force) is *actual* mechanical advantage. If machines were ideal and input work was equal to output work, ideal and actual mechanical advantages would be equal. Because of friction, actual mechanical advantage is always less than ideal mechanical advantage.

FIGURE 4 ··

> REAL-WORLD INQUIRY

An Ideal Machine?

The balls of this Newton's cradle may swing for a long time, but they will eventually come to rest.

✎ **Communicate** With a partner, discuss where in this machine work is lost due to friction. Circle these locations on the photo and explain your reasoning.

Lab zone® Do the Quick Lab *Friction and Efficiency.*

🗝 Assess Your Understanding

2a. Relate Cause and Effect Real machines have an efficiency of less than 100% because some work is wasted to overcome _____

b. Predict What happens to the efficiency of a bicycle as it gets rusty? What must you do to maintain the same amount of output work?

_____

_____

got it? ···

○ I get it! Now I know that efficiency _____

_____

○ I need extra help with _____

Go to MY SCIENCE 🔎 COACH online for help with this subject.

Inclined Planes and Levers

UNLOCK THE BIG ?

🔑 **How Do Inclined Planes Work?**

🔑 **How Are Levers Classified?**

my planeT DiaRY

Is It a Machine?

Which objects in the photo below are machines? If you guessed the truck and the motorbike, you're correct—but not completely! Remember, a device doesn't have to be complicated or motorized in order to be a machine. Look between the truck and the motorbike. The ramp is a machine. Look at the person rolling the bike up the ramp. His hands hold the handlebars. His knees bend to help him walk. These are examples of simple machines. The motorbike and the truck contain many simple machines. There are dozens of machines in this photo, not just the two with motors.

MISCONCEPTIONS

Communicate Discuss these questions with a partner. Then write your answers below.

1. What kind of work is made easier by the ramp in the picture?

_____

_____

_____

2. What are other examples of ramps that you have seen or used?

_____

_____

> PLANET DIARY Go to **Planet Diary** to learn more about everyday machines.

Lab zone® Do the Inquiry Warm-Up *Inclined Planes and Levers.*

Vocabulary
- simple machine • inclined plane • wedge
- screw • lever • fulcrum

Skills
↻ Reading: Relate Cause and Effect
△ Inquiry: Infer

How Do Inclined Planes Work?

Machines can be as simple as chopsticks or as complex as motorbikes. Any complex machine can be broken down into smaller building blocks called simple machines. A **simple machine** is the most basic device for making work easier. Three closely related simple machines—the inclined plane, the wedge, and the screw—form the inclined plane family.

Inclined Plane Lifting a heavy object such as a motorbike is much easier with a ramp. A ramp is an example of a simple machine called an inclined plane. An **inclined plane** is a flat, sloped surface.

How It Works 🔑 **An inclined plane allows you to exert your input force over a longer distance.** As a result, the input force needed is less than the output force. The input force you use on an inclined plane is the force with which you push or pull an object along the slope. The inclined plane's output force is equal to the object's weight.

Mechanical Advantage You can determine the ideal mechanical advantage of an inclined plane by dividing the length of the incline by its height.

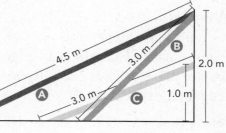

4.5 m   3.0 m   B   2.0 m
Ⓐ   3.0 m   Ⓒ   1.0 m

apply it!

❶ Imagine you were pushing a wheelchair up the ramps in the drawing above. Which would be the hardest to use? Why?

_____

_____

❷ Calculate the ideal mechanical advantage of each ramp using the following formula.

$$\text{Ideal mechanical advantage} = \frac{\text{Length of ramp}}{\text{Height of ramp}}$$

_____

_____

❸ The ramp with the (smallest/greatest) mechanical advantage is the steepest.

FIGURE 1 ·············
Wedges

During a forest fire, select trees are cut down to prevent the fire from spreading.

✎ **Review** In the white circle below, draw and label the input force acting on the wedge and the output forces it exerts.

Input force

Output force   Output force

Wedge

If you've ever sliced an apple with a knife or pulled up a zipper, you are familiar with another simple machine known as a wedge. A **wedge** is a device that is thick at one end and tapers to a thin edge at the other end.

How It Works Think of a wedge as an inclined plane (or two back-to-back inclined planes) that moves. 🔑 **When you use a wedge, instead of moving an object along the inclined plane, you move the inclined plane itself.** For example, when an ax is used to split wood, the ax handle exerts a force on the blade of the ax, which is the wedge. That force pushes the wedge down into the wood. The wedge in turn exerts an output force at a 90° angle to its slope, splitting the wood in two.

Mechanical Advantage The ideal mechanical advantage of a wedge is determined by dividing the length of the wedge by its width. The longer and thinner a wedge is, the greater its mechanical advantage. When you sharpen a knife, you make the wedge thinner. This increases its mechanical advantage. That is why sharp knives cut better than dull knives.

$$\text{Ideal mechanical advantage} = \frac{\text{Length of wedge}}{\text{Width of wedge}}$$

Calculate the ideal mechanical advantage of the firefighter's wedge if it is 4 cm wide and 22 cm long.

_____

_____

Screw

Like a wedge, a **screw** is a simple machine that is related to the inclined plane. A screw can be thought of as an inclined plane wrapped around a cylinder.

How It Works When you twist a screw into a piece of wood, you exert an input force on the screw. 🗝 **The threads of a screw act like an inclined plane to increase the distance over which you exert the input force.** As the threads of the screw turn, they exert an output force on the wood. Friction holds the screw in place. Other examples of screws include bolts, drills, and jar lids.

Mechanical Advantage Think of the length around the threads of a screw as the length of an inclined plane and the length of the screw as the height of an inclined plane. The ideal mechanical advantage of the screw is the length around the threads divided by the length of the screw—just as the ideal mechanical advantage of an inclined plane is its length divided by its height. The closer together the threads of a screw are, the greater the mechanical advantage.

FIGURE 2 ....

Screws

The diagram below shows a screw with ten threads.
✏ **Calculate** What is the mechanical advantage of the screw on the left? CHALLENGE On the smooth screw next to it, draw in the threads to make a screw that is the same length but would be easier to screw into a piece of wood. There is a hint in the text. Find it and circle it.

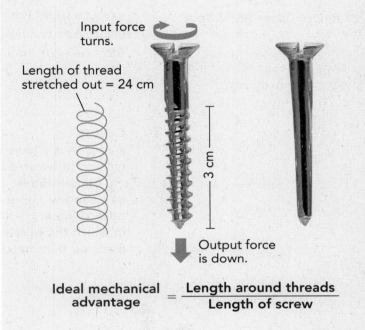

Input force turns.

Length of thread stretched out = 24 cm

3 cm

Output force is down.

$$\text{Ideal mechanical advantage} = \frac{\text{Length around threads}}{\text{Length of screw}}$$

_____

_____

Lab zone® Do the Lab Investigation *Angling for Access.*

🗝 Assess Your Understanding

1a. List List three closely related simple machines in the inclined plane family. _____

_____

b. Explain A simple inclined plane makes work easier by decreasing the input (force/distance) required to move the object.

c. Compare and Contrast Name one way inclined planes and screws are similar and one way they are different.

_____

_____

_____

_____

_____

got it? ....

○ **I get it!** Now I know that inclined planes _____

_____

_____

○ **I need extra help with** _____

Go to **MY SCIENCE** 💬 **COACH** *online for help with this subject.*

How Are Levers Classified?

Have you ever ridden on a seesaw or used a spoon to eat your food? If so, then you are already familiar with another simple machine called a lever. A **lever** is a rigid bar that is free to pivot, or rotate, on a fixed point. The fixed point that a lever pivots around is called the **fulcrum.**

How It Works To understand how levers work, think about using a spoon. Your wrist acts as the fulcrum. The bowl of the spoon is placed near your food. When you turn your wrist, you exert an input force on the handle, and the spoon pivots on the fulcrum. As a result, the bowl of the spoon digs in, exerting an output force on your food.

⟳ Relate Cause and Effect
The How It Works paragraph describes the use of a spoon. Underline the cause and the effect in this paragraph.

FIGURE 3 ···

Levers

A seesaw is a type of lever in which the fulcrum is located halfway between the input and output forces.

✎ **Make Models** In the space to the left, draw a diagram of a seesaw. Label the fulcrum, the input force, and the output force. CHALLENGE The diagrams below show levers in which the fulcrum is not centered. Write the name of a machine that matches each diagram.

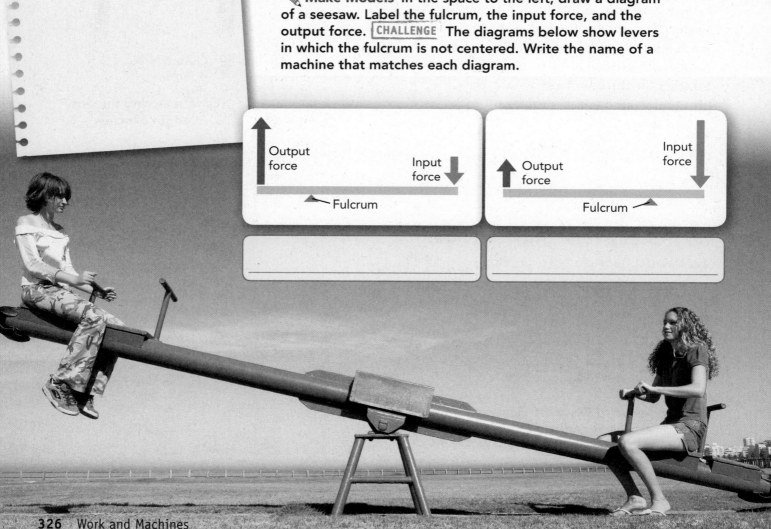

Mechanical Advantage

Using a lever like a spoon doesn't increase your input force or change the direction of your input force. Instead, it increases your input distance. When you use a spoon, you only have to move the handle a short distance in order to scoop up food over a longer distance. However, you need to apply a greater force than you would have without the spoon.

The ideal mechanical advantage of a lever is determined using the following formula.

$$\text{Ideal mechanical advantage} = \frac{\text{Distance from fulcrum to input force}}{\text{Distance from fulcrum to output force}}$$

In the case of the spoon, the distance from the fulcrum to the input force is less than the distance from the fulcrum to the output force. This means that the mechanical advantage is less than 1.

Types of Levers

When a spoon is used as a lever, the input force is located between the fulcrum and the output force. But this is not always the case. **Levers are classified according to the location of the fulcrum relative to the input and output forces.** The three different classes of levers are explained on the next page.

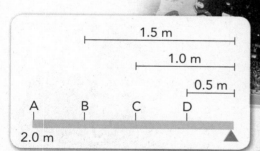

apply it!

A hockey stick is an example of a lever. Your shoulder acts as the fulcrum of the lever. The output force is exerted where the stick hits the puck. You exert the input force where your bottom hand grips the stick. What is the mechanical advantage of a hockey stick

❶ that is gripped at point D and hits the puck at point A? _____

❷ that is gripped at point D and hits the puck at point B? _____

❸ **Infer** Would the mechanical advantage of a hockey stick ever be greater than 1? Explain.

_____

_____

_____

_____

_____

_____

327

FIGURE 4 ·····································

>ART IN MOTION **Three Classes of Levers**

The three classes of levers differ in the positions of the fulcrum, input force, and output force. ✎ **Interpret Diagrams** Draw and label the fulcrum, input force, and output force on the second-class and third-class lever photographs.

Output force

Fulcrum

Input force

First-Class Levers

First-class levers change the direction of the input force. They also increase force or distance. Force increases if the fulcrum is closer to the output force. Distance increases if the fulcrum is closer to the input force. Examples of first-class levers include seesaws and scissors.

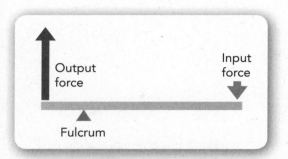

Output force

Input force

Fulcrum

Second-Class Levers

Second-class levers increase force. They do not change the direction of the input force. Examples include doors, nutcrackers, and bottle openers. The mechanical advantage of second-class levers is always greater than 1.

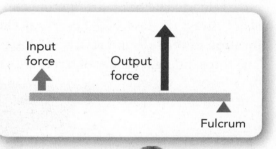

Input force

Output force

Fulcrum

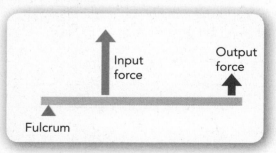

Third-Class Levers

Third-class levers increase distance, but do not change the direction of the input force. Examples include spoons, shovels, and baseball bats. The mechanical advantage of third-class levers is always less than 1.

If you find this one tricky, look for help on the previous page!

Input force

Output force

Fulcrum

FIGURE 5 ···

Levers in the Body

Levers can be found throughout your body. ✎ **Classify** In the last two panels of the diagram, draw an arrow representing the output force. Then identify the class of lever for each part of the body.

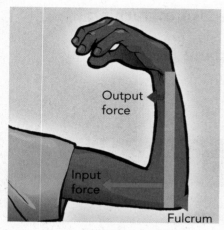

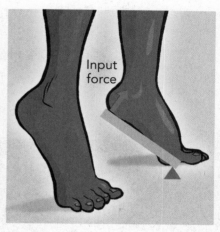

Your biceps muscle provides the input force. The output force is used to lift your arm.

The muscles in the back of your neck provide an input force, and the resulting output force tilts your chin back.

Your calf muscle provides an input force, and the resulting output force raises your body and moves it slightly forward.

Lab zone® Do the Quick Lab *Modeling Levers.*

🗝 Assess Your Understanding

2a. Describe Describe how each class of lever makes work easier.

_____

_____

_____

_____

b. Calculate What is the mechanical advantage of a lever with 2 m between the input force and the fulcrum and 1 m between the output force and the fulcrum? _____

c. Infer What class(es) of lever could the lever from the previous question be? Explain.

_____

_____

_____

_____

_____

_____

_____

_____

got it? ···

O **I get it!** Now I know that levers are classified by _____

_____

O **I need extra help with** _____

Go to **MY SCIENCE COACH** online for help with this subject.

Putting Machines Together

UNLOCK THE BIG ?

🔑 **What Simple Machines Make Use of Turning?**

🔑 **How Does a Compound Machine Do Work?**

my planeт DiaRY

DISCOVERY

Lidar Alert

One of the oldest forms of transportation in the world—the sailboat—may benefit from new technology: a mobile lidar station. Lidar (short for light detection and ranging) stations sense wind speed and direction using laser beams. The new station, developed by Chinese scientists, fits on a bus that can be parked near bodies of water. Sailors need to know about wind speed and direction to position their sails. With the information they gather from these new lidar stations and the simple machines they use to control their sails, sailors can greatly improve their chances of navigating safely and winning races.

Answer the questions below.

1. Why might sailboat makers incorporate simple machines into their designs?

_____

_____

2. What is another example of pairing advanced technology with simple machines?

_____

_____

_____

▶ PLANET DIARY Go to **Planet Diary** to learn more about boating.

Lab zone® Do the Inquiry Warm-Up *Machines That Turn.*

Vocabulary
- pulley
- wheel and axle
- compound machine

Skills
- Reading: Summarize
- Inquiry: Classify

What Simple Machines Make Use of Turning?

If you have ever pulled a suitcase with wheels that were stuck, you know that it is easier to move the suitcase when the wheels can turn. **Two simple machines take advantage of turning: the pulley and the wheel and axle.**

How a Pulley Works When you raise a sail on a sailboat, you are using a pulley. A **pulley** is a simple machine made of a grooved wheel with a rope or cable wrapped around it. You use a pulley by pulling on one end of the rope. This is the input force. At the other end of the rope, the output force pulls up on the object you want to move. The grooved wheel turns. This makes it easier to move the rope than if it had just been looped over a stick. To move an object some distance, a pulley can make work easier in two ways. It can decrease the amount of input force needed to lift the object. It can also change the direction of your input force. For example, when you pull down on a flagpole rope, the flag moves up.

Summarize In one or two sentences, summarize what you have learned on this page.

_____

_____

_____

_____

FIGURE 1 ....

Simple Machines in Sailboats

You can find many simple machines on a sailboat. Below are some diagrams of different parts of a sailboat. **Classify Circle the machines on the diagram that you think are pulleys.**

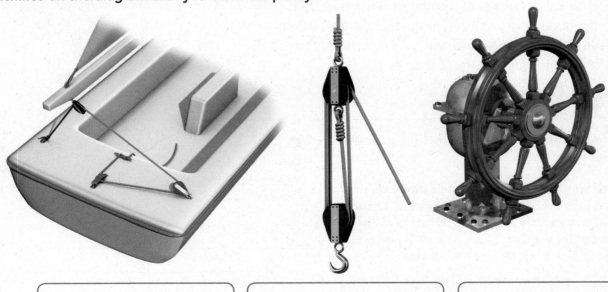

FIGURE 2 ....

> **INTERACTIVE ART** **Types of Pulleys**

Pulley systems are classified by the number and position of the wheels they contain. ✎ Classify Go back to Figure 1 and check your answers. Next to each pulley, label its type.

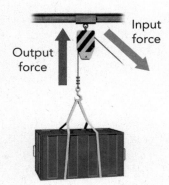

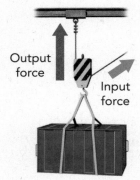

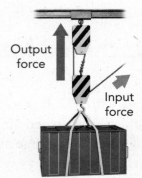

Mechanical advantage = 1

Mechanical advantage = 2

Mechanical advantage = 3

Fixed Pulley

A fixed pulley changes the direction of force but not the amount applied.

Movable Pulley

A movable pulley decreases the amount of input force needed. It does not change the direction of the force.

Block and Tackle

A block and tackle is a pulley system made up of fixed and movable pulleys.

Types of Pulleys A pulley that you attach to a structure is a fixed pulley. Fixed pulleys are used at the tops of flagpoles. A movable pulley is attached directly to the object you are attempting to move. Construction cranes often use movable pulleys. Combining fixed and movable pulleys makes a pulley system called a block and tackle. The direction of the input force of a block and tackle could be either up or down depending on the arrangement of the rope and pulleys. The ideal mechanical advantage of a pulley or pulley system is equal to the number of sections of rope that support the object. Don't include the rope on which you pull downward though, because it does not support the object.

apply it!

The pulley system shown here allows the painter to raise or lower himself.

❶ Label Suppose the painter pulls down on the rope with just enough force to lift himself. Draw and label arrows to indicate the direction of the input and output forces. Draw one of the arrows longer to indicate which force is greater.

❷ Interpret Diagrams The mechanical advantage of this pulley system is _____.

❸ CHALLENGE What is the benefit of combining fixed and movable pulleys in a system like this one?

_____

_____

_____

How a Wheel and Axle Works

You use a screwdriver to tighten screws because it is much easier to turn the handle instead of turning the screw itself. A simple machine made of two connected objects that rotate about a common axis is called a **wheel and axle**. The object with the larger radius is the wheel. In a screwdriver, the handle is the wheel and the shaft is the axle. When you turn the wheel, the axle rotates. The axle exerts a larger output force over a shorter distance.

If you apply force to the axle, your output force will be less than your input force. However, it will be exerted over a greater distance. This is how a paddle wheel on a boat works. The boat's motor turns an axle that turns the boat's wheel, pushing the boat forward a greater distance.

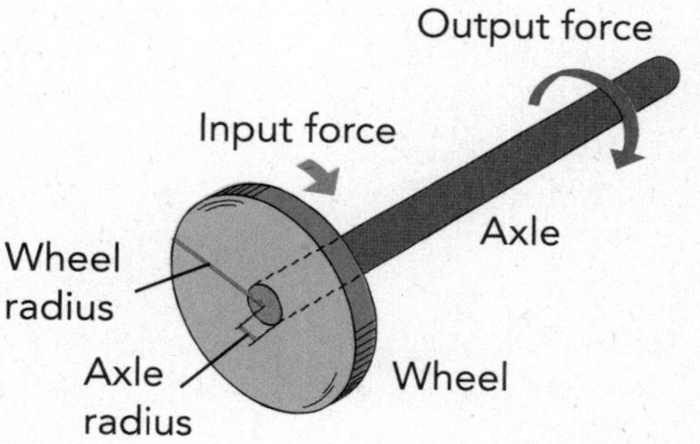

Mechanical Advantage

The ideal mechanical advantage of a wheel and axle is the radius of the wheel divided by the radius of the axle. (A radius is the distance from the outer edge of a circle to the circle's center.) The greater the ratio of the wheel radius to the axle radius, the greater the advantage.

> Ideal mechanical advantage = $\dfrac{\text{Radius of wheel}}{\text{Radius of axle}}$
>
> The blue screwdriver has a handle radius of 1.5 cm and a shaft radius of 0.25 cm. What is its mechanical advantage?_____
>
> ◁ Classify Go back to Figure 1 and recheck your answers. If you spot a wheel and axle, draw a box around it.

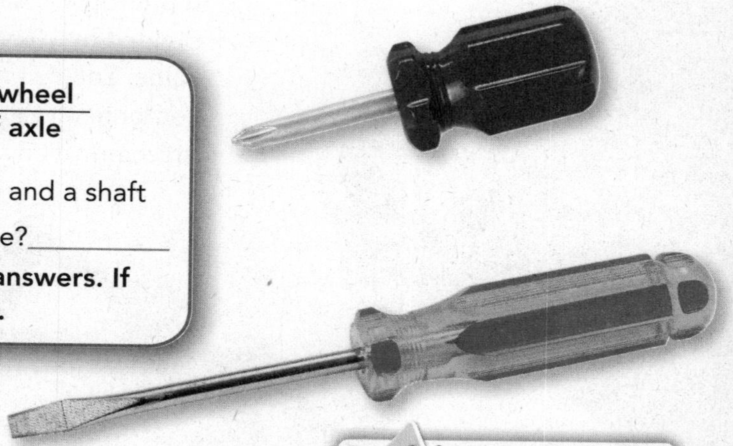

FIGURE 3 ·········

Wheel and Axle

The screwdrivers have the same shaft radius. The blue screwdriver has a larger handle radius.

✎ **Infer** Circle the screwdriver with the greater mechanical advantage.

Output force

Input force

Wheel radius

Axle radius

Axle

Wheel

Lab zone ® Do the Quick Lab *Building Pulleys*.

🔑 Assess Your Understanding

1a. List List two examples of a wheel and axle. Which of your examples has the greater mechanical advantage?

_____

_____

b. Apply Concepts You exert a 100-N force on a pulley system to lift 300 N. What's the mechanical advantage of this system? How many sections of rope support the weight?

_____

_____

got it? ···

○ **I get it!** Now I know that pulleys and wheels and axles _____

_____

○ **I need extra help with** _____

Go to **MY SCIENCE 🔊 COACH** *online for help with this subject.*

How Does a Compound Machine Do Work?

Suppose you and your neighbors volunteer to clean up a local park. Will the job be easier if just a few people help or if everyone in the neighborhood works together? Getting a job done is usually easier if many people work on it. Similarly, doing work can be easier if more than one simple machine is used. A machine that combines two or more simple machines is called a **compound machine.**

 **Within a compound machine, the output force of one simple machine becomes the input force of another simple machine.** Think about a stapler. The handle is a lever. Each tip of a staple acts as a wedge. Suppose the lever has a mechanical advantage of 0.8 and the wedge has mechanical advantage of 2. If you input a force of 10 N on the lever, the output force of the lever will be 8 N. That 8 N becomes the input force of the wedge, and the final output force is 8 N times 2, or 16 N.

Recall that mechanical advantage is output force divided by input force. The mechanical advantage of the stapler is 16 N divided by 10 N, or 1.6. There is another way to calculate this value. You can multiply the mechanical advantages of the stapler's component machines, the lever (0.8) and the wedge (2). The ideal mechanical advantage of a compound machine is the product of the ideal mechanical advantages of the simple machines that it consists of.

FIGURE 4 ·······················

Compound Machines

A compound machine consists of two or more simple machines. ✎ **Identify** In the photo at the left, circle and identify three simple machines that make up the apple peeler.

> If the mechanical advantages of the component machines in the peeler are 2, 3, and 12, what is the overall mechanical advantage of the apple peeler?
>
> _____

How Can I Get That Up There?

EXPLORE THE BIG ?

How do machines make it easier to do work?

FIGURE 5 ·

Piano movers use compound machines to get their
job done. ✎ Calculate the mechanical advantage
(MA) of each simple machine in the compound machine.
(The simple machine mounted on the truck has an inner
radius of 0.05 m and an outer radius of 0.25 m.) What
is the overall mechanical advantage?

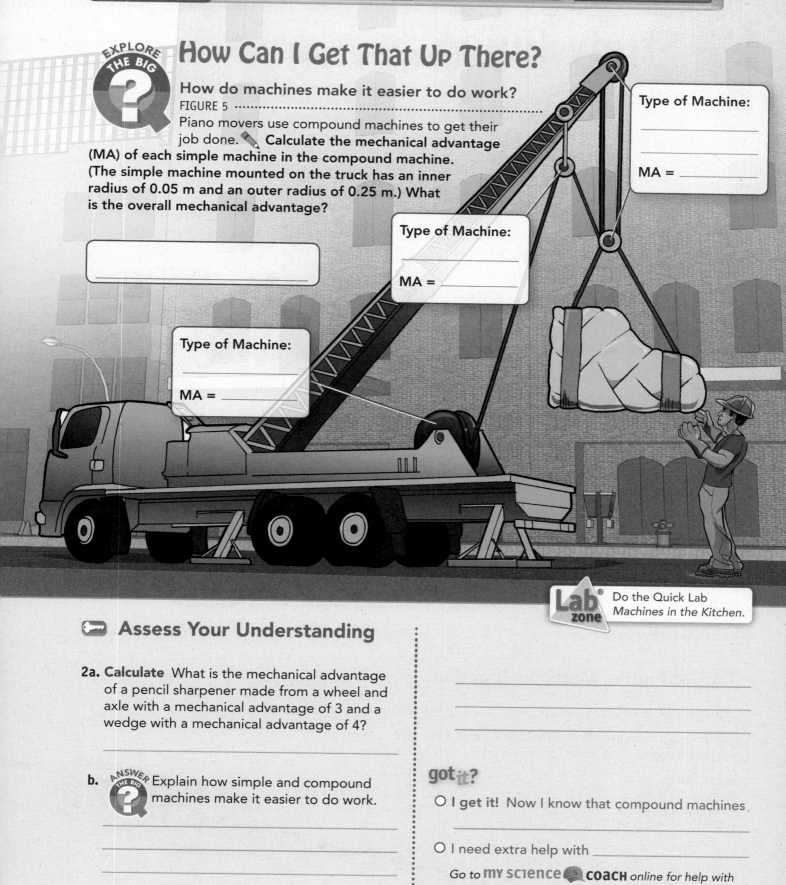

Type of Machine:
_____
MA = _____

Type of Machine:
_____
MA = _____

Type of Machine:
_____
MA = _____

Lab zone® Do the Quick Lab
Machines in the Kitchen.

Assess Your Understanding

2a. Calculate What is the mechanical advantage
of a pencil sharpener made from a wheel and
axle with a mechanical advantage of 3 and a
wedge with a mechanical advantage of 4?

_____

b. ANSWER THE BIG ? Explain how simple and compound
machines make it easier to do work.

_____
_____
_____

got it?

○ I get it! Now I know that compound machines
_____

○ I need extra help with _____

Go to MY SCIENCE ⓢ COACH online for help with
this subject.

Work is done when a _____ is applied in the direction of motion.

_____ make it easier to do work.

LESSON 1 Work and Power

🔑 Work is done on an object when the object moves in the same direction in which the force is exerted.

🔑 The amount of work done on an object can be determined by multiplying force times distance.

🔑 Power equals the amount of work done on an object in a unit of time.

Vocabulary
• work • joule • power • watt

LESSON 2 Understanding Machines

🔑 A machine makes work easier by changing force, distance, or direction.

🔑 The ratio of output force to input force is the mechanical advantage of a machine.

🔑 To calculate the efficiency of a machine, divide the output work by the input work and multiply the result by 100 percent.

Vocabulary
• machine • input force • output force
• mechanical advantage • efficiency

LESSON 3 Inclined Planes and Levers

🔑 Three closely related simple machines—the inclined plane, the wedge, and the screw—form the inclined plane family.

🔑 Levers are classified according to the location of the fulcrum relative to the input and output forces.

Vocabulary
• simple machine • inclined plane
• wedge • screw • lever • fulcrum

LESSON 4 Putting Machines Together

🔑 Two simple machines make use of turning: the pulley and the wheel and axle.

🔑 Within a compound machine, the output force of one simple machine becomes the input force of another simple machine.

Vocabulary
• pulley
• wheel and axle
• compound machine

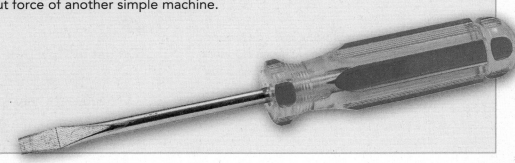

Review and Assessment

LESSON 1 Work and Power

1. The amount of work done on an object is found by multiplying

    a. force times distance.   **b.** force times time.

    c. power times efficiency. **d.** speed times time.

2. The rate at which work is done is called

    _____

3. Calculate You go rock climbing with a pack that weighs 70 N and you reach a height of 30 m. How much work did you do to lift your pack? If you finished the climb in 10 minutes (600 s), what was your power?

    _____

    _____

    _____

4. Apply Concepts What do automobile makers mean when they say their cars are more powerful than their competitors' cars?

    _____

    _____

    _____

5. **Write About It** Your friend's parents tell him that he needs to do more work around the house. How can your friend use science to explain to them that he does plenty of work just by going through his daily activities?

LESSON 2 Understanding Machines

6. One way a machine can make work easier is by

    a. increasing force   **b.** decreasing time

    c. increasing work   **d.** reducing work

7. The actual mechanical advantage of any machine is its _____ divided by its _____

8. Solve Problems You and your friends are building a treehouse, and you need a machine to get a heavy load of wood from the ground to the top of the tree. You set up a pulley system that allows you to pull down on a rope to lift the wood up. You end up able to lift a load you normally couldn't. In what way(s) does your machine make work easier?

    _____

    _____

    _____

    _____

9. Control Variables You are designing an experiment to test the efficiency of different bikes. What variables do you have to control?

    _____

    _____

    _____

10. Relate Cause and Effect You push on an old skateboard with a force of 20 N. The output force is only 10 N. What is the skateboard's efficiency? How would the efficiency change if the old, rusty ball bearings were replaced with new ones?

    _____

    _____

    _____

LESSON 3 Inclined Planes and Levers

11. Which of these is an example of a simple machine from the inclined plane family?

a. baseball bat   b. jar lid

c. bottle opener   d. wheelbarrow

12. The fixed point that a lever pivots around is called the _____

13. Interpret Diagrams Which ramp has the greater ideal mechanical advantage?

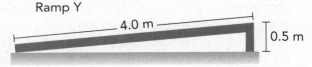
Ramp Y — 4.0 m — 0.5 m

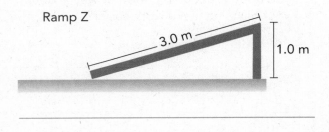
Ramp Z — 3.0 m — 1.0 m

_____
_____
_____

14. Make Judgments Your friend wants to design a wheelbarrow with an ideal mechanical advantage of 5,000. Do you think your friend should consider a different design? Explain.

_____
_____
_____

15. math! On a separate sheet of paper, draw one example of each of the three different classes of levers. For each lever, measure the distance between the fulcrum and the input force, the distance between the fulcrum and the output force, and calculate the ideal mechanical advantage.

LESSON 4 Putting Machines Together

16. Which of these is an example of a wheel and axle?

a. axe   b. seesaw

c. doorknob   d. flagpole rigging

17. A _____ is a system that consists of at least one fixed pulley and one movable pulley.

18. Apply Concepts A circular faucet handle is an example of a wheel and axle. How could you increase the mechanical advantage of a circular faucet handle?

_____
_____
_____

How do machines make it easier to do work?

19. This paper cutter is a compound machine. How does it make cutting paper easier? What simple machines make up the paper cutter? Describe how they interact.

_____
_____
_____
_____
_____
_____
_____

Standardized Test Prep

Multiple Choice

Circle the letter of the best answer.

1. The table below shows the input work and output work for four different pulleys. Which pulley has the highest efficiency?

Work of Different Pulleys		
Pulley	**Input Work**	**Output Work**
Fixed pulley A	20,000 J	8,000 J
Fixed pulley B	20,000 J	10,000 J
Movable pulley	20,000 J	12,000 J
Block and tackle	20,000 J	16,000 J

   A Fixed pulley A
   B Fixed pulley B
   C Movable pulley
   D Block and tackle

2. Why does it take more work to carry a 22-N bag of birdseed to the third floor of a house than it takes to move a 16-N bag of cat food to the second floor of a house?

   A Work equals distance divided by force and the birdseed requires less force to lift it.
   B The force exerted on the birdseed is not in the direction of motion.
   C The cat food has less mass than the birdseed.
   D The birdseed has greater mass and has to be moved farther.

3. Which is the best scientific definition of a machine?

   A A machine is a timesaving device that uses motors and gears.
   B A machine changes the amount of input force.
   C A machine makes work easier by changing force, distance, or direction.
   D A machine can either be simple or compound.

4. Which of the following will increase the efficiency of a machine by reducing friction?

   A greasing the axles on a bicycle
   B decreasing a bicycle wheel's radius
   C increasing a wheel axle's radius
   D increasing the length of scissors' blades

5. Which activity describes work being done on an object?

   A walking a dog on a leash
   B lifting a bag of groceries
   C holding an umbrella still
   D pressing a stamp onto an envelope

Constructed Response

Use your knowledge of science to help you answer Question 6. Write your answer on a separate sheet of paper.

6. Explain why an engineer would design a road to wind around a mountain rather than go straight up the side. Explain how this design would be better.

Good Things Come in Small Packages

Imagine a tiny machine that works right inside your cells, delivering medication to specific sites. Scientists are working to build just such machines. Nanomachines, or nanites, are machines whose size is measured in nanometers. One nanometer is equivalent to one billionth (10^{-9}) of a meter. That's pretty tiny—smaller than most people can imagine. In comparison with these tiny machines, red blood cells, which have a diameter of about 7 micrometers (7×10^{-6} of a meter), look huge!

So how do these tiny machines work? Most nanomachines are made of gold or platinum. They use cylindrical carbon molecules or hydrogen peroxide for fuel. Scientists hope that nanomachines will one day use the fuel of a patient's cell to do work.

Some tube-shaped nanomachines convert energy from light into chemical energy and then into mechanical energy to do work. These machines are injected into human cancer cells in the dark. Before they are injected, the tiny machines are loaded with medicine. When scientists expose the machines to light, a chemical reaction causes a wagging motion inside the tube, which releases the medication in exactly the right spot.

Research It Scientists are working to develop a "submarine" nanomachine. How is this new machine different from other medical nanomachines? Draw the submarine and describe its functions.

This image shows an artist's idea of how a nanite might look as it helps fight cancer in the body. ▼

A new SET OF WHEELS

Students at the Massachusetts Institute of Technology (MIT) have the chance to help 20 million people by taking a class called Wheelchair Design in Developing Countries.

Over the semester, students will learn how to build a wheelchair. They will also study the needs of people who use wheelchairs in developing countries. What's the real test? Designing devices that will actually improve people's lives!

Analyze It Look at the wheelchairs in the photo. Create a graphic organizer in which you identify things someone would need a wheelchair to do, and how a wheelchair feature could meet that need. For example, the user might need to go up or down a steep hill, so the chair should have good brakes and should not be too heavy. Identify and evaluate the scientific knowledge and concepts students may need to apply when creating their wheelchairs.

SCIENC ATHLETES
Let the Games Begin

Every year, students from all over the country compete to be the best at everything from chemistry to robot building. What is this scientific pageant of skill and achievement? It's the Science Olympiad™!

In the Mission Possible event, teams of students work all year to invent, design, and build a Rube Goldberg® machine. A Rube Goldberg® machine is a compound machine designed to accomplish a very simple task—and makes you laugh in the process.

This Rube Goldberg® machine takes over 20 steps to perform three tasks. It selects, crushes, and pitches a can into a recycling bin.

Make It Work Divide your class into teams and compete in your own Mission Possible event in which you invent a complex machine to perform a simple task. Score each team's creation!

WHAT MAKES THESE SNOWBOARDERS "FLY" DOWNHILL?

 How is energy conserved in a transformation?

These women are competing in the sport of snowboard cross. They "fly" down a narrow course, filled with jumps, steep sections, and ramps. Disaster looms at every turn. If they don't crash into each other or fall, then the first one across the finish line wins.

△ Develop Hypotheses **What do you think makes these snowboarders go so fast?**

_____

_____

_____

_____

_____

_____

▷ UNTAMED SCIENCE Watch the **Untamed Science** video to learn more about energy.

Energy

Check Your Understanding

1. **Background** Read the paragraph below and then answer the question.

Michael pulls his brother in a wagon. Suddenly, Michael's dog jumps on his brother's lap. Michael continues to pull the wagon, but it is more difficult now. The added **mass** of the dog means that Michael has to generate more **force** to accelerate the wagon to the same **speed**.

Mass is a measure of the amount of matter in an object.

A **force** is a push or pull.

The **speed** of an object is the distance the object travels per unit of time.

- Why is it harder to pull the wagon with the dog in it?

_____

_____

▶ MY READING WEB If you had trouble completing the question above, visit **My Reading Web** and type in *Energy.*

Vocabulary Skill

Identify Multiple Meanings Some familiar words may have different meanings in science. Look at the different meanings of the words below.

Word	Everyday Meaning	Scientific Meaning
energy	*n.* the ability to be active or take part in a vigorous activity **Example:** She had enough *energy* to run for miles.	*n.* the ability to do work or cause change **Example:** The wind can move objects because it has *energy.*
power	*n.* the ability to influence others **Example:** The coach has a lot of *power* over his young athletes.	*n.* the rate at which work is done **Example:** A truck's engine has more *power* than a car's engine.

2. **Quick Check** Review the sentences below. Then circle the sentence that uses the scientific meaning of the word *energy.*

- A puppy has too much *energy* to be inside the house all day.
- A wrecking ball has enough *energy* to knock down a building.

kinetic energy

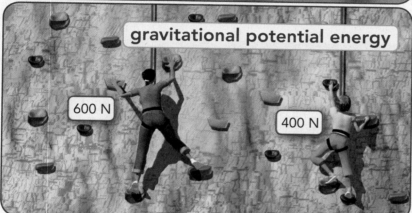

gravitational potential energy

600 N

400 N

mechanical energy

energy transformation

Chapter Preview

LESSON 1
- energy
- kinetic energy
- potential energy
- gravitational potential energy
- elastic potential energy

↻ **Relate Cause and Effect**
△ **Calculate**

LESSON 2
- mechanical energy
- nuclear energy
- thermal energy
- electrical energy
- electromagnetic energy
- chemical energy

↻ **Identify the Main Idea**
△ **Classify**

LESSON 3
- energy transformation
- law of conservation of energy

↻ **Identify Supporting Evidence**
△ **Infer**

> **VOCAB FLASH CARDS** For extra help with vocabulary, visit **Vocab Flash Cards** and type in *Energy.*

What Is Energy?

UNLOCK THE BIG ?

🔑 **How Are Energy, Work, and Power Related?**

🔑 **What Are Two Types of Energy?**

my PLANET DiARY

FUN FACT

Wind Farms

Did you know that wind can be used to produce electricity? A wind farm is a group of very large windmills, or turbines, placed in a location that gets a lot of wind. The energy of the wind causes the propellers of the turbines to spin. The turbines are connected to generators. When the turbines are spinning, the generators produce electricity. The amount of electricity produced depends on the size of the propellers, the number of turbines, and the strength of the wind.

Write your answer to the question below.

Analyze Costs and Benefits What are some advantages and disadvantages of using wind energy to create electricity?

_____
_____
_____
_____
_____
_____
_____

> PLANET DIARY Go to **Planet Diary** to learn more about energy.

 Do the Inquiry Warm-Up *How High Does a Ball Bounce?*

How Are Energy, Work, and Power Related?

Did you put a book in your backpack this morning? If so, then you did work on the book. Recall that work is done when a force moves an object. The ability to do work or cause change is called **energy**.

Work and Energy When you do work on an object, some of your energy is transferred to that object. You can think of work as the transfer of energy. When energy is transferred, the object upon which the work is done gains energy. Energy is measured in joules—the same units as work.

Vocabulary

- energy • kinetic energy • potential energy
- gravitational potential energy • elastic potential energy

Skills

↺ Reading: Relate Cause and Effect

△ Inquiry: Calculate

Power and Energy You may recall that power is the rate at which work is done. **Since the transfer of energy is work, then power is the rate at which energy is transferred, or the amount of energy transferred in a unit of time.**

$$\text{Power} = \frac{\text{Energy Transferred}}{\text{Time}}$$

Different machines have different amounts of power. For example, you could use either a hand shovel or a snowblower, like the one in **Figure 1**, to remove snow from your driveway. Each transfers the same amount of energy when it moves the snow the same distance. However, you could move the snow faster using a snowblower than a hand shovel. The snowblower has more power because it transfers the same amount of energy to the snow in less time.

FIGURE 1 ··········

Power

The snowblower has more power than the person with the hand shovel.

✎ **Apply Concepts** You could use an elevator or the stairs to lift a box to the tenth floor. Which has greater power? Why?

_____

_____

_____

_____

_____

_____

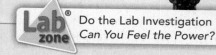

Lab zone ® Do the Lab Investigation *Can You Feel the Power?*

Assess Your Understanding

got it? ···

○ **I get it!** Now I know that since the transfer of energy is work, then power is _____

_____

○ **I need extra help with** _____

Go to my science ⑤ coach *online for help with this subject.*

What Are Two Types of Energy?

Moving objects, such as the vehicles shown in **Figure 2,** have one type of energy. A rock perched on the edge of a cliff or a stretched rubber band has another type of energy. 🔑 **The two basic types of energy are kinetic energy and potential energy.** Whether energy is kinetic or potential depends on the motion, position, and shape of the object.

Kinetic Energy A moving object can do work when it strikes another object and moves it. For example, a swinging hammer does work on a nail as it drives the nail into a piece of wood. The hammer has energy because it can do work. The energy an object has due to its motion is called **kinetic energy.**

Factors Affecting Kinetic Energy The kinetic energy of an object depends on both its speed and its mass. Suppose you are hit with a tennis ball that has been lightly tossed at you. It probably would not hurt much. What if you were hit with the same tennis ball traveling at a much greater speed? It would hurt! The faster an object moves, the more kinetic energy it has.

Kinetic energy also increases as mass increases. Suppose a tennis ball rolls across the ground and hits you in the foot. Compare this with getting hit in the foot with a bowling ball moving at the same speed as the tennis ball. The bowling ball is much more noticeable because it has more kinetic energy than a tennis ball. The bowling ball has more kinetic energy because it has a greater mass.

FIGURE 2 ·······························
> ART IN MOTION **Kinetic Energy**
The kinetic energy of an object depends on its speed and mass.

✏️ **Use the diagram to answer the questions.**

1. **Interpret Diagrams** List the vehicles in order of increasing kinetic energy.

_____

_____

_____

2. **Explain** Describe another example of two objects that have different kinetic energies. Explain why their kinetic energies are different.

_____

_____

_____

_____

_____

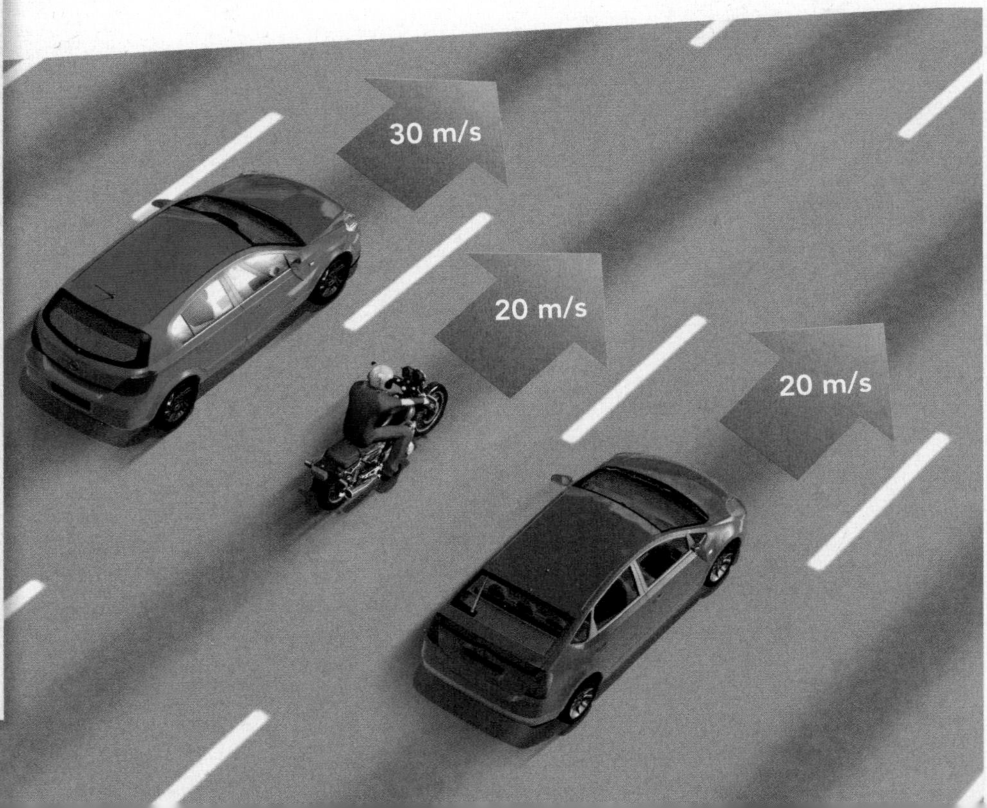

30 m/s

20 m/s

20 m/s

Calculating Kinetic Energy You can use the following equation to solve for the kinetic energy of an object.

$$\text{Kinetic energy} = \tfrac{1}{2} \times \text{Mass} \times \text{Speed}^2$$

For example, suppose a boy is pulling a 10-kg wagon at a speed of 1 m/s.

$$\text{Kinetic energy of wagon} = \tfrac{1}{2} \times 10 \text{ kg} \times (1 \text{ m/s})^2$$

$$= 5 \text{ kg·m}^2/\text{s}^2 = 5 \text{ joules}$$

$$\text{Note that } 1 \text{ kg·m}^2/\text{s}^2 = 1 \text{ joule}$$

Do changes in speed and mass have the same effect on the kinetic energy of the wagon? No—changing the speed of the wagon will have a greater effect on its kinetic energy than changing its mass by the same factor. This is because speed is squared in the kinetic energy equation. For example, doubling the mass of the wagon will double its kinetic energy. Doubling the speed of the wagon will quadruple its kinetic energy.

⟳ Relate Cause and Effect
What has a greater effect on an object's kinetic energy— doubling its mass or doubling its speed? Explain.

_____
_____
_____
_____
_____
_____

do the
math!

A girl and her dog are running. The dog has a mass of 20 kg. The girl has a mass of 60 kg.

1 Calculate Suppose both the dog and the girl run at a speed of 2 m/s. Calculate both of their kinetic energies.

Kinetic energy of dog =

Kinetic energy of girl =

2 Calculate Suppose the dog speeds up and is now running at a speed of 4 m/s. Calculate the dog's kinetic energy.

Kinetic energy of dog =

3 Draw Conclusions Are your answers to Questions 1 and 2 reasonable? Explain.

_____
_____
_____
_____

✏️ **Review** Write the SI unit for each quantity in the table.

Quantity	SI Unit
Force	_____
Height	_____
Work	_____
Mass	_____
Energy	_____

Potential Energy

Potential Energy An object does not have to be moving to have energy. Some objects have energy as a result of their shapes or positions. When you lift a book up to your desk from the floor or compress a spring by winding a toy, you transfer energy to it. The energy you transfer is stored, or held in readiness. It might be used later if the book falls or the spring unwinds. Energy that results from the position or shape of an object is called **potential energy.** This type of energy has the potential to do work.

Gravitational Potential Energy Potential energy related to an object's height is called **gravitational potential energy.** The gravitational potential energy of an object is equal to the work done to lift it to that height. Remember that work is equal to force multiplied by distance. The force you use to lift the object is equal to its weight. The distance you move the object is its height above the ground. You can calculate an object's gravitational potential energy using this equation.

$$\text{Gravitational potential energy} = \text{Weight} \times \text{Height}$$

For example, suppose a book has a weight of 10 newtons (N). If the book is lifted 2 meters off the ground, the book has 10 newtons times 2 meters, or 20 joules, of gravitational potential energy.

FIGURE 3 ·······················

Gravitational Potential Energy

The rock climbers have gravitational potential energy.

✏️ **Use the diagram to answer the questions.**

1. **Identify** Circle the rock climber with the greatest potential energy. Calculate this potential energy. The height to be used is at the rock climber's lowest foot.

_____

_____

_____

_____

2. [CHALLENGE] Where would the rock climbers at the top have to be to have half as much potential energy?

_____

_____

_____

Elastic Potential Energy An object has a different type of potential energy due to its shape. **Elastic potential energy** is the energy associated with objects that can be compressed or stretched. For example, when the girl in **Figure 4** presses down on the trampoline, the trampoline changes shape. The trampoline now has potential energy. When the girl pushes off of the trampoline, the stored energy sends the girl upward.

FIGURE 4 ···

Elastic Potential Energy
The energy stored in a stretched object, such as the trampoline, is elastic potential energy.

✎ **Interpret Diagrams** Rank the amount of elastic potential energy of the trampoline from greatest to least. A ranking of one is the greatest. Write your answers in the circles. Then explain your answers in the space to the right.

Do the Quick Lab *Mass, Velocity, and Kinetic Energy.*

🔑 Assess Your Understanding

1a. Identify The energy an object has due to its motion is called (kinetic/potential) energy. Stored energy that results from the position or shape of an object is called (kinetic/potential) energy.

b. Summarize What are the two factors that affect an object's kinetic energy?

_____

c. Apply Concepts What type of energy does a cup sitting on a table have? Why?

_____

_____

_____

_____

got it? ···

○ **I get it!** Now I know that the two basic types of energy are _____

_____

○ **I need extra help with** _____

Go to MY SCIENCE ⬤ COACH *online for help with this subject.*

Forms of Energy

UNLOCK
THE BIG
?

🔑 **How Can You Find an Object's Mechanical Energy?**

🔑 **What Are Other Forms of Energy?**

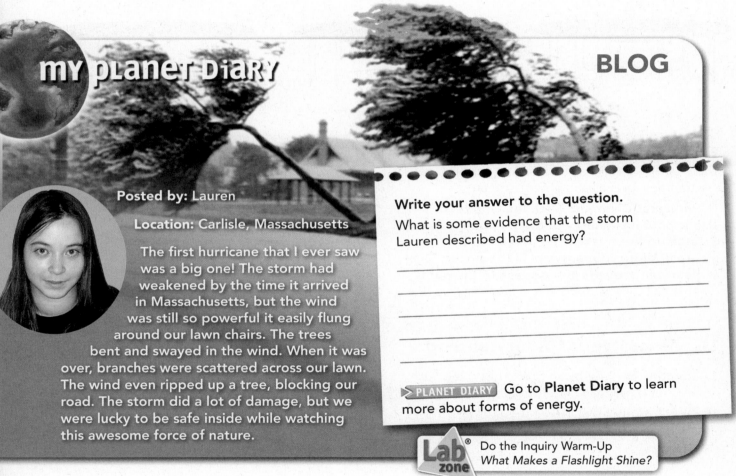

MY PLANET DIARY

BLOG

Posted by: Lauren

Location: Carlisle, Massachusetts

The first hurricane that I ever saw was a big one! The storm had weakened by the time it arrived in Massachusetts, but the wind was still so powerful it easily flung around our lawn chairs. The trees bent and swayed in the wind. When it was over, branches were scattered across our lawn. The wind even ripped up a tree, blocking our road. The storm did a lot of damage, but we were lucky to be safe inside while watching this awesome force of nature.

Write your answer to the question.

What is some evidence that the storm Lauren described had energy?

_____

_____

_____

_____

_____

> PLANET DIARY Go to **Planet Diary** to learn more about forms of energy.

Lab zone® Do the Inquiry Warm-Up
What Makes a Flashlight Shine?

How Can You Find an Object's Mechanical Energy?

What do a falling basketball, a moving car, and a trophy on a shelf all have in common? They all have mechanical energy. The form of energy associated with the motion, position, or shape of an object is called **mechanical energy**.

Vocabulary
- mechanical energy
- electrical energy
- chemical energy
- nuclear energy
- electromagnetic energy
- thermal energy

Skills
- Reading: Identify the Main Idea
- Inquiry: Classify

Calculating Mechanical Energy An object's mechanical energy is a combination of its potential energy and its kinetic energy. For example, the basketball in **Figure 1** has both potential energy and kinetic energy. The higher the basketball moves, the greater its potential energy. The faster the basketball moves, the greater its kinetic energy. You can find an object's mechanical energy by adding together the object's kinetic energy and potential energy.

Mechanical energy = Potential energy + Kinetic energy

Sometimes an object's mechanical energy is its kinetic energy or potential energy only. A car moving along a flat road has kinetic energy only. A trophy resting on a shelf has gravitational potential energy only. But both have mechanical energy.

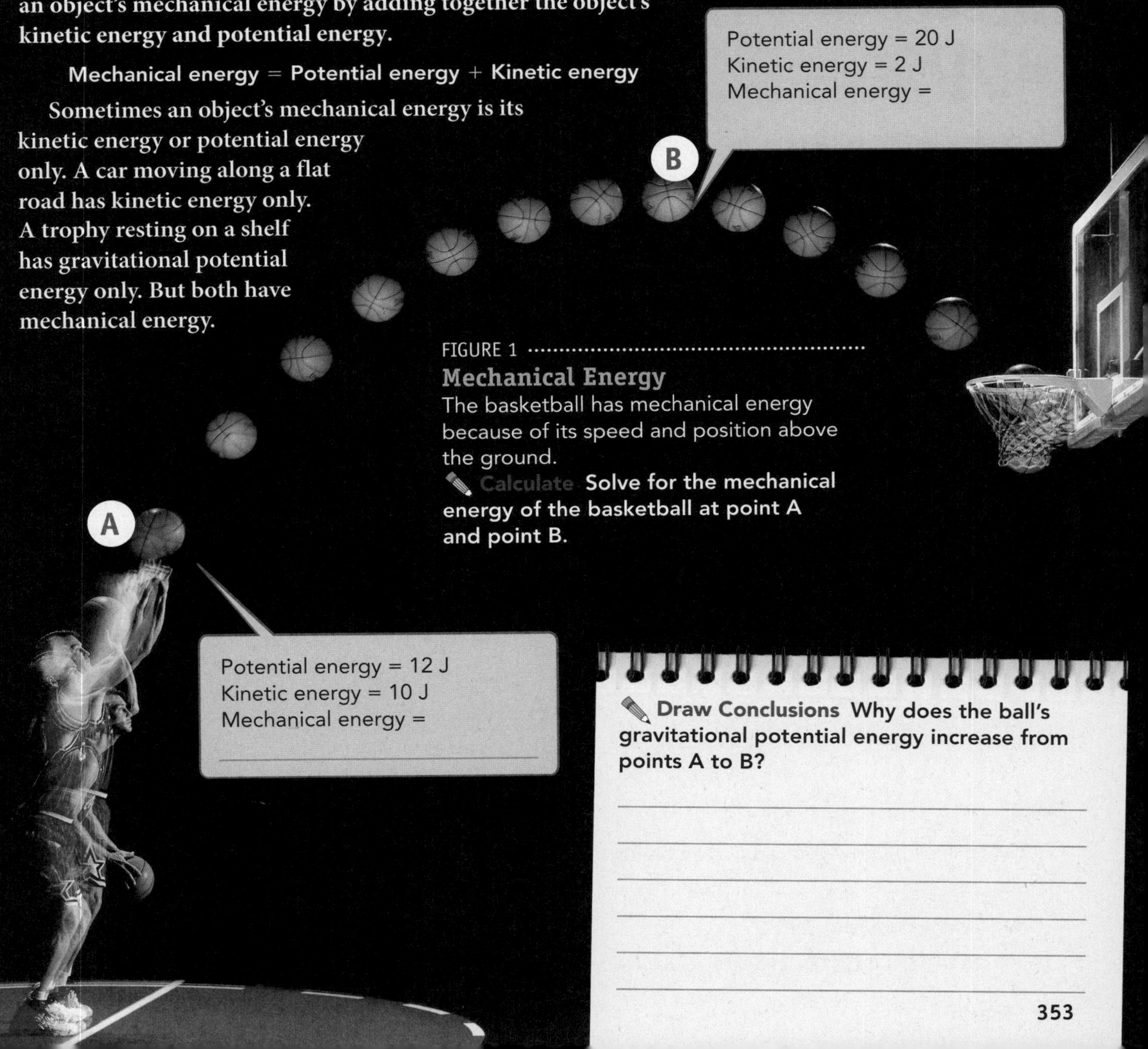

Potential energy = 20 J
Kinetic energy = 2 J
Mechanical energy =

B

A

FIGURE 1

Mechanical Energy
The basketball has mechanical energy because of its speed and position above the ground.

Calculate Solve for the mechanical energy of the basketball at point A and point B.

Potential energy = 12 J
Kinetic energy = 10 J
Mechanical energy =
_____

Draw Conclusions Why does the ball's gravitational potential energy increase from points A to B?

_____
_____
_____
_____

Mechanical Energy and Work An object with mechanical energy can do work on another object. In fact, you can think of mechanical energy, like all forms of energy, as the ability to do work. For example, a basketball does work on the net as it falls through the hoop. The net moves as a result. The more mechanical energy an object has, the more work it can do.

Machines can transfer mechanical energy from one object to another. If you use a crow bar as a lever to pry up a heavy stone, your arms apply mechanical energy to the lever, and the lever transfers that mechanical energy to the stone.

apply it!

The bowling ball does work on the pins when it hits them.

1 Why can the ball do work?

_____

_____

2 How should you throw the ball to maximize the amount of work it does on the pins?

_____

_____

_____

_____

_____

3 [CHALLENGE] The bowling ball in the photo has a mass of 7.0 kg. A candlepin bowling ball has a mass of about 1.0 kg. Does the 7 kg ball always have the greater mechanical energy? Explain.

_____

_____

_____

_____

 Do the Quick Lab *Determining Mechanical Energy.*

Assess Your Understanding

1a. Define Mechanical energy is the form of energy associated with the_____ , _____ , or _____ of an object.

b. Calculate At a certain point the kinetic energy of a falling apple is 5.2 J and its potential energy is 3.5 J. What is its mechanical energy?

_____

c. Infer If an object's mechanical energy is equal to its potential energy, how much kinetic energy does the object have? Explain.

_____

_____

_____

_____

_____

got it?

○ **I get it!** Now I know you can find an object's mechanical energy by _____

_____

○ **I need extra help with** _____

Go to **MY SCIENCE COACH** *online for help with this subject.*

What Are Other Forms of Energy?

So far, you have read about energy that involves the motion, position, or shape of an object. But an object can have other forms of kinetic and potential energy. These other forms are associated with the particles that make up objects. These particles are far too small to see with the naked eye. ⚙ **Forms of energy associated with the particles of objects include nuclear energy, thermal energy, electrical energy, electromagnetic energy, and chemical energy.**

Nuclear Energy All objects are made up of particles called atoms. The region in the center of an atom is called the nucleus. A type of potential energy called **nuclear energy** is stored in the nucleus of an atom. Nuclear energy is released during a nuclear reaction. One kind of nuclear reaction, known as nuclear fission, occurs when a nucleus splits. A nuclear power plant, like the one shown in **Figure 2,** uses fission reactions to produce electricity. Another kind of reaction, known as nuclear fusion, occurs when the nuclei of atoms fuse, or join together. Nuclear fusion reactions occur constantly in the sun, releasing huge amounts of energy. Only a tiny portion of this energy reaches Earth as heat and light.

✏️ **Identify the Main Idea**
Underline the main idea under the red heading Nuclear Energy.

FIGURE 2 ···········
Nuclear Energy
Controlled nuclear fission reactions occur at some power plants. Nuclear fusion reactions occur in the sun.

✏️ **Compare and Contrast** Use the Venn diagram to compare and contrast nuclear fission and nuclear fusion.

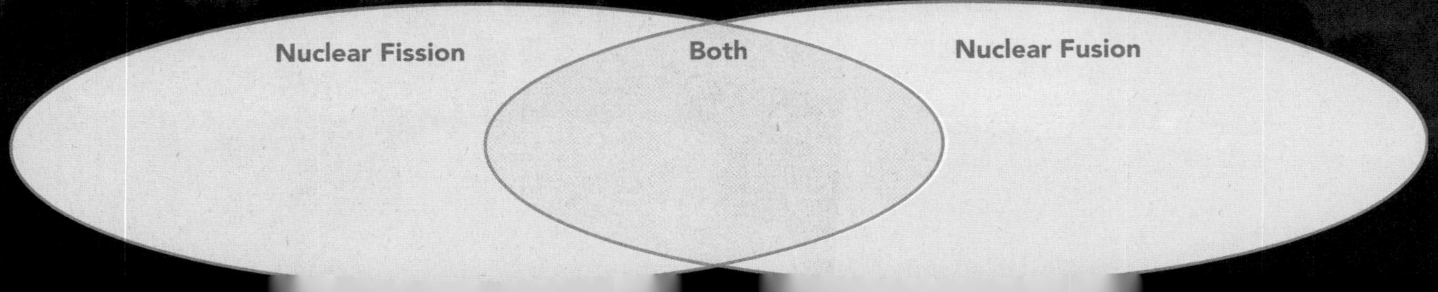

Nuclear Fission   Both   Nuclear Fusion

Thermal Energy

The particles that make up objects are constantly in motion. This means that they have kinetic energy. These particles are arranged in specific ways in different objects, so they also have potential energy. The total kinetic and potential energy of the particles in an object is called **thermal energy.**

The higher the temperature of an object, the more thermal energy the object has. For example, suppose you heat a pot of water. As heat is applied to the water, the particles in the water move faster on average. The faster the particles move, the greater their kinetic energy and the higher the temperature. Therefore, a pot of water at 75°C, for example, has more thermal energy than the same amount of water at 30°C.

Electrical Energy

When you receive a shock from a metal doorknob, you experience electrical energy. The energy of electric charges is **electrical energy.** Depending on whether the charges are moving or stored, electrical energy can be a form of kinetic or potential energy. Lightning is a form of electrical energy. You rely on electrical energy from batteries or electrical lines to run devices such as computers, handheld games, and digital audio players.

FIGURE 3 ·····································

> INTERACTIVE ART **Forms of Energy**

Many objects in this restaurant have more than one form of energy.

✎ **Classify Circle three objects. Describe two forms of energy each object has.**

Electromagnetic Energy

The light you see is one type of electromagnetic energy. **Electromagnetic energy**, also called radiant energy, is a form of energy that travels through space in waves. The source of these waves is vibrating electric charges. These waves do not require a medium, so they can travel through a vacuum, or empty space. This is why you can see the sun and stars.

The microwaves you use to cook your food and the X-rays doctors use to examine patients are also types of electromagnetic energy. Other forms of electromagnetic energy include ultraviolet rays, infrared (or heat) waves, and radio waves. Cell phones send and receive messages using microwaves.

Chemical Energy

Chemical energy is in the foods you eat, in the matches you use to light a candle, and even in the cells of your body. **Chemical energy** is potential energy stored in chemical bonds. Chemical bonds are what hold atoms together. Often when these bonds are broken, this stored energy is released. For example, bonds are broken in your cells and release energy for your body to use.

Vocabulary Identify Multiple Meanings Review the multiple meaning words in the Getting Started section and complete the sentence. During a lightning storm, electric charges move between the clouds and the ground, releasing stored

_____

Lab zone Do the Quick Lab *Sources of Energy.*

🔑 Assess Your Understanding

2a. Explain Why do the particles of objects have both kinetic and potential energy?

_____

_____

_____

_____

_____

_____

_____

b. Classify The energy you get from eating a peanut butter and jelly sandwich is in the form of _____ energy.

got it?

○ **I get it!** Now I know the forms of energy associated with the particles of objects include _____

_____

_____

○ **I need extra help with** _____

Go to **my science ⑤ coach** *online for help with this subject.*

357

Energy Transformations and Conservation

How Are Different Forms of Energy Related?

What Is the Law of Conservation of Energy?

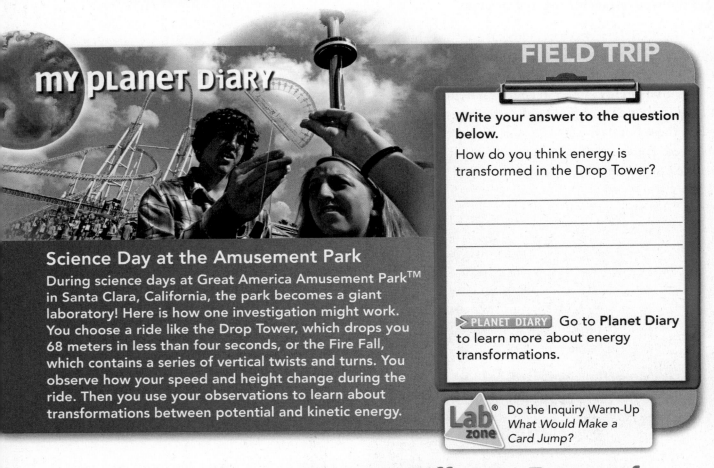

my planet Diary

Science Day at the Amusement Park

During science days at Great America Amusement Park™ in Santa Clara, California, the park becomes a giant laboratory! Here is how one investigation might work. You choose a ride like the Drop Tower, which drops you 68 meters in less than four seconds, or the Fire Fall, which contains a series of vertical twists and turns. You observe how your speed and height change during the ride. Then you use your observations to learn about transformations between potential and kinetic energy.

FIELD TRIP

Write your answer to the question below.

How do you think energy is transformed in the Drop Tower?

_____

_____

_____

_____

_____

> PLANET DIARY Go to **Planet Diary** to learn more about energy transformations.

Lab® Do the Inquiry Warm-Up
zone *What Would Make a Card Jump?*

How Are Different Forms of Energy Related?

What does flowing water have to do with electricity? In a hydro-electric power plant, the mechanical energy of moving water is transformed into electrical energy. **All forms of energy can be transformed into other forms of energy.** A change from one form of energy to another is called an **energy transformation**. Some energy changes involve single transformations, while others involve many transformations.

Vocabulary
- energy transformation
- law of conservation of energy

Skills
- ⊙ Reading: Identify Supporting Evidence
- △ Inquiry: Infer

Single Transformations Sometimes, one form of energy needs to be transformed into another to get work done. For example, a toaster transforms electrical energy to thermal energy to toast your bread. A cell phone transforms electrical energy to electromagnetic energy that travels to other phones.

Your body transforms the chemical energy in food to the mechanical energy you need to move your muscles. Chemical energy in food is also transformed to the thermal energy your body uses to maintain its temperature.

Multiple Transformations Often, a series of energy transformations is needed to do work. In a car engine, a series of energy conversions occurs. Electrical energy produces a spark. The thermal energy of the spark releases chemical energy in the fuel.

The chemical energy in the fuel originated with nuclear reactions within the sun that reached Earth as electromagnetic energy. Plants transformed the energy in sunlight into chemical energy, which was stored in the fossilized remains of living organisms that made up the fuel. As the fuel burns, it expands as it is broken down into smaller particles. The expansion of the fuel produces pressure on parts of the car. The increased pressure eventually causes the wheels to turn, transforming chemical energy into mechanical energy.

⊙ **Identify Supporting Evidence**
Underline the energy transformation that must occur for you to talk on your cell phone.

apply it!

A series of energy transformations must occur for you to ride your bike. Write the forms of energy involved in each transformation.

Reactions occur within the sun to transform _____ energy into _____ energy.

Plants transform _____ energy into _____ energy.

Your body transforms _____ energy into _____ energy to maintain your body temperature.

Your body also transforms _____ energy into _____ energy when you ride your bike.

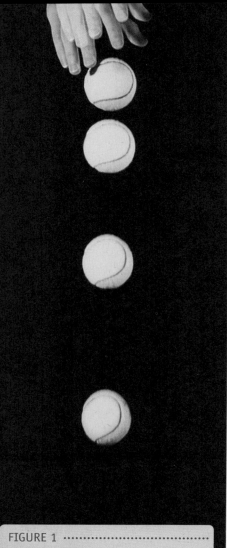

Kinetic and Potential Energy

The transformation between potential and kinetic energy is one of the most common energy transformations. For example, when you stretch a rubber band, you give it elastic potential energy. If you let it go, the rubber band flies across the room. When the rubber band is moving, it has kinetic energy. The potential energy of the stretched rubber has transformed to the kinetic energy of the moving rubber band. Transformations between kinetic and potential energy can also occur in any object that rises or falls. A falling object, a pendulum, and a pole vault are all examples of these transformations.

Falling Object A transformation between potential and kinetic energy occurs in the ball in **Figure 1.** As the height of the ball decreases, it loses potential energy. At the same time, its kinetic energy increases because its speed increases. Its potential energy is transformed into kinetic energy.

Pendulum A pendulum like the one in **Figure 2** swings back and forth. At the highest point in its swing, the pendulum has no movement. As it swings downward, it speeds up. The pendulum is at its greatest speed at the bottom of its swing. As the pendulum swings to the other side, its height increases and its speed decreases. At the top of its swing, it comes to a stop again.

FIGURE 1 ·····································
Falling Ball
The ball was photographed at equal time intervals as it fell.

✎ **Interpret Photos** How can you tell that the ball's kinetic energy is increasing?

_____

_____

_____

_____

_____

_____

FIGURE 2 ·····································
▶ INTERACTIVE ART **Pendulum**
A continuous transformation between potential and kinetic energy occurs in a pendulum. ✎ **Interpret Diagrams** Label the type of energy the pendulum has at positions A, B, and C.

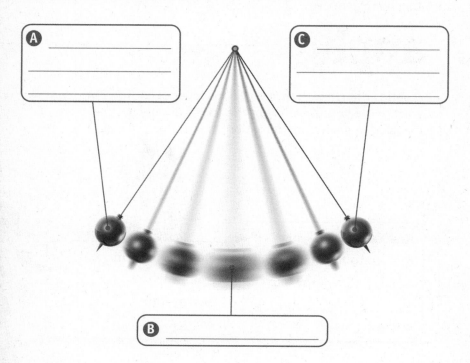

Ⓐ _____

Ⓒ _____

Ⓑ _____

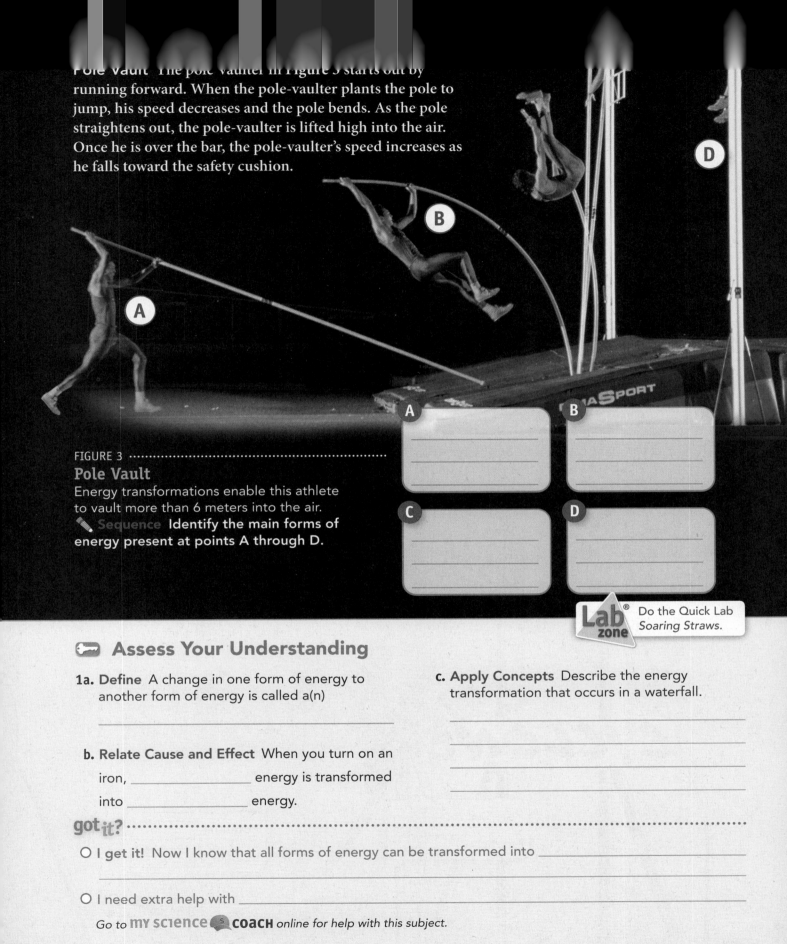

Pole Vault The pole-vaulter in Figure 3 starts out by running forward. When the pole-vaulter plants the pole to jump, his speed decreases and the pole bends. As the pole straightens out, the pole-vaulter is lifted high into the air. Once he is over the bar, the pole-vaulter's speed increases as he falls toward the safety cushion.

FIGURE 3 ··
Pole Vault
Energy transformations enable this athlete to vault more than 6 meters into the air.

✎ Sequence **Identify the main forms of energy present at points A through D.**

A

B

C

D

Lab® **Do the Quick Lab**
zone *Soaring Straws.*

🔑 Assess Your Understanding

1a. Define A change in one form of energy to another form of energy is called a(n)

_____

b. Relate Cause and Effect When you turn on an iron, _____ energy is transformed into _____ energy.

c. Apply Concepts Describe the energy transformation that occurs in a waterfall.

_____

_____

_____

_____

got it? ···

○ **I get it!** Now I know that all forms of energy can be transformed into _____

_____

○ **I need extra help with** _____

Go to MY SCIENCE ⓢ COACH *online for help with this subject.*

What Is the Law of Conservation of Energy?

Once you set a pendulum in motion, does it swing forever? No, it does not. Then what happens to its energy? Is the energy destroyed? Again, the answer is no. The **law of conservation of energy** states that when one form of energy is transformed to another, no energy is lost in the process. 🔑 **According to the law of conservation of energy, energy cannot be created or destroyed.** The total amount of energy is the same before and after any transformation. If you add up all of the new forms of energy after a transformation, all of the original energy will be accounted for. So what happens to the energy of the pendulum once it stops moving?

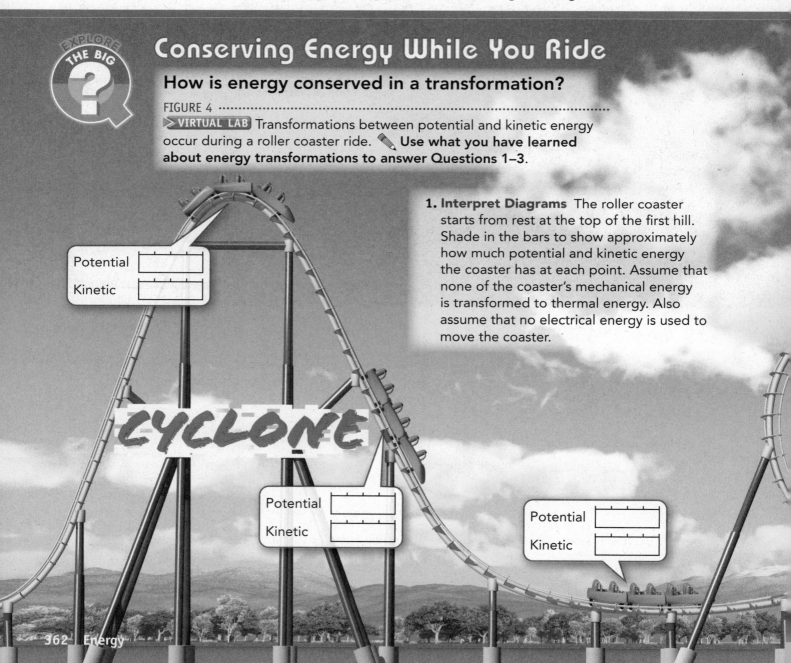

EXPLORE THE BIG ?

Conserving Energy While You Ride

How is energy conserved in a transformation?

FIGURE 4

> VIRTUAL LAB Transformations between potential and kinetic energy occur during a roller coaster ride. ✏️ **Use what you have learned about energy transformations to answer Questions 1–3.**

1. **Interpret Diagrams** The roller coaster starts from rest at the top of the first hill. Shade in the bars to show approximately how much potential and kinetic energy the coaster has at each point. Assume that none of the coaster's mechanical energy is transformed to thermal energy. Also assume that no electrical energy is used to move the coaster.

Potential
Kinetic

CYCLONE

Potential
Kinetic

Potential
Kinetic

As the pendulum swings, it encounters friction at the pivot of the string and from the air through which it moves. Whenever a moving object experiences friction, some of its kinetic energy is transformed into thermal energy. So the mechanical energy of the pendulum is not destroyed. It is transformed to thermal energy.

The fact that friction transforms mechanical energy to thermal energy should not surprise you. After all, you take advantage of such thermal energy when you rub your cold hands together to warm them up. Friction is also the reason why no machine is 100 percent efficient. You may recall that the output work of any real machine is always less than the input work. This reduced efficiency occurs because some mechanical energy is always transformed into thermal energy due to friction.

did you know?

When ancient animals and plants died, the chemical energy they had stored was trapped within their remains. This trapped energy is the chemical energy found in coal.

2. **Infer** Suppose you had taken thermal energy into account in Step 1. Would the total length of the shaded portion of the bars increase, decrease, or stay the same as as result?

   ○ Increase   ○ Decrease   ○ Stay the same

3. **[CHALLENGE]** Why is the first hill of a roller coaster always the tallest?

_____

_____

_____

_____

Potential [ ]

Kinetic [ ]

Potential [ ]

Kinetic [ ]

Lab zone ®   Do the Quick Lab
Law of Conservation of Energy.

Assess Your Understanding

2. **ANSWER THE BIG ?** How is energy conserved in a transformation?

_____

_____

_____

_____

_____

got it? ....

○ **I get it!** Now I know that according to the law of conservation of energy, energy _____

_____

○ **I need extra help with** _____

   Go to **my science** ⑤ **coach** *online for help with this subject.*

10 Study Guide

The total amount of _____ is the same before and after any transformation.

LESSON 1 What Is Energy?

🔑 Since the transfer of energy is work, then power is the rate at which energy is transferred, or the amount of energy transferred in a unit of time.

🔑 The two basic types of energy are kinetic energy and potential energy.

Vocabulary
- energy
- kinetic energy
- potential energy
- gravitational potential energy
- elastic potential energy

LESSON 2 Forms of Energy

🔑 You can find an object's mechanical energy by adding together the object's kinetic energy and potential energy.

🔑 Forms of energy associated with the particles of objects include nuclear energy, thermal energy, electrical energy, electromagnetic energy, and chemical energy.

Vocabulary
- mechanical energy
- electrical energy
- chemical energy
- nuclear energy
- electromagnetic energy
- thermal energy

LESSON 3 Energy Transformations and Conservation

🔑 All forms of energy can be transformed into other forms of energy.

🔑 According to the law of conservation of energy, energy cannot be created or destroyed.

Vocabulary
- energy transformation
- law of conservation of energy

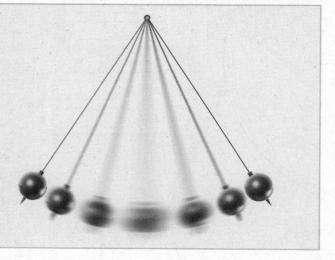

Review and Assessment

What Is Energy?

1. When you stretch a rubber band, you give it
   a. kinetic energy.   **b.** electrical energy.
   c. potential energy.   **d.** chemical energy.

2. To calculate power, divide the amount of energy transferred by _____

3. **Compare and Contrast** In the illustration below, which vehicle has the greatest kinetic energy? Explain your answer.

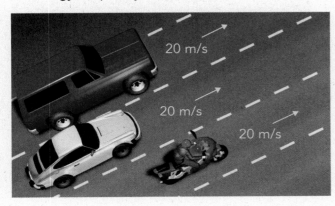

20 m/s

20 m/s

20 m/s

_____

_____

_____

4. **Apply Concepts** If a handsaw does the same amount of work on a log as a chainsaw does, which has more power? Why?

_____

_____

_____

_____

_____

5. **math!** A 1,350-kg car travels at 12 m/s. What is its kinetic energy?

_____

_____

_____

Forms of Energy

6. What is the energy stored in the nucleus of an atom called?
   a. electrical energy   **b.** chemical energy
   c. thermal energy   **d.** nuclear energy

7. An object's mechanical energy is the sum of its

_____

8. **Classify** When you heat a pot of water over a flame, what form of energy is added to the water?

_____

The graph shows the kinetic energy of a 500-N diver during a dive from a 10-m platform. Use the graph to answer Questions 9 and 10.

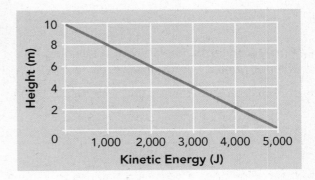

9. **Read Graphs** How does the diver's kinetic energy change as the diver falls? Why?

_____

_____

_____

10. **Calculate** What is the diver's gravitational potential energy just before the dive?

_____

_____

_____

LESSON 3 Energy Transformations and Conservation

11. As a car skids to a stop, friction transforms kinetic energy to

a. thermal energy. b. potential energy.

c. chemical energy. d. electrical energy.

12. The law of conservation of energy states that

_____

_____

_____

_____

13. Classify Describe the energy transformation that occurs in a digital clock.

_____

_____

_____

14. Apply Concepts Explain why a spinning top will not remain in motion forever.

_____

_____

_____

15. Infer Why does a bouncing ball rise to a lower height with each bounce?

_____

_____

_____

_____

_____

16. Write About It An eagle flies from its perch in a tree to the ground to capture and eat its prey. Describe its energy transformations.

 APPLY THE BIG ? **How is energy conserved in a transformation?**

17. The golfer in the photo is taking a swing. The golf club starts at point A and ends at point E. (1) Describe the energy transformations of the club from points A to E. (2) The kinetic energy of the club at point C is more than the potential energy of the club at point B. Does this mean that the law of conservation of energy is violated? Why or why not?

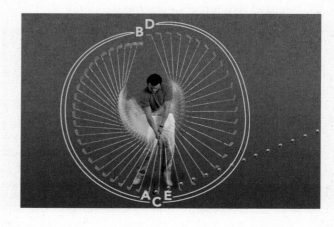

_____

_____

_____

_____

_____

_____

_____

_____

_____

_____

_____

_____

Standardized Test Prep

Multiple Choice

Circle the letter of the best answer.

1. The table gives the kinetic and potential energy of a 6-kg cat doing various activities.

Activity	Kinetic Energy (J)	Potential Energy (J)
Running	200	0
Leaping	150	100
Climbing a tree	3	300
Sleeping on a chair	0	30

During which activity does the cat have the greatest mechanical energy?

A climbing a tree **B** leaping
C running **D** sleeping on a chair

2. Why does wind have energy?

A It can change direction.
B It can do work.
C It moves through space as waves.
D It is electrically charged.

3. A gardener uses a wheelbarrow to haul a load of mulch. How does the wheelbarrow transfer energy to the mulch?

A The wheelbarrow applies potential energy to the mulch.
B The mulch applies gravitational force to the wheelbarrow.
C The gardener uses chemical energy to move the wheelbarrow.
D The wheelbarrow transfers energy of motion to the mulch.

4. Why does a pendulum eventually slow down and stop swinging?

A Friction transforms some of the mechanical energy to thermal energy.
B Kinetic energy changes to potential energy.
C Gravity pulls the pendulum toward Earth's center.
D Potential energy changes to kinetic energy.

5. Which energy transformation takes place when wood is burned?

A Nuclear energy is transformed to thermal energy.
B Thermal energy is transformed to electrical energy.
C Chemical energy is transformed to thermal energy.
D Mechanical energy is transformed to thermal energy.

Constructed Response

Use the table below to answer Question 6. Write your answer on a separate sheet of paper.

Time	Speed at Bottom of Swing (m/s)
8:00 a.m.	2.2
10:00 a.m.	1.9
12:00 p.m.	1.7
2:00 p.m.	1.6

6. A large pendulum at a science museum is set in motion at the beginning of the day. The table shows how its speed at the bottom of the swing changes during the day. Use this data to determine how the height of the pendulum's swing changes. Explain your answer.

CHARGE IT!

Have you ever noticed how many batteries you use every day? There are batteries in cars, flashlights, cell phones, laptop computers, and even bug zappers! Discarded batteries add up to a lot of waste. Fortunately, rechargeable batteries can help keep the energy flowing and reduce the number of batteries that get thrown out. Can you imagine how many nonrechargeable batteries a cell phone would go through in a month?

Batteries transform chemical energy into electrical energy. To refuel a rechargeable battery, you plug it into a power source— such as an outlet in the wall. The electrical energy reverses the chemical changes, storing the electrical energy as chemical energy. The battery is once again "charged up" and ready to go!

Research It Gasoline-powered cars and hybrid cars have rechargeable batteries. Research how the batteries in gasoline-powered cars and hybrid cars are recharged.

Top Cap
(Positive Terminal)

Cathode Tab

Separator

Steel Can
(Negative Terminal)

Anode

Cathode

Anode Tab

▲ The inside of this rechargeable battery has three long thin layers. A separator separates a positive electrode from a negative electrode. Using the battery causes lithium ions to move from the positive material to the negative one. Applying an electrical charge moves the ions back to the positive electrode.

Museum of Science.

Power It Up!

When you turn on the TV, are you using solar energy for power? You may be surprised to learn that the answer is probably "Yes (at least, technically)!" Almost 85 percent of the energy we use comes from fossil fuels—oil, coal, or natural gas. When these fuels are burned, they release solar energy that was stored in them millions of years ago as plants and animals decayed. Fossil fuels are easy to use and reliable. The problem is, they're also nonrenewable. That means they are in limited supply and will one day be used up.

The sun is the source of other energy resources. Weather is influenced by the sun. Changes in weather result in wind and water movement. Both wind and moving water can turn turbines to make electricity. The sun provides the energy for plants to grow, producing biomass, an energy source that can be burned like fossil fuels. These resources are known as renewable energy sources. They will never be used up, or they can be replaced quickly.

Some fuels don't originate with the sun. There are more than 100 nuclear power plants in the United States. In these power plants, the decay of radioactive atoms produces great amounts of energy. But the use of nuclear power is not increasing. Many people fear accidents, and these power plants also produce dangerous radioactive waste. Geothermal energy comes from Earth's interior. This renewable source of energy is nonpolluting and will never run out. But it is only economical to generate electricity in areas where magma heats rock or water near Earth's surface.

Research It How much energy do you use in a day, and what are the sources of this energy? Keep a log of one day of your personal energy use. Write down everything—from running your computer (electricity from a plant that burns coal?) to your hot shower (solar collectors on your roof?) to your bus ride to school (diesel fuel from petroleum?). Compare your log with others' logs in class. Are most of your energy needs met with renewable or nonrenewable sources? How do you think this might change in the future?

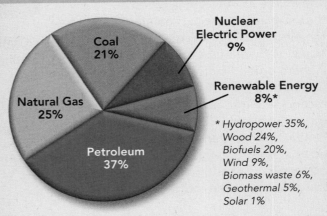

Where Our Energy Comes From

Coal 21%

Nuclear Electric Power 9%

Natural Gas 25%

Renewable Energy 8%*

Petroleum 37%

* Hydropower 35%,
Wood 24%,
Biofuels 20%,
Wind 9%,
Biomass waste 6%,
Geothermal 5%,
Solar 1%

▲ Today, renewable sources supply only about 8 percent of our energy needs. That's a fraction of the energy we use, but the percentage is gradually increasing.
Source: U.S. Energy Information Administration

WHAT
MIGHT THESE
COLORS
MEAN?

 How does heat flow from one object to another?

The image at the right is called a thermogram. A special camera measures the electromagnetic radiation of an object and creates a temperature "map." A thermographic camera can be used to find people in a fire, detect when a racehorse might be injured, and spot tumors in humans. By noticing excessive heat in motors, transformers, and pumps, the camera can detect equipment problems before they fail, saving millions of dollars. **Infer Since a thermogram shows temperature, what might the colors you see indicate?**

_____

_____

_____

_____

> **UNTAMED SCIENCE** Watch the **Untamed Science** video to learn more about heat.

Thermal Energy and Heat

Check Your Understanding

1. Background Read the paragraph below and then answer the question.

Kiera is swimming in the ocean. Since she is moving, she has **kinetic energy.** Energy is measured in **joules.** Her brother, who swims at the same speed but has more mass, has more kinetic energy. If he slows down, he will have the same amount of kinetic energy as Kiera. While swimming, she notices that it is easier to float in salt water because it has a higher **density** than fresh water.

Kinetic energy is energy an object has due to its motion.

A **joule** is a unit of work equal to one newton-meter.

Density is the ratio of the mass of a substance to its volume.

• What are the two ways you can increase kinetic energy?

_____

▶ MY READING WEB If you had trouble completing the question above, visit **My Reading Web** and type in *Thermal Energy and Heat.*

Vocabulary Skill

Identify Multiple Meanings Some words have several meanings. Words you use every day may have different meanings in science.

Word	Everyday Meaning	Scientific Meaning
conductor	*n.* the director of an orchestra **Example:** The *conductor* signaled to the musicians to begin playing.	*n.* a material that conducts heat well **Example:** Metal is a good *conductor.*
heat	*v.* to make warm or hot **Example:** The fireplace began to *heat* the room.	*n.* thermal energy moving from a warmer object to a cooler object **Example:** When the door was left open, *heat* transferred from the warm room to the cool air outside.

2. Quick Check Circle the sentence below that uses the scientific meaning of the word *conductor.*

• The *conductor* got a standing ovation after the concert.

• It is easier to cook eggs in a pan that is a good *conductor.*

MON	TUES	WED
25°	26°	temperature 24°
18°	19°	17°

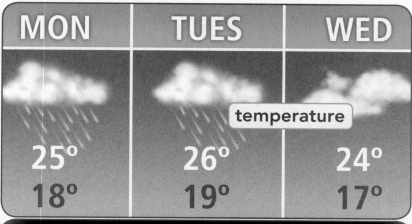

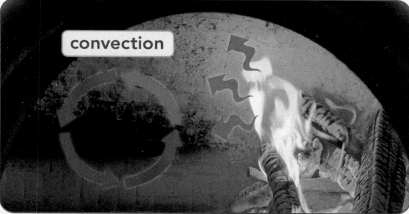

convection

radiation

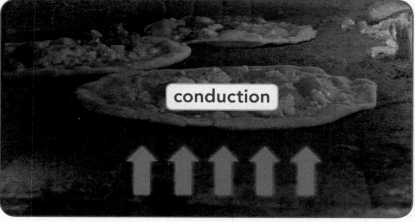

conduction

Chapter Preview

LESSON 1
- temperature
- Fahrenheit scale
- Celsius scale
- Kelvin scale
- absolute zero
- heat

↻ **Identify Supporting Evidence**
△ **Communicate**

LESSON 2
- convection
- convection current
- radiation
- conduction

↻ **Compare and Contrast**
△ **Infer**

LESSON 3
- conductor
- insulator
- specific heat
- thermal expansion

↻ **Identify the Main Idea**
△ **Calculate**

▶ VOCAB FLASH CARDS For extra help with vocabulary, visit **Vocab Flash Cards** and type in *Thermal Energy and Heat.*

Temperature, Thermal Energy, and Heat

LESSON 1

UNLOCK THE BIG Q?

🗝 **What Determines the Temperature of an Object?**

🗝 **What Is Thermal Energy?**

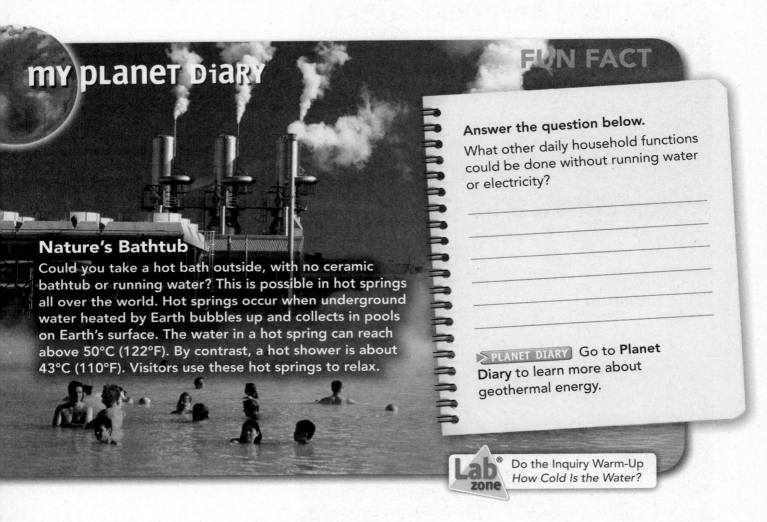

MY PLANET DIARY

FUN FACT

Nature's Bathtub

Could you take a hot bath outside, with no ceramic bathtub or running water? This is possible in hot springs all over the world. Hot springs occur when underground water heated by Earth bubbles up and collects in pools on Earth's surface. The water in a hot spring can reach above 50°C (122°F). By contrast, a hot shower is about 43°C (110°F). Visitors use these hot springs to relax.

Answer the question below.

What other daily household functions could be done without running water or electricity?

_____

_____

_____

_____

_____

> PLANET DIARY Go to **Planet Diary** to learn more about geothermal energy.

Lab zone Do the Inquiry Warm-Up *How Cold Is the Water?*

What Determines the Temperature of an Object?

You may have used a thermometer to take your temperature when you were sick. **Temperature** is a measure of how hot or cold something is compared to a reference point. (One reference point is the freezing point of water.) What makes an object hot or cold?

Vocabulary

- temperature
- Celsius scale
- absolute zero
- Fahrenheit scale
- Kelvin scale
- heat

Skills

- **Reading:** Identify Supporting Evidence
- **Inquiry:** Communicate

Recall that all moving objects have kinetic energy. Matter is made up of tiny particles that are always moving, so these particles have kinetic energy. **Temperature is a measure of the average kinetic energy of the particles in an object.** As an object heats up, its particles move faster. As a result, both the average kinetic energy of the particles and the temperature increase.

The United States uses the **Fahrenheit scale** to measure temperature. Most countries use the **Celsius scale.** You can use an equation to convert between scales, but it's simpler to estimate using thermometers like the one in **Figure 1.** Temperatures that line up, like 32°F and 0°C, are equivalent. Many scientists use the **Kelvin scale.** Celsius and Fahrenheit scales are divided into degrees. The Kelvin scale is divided into kelvins (K). A temperature change of 1 K is the same temperature change as 1°C. Zero kelvins, or **absolute zero,** is the lowest temperature possible. At absolute zero, particles have no kinetic energy. Zero K is equal to −273°C.

did you know?

When Anders Celsius invented the Celsius scale, he had 100°C as the *freezing* point of water and 0°C as its *boiling* point.

MON	TUES	WED	THURS	FRI
25°	26°	24°	25°	24°
18°	19°	17°	17°	18°

FIGURE 1 ....

> ART IN MOTION **Temperature Scales**

The chart above shows a weather report, but it does not identify the temperature scale.

✎ **Interpret Diagrams** Explain why this report would mean something different in Japan than it would in the United States. Fill in the thermometer to show one of the temperatures in Celsius. What is this equivalent to in Fahrenheit?

_____

_____

_____

_____

_____

 Lab zone Do the Lab Investigation
Build Your Own Thermometer.

🔑 Assess Your Understanding

got it? ....

○ **I get it!** Now I know that temperature is related to _____

_____

○ **I need extra help with** _____

Go to **my science** ⓢ **coach** online for help with *this subject.*

What Is Thermal Energy?

Different objects at the same temperature can have different amounts of energy. To understand this, you need to know about thermal energy and about heat. Temperature, thermal energy, and heat are closely related, but they are not the same thing.

Thermal Energy Temperature is a measure of the average kinetic energy of the individual particles in an object. However, it is not a measure of the total amount of energy in an object. **Thermal energy is the total energy of all the particles in an object.** It depends on the temperature of an object, the number of particles in it, and how those particles are arranged. This lesson will focus on the first two factors.

The more particles an object has at a given temperature, the more thermal energy it has. For example, a 1-liter pot of tea at 75°C has more thermal energy than a 0.2-liter mug of tea at 75°C because the pot contains more tea particles. On the other hand, the higher the temperature of an object, the more thermal energy the object has. Therefore, if two 1-liter pots of tea have different temperatures, the pot with the higher temperature has more thermal energy.

⟲ **Identify Supporting Evidence** Since thermal energy is the total energy of all the particles in an object, it depends on multiple factors. Underline sentences that support this idea.

apply it!

The total amount of thermal energy an object has depends on its temperature and how many particles it contains.

❶ **Identify** In the top two panels, circle the chicken pot pie that contains more thermal energy.

❷ **Apply Concepts** In the last panel, draw in and record the temperature of three pies that have more thermal energy than the one on the left.

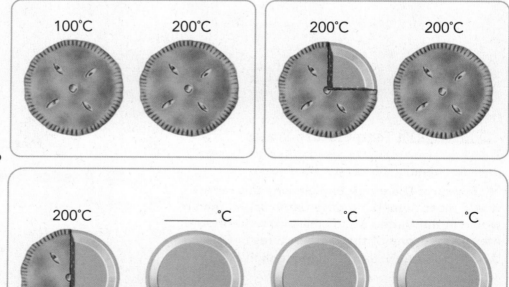

100°C   200°C   200°C   200°C

200°C   _____°C   _____°C   _____°C

Heat You might say that an object contains heat, but, strictly speaking, it does not. Objects contain thermal energy. **Heat** is the *transfer* of thermal energy from a warmer object to a cooler object. The warmer object will cool down, and the cooler object will warm up until they are the same temperature. When this happens, heat stops transferring. Heat is measured in the units of energy—joules.

Vocabulary Write a sentence that uses the scientific meaning of *heat*.

_____

_____

_____

FIGURE 2 ····································

▶ VIRTUAL LAB **Heat**
When you hold your hand over a plate of food, you will feel warmth if heat transfers into you and cold if heat transfers out of you.

✏ **Communicate** In the photo, draw arrows to show the direction of heat transfer for at least two foods. Would your hand feel warmer over some foods than over others? What characteristics of the food might affect how warm or cold your hand feels? Discuss your ideas with a partner.

_____

_____

_____

Lab zone ® Do the Quick Lab *Temperature and Thermal Energy.*

🔑 **Assess Your Understanding**

1a. List What are two factors that determine an object's thermal energy?

_____

_____

b. CHALLENGE Object A has less thermal energy than Object B, but heat flows from Object A to Object B. What conditions would make this possible?

_____

_____

_____

got it?

○ **I get it!** Now I know that the thermal energy in an object is defined as _____

_____

_____

_____

○ **I need extra help with** _____

Go to **MY SCIENCE** ⓢ **COACH** online for help with this subject.

377

The Transfer of Heat

🔑 How Is Heat Transferred?

my planeT DiaRY

DISASTER

Wild Weather

Hurricanes are intense storms that can cause billions of dollars in damage. These storms form when very warm, moist air rises quickly, creating an area of lower air pressure below. As the air rises, the water vapor in the air condenses, releasing a huge amount of thermal energy. This energy causes swirling winds, which draw in more warm water, feeding the storm. If a hurricane's path takes it over land, the storm can cause massive destruction. However, as the storm moves over land, its energy source—the warm ocean water—is depleted, and the storm eventually fizzles out.

Answer the question below.
Why do hurricanes tend to form in warmer climates?

_____

_____

_____

_____

_____

_____

> PLANET DIARY Go to **Planet Diary** to learn more about hurricanes.

Lab zone® Do the Inquiry Warm-Up *What Does It Mean to Heat Up?*

How Is Heat Transferred?

Heat is transferring around you all the time. If it wasn't, nothing would ever change temperature. Heat doesn't transfer randomly. It travels only in one direction and by three different methods. 🔑 **Heat is transferred from warmer areas to cooler areas by conduction, convection, and radiation.**

Vocabulary
- convection
- convection current
- radiation
- conduction

Skills
⟳ **Reading:** Compare and Contrast
△ **Inquiry:** Infer

Convection

Convection is a type of heat transfer that occurs only in fluids, such as water and air. When air is heated, its particles speed up and move farther apart. This makes the heated air less dense. The heated air rises to float on top of the denser, cooler air. Cooler air flows into its place, heats up, and rises. Previously heated air cools down, sinks, and the cycle repeats. This flow creates a circular motion known as a **convection current.** Convection currents in air cause wind and weather changes.

Radiation

Radiation is the transfer of energy by electromagnetic waves. Radiation is the only form of heat transfer that does not require matter. You can feel the radiation from a fire without touching the flames. The sun's energy travels to Earth through 150 million kilometers of empty space.

Conduction

Conduction transfers heat from one particle of matter to another within an object or between two objects. The fast-moving particles in the floor of the oven collide with the slow-moving particles in the uncooked pizza. This causes the pizza's particles to move faster, making the pizza hotter.

FIGURE 1 ....

Heat Transfer

A wood-fire pizza oven demonstrates three types of heat transfer.

✎ **Apply Concepts** Describe a heat transfer that occurs after the pizza comes out of the oven. What kind of transfer is it?

_____

_____

⟳ **Compare and Contrast** Circle statements on the previous page that describe what the different types of heat transfer have in common. Underline their differences on this page.

379

EXPLORE THE BIG Q

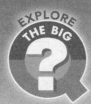

Where Does Heat Transfer on This Beach?

How does heat flow from one object to another?

FIGURE 2

INTERACTIVE ART Heat transfer goes on all around you all the time, even on the beach. **Apply Concepts Fill in the chart below to review the different types of heat transfer. Then, in the illustration, label at least one example of each type of heat transfer. Draw arrows to show how heat is being transferred in each example.**

Type of Heat Transfer	Explanation
Conduction	
Convection	
Radiation	

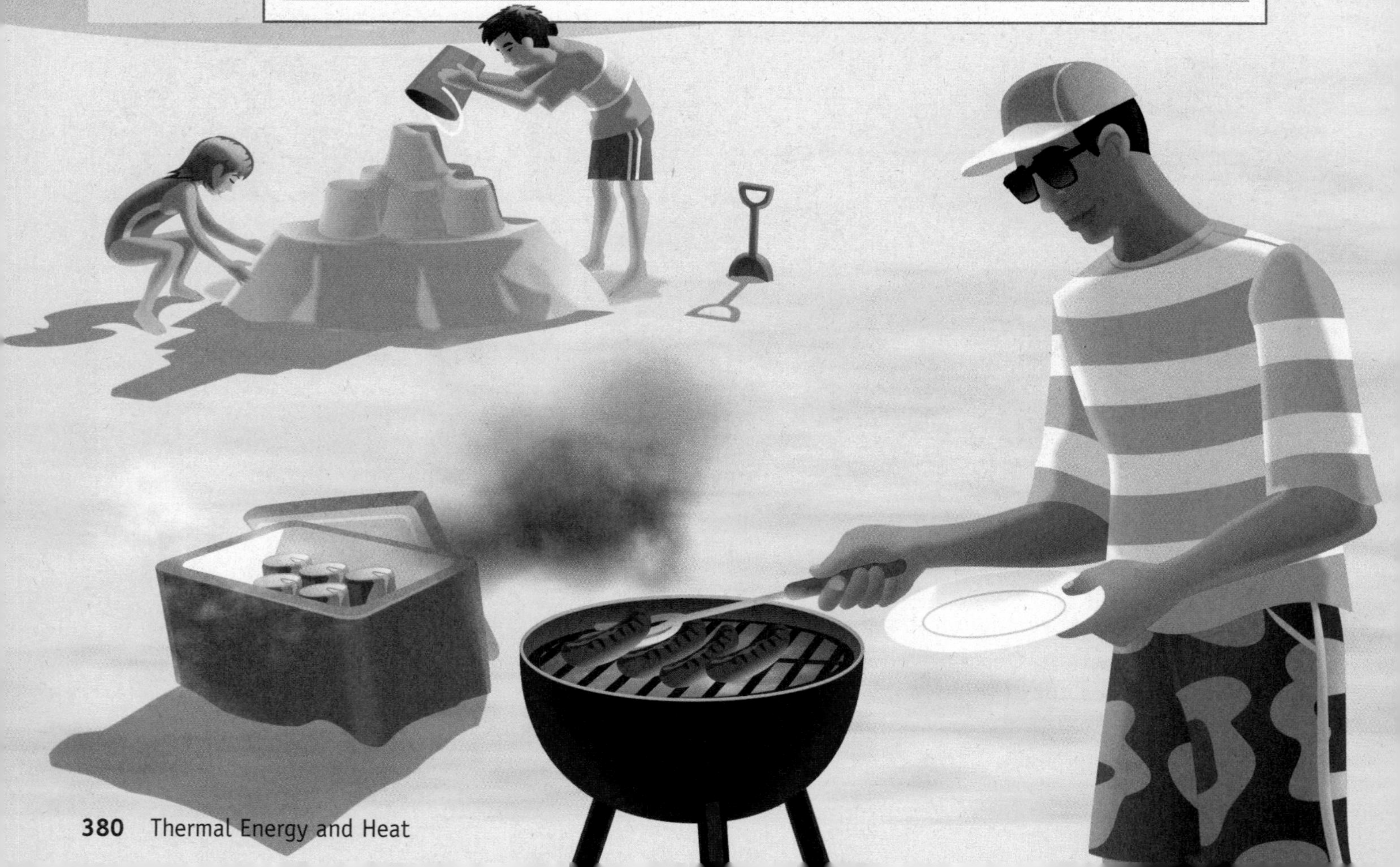

Cooking pots come in a variety of shapes and sizes, but you're much more likely to see a wide, squat pot like this

than a tall, narrow pot like this.

Infer Use conduction to explain why this is the case.

_____
_____
_____
_____
_____
_____
_____

Lab zone ® Do the Quick Lab *Visualizing Convection Currents.*

🔑 Assess Your Understanding

1a. Classify What type of heat transfer occurs when eggs cook in a hot pan? Before toasters, people toasted bread by holding it over a fire. What type of heat transfer occurred then? Name the third type of heat transfer and an example of a food cooked by it.

_____
_____

b. ANSWER THE BIG **?** How does heat flow from one object to another?

_____
_____
_____
_____
_____

got it? ....

○ **I get it!** Now I know that the three methods of heat transfer are _____
_____

○ **I need extra help with** _____

Go to **MY SCIENCE** 🔍 **COACH** online for help with this subject.

Thermal Properties

UNLOCK THE BIG ?

🔑 **How Do Different Materials Respond to Heat?**

my planet Diary

CAREER

Suiting Up

Comic book superheroes often wear special suits that allow them to fly or protect them from enemies. But there are some everyday heroes who wear suits that give them similar super-powers: astronauts! Whenever astronauts go outside a space station or ship, they put on suits that weigh hundreds of pounds. The suits enable them to survive in the wide temperature swings that occur in space. The suits are designed with a flexible insulating material to protect astronauts from extreme temperature swings, radiation, and low pressure in space. They also provide air to breathe, radio communication, and protection from micrometeoroids.

Communicate Answer the question below. Then discuss your answer with a partner.

You also use special clothing to stay warm. What materials do you use to stay warm?

_____

_____

_____

_____

▶ PLANET DIARY Go to **Planet Diary** to learn more about spacesuits.

Lab zone® Do the Inquiry Warm-Up *Thermal Properties.*

How Do Different Materials Respond to Heat?

When you bake something in the oven, you use dishes made of glass, ceramics, or metal instead of plastic. Some materials can stand up to the heat of an oven better than others. Materials respond to heat in different ways. The thermal properties of an object determine how it will respond to heat.

Vocabulary

- conductor
- insulator
- specific heat
- thermal expansion

Skills

- Reading: Identify the Main Idea
- Inquiry: Calculate

Conductors and Insulators If you walk barefoot from your living room rug to the tile floor of your kitchen, you will notice that the tile feels colder than the rug. But the temperature of the rug and the tile are the same—room temperature! The difference has to do with how materials conduct heat. **Some materials conduct heat well, while other materials do not.**

Conductors A material that conducts heat well is called a **conductor.** Metals such as silver are good conductors. Some materials are good conductors because of the particles they contain and how those particles are arranged. A good conductor, such as the tile floor, feels cold to the touch because heat easily transfers out of your skin and into the tile. However, heat also transfers out of conductors easily. A metal flagpole feels much hotter on a summer day than a wooden pole would in the same place because heat easily transfers out of the metal pole and into your hand.

Insulators A wooden pole and your living room rug are good insulators. **Insulators** are materials that do not conduct heat well. Other good insulators include air and wool. For example, wool blankets slow the transfer of heat out of your body.

FIGURE 1 ....

> ART IN MOTION **Conductors and Insulators**
Both conductors and insulators are useful in a kitchen. Conductors easily transfer heat to cook your food. Insulators stay cool enough to be handled.
✎ **Classify** Circle the conductors in the photo. Below, list objects in a kitchen that can act as insulators.

_____

_____

_____

_____

_____

Specific Heat Imagine running across hot sand toward the ocean. You run to the water's edge, but you don't go any farther—the water is too cold. How can the sand be so hot and the water so cold? After all, the sun heats both of them. The answer is that water requires more heat to raise its temperature than sand does.

When an object is heated, its temperature rises. But the temperature does not rise at the same rate for all objects. The amount of heat required to raise the temperature of an object depends on the object's chemical makeup. 🔑 **To change the temperature of different objects by the same amount, different amounts of thermal energy are required.**

The amount of energy required to raise the temperature of 1 kilogram of a material by 1 kelvin is called its **specific heat.** It is measured in joules per kilogram-kelvin, or J/(kg·K). A material with a high specific heat can absorb a great deal of thermal energy without a great change in temperature.

You can calculate thermal energy changes with a formula.

Energy Change = Mass × Specific Heat × Temperature Change

✏️
🔁 **Identify the Main Idea**
Circle the main idea on this page. Underline the sentences that support the main idea.

do the math!

You can calculate the amount of thermal energy gained by 2 kg of water as its temperature increases by 3 K.

Energy Change = Mass × Specific Heat × Temp. Change

Energy Change = 2 kg × 4,180 J/(kg·K) × 3 K

Energy Change = 25,080 J

Material	Specific Heat (J/(kg·K))
Copper	385
Water	4,180
Glass	837
Silver	235
Iron	450

1 Calculate Use the formula and the table at the right to calculate how much energy is lost by 0.5 kg of silver that cools off by 2 K.

_____

2 Interpret Tables How many times more energy must you transfer into a kilogram of glass than a kilogram of silver to raise their temperatures by the same amount?

_____

3 Draw Conclusions The seawater at a beach heats up more slowly than the sand on the beach does. The specific heat of water must be (greater than/less than) the specific heat of sand.

Thermal Expansion To loosen a jar lid, you can hold it under a stream of hot water. This works because the metal lid expands more than the glass does as it gets hotter. ⚏ **As the thermal energy of matter increases, its particles usually spread out, causing the substance to expand.** This is true for almost all matter. The expanding of matter when it is heated is known as **thermal expansion**. When matter is cooled, the opposite happens. Thermal energy is released. This causes the particles to slow down and move closer together. As matter cools, it usually decreases in volume, or contracts. One exception is water. Water expands slightly when it freezes. This is why solid ice floats in a glass of liquid water.

Power Lines

Road Joint

Train Track

FIGURE 2 ···
Thermal Expansion
Many objects are specifically designed to allow extra space for thermal expansion.
✎ **Predict** Pick one of the examples. What might happen if thermal expansion was not considered when this object was designed?

_____
_____
_____
_____
_____

Lab ® Do the Quick Lab
zone Frosty Balloons.

⚏ Assess Your Understanding

1a. Classify Foam picnic coolers keep food cold on a hot day. Is foam a conductor or an insulator? Explain.

_____
_____
_____

b. ◢ **Calculate** The specific heat of foam is about 1,200 J/(kg·K). How much heat does it take to raise the temperature of 1 kg of foam by 2 K?

_____
_____
_____

got it? ···

○ **I get it!** Now I know that the way a material responds to heat depends on _____
_____

○ **I need extra help with** _____

Go to **MY SCIENCE 🔵 COACH** online for help with this subject.

11 Study Guide

Heat flows from _____ objects to _____ objects. The three methods of heat transfer are _____ .

LESSON 1 Temperature, Thermal Energy, and Heat

🔑 Temperature is a measure of the average kinetic energy of the particles in an object.

🔑 Thermal energy is the total energy of all the particles in an object.

Vocabulary
- temperature • Fahrenheit scale • Celsius scale
- Kelvin scale • absolute zero • heat

LESSON 2 The Transfer of Heat

🔑 Heat is transferred from warmer areas to cooler areas by conduction, convection, and radiation.

Vocabulary
- convection • convection current
- radiation • conduction

LESSON 3 Thermal Properties

🔑 Some materials conduct heat well, while other materials do not.

🔑 To change the temperature of different objects by the same amount, different amounts of thermal energy are required.

🔑 As the thermal energy of matter increases, its particles usually spread out, causing the substance to expand.

Vocabulary
- conductor • insulator • specific heat • thermal expansion

Review and Assessment

LESSON 1 Temperature, Thermal Energy, and Heat

1. What is the total energy of all the particles in an object called?

   a. chemical energy   **b.** thermal energy

   c. potential energy   **d.** mechanical energy

2. The temperature scale used in most of the world is the _____

3. **Apply Concepts** How does heat flow when you place an ice cube in your hand?

   _____

   _____

Use the illustration to answer the questions below.

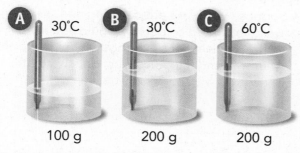

A   30°C   B   30°C   C   60°C

100 g   200 g   200 g

4. **Interpret Data** Compare the average motion of the particles in the three containers. Explain your answer.

   _____

   _____

   _____

   _____

   _____

5. **Draw Conclusions** Compare the total amount of thermal energy in containers A and B. Explain your answer.

   _____

   _____

   _____

   _____

LESSON 2 The Transfer of Heat

6. What is the process by which heat transfers from one particle of matter to another when the particles collide?

   a. conduction   **b.** convection

   c. expansion   **d.** radiation

7. A convection current is _____

   _____

   _____

   _____

8. **Classify** Identify each example of heat transfer as conduction, convection, or radiation: opening the windows in a hot room; a lizard basking in the sun; putting ice on a sprained ankle.

   _____

   _____

9. **Infer** How can heat be transferred across empty space? Explain your answer.

   _____

   _____

   _____

10. **Make Judgments** Suppose you try to heat your home using a fireplace in one of the rooms. Would a fan be helpful? Explain.

   _____

   _____

   _____

   _____

11. **Write About It** Explain why a school might ask teachers to keep the windows closed and the shades down during a heat wave.

11 Review and Assessment

LESSON 3 Thermal Properties

12. Suppose you want to know the amount of heat needed to raise the temperature of 2 kg of copper by 10°C. What property of the copper do you need to know?

 a. the thermal energy of the copper

 b. the temperature of the copper

 c. the specific heat of copper

 d. the melting point of copper

13. Wool is a good insulator, which means _____

_____

14. **Apply Concepts** When they are hung, telephone lines are allowed to sag. Explain why.

_____

_____

_____

15. **Interpret Diagrams** Why are two panes of glass used in the window shown below? (*Hint*: Air is an insulator.)

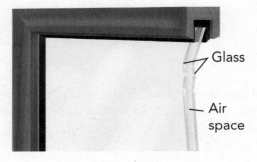

Glass

Air space

_____

_____

_____

16. **math!** Iron has a specific heat of 450 J/(kg·K). Design a set of three iron cooking pots. How much heat is required to increase the temperature of each pot by 100 K?

 APPLY THE BIG ? How does heat flow from one object to another?

17. Suppose you were out camping and the weather turned cold. How would you keep warm? Explain each action you would take. Tell whether conduction, convection, or radiation is involved with each heat transfer.

_____

_____

_____

_____

_____

_____

_____

_____

_____

_____

_____

_____

_____

_____

_____

_____

Standardized Test Prep

Multiple Choice

Circle the letter of the best answer.

1. The temperatures of four pies are shown below.

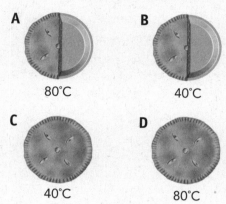

A   B

80°C   40°C

C   D

40°C   80°C

Which statement is true?

A   A and D have the same thermal energy.
B   C and D have the same thermal energy.
C   B has twice the thermal energy as C.
D   D has twice the thermal energy as A.

2. What does a thermometer measure?

A   the average kinetic energy of the particles in an object
B   the movement of heat from one object to another
C   the amount of thermal energy in an object
D   the specific heat of an object

3. Which statement describes the direction of heat flow?

A   Heat flows between two objects at the same temperature.
B   Thermal energy can only be absorbed by cool objects.
C   Heat flows from a warmer object to a cooler object.
D   Heat flows from a cooler object to a warmer object.

4. The specific heat of iron is 450 J/(kg·K). How much thermal energy must be transferred to 15 kg of iron to raise its temperature by 4.0 K?

A   450 J
B   2,700 J
C   5,400 J
D   27,000 J

5. Which of the following can be classified as a good conductor of thermal energy?

A   air
B   wood
C   silver
D   wool

Constructed Response

Use your knowledge of science to help you answer Question 6. Write your answer on a separate sheet of paper.

6. Using the principles of conduction, convection, and radiation, explain how the water in the pot gets hot.

TORNADO ALLEY

Tornadoes are the most intense storms on Earth. With swirling winds that can top 480 km per hour, they can blow down houses, rip up trees, and toss train cars like toys. Tornadoes can occur almost anywhere, but they are more likely in Kansas than in California. Why? Kansas is in Tornado Alley.

Tornado Alley is a zone in the central U.S. where tornadoes touch down more often than at any other place on Earth. Warm, moist air moving north from the Gulf of Mexico clashes there with cool, dry air moving in from the north and west. Where the air masses meet, the cool air forces the warm, moist air aloft.

The warm air has water vapor that changes from a liquid to a gas during evaporation. Thermal energy from the sun is absorbed by and stored in the water vapor. As the moist air rises, the water vapor in it cools and condenses into droplets that form clouds. As the water vapor condenses, the water releases its stored thermal energy. The thermal energy warms the air and allows the moist air that follows to rise higher before cooling, which builds up as huge storm clouds. Under the right conditions, the air inside these clouds can begin to rotate and form tornadoes, the Midwest's most dramatic storms.

Design It Tornado Alley is not the only area where tornadoes form. Research the occurrence of tornadoes over the last five years in the United States. Represent your findings on a map. Caption your map with an explanation of how absorption and release of thermal energy is related to the formation of tornadoes.

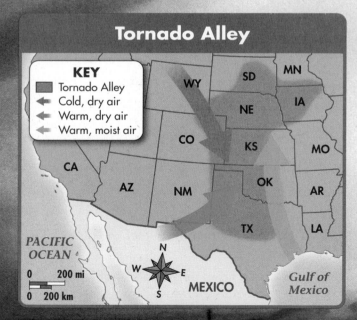

Tornado Alley

KEY
- Tornado Alley
- ← Cold, dry air
- ← Warm, dry air
- ← Warm, moist air

▲ With over 1,000 tornadoes each year, the U.S. ranks first in the world. Canada ranks second, with about 100. Within the U.S., tornadoes are most frequent in Tornado Alley.

HURRICANE WARNING

You jump out of bed, ready for the first day of your family's beach vacation. But wait! What is that red and black flag? The weather report says "Hurricane Watch." Your area may lie in the path of a hurricane.

What provides the power to these severe tropical storms that can cover thousands of kilometers? Well, it all starts with the sun!

1. The sun warms ocean water by radiation. Conduction transfers the thermal energy of the water to the air in contact with it. As surface water evaporates, convection lifts the warm humid air high in the atmosphere, forming thunderstorms.

2. Over several days, the thunderstorms can organize into a system with a low-pressure center. This system is called a tropical depression.

3. As sustained winds increase, the tropical depression can strengthen to become a tropical storm. Thermal energy continues to move from the ocean to the atmosphere. Pressure at the center of the system continues to drop, and winds increase.

4. When winds reach a sustained speed of 119 kph, the storm is classified as a hurricane. But hurricane winds can top 320 kph.

Hurricanes can last for two weeks or more over warm, open water. A hurricane starts to lose strength as it passes over cool water or land because the storm loses its warm-water fuel.

What happens if the temperature of an ocean's surface increases overall? Some scientists say there would be more hurricanes—and they have data to support this prediction. Sea-surface temperature has risen since 1900, and so has the average number of hurricanes each year. This is something to watch out for when planning your next beach getaway!

Analyze It Research the life cycle of a recent hurricane. Draw its track on a map. Then locate and explain each stage of its development along the track. Remember to link the end of the hurricane with its loss of warm-water fuel. Share your diagram in class.

HOW WOULD YOU DESCRIBE WAVES?

What are the properties of waves?

Imagine a sunny day on a calm sea. It seems as if you can see to the edge of the world. Suddenly, the clouds roll in, and the waves begin to get larger and faster. Soon, you can barely see past the next wave. One after another, they batter the sailboat, making it pitch and roll like a wild roller coaster. **Draw Conclusions** What are some features of waves?

_____

_____

_____

_____

_____

> **UNTAMED SCIENCE** Watch the **Untamed Science** video to learn more about waves.

Characteristics of Waves

Check Your Understanding

1. **Background** Read the paragraph below and then answer the question.

At a public pond, Lionel skips stones and tosses rocks into the water, sending waves in all directions. Nearby, Ali **floats** a wooden boat. Both boys observe the **properties** of the waves. The rocks make higher waves than the stones. They watch the **interaction** of the waves and the boat. The boat bounces violently as the higher waves travel under it.

Something **floats** if it moves or rests on the surface of a liquid without sinking.

The **properties** of something are its characteristic qualities or features.

Interaction is the combined action or effect that things have on each other.

- What example in the paragraph suggests that the properties of waves might affect a floating object?

_____

_____

_____

> **MY READING WEB** If you had trouble completing the question above, visit **My Reading Web** and type in *Characteristics of Waves.*

Vocabulary Skill

Identify Multiple Meanings Some words have more than one meaning. Consider the everyday and scientific meanings of the words below.

Word	Everyday Meaning	Scientific Meaning
reflection	*n.* serious thought or consideration	*n.* the bouncing back of a wave from a surface
frequency	*n.* the rate at which something occurs	*n.* the number of waves that pass a point in a certain time

2. **Quick Check** Circle in the chart the meaning of *reflection* as it is used in the following sentence: An echo is the *reflection* of a sound wave.

wave

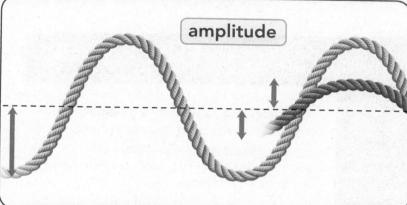

amplitude

reflection

refraction

Chapter Preview

LESSON 1

- wave
- energy
- medium
- mechanical wave
- vibration
- transverse wave
- crest
- trough
- longitudinal wave
- compression
- rarefaction

⟳ **Summarize**
△ **Predict**

LESSON 2

- amplitude
- wavelength
- frequency
- hertz

⟳ **Identify the Main Idea**
△ **Calculate**

LESSON 3

- reflection
- refraction
- diffraction
- interference
- constructive interference
- destructive interference
- standing wave
- node
- antinode
- resonance

⟳ **Relate Cause and Effect**
△ **Observe**

▶ **VOCAB FLASH CARDS** For extra help with vocabulary, visit **Vocab Flash Cards** and type in *Characteristics of Waves.*

What Are Waves?

UNLOCK THE BIG ?

🔑 **What Forms Mechanical Waves?**

🔑 **What Are the Types of Mechanical Waves?**

MY PLANET DiaRY

The Power of Waves

Where does the energy that powers your school come from? It may be from oil, gas, or coal. You also may have heard of using the sun or wind as energy sources. But did you know that ocean waves could be used as an energy source, too? Mechanical systems placed in the ocean or along the shore transform the energy from waves into electricity. Unlike oil, gas, or coal, the energy from ocean waves will not run out. Although wave energy technology is still very new, many scientists are optimistic about its possible use around the world.

FUN FACTS

Communicate Discuss this question with a partner. Write your answer below.

How might wave energy impact the environment? Consider both intended and unintended consequences.

_____

_____

_____

_____

_____

_____

▶ PLANET DIARY Go to **Planet Diary** to learn more about waves.

 Lab zone® Do the Inquiry Warm-Up *What Are Waves?*

Vocabulary

- wave
- energy
- medium
- mechanical wave
- vibration
- transverse wave
- crest
- trough
- longitudinal wave
- compression
- rarefaction

Skills

↻ Reading: Summarize

△ Inquiry: Predict

What Forms Mechanical Waves?

You have probably seen and felt water waves while swimming. But did you know that many kinds of waves affect you daily? Sound and light are very different from water waves, but they are waves, too.

Characteristics of Waves What is a wave? A **wave** is a disturbance involving the transfer of energy from place to place. In science, **energy** is defined as the ability to do work. For example, the energy of a water wave can lift an object on the water's surface as the wave passes under it. But after the wave passes, the water is calm again.

Most waves need something to travel through. For example, sound waves can travel through air, water, and even solid materials. Water waves travel along the surface of the water. A wave can even travel along an object, such as a rope. The material through which a wave travels is called a **medium.** Gases (such as air), liquids (such as water), and solids (such as ropes) can all act as mediums. Waves that require a medium to travel are called **mechanical waves.**

✏️

↻ **Summarize** On the notebook paper, summarize the text on this page in your own words.

CHALLENGE The news media, such as newspapers and television stations, carry current events worldwide. Explain how the way news travels is similar to the way a wave travels.

_____

_____

_____

_____

_____

Waves and Energy
Energy is needed to make a wave. **Mechanical waves form when a source of energy causes a medium to vibrate.** A **vibration** is a repeated back-and-forth or up-and-down motion. Moving objects have energy, which they can transfer to a medium to produce waves. For example, as you see in **Figure 1,** a motorboat's propeller can transfer energy to calm water. As a result, the particles that make up the water start to vibrate. The vibrations move through the water, resulting in a wave.

FIGURE 1 ....

Forming a Mechanical Wave
A source of energy in a medium can cause a mechanical wave to form.

Explain Draw an arrow from each box to the correct part of the photo. Then tell your reason for each choice in the boxes.

Energy Source
Moving objects have energy.

_____

_____

_____

Vibration
When a vibration moves through a medium, a wave results.

_____

_____

_____

_____

_____

Medium
Mechanical waves form in mediums.

_____

_____

_____

Lab zone® Do the Quick Lab *What Causes Mechanical Waves?*

Assess Your Understanding

got it? ....

○ I get it! Now I know that a mechanical wave forms when _____

_____

○ I need extra help with _____

Go to MY SCIENCE COACH online for help with this subject.

What Are the Types of Mechanical Waves?

Waves move through mediums in different ways. 🔑 **The three types of mechanical waves are transverse waves, longitudinal waves, and surface waves.** These waves are classified by how they move through mediums.

Transverse Waves When you make a wave on a rope, the wave moves from one end of the rope to the other. However, the rope itself moves up and down or from side to side, at right angles to the direction in which the wave travels. A wave that vibrates the medium at right angles, or perpendicular, to the direction in which the wave travels is called a **transverse wave.**

Making a transverse wave on a rope forms high and low points along the rope. A high point on a transverse wave is called a **crest,** and a low point is called a **trough** (trawf). In **Figure 2,** you can see that the red ribbon on the rope is first at a crest and then at a trough. As the wave moves through the rope, the ribbon moves up and down between crests and troughs. The dashed line shows the rope's position before it was moved. It is called the rest position.

Vocabulary Identify Multiple Meanings The word *trough* has more than one meaning. Write two sentences that use the word, one showing its everyday meaning and one showing its scientific meaning.

_____

_____

_____

_____

_____

FIGURE 2 ....

Motion in a Transverse Wave
When you shake out a bedsheet or move a rope up and down, you create a transverse wave.

✎ **Complete the tasks.**

1. **Identify** Label the crest, trough, and rest position.

2. **Relate Text and Visuals** Draw a vertical line through the purple arrows and a horizontal line through the blue arrow until it touches the vertical line. What angle did you draw?

_____

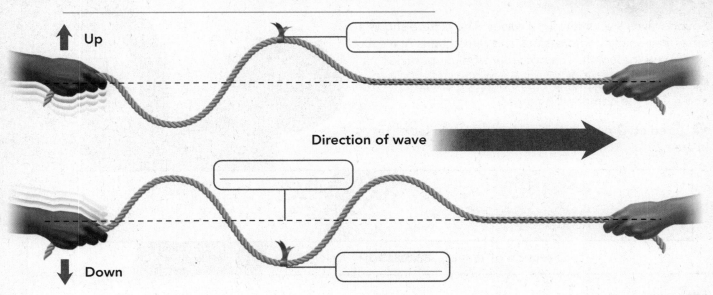

Up

Direction of wave

Down

Longitudinal Waves

If you push and pull one end of a spring toy, you can produce a longitudinal wave like the one shown in **Figure 3.** Notice that the coils in the spring move back and forth in the same direction, or parallel, to the wave's motion. A **longitudinal wave** (lawn juh TOO duh nul) vibrates the medium in the same direction in which the wave travels. Also, notice how the spacing between the coils varies. Some coils are close together, while others are farther apart. An area where the coils are close together is called a **compression** (kum PRESH un). An area where the coils are spread out is called a **rarefaction** (rair uh FAK shun).

As compressions and rarefactions travel along the spring toy, each coil moves forward and then back. The energy travels from one end of the spring to the other, in the form of a wave. After the wave passes, each coil returns to its starting position.

FIGURE 3 ·····················

Motion in a Longitudinal Wave

Fixed points on a transverse wave vibrate up and down. Fixed points on a longitudinal wave, such as the one marked by the red ribbon, vibrate back and forth.

✎ **Interpret Diagrams** Label the areas of compression and rarefaction in the diagram.

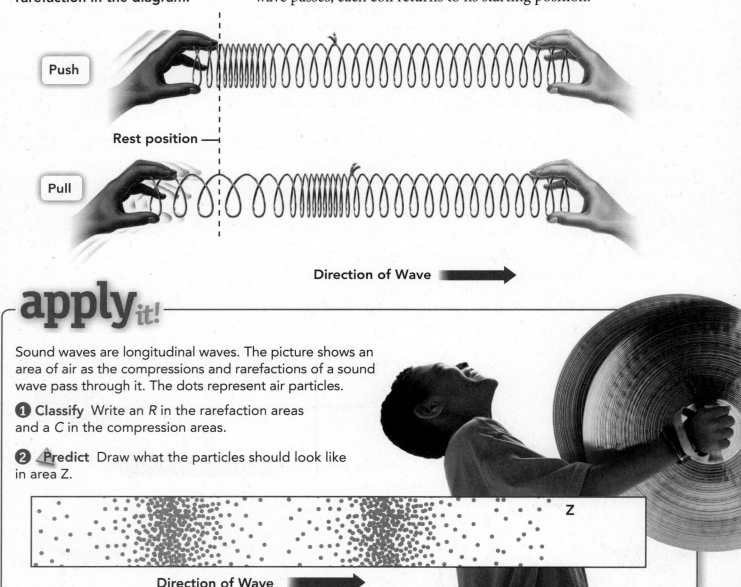

Push

Rest position —

Pull

Direction of Wave ➡

apply it!

Sound waves are longitudinal waves. The picture shows an area of air as the compressions and rarefactions of a sound wave pass through it. The dots represent air particles.

❶ **Classify** Write an *R* in the rarefaction areas and a *C* in the compression areas.

❷ **Predict** Draw what the particles should look like in area Z.

Z

Direction of Wave ➡

Surface Waves

Surface Waves Surface waves are combinations of transverse and longitudinal waves. This type of wave travels along a surface that separates two mediums. Ocean waves are the most familiar surface wave. An ocean wave travels at the surface between water and air. When a wave passes through water, the water (and anything on it) vibrates up and down, like a transverse wave on a rope. The water also moves back and forth slightly in the direction that the wave is traveling, like the coils of a spring. But unlike the coils of a spring, water does not compress. The up-and-down and back-and-forth movements combine to make each particle of water move in a circle, as you see in **Figure 4.**

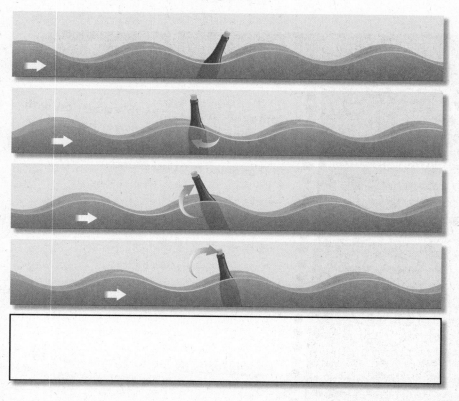

FIGURE 4 ·····················

> **ART IN MOTION** **Waves Transfer Energy**
A wave moves the bottle in a circular motion. After the wave passes, the bottle returns to where it started.

✏️ **Predict** In the empty box, draw what the next picture should look like.

Lab zone® Do the Quick Lab
Three Types of Waves.

Assess Your Understanding

1a. Review Compared to the direction it travels, at what angle does a transverse wave vibrate a medium?

_____

_____

b. Compare and Contrast How are transverse and longitudinal waves alike and different?

_____

_____

got it?

○ **I get it!** Now I know that the three types of mechanical waves are _____

_____

_____

_____

○ **I need extra help with** _____

Go to **MY SCIENCE** Ⓢ **COACH** *online for help with this subject.*

Properties of Waves

🔑 **What Are the Amplitude, Wavelength, Frequency, and Speed of a Wave?**

🔑 **How Are Frequency, Wavelength, and Speed Related?**

my planet Diary

DISCOVERY

The Sound of Romance

Bzzzzzzzzz! Bzzzzzzzzz! What's that noise? It's the sound of a mosquito buzzing in your ear. This distinct buzzing sound comes from sound waves formed as a mosquito beats its wings. Researchers recently discovered that the buzzing sound of female mosquitoes attracts male mosquitoes. When a male mosquito meets a female, he quickly adjusts his own buzz to match the frequency of the sound waves created by the female. Researchers think that this matched buzzing frequency aids in mosquito mating.

Communicate Discuss this question with a partner. Write your answer below.

What are two other animals you know of that make buzzing sounds?

_____

_____

_____

_____

_____

_____

▶ **PLANET DIARY** Go to **Planet Diary** to learn more about wave properties.

Lab zone Do the Inquiry Warm-Up *What Do Waves Look Like?*

Vocabulary
- amplitude - wavelength - frequency - hertz

Skills
- Reading: Identify the Main Idea
- Inquiry: Calculate

What Are the Amplitude, Wavelength, Frequency, and Speed of a Wave?

Waves may vary greatly. For example, waves can be long or short. They can carry a little energy or a lot of energy. They can be transverse or longitudinal. However, all waves have common properties—amplitude, wavelength, frequency, and speed. **Amplitude describes how far the medium in a wave moves. Wavelength describes a wave's length, and frequency describes how often it occurs. Speed describes how quickly a wave moves.**

Amplitude The height of a wave's crest depends on its amplitude. **Amplitude** is the maximum distance the medium vibrates from the rest position. For a water wave, this distance is how far the water particles move above or below the surface level of calm water. High waves have more energy than low waves. The more energy a wave has, the greater its amplitude.

A transverse wave is shown in **Figure 1.** Its amplitude is the maximum distance the medium moves up or down from its rest position. The amplitude of a longitudinal wave is a measure of how compressed or rarefied the medium becomes. When the compressions are dense, it means the wave's amplitude is large.

FIGURE 1 ··

Amplitude
The amplitude of a transverse wave is the maximum distance the medium vibrates from the rest position.

✏ **Label the parts of the wave. Then answer the question.**

Measure What is the amplitude of the wave in centimeters?

_____

Rest position

FIGURE 2 ··························

Properties of Waves

All waves have amplitude, wavelength, frequency, and speed.

✎ **Read the text on these pages before filling in the boxes and answering these questions.**

1. **Name** Which transverse wave has the shortest wavelength?

   _____
   _____

2. **Apply Concepts** If a transverse wave travels 10 meters in 5 seconds, what is its speed?

   _____

3. **Draw Conclusions** How does a shorter wavelength affect the frequency of a wave?

   _____
   _____
   _____
   _____
   _____
   _____
   _____
   _____

✎ **⟳ Identify the Main Idea** Read the text. Underline the main idea in each of the three sections.

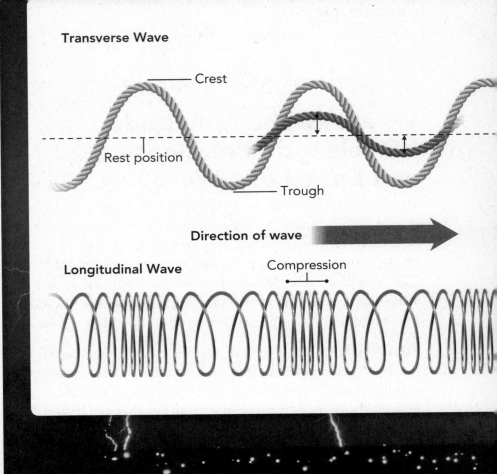

Transverse Wave

— Crest

Rest position

— Trough

Direction of wave

Longitudinal Wave   Compression

Wavelength A wave travels a certain distance before it starts to repeat. The distance between two corresponding parts of a wave is its **wavelength.** You can find the wavelength of a transverse wave by measuring the distance from crest to crest as shown in **Figure 2.** For a longitudinal wave, the wavelength is the distance between compressions.

Frequency The **frequency** of a wave is the number of waves that pass a given point in a certain amount of time. For example, if you make waves on a rope so that one wave passes by a point every second, the frequency is 1 wave per second. Move your hand up and down more quickly and you increase the frequency.

Frequency is measured in units called **hertz** (Hz), and is defined as the number of waves per second. A wave that occurs every second has a frequency of 1 wave per second (1/s) or 1 Hz. If two waves pass every second the frequency is 2 waves per second (2/s) or 2 Hz.

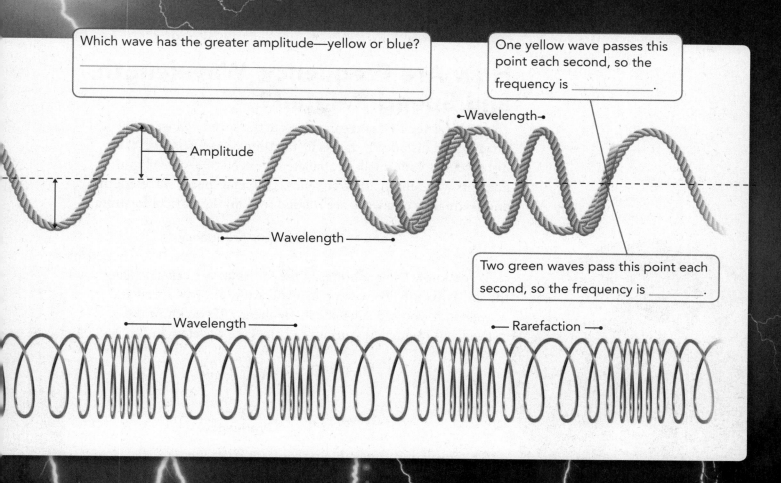

Which wave has the greater amplitude—yellow or blue?

_____

_____

One yellow wave passes this point each second, so the frequency is _____.

Amplitude

←Wavelength→

←————Wavelength————→

Two green waves pass this point each second, so the frequency is _____.

←————Wavelength————→

←— Rarefaction —→

Speed Different waves travel at different speeds. Think about watching a distant thunder-storm on a hot summer day. The thunder occurs the instant the lightning flashes, but the light and sound reach you seconds apart. This happens because light waves travel much faster than sound waves. In fact, light waves travel about a million times faster than sound waves!

The speed of a wave is how far the wave travels in a given amount of time. You can determine a wave's speed by dividing the distance it travels by the time it takes to travel that distance. Sound, for example, travels about 990 meters in 3 seconds in air when the temperature is 0°C. Therefore, its speed is 330 m/s in these conditions. As long as the temperature of the medium (air) doesn't change, the speed of sound will stay the same.

Do the Quick Lab
Properties of Waves.

Assess Your Understanding

got it? ··································

O **I get it!** Now I know that for any wave,

amplitude describes _____

_____,

wavelength describes _____,

frequency describes _____

_____,

and speed describes _____

_____

O **I need extra help with** _____

Go to MY SCIENCE ⓢ COACH *online for help with this subject.*

How Are Frequency, Wavelength, and Speed Related?

You just learned that you can calculate the speed of a wave by dividing the distance it travels by the time it takes to travel that distance. But you can also calculate the speed of a wave if you know its wavelength and frequency.  **The speed, wavelength, and frequency of a wave are related by a mathematical formula.**

$$\text{Speed} = \text{Wavelength} \times \text{Frequency}$$

If you know two quantities in the formula, you can calculate the third quantity. For example, if you know a wave's speed and wavelength, you can calculate its frequency. If you know the speed and frequency, you can calculate the wavelength.

$$\text{Frequency} = \frac{\text{Speed}}{\text{Wavelength}}$$

$$\text{Wavelength} = \frac{\text{Speed}}{\text{Frequency}}$$

The speed of a wave remains constant if the medium, temperature, and pressure do not change. For example, all sound waves travel at the same speed in air at a given temperature and pressure. Even if a sound wave's frequency changes, its speed stays the same. So, if the frequency of a sound wave increases, its wavelength must decrease to maintain a constant speed.

do the math!

The table shows measurements of some properties of a sound wave in water and in air.

❶ **Calculate** Using what you know about the relationship between wavelength, frequency, and speed, fill in the table.

❷ **CHALLENGE** What can this table tell you about the speed of a wave?

Medium	Wavelength	Frequency	Speed
Water	_____	200 Hz	1500 m/s
Water	3.75 m	400 Hz	_____
Air (20°C)	10 m	_____	343 m/s
Air (20°C)	_____	17.15 Hz	343 m/s

_____

_____

_____

THE BIG ? Ride the waves

What are the properties of waves?

FIGURE 3 ··········

> INTERACTIVE ART The waves in some amusement park wave pools are controlled by regularly spaced bursts of air. Changing the timing and strength of these air bursts also changes the characteristics of the waves that result.

✎ **Predict** List and describe four wave characteristics. Which characteristic(s) do you think would change if the air bursts were stronger? Which would change if more air bursts came in a shorter amount of time? Explain.

_____

_____

_____

_____

_____

_____

_____

_____

_____

_____

_____

_____

_____

Lab zone® Do the Quick Lab *What Affects the Speed of a Wave?*

🔑 Assess Your Understanding

1a. ANSWER THE BIG ? What are the properties of waves?

_____

_____

b. Calculate A wave's frequency is 2 Hz and its wavelength is 4 m. What is the wave's speed?

_____

got it?

○ **I get it!** Now I know that wavelength, frequency, and speed are related by the formula _____

_____

○ **I need extra help with** _____

Go to MY SCIENCE ⓢ COACH online for help with this subject.

Interactions of Waves

UNLOCK
THE BIG
?

🔑 **What Changes the Direction of a Wave?**

🔑 **What Are the Two Types of Wave Interference?**

🔑 **How Do Standing Waves Form?**

my planet diary

DISASTER

The Fall of Galloping Gertie

"My breath was coming in gasps; my knees were raw and bleeding, my hands bruised and swollen.... Safely back at the toll plaza, I saw the bridge in its final collapse and saw my car plunge into the Narrows."

This dramatic piece of writing is a witness's real-life account of the collapse of the Tacoma Narrows Bridge in Tacoma, Washington, on November 7, 1940.

Prior to its collapse, the suspension bridge was known for its swaying and rolling in the wind. This motion happened so regularly that the bridge was nicknamed "Galloping Gertie." Only four months after its construction, the bridge collapsed into the waters of Puget Sound during a windstorm. Although a disaster, Galloping Gertie's collapse became a valuable teaching tool for engineers.

Communicate Discuss the following questions with a partner. Write your answers below.

1. Why is "Galloping Gertie" an appropriate nickname for the bridge?

_____

_____

2. If you were an engineer studying this bridge collapse, what is one thing you would research?

_____

_____

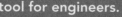
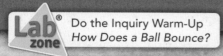
Lab zone® Do the Inquiry Warm-Up How Does a Ball Bounce?

▶ **PLANET DIARY** Go to **Planet Diary** to learn more about waves interacting.

Vocabulary

- reflection • refraction • diffraction • interference
- constructive interference • destructive interference
- standing wave • node • antinode • resonance

Skills

- Reading: Relate Cause and Effect
- Inquiry: Observe

What Changes the Direction of a Wave?

If you toss a ball against a wall, the ball bounces back in a new direction. Like a ball, waves can also change direction. 🔑 **Waves change direction by reflection, refraction, and diffraction.**

Reflection When a wave hits a surface, any part of the wave that cannot pass through the surface bounces back. This interaction with a surface is called **reflection.** Reflection happens often in your everyday life. When you looked in your mirror this morning you used reflected light to see yourself. The echo you hear when you shout in an empty gym is also a reflection.

In **Figure 1** you can see how light waves are reflected. All reflected waves obey the law of reflection.

FIGURE 1 ....

The Law of Reflection
The law of reflection states that the angle of incidence equals the angle of reflection.

✏️ **Explain** Read the sequence of steps, matching each step to its letter in the photo. If the angle of incidence is 45°, explain what the angle of reflection would be.

_____

_____

_____

_____

_____

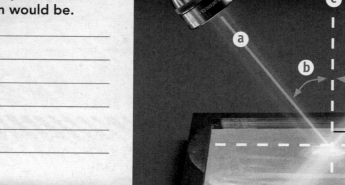

a **Incoming wave** A wave moving toward the surface at an angle.

b **Angle of incidence** The angle between the incoming wave and the normal.

c **Normal** A line perpendicular to the surface at the point where reflection occurs.

d **Angle of reflection** The angle between the reflected wave and the normal.

e **Reflected wave** A wave bouncing off the surface at an angle.

90° angle

Refraction Have you ever ridden a skateboard and gone off the sidewalk onto grass? If so, you know it's hard to keep moving in a straight line. The front wheel on the side moving onto the grass slows down. The front wheel still on the sidewalk continues to move fast. The difference in the speeds of the two front wheels causes the skateboard to change direction.

Like a skateboard that changes direction, changes in speed can cause waves to change direction. Look at **Figure 2.** When a wave enters a new medium at an angle, one side of the wave changes speed before the other side. This causes the wave to bend. Bending occurs because different parts of the wave travel at different speeds. **Refraction** is the bending of waves due to a change in speed.

Waves do not always bend when entering a new medium. No bending occurs if a wave enters a new medium at a right angle. Bending does not occur if the speed of the wave in the new medium is the same as the speed of the wave in the old medium.

⟳ Relate Cause and Effect In the second paragraph, circle the cause of refraction and underline the effect of refraction.

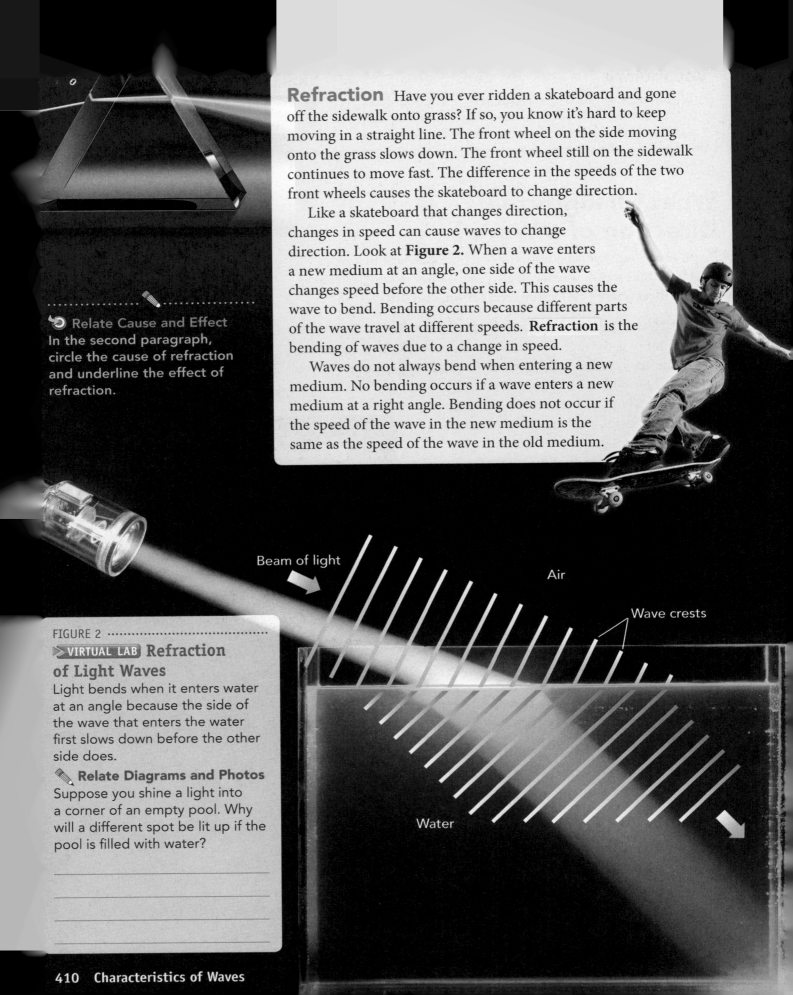

Beam of light

Air

Wave crests

Water

FIGURE 2 ....

⟫VIRTUAL LAB Refraction of Light Waves
Light bends when it enters water at an angle because the side of the wave that enters the water first slows down before the other side does.

✎ **Relate Diagrams and Photos** Suppose you shine a light into a corner of an empty pool. Why will a different spot be lit up if the pool is filled with water?

_____
_____
_____
_____

Diffraction Waves sometimes bend around barriers or pass through openings. When a wave moves around a barrier or through an opening in a barrier, it bends and spreads out. These wave interactions are called **diffraction.** Two examples of diffraction are shown in **Figure 3.**

FIGURE 3 ·····························

The Diffraction of Water Waves
Water waves diffract when they encounter canals or shorelines.

The waves bend around the barrier.

The waves spread out after passing through the narrow opening.

apply it!

Use the three pictures on the right to answer the questions.

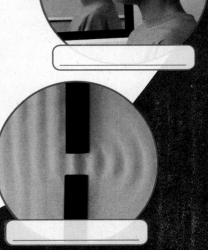

❶ **Observe** Under each picture, write how the waves are changing direction.

❷ **Summarize** In what way are reflection, refraction, and diffraction similar?

_____

_____

_____

Do the Lab Investigation *Making Waves.*

🔑 Assess Your Understanding

1a. Define What is diffraction?

_____

_____

_____

b. Classify A wave bends after entering a new medium. What type of interaction is this?

_____

_____

got it?

○ **I get it!** Now I know that a wave's direction can be changed by _____

_____

_____

○ **I need extra help with** _____

Go to **MY SCIENCE COACH** *online for help with this subject.*

What Are the Two Types of Wave Interference?

Have you ever seen soccer balls collide? The balls bounce off each other because they cannot be in the same place at the same time. Surprisingly, this is not true of waves. Unlike two balls, two waves can overlap when they meet. **Interference** is the interaction between waves that meet. **There are two types of interference: constructive and destructive.**

Constructive Interference
Interference in which waves combine to form a wave with a larger amplitude than any individual wave's amplitude is called **constructive interference.** You can think of constructive interference as waves "helping each other," or adding their energies. For example, in **Figure 4,** when the crests of two waves overlap, they make a higher crest. If two troughs overlap, they make a deeper trough. In both cases, the amplitude of the combined crests or troughs increases.

FIGURE 4 ·····················

Constructive Interference

✎ **Infer** Explain what the black dotted line represents. Then tell what happens to the direction of each wave when the waves meet.

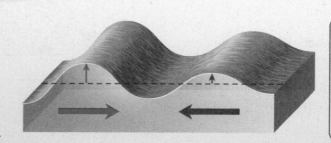

❶ Two waves approach each other. The wave on the left has a greater amplitude.

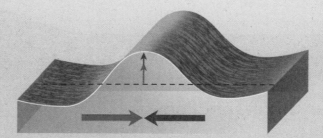

❷ The crest's new amplitude is the sum of the amplitudes of the original crests.

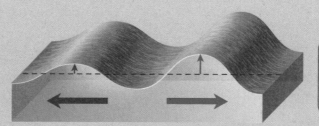

❸ The waves continue on as if they had not met.

Destructive Interference Interference in which two waves combine to form a wave with a smaller amplitude than either original wave had is called **destructive interference**. Destructive interference can occur when the crest of one wave overlaps the trough of another wave. If the crest has a larger amplitude than the trough of the other wave, the crest "wins" and part of it remains. If the original trough had a larger amplitude than the crest of the other wave, the result is a trough. If a crest and trough have equal amplitudes, they will completely cancel as shown in **Figure 5**. Destructive interference is used in noise-canceling headphones to block out distracting noises in a listener's surroundings.

FIGURE 5 ···

▶ INTERACTIVE ART **Destructive Interference**

✎ Observe Look at the pictures below. In the boxes, describe the steps of destructive interference.

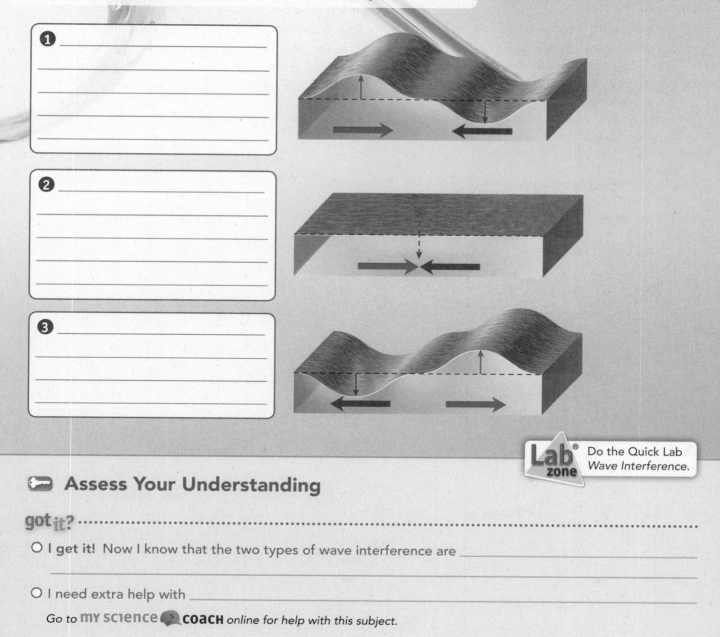

1 _____

2 _____

3 _____

Lab zone ® Do the Quick Lab *Wave Interference.*

⚷ Assess Your Understanding

got it? ···

○ **I get it!** Now I know that the two types of wave interference are _____

_____

○ **I need extra help with** _____

Go to **my science ⑤ coach** online for help with this subject.

How Do Standing Waves Form?

If you tie a rope to a doorknob and shake the free end, waves will travel down the rope, reflect at the end, and come back. The reflected waves will meet the incoming waves and interference occurs. 🔑 **If the incoming wave and reflected wave have just the right frequency, they combine to form a wave that appears to stand still. This wave is called a standing wave.** A standing wave is a wave that appears to stand in one place, even though it is two waves interfering as they pass through each other.

Nodes and Antinodes In a standing wave, destructive interference produces points with zero amplitude, called **nodes,** as shown in **Figure 6.** The nodes are always evenly spaced along the wave. At points in the standing wave where constructive interference occurs, the amplitude is greater than zero. Points of maximum amplitude on a standing wave are called **antinodes.** The antinodes always occur halfway between two nodes.

FIGURE 6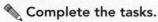

Standing Waves

As the frequency of the standing wave increases, more nodes and antinodes are created.

✏️ **Complete the tasks.**

1. **Identify** In the second box, label the nodes and antinodes.

2. CHALLENGE In the third box, draw the next standing wave in the series, and label its nodes and antinodes.

| 1 Wavelength | $1\frac{1}{2}$ Wavelengths | 2 Wavelengths |

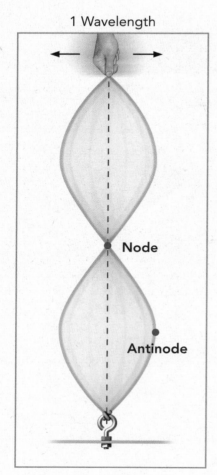

Node

Antinode

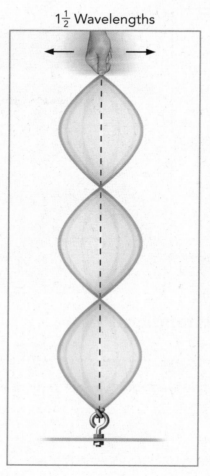

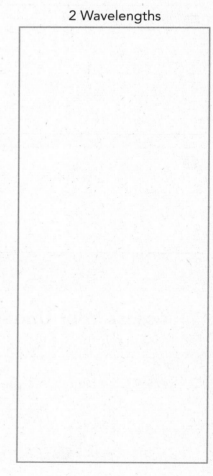

Resonance Have you ever pushed a child on a swing? At first the swing is difficult to push. But once it is going, you need only a gentle push to keep it going. This is because the swing has a natural frequency. Even small pushes that are in rhythm with the swing's natural frequency produce large increases in the swing's amplitude.

Most objects have at least one natural frequency of vibration. Standing waves occur in an object when it vibrates at a natural frequency. If a nearby object vibrates at the same frequency, it can cause resonance. **Resonance** is an increase in the amplitude of a vibration that occurs when external vibrations match an object's natural frequency.

The Tacoma Narrows Bridge, or "Galloping Gertie," may have collapsed because of resonance. Storm winds are said to have resonated with the natural frequency of the bridge. This caused the amplitude of the bridge's sway to increase until the bridge collapsed. You can see the result of the collapse in **Figure 7.**

FIGURE 7 ··

The Power of Resonance
Winds blew as fast as 67 km/h during the storm in which the Tacoma Narrows Bridge collapsed.

✎ **Redesign What might engineers do differently when designing a new bridge for this location?**

_____

_____

_____

Lab zone ®   Do the Quick Lab *Standing Waves.*

🔑 **Assess Your Understanding**

2a. Describe What causes resonance to occur?

_____

_____

_____

b. ↻ **Relate Cause and Effect** What causes nodes to form in a standing wave?

_____

_____

_____

got it?

○ **I get it!** Now I know that standing waves form when _____

_____

_____

_____

_____

○ **I need extra help with** _____

Go to **my science** ⬤ **coach** *online for help with this subject.*

The basic properties of waves are _____, _____, _____, and _____.

LESSON 1 **What Are Waves?**

🔑 Mechanical waves form when a source of energy causes a medium to vibrate.

🔑 The three types of mechanical waves are transverse waves, longitudinal waves, and surface waves.

Vocabulary
- wave • energy • medium • mechanical wave • vibration • transverse wave • crest
- trough • longitudinal wave • compression • rarefaction

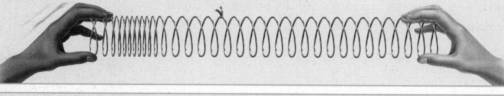

LESSON 2 **Properties of Waves**

🔑 Amplitude describes how far the medium in a wave moves. Wavelength describes a wave's length, and frequency describes how often it occurs. Speed describes how quickly a wave moves.

🔑 The speed, wavelength, and frequency of a wave are related by a mathematical formula:
Speed = Wavelength × Frequency.

Vocabulary
- amplitude • wavelength • frequency • hertz

LESSON 3 **Interactions of Waves**

🔑 Waves change direction by reflection, refraction, and diffraction.

🔑 There are two types of interference: constructive and destructive.

🔑 If the incoming wave and reflected wave have just the right frequency, they combine to form a wave that appears to stand still. This wave is called a standing wave.

Vocabulary
- reflection • refraction • diffraction • interference
- constructive interference • destructive interference • standing wave
- node • antinode • resonance

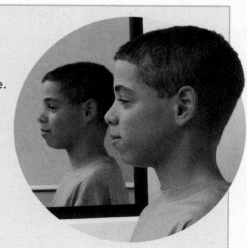

Review and Assessment

LESSON 1 What Are Waves?

1. A wave transfers

  a. energy.   **b.** particles

  c. water.   **d.** air.

2. _____ form when a source of energy causes a medium to vibrate.

3. Classify Label the crest(s) and trough(s) on the transverse wave.

4. Compare and Contrast What is the difference between a transverse wave and a longitudinal wave?

_____

_____

_____

_____

_____

_____

_____

5. Relate Cause and Effect Suppose ripples move from one side of a lake to the other. Does the water move across the lake? Explain.

_____

_____

_____

_____

_____

_____

_____

LESSON 2 Properties of Waves

6. The distance between two crests is a wave's

  a. amplitude.   **b.** wavelength.

  c. frequency.   **d.** speed.

7. The _____ of a wave is the number of waves that pass a given point in a certain amount of time.

This wave in the middle of the ocean was produced by an underwater earthquake. Use the diagram to answer Questions 8–10.

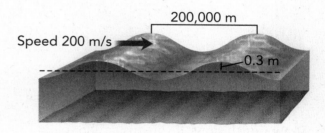

8. Interpret Diagrams What is the amplitude of the wave? What is its wavelength?

_____

_____

9. Calculate Find the frequency of the wave.

_____

_____

_____

10. math! How long would it take this wave to travel 5,000 km?

_____

_____

_____

_____

LESSON 3 **Interactions of Waves**

11. The bending of a wave due to a change in speed is called

    a. interference.   **b.** reflection.

    c. diffraction.   **d.** refraction.

12. _____ occurs when external vibrations match an object's natural frequency.

13. Predict Two waves are traveling toward each other. The crests from the waves meet. Describe what happens.

_____

_____

_____

_____

_____

14. Draw Conclusions If you push a shopping cart and one wheel hits a rough patch of concrete, it is difficult to steer the cart in a straight line. Explain how this is similar to refraction of a wave as it enters a new medium.

_____

_____

_____

_____

_____

_____

_____

15. 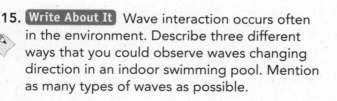 Write About It Wave interaction occurs often in the environment. Describe three different ways that you could observe waves changing direction in an indoor swimming pool. Mention as many types of waves as possible.

 APPLY THE BIG ? **What are the properties of waves?**

16. During a storm, a TV reporter says, "The ocean waves are 3 meters high. They are about 45 m apart and are hitting the shore every 15 seconds." Think about the four basic properties of waves and describe these ocean waves using the correct science words. (*Hint:* You will need to do some calculations first.)

_____

_____

_____

_____

_____

_____

_____

_____

_____

_____

_____

Standardized Test Prep

Multiple Choice

Circle the letter of the best answer.

1. Two waves approach each other as shown in the diagram below. What will be the amplitude of the wave produced when the crests from each wave meet?

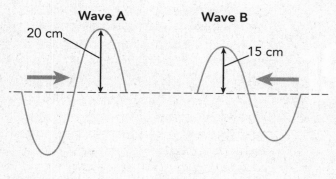

A 20 cm	**B** 35 cm
C 15 cm	**D** 5 cm

2. When a wave enters a new medium at 60° and changes speed, the wave

   A does not bend because one side changes speed before the other side.

   B does not bend because the angle is less than 90°.

   C bends because both sides change speed at the same time.

   D bends because one side changes speed before the other side.

3. The speed of a wave in a spring is 3 m/s. If the wavelength is 0.1 m, what is the frequency?

A 30 Hz	**B** 0.3 Hz
C 30 m/s	**D** 0.3 m/s

4. Which of the following is true about standing waves?

   A Constructive interference produces points with zero amplitude.

   B The nodes are unevenly spaced along the wave.

   C The amplitude of antinodes is greater than nodes.

   D Nodes are points of maximum energy on the wave.

5. What is the angle of incidence if a reflected wave bounces off a mirror at an angle of 65°?

   A 25°

   B 65°

   C 90°

   D 115°

Constructed Response

Use the diagram and your knowledge of science to help you answer Question 6. Write your answer on a separate sheet of paper.

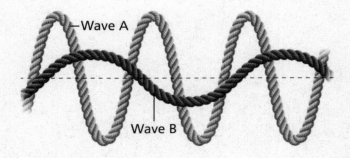

6. The waves shown above travel at the same speed. Which wave has the higher frequency? Which has the longer wavelength? Which has the greater amplitude?

Wall of Water

For as long as humans have sailed on the oceans, ships have disappeared without explanation. People chalked these losses up to bad luck and bad weather. A mysterious phenomenon, proven in 2004 to exist, may finally explain why some large ships are never seen again.

Waves in water usually behave like the other waves around them. Most waves in an area are about the same height and move at the same rate. Ocean waves are rarely more than 15 meters in height and usually form rolling hills of water. But freak monster waves can top 30 meters in height, forming huge walls of water!

Some monster waves form where two currents meet and their waves combine. The weather may be responsible for other monster waves. If an ordinary large wave travels at the same speed and in the same direction as the wind for more than 12 hours, the extra push from the wind can cause the wave to reach monster heights. Some monster waves seem to grow out of normal ocean wave patterns. Physicists theorize that these unstable waves absorb energy from the surrounding waves and grow to vast heights.

Most ships are not designed to withstand 30-meter-high waves, so it's no wonder that little has been found but wreckage. Fortunately, scientists are working on ways to protect ships and sailors in the face of these enormous destructive waves.

Model It Research how so-called monster waves focus and amplify the effects of surrounding waves. Use computer technology to create a diagram or to model the effects. Explain your diagram

An Operatic Superpower

Can someone really break a glass by singing a high note? It may seem like a superpower, but the human voice does have the power to shatter a crystal wine glass! This feat is commonly credited to opera singers because they have very powerful and well-trained voices.

Many wine glasses are made of a type of glass called crystal. The molecules in a crystal glass are arranged in a repeating pattern that forms a repeating internal structure. If you tap a crystal object, you can hear a clear tone. That tone is the natural resonant frequency of vibration for that crystal. When the crystal is exposed to a sound at that frequency, the molecules of the crystal vibrate. When the glass vibrates too much, the shape of the glass distorts, which causes the glass to crack. The cracks expand very rapidly, and the crystal shatters.

A trained singer can reproduce the natural frequency of a crystal glass. If the singer can sing the tone of the crystal's natural frequency loudly enough, the singing can shatter the glass!

Design It Resonant frequencies can also be used to make music. Glass harps use wine glasses filled with varying amounts of water to create different notes. The player runs a moistened finger around the rim of each glass. The size of the glass and the amount of water determine which note sounds. Research to learn more about how glass harps work. Then design an experiment to test the amount of water needed to create different pitches. Create a one-page procedure for your experiment.

HOW DOES MUSIC TRAVEL TO YOUR EARS?

 THE BIG Q

What determines the pitch and loudness of sound?

As these New Orleans musicians play their instruments, vibrations travel through the air as sound waves. The audience hears the music when their ears detect the sound waves. **Infer How do you hear sound from a drum?**

▶ **UNTAMED SCIENCE** Watch the **Untamed Science** video to learn more about sound.

_____

_____

_____

_____

_____

_____

_____

CHAPTER 13

Sound

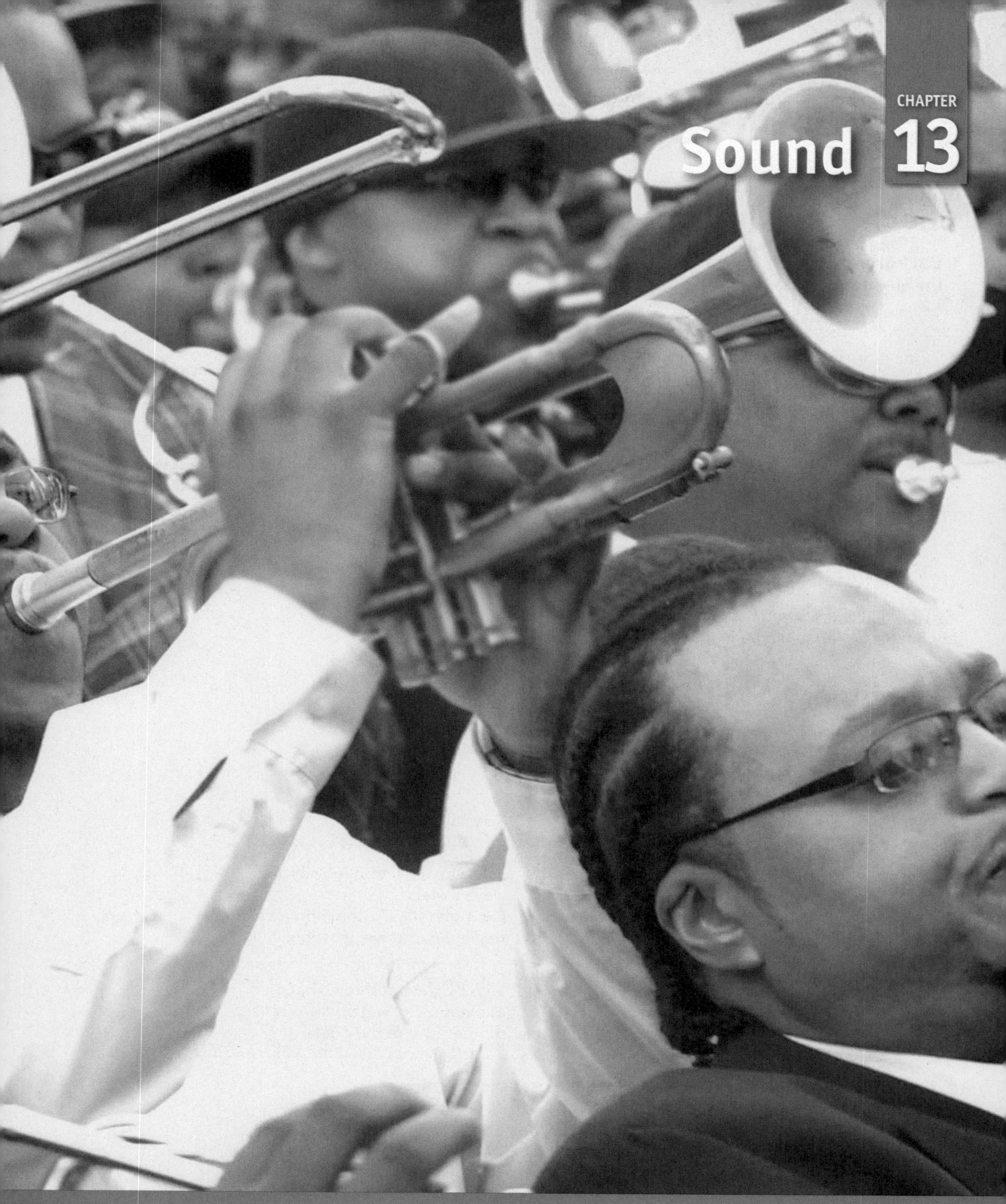

Check Your Understanding

1. Background Read the paragraph below and then answer the question.

One morning, an earthquake occurs in California. The ground **vibrates** as **waves** travel out in all directions from the source of the earthquake. The rocks inside Earth are the **medium** that transmits the waves.

To **vibrate** is to move back and forth.

Waves are disturbances that carry energy from one place to another.

A **medium** is a material through which a wave travels.

• What happens inside Earth during an earthquake?

_____

_____

> MY READING WEB If you had trouble completing the question above, visit **My Reading Web** and type in *Sound.*

Vocabulary Skill

Identify Multiple Meanings Some familiar words have more than one meaning. Words you use every day may have different meanings in science. Look at the different meanings of the words below.

Word	Everyday Meaning	Scientific Meaning
medium	*adj.* in the middle in quality, amount, or size **Example:** The boy is *medium* in size and build.	*n.* the material through which a wave travels **Example:** Air is a common *medium* for sound to travel through.
reflect	*v.* to express or show **Example:** Her skills in basketball *reflect* years of training.	*v.* to be bent or thrown back **Example:** The water waves *reflect* off the sides of the pool.

2. Quick Check Circle the sentence below that uses the scientific meaning of the word *reflect.*

• Her article *reflects* thorough research.
• Light waves *reflect* off the surface of a mirror.

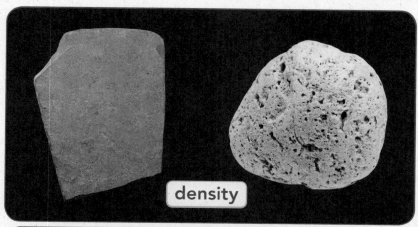

density

pitch

decibel

intensity

Chapter Preview

LESSON 1
- density
  - ↺ Identify the Main Idea
  - ◭ Graph

LESSON 2
- pitch
- loudness
- intensity
- decibel
- Doppler effect
  - ↺ Compare and Contrast
  - ◭ Make Models

LESSON 3
- music
- fundamental tone
- overtone
  - ↺ Identify Supporting Evidence
  - ◭ Predict

LESSON 4
- ear canal
- eardrum
- cochlea
  - ↺ Relate Cause and Effect
  - ◭ Observe

LESSON 5
- echolocation
- ultrasound
- sonar
- sonogram
  - ↺ Ask Questions
  - ◭ Calculate

> VOCAB FLASH CARDS For extra help with vocabulary, visit **Vocab Flash Cards** and type in *Sound.*

The Nature of Sound

UNLOCK THE BIG ?

🗝 **What Is Sound?**

🗝 **What Factors Affect the Speed of Sound?**

MY PLANET DIARY

FUN FACTS

Thunder and Lightning

It's a hot, sticky summer day, and the sky is filled with dark clouds. Suddenly, a flash of light zigzags through the air! A few seconds later, you hear the loud crack of thunder.

The lightning you see causes the thunder you hear. The reason you see lightning before you hear thunder is because light travels much faster than sound. You can use this fact to figure out how close the storm is. After you see a flash of lightning, count off the seconds until you hear the thunder. Divide the number of seconds by five. The result gives the approximate distance (in miles) to the storm.

Write your answer to the question below.
You notice that the time between seeing the lightning and hearing the thunder is increasing. What does this mean?

_____

_____

_____

_____

_____

▶ **PLANET DIARY** Go to **Planet Diary** to learn more about the nature of sound.

 ® Do the Inquiry Warm-Up *What Is Sound?*

What Is Sound?

Here is a riddle: If a tree falls in a forest and no one hears it, does the tree make a sound? To a scientist, a falling tree makes a sound whether someone hears it or not. When a tree falls, the energy with which it strikes the ground causes a disturbance. Particles in the ground and the air begin to vibrate, or move back and forth. The vibrations create a sound wave as the energy travels through two mediums—air and the ground. 🗝 **Sound is a disturbance that travels through a medium as a longitudinal wave.**

Vocabulary
• density

Skills
↻ Reading: Identify the Main Idea
△ Inquiry: Graph

Making Sound Waves A sound wave begins with a vibration. Look at the drum shown in **Figure 1.** When the side of the drum (called the drumhead) is struck, it vibrates rapidly in and out. These vibrations disturb nearby air particles. Each time the drumhead moves outward, it pushes air particles together, creating a *compression*. When the drumhead moves inward, the air particles bounce back and spread out, creating a *rarefaction*. These compressions and rarefactions travel through the air as longitudinal waves.

How Sound Waves Travel Like other mechanical waves, sound waves carry energy through a medium without moving the particles of the medium along. Each particle of the medium vibrates as the disturbance passes. When the disturbance reaches your ears, you hear the sound.

A common medium for sound is air. But sound can travel through solids and liquids, too. For example, when you knock on a solid wooden door, the particles in the wood vibrate. The vibrations make sound waves that travel through the door. When the waves reach the other side of the door, they make sound waves in the air.

Vocabulary Identify Multiple Meanings Review the multiple meanings of the words in the Getting Started section and answer the question. What is the material through which sound waves travel?

_____

FIGURE 1 ·······························
Sound Waves
As the drumheads vibrate, they create sound waves that travel through the air.

✎ **Interpret Diagrams** Label each box as a compression or a rarefaction. Explain how you knew what to label them.

_____
_____
_____
_____

Wavelength

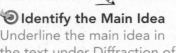

Identify the Main Idea
Underline the main idea in the text under Diffraction of Sound Waves.

FIGURE 2 ······························

Diffraction
Diffraction occurs when sound waves pass through an opening such as a doorway.

Identify Which diagram—A, B, or C—correctly shows what happens to sound waves when they pass through the doorway? Explain your answer.

_____

_____

_____

_____

_____

_____

_____

_____

_____

Diffraction of Sound Waves Have you ever wondered why when you are sitting in a classroom you can hear your friends talking in the hallway before they walk through the doorway? You hear them because sound waves do not always travel in straight lines. Sound waves can diffract, or bend, around the edges of an opening, such as a doorway.

Sound waves can also diffract around obstacles or corners. This is why you can hear someone who is talking in the hallway before the person walks around the corner. The sound waves bend around the corner. Then they spread out so you can hear them even though you cannot see who is talking. Remember this the next time you want to tell a secret!

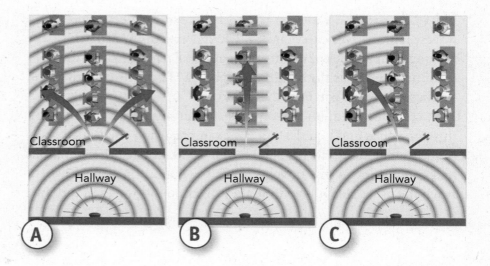

Lab zone — Do the Quick Lab Understanding Sound.

Assess Your Understanding

1a. Identify A sound wave carries _____ through a medium.

b. Compare and Contrast In a sound wave, the particles in the medium are close together in a (compression/rarefaction) and farther apart in a (compression/rarefaction).

c. Apply Concepts Explain why you can hear a ringing telephone through a closed door.

_____

_____

_____

_____

got it? ··

O **I get it!** Now I know sound is _____

_____

O **I need extra help with** _____

Go to MY SCIENCE COACH online for help with this subject.

What Factors Affect the Speed of Sound?

Suppose you were in a stadium watching the baseball player in **Figure 3.** You might see the bat hit the ball before you hear the hit. It is possible to see an action before you hear it because sound travels much more slowly than light. At room temperature, about 20°C, sound travels through air at 342 m/s. This is nearly 900,000 times slower than the speed of light! But the speed of sound is not always 342 m/s. Sound waves travel at different speeds in different media. ▬ **The speed of sound depends on the temperature, stiffness, and density of the medium the sound travels through.**

Temperature In a given liquid or gas, sound travels more slowly at lower temperatures than at higher temperatures. Why? At lower temperatures, the particles of a medium move more slowly than at higher temperatures. It is more difficult for the particles to move, and they return to their original positions more slowly.

FIGURE 3 ···

Speed of Sound in Air

How fast the sound of the bat hitting the ball travels depends on the air temperature. The data in the table show how the speed of sound in air changes with temperature.

✎ **Use the data to answer the questions.**

1. **Graph** Create a line graph. Plot temperature on the horizontal axis and speed on the vertical axis. Give the graph a title.

2. **Predict** What might the speed of sound be at 30°C? _____

Air Temperature (°C)	Speed (m/s)
−20	318
−10	324
0	330
10	336
20	342

Stiffness Years ago, Native Americans put their ears to the ground to find out if herds of bison or other animals were nearby. By listening for sounds in the ground they could hear the herds sooner than if they listened for sounds in the air. What is it about the state of the medium—solid, liquid, or gas—that determines the speed of sound?

The speed of sound depends on the stiffness of the medium. Sound travels more quickly in stiff media because when the particles of the medium are compressed, they quickly spread out again. For example, steel is stiffer than wood. If you knocked on both a wooden and steel door of the same thickness, the steel door would transmit the sound more easily. Sound also travels better over long distances in stiff media because sound waves lose energy more slowly than in less stiff media.

Solids are stiffer than liquids or gases. The particles in a solid are close together, so they bounce back and forth quickly as the compressions and rarefactions of the sound waves pass by. Most liquids are not as stiff as solids. So sound does not travel as fast in liquids as it does in solids. Gases are not very stiff. Sound generally travels the slowest in gases.

do the math! Analyzing Data

The table shows the speed of sound in different media. Use the data to answer the following questions.

1 Interpret Tables In general, does sound travel faster in solids, liquids, or gases?

_____

2 Infer Which substance is stiffer—air or water?

_____

3 Infer What is the stiffest substance in the table?

_____

4 Apply Concepts Suppose you put your ear to a steel fence. You tell your friend to yell and tap the fence at the same time from far away. Which do you think that you will hear first, the yell or the tap? Why?

_____
_____
_____
_____
_____

5 CHALLENGE How many times faster does sound travel in a diamond than in air?

_____
_____

Speed of Sound	
Medium	Speed (m/s)
Gases (20°C)	
Air	342
Helium	977
Liquids (20°C)	
Mercury	1,450
Fresh water	1,482
Solids	
Lead	1,200
Plastic	1,800
Hardwood	4,000
Steel	5,200
Diamond	12,000

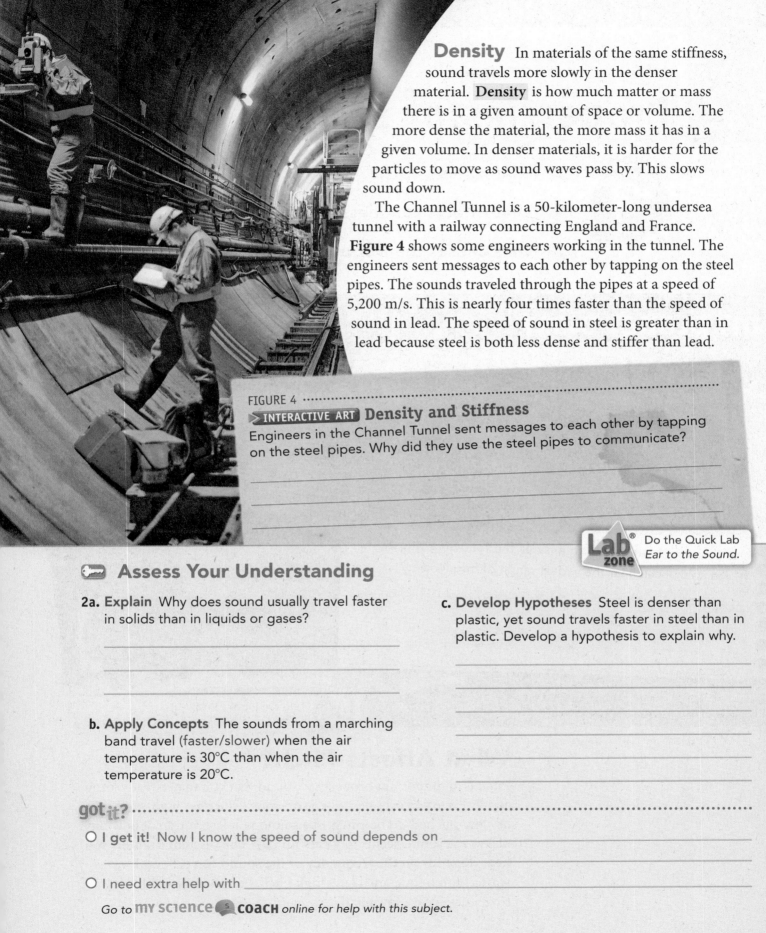

Density In materials of the same stiffness, sound travels more slowly in the denser material. **Density** is how much matter or mass there is in a given amount of space or volume. The more dense the material, the more mass it has in a given volume. In denser materials, it is harder for the particles to move as sound waves pass by. This slows sound down.

The Channel Tunnel is a 50-kilometer-long undersea tunnel with a railway connecting England and France. **Figure 4** shows some engineers working in the tunnel. The engineers sent messages to each other by tapping on the steel pipes. The sounds traveled through the pipes at a speed of 5,200 m/s. This is nearly four times faster than the speed of sound in lead. The speed of sound in steel is greater than in lead because steel is both less dense and stiffer than lead.

FIGURE 4 ···

> **INTERACTIVE ART** **Density and Stiffness**
Engineers in the Channel Tunnel sent messages to each other by tapping on the steel pipes. Why did they use the steel pipes to communicate?

_____

_____

_____

Lab zone® Do the Quick Lab *Ear to the Sound.*

🔑 Assess Your Understanding

2a. Explain Why does sound usually travel faster in solids than in liquids or gases?

_____

_____

_____

b. Apply Concepts The sounds from a marching band travel (faster/slower) when the air temperature is 30°C than when the air temperature is 20°C.

c. Develop Hypotheses Steel is denser than plastic, yet sound travels faster in steel than in plastic. Develop a hypothesis to explain why.

_____

_____

_____

_____

_____

_____

got it? ···

O **I get it!** Now I know the speed of sound depends on _____

_____

O **I need extra help with** _____

Go to **MY SCIENCE COACH** online for help with this subject.

Properties of Sound

UNLOCK THE BIG ?

🔑 **What Affects Pitch?**

🔑 **What Affects Loudness?**

🔑 **What Causes the Doppler Effect?**

my planet diary

Silent Call

To get a dog's attention, a dog trainer blows into a small whistle. But you don't hear a thing. Dogs can hear frequencies well above the human range of hearing. Frequency is measured in hertz (Hz), or the number of sound waves a vibrating object gives off per second. A higher frequency means that the sound has a higher pitch. The table compares the range of frequencies that humans and various animals can hear.

Use the data in the table to answer the following question.

Which animal can hear the widest range of frequencies?

_____

_____

_____

> **PLANET DIARY** Go to **Planet Diary** to learn more about the properties of sound.

SCIENCE STATS

Animal	Range of Hearing (in Hertz)
Human	20–20,000
Dog	67–45,000
Mouse	1,000–91,000
Cat	45–64,000
Bullfrog	100–2,500
Elephant	16–12,000

Lab zone® Do the Inquiry Warm-Up *How Does Amplitude Affect Loudness?*

What Affects Pitch?

Pitch is an important property of sound that you may already know about. Have you ever described someone's voice as "high-pitched" or "low-pitched"? The **pitch** of a sound is a description of how high or low the sound seems to a person. 🔑 **The pitch of a sound you hear depends on the frequency of the sound wave.** Sound waves with a high frequency have a high pitch. Sound waves with a low frequency have a low pitch.

Vocabulary
- pitch • loudness • intensity • decibel
- Doppler effect

Skills
- Reading: Compare and Contrast
- Inquiry: Make Models

The frequency of a sound wave depends on how fast the source of the sound is vibrating. For example, when you speak or sing, air from your lungs rushes past your vocal cords, making them vibrate. This produces sound waves. To sing specific pitches, or notes, you use muscles in your throat to stretch or relax your vocal cords. When your vocal cords stretch, they vibrate more quickly as the air rushes by them. This creates higher-frequency sound waves that have higher pitches. When your vocal cords relax, lower-frequency sound waves with lower pitches are produced.

Frequency is measured in hertz (Hz). For example, a frequency of 50 Hz means 50 vibrations per second. A trained soprano voice can produce frequencies higher than 1,000 Hz. A bass singer can produce frequencies lower than 80 Hz. Young people can normally hear sounds with frequencies between 20 Hz and 20,000 Hz.

FIGURE 1 ·····································

Pitch
The female soprano singer sings high notes and the male bass singer sings low notes.

△ Make Models In the bubble above the bass singer, draw lines to represent the frequency of the sound wave for a low note. Then explain your drawing.

_____

_____

_____

_____

Lab zone® Do the Lab Investigation *Changing Pitch.*

🔑 Assess Your Understanding

got it? ·····································

○ **I get it!** Now I know the pitch of a sound that you hear depends on _____

_____

○ **I need extra help with** _____

Go to **MY SCIENCE** ⓢ **COACH** online for help with this subject.

What Affects Loudness?

Loudness is another important property of sound. You probably already know about loudness. For example, the closer you are to a sound, the louder it is. Also, a whisper in your ear can be just as loud as a shout from a block away. **Loudness** describes your awareness of the energy of a sound.  **The loudness of a sound depends on the energy and intensity of the sound wave.**

Energy If you hit a drum lightly, you hear a sound. If you hit the drum harder, you hear a louder sound. Why? When you hit a drum harder, you transfer more energy to it. This causes the amplitude, or the distance the drumhead moves from its rest position, to increase. A sound source vibrating with a large amplitude produces a sound wave with a large amplitude. Recall that the greater the amplitude of a wave, the more energy it has. So the more energy a sound wave has, the louder it sounds.

Intensity If you were to move closer to the stage shown in **Figure 2,** the voices of the performers would sound louder. Why? Close to the sound source, a sound wave covers a small area. As a wave travels away from the source, it covers more area. The total energy of the wave, however, stays the same. Therefore, the closer a sound wave is to its source, the more energy it has in a given area. The amount of energy a sound wave carries per second through a unit area is its **intensity.** A sound wave of greater intensity sounds louder.

FIGURE 2 ·······························

Intensity
Sound waves spread out as they travel away from the source.

✎ **Interpret Diagrams** Rank the intensity of a sound wave at the three locations. A ranking of 1 is the greatest. Write your answers in the boxes. Explain your answers.

_____

_____

_____

_____

_____

_____

Measuring Loudness The loudness of different sounds is compared using a unit called the **decibel** (dB). The table in the Apply It below compares the loudness of some familiar sounds. The loudness of a sound you can barely hear is about 0 dB. A 10-dB increase in loudness represents a tenfold increase in the intensity of the sound. For example, a 10-dB sound is ten times more intense than a 0-dB sound. A 20-dB sound is 100 times more intense than a 0-dB sound and ten times more intense than a 10-dB sound. Sounds louder than 100 dB can cause damage to your ears, especially if you listen to those sounds for long periods of time. For this reason, airport workers, like the one shown to the right, wear hearing protection.

apply it!

Use the table to answer the questions.

❶ Which sounds louder, a rock concert or a jet plane at takeoff?_____

❷ Which sounds could be dangerous to your ears?

_____

_____

❸ **Calculate** How much more intense is a 20-dB whisper than the threshold of human hearing?

_____

❹ **CHALLENGE** How much more intense is a 90-dB hair dryer than 60-dB street traffic?

_____

Measuring Loudness	
Sound	**Loudness (dB)**
Threshold of human hearing	0
Whisper	15–20
Normal conversation	40–50
Busy street traffic	60–70
Hairdryer	80–90
Rock concert	110–120
Headphones at peak volume	120
Jet plane at takeoff	120–160

 Lab zone ® Do the Quick Lab
Listen to This.

🔑 **Assess Your Understanding**

1a. Review The amount of energy a sound wave carries per second through a unit area is its

_____

b. Describe The intensity of a sound wave (increases/decreases) with distance.

c. Calculate An 80-dB sound is _____ times more intense than a 60-dB sound.

got it?

O **I get it!** Now I know that the loudness of a sound depends on _____

_____

_____

O **I need extra help with** _____

Go to **MY SCIENCE ⓢ COACH** online for help with this subject.

What Causes the Doppler Effect?

Have you ever listened to the siren of a firetruck on its way to a fire? If so, then you probably noticed that as the truck goes by, the pitch of the siren drops. But the pitch of the siren stays constant for the firefighters in the truck. The siren's pitch changes only if it is moving toward or away from a listener.

The change in frequency of a wave as its source moves in relation to an observer is called the **Doppler effect.** If the waves are sound waves, the change in frequency is heard as a change in pitch. The Doppler effect is named after the Austrian scientist Christian Doppler (1803–1853). ⊂ **The Doppler effect occurs because the motion of the source causes the waves to either get closer together or spread out.**

Figure 3 shows how sound waves from a moving source behave. Each time the siren sends out a new wave, the firetruck moves ahead in the same direction as the waves in front of the truck. This causes the waves to get closer together. Because the waves are closer together, they have a shorter wavelength and a higher frequency as they reach observers in front of the truck. As the truck moves away, it travels in the opposite direction of the sound waves behind it. This causes the waves to spread out. Because they spread out, the waves have a longer wavelength and a lower frequency as they reach the observers behind the truck.

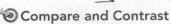

Compare and Contrast
The waves in front of a moving sound source have a (shorter/longer) wavelength. The waves behind a moving sound source have a (shorter/longer) wavelength.

FIGURE 3

▷ ART IN MOTION **The Doppler Effect**

As the firetruck speeds by, observers hear a change in the pitch of the siren. ✎ **Identify** Circle the answer that describes the pitch that the observers hear.

People behind the firetruck hear a (lower/higher) pitch than the firefighters in the truck hear.

People standing in front of the firetruck hear a (lower/higher) pitch than the firefighters in the truck hear.

FIRE DEPARTMENT

EXPLORE THE BIG ?

How Your Headphones Work

What determines the pitch and loudness of sound?

FIGURE 4 ···

> INTERACTIVE ART Headphones turn an electrical signal into sound waves.

1 An electrical signal travels up a wire.

2 The electrical signal causes a magnet to vibrate.

3 The magnet is attached to a thin cone of material. The vibrating cone sends sound waves through the air.

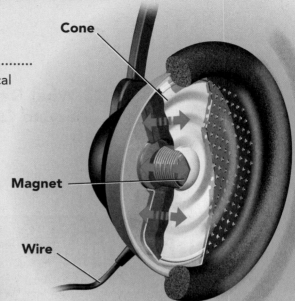

Cone

Magnet

Wire

⟳ **Compare and Contrast** Compare how a drum and headphones produce sounds of higher pitch and greater loudness.

_____

_____

_____

_____

_____

_____

_____

Lab zone® Do the Quick Lab *Pipe Sounds.*

🗝 Assess Your Understanding

2. **ANSWER THE BIG ?** What determines the pitch and loudness of sound?

_____

_____

_____

_____

_____

got it?

O **I get it!** Now I know that the Doppler effect occurs because _____

_____

_____

O **I need extra help with** _____

Go to **my science** 🄼 **coach** online for help with this subject.

3 Music

UNLOCK THE BIG ?

🔑 **What Determines Sound Quality?**

MY PLANET DIARY

Posted by: Jameel

Location: Orlando, Florida

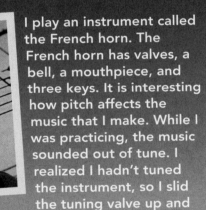

I play an instrument called the French horn. The French horn has valves, a bell, a mouthpiece, and three keys. It is interesting how pitch affects the music that I make. While I was practicing, the music sounded out of tune. I realized I hadn't tuned the instrument, so I slid the tuning valve up and down until I got the right pitch. I like to play my instrument because it enhances my hand/eye coordination. I also love the sound of the music when I play it right.

BLOG

Write your answers to the questions below.

1. What does it mean to tune an instrument?

_____

_____

_____

2. The musicians in a marching band do not tune their instruments until they are outside. Why do you suppose this is?

_____

_____

> PLANET DIARY Go to **Planet Diary** to learn more about music.

Lab zone® Do the Inquiry Warm-Up *What Is Music?*

What Determines Sound Quality?

Most people agree on what is and what is not music. **Music** is a set of notes that combine in patterns that are pleasing. Noise, on the other hand, usually has no pleasing patterns. When you describe a sound as pleasant or unpleasant, you are describing sound quality. The sound quality of music depends on the instruments making the music. 🔑 **The sound quality of musical instruments results from blending a fundamental tone with its overtones.**

Vocabulary
- music • fundamental tone
- overtone

Skills
↻ Reading: Identify Supporting Evidence
△ Inquiry: Predict

Fundamental Tones and Overtones

To understand sound quality, consider the example of a guitar string. As the string vibrates, waves travel along the string and reflect back, setting up a standing wave. Standing waves occur in all musical instruments when they are played. In a trumpet, for example, standing waves occur in a vibrating column of air.

A standing wave can occur only at specific frequencies, which are called natural frequencies. The lowest natural frequency is called the **fundamental tone.** The higher natural frequencies are called overtones. **Overtones** have frequencies that are two, three, or more times the frequency of the fundamental tone.

Most instruments produce several natural frequencies at once. The fundamental tone determines what note you hear. Each instrument produces different overtones, so the blending of the fundamental tones and overtones produces different sound qualities. The size, shape, and material of the instrument determine which overtones are loudest. For example, strumming a guitar's strings forces the guitar's hollow body to vibrate and resonate with the natural frequencies of the guitar strings. Resonance increases the amplitude of the vibration, increasing the loudness of the guitar.

✎
↻ **Identify Supporting Evidence** Underline the reason that the sound quality of a guitar is different from that of a trumpet.

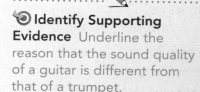

apply it!

A guitar can produce a fundamental tone of 262 Hz. The diagrams show how the fundamental tone and the first two overtones combine to produce the unique sound for a guitar string.

1 Calculate What are the frequencies of the first and second overtones?

Frequency of first overtone = _____

Frequency of second overtone = _____

2 Explain What determines which overtone will be loudest?

_____

_____

3 CHALLENGE Which overtone will be loudest? Why?

_____

_____

Fundamental tone

+

First overtone

+

Second overtone

=

Resulting sound wave

Groups of Musical Instruments

How does a musician control the sounds produced by a musical instrument? To control pitch, the musician changes the fundamental tones. To control loudness, the musician changes the energy of the vibrations. The way pitch and loudness are controlled varies among the groups of instruments.

Stringed Instruments

Stringed instruments include the guitar, violin, cello, and double bass. The strings of these instruments produce sound by vibrating when they are plucked or rubbed with a bow. To create louder sounds, the musicians pluck the strings harder or press the bow harder against the strings. To vary the pitch, the musicians change the length of the vibrating string. They do this by placing their fingers on different places along the string as they play. A short string produces a higher-pitched sound than a long string. The material, thickness, and tightness of a string also affect the pitch it produces.

FIGURE 1 ·······························
Violin
The musician creates sound by rubbing the bow across the strings.

✎ **Interpret Photos** Insert an arrow in the box above to indicate in what direction the musician should move his finger to create a higher-pitched sound.

Percussion Instruments

Percussion instruments include the drums, bells, cymbals, and xylophone. These instruments vibrate when struck. To create louder sounds, the musician hits the instrument harder. The pitch of these instruments depends on the material from which they are made, the size of the instrument, and the part of the instrument that is played. For example, a large drum produces a lower pitch than a small drum.

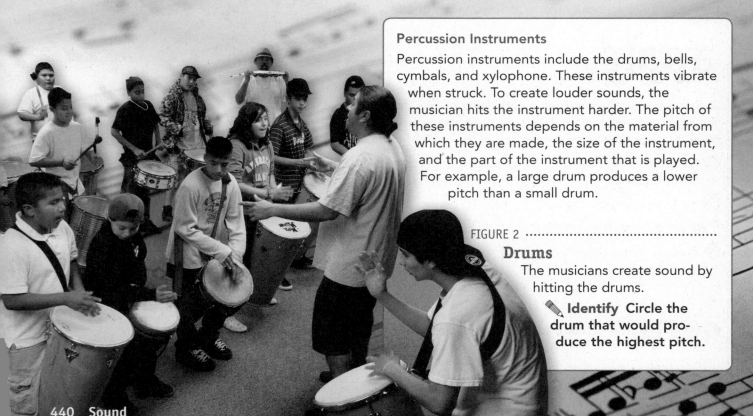

FIGURE 2 ·······························
Drums
The musicians create sound by hitting the drums.

✎ **Identify** Circle the drum that would produce the highest pitch.

Wind Instruments

Wind instruments include the trumpet, trombone, clarinet, and flute. These instruments create sound when the musician blows on or across the mouthpiece. This causes the air column inside the instrument to vibrate. The musician creates a louder sound by blowing harder. The musician changes pitch by changing the length of the air column. A shorter air column produces a higher pitch than a longer air column. In many wind instruments, the musician changes the length of the air column by pressing keys or valves. In the trombone, the musician changes the length of the air column by moving a slide either closer to or farther away from the mouthpiece.

FIGURE 3 ·······················

Trombone

The musician creates sound by blowing into the mouthpiece.

Predict **If the musician pushes the slide away from her, what will happen to the pitch of the trombone? Why?**

_____

_____

_____

_____

Slide

Lab zone Do the Quick Lab *How Can You Change Pitch?*

🔑 Assess Your Understanding

1a. List What are the three groups of musical instruments?

_____

b. Classify What types of instruments are a bell, a whistle, and a banjo?

_____

_____

_____

got it?

○ **I get it!** Now I know the sound quality of a musical instrument results from _____

_____

_____

_____

○ **I need extra help with** _____

Go to **MY SCIENCE COACH** online for help with this subject.

441

Hearing Sound

🔑 **How Do Your Ears Work?**

my planeT DiaRY

MISCONCEPTION

Misconception: Deaf people are not able to sense music.

Did you know that Beethoven composed many great works after he lost his hearing? Like all musicians, Beethoven could read music and hear it being played in his mind. But Beethoven may have been able to appreciate music in ways that musicians with normal hearing cannot. A recent study has shown that deaf people can sense vibrations in the same area of the brain that is used to hear. These vibrations create a pattern that they recognize and enjoy.

Deaf musicians can also feel vibrations in different parts of their bodies. The famous solo percussionist Evelyn Glennie performs barefoot so that she can better feel the vibrations in the floor. She also notices changes in the density of the air around her.

Write your answers to the questions below.

1. What senses are used to feel music?

_____

2. Describe an example of how you have felt the vibrations from music.

_____

_____

_____

▶ **PLANET DIARY** Go to **Planet Diary** to learn more about hearing sound.

Lab **zone** Do the Inquiry Warm-Up *Hearing Sound.*

Vocabulary
- ear canal • eardrum
- cochlea

Skills
↺ **Reading:** Relate Cause and Effect
△ **Inquiry:** Observe

How Do Your Ears Work?

The library is quiet. You are doing your homework. Suddenly, a door slams shut. Startled, you turn in the direction of the sound. Your ears detected the sound waves produced by the slamming door. But how exactly did your brain receive the information? 🔑 **Your ear gathers sound waves and sends information about sound to your brain.** Your ear has three main sections: the outer ear, the middle ear, and the inner ear. Each section has a different function. The outer ear funnels sound waves, the middle ear transmits the waves inward, and the inner ear converts sound waves into a form that travels to your brain.

apply it!

One of the functions of your ears is to locate the direction of sounds.

1 Ask your partner to sit in a chair with eyes closed.

2 △ **Observe** Tap two pencils together in different locations around your partner's head and face. Ask your partner to identify what direction the sounds come from. Record the locations where the taps are easily identified. Record the locations where the taps are harder to identify.

_____
_____
_____
_____
_____
_____

3 Switch places with your partner and repeat steps 1 and 2.

4 **Draw Conclusions** Discuss which sounds were easily located. Suggest an explanation for your observations.

_____
_____
_____
_____
_____
_____
_____
_____
_____
_____
_____
_____
_____

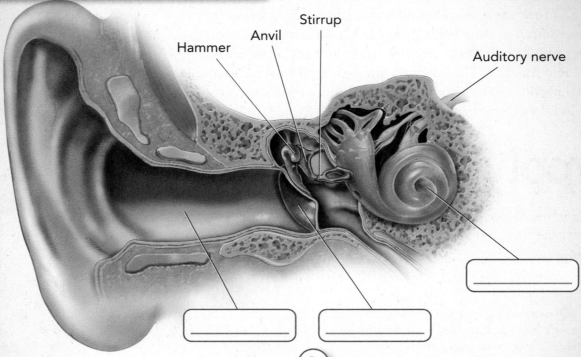

① Outer Ear

The first section of your ear is the outer ear. The outermost part of your outer ear looks and acts like a funnel. It collects sound waves and directs them into a narrow region called the **ear canal.** Your ear canal is a few centimeters long and ends at the eardrum. The **eardrum** is a small, tightly stretched, drumlike membrane. The sound waves make your eardrum vibrate, just as a drum vibrates when you strike it.

② Middle Ear

Behind the eardrum is the middle ear. The middle ear contains the three smallest bones in your body—the hammer, the anvil, and the stirrup. The hammer is attached to the eardrum. When the eardrum vibrates, the hammer does too. The hammer then transmits vibrations first to the anvil and then to the stirrup.

Hammer   Anvil   Stirrup

Auditory nerve

FIGURE 1 ···

The Human Ear

The ear has three main sections: the outer ear, the middle ear, and the inner ear.

✎ **Answer the following questions.**

1. **Name** Label the ear canal, eardrum, and cochlea.
2. **Identify** Circle each section of the ear. Draw a line from each circle to its matching text box.
3. **CHALLENGE** Which structure provides evidence that sound can travel through liquids? Explain.

_____

_____

_____

_____

_____

③ Inner Ear

A membrane separates the middle ear from the inner ear, the third section of the ear. When the stirrup vibrates against this membrane, the vibrations pass into the cochlea. The **cochlea** (KAHK lee uh) is a liquid-filled cavity shaped like a snail shell. The cochlea contains more than 10,000 tiny structures called hair cells. These hair cells have hairlike projections that float in the liquid of the cochlea. When vibrations move through the liquid, the hair cells move, causing messages to be sent to the brain through the auditory nerve. The brain processes these messages and tells you that you've heard sound.

Hearing Loss

When hearing loss occurs, a person may have difficulty hearing soft sounds or high-pitched sounds. Hearing loss can occur suddenly if the eardrum is damaged or punctured. (Imagine trying to play a torn drum!) For this reason, it is dangerous to put objects into your ear, even to clean it. Hearing loss can also occur gradually. As a person gets older, some hair cells in the cochlea die and do not grow back. People with this kind of hearing loss often have difficulty hearing high-frequency sounds. Extended exposure to loud sounds can also damage hair cells.

For some types of hearing loss, hearing aids can restore some ability to hear. Some hearing aids amplify sounds entering the ear. Others can amplify specific frequencies that a person has lost the ability to hear. For severe forms of hearing loss, a cochlear implant replaces the entire function of the ear. A cochlear implant contains a sound processor, an implant, and electrodes, as shown in **Figure 2.** The sound processor turns sound waves into an electrical signal. The implant transmits the signal to the electrodes. The electrodes stimulate the auditory nerve directly instead of the damaged cochlea.

✏️
⟳ Relate Cause and Effect
Underline three causes of hearing loss.

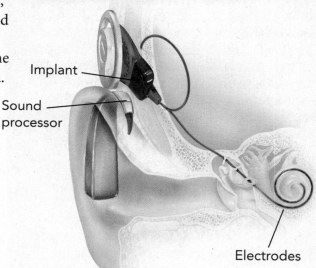

Implant

Sound processor

Electrodes

FIGURE 2 ·····················

A Cochlear Implant

A cochlear implant can restore the ability to hear.

✏️ **Explain** How does a cochlear implant replace the function of the ear?

_____

_____

_____

_____

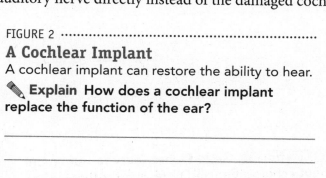

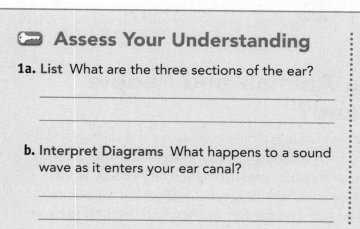

Lab zone® Do the Quick Lab *Design and Build Hearing Protectors.*

🔑 Assess Your Understanding

1a. List What are the three sections of the ear?

_____

_____

b. Interpret Diagrams What happens to a sound wave as it enters your ear canal?

_____

_____

got it?

○ **I get it!** Now I know the function of your ear is

_____

_____

_____

○ **I need extra help with** _____

Go to MY SCIENCE ⓢ COACH *online for help with this subject.*

Using Sound

UNLOCK THE BIG ?

🔑 How Do Animals and People Use Sound?

my planet Diary

CAREERS

Marine Scientist

Why are marine scientists in Sarasota Bay, Florida, spying on dolphins? Dolphins send out a series of high-frequency clicks to navigate and find food. They whistle to communicate with each other. The scientists are recording underwater sounds in the bay. They are also noting dolphin sightings. They will use the data to determine how boat noise in the bay affects dolphin behavior.

Boat noise, underwater drilling, and sonar devices used by the military have all been shown to affect dolphins, porpoises, and whales. For this reason, it is a rich area of research for marine scientists.

Write your answer to the question below.

Make Judgments How do you think boat noise could affect the dolphins in the bay?

_____

_____

_____

_____

_____

_____

_____

> PLANET DIARY Go to **Planet Diary** to learn more about echolocation and ultrasound technologies.

Lab® zone Do the Inquiry Warm-Up *How Can You Use Time to Measure Distance?*

How Do Animals and People Use Sound?

Have you ever shouted into a canyon or a cave and then waited for the echo? An echo is a reflected sound wave. When a sound wave hits a surface that it cannot pass through, it may reflect. Some practical uses of sound, including echolocation and ultrasound technologies, are based on the fact that sound reflects off surfaces.

Vocabulary
- echolocation • ultrasound
- sonar • sonogram

Skills
↻ Reading: Ask Questions
△ Inquiry: Calculate

Echolocation Many animals find it easy to move around in dark places. This is because they use echolocation. **Echolocation** (EK oh loh KAY shun) is the use of reflected sound waves to determine distances or to locate objects. 🔑 **Some animals, including bats and dolphins, use echolocation to navigate and find food.**

Sound waves with frequencies above the normal human range of hearing are called **ultrasound.** The prefix *ultra-* means "beyond." Bats use ultrasound waves with frequencies up to 100,000 Hz to move around and hunt. As a bat flies, it sends out short pulses of ultrasound waves. The waves reflect off objects and return to the bat's ears, as shown in **Figure 1.** The time it takes for the sound waves to return tells the bat how far it is from obstacles or prey.

Dolphins use ultrasound waves with frequencies up to 150,000 Hz to hunt and move around in murky, deep water. The sound waves travel through the water and reflect off fish or other prey. Dolphins sense the reflected sound waves through their jawbones.

FIGURE 1 ·······························
Echolocation
A bat uses echolocation to hunt.
✎ **Answer the following questions.**

1. **Relate Diagrams and Photos** In each of the steps, describe how the bat locates its prey.

2. **Explain** Why would the bat have to continue to send out sound waves as it gets closer to its prey?

_____

_____

1

3

2

✎ **Ask Questions** Before reading about ultrasound technologies, ask yourself a *What* or *How* question. Then answer your question.

_____

_____

_____

_____

_____

✎ **Vocabulary** Identify Multiple Meanings Review the multiple meanings of the words in the Getting Started section and complete the sentence. A sonar device detects sound waves

after they _____

off objects.

Ultrasound Technologies

Unlike animals, people cannot send out pulses of ultrasound to help them move around in the dark. But people sometimes need to explore places they cannot easily reach, such as deep under water or inside the human body. ▬ **People use ultrasound technologies, such as sonar and ultrasound imaging, to observe things that they cannot see directly.**

Sonar A system that uses reflected sound waves to detect and locate objects under water is called **sonar.** The word *sonar* comes from the initial letters of **so**und **n**avigation **a**nd **r**anging. "Navigation" means finding your way around on the ocean (or in the air). "Ranging" means finding the distance between objects. People use sonar to determine the depth of water, to map the ocean floor, and to locate objects such as sunken ships and schools of fish.

A sonar device sends a burst of ultrasound waves that travel through the water. When the sound waves strike an object or the ocean floor, they reflect. The sonar device detects the reflected waves. A computer in the sonar device measures the time it takes for the sound waves to go out and return. Then it uses the following equation to solve for the total distance that sound travels.

Distance = Speed of sound in water × Time

To solve for how far away the object is you must divide the total distance by two. This is because sound waves travel out and return.

apply it!

A sonar device sends out sound waves to detect a sunken ship.

1 ✎ **Calculate** Suppose the sonar device detects the reflected sound waves 10.0 seconds later. The speed of sound in salt water is 1,530 m/s. How far down is the sunken ship?

_____

_____

_____

_____

_____

2 **CHALLENGE** The *Titanic* is located nearly 3,800 meters below the surface of the ocean. How much time would it take for the sound waves to travel to the *Titanic* and back to the surface?

_____

_____

_____

Ultrasound Imaging Doctors use ultrasound imaging to look inside the human body. An ultrasound imaging device sends ultrasound waves into the body. Then it detects the reflected sound waves. Different parts of the body, such as bones, muscles, the liver, or the heart, reflect sound differently. The device uses the reflected waves to create a picture called a **sonogram.** A doctor can use sonograms to diagnose and treat many medical conditions.

The technician in **Figure 2** is using an ultrasound imaging device to examine a fetus. The technician holds a small probe on the pregnant woman's abdomen. The probe sends out very high frequency ultrasound waves (about 4 million Hz). By analyzing the reflected sound waves, the device builds up a sonogram. The sonogram can show the position of the fetus. Sonograms can also show if there is more than one fetus. In addition to a still picture, ultrasound imaging can produce a video of the fetus.

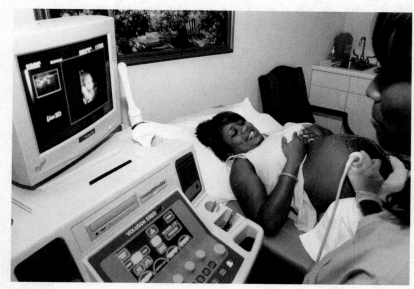

FIGURE 2 ·····························

> REAL-WORLD INQUIRY **Ultrasound in Medicine**
An ultrasound imaging device creates a sonogram of a fetus.

✎ **Explain How does an ultrasound imaging device work?**

_____

_____

_____

_____

_____

 Do the Quick Lab
Designing Experiments.

☞ Assess Your Understanding

1a. Define _____ is the use of reflected sound waves to determine distances or to locate objects.

b. Compare and Contrast How is sonar similar to ultrasound imaging? How is it different?

_____

_____

_____

_____

_____

_____

_____

got it?

○ **I get it!** Now I know that animals use echolocation to _____

_____

_____

and humans use ultrasound technologies to

_____

_____

_____

○ **I need extra help with** _____

Go to **MY SCIENCE** ⓢ **COACH** *online for help with this subject.*

Study Guide

The pitch of a sound depends on the_____ of the sound wave. The loudness of a sound depends on the _____ and _____ of the sound wave.

LESSON 1 The Nature of Sound

🔑 Sound is a disturbance that travels through a medium as a longitudinal wave.

🔑 The speed of sound depends on the temperature, stiffness, and density of the medium the sound travels through.

Vocabulary
• density

LESSON 2 Properties of Sound

🔑 The pitch of a sound you hear depends on the frequency of the sound wave.

🔑 The loudness of a sound depends on the energy and intensity of the sound wave.

🔑 The Doppler effect occurs because the motion of the source causes the waves to either get closer together or spread out.

Vocabulary
• pitch • loudness • intensity • decibel
• Doppler effect

LESSON 3 Music

🔑 The sound quality of musical instruments results from blending a fundamental tone with its overtones.

Vocabulary
• music
• fundamental tone
• overtone

LESSON 4 Hearing Sound

🔑 Your ear gathers sound waves and sends information about sound to your brain.

Vocabulary
• ear canal
• eardrum
• cochlea

LESSON 5 Using Sound

🔑 Some animals, including bats and dolphins, use echolocation to navigate and find food.

🔑 People use ultrasound technologies, such as sonar and ultrasound imaging, to observe things that they cannot see directly.

Vocabulary
• echolocation
• ultrasound
• sonar
• sonogram

Review and Assessment

LESSON 1 The Nature of Sound

1. What term describes how much matter or mass there is in a given volume?

  a. stiffness   **b.** density

  c. temperature   **d.** diffraction

2. If you increase the temperature of a liquid or gas, a sound wave will travel _____

3. Summarize What three properties of a medium affect the speed of sound?

_____

_____

4. Make Models In the circles below, draw the air particles in a compression and rarefaction of the same sound wave.

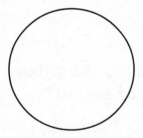 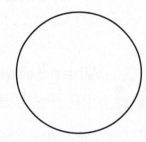

    Compression   Rarefaction

5. Relate Cause and Effect Why is a vibration of an object necessary for a sound wave to form?

_____

_____

_____

_____

_____

6. Infer Thunder and lightning happen at the same time. Explain why you see the lightning before you hear the thunder.

_____

_____

_____

LESSON 2 Properties of Sound

7. What property of sound describes your awareness of the energy of a sound?

  a. loudness   **b.** intensity

  c. pitch   **d.** elasticity

8. As a sound wave travels, its intensity decreases because _____

_____

9. Interpret Diagrams Look at the sound waves coming from the two speakers. Which speaker cone is vibrating faster? How do you know?

_____

_____

_____

10. Relate Cause and Effect As a car drives past a person standing on a sidewalk, the driver keeps a hand on the horn. How does the pitch of the horn differ for the driver and the person standing on the sidewalk?

_____

_____

_____

_____

11. **Write About It** Explain how listening to your headphones at too high a volume can cause just as much damage to your ears as the sounds at a rock concert.

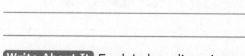

451

LESSON 3 Music

12. What term describes the lowest natural frequency of the source of a sound?

    a. overtone   **b.** standing wave

    c. fundamental tone   **d.** pitch

13. The quality of sound that a musical instrument produces is the result of _____

_____

_____

14. Apply Concepts A trumpet player pushes down on one of the valves to produce a lower note. How did the length of the air column in the trumpet change? Explain.

_____

_____

_____

_____

LESSON 4 Hearing Sound

15. What part of the ear contains thousands of hair cells that transmit sound?

    a. cochlea   **b.** middle ear

    c. ear canal   **d.** eardrum

16. The middle ear contains the three smallest bones in the body, which are called the

_____, the _____,

and the _____

17. Infer Sometimes a very loud sound or physical contact with an object can tear the eardrum. How would this affect hearing? Why?

_____

_____

_____

_____

LESSON 5 Using Sound

18. What system uses reflected sound waves to detect and locate objects under water?

    a. sonogram   **b.** ultrasound imaging

    c. diffraction   **d.** sonar

19. Some animals use _____

to navigate by sensing reflected sound waves.

20. math! Suppose it takes 6.0 seconds for a sound wave to travel to the bottom of the ocean and back to the surface. If the speed of sound in salt water is 1,530 m/s, how deep is the ocean at this point?

_____

_____

_____

What determines the pitch and loudness of sound?

21. How could you make sounds of different pitch and loudness with the two drums?

_____

_____

_____

_____

Standardized Test Prep

Multiple Choice

Circle the letter of the best answer.

1. The table below compares the loudness of several different sounds.

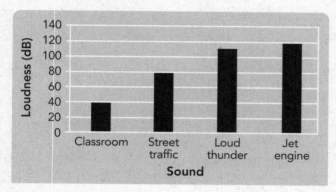

   How many times more intense is the sound of a jet engine than the sound of loud thunder?

A 2		**B** 10	
C 20		**D** 100	

2. Fishing boats use sonar to locate schools of fish. What characteristic of sound is most important for this application of sonar?

   A Sound waves reflect off some surfaces.

   B Sound waves diffract around corners.

   C Sound waves interfere when they overlap.

   D Sound waves spread out from a source.

3. A trumpet and a piano can both play the same note, but the sound qualities are very different. Why does the sound quality depend on the instrument that produces it?

   A Each instrument produces a different fundamental tone.

   B Each instrument produces different overtones.

   C The amplitude of the notes is different.

   D The intensity of the sound is different.

4. Why does sound intensity decrease as the distance from the source increases?

   A Most of the energy is absorbed by the particles of the medium.

   B The same amount of energy is spread out over a larger area.

   C The frequency increases as distance from the source increases.

   D The energy of the sound wave decreases.

5. What is the function of the inner ear?

   A The inner ear vibrates when sound waves strike it.

   B The inner ear converts vibrations into signals that travel to the brain.

   C The inner ear increases the frequency of sound waves.

   D The inner ear transmits sound waves from the ear canal to the cochlea.

Constructed Response

Use the table below to answer Question 6. Draw your graph on a separate sheet of paper.

6. Make a bar graph to compare highest frequencies heard by and produced by each animal listed. Which animal(s) can produce sounds that are too high for humans to hear?

Animal	Highest Frequency Heard (Hz)	Highest Frequency Produced (Hz)
Human	20,000	1,100
Dog	45,000	1,800
Cat	64,000	1,500
Bat	120,000	120,000
Porpoise	150,000	120,000

CAN YOU HEAR ME NOW?

Write About It Write a letter to your town or city council. Identify and explain what the impact of noise pollution is on the people in your town or city. Describe your ideas about how to reduce noise in your area.

CRASH! BANG! BEEP BEEP! In cities all across the world, noise pollution is part of everyday life. Noise pollution is loud, distracting sound.

There are many different types of noise pollution. Some of the most common are residential noise, road traffic noise, and air traffic noise. Residential noise pollution occurs in places where people live. It includes noisy neighbors, high-pitched car alarms, and power tools from renovations. Road traffic noise pollution is common at busy intersections or on highways. Helicopters and airplanes cause air traffic noise pollution. Air traffic noise is especially troublesome for people who live or work near airports.

Too much noise can cause hearing loss, lack of sleep, and increased stress. Studies show that students who go to school in areas that have high levels of noise pollution have lower test scores. The noise affects students' ability to concentrate.

More than 100 million Americans are regularly exposed to noise levels higher than 55 decibels—the common standard for background noise levels. As a result, governments are passing laws to reduce noise pollution.

NOISY Occupations

Settings and costumes can make a film interesting to watch. But think for a moment about watching a car chase without the sounds of traffic, tires squealing, or motors revving. The scene might look great, but it would be less thrilling.

Several people work to create the sound effects in a movie.

Foley artists create the background noises that make a scene convincing. They create everyday sounds such as footsteps or jingling keys. They also create less ordinary noises, such as punching noises. These noises might not be very obvious, but you would notice if they weren't there.

Sound mixers record all sound effects and dialogue. If all of the sounds were recorded at the same time scenes were filmed, you wouldn't be able to hear a thing the actors were saying—the wrong noises would be loud and cover the speech. So sound mixers record the dialogue and effects separately and mix them together in the studio.

Sound effects editors make sure that everyone follows the sound plan for the film, and that all of the noises happen at the right time in a way that works.

Record It Work in a small group to record an audio track. Design a solution for sounds you have to "fake." For example, how would you make a sound for something dropping from the roof? Play your track for the class—can they tell what is happening?

HOW DO SCANS "SEE" YOUR BRAIN?

What kinds of waves make up the electromagnetic spectrum?

It might look like a colorful wig, but this image shows the nerve pathways of the brain. Using machines that read energy from our bodies, doctors can see how and when different areas of the brain are active without surgery or radiation.

When your brain performs a task, such as remembering a phone number, blood circulation to that part of your brain increases. The scan recognizes that activity.

△Infer **What might the colors of this brain scan mean?**

_____

_____

_____

_____

_____

▷ UNTAMED SCIENCE Watch the **Untamed Science** video to learn more about electromagnetic waves.

Electromagnetic Waves

14 Getting Started

Check Your Understanding

1. **Background** Read the paragraph below and then answer the question.

> Have you ever stepped in a large puddle? When your foot hits the water, it transfers energy to the water, creating a wave. The medium, water, vibrates with the transfer of energy. The water ripples around your foot.

A **wave** is a disturbance that transfers energy from place to place.

The material through which a wave travels is the **medium.**

To **vibrate** is to move in a repeated back-and-forth or up-and-down motion.

- What caused the water to vibrate?

_____

_____

> MY READING WEB If you had trouble completing the question above, visit **My Reading Web** and type in *Electromagnetic Waves.*

Vocabulary Skill

Greek Word Origins Some science words in this chapter contain word parts with Greek origins. The table below lists some of the Greek words from which the vocabulary words come.

Greek Word	Meaning of Greek Word	Example
mikro-	small	microwaves, *n.* electromagnetic radiation with short wavelengths and high frequencies
-skopion	for seeing or observing	spectroscope, *n.* instrument used to see different colors of light
photos	light	photon, *n.* packet of light energy

2. **Quick Check** Circle the word part in *spectroscope* that tells you its meaning has to do with viewing.

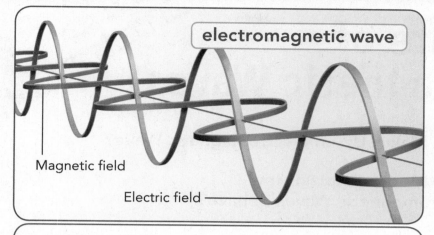

electromagnetic wave

Magnetic field

Electric field

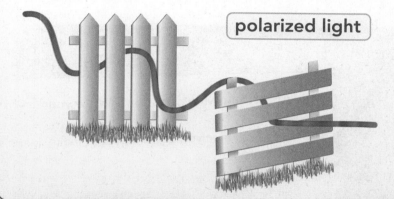

polarized light

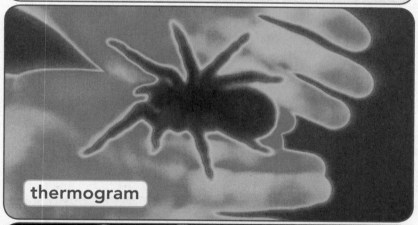

thermogram

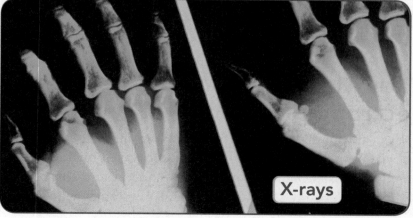

X-rays

Chapter Preview

LESSON 1

- electromagnetic wave
- electromagnetic radiation
- polarized light
- photoelectric effect
- photon

🔄 **Identify the Main Idea**
🔺 **Calculate**

LESSON 2

- electromagnetic spectrum
- radio waves
- microwaves
- radar
- infrared rays
- thermogram
- visible light
- ultraviolet rays
- X-rays
- gamma rays

🔄 **Summarize**
🔺 **Communicate**

LESSON 3

- amplitude modulation
- frequency modulation

🔄 **Compare and Contrast**
🔺 **Interpret Data**

> VOCAB FLASH CARDS For extra help with vocabulary, visit **Vocab Flash Cards** and type in *Electromagnetic Waves.*

The Nature of Electromagnetic Waves

 UNLOCK THE BIG **Q**

🔑 **What Makes Up an Electromagnetic Wave?**

🔑 **What Models Explain How Electromagnetic Waves Behave?**

my planeT DiaRY

BLOG

Posted by: Justin

Location: King George, Virginia

Electromagnetic waves are used in everyday life. Some examples are phones, iPods, scales, and super computers. Imaging machines such as MRIs, CAT Scans, X-rays, and ultrasound allow us to detect abnormalities in the body. Electromagnetic waves help us with jobs, school, and medical problems. They make life easier by shortening time needed to do things. Phones allow us to speak to relatives in different states. Super computers help us monitor the shuttles in space.

Read the following questions. Write your answers below.

1. How do electromagnetic waves make Justin's life easier?

_____

_____

_____

2. How do you use electromagnetic waves in your everyday life?

_____

_____

> PLANET DIARY Go to **Planet Diary** to learn more about electromagnetic waves.

 Lab® zone Do the Inquiry Warm-Up *How Fast Are Electromagnetic Waves?*

What Makes Up an Electromagnetic Wave?

As you sit at your desk and read this book, you are surrounded by waves you cannot see or hear. There are radio waves, microwaves, infrared rays, visible light, ultraviolet rays, and tiny amounts of X-rays and gamma rays. These waves are all electromagnetic waves.

Vocabulary
- electromagnetic wave • electromagnetic radiation
- polarized light • photoelectric effect • photon

Skills
↻ Reading: Identify the Main Idea
△ Inquiry: Calculate

Characteristics of Electromagnetic Waves

An **electromagnetic wave** is a transverse wave that involves the transfer of electric and magnetic energy. **An electromagnetic wave is made up of vibrating electric and magnetic fields that move through space or some medium at the speed of light.**

An electromagnetic wave can begin with the movement of charged particles, all of which have electric fields around them. As the particles change speed or direction, a vibrating electric field is created, which in turn produces a vibrating magnetic field. The vibrating magnetic field creates a vibrating electric field. The electric and magnetic fields produce each other repeatedly. The result is an electromagnetic wave, shown in **Figure 1.** Note that the two fields vibrate at right angles to one another.

Energy The energy that electromagnetic waves transfer through matter or space is called **electromagnetic radiation.** Electromagnetic waves do not require a medium such as air, so they can transfer energy through a vacuum, or empty space.

FIGURE 1 ·····························

Electromagnetic Wave

An electromagnetic wave travels through space at the speed of light—about 300,000 kilometers per second.

✏️ △ Calculate How long will it take sunlight to travel the 150 million kilometers to Earth? Use a calculator to solve the problem.

_____

_____

_____

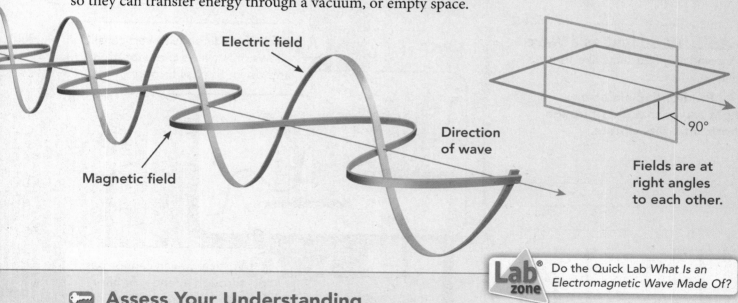

Electric field

Magnetic field

Direction of wave

90°

Fields are at right angles to each other.

Lab® zone Do the Quick Lab *What Is an Electromagnetic Wave Made Of?*

↻ Assess Your Understanding

got it? ···

○ **I get it!** Now I know that electromagnetic waves are made of _____

_____

○ **I need extra help with** _____

Go to **my science** ⓢ **coach** online for help with this subject.

What Models Explain How Electromagnetic Waves Behave?

🔑 **Two different models are needed to explain the behavior of electromagnetic waves. A wave model best explains many of the behaviors, but a particle model best explains others.** Light is an electromagnetic wave. It has many properties of waves but can also act as though it is a stream of particles.

Wave Model of Light When light passes through a polarizing filter, it has the properties of a wave. An ordinary beam of light consists of waves that vibrate in all directions. A polarizing filter acts as though it has tiny slits aligned in only one direction. The slits can be horizontal or vertical. When light enters a polarizing filter, only some waves can pass through it. The light that passes through is called **polarized light.**

To help you understand the wave model, think of light waves like transverse waves on a rope. They vibrate in all directions. If you shake a rope through a fence with vertical slits, only waves that vibrate up and down will pass through, as shown in **Figure 2.** The other waves are blocked. A polarizing filter acts like the slits in a fence. It allows only waves that vibrate in one direction to pass through it.

🔁 **Identify the Main Idea**
Circle the main idea in the first paragraph. Underline the details.

FIGURE 2 ·······························

▶ VIRTUAL LAB **Light as a Wave**
A polarizing filter acts like the slits in a fence.

✎ **Predict** Explain how light waves that pass through horizontal slits vibrate.

_____

_____

_____

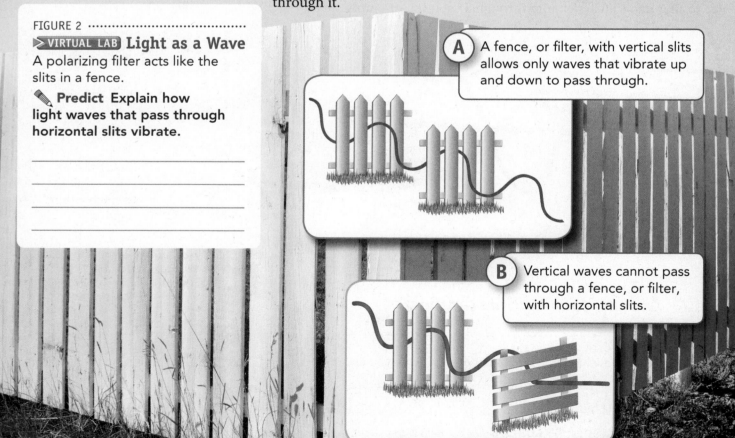

A A fence, or filter, with vertical slits allows only waves that vibrate up and down to pass through.

B Vertical waves cannot pass through a fence, or filter, with horizontal slits.

apply it!

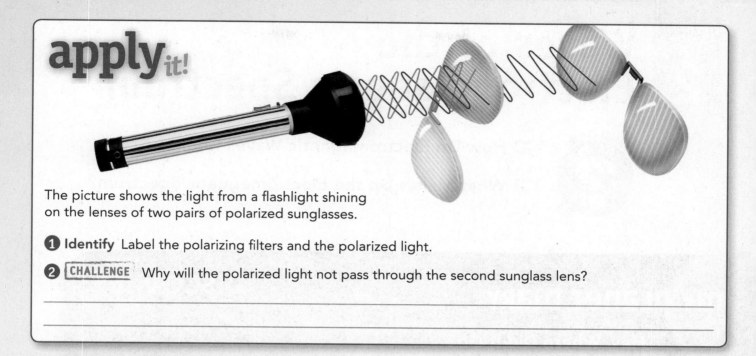

The picture shows the light from a flashlight shining on the lenses of two pairs of polarized sunglasses.

1 Identify Label the polarizing filters and the polarized light.

2 CHALLENGE Why will the polarized light not pass through the second sunglass lens?

_____

_____

Particle Model of Light
Sometimes light behaves like a stream of particles. For example, when a beam of high frequency light shines on some metals, it causes tiny particles to move. These particles are called electrons. Sometimes light can even cause an electron to move so much that it is knocked out of the metal, as shown in **Figure 3**. This is called the **photoelectric effect.** This effect can be explained by thinking of light as a stream of tiny packets, or particles, of energy. Each packet of light energy is called a **photon.** For the effect to occur, each photon must contain enough energy to knock an electron free from the metal.

FIGURE 3 ··
The Photoelectric Effect
Photons hitting a metal surface knock out electrons.

Dim blue light or ultraviolet rays

Metal plate

Lab zone ® Do the Quick Lab
Waves or Particles?

🔑 Assess Your Understanding

1a. Define A _____ is a tiny packet of energy.

b. Describe What does a polarizing filter do?

_____

_____

_____

got it?

○ **I get it!** Now I know that the models that explain how electromagnetic waves behave are _____

_____

○ **I need extra help with** _____

Go to my science ⓢ coach *online for help with this subject.*

Waves of the Electromagnetic Spectrum

UNLOCK THE BIG ?

🔑 How Do Electromagnetic Waves Compare?

🔑 What Makes Up the Electromagnetic Spectrum?

my PLANET DiARY

DISCOVERY

Hey, Where Did It Go?

What would you do if you had an invisibility cloak? This idea might not be as far-fetched as it sounds. Scientists have actually been working on creating a way to make objects invisible! Researchers have created a device that can change the direction of microwaves, so that they flow around a test object. This rerouting causes the object to look invisible at microwave frequencies. Unfortunately, people cannot see microwaves, which means the object isn't invisible to us. But, who knows, maybe one day you'll be able to put on one of these "cloaks" and move around completely unseen!

Answer the question below.

If a device like this is developed for visible light, how do you think a scientist who studies animals in nature might use it?

_____

_____

_____

_____

_____

_____

▶ PLANET DIARY Go to **Planet Diary** to learn more about the electromagnetic spectrum.

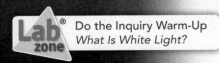

Lab® zone Do the Inquiry Warm-Up *What Is White Light?*

Vocabulary
- electromagnetic spectrum • radio waves • microwaves
- radar • infrared rays • thermogram • visible light
- ultraviolet rays • X-rays • gamma rays

Skills
- Reading: Summarize
- Inquiry: Communicate

How Do Electromagnetic Waves Compare?

Can you imagine trying to take a photo with a radio or heating your food with X-rays? Light, radio waves, and X-rays are all electromagnetic waves. But each has properties that make it more useful for some purposes than others. **All electromagnetic waves travel at the same speed in a vacuum, but they have different wavelengths and different frequencies.** A vacuum is a space that contains no air or other gas.

Visible light is the only range of wavelengths your eyes can see. Your radio detects radio waves, which have much longer wavelengths than visible light. X-rays, on the other hand, have much shorter wavelengths than visible light.

For waves in any medium, as the wavelength decreases, the frequency increases. Waves with the longest wavelengths have the lowest frequencies. Waves with the shortest wavelengths have the highest frequencies. The higher the frequency of a wave, the higher its energy.

FIGURE 1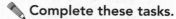

Comparing Electromagnetic Waves
Different types of electromagnetic waves have different wavelengths.

✏ **Complete these tasks.**

1. **Label** Write the names *visible light*, *radio waves*, and *X-rays* in the correct boxes on the diagram.

2. **Draw Conclusions** Which wave has the highest energy? Explain.

_____

_____

_____

_____

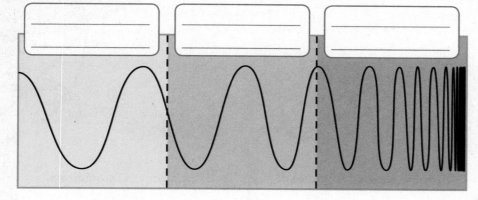

Lab® Do the Quick Lab
zone *Differences Between Waves.*

Assess Your Understanding

got it? ···

O **I get it!** Now I know that electromagnetic waves have different _____

_____ but the same _____

O **I need extra help with** _____

Go to MY SCIENCE 🔵 COACH *online for help with this subject.*

What Makes Up the Electromagnetic Spectrum?

There are many different types of electromagnetic waves. The complete range of electromagnetic waves placed in order of increasing frequency is called the **electromagnetic spectrum.** 🔑 The electromagnetic spectrum is made up of radio waves, microwaves, infrared rays, visible light, ultraviolet rays, X-rays, and gamma rays. The full spectrum is shown in **Figure 2.**

Radio Waves Electromagnetic waves with the longest wavelengths and the lowest frequencies are **radio waves.** Radio waves are used in broadcasting to carry signals for radio programs. A broadcast station sends out radio waves at certain frequencies. Your radio picks up the radio waves and converts them into an electrical signal. The electrical signal is then converted into sound.

FIGURE 2 ···

The Electromagnetic Spectrum
The electromagnetic spectrum can be broken up into different categories.

✏️ **Interpret Diagrams** Use the word bank to fill in the boxes in the diagram. Do microwaves or ultraviolet waves have longer wavelengths? Which have higher frequencies?

_____

_____

_____

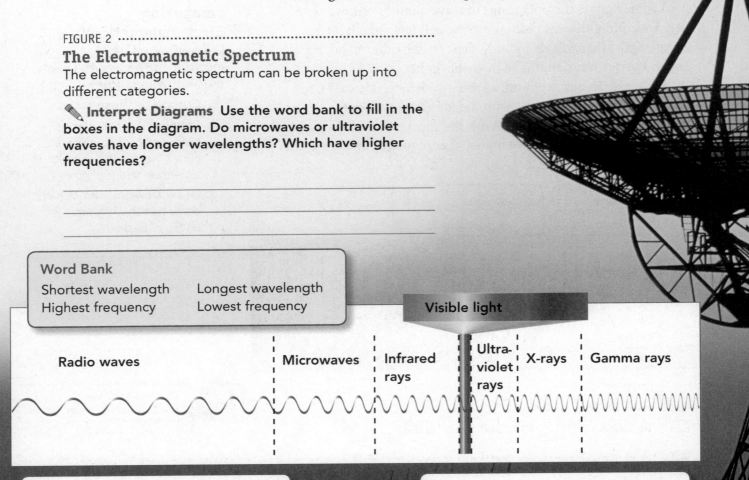

Word Bank
Shortest wavelength   Longest wavelength
Highest frequency   Lowest frequency

Visible light

Radio waves | Microwaves | Infrared rays | Ultra-violet rays | X-rays | Gamma rays

Microwaves

Microwaves have shorter wavelengths and higher frequencies than radio waves do. When you think about microwaves, you probably think of microwave ovens that cook and heat food. But microwaves have many other uses, including cellular phone communication and radar.

Radar stands for **ra**dio **d**etection **and** **r**anging. **Radar** is a system that uses reflected microwaves to detect objects and measure their distance and speed. To measure distance, a radar device sends out microwaves that reflect off an object. The time it takes for the reflected waves to return is used to calculate the object's distance. To measure speed, a radar device uses the Doppler effect. For example, suppose a police radar gun sends out microwaves that reflect off a car. Because the car is moving, the frequency of the reflected waves is different from the frequency of the original waves. The difference in frequency is used to calculate the car's speed.

apply it!

Radio stations are broadcast in two different frequency ranges. The ranges are the kilohertz range (kHz) for AM stations and the megahertz range (MHz) for FM stations. The prefix *kilo-* means "thousand"; *mega-* means "million."

1 **Interpret Data** What is the frequency range of the AM band on the radio? Of the FM band?

_____

_____

2 **Interpret Photos** Approximately what frequencies are being tuned in on each band?

_____

_____

3 [CHALLENGE] The units kHz and MHz stand for kilohertz and megahertz, respectively. If 1 MHz = 1000 kHz and 1 kHz = 1000 Hz, what is the frequency, in Hz, of a signal broadcast on 99.7 FM? Express your answer in scientific notation.

_____

_____

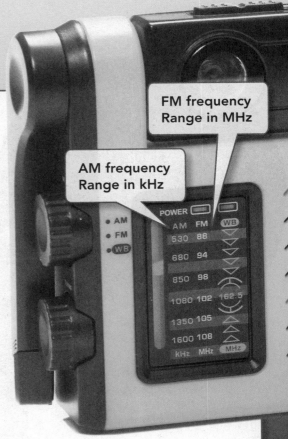

FM frequency Range in MHz

AM frequency Range in kHz

Infrared Rays

Infrared Rays If you turn on an electric stove's burner, you can feel it warm up before the heating element starts to glow. The invisible heat you feel is infrared radiation, or infrared rays. **Infrared rays** are electromagnetic waves with wavelengths shorter than those of microwaves. They have higher frequencies and therefore more energy than microwaves. Because you can feel the energy of infrared rays as heat, these rays are often called heat rays. Heat lamps have bulbs that give off mainly infrared rays. They are used to keep things warm, such as food in a cafeteria or young animals in an incubator.

Most objects give off some infrared rays. Warmer objects give off infrared rays with more energy and higher frequencies than cooler objects. An infrared camera uses infrared rays instead of visible light to take pictures called thermograms. A **thermogram** is an image that shows regions of different temperatures in different colors, as shown in **Figure 3.**

FIGURE 3 ·····································

The Uses of Infrared Rays
Infrared rays are used in devices such as heat lamps and TV remote controls.

✎ **Complete these tasks.**

1. **Interpret Diagrams** List the labeled areas on the thermogram from hottest to coolest.

   _____

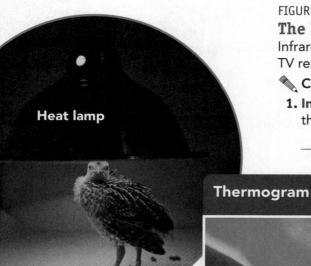

Heat lamp

2. **Identify** Where do you think this heat lamp is being used?

   _____

   _____

   _____

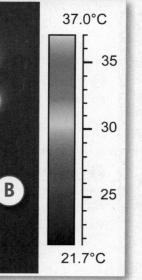

Thermogram

37.0°C

35

30

25

21.7°C

Visible light waves with the longest wavelengths appear red in color.

The shortest wavelengths of visible light appear violet in color.

Sequence What are the colors of the visible spectrum in order, starting with red?

_____

_____

_____

_____

Interpret Photos Which color has the highest frequency?

_____

_____

FIGURE 4 ······································
The Visible Spectrum
Refraction of white light from the sun by raindrops separates the light into the colors of the visible spectrum.

✏ **Answer the questions in the boxes to the left and below.**

◢ **Communicate** Talk with a partner. Describe other times when you have seen the visible spectrum.

_____

_____

_____

_____

_____

_____

Visible Light
Electromagnetic waves that you can see are called **visible light.** They make up only a small part of the electromagnetic spectrum. Visible light waves have shorter wavelengths and higher frequencies than infrared rays.

Visible light that appears white is actually a mixture of many colors. Recall that light waves bend, or refract, when they enter a new medium. So, when white light passes through rain drops, a rainbow can result, like the one in **Figure 4**.

Ultraviolet Rays
Electromagnetic waves with wavelengths just shorter than those of visible light are called **ultraviolet rays.** Ultraviolet rays have higher frequencies than visible light, so they carry more energy. The energy of ultraviolet rays can damage or kill living cells. For example, too much exposure to ultraviolet rays can burn your skin and over time may cause skin cancer. However, small doses of ultraviolet rays are useful. They cause skin cells to produce vitamin D, which is needed for healthy bones and teeth.

did you
know?
The Environmental Protection Agency of the United States tracks ultraviolet light levels in Texas and throughout the country. The agency's UV index rates ultraviolet exposure on a scale of 1 to 11+. High ratings result in UV exposure warnings. These warnings let people know how long they can be out in the sun safely without sunblock.

469

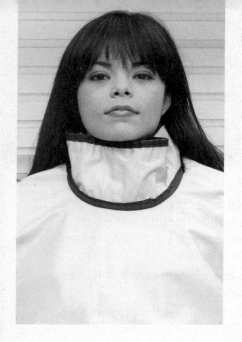

FIGURE 5 ·····························

Lead Apron

X-rays are often used to look at bones and teeth.

✎ **Explain** Why does a dentist cover you with a lead apron to take X-rays of your teeth?

_____

_____

_____

_____

·············· ✎ ··············

↻ **Summarize** In your own words, write a summary of the section about gamma rays.

X-rays

Electromagnetic waves with wavelengths just shorter than those of ultraviolet rays are **X-rays.** Their frequencies are just a little higher than ultraviolet rays. Because of their high frequencies, X-rays carry more energy than ultraviolet rays and can penetrate most matter. Dense matter, such as bone or lead, absorbs X-rays so they do not pass through. Therefore, X-rays are used to make images of bones and teeth. However, too much exposure to X-rays can cause cancer. See **Figure 5.**

X-rays can also be used in industry and engineering. Engineers can use an X-ray image of a steel or concrete structure to find cracks. Dark areas on the X-ray film show the cracks.

Gamma Rays

Electromagnetic waves with the shortest wavelengths and highest frequencies are **gamma rays.** Since they have the greatest amount of energy, gamma rays are the most penetrating of electromagnetic waves. Because of their penetrating ability, these rays are used to examine the body's internal structures. A patient can be injected with a fluid that emits gamma rays. Then, a gamma-ray detector can form an image of the inside of the body.

Some radioactive substances and certain nuclear reactions produce gamma rays. Some objects in space emit bursts of gamma rays. However, these rays are blocked by Earth's atmosphere. Astronomers think that explosions of distant stars produce these gamma rays.

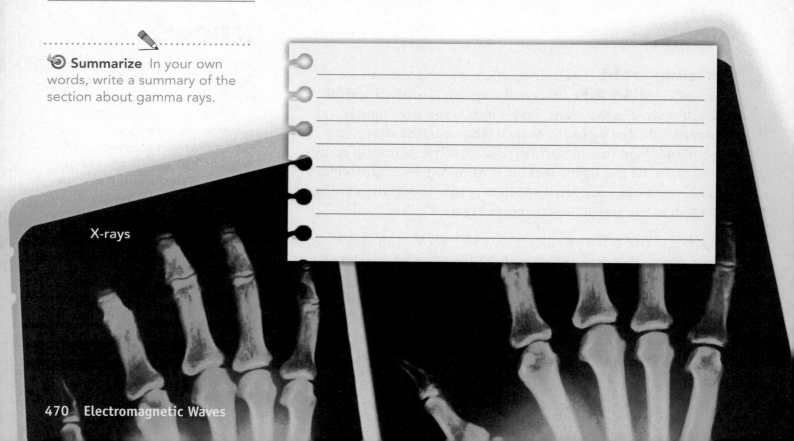

X-rays

Surfing the Spectrum

What kinds of waves make up the electromagnetic spectrum?

FIGURE 6 ·································

> INTERACTIVE ART The electromagnetic spectrum includes many kinds of waves.

✎ **Complete the activities.**

1. **Identify** Label each kind of wave on the electromagnetic spectrum.

2. **Classify** Circle the name of the highest energy waves.

3. **Apply Concepts** On the notebook page, describe the uses of two kinds of waves.

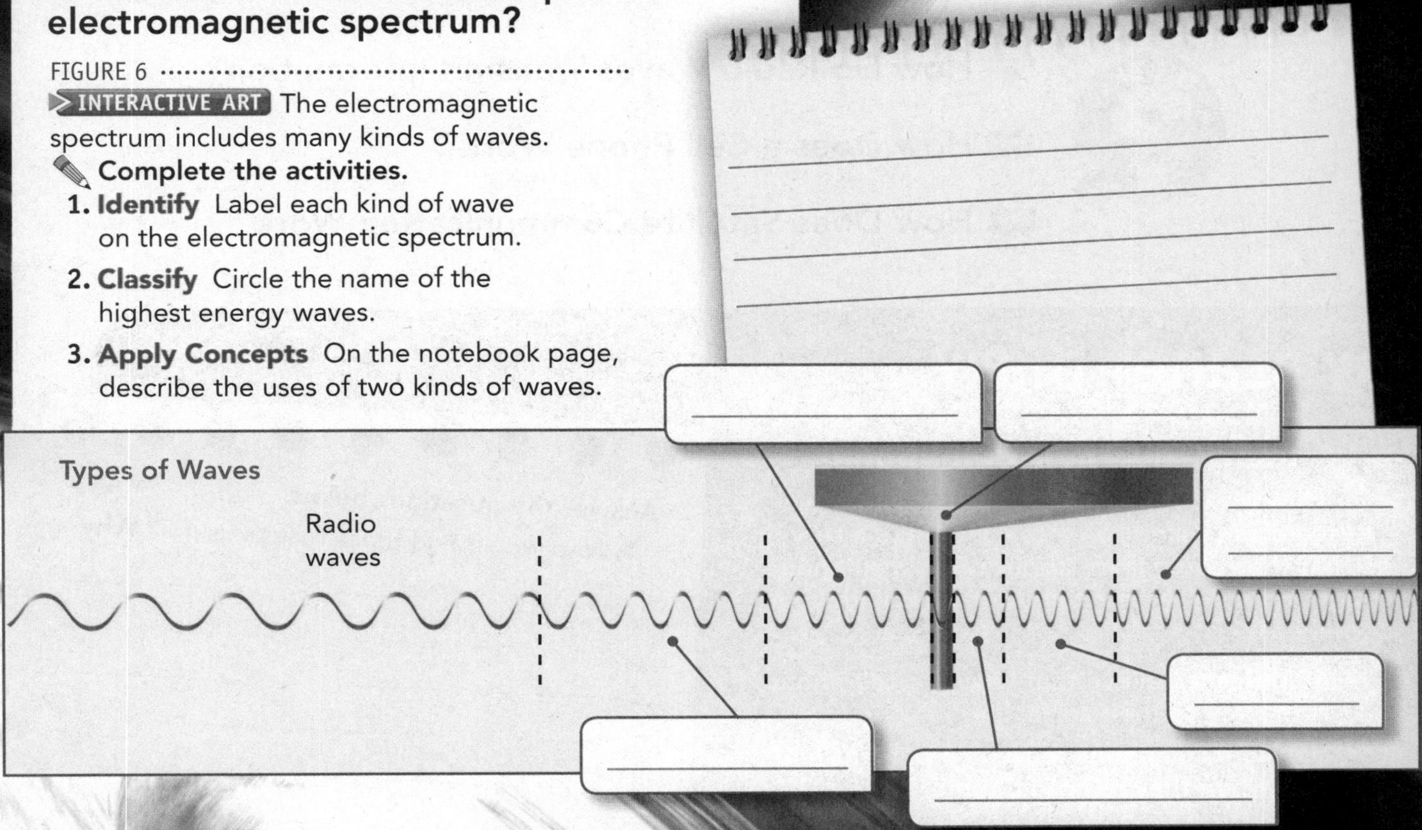

Types of Waves

Radio waves

Do the Quick Lab *Parts of the Electromagnetic Spectrum.*

🔑 Assess Your Understanding

1a. Explain How do ultraviolet rays help your bones and teeth?

_____

_____

_____

b. ANSWER THE BIG ? What kinds of waves make up the electromagnetic spectrum?

_____

_____

_____

got it? ·····································

○ **I get it!** Now I know the electromagnetic spectrum is made up of _____

_____

○ **I need extra help with** _____

Go to MY SCIENCE ⑤ COACH *online for help with this subject.*

Wireless Communication

🔑 **How Do Radio Waves Transmit Information?**

🔑 **How Does a Cell Phone Work?**

🔑 **How Does Satellite Communication Work?**

my planet diary

Teens and Their Cell Phones

How do teens feel about cell phones? Researchers asked some teens to take a survey so that they could learn about teens' cell-phone usage. How do these results compare with your own ideas?

- 45 percent believe that having a cell phone is the key to their social life.

- Having a cell phone makes 78 percent feel safe when they're not at home.

- When asked to select additional features for a basic cell phone, 71 percent chose a music player.

- More than half use cell phones to check e-mail.

- Nearly half said they could send text messages while blindfolded!

FUN FACTS

Answer the questions below.

1. Who would find these results useful? Why?

_____

_____

_____

_____

_____

2. What do you think is the most important use of a cell phone?

_____

_____

> **PLANET DIARY** Go to **Planet Diary** to learn more about wireless communication.

 Do the Inquiry Warm-Up *How Can Waves Change?*

Vocabulary
- amplitude modulation
- frequency modulation

Skills
- Reading: Compare and Contrast
- Inquiry: Interpret Data

How Do Radio Waves Transmit Information?

You are in the car on a long road trip and switch on the radio to listen to some music. In an instant, your favorite song is coming through the car's speakers. How do radio broadcasts reach you?

Broadcasting Radio waves carry, or transmit, signals for radio programs. Charged particles vibrating inside transmission antennas produce radio waves. Transmission antennas send out, or broadcast, radio waves in many directions. 🔑 **Radio waves carry information from the antenna of a broadcasting station to the receiving antenna of your radio.** Look at **Figure 1.**

FIGURE 1 ·····································

How a Radio Works
Radios tune in radio wave signals broadcast by antennas located at radio stations.

✎ **Sequence** In the circles, number the steps to show the correct order of events that results in hearing a broadcast.

The electronic signal comes out of your radio as sound.

Radio waves strike your radio's antenna and are picked up.

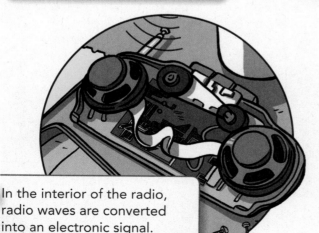

In the interior of the radio, radio waves are converted into an electronic signal.

At the radio station, electronics convert music into radio waves that are then broadcast by a large antenna.

FIGURE 2 ···

> INTERACTIVE ART Radio Waves
Radio stations transmit signals
by changing a radio wave's
amplitude or frequency.

✎ **Interpret Diagrams** Under
each type of wave, write the
wave property that is constant.

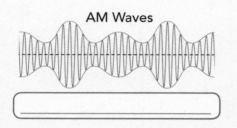

AM Waves

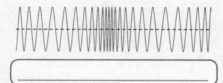

FM Waves

Broadcasting Signals Radio stations broadcast signals in
two frequency bands. These bands are amplitude modulation (AM)
and frequency modulation (FM).

Amplitude Modulation A method of broadcasting signals by
changing the amplitude of a wave is called **amplitude modulation.**
AM signals travel as changes, or modulations, in the amplitude of
the wave. The frequency of an AM wave is constant.

AM radio waves have relatively long wavelengths and low
frequencies and energy. They are easily reflected back to Earth's
surface by Earth's ionosphere, a region of charged particles high
in the atmosphere. Therefore, AM radio stations can be broadcast
over long distances.

Frequency Modulation **Frequency modulation** is a method
of broadcasting signals by changing the frequency of a wave.
FM signals travel as changes in the frequency of the wave. The
amplitude of an FM wave is constant.

FM waves have higher frequencies and more energy than
AM waves. FM waves pass through the ionosphere instead of being
reflected back to Earth. Therefore, they do not travel as far on
Earth's surface as AM waves. However, FM waves usually produce
better sound quality than AM waves. **Figure 2** shows FM waves and
AM waves.

··············· ✎ ···············

↻ **Compare and Contrast**
Complete the Venn diagram
to compare AM and FM
radio waves.

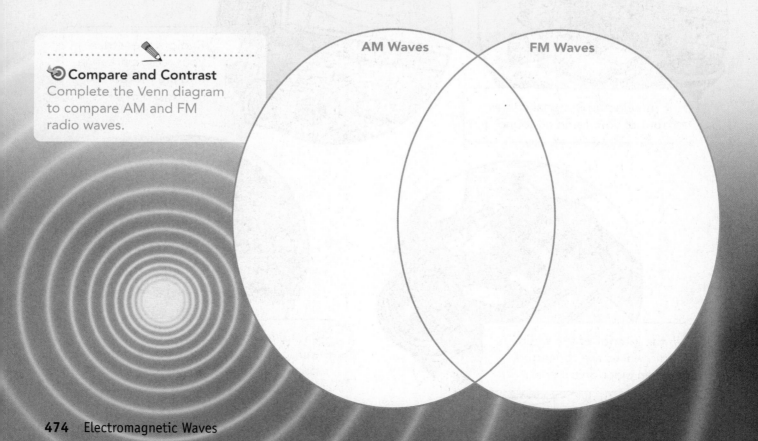

AM Waves   FM Waves

do the math! Analyzing Data

The table shows the frequencies assigned by the Federal Communications Commission (FCC) for various radio channels.

① **Interpret Data** Which broadcast uses the highest-frequency range? Which uses the lowest-frequency range?

_____

_____

_____

_____

_____

Broadcast Frequencies		
Type of Broadcast	Frequency Range	Converted Frequency Range
AM radio	535 kHz to 1,605 kHz	_____ _____
Amateur radio	1,800 kHz to 1,900 kHz	_____ _____
FM radio	88 MHz to 108 MHz	_____ _____

② **CHALLENGE** Convert each given frequency range into units of hertz. (*Hint:* 1 kHz = 1000 Hz, and 1 MHz = 1,000,000 Hz.) Write your answers in the table.

The Radio Spectrum
In addition to AM and FM broadcasts, radio waves are used for many types of communication. The FCC assigns different radio frequencies for different uses. Radio stations use one part of the radio spectrum. Taxi and police radios are assigned separate sets of frequencies. Amateur radio frequencies are assigned for people who operate radios as a hobby. Because the signals all have different assigned frequencies, they travel without interfering.

Lab zone ® Do the Lab Investigation *Build a Crystal Radio.*

🗝 Assess Your Understanding

1a. Identify What wave property is changed when AM radio signals are broadcast?

_____

b. Apply Concepts Longer wavelengths bend more easily around obstacles such as mountains. In a hilly countryside, will you be more likely to hear an AM or FM station?

_____

_____

got it?

○ **I get it!** Now I know that radio waves _____

_____

_____

_____

○ **I need extra help with** _____

Go to **MY SCIENCE** 🅢 **COACH** online for help with this subject.

How Does a Cell Phone Work?

Cellular telephones, or cell phones, are an important part of your daily life. However, they only work if they are in a cellular system. The cellular system works by dividing regions into many small cells, or geographical areas, as shown in **Figure 3**. Each cell has one or more towers that relay signals to a central hub.

🔑 **Cell phones transmit and receive signals using high-frequency microwaves.** Though the process needed to complete a cell phone call looks complicated, the entire process happens so quickly it seems to be instantaneous. In addition to making phone calls, cell phones have many different uses. They can be used to send text messages, browse the Internet, and take photos.

1 When you place a cell-phone call, the phone sends out microwaves, which are tagged with a number unique to your phone.

2 A tower picks up the microwaves and transfers the signal to a hub.

3 The hub channels and transmits the signal to a receiver. The receiver may be another tower or another hub, depending on the distance between the two phones.

4 The tower or hub transmits the signal to the receiving cell phone.

FIGURE 3 ....

> ART IN MOTION **Using a Cell Phone**

The quality of your cell-phone calls depends on the terrain and how close your phone is to a cell-phone tower or a central hub.

✎ **Apply Concepts** Suppose you make a call from location B to a friend at location C. Draw the path the signal could travel to complete the call. Explain what would likely happen if you made a cell call from location A.

_____

_____

_____

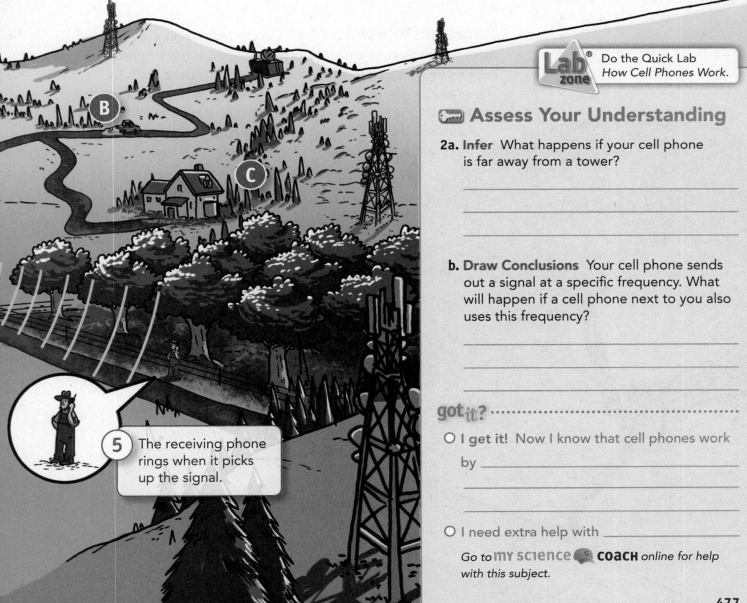

⑤ The receiving phone rings when it picks up the signal.

Lab® zone | Do the Quick Lab *How Cell Phones Work.*

🗝 **Assess Your Understanding**

2a. Infer What happens if your cell phone is far away from a tower?

_____

_____

_____

b. Draw Conclusions Your cell phone sends out a signal at a specific frequency. What will happen if a cell phone next to you also uses this frequency?

_____

_____

_____

got it? ....

○ **I get it!** Now I know that cell phones work by _____

_____

_____

○ **I need extra help with** _____

Go to **my science** coach *online for help with this subject.*

How Does Satellite Communication Work?

Satellites orbiting Earth send information around the world. Communications satellites work like the receivers and transmitters of a cellular phone system. 🔑 **Communications satellites receive radio, television, and telephone signals and relay the signals to receivers on Earth.** Because a satellite can "see" only part of Earth at any time, more than one satellite is needed for any purpose.

✏️ **Compare and Contrast**

In the paragraphs to the right, underline the sentences that compare satellite communication with another form of electronic communication.

Satellite Phone Systems Several companies offer satellite phone systems. Radio waves from one phone are sent up to a communications satellite. The satellite transmits the waves back to the receiving phone on Earth. With this kind of phone, you can call anywhere in the world, but it costs more than using a cell phone.

Satellite Television Systems Television networks and cable companies use communications satellites. Television signals are sent up to satellites. The satellites then relay the signals to places around the world. Television signals from satellites are often scrambled. Customers of satellite companies need a satellite dish antenna like the one shown in **Figure 4** to pick up the signals and a decoding box to unscramble the signals.

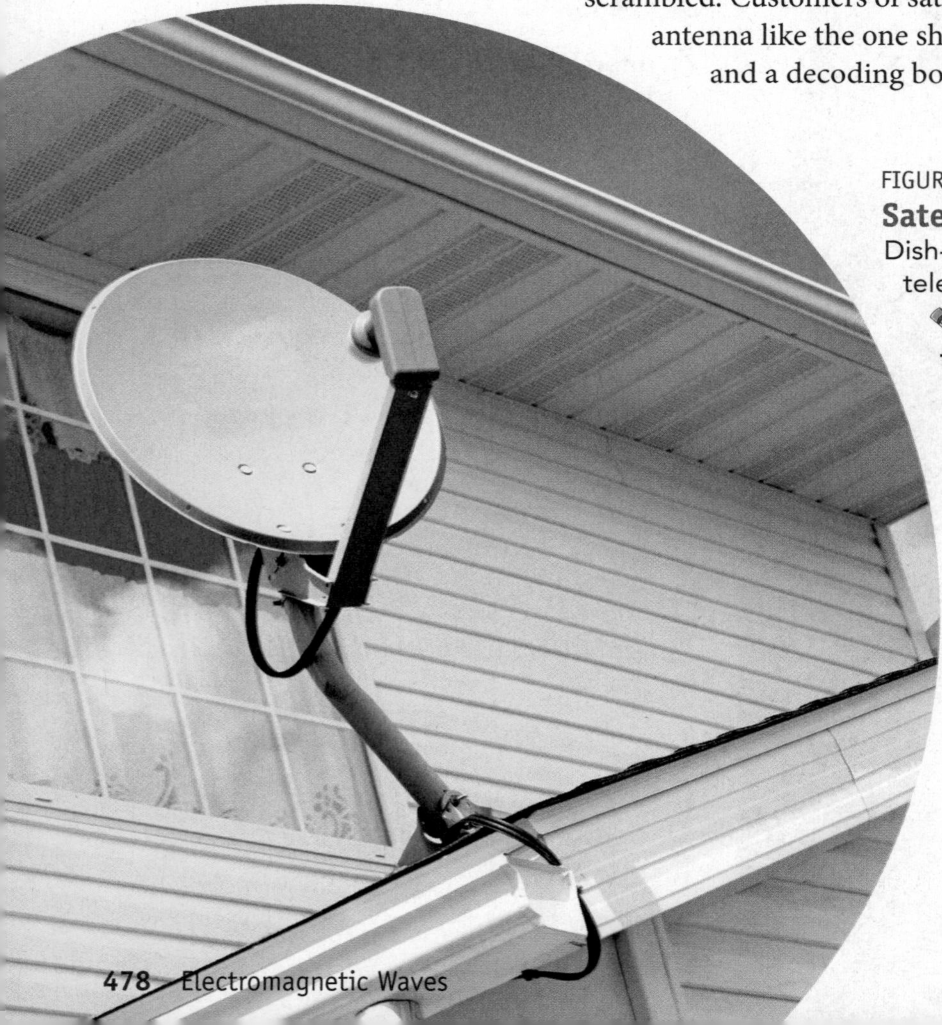

FIGURE 4 ·····························
Satellite Dishes
Dish-shaped antennas receive signals for television programs from satellites.

✒️ **Infer** Satellite dishes point to a fixed location in the sky. What does this tell you about the position of the satellite?

_____

_____

_____

_____

Global Positioning System

Global Positioning System The Global Positioning System (GPS) is a system of navigation originally designed for the military. GPS uses a network of 24 satellites that broadcast radio signals to Earth. These signals carry information that tells you your exact location on Earth's surface, or even in the air. Anybody with a GPS receiver can pick up these signals. GPS receivers can be found in cars, airplanes, boats, and even cell phones.

Signals from four out of 24 GPS satellites are used to determine your position. The signals from three satellites tell you where you are on Earth's surface. The signal from the fourth satellite tells you how far above Earth's surface you are.

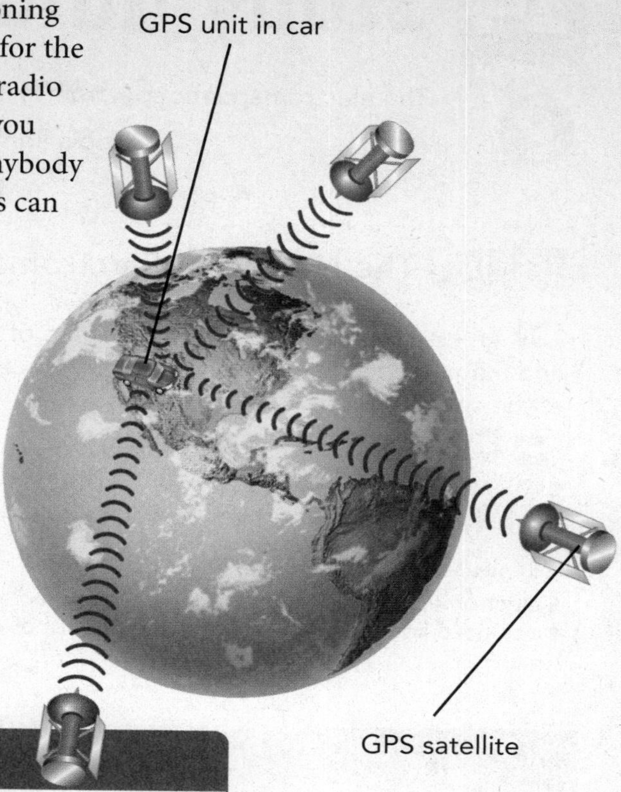

GPS unit in car

GPS satellite

FIGURE 5 ....

> ART IN MOTION **Uses of Satellites**

Modern communication uses satellites in different ways.

✎ **Summarize** Complete the table by summarizing how satellites are used in each type of communication.

System	Summary
Global Positioning System	_____ _____ _____
Satellite Phone System	_____ _____ _____ _____
Television Satellites	_____ _____ _____ _____

Lab zone ® Do the Quick Lab *How Does GPS Work?*

🗝 Assess Your Understanding

got it? ....

○ I get it! Now I know that satellites work by _____
_____

○ I need extra help with _____

Go to MY SCIENCE ⑤ COACH online for help with this subject.

14 | Study Guide

The electromagnetic spectrum is made up of radio waves, _____, _____, visible light, _____, _____, and gamma rays.

LESSON 1 The Nature of Electromagnetic Waves

🔑 An electromagnetic wave is made up of vibrating electric and magnetic fields that move through space or some medium at the speed of light.

🔑 Two different models are needed to explain the behavior of electromagnetic waves. A wave model best explains many of the behaviors, but a particle model best explains others.

Vocabulary
• electromagnetic wave • electromagnetic radiation
• polarized light • photoelectric effect • photon

LESSON 2 Waves of the Electromagnetic Spectrum

🔑 All electromagnetic waves travel at the same speed in a vacuum, but they have different wavelengths and different frequencies.

🔑 The electromagnetic spectrum is made up of radio waves, microwaves, infrared rays, visible light, ultraviolet rays, X-rays, and gamma rays.

Vocabulary
• electromagnetic spectrum • radio waves • microwaves • radar
• infrared rays • thermogram • visible light • ultraviolet rays
• X-rays • gamma rays

LESSON 3 Wireless Communication

🔑 Radio waves carry information from the antenna of a broadcasting station to the receiving antenna of your radio.

🔑 Cell phones transmit and receive signals using high-frequency microwaves.

🔑 Communications satellites receive radio, television, and telephone signals and relay the signals to receivers on Earth.

Vocabulary
• amplitude modulation • frequency modulation

Review and Assessment

LESSON 1 The Nature of Electromagnetic Waves

1. An electromagnetic wave consists of

  a. AM and FM waves.

  b. electrons and protons.

  c. electric and magnetic fields.

  d. particles of a medium.

2. The _____ model of light describes the behavior of light when it acts as a stream of photons.

3. **Compare and Contrast** Explain how polarized light is different from non-polarized light.

_____

_____

_____

_____

_____

4. **Observe** How do you know that electromagnetic waves can travel through a vacuum?

_____

_____

_____

_____

5. 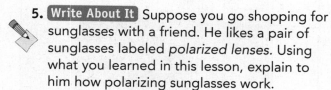 **Write About It** Suppose you go shopping for sunglasses with a friend. He likes a pair of sunglasses labeled *polarized lenses*. Using what you learned in this lesson, explain to him how polarizing sunglasses work.

LESSON 2 Waves of the Electromagnetic Spectrum

6. The electromagnetic waves with the longest wavelengths and lowest frequencies are

  a. radio waves.   **b.** infrared rays.

  c. X-rays.   **d.** gamma rays.

7. _____ is the only type of electromagnetic wave that you can see.

Use the graph below to answer Questions 8 and 9.

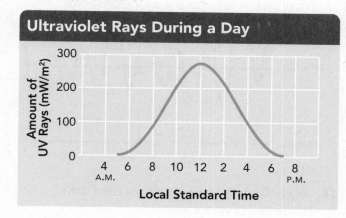

Ultraviolet Rays During a Day

8. **Interpret Graphs** What is the amount of ultraviolet rays at 8 P.M.?

_____

9. **Infer** What is the cause of the peak in the graph line at 12 P.M.?

_____

_____

10. **Classify** Night vision goggles allow you to see warm objects in a dark environment. Which type of electromagnetic wave do they detect?

_____

_____

LESSON 3 **Wireless Communication**

11. What is the ionosphere?

   a. a type of AM radio wave

   b. a region of charged particles in Earth's atmosphere

   c. the region of a cell-phone network

   d. a type of FM radio wave

12. Cell phones transmit and receive signals using

_____

13. Make Models An AM wave is shown below. Draw an FM wave in the space provided.

AM wave

FM wave

14. Apply Concepts Explain how the Global Positioning System works.

_____

_____

_____

_____

_____

15. Write About It You are going on a car trip with your family across the United States. To your brother's surprise, the AM radio station that your family is listening to is coming from a city 1,000 kilometers away. Explain to him how this is possible. Be sure to describe how the ionosphere affects AM radio transmissions.

What kinds of waves make up the electromagnetic spectrum?

16. Many everyday technologies with which you come in contact use electromagnetic waves. Choose four objects from the picture below and describe the kinds of electromagnetic waves that they use. List your answer in order of increasing energy of the waves each object uses.

_____

_____

_____

_____

_____

_____

_____

Standardized Test Prep

Multiple Choice

Circle the letter of the best answer.

1. What would you add to the picture below so that light does not hit the final screen?

   A another light bulb
   B a filter with horizontal slits
   C a filter with vertical slits
   D none of the above

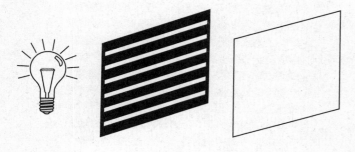

2. Ultraviolet rays from the sun are able to reach Earth's surface because

   A they require air to travel through.
   B they have less energy than infrared rays.
   C they have lower frequency than visible light.
   D they can travel through empty space.

3. Which of the following groups of electromagnetic waves is listed correctly in order of increasing energy?

   A X-rays, visible light, radio waves
   B radio waves, visible light, X-rays
   C infrared rays, visible light, radio waves
   D visible light, gamma rays, X-rays

4. Radar is a system that

   A detects objects and measures their speed.
   B kills bacteria.
   C carries AM signals.
   D searches for hidden objects.

5. AM radio waves are able to travel farther than FM radio waves because

   A AM waves produce better sound quality.
   B AM waves are reflected by Earth's ionosphere.
   C AM waves are faster than FM waves.
   D AM waves have constant amplitude.

Constructed Response

Refer to the image below to answer Question 6. Write your answer on a separate sheet of paper.

6. Explain how the visible spectrum is formed as a rainbow appears after it rains. In your answer, explain what white light is composed of.

Museum of Science **TECH & DESIGN**

Channel Surfin'
on an
Infrared WAVE

You have access to an entire world of entertainment and information at the push of a button, and you don't have to leave your chair. When you push the buttons on your remote control, it uses infrared light (an invisible part of the electromagnetic spectrum) to send signals to an electronic device.

When you press a button on a TV remote control, it sends out pulses of infrared light. These pulses contain a binary code. A binary code consists of a combination of the numbers 1 and 0. Each command on the remote control has a different binary code. For example, on one type of remote the command for "channel up" is 001 0000. The command for "channel down" is 001 0001. The TV's microprocessor, or the brain of the TV, interprets and carries out the correct command.

So why doesn't that remote control turn on the CD player or the microwave? To avoid interference from other infrared light sources, such as the sun and fluorescent light bulbs, each remote control uses a specific wavelength for its signals. As a result, other electronic devices won't respond to the infrared signals from the TV remote control.

Research It Research how a remote control can use both infrared light and radio frequencies. Design a device that uses both types of waves and explain how the device works and how it can be used.

START 0 0 1 0 0 1 0 0 0 0 0 STOP

Volume Up   Device Address

Museum of Science

Puny POWER Plants

How would you like to turn your bedroom window into an invisible power plant? How about the roof of your family car? Or the roof of your home? Or the fabric of your T-shirt? If scientists and engineers have their way, one or more of these questions will have an answer in just a few years. And the answer will be "Why not?"

All electric power plants change some original form of energy into electricity, another form of energy. The starting form of energy might be the motion of water rushing through a dam. It might be thermal energy produced either by burning coal, oil, or natural gas or by the decay of nuclei of radioactive atoms. It could also be a steady wind that spins the blades of a forest of turbines. Power plants that use these methods of producing electricity are large. But new ones may be so tiny, you might have trouble seeing them.

Over the years, scientists and engineers have developed very tiny power plants called photovoltaic cells. These cells are made of materials that give off electrons when they absorb light. These electrons can then be guided to form an electric current. In this way, a photovoltaic cell transforms light energy directly into electrical energy.

Scientists and engineers are now producing photovoltaic cells that are so small, they could be built into a windowpane that still allows you to see through the glass. They are so thin that they can bend like a length of thread. Will these miniature power plants be used some day to make your T-shirt light up in the dark, to help run your family car, or to light the bulbs in your home? You probably won't be shocked if the answer turns out to be "Yes."

▲ Small, thin, and embedded in a plastic sheet, this solar cell is flexible enough to be wrapped around a pen. It also turns sunlight into electricity.

Research It All types of power plants have both benefits and drawbacks. Do research to find out what these benefits and drawbacks are. Then debate the reasons why solar cells should, or should not, be used to replace existing sources of electricity.

WHY CAN YOU SEE A CITY IN THIS SCULPTURE?

How does light interact with matter?

Cloud Gate, a 110-ton sculpture in Chicago, Illinois, is made of highly polished stainless steel. The buildings that you see in the sculpture are a reflection of the city of Chicago.

Predict If you were standing directly in front of this sculpture, what would you see? Explain your answer.

_____

_____

_____

_____

_____

_____

> UNTAMED SCIENCE   Watch the **Untamed Science** video to learn more about light.

Light

15 Getting Started

Check Your Understanding

1. Background Read the paragraph below and then answer the question.

Jamal wakes up early to write a term paper. As the sun rises, it **transmits** sunlight through the window. The light **reflects** off of his computer screen, making it difficult for him to read the words he types. He pulls down the window shade knowing it will **absorb** some of the light.

To **transmit** is to pass something from one place to another.

To **reflect** is to throw something back.

To **absorb** is to take something in or soak it up.

• Why does the window create a problem for Jamal?

_____

_____

> MY READING WEB If you had trouble completing the question above, visit **My Reading Web** and type in *Light.*

Vocabulary Skill

Use Prefixes A prefix is a word part that is added at the beginning of a root or base word to change its meaning. Knowing the meaning of prefixes will help you figure out new words.

Prefix	Meaning	Example
micro-	small, tiny	microscope
tele-	distant, operating at a distance	telescope
con-	together with, jointly	concave mirror, convex mirror
trans-	through	translucent

2. Quick Check Choose the word from the table that best completes the sentence.

You need a _____ to view the planets in any detail.

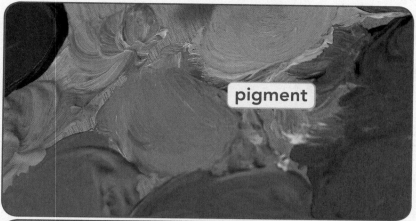

pigment

plane mirror

mirage

convex lens

Chapter Preview

LESSON 1
- transparent • translucent
- opaque • primary color
- secondary color
- complementary color • pigment
- 🔄 **Identify the Main Idea**
- 🔺 **Predict**

LESSON 2
- ray • regular reflection • image
- diffuse reflection • plane mirror
- virtual image • concave mirror
- optical axis • focal point
- real image • convex mirror
- 🔄 **Compare and Contrast**
- 🔺 **Classify**

LESSON 3
- index of refraction • mirage
- lens • concave lens
- convex lens
- 🔄 **Ask Questions**
- 🔺 **Interpret Data**

LESSON 4
- cornea • pupil • iris • retina
- rods • cones • optic nerve
- nearsighted • farsighted
- 🔄 **Sequence**
- 🔺 **Observe**

LESSON 5
- camera • telescope
- refracting telescope • objective
- eyepiece • reflecting telescope
- microscope
- 🔄 **Relate Text and Visuals**
- 🔺 **Infer**

> **VOCAB FLASH CARDS** For extra help with vocabulary, visit **Vocab Flash Cards** and type in *Light*.

Light and Color

UNLOCK THE BIG ?

🔑 **What Determines Color?**

🔑 **How Do Colors Combine?**

MY PLANET DIARY

Why Is the Sky Blue?

Why does the sky look blue on a clear, sunny day? The answer has to do with the nature of light.

The sun gives off white light. White light is made up of many colors. The different colors of light have different wavelengths. Red light has a longer wavelength than blue light. As the sun's light passes through our atmosphere, gas molecules in the air scatter the sunlight. The blue wavelengths get scattered the most, so the sky appears blue!

FUN FACTS

Communicate Discuss this question with a classmate. Then write your answer below.

The water droplets in clouds scatter all of the wavelengths of visible light equally. How does this explain why clouds are white?

_____

_____

_____

_____

> **PLANET DIARY** Go to **Planet Diary** to learn more about color.

Lab zone® Do the Inquiry Warm-Up
How Do Colors Mix?

What Determines Color?

Why is the grass green or a daffodil yellow? To understand why objects have different colors, you need to know how light can interact with an object. When light strikes an object, the light can be reflected, transmitted, or absorbed. Think about a pair of sunglasses. If you hold the sunglasses in your hand, you can see light that reflects off the lenses. If you put the sunglasses on, you see light that is transmitted through the lenses. The lenses also absorb some light. That is why objects appear darker when seen through the lenses.

Vocabulary
- transparent • translucent • opaque • primary color
- secondary color • complementary color • pigment

Skills
⟲ Reading: Identify the Main Idea
△ Inquiry: Predict

Classifying Materials Lenses, like all objects, are made of different materials. Most materials can be classified as transparent, translucent, or opaque based on what happens to light that strikes the material.

A material that transmits most of the light that strikes it is called **transparent.** Light passes through a transparent material without being scattered. This allows you to see clearly what is on the other side. Water, air, and clear glass are all transparent materials. In **Figure 1,** the window shown in the photo is partially fogged up by condensation. The center of the window, where the condensation has been wiped away, is transparent. The fogged-up part of the window is translucent. A **translucent** (trans LOO sunt) material scatters the light that passes through it. You can usually see something behind a translucent object, but the details are blurred. Wax paper and frosted glass are translucent materials.

A material that reflects or absorbs all of the light that strikes it is called **opaque** (oh PAYK). You cannot see through opaque materials because light cannot pass through them. In **Figure 1,** the wood and snow shown in the photo are opaque. Metals and tightly woven fabric are other examples of opaque materials.

✎
⟲ **Identify the Main Idea**
Underline the main idea under the red heading Classifying Materials.

FIGURE 1 ⋯⋯⋯⋯⋯⋯⋯⋯⋯⋯⋯⋯
Types of Materials
The windows contain transparent, translucent, and opaque sections. ✎ **Relate Diagrams and Photos Suppose the ball was placed behind the three-sectional window below. Draw what you would see inside the dashed circle.**

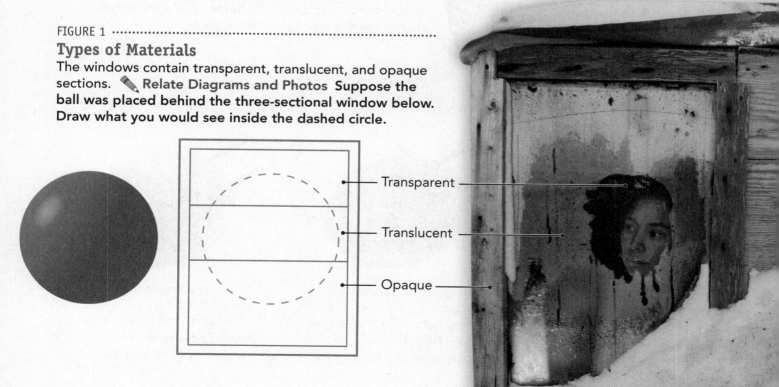

— Transparent —

— Translucent —

— Opaque —

Vocabulary Prefixes How does knowing the meaning of the prefix *trans-* help you remember what happens to light that strikes a translucent object?

_____

_____

_____

_____

Opaque Objects

The color of an opaque object depends on the wavelengths of light that the object reflects. Every opaque object absorbs some wavelengths of light and reflects others. **The color of an opaque object is the color of the light it reflects.** For example, look at the apple shown at the top of **Figure 2**. The apple appears red because it reflects red wavelengths of light. The apple absorbs the other colors of light. The leaf looks green because it reflects green light and absorbs the other colors.

Objects can appear to change color if you view them in a different color of light. In red light, the apple appears red because there is red light for it to reflect. But the leaf appears black because there is no green light to reflect. In green light, the leaf looks green but the apple looks black. And in blue light, both the apple and the leaf look black.

Transparent and Translucent Objects

Materials that are transparent or translucent allow only certain colors of light to pass through them. They reflect or absorb the other colors. **The color of a transparent or translucent object is the color of the light it transmits.** For example, when white light shines through transparent blue glass, the glass appears blue because it transmits blue light.

White light

FIGURE 2 ⋯⋯⋯⋯⋯⋯⋯⋯⋯⋯⋯⋯⋯⋯⋯⋯

▷VIRTUAL LAB **Color of an Opaque Object**
The color an apple appears to be depends on the color of the light that strikes it. **Infer Circle the correct answers in the text below each apple.**

The apple appears red because it (absorbs/reflects) red light. The leaves look black because they (absorb/reflect) red light.

The apple appears black because it (absorbs/reflects) green light. The leaves look green because they (absorb/reflect) green light.

The apple appears black because it (absorbs/reflects) blue light. The leaves look black because they (absorb/reflect) blue light.

Transparent or translucent materials are used to make color filters. For example, a red color filter is red because it allows only red light to pass through it. When you look at an object through a color filter, the color of the object may appear different than when you see the object in white light.

The lenses in sunglasses are often color filters. For example, lenses tinted yellow are yellow filters. When you put on those sunglasses, some objects appear to change color. The color you see depends on the color of the filter and on the color of the object as it appears in white light.

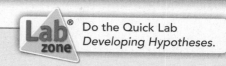
White light

apply it!

Predict Imagine looking at the beach ball at the right through a red, green, or blue filter. Predict how each section of the beach ball would appear. In the diagrams below, label each section of the beach ball with its corresponding color.

Red filter

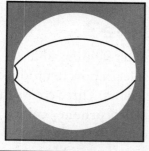

Green filter

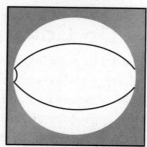

Blue filter

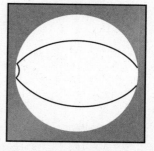

Lab zone Do the Quick Lab Developing Hypotheses.

🔑 Assess Your Understanding

1a. Identify A(n) _____ object reflects or absorbs all the light that strikes it.

b. Apply Concepts A person wearing a blue shirt is standing in sunlight. What color(s) of light does the shirt reflect? What color(s) of light does the shirt absorb?

_____

_____

c. Predict Suppose you are wearing green-tinted glasses. What color would a blue shirt appear through these glasses? _____

got it?

○ **I get it!** Now I know that the color of an opaque object is _____

_____

and the color of a transparent or translucent object is _____

_____

○ **I need extra help with** _____

_____

Go to MY SCIENCE ⓢ COACH online for help with this subject.

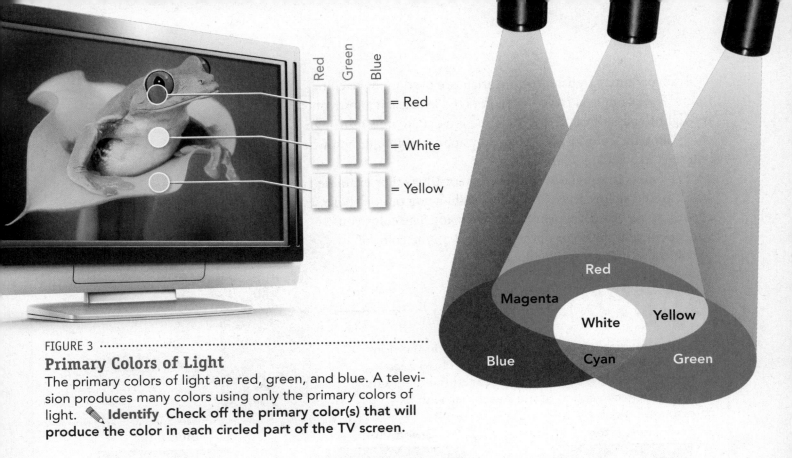

FIGURE 3 ········

Primary Colors of Light

The primary colors of light are red, green, and blue. A television produces many colors using only the primary colors of light. ✎ **Identify** Check off the primary color(s) that will produce the color in each circled part of the TV screen.

How Do Colors Combine?

Color is used in painting, photography, theater lighting, and printing. People who work with color must learn how to produce a wide range of colors using just a few basic colors. Three colors that can combine to make any other color are called **primary colors.** Two primary colors combine in equal amounts to produce a **secondary color.**

Mixing Light The primary colors of light are red, green, and blue. 🔑 **When the three primary colors of light are combined in equal amounts, they produce white light.** If they are combined in different amounts, the primary colors can produce other colors. For example, red and green combine to form yellow light. Yellow is a secondary color of light because two primary colors produce it. The secondary colors of light are yellow (red + green), cyan (green + blue), and magenta (red + blue). **Figure 3** shows the primary and secondary colors of light.

A primary and a secondary color can combine to make white light. Any two colors that combine to form white light are called **complementary colors.** Yellow and blue are complementary colors, as are cyan and red, and magenta and green.

A television produces many colors using only the primary colors of light. The picture on a TV screen is made up of little bars of red, green, and blue light. By varying the brightness of each colored bar, the television can produce thousands of different colors.

Mixing light

List at least three examples of mixing light.

_____

_____

_____

_____

_____

_____

_____

Mixing Pigment

Mixing Pigment How does an artist produce the many shades of colors you see in a painting? Inks, paints, and dyes contain **pigments,** or colored substances that are used to color other materials. Pigments absorb some colors and reflect others. The color you see is the result of the colors that a particular pigment reflects.

Mixing colors of pigments is different from mixing colors of light. As pigments are added together, fewer colors of light are reflected and more are absorbed. The more pigments that are combined, the darker the mixture looks.

Cyan, yellow, and magenta are the primary colors of pigments. **When the three primary colors of pigments are combined in equal amounts, they produce black.** By combining pigments in varying amounts, you can produce many other colors. If you combine two primary colors of pigments, you get a secondary color, as shown in **Figure 4.** The secondary colors of pigments are red, green, and blue.

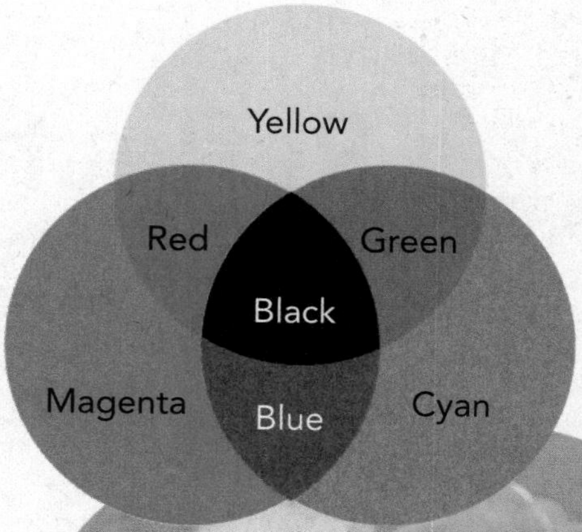

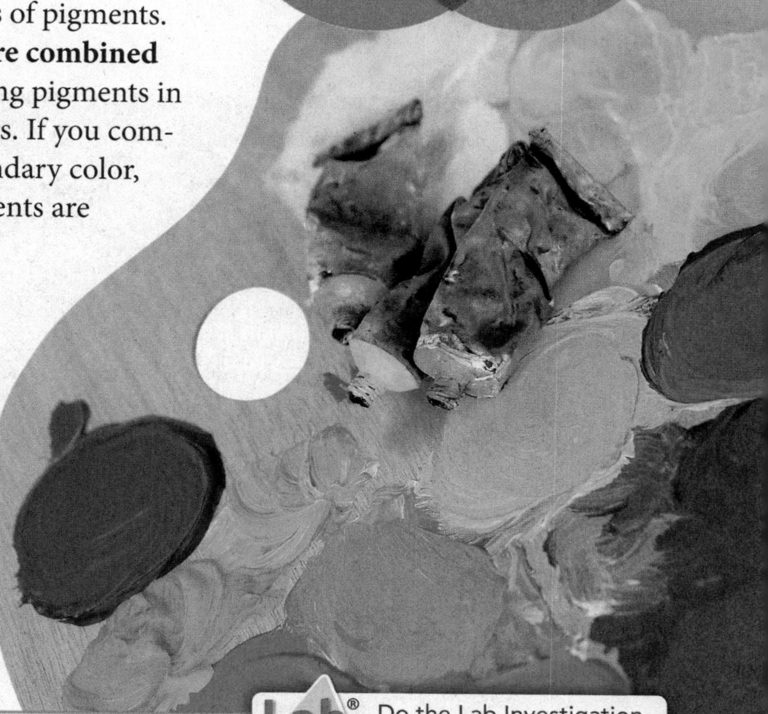

FIGURE 4 ···

Primary Colors of Pigment

Oil painters use a tray called a *palette* to hold and mix pigments. ✎ **Identify Write the names of the primary colors that combine to produce the secondary color at the end of each statement.**

_____ + _____ = red

_____ + _____ = green

_____ + _____ = blue

Lab zone® Do the Lab Investigation *Changing Colors.*

Assess Your Understanding

2a. Identify What are the primary colors of light? What are the primary colors of pigment?

_____

_____

_____

_____

b. Compare and Contrast The result of mixing the primary colors of light in equal amounts is the color _____. The result of mixing the primary colors of pigment in equal amounts is the color _____.

got it? ···

○ **I get it!** Now I know that to produce white light you combine _____

_____

○ **I need extra help with** _____

Go to **my science** ⊙ **coach** *online for help with this subject.*

Reflection and Mirrors

UNLOCK
THE BIG
?

What Are the Kinds of Reflection?

What Types of Images Do Mirrors Produce?

my pLaneT DiaRY

DISCOVERY

Periscope

In a submarine hidden beneath the ocean's surface, a captain peered into a long tube to see possible threats in the sea and air above. This sight tube, called a periscope, was designed by the Frenchman Marie Davey in 1854. Davey's periscope contained two mirrors, one placed at each end of a vertical tube. The mirrors were set parallel to each other and at 45 degrees to the vertical. The reflective surfaces faced each other. When light from an object on the surface reflected downward, an image appeared to the eye. People in submerged submarines could see what was above them!

Write your answer to the question below.

Imagine you are in a submerged submarine looking through a periscope. What are some things you might see?

_____

_____

_____

_____

_____

> PLANET DIARY Go to **Planet Diary** to learn more about mirrors.

Lab® zone Do the Inquiry Warm-Up _How Does Your Reflection Wink?_

What Are the Kinds of Reflection?

Why do you see a reflection of yourself in a mirror but not on a page of your textbook? To answer this question, you need to understand how a surface reflects light. To show how light reflects, you can represent light waves as straight lines called **rays.** You may recall that light obeys the law of reflection—the angle of reflection equals the angle of incidence. 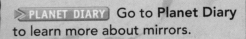 **The two ways in which a surface can reflect light are regular reflection and diffuse reflection.**

Vocabulary
- ray
- regular reflection
- image
- diffuse reflection
- plane mirror
- virtual image
- concave mirror
- optical axis
- focal point
- real image
- convex mirror

Skills
- ↻ Reading: Compare and Contrast
- △ Inquiry: Classify

Regular reflection occurs when parallel rays of light hit a smooth surface. All of the light rays reflect at the same angle because of the smooth surface. So you see a clear image. An **image** is a copy of the object formed by reflected or refracted rays of light. Shiny surfaces such as metal, glass, and calm water produce regular reflection.

Diffuse reflection occurs when parallel rays of light hit an uneven surface. Each light ray obeys the law of reflection but hits the surface at a different angle because the surface is uneven. Therefore, each ray reflects at a different angle. You either don't see an image or the image is not clear. Most objects reflect light diffusely. This is because most surfaces are not smooth. Even surfaces that appear to be smooth, such as a piece of paper, have small bumps that reflect light at different angles.

FIGURE 1 ·····················

Diffuse and Regular Reflection
✎ **Identify** Label the kind of reflection that occurs on each surface.

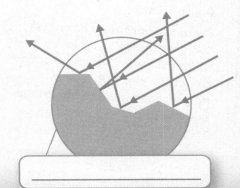

Lab zone ® Do the Quick Lab *Observing.*

🔑 Assess Your Understanding

got it? ·······················

○ **I get it!** Now I know the two kinds of reflection are _____

_____

○ **I need extra help with** _____

    Go to my science ⓢ coach *online for help with this subject.*

What Types of Images Do Mirrors Produce?

Have you ever looked at yourself in the curved mirrors of a fun house? If so, you know that your image looks different than it does in a flat mirror. Your image may look tall and skinny at one point and short and wide at another point. To understand why your image changes, you need to learn about the types of mirrors.

Plane Mirror Did you look into a mirror this morning to brush your teeth? If you did, you probably used a plane mirror. A **plane mirror** is a flat sheet of glass that has a smooth, silver-colored coating on one side. Often this coating is on the back of the glass to protect it from damage. When light strikes a mirror, the coating reflects the light. Because the coating is smooth, regular reflection occurs and a clear image forms. The image you see in a plane mirror is a **virtual image**—an image that forms where light seems to come from. "Virtual" describes something that does not really exist. Your image appears to be behind the mirror, but you can't reach behind the mirror and touch it.

🔑 **A plane mirror produces a virtual image that is upright and the same size as the object.** But the image is not quite the same as the object. The left and right of the image are reversed. For example, when you look in a mirror, your right hand appears to be a left hand in the image.

FIGURE 2 ···

Image in a Plane Mirror

A plane mirror forms a virtual image. The reflected light rays appear to come from behind the mirror, where the image forms.

✏️ **Interpret Photos Is the raised hand in the image an image of the dancer's left hand or her right hand? Explain.**

_____

Image   Plane mirror   Object

Concave Mirrors A mirror with a surface that curves inward like the inside of a bowl is a **concave mirror**. **Figure 3** shows how a concave mirror can reflect parallel rays of light so that they meet at a point. Notice that the rays of light shown are parallel to the optical axis. The **optical axis** is an imaginary line that divides a mirror in half, much like the equator that divides Earth into northern and southern halves. The point at which rays parallel to the optical axis reflect and meet is called the **focal point**.

The type of image that is formed by a concave mirror depends on the location of the object. 🔑 **Concave mirrors can produce real or virtual images.** A **real image** forms when light rays actually meet. If the object is farther away from the mirror than the focal point, the reflected rays form a real image. Unlike a virtual image, a real image can be projected on a surface such as a piece of paper. Real images are upside down. A real image may be smaller, larger, or the same size as the object.

If an object is between the mirror and the focal point, the reflected rays form a virtual image. Virtual images formed by a concave mirror are always larger than the object. Concave mirrors produce the magnified images you see in a makeup mirror.

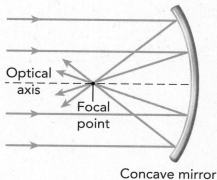

Concave mirror

FIGURE 3 ·······································
Concave Mirror
A concave mirror reflects rays of light parallel to the optical axis back through the focal point. The figures below show how a concave mirror can produce both real and virtual images.

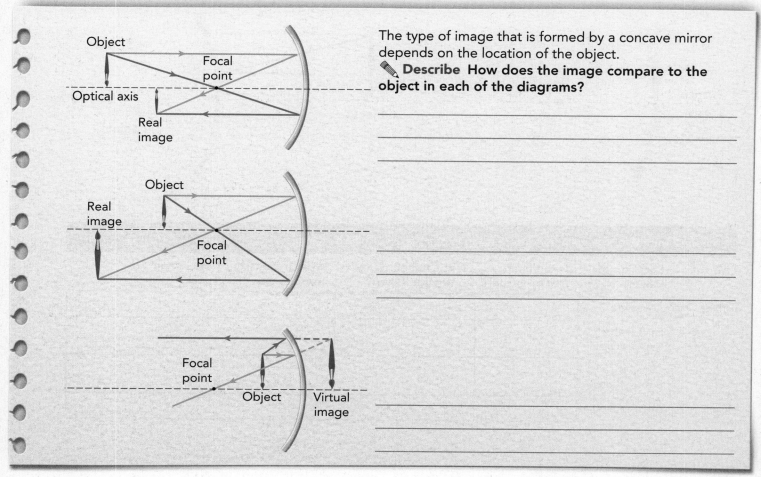

The type of image that is formed by a concave mirror depends on the location of the object.

✏️ **Describe** How does the image compare to the object in each of the diagrams?

_____

_____

_____

_____

_____

_____

_____

_____

_____

_____

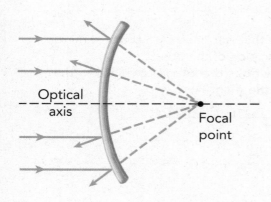

Compare and Contrast

Compare and contrast the shape of a convex mirror and a concave mirror.

_____

_____

_____

_____

Convex Mirrors A mirror with a surface that curves outward is called a **convex mirror.** **Figure 4a** shows how convex mirrors reflect parallel rays of light. The reflected rays spread out but appear to come from a focal point behind the mirror. The focal point of a convex mirror is the point from which the rays appear to come. 🔑 **A convex mirror produces a virtual image that is always smaller than the object.**

Perhaps you have seen this warning on a car mirror: "Objects in mirror are closer than they appear." Convex mirrors are used in cars as passenger-side mirrors. The advantage of a convex mirror is that it allows you to see a larger area than you can with a plane mirror. The disadvantage is that the image is reduced in size. As a result, the image appears to be farther away than it actually is. The driver must understand this and adjust for it.

FIGURE 4 ···

▶ INTERACTIVE ART **Convex Mirror**

a. Light rays parallel to the optical axis reflect as if they came from the focal point behind a convex mirror.

b. ✎ CHALLENGE **Extend the two reflected rays behind the mirror to where they intersect. This is the top of the virtual image. Draw the image.**

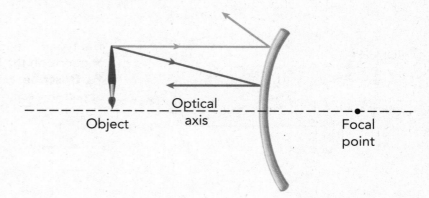

Complete the table to review the different types of images formed by mirrors.

Mirror	Location of Object	Is the image real or virtual?	Is the image upright or upside down?	What is the size of the image compared to the object?
Plane	Anywhere			
Concave	Farther than the focal point			
	Closer than the focal point			
Convex	Anywhere			

apply it!

Each of the photos shows an application of a curved mirror. A bus driver uses the mirror in the top photo to check for traffic. A boy uses the mirror in the bottom photo to put in contact lenses.

1 ◢ **Classify** Which type of curved mirror is in the top photo?_____

2 ◢ **Classify** Which type of curved mirror is in the bottom photo?_____

3 **Explain** Why is the mirror in the top photo more useful than a plane mirror for checking traffic?

_____

_____

_____

4 **Explain** Why is the mirror in the bottom photo more useful than a plane mirror for putting in contact lenses?

_____

_____

_____

Do the Quick Lab
Mirror Images.

🔑 Assess Your Understanding

1a. Define A(n) _____ is a copy of an object formed by reflected or refracted rays of light.

b. ◢ **Classify** A _____ mirror can form real and virtual images. _____ and _____ mirrors form only virtual images.

c. Apply Concepts Which type of mirror would you use if you wanted to project an image on a screen? Why?

_____

_____

_____

got it? ....

○ **I get it!** Now I know that the two types of images produced by mirrors are real _____

_____

○ **I need extra help with** _____

Go to **MY SCIENCE COACH** *online for help with this subject.*

Refraction and Lenses

UNLOCK THE BIG Q?

🔑 **What Causes Light Rays to Bend?**

🔑 **What Determines the Type of Image Formed by a Lens?**

MY PLANET DIARY

BIOGRAPHY

Isaac Newton

Sir Isaac Newton (1642–1727) may be best known as the man who came up with the theory of gravity. But Newton, who was born in England, made numerous other important contributions to both math and science, including defining the laws of motion and co-founding the field of calculus. In the 1660s, Newton investigated the laws of light and color. In his famous book *Opticks*, he describes how he passed sunlight through a prism to prove that white light consists of many colors. Newton was knighted in 1705 and was the first scientist to be buried at Westminster Abbey.

Communicate Write your answers to the questions below. Then discuss your answers with a partner.

1. How did Newton prove that sunlight consists of many colors?

_____

_____

2. Describe a discovery that you made through experimentation.

_____

_____

_____

_____

_____

> PLANET DIARY Go to **Planet Diary** to learn more about lenses.

Lab zone® Do the Inquiry Warm-Up *How Can You Make an Image Appear?*

my science online.com | Refraction | PLANET DIARY | ART IN MOTION

Vocabulary
- index of refraction • mirage • lens
- concave lens • convex lens

Skills
- Reading: Ask Questions
- Inquiry: Interpret Data

What Causes Light Rays to Bend?

A fish tank can play tricks on your eyes. If you look through the side of a fish tank, a fish seems closer than if you look at it from the top. If you look through the corner of the tank, you may see the same fish twice. Look at **Figure 1.** You see one image of the fish through the front of the tank and another through the side. The two images appear in different places! How can this happen?

Refraction can cause you to see something that may not actually be there. As you look at a fish in a tank, the light coming from the fish to your eye bends as it passes through three different mediums. The mediums are water, the glass of the tank, and air. As the light passes from one medium to the next, it is refracted. **When light rays enter a new medium at an angle, the change in speed causes the rays to bend.**

FIGURE 1 ·····················

Optical Illusion in a Fish Tank

There is only one fish in this tank, but refraction makes it look as though there are two.

Communicate Discuss with a classmate some other examples of how the appearance of objects in water is different than in the air. Describe these examples below.

_____

_____

_____

_____

_____

_____

503

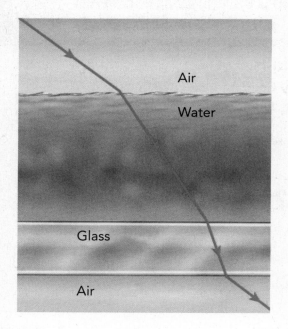

FIGURE 2 ·····················

Refraction of Light

The light ray bends as it passes through different mediums.

✎ **Interpret Diagrams** In which medium does light travel the fastest?

Refraction in Different Mediums

Some mediums cause light to bend more than others. **Figure 2** shows how the path of a light ray changes as it passes from one medium to another. When light passes from air into water, the light slows down. Light slows down again and bends even more when it passes from water into glass. When light passes from glass back into air, the light speeds up. Notice that the ray that leaves the glass is traveling in the same direction as it was before it entered the water. Light travels fastest in air, a little slower in water, and slower still in glass.

Glass causes light to bend more than either air or water does. Another way to say this is that glass has a higher index of refraction than either air or water. The **index of refraction** of a medium is a measure of how much a light ray bends when it enters that medium. The higher the index of refraction of a medium, the more it bends light. The index of refraction of water is 1.33. The index of refraction of glass is about 1.5. So light is bent more by glass than by water.

do the math! Analyzing Data

Bending Light

The table shows the index of refraction of some common mediums. **Use the data to answer the following questions.**

❶ **Interpret Data** Which medium causes the greatest change in the direction of a light ray that enters at an angle?

_____

❷ **Interpret Data** According to the table, which tend to bend light more, solids or liquids?

_____

❸ **Predict** Would you expect light to bend if it entered corn oil at an angle after it traveled through glycerol? Explain.

_____

_____

Index of Refraction

Medium	Index of Refraction
Air (gas)	1.00
Water (liquid)	1.33
Ethyl alcohol (liquid)	1.36
Quartz (solid)	1.46
Corn oil (liquid)	1.47
Glycerol (liquid)	1.47
Glass, crown (solid)	1.52
Sodium chloride (solid)	1.54
Zircon (solid)	1.92
Diamond (solid)	2.42

Prisms and Rainbows Recall that when white light enters a prism, each wavelength is refracted by a different amount. The longer the wavelength, the less the wave is bent by a prism. Red, with the longest wavelength, is refracted the least. Violet, with the shortest wavelength, is refracted the most. This difference in refraction causes white light to spread out into the colors of the spectrum—red, orange, yellow, green, blue, and violet.

The same process occurs in water droplets suspended in the air. When white light from the sun shines through the droplets, a rainbow may appear. The water droplets act like tiny prisms, refracting and reflecting the light and separating the colors.

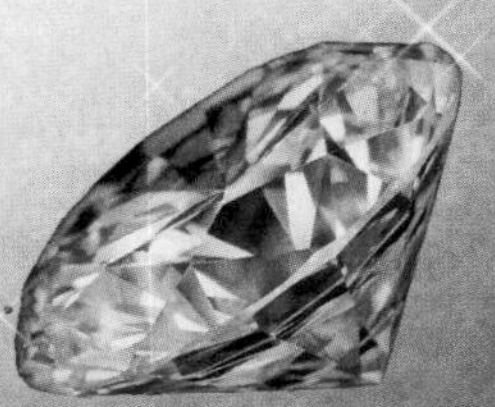

EXPLORE THE BIG ?

Water + Light = A Rainbow

How does light interact with matter?

FIGURE 3 ·······································

> ART IN MOTION

A rainbow forms when light is reflected and refracted by water droplets suspended in the air. The diagram shows the path of a light ray that strikes a water droplet. ✎ **Interpret Diagrams** Use the diagram to answer the questions.

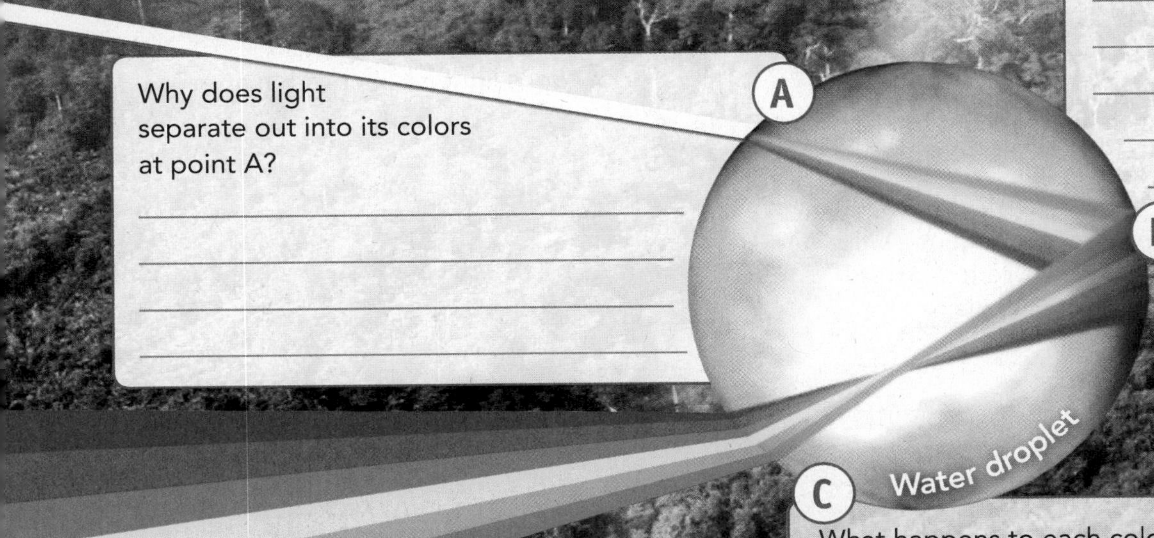

Why does light separate out into its colors at point A?

_____

_____

_____

What happens to each color of light at point B?

_____

_____

_____

_____

_____

_____

A

B

C Water droplet

What happens to each color of light at point C?

_____

_____

_____

✏️
🔄Ask Questions Before reading about mirages, ask a *What* or *How* question. As you read, write the answer to your question below.

_____

_____

_____

FIGURE 4 ································
Mirage
The puddles and reflections on the road are mirages.

Mirages You're traveling in a car on a hot day, and you notice that the road ahead looks wet. Yet when you get there, the road is dry. Did the puddles dry up? No, the puddles were never there! You saw a **mirage** (mih RAHJ)—an image of a distant object caused by refraction of light. The puddles on the road are light rays from the sky that are refracted to your eyes.

Figure 4 shows a mirage. Notice that there appears to be a reflection of the truck in the road. The air just above the road is hotter than the air higher up. Light travels faster in hot air. So light rays from the truck that travel toward the road are bent upward by the hot air. Your brain assumes that these rays traveled in a straight line. So the rays look as if they have reflected off a smooth surface. What you see is a mirage.

Lab® zone
Do the Quick
Lab *Bent Pencil*.

🔑 Assess Your Understanding

1a. Identify A material's _____ is a measure of how much a ray of light bends when it enters that material from air.

b. Predict If a glass prism were in a medium with the same index of refraction, would it separate white light into different colors? Explain.

_____

_____

_____

c. ANSWER THE BIG ❓ How does light interact with matter?

_____

_____

_____

_____

_____

_____

got**it?** ··

○ **I get it!** Now I know that the reason light rays bend when they enter a new medium at an angle is because _____

○ **I need extra help with** _____

Go to MY SCIENCE ⓢ COACH *online for help with this subject.*

What Determines the Type of Image Formed by a Lens?

Any time you look through binoculars, a camera, or eyeglasses, you are using lenses to bend light. A **lens** is a curved piece of glass or other transparent material that refracts light. A lens forms an image by refracting light rays that pass through it. Like mirrors, lenses can have different shapes. 🔑 **The type of image formed by a lens depends on the shape of the lens and the position of the object.**

Concave Lenses A **concave lens** is thinner in the center than at the edges. When light rays traveling parallel to the optical axis pass through a concave lens, they bend away from the optical axis and never meet. A concave lens can produce only virtual images because parallel light rays passing through the lens never meet.

Look at the book to the right. Notice that the words seen through the lens appear smaller than the words outside of the lens. The words seen through the lens are virtual images. A concave lens always produces a virtual image that is upright and smaller than the object. **Figure 5a** shows how a concave lens forms an image. The image is located where the light rays appear to come from.

FIGURE 5 ·······························

Concave Lens

a. A concave lens produces a virtual image that is upright and smaller than the object.

Object   Focal point   Image   Focal point

b. ✏️ **Apply Concepts** Locate this object's image. Extend the two light rays straight back to the same side of the lens as the object. The point where they intersect is the location of the image. Draw the image.

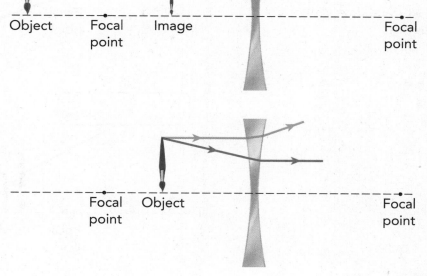

Focal point   Object   Focal point

507

Convex Lenses

A **convex lens** is thicker in the center than at the edges. As light rays parallel to the optical axis pass through a convex lens, they are bent toward the center of the lens. The rays meet at the focal point of the lens and continue to travel beyond. The more curved the lens, the more it refracts light. A convex lens acts like a concave mirror, because it focuses rays of light.

An object's position relative to the focal point determines whether a convex lens forms a real or virtual image. Look at **Figure 6.** Notice that the words seen through the lens are larger than the words outside of the lens. The words seen through the lens are virtual images. When an object is between the lens and the focal point, the refracted rays form a virtual image. The image forms on the same side of the lens as the object and is larger than the object. If the object is outside of the focal point, the refracted rays form a real image on the other side of the lens. The real image can be smaller, larger, or the same size as the object. The diagrams in **Figure 7** show how a convex lens forms real and virtual images.

FIGURE 6 ···

Convex Lens

When an object is inside the focal point, the image seen through a convex lens is larger than the object. ✎ **Identify Name a device that uses this type of lens.**

_____

_____

Lenses

List some devices that use lenses.

_____

_____

_____

_____

_____

_____

_____

FIGURE 7 ···

▷ **INTERACTIVE ART** **How a Convex Lens Works**

The type of image formed by a convex lens depends on the object's position. ✎ **Classify Label which image is virtual and which image is real.**

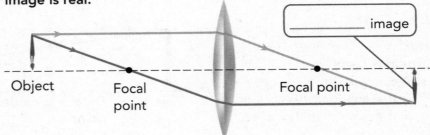

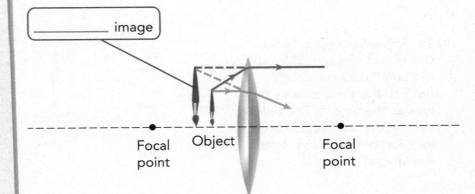

apply it!

① **Interpret Photos** These photos show parallel rays of light passing through a convex lens and a concave lens. Why do you suppose a convex lens is called a converging lens and a concave lens is called a diverging lens?

_____

_____

_____

② **Review** Complete the Lenses and Mirrors table. Use the table to answer Question 3.

③ **Summarize** A convex lens acts like a _____ mirror. A concave lens acts like a _____ mirror.

④ **CHALLENGE** Suppose a convex lens and a concave mirror are underwater. Compared to the way they work in air, which one do you expect will be more affected by the water? Why?

_____

_____

_____

_____

Convex lens

Concave lens

Lenses and Mirrors

Type of Mirror or Lens	Real, Virtual, or Both Types of Images	Upright, Inverted, or Both Types of Images
Concave Mirror	Both	_____
Convex Mirror	_____	Upright
Concave Lens	_____	_____
Convex Lens	_____	_____

Lab zone® Do the Quick Lab
Looking at Images.

⚷ Assess Your Understanding

2a. Define A _____ is a curved piece of glass or other transparent material that refracts light.

b. **Compare and Contrast** Describe the shapes of a concave lens and a convex lens.

_____

_____

_____

c. **Make Generalizations** Use **Figure 7** to explain how you can you tell whether a convex lens will produce a real or virtual image.

_____

_____

_____

_____

_____

got it? •••

○ **I get it!** Now I know that the type of image formed by a lens depends on _____

_____

○ **I need extra help with** _____

Go to **MY SCIENCE COACH** *online for help with this subject.*

Seeing Light

 **UNLOCK THE BIG ?**

🔑 **How Do You See Objects?**

MY PLANET DIARY

Misconception: You can see in total darkness as long as your eyes adjust to the darkness.

Fact: It is impossible to see objects in total darkness. If there is some light, such as light from a street lamp or moonlight, we can see objects because the light reflects off the objects and enters our eyes. In these low light conditions, our eyes adjust to let more light in. It can take 10 to 30 minutes for this to happen.

Evidence: If a person is in a completely dark environment, such as a deep cave, he or she cannot see objects.

MISCONCEPTION

Communicate Write your answers to the questions below. Then discuss your answers with a partner.

1. How do you suppose your eyes adjust to let in more light?

_____

_____

_____

2. Think of an experiment to test whether or not humans can see in complete darkness.

_____

_____

_____

_____

▶ **PLANET DIARY** Go to **Planet Diary** to learn more about the human eye.

 Lab® **zone** Do the Inquiry Warm-Up *Can You See Everything With One Eye?*

Vocabulary
- cornea • pupil • iris • retina • rods • cones
- optic nerve • nearsighted • farsighted

Skills
- Reading: Sequence
- Inquiry: Observe

How Do You See Objects?

The first rule of baseball or softball is to keep your eye on the ball. As the ball moves near or far, your eyes must adjust continuously to keep it in focus. Fortunately, your eyes can change focus automatically. The eye is a complex structure with many parts. Each part plays a role in vision. **You see objects when a process occurs that involves both your eyes and your brain.**

Light Enters the Eye Light enters the eye through the transparent front surface called the **cornea** (KAWR nee uh). The cornea protects the eye. It also acts as a lens to help focus light rays.

After passing through the cornea, light enters the pupil, the part of the eye that looks black. The **pupil** is an opening through which light enters the inside of the eye. In dim light, the pupil becomes larger to allow in more light. In bright light, the pupil becomes smaller to allow in less light. The **iris** is a ring of muscle that contracts and expands to change the size of the pupil. The iris gives the eye its color. In most people the iris is brown; in others it is blue, green, or hazel.

apply it!

The photographs show the same pupil exposed to different amounts of light.

❶ Identify Label which pupil is in dim light and which pupil is in bright light.

❷ Explain Why does the size of the pupil change?

_____

_____

❸ Observe Work with a classmate. Cover one of your eyes with your hand for several seconds. Then remove your hand. Your classmate should observe what happens to your pupil. Switch roles. Record your observations.

_____

_____

_____

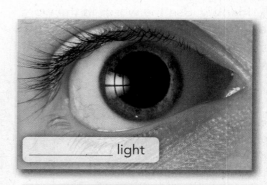
_____ light

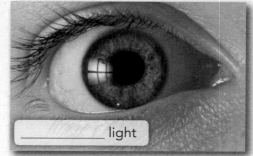
_____ light

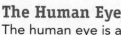 **Sequence** A sequence is the order in which the steps in a process occur. As you read, complete the flowchart to show how you see objects.

How You See Objects

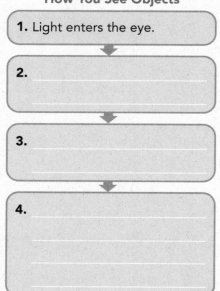

1. Light enters the eye.

2. _____

3. _____

4. _____

An Image Forms

After entering the pupil, the light passes through the lens. The lens is a convex lens that refracts light to form an image on the lining of your eyeball. Muscles, called ciliary muscles, hold the lens in place behind the pupil. When you focus on a distant object, the ciliary muscles relax, and the lens becomes longer and thinner. When you focus on a nearby object, the muscles contract, and the lens becomes shorter and fatter.

When the cornea and the lens refract light, an upside-down image is formed on the retina. The **retina** is a layer of cells that lines the inside of the eyeball. (Cells are the tiny structures that make up living things.) **Rods** are cells that contain a pigment that responds to small amounts of light. The rods allow you to see in dim light. **Cones** are cells that respond to color. They may detect red light, green light, or blue light. Cones respond best in bright light. Both rods and cones help change images on the retina into signals that then travel to the brain.

A Signal Goes to the Brain

The rods and cones send signals to the brain along a short, thick nerve called the **optic nerve.** The optic nerve begins at the blind spot, an area of the retina that has no rods or cones. Your brain interprets the signals from the optic nerve as an upright image. It also combines the two images from your eyes into a single three-dimensional image.

FIGURE 1

The Human Eye

The human eye is a complex structure with many parts that allow you to see.

Identify Use the words in the word bank to identify the parts of the eye.

Word Bank

Ciliary muscles
Cornea
Iris
Lens
Optic nerve
Pupil
Retina

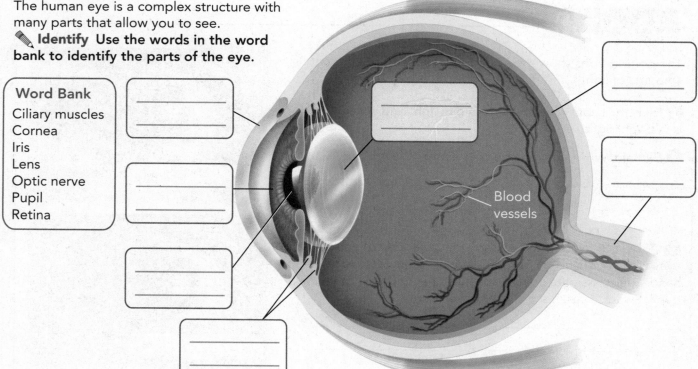

Blood vessels

Correcting Vision If the eyeball is slightly too long or too short, the image on the retina is out of focus. Fortunately, wearing glasses or contact lenses can correct this type of vision problem.

A **nearsighted** person can see nearby things clearly, but objects at a distance are blurred. The eyeball is too long, so the lens focuses the image in front of the retina. To correct this, a concave lens in front of the eye spreads out light rays before they enter the eye. As a result, the image forms on the retina.

A **farsighted** person can see distant objects clearly, but nearby objects appear blurry. The eyeball is too short, so the image that falls on the retina is out of focus. A convex lens corrects this by bending light rays toward each other before they enter the eye. An image then focuses on the retina.

 Diagnose the Patient! Read each patient's chart. Circle the diagnosis. Write in the type of lens needed in each case.

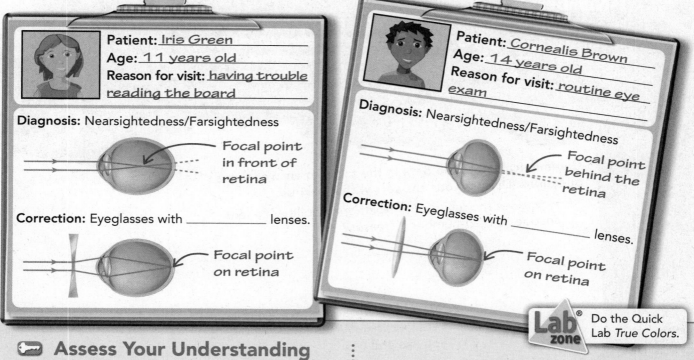

Patient: Iris Green
Age: 11 years old
Reason for visit: having trouble reading the board

Diagnosis: Nearsightedness/Farsightedness

Focal point in front of retina

Correction: Eyeglasses with _____ lenses.

Focal point on retina

Patient: Cornealis Brown
Age: 14 years old
Reason for visit: routine eye exam

Diagnosis: Nearsightedness/Farsightedness

Focal point behind the retina

Correction: Eyeglasses with _____ lenses.

Focal point on retina

Lab zone® Do the Quick Lab *True Colors.*

🔑 Assess Your Understanding

1a. Sequence The part of the eye that light enters first is called the _____

b. Explain How is an image formed on the retina?

_____

_____

_____

_____

got it?

○ **I get it!** Now I know that seeing objects is a process that involves both _____

_____

○ **I need extra help with** _____

_____

Go to my science ⓢ coach *online for help with this subject.*

Using Light

🔑 How Do Cameras, Telescopes, and Microscopes Work?

my PLANET DiaRY

SCIENCE STATS

F-Numbers

Have you ever seen numbers such as F1.0, F1.4, or F2.8 on the LCD screen of a digital camera? These numbers are called *f-numbers*. F-numbers tell the size of the lens opening on the camera. The larger the f-number is, the smaller the lens opening is. By changing the f-number, a photographer can change the amount of light the lens lets in. The table shows the amount of light let in (relative ability to gather light) for different f-numbers.

Communicate Use the data in the table to answer these questions. Discuss your answers with a partner.

1. How does the relative light-gathering ability of a lens change as the f-number increases?

_____

_____

2. Suppose you want to take a picture in very low light. Which f-number would you use and why?

_____

_____

_____

F-number	Relative Ability to Gather Light
1.0	32×
1.4	16×
2.0	8×
2.8	4×
4.0	2×
5.6	1

▶ **PLANET DIARY** Go to **Planet Diary** to learn more about optical instruments.

Lab zone® Do the Inquiry Warm-Up *How Does a Pinhole Camera Work?*

Vocabulary

- camera • telescope • refracting telescope • objective
- eyepiece • reflecting telescope • microscope

Skills

↻ **Reading: Relate Text and Visuals**

△ **Inquiry: Infer**

How Do Cameras, Telescopes, and Microscopes Work?

A microscope helps you see objects that are nearby. But another type of optical (or light-using) instrument, a telescope, helps you see objects that are far away. Three common types of optical instruments are cameras, telescopes, and microscopes.

Cameras A **camera** records an image of an object. A film camera records the image on film. A digital camera records the image electronically on a sensor. Both types of cameras follow the same basic principle. ⟳ **The lenses in a camera focus light to form a real, upside-down image in the back of the camera.** In many cameras, the lenses automatically move closer to or away from the film or sensor until the image is focused.

To take a photo with a digital camera, you press halfway down on a button called the shutter release. The camera automatically adjusts the amount of light that hits the sensor by changing the size of its opening. The camera also adjusts the amount of time that the sensor is exposed to light. When you press all the way down on the shutter release, the camera records the final image. The camera stores the final images so that you can transfer them to a computer.

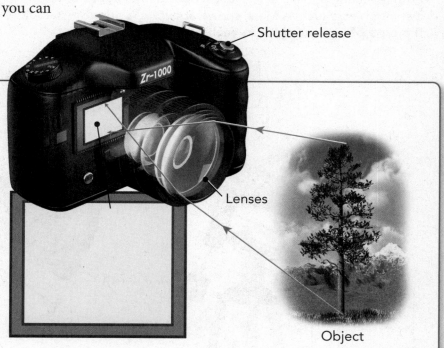

Shutter release

Zr-1000

Lenses

Object

apply it!

The diagram shows the structure of a digital camera.

1 Interpret Diagrams What happens to each light ray as it passes through the lenses?

_____

2 Identify On what part of the camera does an image form?

_____

3 △ Infer Draw the image of the tree in the box to the right.

What is the purpose of the eyepiece in both types of telescopes and the microscope?

- to shrink the image
- to magnify the image
- to gather light
- to reflect light

Telescopes Distant objects are difficult to see because light from them has spread out by the time it reaches your eyes. Your eyes are too small to gather much light. A **telescope** forms enlarged images of distant objects. 🔑 Telescopes use lenses or mirrors to collect and focus light from distant objects. The most common use of telescopes is to study objects in space.

Figure 1 shows the two main types of telescopes: refracting telescopes and reflecting telescopes. A **refracting telescope** consists of two convex lenses, one at each end of a tube. The larger lens is called the objective. The **objective** gathers the light coming from an object and focuses the rays to form a real image. The convex lens close to your eye is called the eyepiece. The **eyepiece** magnifies the image so you can see it clearly. The image seen through the refracting telescope is upside down.

A **reflecting telescope** uses a large concave mirror to gather light. The mirror collects light from distant objects and focuses the rays to form a real image. A small, plane mirror inside the telescope reflects the image to the eyepiece. The images you see through a reflecting telescope are upside down, just like the images seen through a refracting telescope.

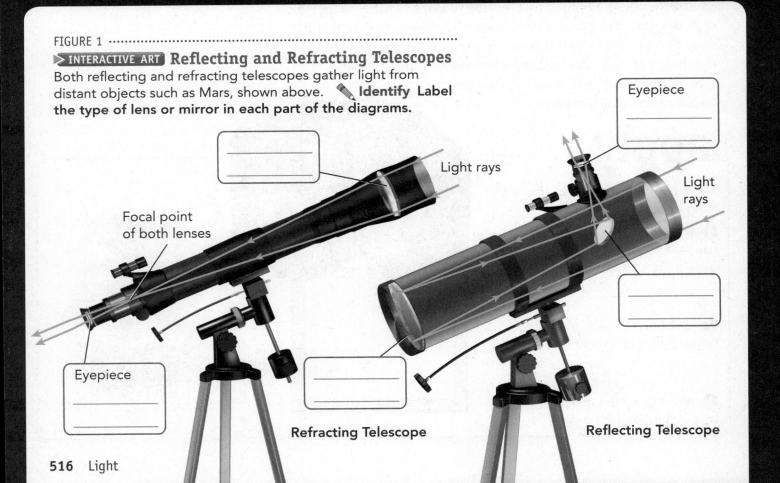

FIGURE 1 ·······································

▶ **INTERACTIVE ART** **Reflecting and Refracting Telescopes**
Both reflecting and refracting telescopes gather light from distant objects such as Mars, shown above. ✏️ **Identify** Label the type of lens or mirror in each part of the diagrams.

Eyepiece
_____
_____

Light rays

Focal point of both lenses

Light rays

Eyepiece
_____
_____

_____
_____

_____
_____

Refracting Telescope

Reflecting Telescope

Microscopes To look at small, nearby objects, you would use a microscope. A **microscope** forms enlarged images of tiny objects. 🔑 **A microscope uses a combination of lenses to produce and magnify an image.** For example, the microscope that is shown in **Figure 2** uses two convex lenses to magnify an object, or specimen. The specimen is placed near the objective. The objective forms a real, enlarged image of the specimen. Then the eyepiece enlarges the image even more.

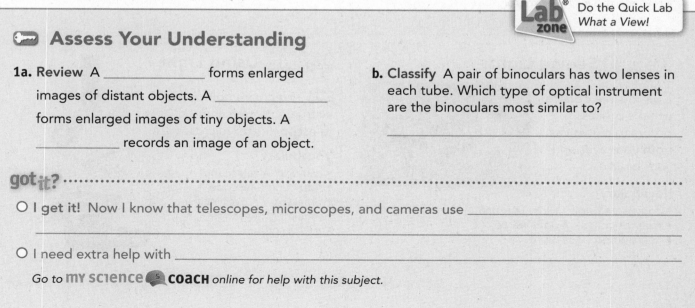

Eyepiece (convex lens)

Light rays

Objective (convex lens)

Slide with specimen

Light source

FIGURE 2 ·····························

Microscope
This microscope uses a combination of lenses to form enlarged images of tiny objects.

✎ CHALLENGE **The objects below have been enlarged by a microscope. Try to guess what they are.** *(The answers are upside down below.)*

From left to right: human hair, leaf, insect (louse)

🔑 **Assess Your Understanding**

Lab zone® Do the Quick Lab
What a View!

1a. Review A _____ forms enlarged images of distant objects. A _____ forms enlarged images of tiny objects. A _____ records an image of an object.

b. Classify A pair of binoculars has two lenses in each tube. Which type of optical instrument are the binoculars most similar to?

_____

_____

got it? ···

○ I get it! Now I know that telescopes, microscopes, and cameras use _____

_____

○ I need extra help with _____

Go to MY SCIENCE ⑤ COACH *online for help with this subject.*

15 Study Guide

When light interacts with matter, it can be _____ , _____ , or _____ .

LESSON 1 Light and Color

🔑 The color of an opaque object is the color of the light it reflects. The color of a transparent or translucent object is the color of the light it transmits.

🔑 When the three primary colors of light are combined in equal amounts, they produce white light. When the three primary colors of pigment are combined in equal amounts, they produce black.

Vocabulary
- transparent • translucent • opaque • primary color
- secondary color • complementary color • pigment

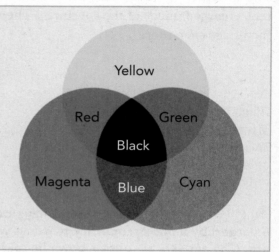

LESSON 2 Reflection and Mirrors

🔑 The two ways in which a surface can reflect light are regular reflection and diffuse reflection.

🔑 The three common types of mirrors are plane, concave, and convex.

Vocabulary
- ray • regular reflection • image
- diffuse reflection • plane mirror
- virtual image • concave mirror
- optical axis • focal point
- real image • convex mirror

LESSON 3 Refraction and Lenses

🔑 When light rays enter a new medium at an angle, the change in speed causes them to bend.

🔑 The type of image formed by a lens depends on the shape of the lens and the position of the object.

Vocabulary
- index of refraction • mirage • lens
- concave lens • convex lens

LESSON 4 Seeing Light

🔑 You see objects when a process occurs that involves both your eyes and your brain.

Vocabulary
- cornea • pupil • iris • retina
- rods • cones • optic nerve
- nearsighted • farsighted

LESSON 5 Using Light

🔑 Three common optical instruments are cameras, telescopes, and microscopes.

Vocabulary
- camera • telescope
- refracting telescope
- objective • eyepiece
- reflecting telescope
- microscope

Review and Assessment

LESSON 1 Light and Color

1. A type of material that reflects or absorbs all of the light that strikes it is called

a. translucent. b. transparent.

c. reflective. d. opaque.

2. Colors that combine to make any other color are called _____

3. Classify Do the colors shown below represent colors of pigments or light? Explain.

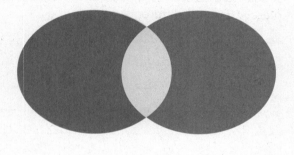

_____
_____
_____

4. Compare and Contrast Why do you see the petals of a rose as red and the leaves as green? Explain.

_____
_____
_____
_____

5. **Write About It** Helena works in the lighting crew for a theater. She needs to create a red spotlight on the stage. Kimi is a painter. He wants to create red paint for the background in a new painting. Use the terms *primary color* and *complementary color* to explain what color or combinations of colors each person must use. Explain any differences you note.

LESSON 2 Reflection and Mirrors

6. What type of reflection describes how light reflects off an uneven surface?

a. real reflection b. concave reflection

c. diffuse reflection d. regular reflection

7. Light rays obey the law of reflection, which states that _____

_____
_____

8. Draw Use a ruler to draw how the parallel light rays reflect off each mirror below.

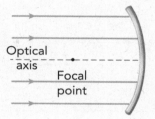

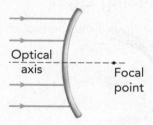

9. Classify Name the kind(s) of mirror(s) that can produce only virtual images.

_____

10. Apply Concepts Can a plane mirror produce a real image? Explain.

_____
_____
_____
_____

15 Review and Assessment

LESSON 3 Refraction and Lenses

11. A curved piece of glass or other transparent material that is used to refract light is called a

   a. prism.   **b.** lens.

   c. mirage.   **d.** mirror.

12. A _____ lens can produce only virtual images because parallel light rays passing through the lens never meet.

13. **math!** Quartz has an index of refraction of 1.46. Diamond has an index of refraction of 2.42. In which material does a light ray entering from air slow down more? Explain.

_____

_____

_____

_____

LESSON 4 Seeing Light

14. What is the ring of muscle that changes the size of the eye's pupil?

   a. iris   **b.** retina

   c. cornea   **d.** cone

15. A _____ person has trouble seeing things nearby.

16. **Apply Concepts** How are your eyes able to clearly see both near and distant objects?

_____

_____

_____

_____

_____

LESSON 5 Using Light

17. What is a device that helps you see very small, nearby objects more clearly?

   a. telescope   **b.** camera

   c. microscope   **d.** binoculars

18. A _____ telescope gathers light with a concave mirror.

19. **Compare and Contrast** How is a microscope similar to a convex lens used as a magnifying glass? How is it different?

_____

_____

_____

_____

_____

How does light interact with matter?

20. Explain why the beam of light changes direction when it enters the water.

_____

_____

_____

_____

Standardized Test Prep

Multiple Choice

Circle the letter of the best answer.

1. The diagram below shows a periscope, a tool used to see objects not in the viewer's direct line of sight.

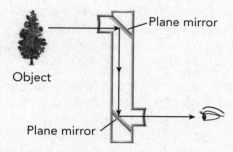

   If you want to build a periscope, what measurement is most important?

   A the width of the two mirrors
   B the distance between the two mirrors
   C the angle of the two mirrors
   D the length of the tube

2. The index of refraction for water is 1.33 and for glass it is 1.5. What happens to the speed of light when light travels from glass into water?

   A It increases.
   B It decreases.
   C It remains the same.
   D It depends on the angle of incidence.

3. A convex lens can produce a real or a virtual image. Which type of mirror is most similar to a convex lens?

   A concave mirror
   B convex mirror
   C plane mirror
   D none of the above

4. You view an American flag through sunglasses that are tinted green. What colors do you see?

   A green and blue
   B red and black
   C blue and red
   D black and green

5. Which of the following describes looking at an object through a translucent material?

   A You see the object clearly but it is upside down.
   B You do not see the object at all.
   C You see the object but its details are blurred.
   D You see the object very clearly.

Constructed Response

Use the diagram below and your knowledge of science to help you answer Question 6. Write your answer on a separate sheet of paper.

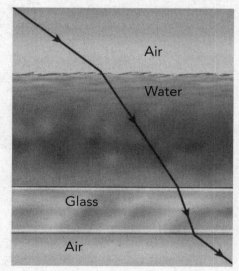

6. Explain why the path of the light ray changes as it travels through the different mediums.

Seeing Double

Binoculars are really a set of two telescopes—one for each eye—that magnify distant objects. When scientists want to look at something even farther away, they can now turn to the world's largest pair of binoculars: the Large Binocular Telescope (LBT) on Mount Graham in Arizona.

The 120-million-dollar LBT is the world's most powerful optical telescope. It provides scientists with pictures and data of a huge area of space. The LBT has two massive mirrors that work together. Each mirror has a diameter of 8.4 meters! The mirrors gather light and allow scientists to look deeper into the universe than ever before. In fact, the LBT provides the same resolution as a 22.8-meter telescope—that's about as big as two school buses! It also has a larger field for collecting images than any single telescope, allowing scientists to see more.

Design It Research how mirrors work in a reflecting telescope. Make a model or draw a diagram of how a reflecting telescope works. Show how the angles of reflection would work with the mirrors placed at two different angles. Which angles will work best? Present your model or drawing to your class.

Lens

Light from star

Viewing mirror reflects light to eyepiece.

Concave mirror reflects light.

▲ Isaac Newton built the first model for a reflecting telescope in 1688.

The world's largest binoculars peer into space. ▶

Hiding in Plain Sight

The third layer of the dwarf chameleon's skin reflects blue light, which combines with the yellow in the second layer to make the chameleon appear bright green. ▼

The South African dwarf chameleon has mastered the art of the quick change! This lizard can change the color of its skin in response to light, temperature, and other environmental factors.

Each of the four layers of the dwarf chameleon's skin plays a role in its brilliant appearance. The top layer is clear, so light passes right through it. The second layer has cells that contain a yellow pigment. The third layer doesn't have a specific color—it has cells that scatter light. The way these cells scatter light is similar to the way Earth's atmosphere scatters light, reflecting blue light especially well. The bottom layer of a dwarf chameleon's skin contains a pigment called melanin, which absorbs red light. Hormones control how the melanin is arranged in this layer. The melanin moves in response to light, temperature, and other environmental factors. As the melanin moves, the color of the chameleon's skin changes.

The chameleon's color results from the combination of the reflected light from the underlying layers of skin. When mostly blue light reflected from the third layer combines with light from the yellow layer, the chameleon is bright green.

Model It Use a piece of clear plastic wrap, yellow plastic wrap, a small prism, and white or blue paper to model the top three layers of the chameleon's skin. Does changing the angle of the prism change the color you see through the layers of "skin"? Draw a diagram of your model, and describe how changing the color of the bottom layer and the angle of the prism change the colors you see.

WHY ARE THE PEOPLE IN THIS BUILDING SAFE FROM LIGHTNING?

How does an electric circuit work?

Lightning strikes Earth more than 100 times every second. Buildings can be protected from lightning strikes with tall metal poles called lightning rods. When lightning strikes, it is more likely to hit the rod than the building. A lightning strike can flow through the rod and into metal wires that are connected to the ground. This prevents the building from being damaged and anyone inside from being injured.

Communicate **How is a lightning bolt like the electricity that runs through power lines? Discuss this with a partner.**

> **UNTAMED SCIENCE** Watch the **Untamed Science** video to learn more about electricity.

_____
_____
_____
_____

16 Getting Started

Check Your Understanding

1. **Background** Read the paragraph below and then answer the question.

When you lift up a basketball, you apply a **force** to it. The **energy** you use to lift it gets transferred to the ball as gravitational **potential energy.** The higher you lift the ball, the more energy you use and the more gravitational potential energy the ball gains.

> A **force** is a push or pull exerted on an object.
>
> **Energy** is the ability to do work or cause change.
>
> **Potential energy** is the stored energy that results from the position or shape of an object.

- What happens to the ball's gravitational potential energy if it is dropped?

_____

> MY READING WEB If you had trouble completing the question above, visit **My Reading Web** and type in *Electricity*.

Vocabulary Skill

Latin Word Origins Many science words in English come from Latin. For example, the word *solar*, which means "of the sun," comes from the Latin *sol*, which means "sun."

Latin Word	Meaning of Latin Word	Example
circuitus	going around	circuit, *n.* a complete, unbroken path
currere	to run	current, *n.* a continuous flow
insula	island	insulator, *n.* a material through which charges cannot flow

2. **Quick Check** Choose the word that best completes the sentence.

- An electric _____ is formed by the movement of electric charges from one place to another.

static electricity

static discharge

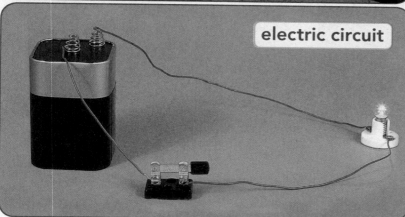

electric circuit

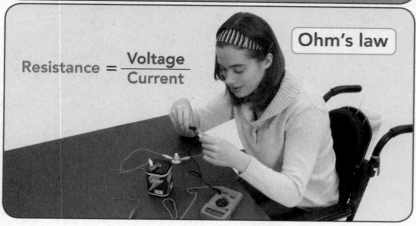

Ohm's law

$$Resistance = \frac{Voltage}{Current}$$

Chapter Preview

LESSON 1

- electric force
- electric field
- static electricity
- conservation of charge
- friction
- conduction
- induction
- polarization
- static discharge
- ↺ **Relate Cause and Effect**
- △ **Draw Conclusions**

LESSON 2

- electric current
- electric circuit
- conductor
- insulator
- voltage
- resistance
- ↺ **Ask Questions**
- △ **Classify**

LESSON 3

- Ohm's law
- series circuit
- parallel circuit
- ↺ **Compare and Contrast**
- △ **Make Models**

LESSON 4

- power
- short circuit
- third prong
- grounded
- fuse
- circuit breaker
- ↺ **Summarize**
- △ **Calculate**

> VOCAB FLASH CARDS For extra help with vocabulary, visit **Vocab Flash Cards** and type in *Electricity.*

527

Electric Charge and Static Electricity

🔑 **How Do Charges Interact?**

🔑 **How Does Charge Build Up?**

my planeT DiaRY

Force Fields

Misconception: Force fields exist only in science fiction stories.

Fact: Force fields are an important part of your everyday life.

You're actually sitting in a force field right now! A force field exists around any object that repels or attracts other objects. A giant gravitational force field surrounds Earth. This field keeps you from floating off into space. Earth's magnetic field makes compass needles point north. You make your own force field every time you get shocked when you reach for a doorknob!

MISCONCEPTIONS

Answer the questions below.

1. A gravitational field keeps you on Earth. What other uses might force fields have?

_____

_____

2. Describe how a different science fiction invention could be rooted in real science.

_____

_____

▶ **PLANET DIARY** Go to **Planet Diary** to learn more about force fields.

Lab zone® Do the Inquiry Warm-Up *Can You Move a Can Without Touching It?*

Vocabulary
- electric force • electric field • static electricity
- conservation of charge • friction • conduction
- induction • polarization • static discharge

Skills
Reading: Relate Cause and Effect

Inquiry: Draw Conclusions

How Do Charges Interact?

You're already late for school and one of your socks is missing! You finally find it sticking to the back of your blanket. How did that happen? The explanation has to do with electric charges.

Types of Charge Atoms contain charged particles called electrons and protons. If two electrons come close together, they push each other apart. In other words, they repel each other. Two protons behave the same way. If a proton and an electron come close together, they attract one another. Protons attract electrons because the two have opposite electric charges. The charge on a proton is positive (+). The charge on an electron is negative (−).

The two types of electric charges interact in specific ways, as you see in **Figure 1.** 🔑 **Charges that are the same repel each other. Charges that are different attract each other.** The interaction between electric charges is called electricity. The force between charged objects is called **electric force.**

FIGURE 1 ·····························

Repel or Attract?
✏️ △ **Draw Conclusions** On each sphere, write if it has a positive (+) or a negative (−) charge. Compare your answers with a group. Can you tell for sure which spheres are positively charged and which are negatively charged? What conclusions can you draw?

_____

_____

_____

_____

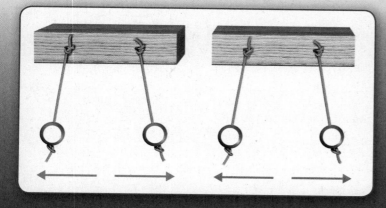

Electric Fields

You may have heard of a gravitational field, which is the space around an object (such as a planet) where the object's gravitational force is exerted. Similarly, an electric field extends around a charged object. An **electric field** is a region around a charged object where the object's electric force is exerted on other charged objects. Electric fields and forces get weaker the farther away they are from the charge.

An electric field is invisible. You can use field lines to represent it, as shown in **Figure 2**. A field line shows the force that would be exerted on a positive charge at any point along that line. Positive charges are repelled by positive charges and attracted to negative charges, so field lines point away from positive charges and toward negative charges. Single charges have straight field lines, since a positive charge will be repelled away from or attracted to it in a straight line. When multiple charges are present, each charge exerts a force. These forces combine to make more complicated field lines.

FIGURE 2 ·······
Electric Fields
Field lines show the direction of the force acting on a positive charge.

✎ **Answer the questions.**

1. **Identify** Identify which charge is positive and which charge is negative.

2. **Interpret Diagrams** The boxes on the electric field are the same size. How many field lines are inside the white box?

_____

3. **Interpret Diagrams** The blue box is closer to the charges. How many field lines are in this box?

_____

4. **Draw Conclusions** What is the relationship between the number of field lines in an area and the strength of the electric force?

_____

_____

_____

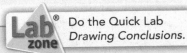

Do the Quick Lab
Drawing Conclusions.

🔑 Assess Your Understanding

got it? ·······

○ **I get it!** Now I know that the way electric charges interact depends on _____

_____

○ **I need extra help with**_____

Go to **MY SCIENCE COACH** online for help with this subject.

How Does Charge Build Up?

Most objects have no overall charge. An atom usually has as many electrons as it has protons, so each positive charge is balanced by a negative charge. This leaves the atom uncharged, or neutral.

An uncharged object can become charged by gaining or losing electrons. If an object loses electrons, it is left with more protons than electrons. It has an overall positive charge. If an object gains electrons, it will have an overall negative charge. The buildup of charges on an object is called **static electricity.** In static electricity, charges build up on an object, but they do not flow continuously.

FIGURE 3 ·······························

Charge Buildup

Rubbing two objects together can produce static electricity.

✎ **Interpret Photos** Circle the phrases that best complete the statements. Follow the directions to draw how the charges are arranged in each photo.

❶ The balloon is (positively/ negatively/not) charged. The balloon (attracts/repels/neither attracts nor repels) the girl's hair.

❷ Rubbing the balloon allows more electrons to move onto the balloon. The balloon is now (positively/negatively) charged. **Draw what the charges on the balloon look like now.**

❸ The (positive/negative) charges in the girl's hair are now attracted to the negative charges on the balloon. **Draw how the charges on the balloon are arranged now.**

Charging Objects

Charges are neither created nor destroyed. This is a rule known as the law of **conservation of charge.** An object can't become charged by destroying or creating its own electrons. If one object loses electrons, another object must pick them up. 🔑 **There are four methods by which charges can redistribute themselves to build up static electricity: by friction, by conduction, by induction, and by polarization.**

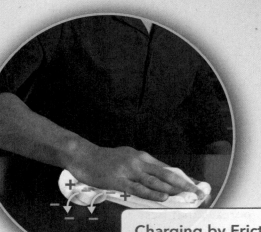

Charging by Friction

When two uncharged objects are rubbed together, some electrons from one object can move onto the other object. The object that gains electrons becomes negatively charged. The object that loses electrons becomes positively charged. Charging by **friction** is the transfer of electrons from one uncharged object to another by rubbing the objects together.

Charging by Conduction

When a charged object touches another object, electrons can be transferred. Charging by **conduction** is the transfer of electrons from one object to another by direct contact. Electrons transfer from the object that has more negative charge to the object that has more positive charge. A positively charged object, like the metal ball, gains electrons when an uncharged person touches it. The girl starts out neutral, but electrons move from her hair, through her arm, to the ball. This leaves her hair positively charged, and the strands repel each other.

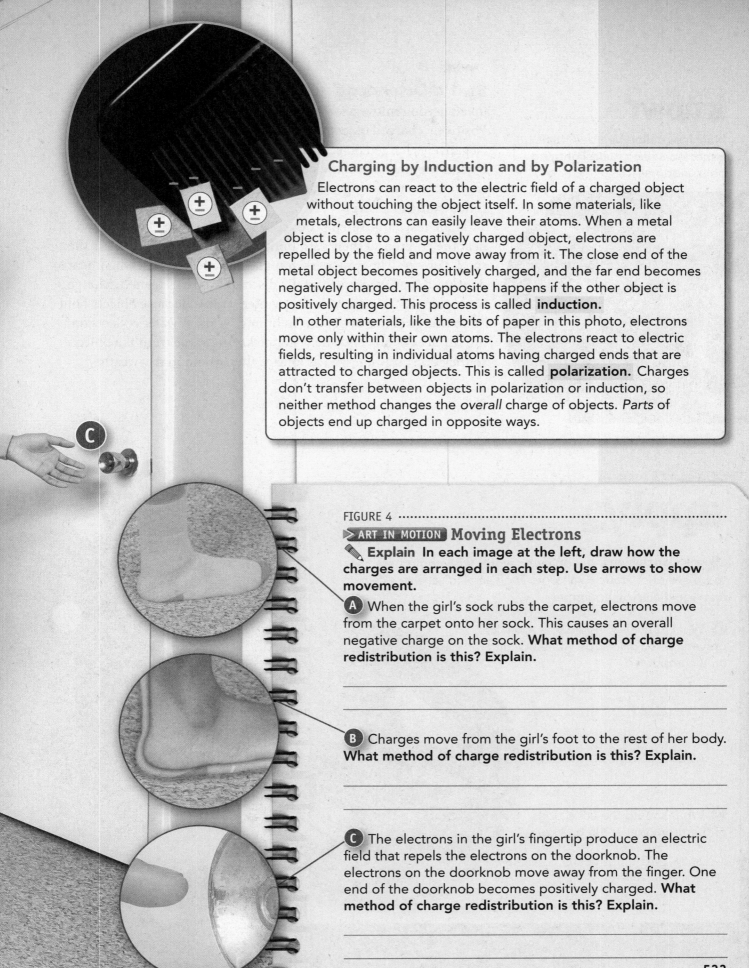

Charging by Induction and by Polarization

Electrons can react to the electric field of a charged object without touching the object itself. In some materials, like metals, electrons can easily leave their atoms. When a metal object is close to a negatively charged object, electrons are repelled by the field and move away from it. The close end of the metal object becomes positively charged, and the far end becomes negatively charged. The opposite happens if the other object is positively charged. This process is called **induction.**

In other materials, like the bits of paper in this photo, electrons move only within their own atoms. The electrons react to electric fields, resulting in individual atoms having charged ends that are attracted to charged objects. This is called **polarization.** Charges don't transfer between objects in polarization or induction, so neither method changes the *overall* charge of objects. *Parts* of objects end up charged in opposite ways.

FIGURE 4 ···

> ART IN MOTION **Moving Electrons**

✎ **Explain** In each image at the left, draw how the charges are arranged in each step. Use arrows to show movement.

Ⓐ When the girl's sock rubs the carpet, electrons move from the carpet onto her sock. This causes an overall negative charge on the sock. **What method of charge redistribution is this? Explain.**

_____

_____

Ⓑ Charges move from the girl's foot to the rest of her body. **What method of charge redistribution is this? Explain.**

_____

_____

Ⓒ The electrons in the girl's fingertip produce an electric field that repels the electrons on the doorknob. The electrons on the doorknob move away from the finger. One end of the doorknob becomes positively charged. **What method of charge redistribution is this? Explain.**

_____

_____

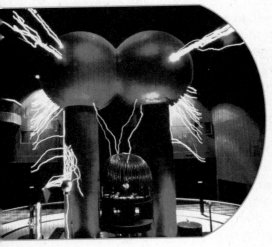

Static Discharge If your hair becomes charged and sticks up after you remove a sweater, it doesn't stay that way forever. Positively charged objects gradually gain electrons from the air. Negatively charged objects gradually lose electrons to the air. The objects eventually become neutral again. The loss of static electricity as electric charges transfer from one object to another is called **static discharge.**

Static discharge often produces a spark. Moving electrons can heat the air around their path until it glows. The glowing air is the spark you see. The tiny spark you may have felt or seen when near a doorknob is an example of static discharge. Sparks from discharge happen more frequently during winter. This is because objects hold on to charge better in dry air. In humid weather, water collects on the surfaces of objects. The water picks up charge from the objects, so they don't stay charged as long as they would in dry weather.

apply it!

⚠ **Draw Conclusions** Anyone who works with computers has to be aware of static discharge. Even small discharges can damage electrical equipment.

❶ What activities should you avoid to prevent static discharge while working on a computer?

_____

_____

_____

_____

❷ What should the conditions of the room you are in be like?

_____

_____

_____

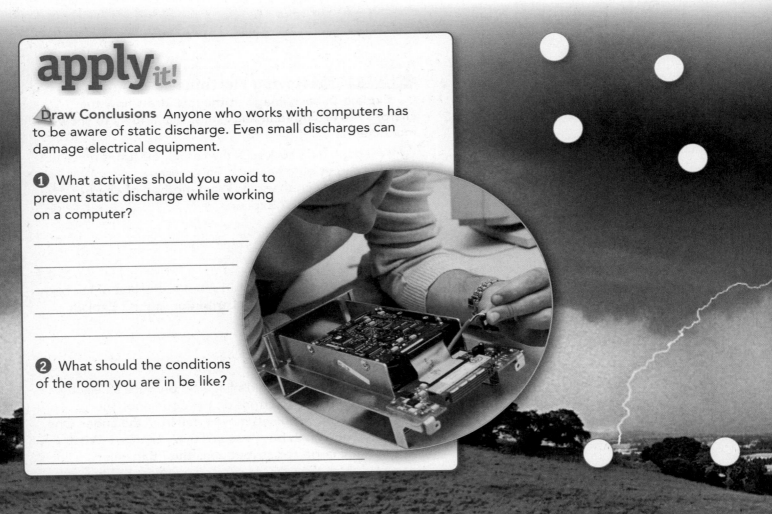

Lightning bolts are an example of static discharge. During thunderstorms, air swirls violently. Water droplets within the clouds become charged. Electrons move from areas of negative charge to areas of positive charge, producing an intense spark. That spark is lightning.

Some lightning reaches Earth. Negative charges at the bottoms of storm clouds create an electric field. This causes Earth's surface to become positively charged through induction. Electrons jump between the clouds and Earth's surface, producing a giant spark of lightning as they travel through the air.

Relate Cause and Effect
Pick one example of cause and effect in this section. Underline the cause, and then circle the effect that results.

FIGURE 5 ···

Static Discharge
Lightning is just a much bigger version of the sparks you feel when you shock yourself on a doorknob.

✏ **Relate Text and Visuals** In the white circles, draw how positive and negative charges are arranged during a lightning strike.

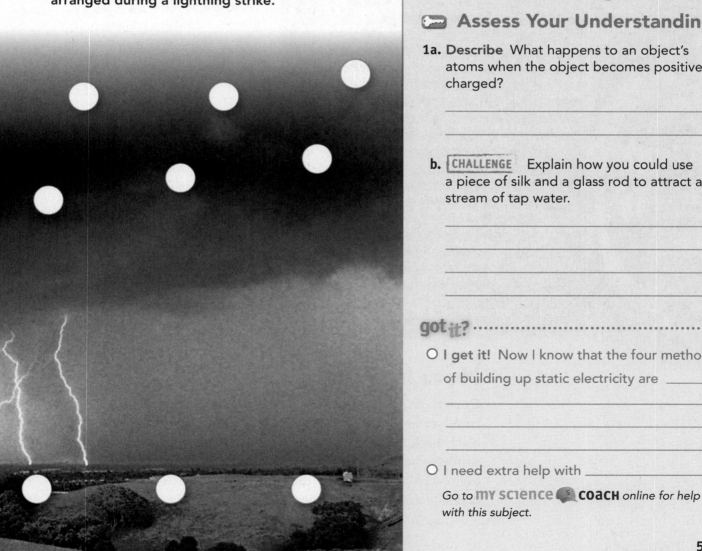

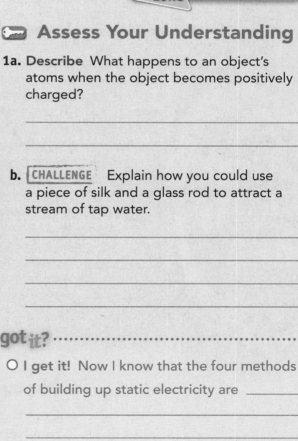
Do the Quick Lab
Sparks Are Flying.

🔲 Assess Your Understanding

1a. Describe What happens to an object's atoms when the object becomes positively charged?

_____

_____

b. [CHALLENGE] Explain how you could use a piece of silk and a glass rod to attract a stream of tap water.

_____

_____

_____

_____

got it? ···

○ **I get it!** Now I know that the four methods of building up static electricity are _____

_____

_____

○ **I need extra help with** _____

Go to MY SCIENCE ⓢ COACH *online for help with this subject.*

535

Electric Current

UNLOCK THE BIG **Q?**

🔑 **How Is Electric Current Made?**

🔑 **How Do Conductors Differ From Insulators?**

🔑 **What Affects Current Flow?**

MY PLANET DiARY

Be a Superconductor—of Science!

John Vander Sande wants your city to run more efficiently. A company he cofounded is working to replace old power lines with materials that let electric current flow more efficiently. These materials are called superconductors. Superconductors are often found in lab equipment, as shown at the left, but companies like Vander Sande's are finding other uses for them. Vander Sande didn't start his career working with power lines. He began his work in materials science as a professor at the Massachusetts Institute of Technology (MIT). He got into superconducting by chance after hearing about discoveries at a lecture by one of his colleagues. He encourages everyone to stay open to opportunities in science, because they can pop up anywhere at any time.

Answer the question below.

Describe an instance in your life when hearing something by chance led to a new opportunity.

_____

_____

_____

_____

_____

▶ PLANET DIARY Go to **Planet Diary** to learn more about superconductors.

Lab zone® Do the Inquiry Warm-Up *How Can Current Be Measured?*

How Is Electric Current Made?

Dozens of sushi dishes ride along a conveyor belt in **Figure 1.** The conveyer belt carries full dishes past customers and carries empty plates back to the kitchen. You might be wondering what a conveyor belt of rice, vegetables, and fish could possibly have to do with electricity. Like the sushi plates, electric charges can be made to move in a confined path.

Vocabulary
- electric current • electric circuit
- conductor • insulator
- voltage • resistance

Skills
⟲ **Reading:** Ask Questions
△ **Inquiry:** Classify

Flow of Electric Charges Lightning releases a large amount of electrical energy. However, the electric charge from lightning doesn't last long enough to power your radio or your TV. These devices need electric charges that flow continuously. They require electric current.

Recall that static electric charges do not flow continuously. ⚷ **When electric charges are made to flow through a material, they produce an electric current.** Electric current is the continuous flow of electric charges through a material. The amount of charge that passes through a wire in a given period of time is the rate of electric current. The unit for the rate of current is the ampere, named for André Marie Ampère, an early investigator of electricity. The name of the unit is often shortened to amp or A. The number of amps describes the amount of charge flowing past a given point each second.

FIGURE 1 ·····························

Electric Current

The conveyor belt represents a current. If it represented a greater current, more plates would pass by you in the same amount of time. One way for this to occur would be for the belt to go faster.

✎ **Make Models** Suppose the belt couldn't go faster. Draw a different way a greater current could be represented.

Current in a Circuit

The electric currents that power your computer and music player need very specific paths to work. In order to maintain an electric current, charges must be able to flow continuously in a loop. A complete, unbroken path that charges can flow through is called an **electric circuit.**

Someone jogging along the roads in **Figure 2** is moving like a charge in an electric circuit. If the road forms a complete loop, the jogger can move in a continuous path. However, the jogger cannot continue if any section of the road is closed. Similarly, if an electric circuit is complete, charges can flow continuously. If an electric circuit is broken, charges will not flow.

Electric circuits are all around you. All electrical devices, from toasters to televisions, contain electric circuits.

FIGURE 2 ·····························

Circuits

Just like charges in a wire, people can move around in circuits. One possible jogging circuit is outlined in this photo.

✎ **Interpret Photos** Trace another possible circuit. What could break this circuit?

_____

_____

_____

Lab® Do the Quick Lab
zone *Producing Electric Current.*

🔑 Assess Your Understanding

1a. Review What is the unit of current?

_____

b. Predict What could break the circuit between your home and an electric power plant?

_____

got it?

○ **I get it!** Now I know that electric current is made of _____

_____

○ **I need extra help with** _____

Go to **MY SCIENCE** 🌐 **COACH** *online for help with this subject.*

How Do Conductors Differ From Insulators?

Charges can flow more easily through some materials than others. A **conductor** is a material through which charge can flow easily. Electrons can move freely, allowing conductors to be charged by induction. Metals, such as copper, are good conductors.

Wires are surrounded by insulators. **Insulators** are materials, such as rubber, that do not allow charges to flow. However, electrons can move around within their own atoms, allowing for polarization. They can also be stripped off when charging by friction.

Semiconductors are materials that behave sometimes as conductors and sometimes as insulators. Pure silicon acts like an insulator, but when other elements are added, it behaves like a conductor. Silicon is a semiconductor found in most electronic devices.

The difference between conductors and insulators comes from how strongly electrons are attached to atoms. 🔑 **The atoms in conductors have loosely bound electrons that can move freely. Electrons in insulators cannot move freely among atoms.**

✏️ **Ask Questions** Current, conductors, and insulators all show up in your daily life. Write down a question about one of these topics that you would like answered.

_____

_____

_____

apply it!

All objects are made up of conductors or insulators, not just the ones you usually see in electronic devices.

❶ **Identify** The gloves that electricians wear when working on power lines should be made out of (insulating/conducting) materials.

❷ **Classify** Circle the conductors in these photos. Be careful—only parts of some items are conductors!

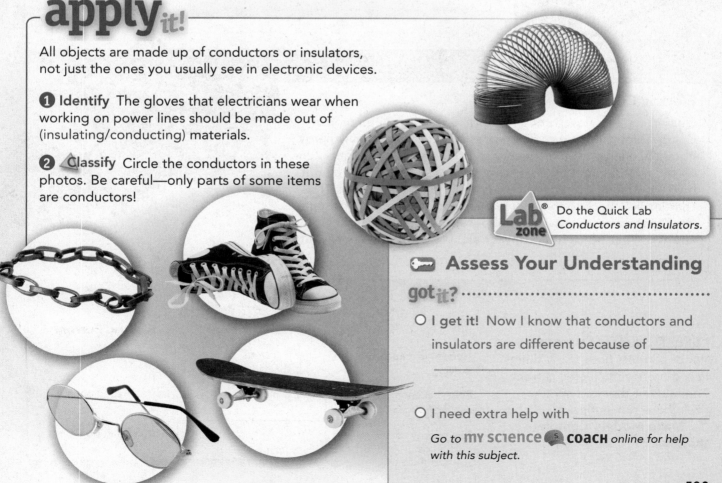

Lab zone Do the Quick Lab *Conductors and Insulators.*

🔑 **Assess Your Understanding**

got it? ....

○ **I get it!** Now I know that conductors and insulators are different because of _____

_____

○ **I need extra help with** _____

Go to **MY SCIENCE COACH** *online for help with this subject.*

What Affects Current Flow?

Suppose you are on a water slide at an amusement park. You climb the steps, sit down, and whoosh! The water current carries you down the slide. Electric charges flow in much the same way water moves down the slide.  **Current flow is affected by the energy of the charges and the properties of the objects that the charges flow through.**

Water Currents

A completely horizontal water slide wouldn't be much fun. A water slide that was only a few centimeters tall wouldn't be much better. Water slides are exciting because of gravitational potential energy. (Remember that gravitational potential energy is the energy an object has because of its height above the ground.) As the water falls down the slide, its potential energy is converted into kinetic energy. The water speeds up, since speed increases as kinetic energy increases. The higher the slide, the more potential energy the water starts with and the faster it will end up moving. At the bottom of the slide, the water has no potential energy. It has all been converted to kinetic energy. The water gains potential energy as it is pumped back to the top, starting the ride again.

✎ **How could the current through a water slide be interrupted?**

_____

_____

Electric Currents

Electric currents flow through wires like water through pipes. Charges flow because of differences in electric potential energy. Potential energy from an energy source (like a battery) gets converted into different forms of energy. If a circuit contains a light bulb, its potential energy is converted into light and heat. The charges flow back to the energy source and the process restarts.

✎ **Slides convert gravitational potential energy into kinetic energy. What do circuits convert electric potential energy into?**

_____

FIGURE 3 ·······························
> **INTERACTIVE ART** **Currents**
Water currents have many things in common with electric currents. The table at the right summarizes these similarities.

✎ **Make Models Complete the table.**

	Water Current	Electric Current
Current is made up of moving	water	charges
Potential energy is converted into	_____	heat, light
The energy source for the circuit is a	_____	battery

Voltage

The *V* on a battery stands for volts, which is the unit of voltage. **Voltage** is the difference in electric potential energy *per charge* between two points in a circuit. (Electric potential energy per charge is also called electric potential.) This energy difference causes charges to flow. Because the voltage of a battery is related to energy per charge, it doesn't tell you how much total energy the battery supplies. A car battery and eight watch batteries both supply 12 volts, but eight watch batteries can't run a car. Each charge has the same amount of energy, but the car battery can provide that energy to many more charges. This results in a higher *total* energy. You can compare voltage to gravitational potential energy *per kilogram*. **Figure 4** shows the difference between total energy and energy per kilogram.

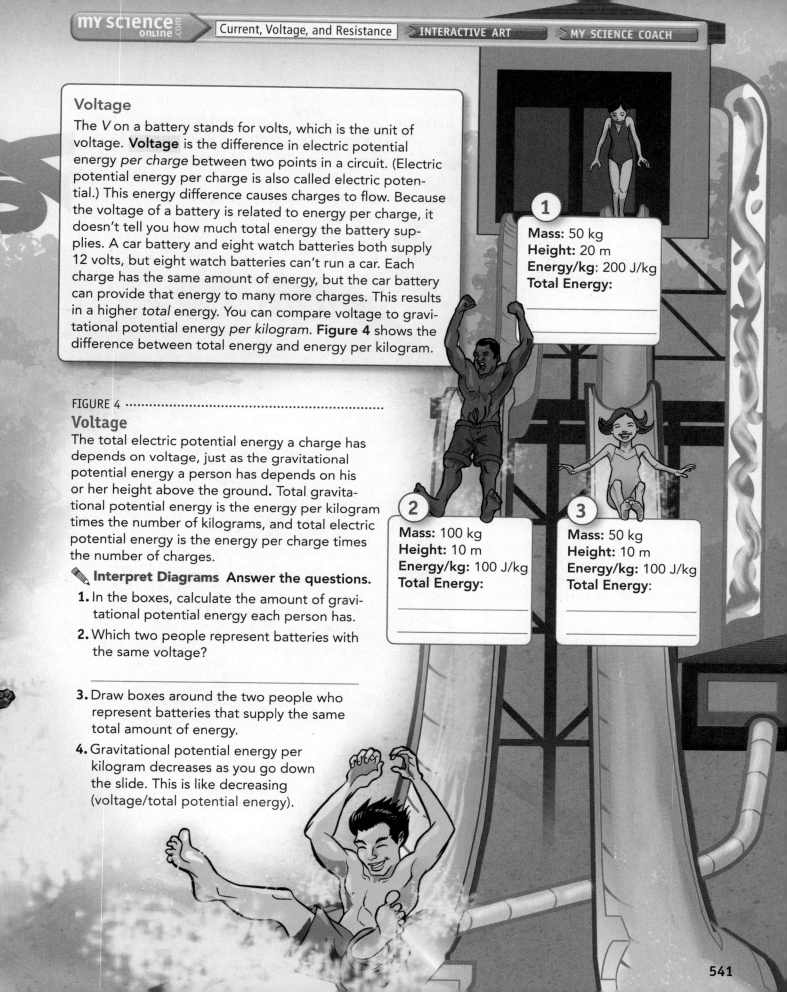

1
Mass: 50 kg
Height: 20 m
Energy/kg: 200 J/kg
Total Energy:
_____
_____

FIGURE 4 ···

Voltage

The total electric potential energy a charge has depends on voltage, just as the gravitational potential energy a person has depends on his or her height above the ground. Total gravitational potential energy is the energy per kilogram times the number of kilograms, and total electric potential energy is the energy per charge times the number of charges.

✎ **Interpret Diagrams** Answer the questions.

1. In the boxes, calculate the amount of gravitational potential energy each person has.

2. Which two people represent batteries with the same voltage?

   _____

3. Draw boxes around the two people who represent batteries that supply the same total amount of energy.

4. Gravitational potential energy per kilogram decreases as you go down the slide. This is like decreasing (voltage/total potential energy).

2
Mass: 100 kg
Height: 10 m
Energy/kg: 100 J/kg
Total Energy:
_____
_____

3
Mass: 50 kg
Height: 10 m
Energy/kg: 100 J/kg
Total Energy:
_____
_____

541

FIGURE 5 ·····························

Dimensions and Resistance

The length and diameter of a straw determine how difficult it is to drink through it. Similarly, the length and diameter of a wire determine how difficult it is for charge to flow through it.

✎ **Interpret Photos** Which of the straws in the photo would be the hardest to drink with? Explain. Is this straw like a wire with high or low resistance?

_____

_____

_____

_____

_____

Resistance The amount of current in a circuit depends on more than voltage. Current also depends on the resistance of the circuit. **Resistance** is the measure of how difficult it is for charges to flow through an object. The greater the resistance, the less current there is for a given voltage. The unit of measure of resistance is the ohm (Ω).

The four factors that determine the resistance of an object are diameter, length, material, and temperature. Objects with different characteristics have different resistances. If more than one path is available, more current will flow through the path that has the lower resistance.

Diameter

Milk flows more easily through a wide straw than it does through a narrow straw. Current flows more easily through a wide wire than through a narrow wire.

✎ **How does a wire's diameter affect its electrical resistance? Explain.**

_____

_____

_____

_____

_____

Length

You may have noticed that it is easier to drink milk through a short straw than through a long straw. Similarly, short wires have less resistance than long wires.

✎ **How does an object's length affect its electrical resistance?**

_____

_____

_____

_____

FIGURE 6

Materials and Resistance

When power lines fall down during storms, the workers repairing them must be careful to avoid electric shocks.

✏️ **Solve Problems** What should workers wear while doing the job? What should they avoid wearing?

_____

_____

_____

_____

Word Origins *Resistance* comes from the word *resist*, which comes from the Latin word *resistere*. What do you think *resistere* means?

○ to be opposed to

○ to run

○ to speed up

Temperature

The electrical resistance of most materials increases as temperature increases. As the temperature of most materials decreases, resistance decreases as well.

✏️ **Why would it be useful to keep power lines cool in the summer?**

_____

_____

_____

_____

Material

Some materials have electrons that are tightly held to their atoms. They have a high resistance because it is difficult for charges to move. Other materials have electrons that are loosely held to their atoms. They have a low resistance because charges can move through them easily.

✏️ **Do conductors or insulators have a lower resistance? Explain.**

_____

_____

_____

_____

 Do the Quick Lab *Modeling Potential Difference.*

🔑 Assess Your Understanding

2a. List List the four factors that determine the resistance of an object.

_____

_____

b. **CHALLENGE** Battery A supplies 500 charges. Each charge has 2 J of energy. Battery B supplies 50 charges, each of which has 4 J of energy. Which battery supplies more total energy? Which has a higher voltage?

_____

_____

got it? ·······································

○ I get it! Now I know that current is affected by _____

○ I need extra help with _____

Go to **MY SCIENCE COACH** online for help with this subject.

543

Electric Circuits

UNLOCK THE BIG ?

🔑 **What Did Ohm Discover?**

🔑 **What Is a Circuit Made Of?**

my planet diary

Lights Out

One winter night, a string of bright lights adorning a store window catches your eye. As you look, one bulb suddenly goes out, yet the others stay on! How can that be?

Normally, when a light bulb burns out, it breaks the flow of current through a circuit. But many holiday lights are on circuits that provide more than one possible path for the electric current to follow. This type of circuit provides a path for the current to flow even if one component goes bad. So if one light bulb burns out, the rest of the lights remain lit.

FUN FACTS

Communicate Discuss these questions with a partner and then answer them below.

1. What other devices have you used that can keep working even if one part stops working?

_____

_____

_____

2. When could it be useful to have a device turn off completely if one part breaks?

_____

_____

_____

> PLANET DIARY Go to **Planet Diary** to learn more about circuits.

Lab zone® **Do the Inquiry Warm-Up** *Do the Lights Keep Shining?*

Vocabulary
• Ohm's law
• series circuit
• parallel circuit

Skills
Reading: Compare and Contrast
Inquiry: Make Models

What Did Ohm Discover?

In the 1800s, Georg Ohm performed many experiments on electrical resistance. **Ohm found that the current, voltage, and resistance in a circuit are always related in the same way.**

Ohm's Observations Ohm set up a circuit with a voltage between two points on a conductor. He measured the resistance of the conductor and the current between those points. Then he changed the voltage and took new measurements.

Ohm found that if the factors that affect resistance are held constant, the resistance of most conductors does not depend on the voltage across them. Changing the voltage in a circuit changes the current but does not change the resistance. Ohm concluded that conductors and most other devices have a constant resistance regardless of the applied voltage.

FIGURE 1 ···

> VIRTUAL LAB **Circuit Relationships**
The work Ohm did on circuits in the 1800s still applies to almost all electric circuits today. The mathematical relationship he found between the components in a circuit holds true for circuits in everyday devices such as cell phones.

Interpret Data Suppose you use various cell phone parts to perform experiments similar to Ohm's. You come up with the following data table. Use the data to predict the relationship that Ohm found.

Voltage (V)	Current (A)	Resistance (Ω)
6.0	2.0	3.0
6.0	1.5	4.0
6.0	1.0	6.0
4.2	2.0	2.1
4.2	0.7	6.0
4.2	1.4	3.0

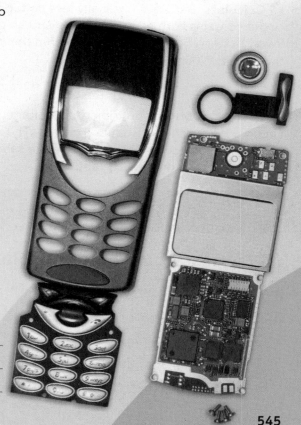

_____

_____

Ohm's Law Ohm created a law that describes how voltage, current, and resistance are related. **Ohm's law** says that resistance in a circuit is equal to voltage divided by current. This relationship can be represented by an equation.

$$\text{Resistance} = \frac{\text{Voltage}}{\text{Current}}$$

The units are ohms (Ω) = volts (V) $\div$ amps (A). One ohm is equal to one volt per amp. You can rearrange Ohm's law to solve for voltage when you know current and resistance.

Voltage = Current × Resistance

You can use the formula to see how changes in resistance, voltage, and current are related. For example, what happens to current if voltage is doubled without changing the resistance? For a constant resistance, if voltage is doubled, current doubles as well.

do the math!

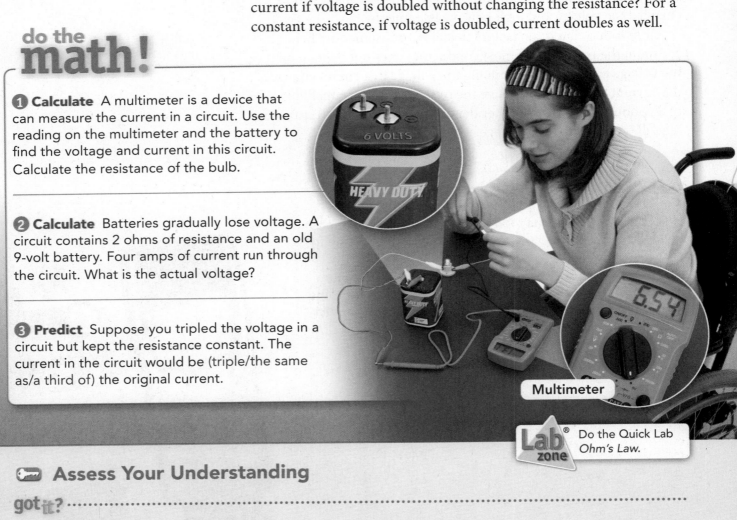

❶ **Calculate** A multimeter is a device that can measure the current in a circuit. Use the reading on the multimeter and the battery to find the voltage and current in this circuit. Calculate the resistance of the bulb.

❷ **Calculate** Batteries gradually lose voltage. A circuit contains 2 ohms of resistance and an old 9-volt battery. Four amps of current run through the circuit. What is the actual voltage?

❸ **Predict** Suppose you tripled the voltage in a circuit but kept the resistance constant. The current in the circuit would be (triple/the same as/a third of) the original current.

Multimeter

Lab zone   Do the Quick Lab
Ohm's Law.

🔑 Assess Your Understanding

got it? ....

○ **I get it!** Now I know that Ohm's Law _____

_____

○ **I need extra help with** _____

Go to **MY SCIENCE ⓢ COACH** *online for help with this subject.*

What Is a Circuit Made Of?

Objects that use electricity contain circuits. 🔌 **All electric circuits have these basic features: devices that run on electrical energy, sources of electrical energy, and conducting wires.**

- Batteries and power plants are examples of energy sources. They supply the voltage that causes current to flow. When the energy source is a battery, current flows from the positive end to the negative end.

- Energy is always conserved in a circuit. Electrical energy doesn't get used up. It gets transformed into other forms of energy, such as heat, light, mechanical, and sound energy. Appliances such as toasters transform electrical energy. These devices resist current, so they are represented in a circuit as resistors.

- Electric circuits are connected by conducting wires. The conducting wires complete the path of the current. They allow charges to flow from the energy source to the device that runs on electric current and back to the energy source.

- A switch is often included to control the current. Opening a switch breaks the circuit, which shuts off the device.

All the parts of a circuit are shown in **Figure 2.** Each part in the photograph is represented in the diagram by a simple symbol.

FIGURE 2 ·····················

Circuit Diagrams
A symbol in a circuit diagram represents a part of the circuit.

✏️ **Make Models Draw the circuit diagram for a circuit with two resistors, two batteries, and a switch.**

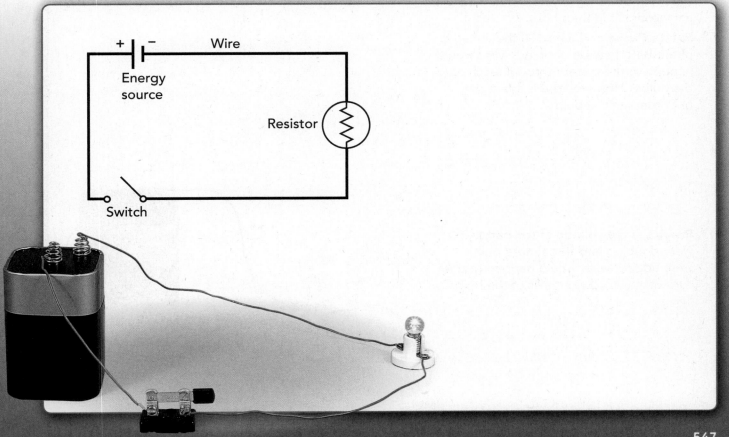

547

.... ✏ ....

⟳ Compare and Contrast On these two pages, underline differences between series and parallel circuits. Below, list their similarities.

_____

_____

_____

_____

_____

Series Circuits If all the parts of an electric circuit are connected one after another along one path, the circuit is called a **series circuit.** A series circuit has only one path for the current to take.

A series circuit is very simple to design and build, but it has some disadvantages. What happens if a light bulb in a series circuit burns out? A burned-out bulb is a break in the circuit, and there is no other path for the current to take. So if one light goes out, the other lights go out as well.

Another disadvantage of a series circuit is that the light bulbs in the circuit become dimmer as more bulbs are added. Think about what happens to the overall resistance of a series circuit as you add more bulbs. The resistance increases. Remember that for a constant voltage, if resistance increases, current decreases. If you add light bulbs to a series circuit without changing the voltage, the current decreases. The bulbs burn less brightly.

FIGURE 3 ···

Series Circuits

The number of bulbs in a series circuit affects each bulb's brightness. Remember that voltage = current × resistance.

✏ **Answer the questions below.**

1. **Make Models** Draw the circuit diagram for the circuit in the photo.

2. **Relate Cause and Effect** If the voltage of the battery were doubled, what would happen to the current through each of the bulbs? How would this affect the brightness of the bulbs?

   _____

   _____

   _____

   _____

3. **Predict** If the voltage of the battery were doubled **and** three more bulbs were added, what would happen to the current and the brightness of the bulbs?

   _____

   _____

   _____

   _____

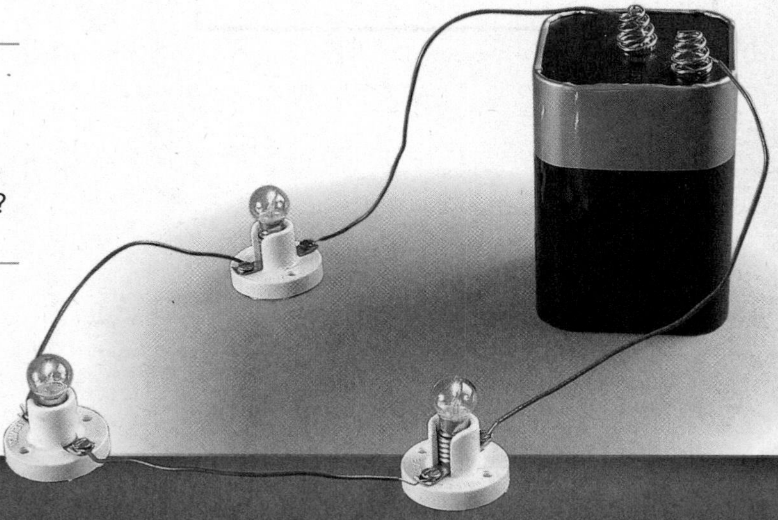

Parallel Circuits In a **parallel circuit,** different parts of the circuit are on separate branches. There are several paths for current to take. Each bulb is connected by a separate path from the battery and back to the battery.

What happens if a light burns out in a parallel circuit? If there is a break in one branch, charges can still move through the other branches. So if one bulb goes out, the others remain lit. Switches can be added to each branch to turn lights on and off without affecting the other branches.

What happens to the resistance of a parallel circuit when you add a branch? The overall resistance actually *decreases*. As new branches are added to a parallel circuit, the electric current has more paths to follow, so the overall resistance decreases. Remember that for a given voltage, if resistance decreases, current increases. The additional current travels along each new branch without affecting the original branches. So as you add branches to a parallel circuit, the brightness of the light bulbs does not change.

FIGURE 4 ·····················

Parallel Circuits

A floor lamp with multiple bulbs can be represented with the same circuit diagram as the circuit at the left. You can turn each bulb on and off individually.

✎ **Make Models** **On the circuit diagram, draw where the switches must be for a lamp like this. If the lamp is lit as it is in the photo below, trace the path(s) in the circuit through which current flows.**

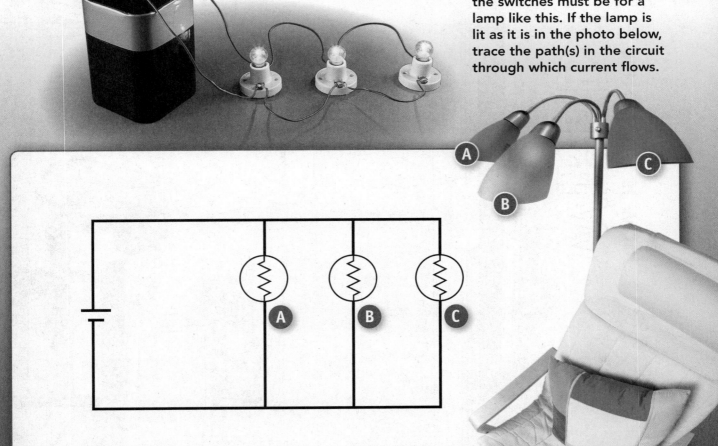

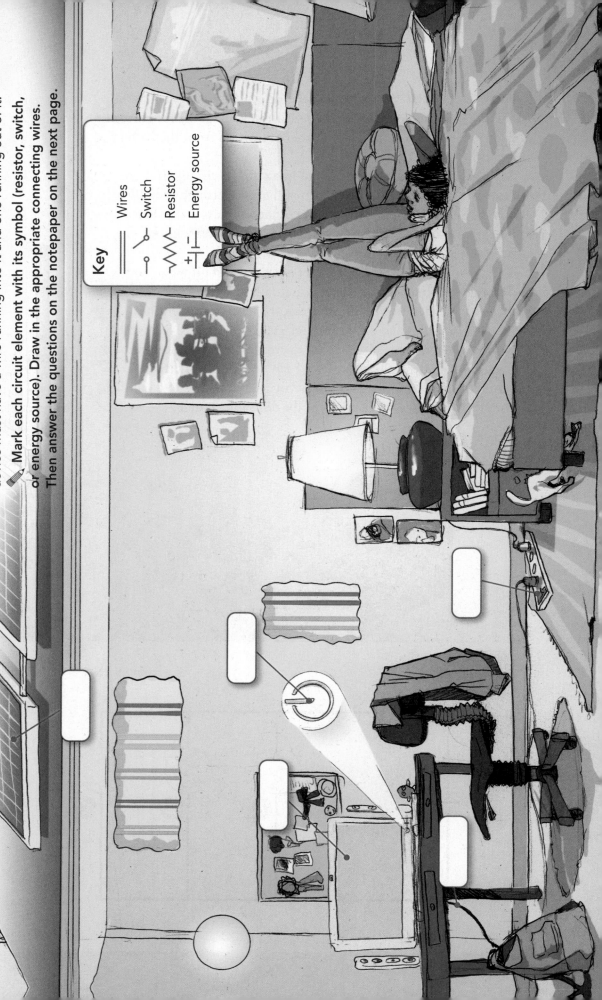

How does an electric circuit work?

FIGURE 5 **INTERACTIVE ART** Your home is full of electrical devices. When you turn one device on or off, it does not affect other appliances. This means that your home contains a (series/parallel) circuit. Since the devices in your home are part of complete circuits, each device must have a wire running into it and one running out of it.

✏ Mark each circuit element with its symbol (resistor, switch, or energy source). Draw in the appropriate connecting wires. Then answer the questions on the notepaper on the next page.

How is my house WIRED?

EXPLORE THE BIG ?

Key

————	Wires
⌐o o—	Switch
⋀⋀⋀	Resistor
⊣⊢	Energy source

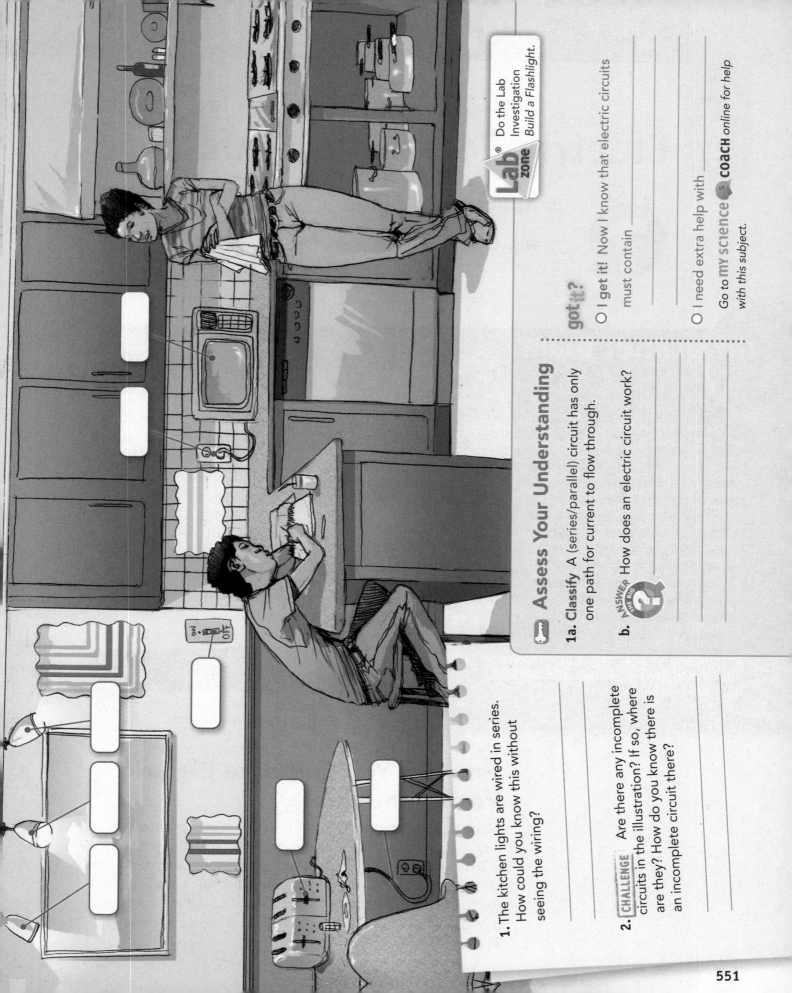

1. The kitchen lights are wired in series. How could you know this without seeing the wiring?

_____

2. **CHALLENGE** Are there any incomplete circuits in the illustration? If so, where are they? How do you know there is an incomplete circuit there?

_____

Lab zone® Do the Lab Investigation *Build a Flashlight.*

🔑 Assess Your Understanding

1a. Classify A (series/parallel) circuit has only one path for current to flow through.

b. **ANSWER THE BIG** How does an electric circuit work?

_____

got it?

○ I get it! Now I know that electric circuits must contain _____

_____

○ I need extra help with _____

Go to **MY SCIENCE COACH** online for help with this subject.

Electric Power and Safety

🔑 **How Do You Calculate Electric Power and Energy?**

🔑 **How Can Electric Shocks Be Prevented?**

MY PLANET DIARY

A Bright Idea

Forget about being *in* the spotlight—with LED clothing you can *be* the spotlight! LEDs, or light-emitting diodes, are small light bulbs. What's special about LEDs is that they can be just as bright as the regular bulbs in your home while using much less energy. Regular bulbs waste a lot of electrical energy by converting it into heat. A dress like this one made out of regular bulbs would be much too hot to wear! As scientists work to make LEDs cheaper, they could go from dresses in fashion shows to lamps in your house. This would lower your electric bill and help the environment.

Answer the question below.
What other electrical devices could be made more efficient with LEDs?

_____

_____

_____

_____

> **PLANET DIARY** Go to **Planet Diary** to learn more about LEDs.

Lab zone Do the Inquiry Warm-Up *How Can You Make a Bulb Burn More Brightly?*

How Do You Calculate Electric Power and Energy?

All electrical appliances transform electrical energy into other forms. Hair dryers transform electrical energy into thermal energy to dry your hair. An amplifier that a guitar player uses transforms electrical energy into sound. A washing machine transforms electrical energy into mechanical energy. The rate at which energy is transformed from one form to another is known as **power.** The unit of power is the watt (W).

Vocabulary
- power
- third prong
- fuse
- short circuit
- grounded
- circuit breaker

Skills
- Reading: Summarize
- Inquiry: Calculate

Power Ratings You are already familiar with different amounts of electric power. The power rating of a bright light bulb, for example, might be 100 W. The power rating of a dimmer bulb might be 60 W. The brighter bulb transforms (or uses) electrical energy at a faster rate than the dimmer bulb.

Calculating Power The power of a light bulb or appliance depends on two factors: voltage and current. **Power is calculated by multiplying voltage by current.**

$$Power = Voltage \times Current$$

The units are watts (W) = volts (V) × amperes (A). The equation can also be rearranged to let you solve for current if you know power and voltage.

$$Current = \frac{Power}{Voltage}$$

Summarize Summarize what you have learned from these two pages.

_____

_____

_____

_____

_____

_____

_____

do the math! — TECH & DESIGN

Many appliances around your home are labeled with their power ratings. In the United States, standard wall outlets supply 120 volts.

Calculate Determine the current running through each of these appliances. (The toaster has been done for you.)

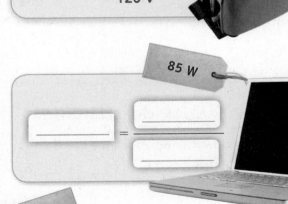

850 W

$$Current = \frac{Power}{Voltage}$$

$$7.08\ A = \frac{850\ W}{120\ V}$$

4000 W

85 W

300 W

Paying for Electrical Energy

The electric bill that comes to your home charges for the month's energy use, not power. Power tells you how much energy an appliance uses in a certain amount of time. **The total amount of energy used is equal to the power of the appliance multiplied by the amount of time the appliance is used.**

$$\text{Energy} = \textbf{Power} \times \text{Time}$$

Electric power is usually measured in thousands of watts, or kilowatts (kW). To go from watts to kilowatts, you divide by 1,000. Time is measured in hours. A common unit of electrical energy is the kilowatt-hour (kWh).

$$\text{Kilowatt-hours} = \textbf{Kilowatts} \times \text{Hours}$$

A refrigerator averages a power of 0.075 kW (75 W). Knowing that, you can calculate how much energy it will use in one month (about 720 hours).

$$\text{Energy} = \textbf{0.075 kW} \times 720 \text{ hours}$$

$$\text{Energy} = \textbf{54 kWh}$$

FIGURE 1 ·······························

> REAL-WORLD INQUIRY

Electrical Energy

There are devices that let you measure the energy usage of electronic devices.

✎ **Apply Concepts** Pick an appliance from the previous page. Use the notebook to answer the questions.

1. What would the monitor display if the appliance you picked was plugged in for three hours?

2. CHALLENGE Calculate the power rating for the appliance that is plugged into the meter at the left. Assume that it has been running for three hours.

 Do the Quick Lab **Calculating Electric Power and Energy Use.**

Assess Your Understanding

1a. Review The power of an appliance can be found by multiplying _____ by _____

b. Calculate How much energy does an 850 W toaster consume if it is used for 1.5 hours over the course of a month?

_____

_____

got it?

○ **I get it!** Now I know that electric power and energy depend on _____

_____

○ **I need extra help with** _____

Go to MY SCIENCE ⑤ COACH *online for help with this subject.*

How Can Electric Shocks Be Prevented?

A **short circuit** is a connection that allows current to take the path of least resistance. Touching a frayed wire causes a short circuit, since current can flow through the person rather than through the wire. Since the new path has less resistance, the current can be very high. Many bodily functions, such as heartbeat, breathing, and muscle movement, are controlled by electrical signals. Because of this, electric shocks can be fatal.

🔑 **Shocks can be prevented with devices that redirect current or break circuits.** Ground wires connect the circuits in a building directly to Earth, giving charges an alternate path in the event of a short circuit. The **third prong** you may have seen on electrical plugs connects the metal parts of appliances to the building's ground wire. Any circuit connected to Earth in this way is **grounded.**

The circuits in your home also contain devices that prevent circuits from overheating, since overheated circuits can result in fires. **Fuses** are devices that melt if they get too hot. This breaks the circuit. **Circuit breakers** are switches that will bend away from circuits as they heat up. Unlike fuses, which break when they are triggered, circuit breakers can be reset.

FIGURE 2 ···

Fuses

Fuses are often found in appliances such as coffee makers. A fuse will melt and break, cutting off the circuit, before the appliance can get so hot that it catches fire.

✎ **Infer** What other electronic devices may contain fuses? Explain your reasoning.

_____

_____

_____

Do the Quick Lab
Electric Shock and Short Circuit Safety.

🔑 **Assess Your Understanding**

got it? ···

○ **I get it!** Now I know that electric safety devices _____

_____

_____

○ **I need extra help with** _____

Go to MY SCIENCE ⑤ COACH *online for help with this subject.*

REVIEW THE BIG ?

The basic features of an electric circuit are _____

_____

_____

LESSON 1 Electric Charge and Static Electricity

🔑 Charges that are the same repel each other. Charges that are different attract each other.

🔑 There are four methods by which charges can redistribute themselves to build up static electricity: by friction, by conduction, by induction, and by polarization.

Vocabulary
- electric force • electric field
- static electricity • conservation of charge
- friction • conduction
- induction • polarization • static discharge

LESSON 2 Electric Current

🔑 When electric charges are made to flow through a material, they produce an electric current.

🔑 The atoms in conductors have loosely bound electrons that can move freely. Electrons in insulators cannot move freely among atoms.

🔑 Current flow is affected by the energy of the charges and the properties of the objects that the charges flow through.

Vocabulary
- electric current • electric circuit
- conductor • insulator • voltage • resistance

LESSON 3 Electric Circuits

🔑 Ohm found that the current, voltage, and resistance in a circuit are always related in the same way.

🔑 All electric circuits have the same basic features: devices that are run by electrical energy, sources of electrical energy, and conducting wires.

Vocabulary
- Ohm's law • series circuit • parallel circuit

LESSON 4 Electric Power and Safety

🔑 Power is calculated by multiplying voltage by current.

🔑 The total amount of energy used is equal to the power of the appliance multiplied by the amount of time the appliance is used.

🔑 Shocks can be prevented with devices that redirect current or break circuits.

Vocabulary
- power • short circuit • third prong
- grounded • fuse • circuit breaker

Review and Assessment

LESSON 1 Electric Charge and Static Electricity

1. What type of charge transfer occurs when two objects are rubbed together?

   a. friction   **b.** induction

   c. conduction   **d.** polarization

2. The transfer of electrons from a cloud to the ground during a lightning strike is an example of _____

3. Apply Concepts Draw the electric field for a single positive charge. Be sure to show which way the field lines point.

4. Relate Cause and Effect Explain what happens to the electrons in a metal object when it is held near a negatively charged object. What happens to the overall charge of the metal object?

_____

_____

_____

_____

_____

5. **Write About It** A park needs a sign to tell visitors what to do during a thunderstorm. Write a paragraph that explains why standing under a tall tree during a thunderstorm is dangerous.

LESSON 2 Electric Current

6. Which of these objects is an insulator?

   a. gold ring   **b.** copper coin

   c. glass rod   **d.** steel fork

7. An electric current is _____

_____

8. Classify The appliances in your home can be made of several different materials. What kinds of materials are the wires made of? What kinds of materials surround the wire for safety?

_____

_____

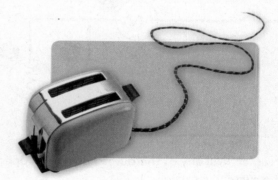

9. Infer Copper wires carry electric current from power plants to users. How is the resistance of these power lines likely to vary during the year in an area that has very hot summers? Explain.

_____

_____

_____

10. Make Models Water will not flow down a flat slide because there is no potential energy difference between the two ends. How could this situation be represented in an electric circuit? Explain your reasoning.

_____

_____

_____

_____

LESSON 3 Electric Circuits

11. Lisa built an electric circuit. When she added a second light bulb, the first bulb became dimmer. What type of circuit did Lisa build?

 a. series   **b.** parallel

 c. open   **d.** short

12. According to Ohm's law, the resistance in a circuit can be determined by _____

_____

Use the diagram below to answer Questions 13 and 14.

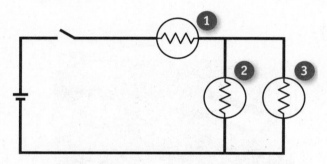

13. Predict Will any of the bulbs light if you open the switch? Explain.

_____

_____

14. Control Variables Which bulbs would continue to shine if Bulb 1 broke? Which would shine if Bulb 2 broke instead? Explain.

_____

_____

_____

_____

15. math! Most homes contain 120-V outlets. Suppose you have lamps with resistances of 120 Ω, 144 Ω, and 240 Ω. Predict which one will draw the most current. Check your prediction by calculating the current that runs through each lamp.

LESSON 4 Electric Power and Safety

16. What unit is used to measure electric power?

 a. ampere (A)   **b.** volt (V)

 c. watt (W)   **d.** ohm (Ω)

17. An appliance's total electrical energy consumption is calculated by _____

_____

18. Infer If you touch an electric wire and get a shock, what can you infer about the resistance of your body compared to the resistance of the circuit?

_____

_____

19. Calculate A device draws 40 A of current and has a 12-V battery. What is its power?

_____

APPLY THE BIG ? How does an electric circuit work?

20. Identify the parts that make up the circuit in a laptop computer. Describe what happens inside the circuit when the computer is on.

_____

_____

_____

_____

_____

_____

_____

_____

_____

_____

_____

_____

Standardized Test Prep

Multiple Choice

Circle the letter of the best answer.

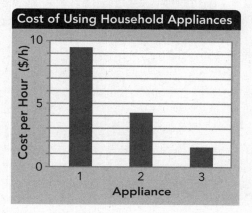

Cost of Using Household Appliances

1. Which of the following is a valid interpretation of the graph?

    A The voltage is highest in Appliance 1.

    B Appliance 1 uses the most power.

    C During one month, a family pays more to run Appliance 1 than Appliance 2.

    D Appliance 1 draws the least current.

2. Your alarm clock has a voltage of 120 V and a resistance of 1200 Ω. What current does the alarm clock draw?

    A 0.10 A

    B 10.0 A

    C 12.0 A

    D 100 A

3. You want to build a device that can conduct current but will be safe if touched by a person. Which of the following pairs of materials could you use?

    A glass to conduct and rubber to insulate

    B copper to conduct and silver to insulate

    C sand to conduct and plastic to insulate

    D silver to conduct and plastic to insulate

4. How does a fuse prevent electrical fires?

    A by providing a path for excess charges to get to the ground

    B by melting if the current gets too high

    C by reducing the voltage supplied to electrical devices

    D by storing potential energy for later use

5. What happens when an object is rubbed against another object to charge by friction?

    A Electrons are transferred from one object to another.

    B Electrons in one of the objects disappear.

    C Electrons in one object suddenly become negatively charged.

    D Electrons are created by the friction between the objects.

Constructed Response

Use your knowledge of science to help you answer Question 6. Write your answer on a separate sheet of paper.

6. A lightning bolt can have a voltage of over 100 million volts. Explain why lightning cannot power your cell phone but a 6-volt battery can. Then explain what would happen if a 100-million-volt battery was plugged into a cell phone. Use Ohm's law in your answer.

SOMETHING for NOTHING

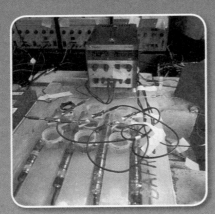

▲ This complicated device can supposedly harness free energy.

The race is on to find a new, cheap energy source. Any online search for "free energy" will find a lot of Web sites. These sites promise clean, free electricity if you buy or invest in their devices.

But can they back up their promises? Many sites suggest that the power companies have conspired against the people who have discovered and invented these free-energy devices. One site even claims that there is a fourth law of motion. This fourth law is an extension of Newton's Third Law of Motion. If every action has an equal and opposite reaction, the site claims, then that reaction can power the original action.

Debate It Some free-energy devices claim to be able to generate electricity using a perpetual motion machine. Some claim to harness latent heat from the air. Some claim to use magnets. Research how energy is generated, and evaluate these claims. Debate as a class whether it is possible to have truly free energy.

Does free electricity really exist? Some people say yes.

▽ In 1913, Nikola Tesla patented a turbine that ran off of steam. Many people have tried to find a way to use Tesla's engine to generate free electricity.

Going GREEN

Every time you turn on a light, you are using energy. We know this, but we don't always think about where the energy comes from. In most cases, that energy has come from fossil fuels, extracted from the ground, refined, and burned for their energy, in a process that causes a lot of pollution. Some scientists and government policymakers are exploring green (environmentally friendly) sources of energy.

According to the U.S. Environmental Protection Agency (EPA), green energy comes from technologies that don't produce waste products that will harm the environment. This includes resources like solar power and wind power, as well as geothermal energy from hot springs under the Earth's crust.

Reduced air pollution is just one of many benefits of green energy. Green energy also lowers greenhouse gas emissions and can cost less for consumers—like your family! Going green also creates jobs. Having many different sources makes the energy grid more stable. If one source stops working, we will still be able to get energy from other sources. What's not to love? Unfortunately, green energy technologies are expensive to develop.

▲ The flow of water is a renewable resource. But hydroelectric dams can damage habitats by changing the course of rivers.

Debate It Research the benefits and costs of developing green energy technologies. Organize a classroom debate about the costs and benefits of green energy. Be prepared to argue both sides of the issue.

HOW CAN THIS TRAIN MOVE WITHOUT TOUCHING THE TRACK?

 THE BIG Q

How are electricity and magnetism related?

This type of train is called a maglev, or magnetic levitation train, and operates at speeds of 430 km/h (about twice as fast as a conventional train). It does not have a traditional engine, which means it does not give off any pollutants. Instead, the maglev train uses electricity in the track to power magnets that propel the train forward and levitation magnets to keep the train floating about 10 mm above the track.

Draw Conclusions How can this train move without touching the track?

_____

_____

_____

_____

> **UNTAMED SCIENCE** Watch the **Untamed Science** video to learn more about magnetism and electromagnetism.

Magnetism and Electromagnetism

17 Getting Started

Check Your Understanding

1. **Background** Read the paragraph below and then answer the question.

While Chung works, his computer shuts down. Both the street and his house are dark, so he knows there is no **electricity**. A fallen tree has snapped an electric wire. The wire was the **conductor** that brought him power. Chung reaches for the light switch, but then remembers that no **electric current** will flow when he turns it on.

Electricity is a form of energy sometimes created by the movement of charged particles.

A material through which charges can easily flow is a **conductor.**

Electric current is the continuous flow of electric charges through a material.

• How can electricity be restored to Chung's house?

_____

_____

> **MY READING WEB** If you had trouble completing the question above, visit **My Reading Web** and type in *Magnetism and Electromagnetism.*

Vocabulary Skill

Use Context to Determine Meaning Science books often use unfamiliar words. Look for context clues in surrounding words and phrases to figure out the meaning of a new word. In the paragraph below, look for clues to the meaning of *magnetic force.*

The attraction or repulsion between magnetic poles is **magnetic force.** A force is a push or pull that can cause an object to change its motion. A magnetic force is produced when magnetic poles interact.

Example	Magnetic force
Definition	*n.* attraction or repulsion between magnetic poles
Explanation	Force is a push or pull.
Other Information	Magnetic force is produced when magnetic poles interact.

2. **Quick Check** In the paragraph above, circle the explanation of the word *force.*

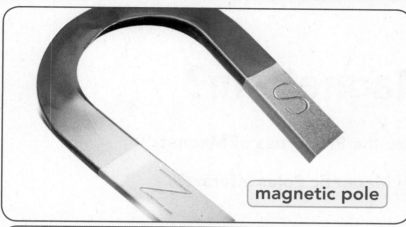

magnetic pole

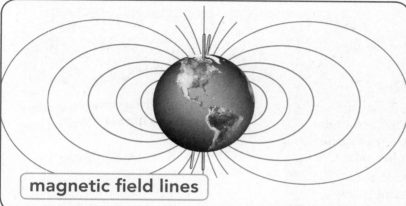

magnetic field lines

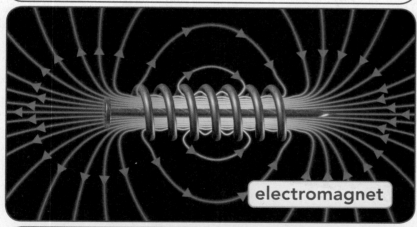

electromagnet

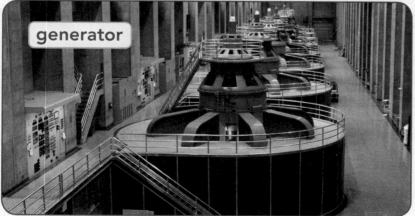

generator

Chapter Preview

LESSON 1
- magnet
- magnetism
- magnetic pole
- magnetic force
- ↻ Summarize
- △ Infer

LESSON 2
- magnetic field
- magnetic field lines
- compass
- magnetic declination
- ↻ Identify the Main Idea
- △ Observe

LESSON 3
- electromagnetism
- solenoid
- electromagnet
- ↻ Relate Cause and Effect
- △ Predict

LESSON 4
- galvanometer
- electric motor
- ↻ Sequence
- △ Graph

LESSON 5
- electromagnetic induction
- direct current
- alternating current
- generator
- transformer
- ↻ Ask Questions
- △ Make Models

> VOCAB FLASH CARDS   For extra help with vocabulary, visit **Vocab Flash Cards** and type in *Magnetism and Electromagnetism.*

What Is Magnetism?

UNLOCK THE BIG

🔑 **What Are the Properties of Magnets?**

🔑 **How Do Magnetic Poles Interact?**

MY PLANET DIARY

FUN FACTS

Crocodile Sense

Crocodiles are threatened animals. So, if they are not protected, they may become endangered and then disappear altogether. However, in Florida, many crocodiles live where people do, so they threaten people's safety.

To keep both people and crocodiles safe, biologists tried to move crocodiles away from people. But there was a problem. Crocodiles use Earth's magnetic field to help them navigate. Whenever they relocated a crocodile, it eventually returned, if it was not killed on the way back. But then the biologists heard that scientists in Mexico had taped a magnet to each side of a crocodile's head before relocating it. They thought that the magnets would interfere with the crocodile's ability to use Earth's magnetic field to find its way back. Biologists here did the same thing. So far, it has been successful.

Communicate Discuss the following questions with a partner. Write your answers below.

Why do you think it is important to relocate crocodiles?

_____

_____

_____

_____

_____

_____

> **PLANET DIARY** Go to **Planet Diary** to learn more about magnetism.

Lab zone® Do the Inquiry Warm-Up *Natural Magnets.*

What Are the Properties of Magnets?

Imagine that you're in Shanghai, China, zooming along in a maglev train propelled by magnets. Your 30-kilometer trip from the airport to the city station takes less than eight minutes. The same trip in a taxi would take about an hour.

Vocabulary
- magnet   • magnetism
- magnetic pole   • magnetic force

Skills
↻ **Reading:** Summarize
△ **Inquiry:** Infer

Magnets When you think of magnets, you might think about the objects that hold notes to your refrigerator. But magnets can be large, like the one in **Figure 1**. They can be small like those on your refrigerator, in your wallet, on your kitchen cabinets, or on security tags at a store. A **magnet** is any material that attracts iron and materials that contain iron.

Discovering Magnets Magnets have many modern uses, but they are not new. The ancient Greeks discovered that a rock called magnetite attracted materials containing iron. The rocks also attracted or repelled other magnetic rocks. The attraction or repulsion of magnetic materials is called **magnetism.**

Magnets have the same properties as magnetite rocks. ◀━ Magnets attract iron and materials that contain iron. Magnets attract or repel other magnets. In addition, one end of a magnet will always point north when allowed to swing freely.

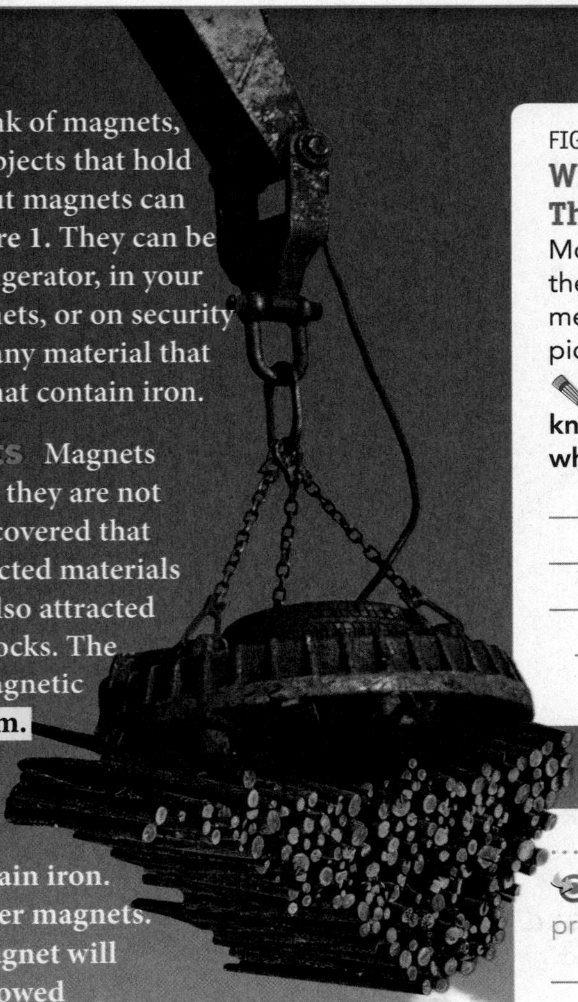

FIGURE 1 ···················
What's Wrong With This Picture?
Most people would not expect the powerful magnet used at a metal scrap yard to be able to pick up wood.

✎ **Explain** Use what you know about magnets to explain why this scene is impossible.

_____
_____
_____
_____
_____

✎
↻ **Summarize** Summarize the properties of magnetite.

_____
_____
_____
_____

Lab zone® Do the Lab Investigation _Detecting Fake Coins._

🗝 Assess Your Understanding

got it? ··

○ **I get it!** Now I know that three properties of magnets are that magnets _____
_____
_____

○ **I need extra help with** _____

_Go to_ **MY SCIENCE** ⬤ₛ **COACH** _online for help with this subject._

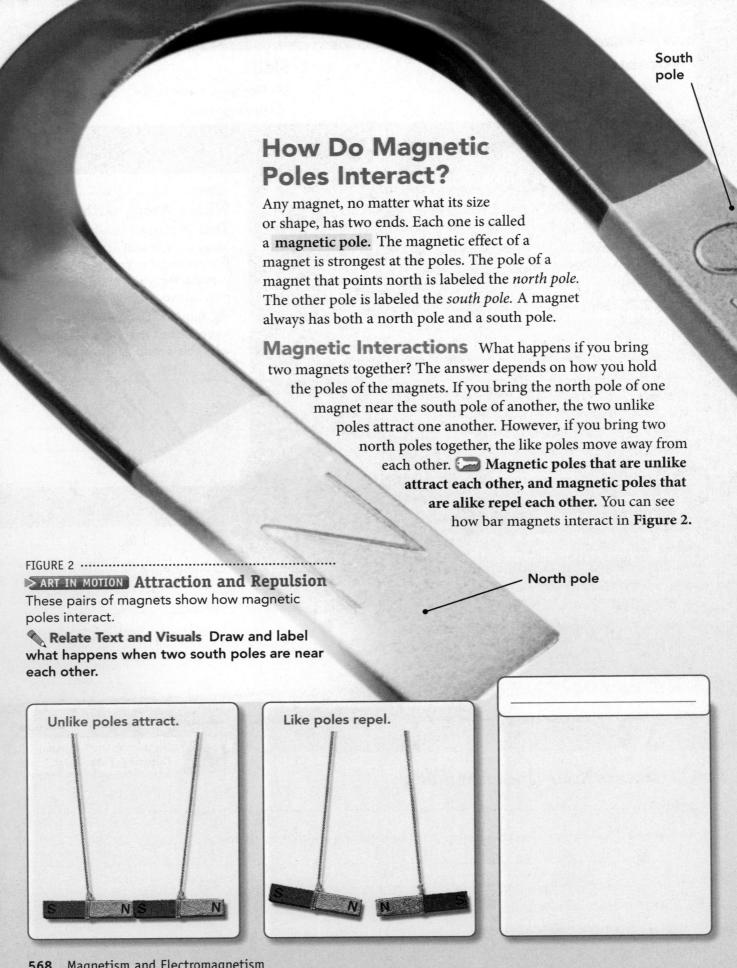

How Do Magnetic Poles Interact?

Any magnet, no matter what its size or shape, has two ends. Each one is called a **magnetic pole.** The magnetic effect of a magnet is strongest at the poles. The pole of a magnet that points north is labeled the *north pole.* The other pole is labeled the *south pole.* A magnet always has both a north pole and a south pole.

Magnetic Interactions What happens if you bring two magnets together? The answer depends on how you hold the poles of the magnets. If you bring the north pole of one magnet near the south pole of another, the two unlike poles attract one another. However, if you bring two north poles together, the like poles move away from each other. **Magnetic poles that are unlike attract each other, and magnetic poles that are alike repel each other.** You can see how bar magnets interact in **Figure 2.**

South pole

North pole

FIGURE 2 ·······························
> ART IN MOTION **Attraction and Repulsion**
These pairs of magnets show how magnetic poles interact.

✎ **Relate Text and Visuals** Draw and label what happens when two south poles are near each other.

Unlike poles attract.

S   S   N

Like poles repel.

S   N   N   S

Magnetic Force

Magnetic Force The attraction or repulsion between magnetic poles is **magnetic force.** A force is a push or a pull that can cause an object to move. A magnetic force is produced when magnetic poles come near each other and interact. Any material that exerts a magnetic force is a magnet.

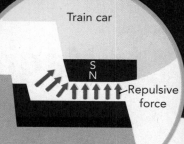

Train car

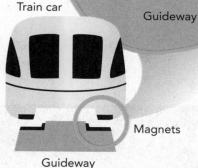

Repulsive force

Guideway

apply it!

Train car

Magnets

Guideway

The maglev train you read about earlier depends on magnetic force to float above the guideway, or track. The magnetic force is produced by magnets in the bottom of the train and in the guideway.

1 Infer For the train to float, which pole of the guideway's magnet should face the north pole of the train car's magnet?

_____

2 CHALLENGE List some advantages of the fact that the train does not touch the guideway.

_____

_____

Lab zone Do the Quick Lab *Magnetic Poles.*

Assess Your Understanding

1a. Identify What areas of a magnet have the strongest magnetic effect?

_____

_____

_____

b. Relate Cause and Effect How can two magnets demonstrate magnetic force?

_____

_____

_____

got it?

○ **I get it!** Now I know that magnetic poles that are unlike _____

and magnetic poles that are alike _____

○ **I need extra help with** _____

Go to MY SCIENCE **COACH** *online for help with this subject.*

Magnetic Fields

UNLOCK THE BIG **?**

🔑 **What Is a Magnetic Field's Shape?**

🔑 **What Is Earth's Magnetic Field Like?**

my planet diary

Cow Magnets

You probably know that cows eat grass. Did you know that they also eat metal? When cows graze, they may ingest metal objects that contain iron such as nails, wires, and old cans. If the metal is sharp, it could pierce the cow's stomach, causing infection, illness, or even death.

To ensure that their cows are safe, farmers have their cows swallow a magnet. Once inside the cow's stomach, the magnet attracts the iron in the metal that the cow eats. This keeps the metal from moving around and possibly puncturing other organs. One magnet can protect a cow for life.

FUN FACTS

Read the following questions. Write your answers below.

1. Why is it dangerous for a cow to eat metal?

_____

_____

_____

_____

2. As a farmer, what else could you do to keep metal objects from harming the cows?

_____

_____

> PLANET DIARY Go to **Planet Diary** to learn more about magnetic fields.

Lab zone® Do the Inquiry Warm-Up *Predict the Field.*

Vocabulary
- magnetic field • magnetic field lines
- compass • magnetic declination

Skills
- Reading: Identify the Main Idea
- Inquiry: Observe

What Is a Magnetic Field's Shape?

You know that a magnetic force is strongest at the poles of a magnet. But magnetic force is not limited to the poles. It is exerted all around a magnet. The area of magnetic force around a magnet is known as its **magnetic field.** Because of magnetic fields, magnets can interact without even touching.

Representing Magnetic Field Lines **Figure 1** shows the magnetic field of a bar magnet. The **magnetic field lines** are shown in purple. Magnetic field lines are lines that map out the invisible magnetic field around a magnet. **Magnetic field lines spread out from one pole, curve around the magnet, and return to the other pole.** The lines form complete loops from pole to pole and never cross. Arrowheads indicate the direction of the magnetic field lines. They always leave the north pole and enter the south pole. The closer together the lines are, the stronger the field. Magnetic field lines are closest together at the poles.

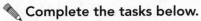

FIGURE 1 ·······················
Magnetic Field Lines
Magnetic fields are invisible, but you can represent a field using magnetic field lines.

✎ **Complete the tasks below.**

1. **Relate Text and Visuals** In the boxes, identify where the magnetic field is strong and where it is weak.

2. CHALLENGE Forces that affect objects without touching them are called *field* forces. Is gravity a field force? Explain.

_____
_____
_____
_____

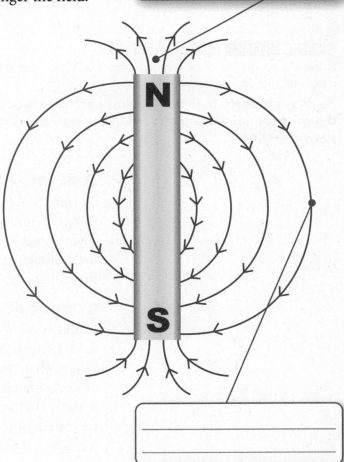

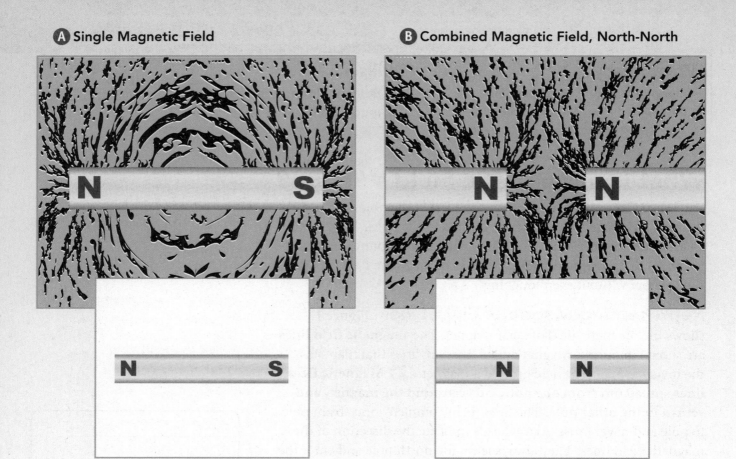

FIGURE 2 ···

INTERACTIVE ART **Magnetic Fields**
Different magnetic pole arrangements will produce different
magnetic fields.

✎ **Make Models** **In the box below each diagram, draw**
the corresponding magnetic field lines with arrowheads to
show direction.

A Single Magnetic Field Although you cannot see
a magnetic field, you can see its effects. **Figure 2A** shows iron
filings sprinkled on a sheet of clear plastic that covers one magnet.
The magnetic forces of the magnet act on the iron filings and align
them along the invisible magnetic field lines. The result is that the
iron filings form a pattern similar to magnetic field lines.

Combined Magnetic Fields When the magnetic
fields of two or more magnets overlap, the result is a combined
field. **Figures 2B** and **2C** show the effects of magnetic force on iron
filings when the poles of two bar magnets are brought near each
other. Compare the pattern of a north-north pole arrangement and
a north-south pole arrangement. The fields from two like poles
repel each other. But the fields from unlike poles attract each other,
forming a strong field between the magnets.

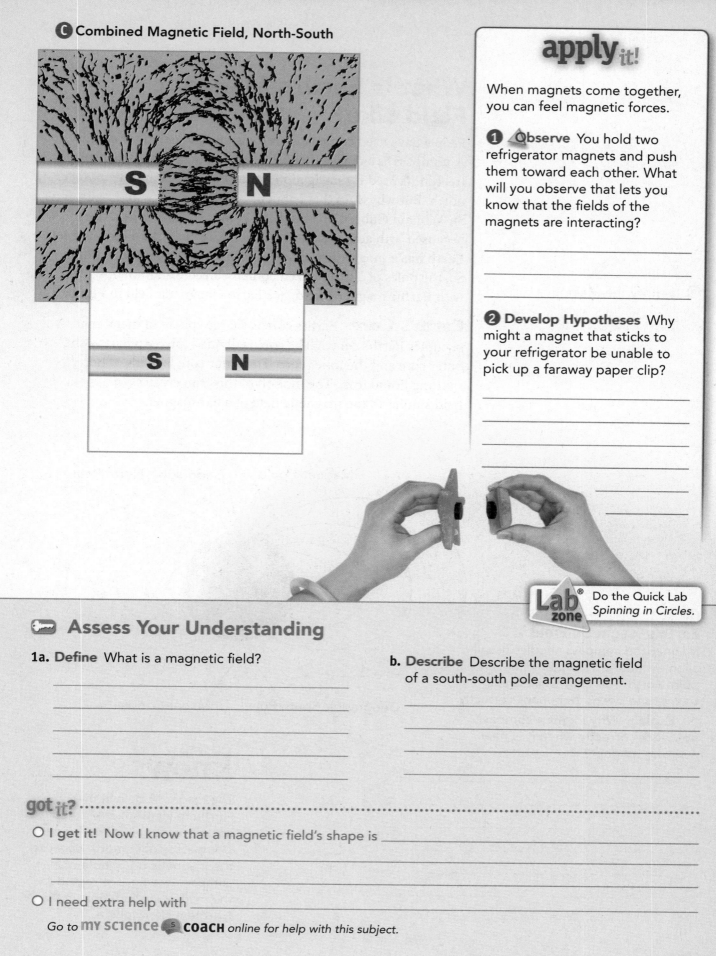

C Combined Magnetic Field, North-South

apply it!

When magnets come together, you can feel magnetic forces.

1 **Observe** You hold two refrigerator magnets and push them toward each other. What will you observe that lets you know that the fields of the magnets are interacting?

_____

_____

_____

2 **Develop Hypotheses** Why might a magnet that sticks to your refrigerator be unable to pick up a faraway paper clip?

_____

_____

_____

_____

_____

Lab zone® Do the Quick Lab *Spinning in Circles.*

Assess Your Understanding

1a. Define What is a magnetic field?

_____

_____

_____

_____

b. Describe Describe the magnetic field of a south-south pole arrangement.

_____

_____

_____

_____

got it?

O **I get it!** Now I know that a magnetic field's shape is _____

_____

O **I need extra help with** _____

Go to **MY SCIENCE** **COACH** *online for help with this subject.*

What Is Earth's Magnetic Field Like?

People have used compasses as tools for navigation for centuries. A **compass** is a device that has a magnet on a needle that spins freely. It is used for navigation because its needle usually points north. But why does that happen? In the late 1500s an Englishman, Sir William Gilbert, proved that a compass behaves as it does because Earth acts as a giant magnet. **Just like a bar magnet, Earth has a magnetic field around it and two magnetic poles.** So, the poles of a magnetized compass needle align themselves with Earth's magnetic field. See Earth's magnetic field in **Figure 3**.

Earth's Core   Earth's core is a large sphere of metal that occupies Earth's center. The core is divided into two parts—the outer core and the inner core. The outer core is made of hot swirling liquid iron. The motion of this iron creates a magnetic field similar to the magnetic field of a bar magnet.

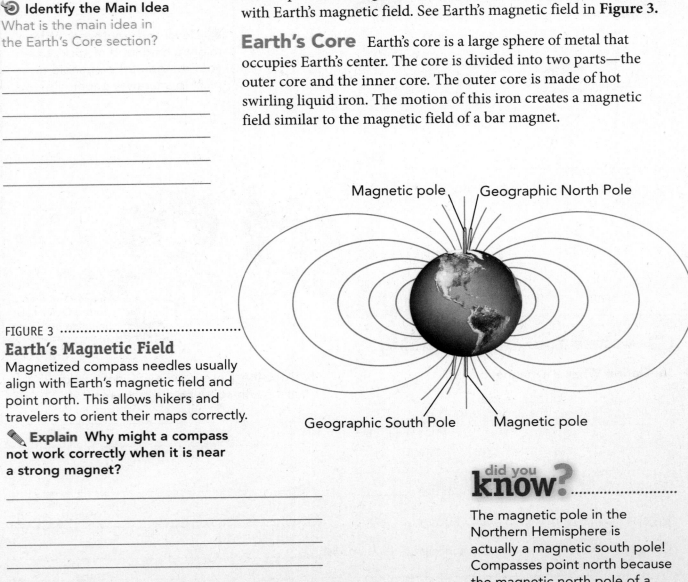

FIGURE 3
Earth's Magnetic Field
Magnetized compass needles usually align with Earth's magnetic field and point north. This allows hikers and travelers to orient their maps correctly.

✏️ **Explain** Why might a compass not work correctly when it is near a strong magnet?

_____

_____

_____

_____

_____

_____

did you know?

The magnetic pole in the Northern Hemisphere is actually a magnetic south pole! Compasses point north because the magnetic north pole of a compass needle is attracted to the magnetic south pole in the Northern Hemisphere.

Earth's Magnetic Poles You know that Earth has geographic poles. But Earth also has magnetic poles that are located on Earth's surface where the magnetic force is strongest. As you just saw in **Figure 3,** the magnetic poles are not in the same place as the geographic poles. Suppose you could draw a line between you and the geographic North Pole. Then imagine a second line drawn between you and the magnetic pole in the Northern Hemisphere. The angle between these two lines is the angle between geographic north and the north to which a compass needle points. This angle is known as **magnetic declination.**

The magnetic declination of a location changes. Earth's magnetic poles do not stay in one place as the geographic poles do.

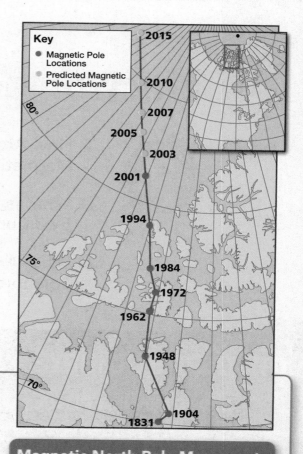

Key
● Magnetic Pole Locations
● Predicted Magnetic Pole Locations

do the math!

The last expedition to directly observe the pole's location was in May 2001. The map shows estimated positions after 2001.

1 Calculate What is the total distance the pole traveled from 1948 to 2001?

_____

_____

_____

2 Interpret Data What was the mean speed of the pole's movement from 1948 to 2001? What was the mode?

_____

_____

Magnetic North Pole Movement

Year of Reading	Distance Moved Since Previous Reading (km)
1948	420
1962	150
1972	120
1984	120
1994	180
2001	287

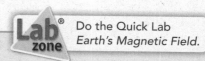

Lab zone   Do the Quick Lab
Earth's Magnetic Field.

📖 Assess Your Understanding

got **it?** ....

○ **I get it!** Now I know that Earth has a magnetic field _____

_____

○ I need extra help with _____

Go to **MY SCIENCE** ⑤ **COACH** *online for help with this subject.*

Electromagnetic Force

🔑 **How Are Electric Currents and Magnetic Fields Related?**

🔑 **What Is a Magnetic Field Produced by a Current Like?**

🔑 **What Are the Characteristics of Solenoids and Electromagnets?**

my PLaNeT DiaRY

More Than Just Plastic

How do plastic cards with stripes, such as your library card, work? The black stripe on the back of the card is made up of tiny magnetic particles. Information can be recorded on the stripe. When a card is swiped through a card-reading machine, the cardholder's information is relayed from the card to a computer or sent to a place for verification.

If the card is placed near magnetic material, the arrangement of the magnetic particles on the stripe can get rearranged. Once this happens, the card becomes useless because it no longer holds the cardholder's information. If you are ever given a credit card to use, make sure you keep it away from magnets or else you may leave the store empty-handed!

FUN FACTS

Communicate Discuss the question with a partner. Then write your answer below.

List types of cards that have a magnetic stripe.

_____

_____

_____

_____

_____

_____

▶ **PLANET DIARY** Go to **Planet Diary** to learn more about electromagnetic force.

Lab zone® Do the Inquiry Warm-Up *Electromagnetism.*

Vocabulary
- electromagnetism
- electromagnet
- solenoid

Skills
- 🔄 Reading: Relate Cause and Effect
- ⚠ Inquiry: Predict

How Are Electric Currents and Magnetic Fields Related?

You know that a magnet has a magnetic field. But did you know that an electric current produces a magnetic field? In 1820, the Danish scientist Hans Christian Oersted (UR STED) accidentally discovered this fact. He was teaching a class at the University of Copenhagen. During his lecture he produced a current in a wire just like the current in a battery-powered flashlight. When he brought a compass near the wire, he observed that the compass needle changed direction.

Oersted's Experiment Oersted could have assumed that something was wrong with his equipment, but instead he decided to investigate further. So he set up several compasses around a wire. With no current in the wire, all of the compass needles pointed north. When he produced a current in the wire, he observed that the compass needles pointed in different directions to form a circle. Oersted concluded that the current had produced a magnetic field around the wire. Oersted's results showed that magnetism and electricity are related.

Cause	Effect
There is no current in the wire.	_____ _____ _____ _____
_____ _____ _____	The compass needles pointed in different directions to form a circle.

🔄 **Relate Cause and Effect**
Use the information about Oersted's experiment to complete the chart.

Electric Current and Magnetism Oersted's experiment showed that wherever there is electricity, there is magnetism. 🔑 **An electric current produces a magnetic field.** This relationship between electricity and magnetism is called **electromagnetism.** Although you cannot see electromagnetism directly, you can see its effect. That is, a compass needle moves when it is in a magnetic field produced by an electric current, as you can see in **Figure 1**.

FIGURE 1 ·····················
Moving Compass Needles
These photographs show you how an electric current produces a magnetic field.

✏️ **Interpret Photos In the boxes, explain what is happening to the compass needles when the current in the wire is turned on or off.**

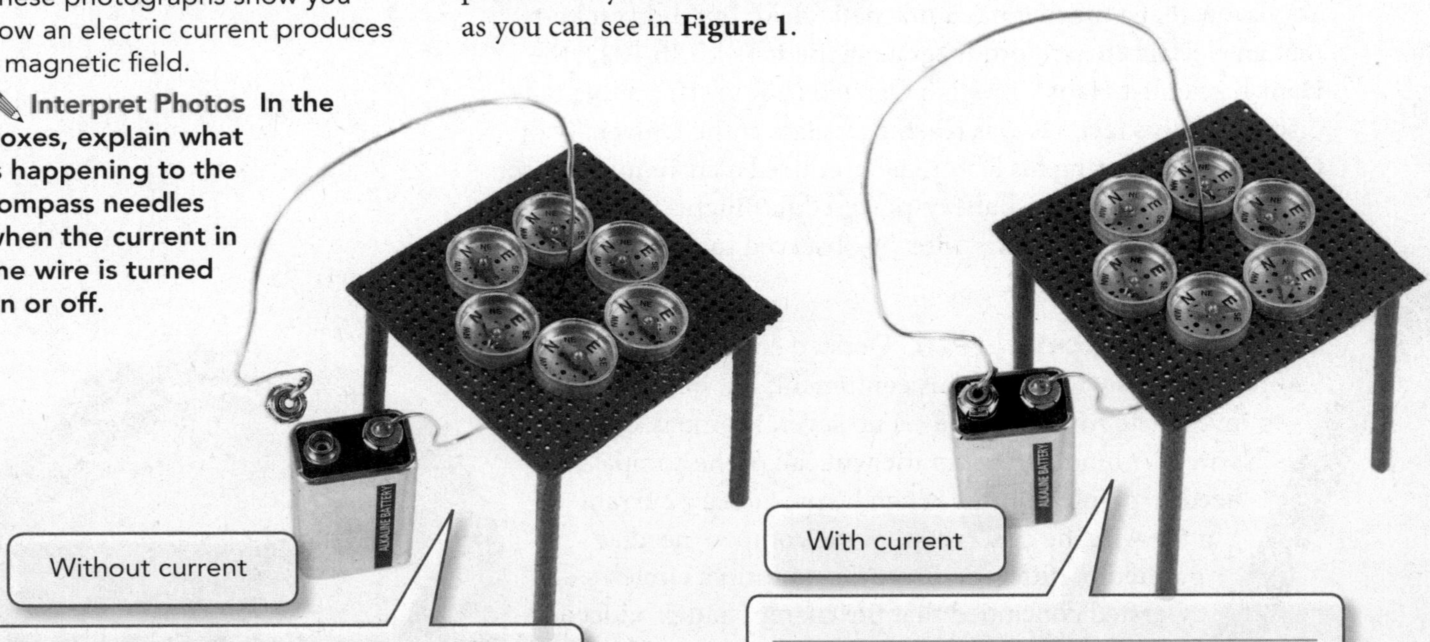

Without current

With current

🔑 Do the Quick Lab *Electric Current and Magnetism.*

🔑 **Assess Your Understanding**

1a. Explain What did Oersted conclude?

_____

_____

_____

b. 🔄 **Relate Cause and Effect** How does a current affect a compass?

_____

_____

got it? ··

○ **I get it!** Now I know that an electric current produces a _____

○ **I need extra help with** _____

    Go to **my science COACH** online for help with this subject.

What Is a Magnetic Field Produced by a Current Like?

🔑 **The magnetic field produced by a current has a strength and a direction. The field can be turned on or off, have its direction reversed, or have its strength changed.** To turn a magnetic field produced by a current on or off, you turn the current on or off. To change the direction of the magnetic field, you reverse the direction of the current.

There are two ways to change the strength of a magnetic field. First, you can increase the amount of current in the wire. Second, you can make a loop or coil in the wire. The magnetic field around the wire forms a circle. When you make a loop in a wire, the magnetic field lines bunch close together inside the loop. This strengthens the magnetic field. Every additional loop strengthens the magnetic field even more. **Figure 2** shows three different ways to change the characteristics of a magnetic field.

FIGURE 2 ···

Change Magnetic Field Characteristics

✎ **Interpret Diagrams** Write the ways used to change the magnetic fields in diagrams A and B. In diagram C, draw a picture to show a third way to change magnetic fields and describe it.

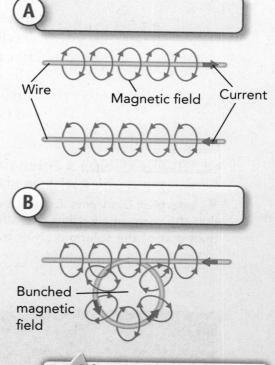

🔑 **Assess Your Understanding**

got it? ···

○ I get it! Now I know that the magnetic field produced by a current can be changed by _____

_____

○ I need extra help with _____

Go to MY SCIENCE ⬤ COACH online for help with this subject.

 Do the Quick Lab *Magnetic Fields From Electric Current.*

What Are the Characteristics of Solenoids and Electromagnets?

You know that you can strengthen the magnetic field around a wire with a current by coiling the wire. 🔌 **Both solenoids and electromagnets use electric current and coiled wires to produce strong magnetic fields.**

Solenoids By running current through a wire which is wound into many loops, you strengthen the magnetic field in the center of the coil as shown in **Figure 3**. A coil of wire with a current is called a **solenoid.** The two ends of a solenoid act like the poles of a magnet. However, the north and south poles change when the direction of the current changes.

Electromagnets If you place a material with strong magnetic properties inside a solenoid, the strength of the magnetic field increases. This is because the material, called a ferromagnetic material, becomes a magnet. A solenoid with a ferromagnetic core is called an **electromagnet.** Both the current in the wire and the magnetized core produce the magnetic field of an electromagnet. Therefore, the overall magnetic field of an electromagnet is much stronger than that of a solenoid. An electromagnet is turned on and off by turning the current on and off.

FIGURE 3 ···

▷ REAL-WORLD INQUIRY **A Solenoid and an Electromagnet**
An electromagnet is a solenoid with a ferromagnetic core.

✎ Interpret Diagrams **Explain how the diagram shows you that the magnetic field of the electromagnet is stronger than that of the solenoid on its own.**

_____

_____

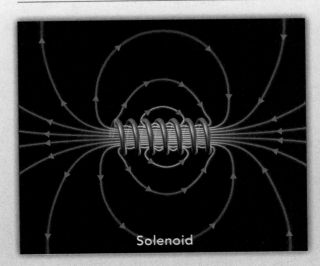
Solenoid

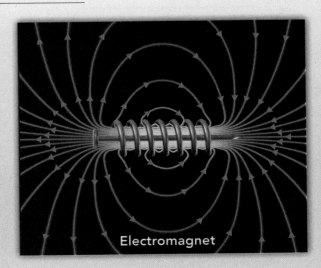
Electromagnet

Regulating Strength You can increase the strength of an electromagnet in four ways. First, you can increase the current in the solenoid. Second, you can add more loops of wire to the solenoid. Third, you can wind the coils of the solenoid closer together. Finally, you can use a material that is more magnetic than iron for the core. Alnico is such a material.

Using Electromagnets Electromagnets are very common. They are used in electric motors, earphones, and many other everyday objects. Electromagnets are even used in junkyards to lift old cars and other heavy steel objects.

Vocabulary Use Context to Determine Meaning Underline clues in the text that help you determine the meaning of *alnico*.

apply it!

An electromagnet makes a doorbell ring. A pushed button closes the circuit and turns on the electromagnet. Current flows through the electromagnet, producing a strong magnetic field.

1 **Predict** What effect will the magnetic field have on the steel bar? The clapper?

_____

_____

_____

2 CHALLENGE What turns off the electromagnet?

_____

Diagram labels: Energy source, Current, Electromagnet, Bell, Steel bar, Button, Spring, Clapper

Lab zone ® Do the Quick Lab *Electromagnet.*

🔑 Assess Your Understanding

2a. Define What is a solenoid?

_____

_____

b. Apply Concepts What are four ways to make an electromagnet stronger?

_____

_____

_____

got it?

○ **I get it!** Now I know that both solenoids and electromagnets _____

_____

_____

_____

_____

○ **I need extra help with** _____

Go to **my science** ⓢ **coach** online for help with this subject.

LESSON
4

Electricity, Magnetism, and Motion

UNLOCK THE BIG ?

🔑 **How Is Electrical Energy Transformed Into Mechanical Energy?**

🔑 **How Does a Galvanometer Work?**

🔑 **What Does an Electric Motor Do?**

my pLaneT DiaRY

DISCOVERY

Miniature Motor

In 1960, scientist and California Institute of Technology (Caltech) professor Richard Feynman publicly offered a prize of $1,000 to the first person to build an electric motor no larger than 0.3969 cubic millimeters. A Caltech graduate named William McLellan accepted the challenge. He used a toothpick, microscope slides, fine hairs from a paintbrush, and wires only 1/80th of a millimeter wide to build the world's smallest motor. McLellan showed his tiny motor to Feynman and collected the $1,000 prize. Scientists today have found many uses for tiny motors in products such as high-definition tele-visions, cars, and ink-jet printers.

A tiny motor capable of producing high-resolution, DVD-quality images.

Communicate Work with a partner to answer the question.
What might be some other uses of tiny motors?

_____

_____

_____

_____

_____

> PLANET DIARY Go to **Planet Diary** to learn more about electric motors.

Lab zone® Do the Inquiry Warm-Up *How Are Electricity, Magnets, and Motion Related?*

How Is Electrical Energy Transformed Into Mechanical Energy?

What do trains, fans, microwave ovens, and clocks have in common? The answer is that these objects, along with many other everyday objects, use electricity. In addition, all these objects move or have moving parts. How does electricity produce motion?

Vocabulary

- galvanometer • electric motor

Skills

- Reading: Sequence
- Inquiry: Graph

Energy and Motion As you know, magnetic force can produce motion. For example, magnets move together or apart when they are close. You also know that an electric current in a wire produces a magnetic field. So, a magnet can move a wire with a current, just as it would move another magnet. The direction of movement depends on the direction of the current. See **Figure 1**.

The ability to move an object over a distance is called energy. The energy associated with electric currents is called electrical energy. The energy an object has due to its movement or position is called mechanical energy.

Energy Transformation Energy can be transformed from one form into another. **When a wire with a current is placed in a magnetic field, electrical energy is transformed into mechanical energy.** This transformation happens when the magnetic field produced by the current causes the wire to move.

FIGURE 1 ....
Producing Motion
A wire with a current can be moved by a magnet.

✎ **Complete the tasks.**

1. **Identify** What affects the direction of the wire's movement?

_____

_____

2. **Classify** In each box, write down the type of energy that is being pointed out.

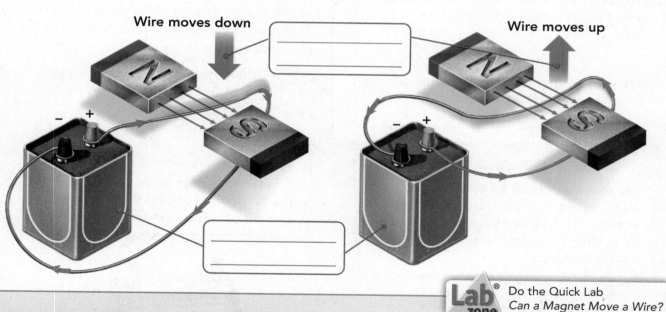

Wire moves down

Wire moves up

Lab zone | Do the Quick Lab *Can a Magnet Move a Wire?*

Assess Your Understanding

got it? ....

○ **I get it!** Now I know that when a wire with a current is placed in a magnetic field, electrical energy

_____

○ **I need extra help with** _____

Go to MY SCIENCE ⑤ COACH online for help with this subject.

How Does a Galvanometer Work?

You have learned that a straight wire with a current moves when it is placed in a magnetic field. But what happens if you place a loop of wire with a current in a magnetic field? Look at **Figure 2.** The current in one side of the loop flows in the opposite direction than the current in the other side of the loop. The direction of the current determines the direction in which the wire moves. Therefore, the sides of the loop move in opposite directions. Once each side has moved as far up or down as it can go, it will stop moving. As a result, the loop can rotate only a half turn.

Inside a Galvanometer
The rotation of a wire loop in a magnetic field is the basis of a galvanometer. A **galvanometer** is a device that measures small currents. **An electric current turns the pointer of a galvanometer.** In a galvanometer, an electromagnet is suspended between opposite poles of two permanent magnets. The electromagnet's coil is attached to a pointer, as you can see in **Figure 2.** When a current is in the electromagnet's coil, it produces a magnetic field. This field interacts with the permanent magnet's field, causing the coil and the pointer to rotate. The distance the loops and the pointer rotate depends on the amount of current in the wire.

Sequence In the second paragraph on this page, underline and number the steps that explain how a galvanometer works.

FIGURE 2 ·······················

How a Galvanometer Works
Answer the questions about a galvanometer.

1. **Predict** What would happen if the current flowed in the opposite direction?

_____

_____

2. **Interpret Diagrams** Where does the needle point when there is no current?

_____

_____

A Because the current on each side of the wire loop flows in different directions, one side of the loop moves down as the other side moves up. This causes the loop to rotate.

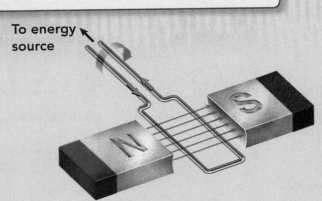

To energy source

B An electromagnet turns the pointer to indicate the amount of current present.

Uses of Galvanometers

A galvanometer has a scale that is marked to show how much the pointer turns for a known current. You can use the galvanometer to measure an unknown current. Galvanometers are useful in everyday life. For example, electricians use them in their work. Some cars use them as fuel gauges. Galvanometers are also used in lie detectors to measure how much current a person's skin conducts. People who are stressed sweat more. Water conducts electricity. Therefore, their moist skin conducts more electric current.

do the math!

This data from a galvanometer show the current conducted by a person's skin. The current is measured in microsiemens, a unit used to measure small amounts of electricity.

Minutes	0	4	8	12	16	20
Microsiemens	5	7	3	1	8	10

❶ **Graph** Use the data in the table to plot points on the graph.

❷ **CHALLENGE** What would a point at (24, 12) tell you about the person?

_____
_____
_____
_____
_____
_____

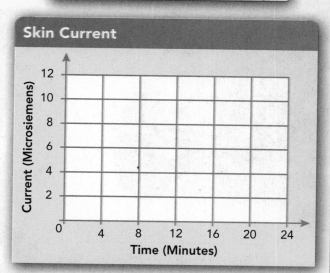

Skin Current

Current (Microsiemens) vs. Time (Minutes)

Do the Quick Lab
How Galvanometers Work.

🔑 Assess Your Understanding

1a. Review What does a galvanometer measure?

_____

b. Relate Cause and Effect What causes the pointer to move in a galvanometer?

_____
_____

got it?

○ **I get it!** Now I know that a galvanometer works by using _____
_____

○ **I need extra help with** _____

Go to **my science** 🅢 **coach** *online for help with this subject.*

What Does an Electric Motor Do?

Have you ever wondered how a remote-controlled car moves? A remote-controlled car's wheels are turned by a rod, or axle, which is connected to an electric motor. An **electric motor** is a device that uses an electric current to turn an axle. 🔑 **An electric motor transforms electrical energy into mechanical energy.**

Look at **Figure 3** to read about the parts of a motor.

If current only flowed in one direction through the armature, the armature could only rotate a half a turn. However, the brushes and commutator enable the current in the armature to change direction. Current always flows from the positive to the negative terminal of a battery. The current in the armature is reversed each time the commutator moves to a different brush. This causes the side of the armature that just moved up to move down. The side that just moved down will move up. The armature rotates continuously. See **Figure 4**.

FIGURE 3 ·····································

Parts of a Motor
A simple electric motor contains four parts.

✏️ **Observe** Which part of an electric motor must be attached directly to the energy source?

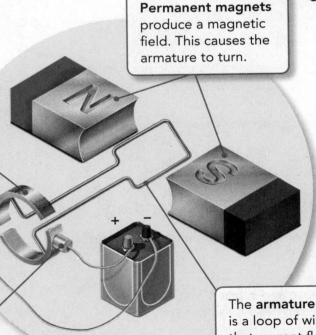

Permanent magnets produce a magnetic field. This causes the armature to turn.

The **commutator** consists of two semicircular pieces of metal. It conducts current from the brushes to the armature.

Brushes conduct current to the rest of the commutator. They do not move.

The **armature** is a loop of wire that current flows through.

FIGURE 4 ·········

> **INTERACTIVE ART** **How a Motor Works**

The magnetic field around the armature interacts with the field of the permanent magnet, allowing the armature to turn continuously. The direction of the current determines which way the armature turns.

✎ **Infer** Based on the direction the armature is turning in each diagram, draw arrows showing the direction of the current.

The current is in opposite directions on each side of the armature causing one side to move up while the other side moves down.

The commutator rotates with the armature. The direction of current reverses with each half turn so the armature spins continuously.

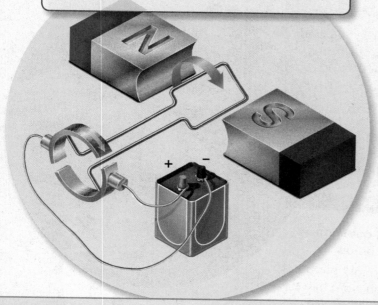

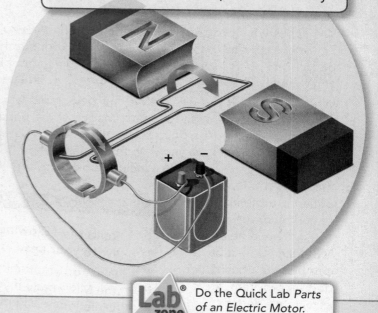

Lab zone® Do the Quick Lab *Parts of an Electric Motor.*

🗝 Assess Your Understanding

2a. Define What is an electric motor?

_____

_____

_____

_____

b. Summarize What makes the armature turn continuously?

_____

_____

got it?

○ **I get it!** Now I know that an electric motor transforms _____

_____

_____

○ **I need extra help with** _____

Go to **MY SCIENCE** 🔎 **COACH** online for help with this subject.

Electricity From Magnetism

UNLOCK THE BIG ?

🔑 **How Can an Electric Current Be Produced in a Conductor?**

🔑 **How Does a Generator Work?**

🔑 **What Does a Transformer Do?**

MY PLANET DIARY

CAREERS

MRI Technologist

Does working in the medical field interest you? Are you good at operating devices? Do you have a knack for soothing anxious people? If you answered yes, you should think about becoming an Magnetic Resonance Imaging (MRI) technologist.

When a patient is put into an MRI machine, radio waves and magnetic fields are used to create images of the patient's internal structures. The doctors use these detailed pictures to determine what is wrong with the patient. The MRI technologist's responsibilities include operating the MRI machine, comforting nervous patients, and maintaining patient confidentiality. You can become an MRI technologist by completing a bachelor's degree program, an associate's degree program, or a certificate program.

Read the following question. Write your answer below.

What do you think might happen to the MRI image if you wore metal jewelry while in the MRI machine? Why?

_____

_____

_____

_____

▶ **PLANET DIARY** Go to **Planet Diary** to learn more about electricity from magnetism.

Lab zone® Do the Inquiry Warm-Up *Electric Current Without a Battery.*

Vocabulary
- electromagnetic induction • direct current
- alternating current • generator • transformer

Skills
- Reading: Ask Questions
- Inquiry: Make Models

How Can an Electric Current Be Produced in a Conductor?

An electric motor uses electrical energy to produce motion. Can motion produce electrical energy? In 1831, scientists discovered that moving a wire in a magnetic field can cause an electric current. This current allows electrical energy to be supplied to homes, schools, and businesses all over the world.

To understand how electrical energy is supplied by your electric company, you need to know how current is produced. A magnet can make, or induce, current in a conductor, such as a wire, as long as there is motion. ☞ An electric current is induced in a conductor when the conductor moves through a magnetic field. Generating electric current from the motion of a conductor through a magnetic field is called **electromagnetic induction.** Current that is generated in this way is called induced current.

Ask Questions Read the paragraph. Then write two questions that you still have about producing electric current.

_____

_____

_____

_____

_____

_____

_____

_____

_____

_____

_____

Induction of Electric Current

Michael Faraday and Joseph Henry each found that motion in a magnetic field will induce a current. Either the conductor can move through the magnetic field, or the magnet can move. In **Figure 1,** a conductor, the coil of wire, is connected to a galvanometer, forming a closed circuit. If the coil and the magnet do not move, the galvanometer's pointer does not move. However, when either the wire coil or the magnet moves, the galvanometer registers a current. Moving the coil or the magnet induces the current without any voltage source. The direction of an induced current depends on the direction that the coil or magnet moves. When the motion is reversed, the direction of the current also reverses.

FIGURE 1 ·······································

Motion Produces a Current

Electric current is induced in a wire whenever the magnetic field around it is changing. The field changes when either the magnet or the wire moves.

 **Complete the tasks.**

1. **Describe** Under each diagram, label the direction of the current using *clockwise* or *counterclockwise*.

2. CHALLENGE Make a general statement that relates the motion of the circuit (up or down) to the direction of the current (clockwise or counterclockwise).

_____

_____

_____

_____

_____

_____

_____

_____

_____

Moving Coil

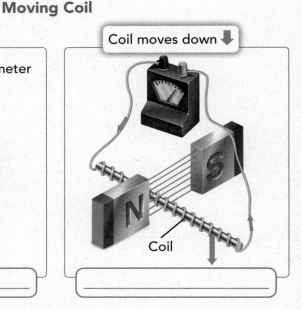

Coil moves up ⬆

Galvanometer

Magnetic field

Coil moves down ⬇

Coil

Moving Magnet

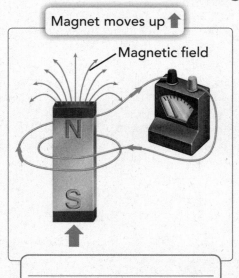

Magnet moves up ⬆

Magnetic field

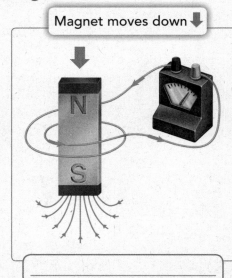

Magnet moves down ⬇

Alternating and Direct Current

A current with charges that flow in one direction is called **direct current**, or DC. A battery produces direct current when a battery is placed in a circuit and charges flow in one direction. They move from one end of the battery, around the circuit, and into the other end of the battery.

If a wire in a magnetic field changes direction repeatedly, the induced current also keeps changing direction. A constantly reversing current is called **alternating current**, or AC. You could induce alternating current by moving either the coil or the magnet up and down repeatedly in the **Figure 1** circuit.

Alternating current has a major advantage over direct current. An AC voltage can be easily raised or lowered. This means that a high voltage can be used to send electrical energy over great distances. Then the voltage can be reduced to a safer level for everyday use. The electric current in the circuits in homes, schools, and other buildings is alternating current. Look at **Figure 2** to learn about how electricity has changed over time.

1860

1882
Direct Current

Thomas Edison opens a generating plant in New York City. It serves an area of about 2.6 square kilometers.

1880

1888
Alternating Current

Nikola Tesla receives patents for a system of distributing alternating current.

Today
Direct and Alternating Current

An electric car runs on direct current from its battery. However, alternating current is needed to charge the battery.

Today

FIGURE 2 ·········

The History of Electricity
The work of several scientists brought electricity from the laboratory into everyday use.

✎ **Draw Conclusions** Why do you think we use alternating current today?

_____

_____

Lab zone ® Do the Quick Lab *Inducing an Electric Current.*

🔑 Assess Your Understanding

1a. Describe How can you use a magnet to induce a current?

_____

_____

b. Classify Give an example of an electronic appliance that runs on AC and one that runs on DC.

_____

_____

got it? ···

○ **I get it!** Now I know that electric current is induced when _____

_____

○ **I need extra help with** _____

Go to **MY SCIENCE COACH** online for help with this subject.

How Does a Generator Work?

An electric **generator** is a device that transforms mechanical energy into electrical energy. ⟾ **A generator uses motion in a magnetic field to produce current.**

In **Figure 3,** you can see how an AC generator works. Turn the crank, and the armature rotates in the magnetic field. As the armature rotates, one side of it moves up as the other moves down. This motion induces a current in the armature. Slip rings turn with the armature. The turning slip rings allow current to flow into the brushes. When the brushes are connected to a circuit, the generator can be used as an energy source.

The electric company uses giant generators to produce most of the electrical energy you use each day. Huge turbines turn the armatures of the generators. Turbines are circular devices with many blades. They spin when water, steam, or hot gas flows through them. This turns the armatures, which generates electric current.

FIGURE 3 ·······························
> **INTERACTIVE ART** **How a Generator Works**
In a generator, an armature rotates in a magnetic field to induce a current.

✎ **Describe** Write what each part of the generator does in the boxes.

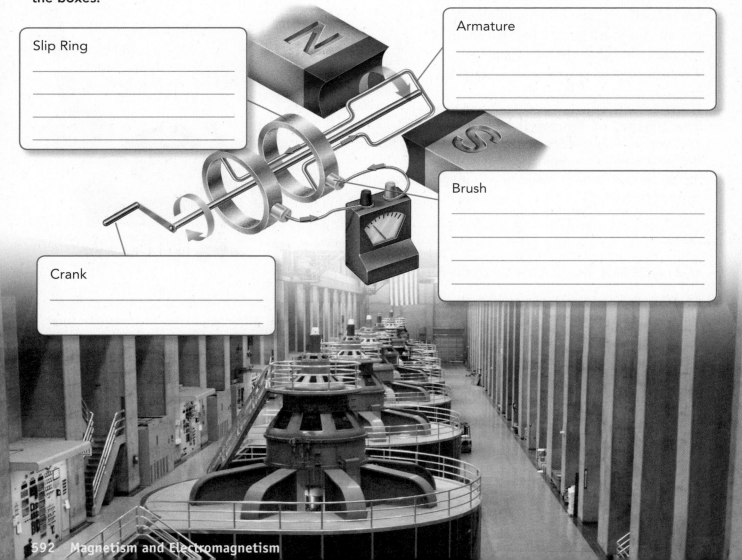

Slip Ring
_____
_____
_____

Crank
_____
_____

Armature
_____
_____
_____

Brush
_____
_____
_____

EXPLORE THE BIG **?**

How are electricity and magnetism related?

FIGURE 4 ....
Wind-up cell phone chargers are small generators that let you charge your cell phone anywhere.

✎ **Analyze Models and Systems** Complete the tasks below.

If you connect the output wires of the charger to a battery, _____ will flow through the armature, producing a _____. The permanent magnet in the charger will then cause the armature to _____. Draw what you will observe that lets you know this is happening.

When I turn the crank of the wind-up cell phone charger, or generator, I turn an armature in a(n) _____. This generates a(n) _____ in the wire, which powers the phone.

Lab zone ® Do the Quick Lab *How Generators Work.*

🔑 **Assess Your Understanding**

2a. Review What is one way to induce an electric current?

_____
_____
_____

b. ANSWER THE BIG **?** How are electricity and magnetism related?

_____
_____
_____
_____

got**it?** ....

○ **I get it!** Now I know a generator produces current by _____
_____

○ **I need extra help with** _____

Go to **MY SCIENCE** Ⓢ **COACH** *online for help with this subject.*

What Does a Transformer Do?

The electrical energy generated by electric companies is transmitted over long distances at very high voltages. However, in your home, electrical energy is used at much lower voltages. Transformers change the voltage so you can use electricity.

🔑 **A transformer is a device that increases or decreases voltage.** A **transformer** consists of two separate coils of insulated wire wrapped around an iron core. The primary coil is connected to a circuit with a voltage source and alternating current. The secondary coil is connected to a separate circuit that does not contain a voltage source. The changing current in the primary coil produces a changing magnetic field. This changing magnetic field induces a current in the secondary coil.

The change in voltage from the primary coil to the secondary coil depends on the number of loops in each coil. In step-up transformers, as shown in **Figure 5,** the primary coil has fewer loops than the secondary coil. Step-up transformers increase voltage. In step-down transformers, the primary coil has more loops. Voltage is reduced. The greater the difference between the number of loops in the primary and secondary coils in a transformer, the more the voltage will change. The relationship is a ratio.

$$\frac{\text{voltage}_{\text{primary}}}{\text{voltage}_{\text{secondary}}} = \frac{\text{coils}_{\text{primary}}}{\text{coils}_{\text{secondary}}}$$

$$\frac{120 \text{ v}}{6 \text{ v}} = 20$$

In this transformer, the voltage in the primary coil is twenty times higher than the voltage in the secondary coil. This means there are twenty times as many loops in the primary coil as there are in the secondary coil. If the primary coil has forty loops, then the secondary coil has two.

FIGURE 5 ·······························

Transformers
A step-up transformer, like the one shown below, is used to help transmit electricity from generating plants. Step-down transformers are used in power cords for some small electronics.

✎ **Make Models** Draw wire loops to show both the primary and secondary coils of this step-down transformer.

This kind of plug contains a step-down transformer.

Step-Up Transformer

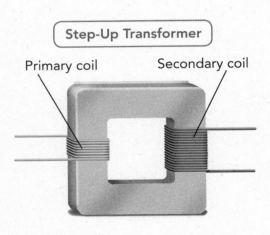

Primary coil   Secondary coil

Step-Down Transformer

do the **math!**

Transforming Electricity

The illustration shows how transformers change voltage between the generating plant and your home. For each transformer in the illustration below, state whether it is a step-up or step-down transformer.

In the boxes, calculate the ratio of loops in the primary coil to loops in the secondary coil.

[box] [box] [box]

_____ Transformer   _____ Transformer   _____ Transformer

Generating plant

11,000 V   240,000 V   High-voltage transmission lines   2,400 V   120 V

Lab zone® Do the Quick Lab *How Transformers Work.*

🗝 Assess Your Understanding

3a. Identify Which coil has more loops in a step-down transformer?

_____

_____

_____

b. Infer Why do some appliances have step-down transformers built in?

_____

_____

_____

got it? ··

○ **I get it!** Now I know a transformer is a device used to _____

_____

○ **I need extra help with** _____

Go to **MY SCIENCE** 🌐 **COACH** *online for help with this subject.*

_____ in a wire produces a _____

and movement of a wire through a _____

produces _____.

LESSON 1 What Is Magnetism?

🔑 Magnets attract iron and materials that contain iron. Magnets attract or repel other magnets. In addition, one end of a magnet will always point north when allowed to swing freely.

🔑 Magnetic poles that are unlike attract each other, and magnetic poles that are alike repel each other.

Vocabulary
• magnet
• magnetism
• magnetic pole
• magnetic force

LESSON 2 Magnetic Fields

🔑 Magnetic field lines spread out from one pole, curve around the magnet, and return to the other pole.

🔑 Like a bar magnet, Earth has a magnetic field around it and two magnetic poles.

Vocabulary
• magnetic field
• magnetic field lines
• compass
• magnetic declination

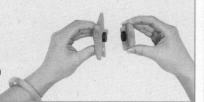

LESSON 3 Electromagnetic Force

🔑 An electric current produces a magnetic field.

🔑 The magnetic field produced by a current can be turned on or off, reverse direction, or change its strength.

🔑 Both solenoids and electromagnets use electric current and coiled wires to produce strong magnetic fields.

Vocabulary
• electromagnetism   • solenoid   • electromagnet

LESSON 4 Electricity, Magnetism, and Motion

🔑 By placing a wire with a current in a magnetic field, electrical energy can be transformed into mechanical energy.

🔑 An electric current turns the pointer of a galvanometer.

🔑 An electric motor transforms electrical energy into mechanical energy.

Vocabulary
• galvanometer   • electric motor

LESSON 5 Electricity From Magnetism

🔑 An electric current is induced in a conductor when the conductor moves through a magnetic field.

🔑 A generator uses motion in a magnetic field to produce current.

🔑 A transformer is a device that increases or decreases voltage.

Vocabulary
• electromagnetic induction   • direct current
• alternating current   • generator   • transformer

Review and Assessment

LESSON 1 What Is Magnetism?

1. A magnet is attracted to a soup can because the can has

   a. a south pole.   **b.** a north pole.

   c. a magnetic field.   **d.** iron in it.

2. Any magnet, no matter its shape, has two ends, and each one is called

a _____

3. **Predict** What will happen to a bar magnet suspended from a string when it swings freely?

_____

_____

_____

4. **Interpret Diagrams** In the diagram, what do the arrows represent? Explain your answer.

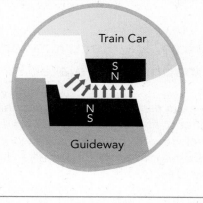

_____

_____

_____

_____

5. **Design Experiments** If two magnets' poles are not labeled, how can you tell which poles are the same and which are different?

_____

_____

_____

_____

LESSON 2 Magnetic Fields

6. A compass works because its magnetic needle

   a. points east.   **b.** spins freely.

   c. points west.   **d.** repels magnets.

7. _____ map out the magnetic field around a magnet.

8. **Make Models** How is Earth like a magnet?

_____

_____

_____

9. **Draw Conclusions** Look at the diagram below. Is the left magnetic pole a north or south pole? Explain your answer.

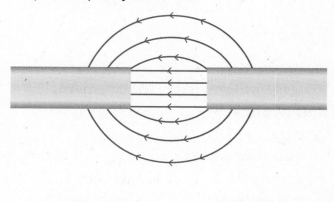

_____

_____

_____

_____

10. **Write About It** Imagine that you are the early inventor of the compass. Write an advertisement for your product that tells explorers how a compass works.

17 Review and Assessment

LESSON 3 Electromagnetic Force

11. The relationship between electricity and magnetism is called

    a. electrical energy.   **b.** induced current.

    c. electromagnetism. **d.** ferromagnetism.

12. A coil of wire with a current is called

    a _____

13. Relate Cause and Effect You have a magnetic field produced by a current. What would you do to change the direction and increase the strength of the field?

_____

_____

_____

_____

_____

_____

LESSON 4 Electricity, Magnetism, and Motion

14. Electrical energy is transformed into mechanical energy in a

    a. motor.   **b.** solenoid.

    c. transformer. **d.** electromagnet.

15. A galvanometer is a device that

    measures _____

16. Compare and Contrast How is a motor similar to a galvanometer? How is it different?

_____

_____

_____

_____

_____

LESSON 5 Electricity From Magnetism

17. A device that changes the voltage of alternating current is a

    a. transformer.   **b.** motor.

    c. generator.   **d.** galvanometer.

18. Generating a current by moving a conductor in a magnetic field is _____

_____

19. Write About It You are a television news reporter covering the opening of a new dam that will help to generate electrical energy. Write a short news story describing how the dam transforms mechanical energy from the motion of the water into electrical energy.

APPLY THE BIG ❓ How are electricity and magnetism related?

20. A crane in a junkyard may have an electromagnet to lift heavy metal objects. Explain how electricity and magnetism work in an electromagnet so that a crane can lift heavy metal objects.

_____

_____

_____

_____

_____

_____

_____

_____

Standardized Test Prep

Multiple Choice

Circle the letter of the best answer.

The graph below shows how a solenoid's loops affect its magnetic field strength. Use the graph to answer Question 1.

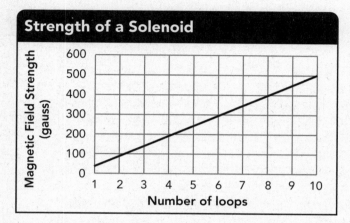

Strength of a Solenoid

1. Predict the strength of a 12-loop solenoid.

   A   300 gauss   B   600 gauss
   C   700 gauss   D   1200 gauss

2. You can increase a step-up transformer's voltage with

   A   a power source connected to the primary coil.
   B   a source connected to the secondary coil.
   C   increasing the number of loops in the primary coil.
   D   increasing the number of loops in the secondary coil.

3. To measure the current induced by moving a wire through a magnetic field, which piece of equipment would a scientist need?

   A   a galvanometer
   B   a transformer
   C   an insulated wire
   D   an LED

4. What happens when a magnet moves through a coil of wire?

   A   The magnet loses magnetism.
   B   A current is induced in the wire.
   C   A current is induced in the magnet.
   D   Electrical energy is transformed into mechanical energy.

5. How does Earth's magnetic field compare with that of a bar magnet?

   A   Their magnetic fields increase with size.
   B   The attractive force of their magnetic fields is greatest at the poles.
   C   The attractive force of their magnetic fields is greatest at the center.
   D   Electric current causes them to lose magnetism.

Constructed Response

Use the diagram below and your knowledge of science to help you answer Question 6. Write your answer on a separate sheet of paper.

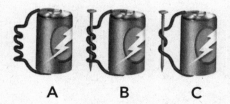

A   B   C

6. Three electromagnets are illustrated in the diagram above. Will the electromagnet labeled A or B produce a stronger magnetic field? Will the electromagnet B or C produce a stronger field? Explain your answers.

MAGNETIC PICTURES

Doctors can look inside your body to detect infection, bleeding, or tumors in the brain—without surgery or high-energy radiation that can damage tissues. They can get very detailed views of ligaments, tendons, and muscles that reveal injuries. They can find breast cancers that mammograms miss, and they can map areas of low blood flow after a heart attack. How do they do this? They use Magnetic Resonance Imaging (MRI).

MRI machines use powerful electromagnets, radio waves, and computers to take pictures of the inside of bodies. This process works because human bodies contain so much water. First, the large magnet in the MRI machine aligns the hydrogen atoms in the water molecules within the field. Then, the machine emits a radio frequency pulse that spins all of the hydrogen atoms the same way. The hydrogen atoms release energy in the form of a radio signal as they return to their normal positions, and computers can turn that signal into pictures. Healthy tissues respond differently to the magnet than unhealthy or damaged tissues.

Research It MRI scanning rooms have strict rules about what is allowed inside because metal objects can become deadly. Research the safety concerns for MRI use on humans. Then write a safety brochure to share your findings.

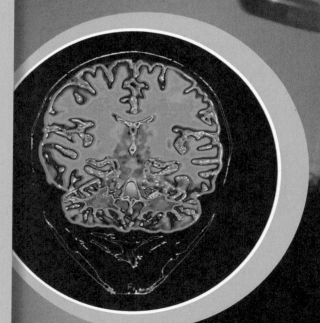

Now, instead of using X-rays, doctors use magnets to look in detail at systems inside the body. ▼

▲ This MRI of a healthy brain shows both hemispheres in bright pink and the cerebellum in green.

A SHOCKING MESSAGE!

In the 1830s, before the telephone had been invented, people were experimenting with ways to communicate across long distances. Samuel Morse and Alfred Vail discovered that it was possible to use an electromagnet to send a signal through cheap wire.

The electromagnet is part of an electric circuit. On one end of the wire is a telegraph switch. Closing the switch completes the circuit, sending an electric current through the wire. Opening the switch stops the current. On the other end of the wire is a telegraph with an electromagnet, a metal key, and a metal plate. As the electric current flows through the electromagnet, a magnetic field forms.

The metal key is then attracted to the metal plate. The sender can close and open the switch quickly, making a short clicking sound called a "dot" on the other end. Or, the sender can hold the switch closed and create a longer sound, called a "dash." Leaving the switch open for a moment comes across as a "space," or a break in the sounds.

This pattern of dots, dashes, and spaces became a new tool for communicating without using voices—Morse code. Telegraph operators could spell out words and phrases. Three dots, followed by three dashes, followed by three dots, for example, is the Morse code signal for SOS, or help!

Signal It Work with a partner to find resources that will help you construct your own electromagnetic telegraph machine! Predict which materials will best conduct a signal, and then verify your predictions by building a model.

APPENDIX A

Using a Laboratory Balance

The laboratory balance is an important tool in scientific investigations. Different kinds of balances are used in the laboratory to determine the masses and weights of objects. You can use a triple-beam balance to determine the masses of materials that you study or experiment with in the laboratory. An electronic balance, unlike a triple-beam balance, is used to measure the weights of materials.

The triple-beam balance that you may use in your science class is probably similar to the balance illustrated in this Appendix. **To use the balance properly, you should learn the name, location, and function of each part of the balance you are using. What kind of balance do you have in your science class?**

The Triple-Beam Balance

The triple-beam balance is a single-pan balance with three beams calibrated in grams. The back, or 100-gram, beam is divided into ten units of 10 grams each. The middle, or 500-gram, beam is divided into five units of 100 grams each. The front, or 10-gram, beam is divided into ten units of 1 gram each. Each of the units on the front beam is further divided into units of 0.1 gram. What is the largest mass you could find with a triple-beam balance?

The following procedure can be used to find the mass of an object with a triple-beam balance:

1. Place the object on the pan.
2. Move the rider on the middle beam notch by notch until the horizontal pointer on the right drops below zero. Move the rider back one notch.
3. Move the rider on the back beam notch by notch until the pointer again drops below zero. Move the rider back one notch.
4. Slowly slide the rider along the front beam until the pointer stops at the zero point.
5. The mass of the object is equal to the sum of the readings on the three beams.

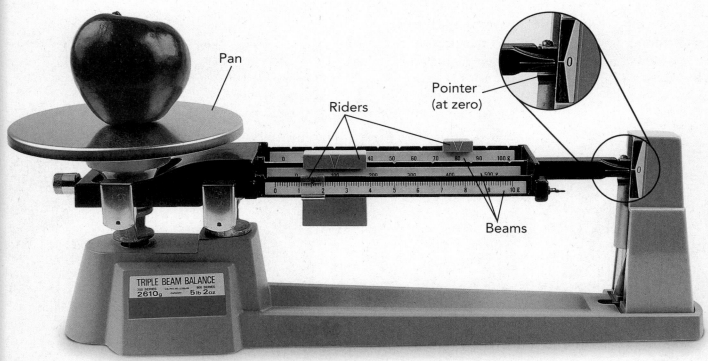

Pan

Riders

Pointer
(at zero)

Beams

TRIPLE BEAM BALANCE
700 SERIES   800 SERIES
2610g   CAPACITY   5 lb 2 oz

APPENDIX B

List of Chemical Elements

Name	Symbol	Atomic Number	Atomic Mass†
Actinium	Ac	89	(227)
Aluminum	Al	13	26.982
Americium	Am	95	(243)
Antimony	Sb	51	121.75
Argon	Ar	18	39.948
Arsenic	As	33	74.922
Astatine	At	85	(210)
Barium	Ba	56	137.33
Berkelium	Bk	97	(247)
Beryllium	Be	4	9.0122
Bismuth	Bi	83	208.98
Bohrium	Bh	107	(264)
Boron	B	5	10.81
Bromine	Br	35	79.904
Cadmium	Cd	48	112.41
Calcium	Ca	20	40.08
Californium	Cf	98	(251)
Carbon	C	6	12.011
Cerium	Ce	58	140.12
Cesium	Cs	55	132.91
Chlorine	Cl	17	35.453
Chromium	Cr	24	51.996
Cobalt	Co	27	58.933
Copernicium	Cn	112	(277)
Copper	Cu	29	63.546
Curium	Cm	96	(247)
Darmstadtium	Ds	110	(269)
Dubnium	Db	105	(262)
Dysprosium	Dy	66	162.50
Einsteinium	Es	99	(252)
Erbium	Er	68	167.26
Europium	Eu	63	151.96
Fermium	Fm	100	(257)
Flerovium	Fl	114	(289)
Fluorine	F	9	18.998
Francium	Fr	87	(223)
Gadolinium	Gd	64	157.25
Gallium	Ga	31	69.72
Germanium	Ge	32	72.59
Gold	Au	79	196.97
Hafnium	Hf	72	178.49
Hassium	Hs	108	(265)
Helium	He	2	4.0026
Holmium	Ho	67	164.93
Hydrogen	H	1	1.0079
Indium	In	49	114.82
Iodine	I	53	126.90
Iridium	Ir	77	192.22
Iron	Fe	26	55.847
Krypton	Kr	36	83.80
Lanthanum	La	57	138.91
Lawrencium	Lr	103	(262)
Lead	Pb	82	207.2
Lithium	Li	3	6.941
Livermorium	Lv	116	(292)
Lutetium	Lu	71	174.97
Magnesium	Mg	12	24.305
Manganese	Mn	25	54.938
Meitnerium	Mt	109	(268)

Name	Symbol	Atomic Number	Atomic Mass†
Mendelevium	Md	101	(258)
Mercury	Hg	80	200.59
Molybdenum	Mo	42	95.94
Moscovium	Mc	115	(288)
Neodymium	Nd	60	144.24
Neon	Ne	10	20.179
Neptunium	Np	93	(237)
Nickel	Ni	28	58.71
Nihonium	Nh	113	(284)
Niobium	Nb	41	92.906
Nitrogen	N	7	14.007
Nobelium	No	102	(259)
Oganesson	Og	118	(294)
Osmium	Os	76	190.2
Oxygen	O	8	15.999
Palladium	Pd	46	106.4
Phosphorus	P	15	30.974
Platinum	Pt	78	195.09
Plutonium	Pu	94	(244)
Polonium	Po	84	(209)
Potassium	K	19	39.098
Praseodymium	Pr	59	140.91
Promethium	Pm	61	(145)
Protactinium	Pa	91	231.04
Radium	Ra	88	(226)
Radon	Rn	86	(222)
Rhenium	Re	75	186.21
Rhodium	Rh	45	102.91
Roentgenium	Rg	111	(272)
Rubidium	Rb	37	85.468
Ruthenium	Ru	44	101.07
Rutherfordium	Rf	104	(261)
Samarium	Sm	62	150.4
Scandium	Sc	21	44.956
Seaborgium	Sg	106	(263)
Selenium	Se	34	78.96
Silicon	Si	14	28.086
Silver	Ag	47	107.87
Sodium	Na	11	22.990
Strontium	Sr	38	87.62
Sulfur	S	16	32.06
Tantalum	Ta	73	180.95
Technetium	Tc	43	(98)
Tellurium	Te	52	127.60
Tennessine	Ts	117	(294)
Terbium	Tb	65	158.93
Thallium	Tl	81	204.37
Thorium	Th	90	232.04
Thulium	Tm	69	168.93
Tin	Sn	50	118.69
Titanium	Ti	22	47.90
Tungsten	W	74	183.85
Uranium	U	92	238.03
Vanadium	V	23	50.941
Xenon	Xe	54	131.30
Ytterbium	Yb	70	173.04
Yttrium	Y	39	88.906
Zinc	Zn	30	65.38
Zirconium	Zr	40	91.22

†Numbers in parentheses give the mass number of the most stable isotope.

APPENDIX C

Periodic Table of the Elements

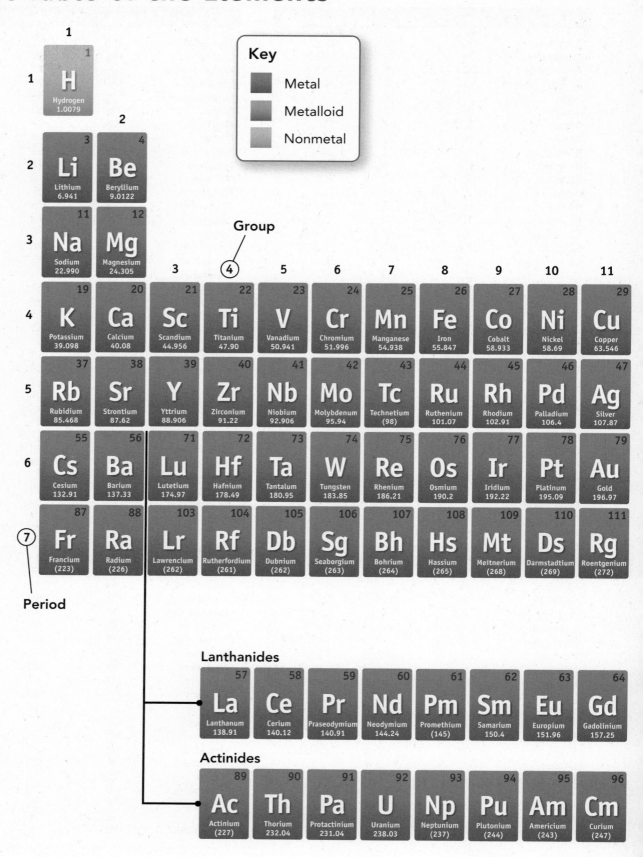

Key

Metal

Metalloid

Nonmetal

Group

Period

1									
1 **H** Hydrogen 1.0079									

2									
3 **Li** Lithium 6.941	**4** **Be** Beryllium 9.0122								

11 **Na** Sodium 22.990	**12** **Mg** Magnesium 24.305

	3	4	5	6	7	8	9	10	11
4	**19** **K** Potassium 39.098	**20** **Ca** Calcium 40.08	**21** **Sc** Scandium 44.956	**22** **Ti** Titanium 47.90	**23** **V** Vanadium 50.941	**24** **Cr** Chromium 51.996	**25** **Mn** Manganese 54.938	**26** **Fe** Iron 55.847	**27** **Co** Cobalt 58.933
5	**37** **Rb** Rubidium 85.468	**38** **Sr** Strontium 87.62	**39** **Y** Yttrium 88.906	**40** **Zr** Zirconium 91.22	**41** **Nb** Niobium 92.906	**42** **Mo** Molybdenum 95.94	**43** **Tc** Technetium (98)	**44** **Ru** Ruthenium 101.07	**45** **Rh** Rhodium 102.91
6	**55** **Cs** Cesium 132.91	**56** **Ba** Barium 137.33	**71** **Lu** Lutetium 174.97	**72** **Hf** Hafnium 178.49	**73** **Ta** Tantalum 180.95	**74** **W** Tungsten 183.85	**75** **Re** Rhenium 186.21	**76** **Os** Osmium 190.2	**77** **Ir** Iridium 192.22
7	**87** **Fr** Francium (223)	**88** **Ra** Radium (226)	**103** **Lr** Lawrencium (262)	**104** **Rf** Rutherfordium (261)	**105** **Db** Dubnium (262)	**106** **Sg** Seaborgium (263)	**107** **Bh** Bohrium (264)	**108** **Hs** Hassium (265)	**109** **Mt** Meitnerium (268)

Continued columns 10, 11 and group numbers 28, 29:

Period 4: **28 Ni** Nickel 58.69, **29 Cu** Copper 63.546
Period 5: **46 Pd** Palladium 106.4, **47 Ag** Silver 107.87
Period 6: **78 Pt** Platinum 195.09, **79 Au** Gold 196.97
Period 7: **110 Ds** Darmstadtium (269), **111 Rg** Roentgenium (272)

Lanthanides

57 **La** Lanthanum 138.91	**58** **Ce** Cerium 140.12	**59** **Pr** Praseodymium 140.91	**60** **Nd** Neodymium 144.24	**61** **Pm** Promethium (145)	**62** **Sm** Samarium 150.4	**63** **Eu** Europium 151.96	**64** **Gd** Gadolinium 157.25

Actinides

89 **Ac** Actinium (227)	**90** **Th** Thorium 232.04	**91** **Pa** Protactinium 231.04	**92** **U** Uranium 238.03	**93** **Np** Neptunium (237)	**94** **Pu** Plutonium (244)	**95** **Am** Americium (243)	**96** **Cm** Curium (247)

Many periodic tables include a zigzag line that separates the metals from the nonmetals. Metalloids, found on either side of the line, share properties of both metals and nonmetals.

18

| | | | | | 2
He
Helium
4.0026 |

13 **14** **15** **16** **17**

| 5
B
Boron
10.81 | 6
C
Carbon
12.011 | 7
N
Nitrogen
14.007 | 8
O
Oxygen
15.999 | 9
F
Fluorine
18.998 | 10
Ne
Neon
20.179 |

| 13
Al
Aluminum
26.982 | 14
Si
Silicon
28.086 | 15
P
Phosphorus
30.974 | 16
S
Sulfur
32.06 | 17
Cl
Chlorine
35.453 | 18
Ar
Argon
39.948 |

12

| 30
Zn
Zinc
65.38 | 31
Ga
Gallium
69.72 | 32
Ge
Germanium
72.59 | 33
As
Arsenic
74.922 | 34
Se
Selenium
78.96 | 35
Br
Bromine
79.904 | 36
Kr
Krypton
83.80 |

| 48
Cd
Cadmium
112.41 | 49
In
Indium
114.82 | 50
Sn
Tin
118.69 | 51
Sb
Antimony
121.75 | 52
Te
Tellurium
127.60 | 53
I
Iodine
126.90 | 54
Xe
Xenon
131.30 |

| 80
Hg
Mercury
200.59 | 81
Tl
Thallium
204.37 | 82
Pb
Lead
207.2 | 83
Bi
Bismuth
208.98 | 84
Po
Polonium
(209) | 85
At
Astatine
(210) | 86
Rn
Radon
(222) |

| 112
Cn
Copernicium
(277) | 113
Nh
Nihonium
(284) | 114
Fl
Flerovium
(289) | 115
Mc
Moscovium
(288) | 116
Lv
Livermorium
(292) | 117
Ts
Tennessine
(294) | 118
Og
Oganesson
(294) |

Atomic masses in parentheses are those of the most stable isotopes.

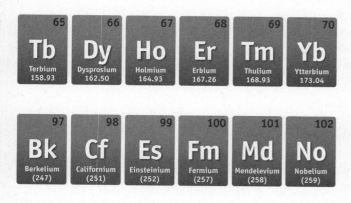

| 65
Tb
Terbium
158.93 | 66
Dy
Dysprosium
162.50 | 67
Ho
Holmium
164.93 | 68
Er
Erbium
167.26 | 69
Tm
Thulium
168.93 | 70
Yb
Ytterbium
173.04 |

| 97
Bk
Berkelium
(247) | 98
Cf
Californium
(251) | 99
Es
Einsteinium
(252) | 100
Fm
Fermium
(257) | 101
Md
Mendelevium
(258) | 102
No
Nobelium
(259) |

APPENDIX D
The Design Process

Engineers are people who use scientific and technological knowledge to solve practical problems. To design new products, engineers usually follow the process described here, even though they may not follow these steps in the same order each time.

Identify a Need

Before engineers begin designing a new product, they must first identify the need they are trying to meet or the problem they want to solve. For example, suppose you are a member of a design team in a company that makes model cars. Your team has identified a need: a model car that is inexpensive and easy to assemble.

Research the Problem

Engineers often begin by gathering information that will help them with their new design. This research may include finding articles in books, magazines, or on the Internet. It may also involve talking to other engineers who have solved similar problems. Engineers often perform experiments related to the product they want to design.

For your model car, you could look at cars that are similar to the one you want to design. You might do research on the Internet. You could also test some materials to see whether they will work well in a model car.

Design a Solution

Brainstorm Ideas When engineers design new products, they usually work in teams. Design teams often hold brainstorming meetings in which any team member can contribute ideas. Brainstorming is a creative process in which one team member's suggestions often spark ideas in other group members. Brainstorming can lead to new approaches to solving a design problem.

Document the Process As the design team works, its members document, or keep a record of, the process. Having access to documentation enables others to repeat, or replicate, the process in the future. Design teams document their research sources, ideas, lists of materials, and so on because any part of the process may be a helpful resource later.

Identify Constraints During brainstorming, a design team may come up with several possible designs. To better focus their ideas, team members consider constraints. A constraint is a factor that limits a product design. Physical characteristics, such as the properties of materials used to make your model car, are constraints. Money and time are also constraints. If the materials in a product cost a lot or if the product takes a long time to make, the design may be impractical.

Make Trade-offs Design teams usually need to make trade-offs. In a trade-off, engineers give up one benefit of a proposed design in order to obtain another. In designing your model car, you might have to make trade-offs. For example, you might decide to give up the benefit of sturdiness in order to obtain the benefit of lower cost.

Select a Solution After considering the constraints and trade-offs of the possible designs, engineers then select one idea to develop further. That idea represents the solution that the team thinks best meets the need or solves the problem that was identified at the beginning of the process. The decision includes selecting the materials that will be used in the first attempt to build a product.

Create, Test, and Evaluate a Prototype

Once the team has chosen a design plan, the engineers build a prototype. A prototype is a working model used to test a design. Engineers evaluate the prototype to see whether it meets the goal. They must determine whether it works well, is easy to operate, is safe to use, and holds up to repeated use.

Part of the evaluation includes collecting data in the form of measurements. For example, think of your model car. Once you decide how to build your prototype, what would you want to know about it? You might want to measure how much baggage it could carry or how its shape affects its speed.

Troubleshoot and Redesign

Few prototypes work perfectly, which is why they need to be tested. Once a design team has tested a prototype, the members analyze the results and identify any problems. The team then tries to troubleshoot, or fix the design problems. Troubleshooting allows the team to redesign the prototype to improve on how well the solution meets the need.

Communicate the Solution

A team needs to communicate the final design to the people who will manufacture and use the product. To do this, teams may use sketches, detailed drawings, computer simulations, and word descriptions. The team may also present the evidence that was collected when the prototype was tested. This evidence may include mathematical representations, such as graphs and data tables, that support the choice for the final design.

607

GLOSSARY

A

absolute zero The temperature at which no more energy can be removed from matter. (375)
cero absoluto Temperatura a cuyo punto ya no se puede extraer energía de la materia.

acceleration The rate at which velocity changes. (246)
aceleración Ritmo al que cambia la velocidad.

acid A substance that tastes sour, reacts with metals and carbonates, and turns blue litmus paper red. (213)
ácido Sustancia de sabor agrio que reacciona con metales y carbonatos, y que vuelve rojo el papel de tornasol azul.

activation energy The minimum amount of energy needed to start a chemical reaction. (183)
energía de activación Cantidad mínima de energía que se necesita para iniciar una reacción química.

alkali metal An element in Group 1 of the periodic table. (92)
metal alcalino Elemento en el Grupo 1 de la tabla periódica.

alkaline earth metal An element in Group 2 of the periodic table. (92)
metal alcalinotérreo Elemento en el Grupo 2 de la tabla periódica.

alloy A mixture of two or more elements, at least one of which is a metal. (151)
aleación Mezcla de dos o más elementos, uno de los cuales es un metal.

alpha particle A particle given off during radioactive decay that consists of two protons and two neutrons. (109)
partícula alfa Partícula liberada durante la desintegración radiactiva que tiene dos protones y dos neutrones.

alternating current Current consisting of charges that move back and forth in a circuit. (591)
corriente alterna Corriente de cargas eléctricas que se mueven hacia delante y hacia atrás en un circuito.

amorphous solid A solid made up of particles that are not arranged in a regular pattern. (42)
sólido amorfo Sólido constituido por partículas que no están dispuestas en un patrón regular.

amplitude 1. The height of a transverse wave from the center to a crest or trough. **2.** The maximum distance the particles of a medium move away from their rest positions as a longitudinal wave passes through the medium. (403)

amplitud 1. Altura de una onda transversal desde el centro a una cresta o un valle. **2.** Máxima distancia del desvío de las partículas de un medio, desde sus posiciones de reposo, al ser atravesado por una onda longitudinal.

amplitude modulation A method of transmitting signals by changing the amplitude of a radio wave. (474)
amplitud modulada Método de transmisión de señales al cambiar la amplitud de una onda de radio.

antinode A point of maximum amplitude on a standing wave. (414)
antinodo Punto de máxima amplitud de una onda estacionaria.

atom The basic particle from which all elements are made; the smallest particle of an element that has the properties of that element. (10, 73)
átomo Partícula básica de la que todos los elementos están formados; partícula más pequeña de un elemento, que tiene las propiedades de ese elemento.

atomic mass The average mass of all the isotopes of an element. (81)
masa atómica Promedio de la masa de todos los isótopos de un elemento.

atomic number The number of protons in the nucleus of an atom. (78)
número atómico Número de protones en el núcleo de un átomo.

average speed The overall rate of speed at which an object moves; calculated by dividing the total distance an object travels by the total time. (240)
velocidad media Índice de velocidad general de un objeto en movimiento; se calcula dividiendo la distancia total recorrida por el tiempo total empleado.

B

base A substance that tastes bitter, feels slippery, and turns red litmus paper blue. (215)
base Sustancia de sabor amargo, escurridiza y que vuelve azul el papel de tornasol rojo.

beta particle A fast-moving electron that is given off as nuclear radiation. (109)
partícula beta Electrón de movimiento rápido producido como radiación nuclear.

boiling Vaporization that occurs at and below the surface of a liquid. (51)
ebullición Evaporación que ocurre en y bajo la superficie de un líquido.

boiling point The temperature at which a liquid boils. (51)

punto de ebullición Temperatura a la cual hierve un líquido.

Boyle's law A principle that describes the relationship between the pressure and volume of a gas at constant temperature. (60)

ley de Boyle Principio que describe la relación entre la presión y el volumen de un gas a una temperatura constante.

buoyant force The upward force exerted by a fluid on a submerged object. (291)

fuerza de flotación Fuerza ascendente que ejerce un fluido sobre un objeto sumergido.

C

camera An optical instrument that uses lenses to focus light and film or an electronic sensor to record an image of an object. (515)

cámara Instrumento óptico que usa lentes para enfocar la luz, y película o un sensor electrónico para grabar la imagen de un objeto.

catalyst A material that increases the rate of a reaction by lowering the activation energy. (187)

catalizador Material que aumenta la velocidad de una reacción al disminuir la energía de activación.

Celsius scale The temperature scale on which water freezes at 0°C and boils at 100°C. (375)

escala Celsius Escala de temperatura en la que el punto de congelación del agua es 0°C y el punto de ebullición es 100°C.

centripetal force A force that causes an object to move in a circle. (289)

fuerza centrípeta Fuerza que hace que un objeto se mueva circularmente.

Charles's law A principle that describes the relationship between the temperature and volume of a gas at constant pressure. (58)

ley de Charles Principio que describe la relación entre la temperatura y el volumen de un gas a una presión constante.

chemical bond The force of attraction that holds two atoms together. (10, 125)

enlace químico Fuerza de atracción que mantiene juntos a dos átomos.

chemical change A change in which one or more substances combine or break apart to form new substances. (23, 164)

cambio químico Cambio en el cual una o más sustancias se combinan o se descomponen para formar sustancias nuevas.

chemical energy A form of potential energy that is stored in chemical bonds between atoms. (27, 357)

energía química Forma de energía potencial almacenada en los enlaces químicos de los átomos.

chemical equation A short, easy way to show a chemical reaction using symbols. (170)

ecuación química Forma corta y sencilla de mostrar una reacción química usando símbolos.

chemical formula Symbols that show the elements in a compound and the ratio of atoms. (11, 134)

fórmula química Símbolos que muestran los elementos de un compuesto y la cantidad de átomos.

chemical property A characteristic of a substance that describes its ability to change into different substances. (6)

propiedad química Característica de una sustancia que describe su capacidad de convertirse en sustancias diferentes.

chemical symbol A one- or two-letter representation of an element. (83)

símbolo químico Representación con una o dos letras de un elemento.

chemistry The study of the properties of matter and how matter changes. (5)

química Estudio de las propiedades de la materia y de sus cambios.

circuit breaker A reusable safety switch that breaks the circuit when the current becomes too high. (555)

interruptor de circuito Interruptor de seguridad reutilizable que corta un circuito cuando la corriente es demasiado alta.

closed system A system in which no matter is allowed to enter or leave. (175)

sistema cerrado Sistema en el cual la materia no puede entrar ni salir.

cochlea A fluid-filled cavity in the inner ear that is shaped like a snail shell and lined with receptor cells that respond to sound. (444)

cóclea Cavidad llena de fluido situada en el oído interno, con forma de caracol, forrada de células receptoras que responden a los sonidos.

GLOSSARY

coefficient A number in front of a chemical formula in an equation that indicates how many molecules or atoms of each reactant and product are involved in a reaction. (177)
coeficiente En un ecuación, número delante de una fórmula química que indica cuántas moléculas o átomos de cada reactante y producto intervienen en una reacción.

colloid A mixture containing small, undissolved particles that do not settle out. (201)
coloide Mezcla que contiene partículas pequeñas y sin disolver que no se depositan.

compass A device with a magnetized needle that can spin freely; a compass needle always points north. (574)
brújula Instrumento con una aguja imantada que puede girar libremente; la aguja siempre apunta hacia el norte.

complementary colors Any two colors that combine to form white light. (494)
colores complementarios Dos colores cualesquiera que se combinan para crear luz blanca.

compound A substance made of two or more elements chemically combined in a specific ratio, or proportion. (11)
compuesto Sustancia formada por dos o más elementos combinados químicamente en una razón o proporción específica.

compound machine A device that combines two or more simple machines. (334)
máquina compuesta Dispositivo que combina dos o más máquinas simples.

compression 1. Stress that squeezes rock until it folds or breaks. **2.** The part of a longitudinal wave where the particles of the medium are close together. (400)
compresión 1. Fuerza que oprime una roca hasta que se pliega o se rompe. **2.** Parte de una onda longitudinal en la que las partículas del medio están muy próximas unas con otras.

concave lens A lens that is thinner in the center than at the edges. (507)
lente cóncava Lente que es más fina en el centro que en los extremos.

concave mirror A mirror with a surface that curves inward. (499)
espejo cóncavo Espejo cuya superficie se curva hacia dentro.

concentrated solution A mixture that has a lot of solute dissolved in it. (205)
solución concentrada Mezcla que tiene muchos solutos disueltos en ella.

concentration The amount of one material in a certain volume of another material. (186)
concentración Cantidad de un material en cierto volumen de otro material.

condensation The change in state from a gas to a liquid. (52)
condensación Cambio del estado gaseoso al estado líquido.

conduction 1. The transfer of thermal energy from one particle of matter to another. **2.** A method of charging an object by allowing electrons to flow from one object to another object through direct contact. (379, 532, 539)
conducción 1. Transferencia de energía térmica de una partícula de materia a otra. **2.** Método de transferencia de electricidad que consiste en permitir que los electrones fluyan por contacto directo de un cuerpo a otro.

conductor 1. A material that conducts heat well. **2.** A material that allows electric charges to flow. (383)
conductor 1. Material que puede conducir bien el calor. **2.** Material que permite que las cargas eléctricas fluyan.

cones Cells in the retina that respond to and detect color. (512)
conos Células en la retina que responden y detectan el color.

conservation of charge The law that states that charges are neither created nor destroyed. (532)
conservación de carga eléctrica Ley que establece que las cargas no se crean ni se destruyen.

constructive interference The interference that occurs when two waves combine to make a wave with an amplitude larger than the amplitude of either of the individual waves. (412)
interferencia constructiva Interferencia que ocurre cuando se combinan ondas para crear una onda con una amplitud mayor a la de cualquiera de las ondas individuales.

convection The transfer of thermal energy by the movement of a fluid. (379)
convección Transferencia de energía térmica por el movimiento de un líquido.

convection current The movement of a fluid, caused by differences in temperature, that transfers heat from one part of the fluid to another. (379)
corriente de convección Movimiento de un líquido ocasionado por diferencias de temperatura y que transfiere calor de un área del líquido a otra.

convex lens A lens that is thicker in the center than at the edges. (508)

lente convexa Lente que es más gruesa en el centro que en los extremos.

convex mirror A mirror with a surface that curves outward. (500)

espejo convexo Espejo cuya superficie se curva hacia fuera.

cornea The transparent tissue that covers the front of the eye. (511)

córnea Tejido transparente que cubre la parte delantera del ojo.

corrosion The gradual wearing away of a metal element due to a chemical reaction. (91)

corrosión Desgaste progresivo de un elemento metal debido a una reacción química.

corrosive The way in which acids react with some metals so as to wear away the metal. (213)

corrosivo Forma en que los ácidos reaccionan con algunos metales y los desgastan.

covalent bond A chemical bond formed when two atoms share electrons. (139)

enlace covalente Enlace químico que se forma cuando dos átomos comparten electrones.

crest The highest part of a transverse wave. (399)
cresta Parte más alta de una onda transversal.

crystal A solid in which the atoms are arranged in a pattern that repeats again and again. (136)
cristal Cuerpo sólido en el que los átomos siguen un patrón que se repite una y otra vez.

crystalline solid A solid that is made up of crystals in which particles are arranged in a regular, repeating pattern. (42)
sólido cristalino Sólido constituido por cristales en los que las partículas están colocadas en un patrón regular repetitivo.

D

decibel (dB) A unit used to compare the loudness of different sounds. (435)
decibelio (dB) Unidad usada para comparar el volumen de distintos sonidos.

decomposition A chemical reaction that breaks down compounds into simpler products. (180)
descomposición Reacción química que descompone los compuestos en productos más simples.

density The measurement of how much mass of a substance is contained in a given volume. (18, 431)
densidad Medida de la masa de una sustancia que tiene un volumen dado.

destructive interference The interference that occurs when two waves combine to make a wave with an amplitude smaller than the amplitude of either of the individual waves. (413)
interferencia destructiva Interferencia que ocurre cuando dos ondas se combinan para crear una onda con una amplitud menor a la de cualquiera de las ondas individuales.

diatomic molecule A molecule consisting of two atoms. (100)
molécula diatómica Molécula que tiene dos átomos.

diffraction The bending or spreading of waves as they move around a barrier or pass through an opening. (411)
difracción Desviación de las ondas al desplazarse alrededor de una barrera o atravesar una abertura.

diffuse reflection Reflection that occurs when parallel rays of light hit an uneven surface and all reflect at different angles. (497)
reflexión difusa Reflexión que ocurre cuando rayos de luz paralelos tocan una superficie rugosa y se reflejan en diferentes ángulos.

dilute solution A mixture that has only a little solute dissolved in it. (205)
solución diluida Mezcla que sólo tiene un poco de soluto disuelto en ella.

direct current Current consisting of charges that flow in only one direction in a circuit. (591)
corriente directa Corriente de cargas eléctricas que fluyen en una sola dirección en un circuito.

directly proportional A term used to describe the relationship between two variables whose graph is a straight line passing through the point (0, 0). (59)
directamente proporcional Término empleado para describir la relación entre dos variables cuya gráfica forma una línea recta que pasa por el punto (0, 0).

distance The length of the path between two points. (237)
distancia Medida del espacio entre dos puntos.

Doppler effect The change in frequency of a wave as its source moves in relation to an observer. (436)
efecto Doppler Cambio en la frecuencia de una onda a medida que la fuente se mueve en relación al observador.

GLOSSARY

double bond A chemical bond formed when atoms share two pairs of electrons. (140)
enlace doble Enlace químico formado cuando los átomos comparten dos pares de electrones.

ductile A term used to describe a material that can be pulled out into a long wire. (90)
dúctil Término usado para describir un material que se puede estirar hasta crear un alambre largo.

——————— **E** ———————

ear canal A narrow region leading from the outside of the human ear to the eardrum. (444)
canal auditivo Región estrecha que conecta el exterior del oído humano con el tímpano.

eardrum The small, tightly stretched drumlike membrane that separates the outer ear from the middle ear, and that vibrates when sound waves strike it. (444)
tímpano Membrana pequeña, extendida y tensa como la de un tambor que separa el oído externo del oído medio y que vibra cuando la golpean las ondas sonoras.

echolocation The use of reflected sound waves to determine distances or to locate objects. (447)
ecolocación Uso de ondas sonoras reflejadas para determinar distancias o para localizar objetos.

efficiency The percentage of input work that is converted to output work. (320)
eficacia Porcentaje de trabajo aportado que se convierte en trabajo producido.

elastic potential energy The energy of stretched or compressed objects. (351)
energía elástica potencial Energía de los cuerpos estirados o comprimidos.

electric circuit A complete, unbroken path through which electric charges can flow. (538)
circuito eléctrico Trayecto completo y continuo a través del cual pueden fluir las cargas eléctricas.

electric current The continuous flow of electric charges through a material. (537)
corriente eléctrica Flujo continuo de cargas eléctricas a través de un material.

electric field The region around a charged object where the object's electric force is exerted on other charged objects. (530)
campo eléctrico Región alrededor de un objeto cargado, donde su fuerza eléctrica interactúa con otros objetos cargados eléctricamente.

electric force The force between charged objects. (529)
fuerza eléctrica Fuerza entre cuerpos cargados eléctricamente.

electric motor A device that transforms electrical energy to mechanical energy. (586)
motor eléctrico Instrumento que convierte la energía eléctrica en energía mecánica.

electrical conductivity The ability of an object to carry electric current. (90)
conductividad eléctrica Capacidad de un objeto para cargar corriente eléctrica.

electrical energy The energy of electric charges. (356)
energía eléctrica Energía de las cargas eléctricas.

electromagnet A magnet created by wrapping a coil of wire with a current running through it around a core of material that is easily magnetised. (580)
electroimán Imán creado al enrollar una espiral de alambre, por la cual fluye una corriente eléctrica, alrededor de un núcleo de material que se magnetiza fácilmente.

electromagnetic energy The energy of light and other forms of radiation, which travels through space as waves. (357)
energía electromagnética Energía de la luz y otras formas de radiación, que viaja a través del espacio en forma de ondas.

electromagnetic induction The process of generating an electric current from the motion of a conductor through a magnetic field. (589)
inducción electromagnética Proceso por el cual se genera una corriente eléctrica a partir del movimiento de un conductor a través de un campo magnético.

electromagnetic radiation The energy transferred through space by electromagnetic waves. (461)
radiación electromagnética Energía transferida a través del espacio por ondas electromagnéticas.

electromagnetic spectrum The complete range of electromagnetic waves placed in order of increasing frequency. (466)
espectro electromagnético Gama completa de ondas electromagnéticas organizadas de menor a mayor frecuencia.

electromagnetic wave 1. A wave made up of a combination of a changing electric field and a changing magnetic field. 2. A wave that can transfer electric and magnetic energy through the vacuum of space. (461)
onda electromagnética 1. Onda formada por la combinación de un campo eléctrico cambiante y un campo magnético cambiante. 2. Onda que puede transferir energía eléctrica y magnética a través del vacío del espacio.

electromagnetism The relationship between electricity and magnetism. (578)
electromagnetismo Relación entre la electricidad y el magnetismo.

electron A tiny, negatively charged particle that moves around the outside of the nucleus of an atom. (74)
electrón Partícula pequeña de carga negativa que se mueve alrededor del núcleo de un átomo.

electron dot diagram A representation of the valence electrons in an atom, using dots. (125)
esquema de puntos por electrones Representación del número de electrones de valencia de un átomo, usando puntos.

element A pure substance that cannot be broken down into other substances by chemical or physical means. (9)
elemento Sustancia que no se puede descomponer en otras sustancias por medios químicos o físicos.

endothermic change A change in which energy is absorbed. (27)
cambio endotérmico Cambio en el que se absorbe energía.

endothermic reaction A reaction that absorbs energy. (168)
reacción endotérmica Reacción que absorbe energía.

energy The ability to do work or cause change. (346, 397)
energía Capacidad para realizar un trabajo o producir cambios.

energy level A region of an atom in which electrons of the same energy are likely to be found. (76)
nivel de energía Región de un átomo en la que es probable que se encuentren electrones con la misma energía.

energy transformation A change from one form of energy to another; also called an energy conversion. (358)
transformación de la energía Cambio de una forma de energía a otra; también se le llama conversión de energía.

enzyme 1. A type of protein that speeds up a chemical reaction in a living thing. **2.** A biological catalyst that lowers the activation energy of reactions in cells. (187)
enzima 1. Tipo de proteína que acelera una reacción química de un ser vivo. **2.** Catalizador biológico que disminuye la energía de activación de las reacciones celulares.

evaporation The process by which molecules at the surface of a liquid absorb enough energy to change to a gas. (51)
evaporación Proceso mediante el cual las moléculas en la superficie de un líquido absorben suficiente energía para pasar al estado gaseoso.

exothermic change A change in which energy is released. (27)
cambio exotérmico Cambio en el que se libera energía.

exothermic reaction A reaction that releases energy, usually in the form of heat. (168)
reacción exotérmica Reacción que libera energía generalmente en forma de calor.

eyepiece A lens that magnifies the image formed by the objective. (516)
ocular Lente que aumenta la imagen formada por el objetivo.

F

Fahrenheit scale The temperature scale on which water freezes at 32°F and boils at 212°F. (375)
escala Fahrenheit Escala de temperatura en la que el punto de congelación del agua es 32°F y el punto de ebullición es 212°F.

farsighted Having the condition in which a person can see distant objects clearly and nearby objects as blurry. (513)
hipermetropía Condición en la que una persona ve con claridad los objetos lejanos y ve borrosos los objetos cercanos.

fluid Any substance that can flow. (43)
fluido Cualquier sustancia que puede fluir.

fluid friction Friction that occurs as an object moves through a fluid. (269)
fricción de fluido Fricción que ocurre cuando un cuerpo se mueve a través de un fluido.

focal point The point at which light rays parallel to the optical axis meet, or appear to meet, after being reflected (or refracted) by a mirror (or a lens). (499)
punto de enfoque Punto en el que se encuentran, o parecen encontrarse, los rayos de luz paralelos al eje óptico después de reflejarse (o refractarse) en un espejo (o lente).

force A push or pull exerted on an object. (263)
fuerza Empuje o atracción que se ejerce sobre un cuerpo.

GLOSSARY

free fall The motion of a falling object when the only force acting on it is gravity. (287)
caída libre Movimiento de un objeto que cae cuando la única fuerza que actúa sobre éste es la gravedad.

freezing The change in state from a liquid to a solid. (50)
congelación Cambio del estado líquido al sólido.

frequency The number of complete waves that pass a given point in a certain amount of time. (404)
frecuencia Número de ondas completas que pasan por un punto dado en cierto tiempo.

frequency modulation A method of transmitting signals by changing the frequency of a wave. (474)
frecuencia modulada Método de transmisión de señales mediante el cambio de la frecuencia de una onda.

friction 1. The force that two surfaces exert on each other when they rub against each other. **2.** The transfer of electrons from one uncharged object to another uncharged object by rubbing. (267, 532)
fricción 1. Fuerza que dos superficies ejercen una sobre la otra al frotarse. **2.** Transferencia de electrones al frotarse un cuerpo no cargado con otro cuerpo no cargado.

fulcrum The fixed point around which a lever pivots. (326)
fulcro Punto fijo en torno al cual gira una palanca.

fundamental tone The lowest natural frequency of an object. (439)
tono fundamental Frecuencia natural más baja de un cuerpo.

fuse A safety device with a thin metal strip that will melt if too much current passes through a circuit. (555)
fusible Elemento de seguridad que tiene una tira metálica delgada que se derrite si una corriente demasiado fuerte pasa por un circuito.

G

galvanometer A device that uses an electromagnet to detect small amounts of current. (584)
galvanómetro Instrumento que usa un electroimán para detectar la intensidad de una pequeña corriente.

gamma rays Electromagnetic waves with the shortest wavelengths and highest frequencies. (109, 470)
rayos gamma Ondas electromagnéticas con la menor longitud de onda y la mayor frecuencia.

gas A state of matter with no definite shape or volume. (45)
gas Estado de la materia sin forma ni volumen definidos.

generator A device that transforms mechanical energy into electrical energy. (592)
generador eléctrico Instrumento que convierte la energía mecánica en energía eléctrica.

gravitational potential energy Potential energy that depends on the height of an object. (350)
energía gravitatoria potencial Energía potencial que depende de la altura de un cuerpo.

gravity The attractive force between objects; the force that moves objects downhill. (271)
gravedad Fuerza que atrae a los cuerpos entre sí; fuerza que mueve un cuerpo cuesta abajo.

grounded Allowing charges to flow directly from the circuit into the building's ground wire and then into Earth in the event of a short circuit. (555)
conectado a tierra Permitir que las cargas eléctricas fluyan directamente del circuito al cable a tierra del edificio y luego a la Tierra en caso de un cortocircuito.

group Elements in the same vertical column of the periodic table; also called family. (87)
grupo Elementos en la misma columna vertical de la tabla periódica; también llamado familia.

H

half-life The time it takes for half of the atoms of a radioactive element to decay. (111)
vida media Tiempo que toma descomponer la mitad de los átomos de un elemento radiactivo.

halogen An element found in Group 17 of the periodic table. (101)
halógeno Elemento del Grupo 17 de la tabla periódica.

heat The transfer of thermal energy from a warmer object to a cooler object. (377)
calor Transferencia de energía térmica de un cuerpo más cálido a uno menos cálido.

hertz (Hz) Unit of measurement for frequency. (404)
hercio (Hz) Unidad de medida de la frecuencia.

hydrogen ion A positively charged ion (H^+) formed of a hydrogen atom that has lost its electron. (219)
ión hidrógeno Ión de carga positiva (H^+) formado por un átomo de hidrógeno que ha perdido su electrón.

hydroxide ion A negatively charged ion made of oxygen and hydrogen (OH⁻). (220)
ión hidróxido Ión de carga negativa formado de oxígeno e hidrógeno (OH⁻).

--- **I** ---

image A copy of an object formed by reflected or refracted rays of light. (497)
imagen Copia de un objeto formada por rayos de luz que se reflejan y se refractan.

inclined plane A simple machine that is a flat, sloped surface. (323)
plano inclinado Máquina simple que consiste en una superficie plana con pendiente.

indicator A compound that changes color in the presence of an acid or a base. (214)
indicador Compuesto que cambia de color en presencia de un ácido o una base.

index of refraction A measure of the amount a ray of light bends when it passes from one medium to another. (504)
índice de refracción Medida de la inclinación de un rayo de luz cuando pasa de un medio a otro.

induction A method of redistributing the charge on an object by means of the electric field of another object; the objects have no direct contact. (533)
inducción Método de redistribuir la carga de un cuerpo haciendo uso del campo eléctrico de otro; los cuerpos no están en contacto directo.

inertia The tendency of an object to resist a change in motion. (275)
inercia Tendencia de un cuerpo de resistirse a cambios de movimiento.

infrared rays Electromagnetic waves with shorter wavelengths and higher frequencies than microwaves. (468)
rayos infrarrojos Ondas electromagnéticas con longitudes de onda más cortas y frecuencias más altas que las microondas.

inhibitor A material that decreases the rate of a reaction. (187)
inhibidor Material que disminuye la velocidad de una reacción.

input force The force exerted on a machine. (315)
fuerza aplicada Fuerza que se ejerce sobre una máquina.

instantaneous speed The speed of an object at one instant of time. (241)
velocidad instantánea Velocidad de un objeto en un instante del tiempo.

insulator 1. A material that does not conduct heat well. **2.** A material that does not easily allow electric charges to flow. (383, 539)
aislante 1. Material que no conduce bien el calor. **2.** Material que no permite fácilmente que las cargas eléctricas fluyan.

intensity The amount of energy per second carried through a unit area by a wave. (434)
intensidad Cantidad de energía por segundo que transporta una onda a través de una unidad de área.

interference The interaction between waves that meet. (412)
interferencia Interacción entre dos o más ondas que se encuentran.

International System of Units (SI) A system of units used by scientists to measure the properties of matter. (16, 237)
Sistema Internacional de Unidades (SI) Sistema de unidades que los científicos usan para medir las propiedades de la materia.

inversely proportional A term used to describe the relationship between two variables whose product is constant. (61)
inversamente proporcional Término usado para describir la relación entre dos variables cuyo producto es constante.

ion An atom or group of atoms that has become electrically charged. (131)
ión Átomo o grupo de átomos que está cargado eléctricamente.

ionic bond The attraction between oppositely charged ions. (132)
enlace iónico Atracción entre iones con cargas opuestas.

ionic compound A compound that consists of positive and negative ions. (132)
compuesto iónico Compuesto que tiene iones positivos y negativos.

iris The ring of muscle that surrounds the pupil and regulates the amount of light entering the eye; gives the eye its color. (511)
iris Disco de músculo que rodea la pupila y regula la cantidad de luz que entra al ojo; da color al ojo.

GLOSSARY

isotope An atom with the same number of protons and a different number of neutrons from other atoms of the same element. (79)
isótopo Átomo con el mismo número de protones y un número diferente de neutrones que otros átomos del mismo elemento.

-------------------- J --------------------

joule The amount of work you do when you exert a force of 1 newton to move an object a distance of 1 meter. (311)
julio Cantidad de trabajo que se produce al aplicar una fuerza de 1 newton para mover un objeto una distancia de 1 metro.

-------------------- K --------------------

Kelvin scale The temperature scale on which zero is the temperature at which no more energy can be removed from matter. (375)
escala Kelvin Escala de temperatura en la cual el cero es la temperatura a cuyo punto no se puede extraer más energía de la materia.

kinetic energy Energy that an object has due to its motion. (348)
energía cinética Energía que tiene un cuerpo debido a su movimiento.

-------------------- L --------------------

law of conservation of energy The rule that energy cannot be created or destroyed. (362)
ley de conservación de la energía Regla que dice que la energía no se puede crear ni destruir.

law of conservation of mass The principle that the total amount of matter is neither created nor destroyed during any chemical or physical change. (25, 174)
ley de conservación de la masa Principio que establece que la cantidad total de materia no se crea ni se destruye durante cambios químicos o físicos.

law of conservation of momentum The rule that in the absence of outside forces the total momentum of objects that interact does not change. (284)
principio de la conservación del momento Regla que establece que, en ausencia de fuerzas externas, la cantidad de movimiento total de los cuerpos que se relacionan no cambia.

lens 1. The flexible structure that focuses light that has entered the eye. **2.** A curved piece of glass or other transparent material that is used to refract light. (507)
lente 1. Estructura flexible que enfoca la luz que entra al ojo. **2.** Trozo curvo de vidrio u otro material transparente que se usa para refractar la luz.

lever A simple machine that consists of a rigid bar that pivots about a fixed point. (326)
palanca Máquina simple que consiste en una barra rígida que gira en torno a un punto fijo.

liquid A state of matter that has no definite shape but has a definite volume. (43)
líquido Estado de la materia que no tiene forma definida pero sí volumen definido.

longitudinal wave A wave that moves the medium in a direction parallel to the direction in which the wave travels. (400)
onda longitudinal Onda que mueve al medio en una dirección paralela a la dirección en la que se propaga la onda.

loudness Perception of the energy of a sound. (434)
volumen Percepción de la energía de un sonido.

luster The way a mineral reflects light from its surface. (90)
lustre Manera en la que un mineral refleja la luz en su superficie.

-------------------- M --------------------

machine A device that changes the amount of force exerted, the distance over which a force is exerted, or the direction in which force is exerted. (315)
máquina Dispositivo que altera la cantidad de fuerza ejercida, la distancia sobre que se ejerce la fuerza, o la dirección en la que se ejerce la fuerza.

magnet Any material that attracts iron and materials that contain iron. (567)
imán Material que atrae hierro o materiales que contienen el hierro.

magnetic declination The angle between geographic north and the north to which a compass needle points. (575)
declinación magnética Ángulo (en una ubicación particular) entre el norte geográfico y el polo magnético ubicado en el hemisferio norte de la Tierra.

magnetic field The region around a magnet where the magnetic force is exerted. (571)
campo magnético Área alrededor de un imán donde actúa la fuerza magnética.

magnetic field lines Lines that map out the magnetic field around a magnet. (571)
líneas del campo magnético Líneas que representan el campo magnético alrededor de un imán.

magnetic force A force produced when magnetic poles interact. (569)
fuerza magnética Fuerza que se produce cuando hay actividad entre los polos magnéticos.

magnetic pole The ends of a magnetic object, where the magnetic force is strongest. (568)
polo magnético Extremo de un cuerpo magnético, donde la fuerza magnética es mayor.

magnetism The force of attraction or repulsion of magnetic materials. (567)
magnetismo Poder de atracción o repulsión de los materiales magnéticos.

malleable A term used to describe material that can be hammered or rolled into flat sheets. (90)
maleable Término usado para describir materiales que se pueden convertir en láminas planas por medio de martillazos o con un rodillo.

mass A measure of how much matter is in an object. (16, 272)
masa Medida de cuánta materia hay en un cuerpo.

mass number The sum of protons and neutrons in the nucleus of an atom. (79)
número de masa Suma de los protones y neutrones en el núcleo de un átomo.

matter Anything that has mass and takes up space. (5)
materia Cualquier cosa que tiene masa y ocupa un espacio.

mechanical advantage The number of times a machine increases a force exerted on it. (318)
ventaja mecánica Número de veces que una máquina amplifica la fuerza que se ejerce sobre ella.

mechanical energy Kinetic or potential energy associated with the motion or position of an object. (352)
energía mecánica Energía cinética o potencial asociada con el movimiento o la posición de un cuerpo.

mechanical wave A wave that requires a medium through which to travel. (397)
onda mecánica Onda que necesita un medio por el cual propagarse.

medium The material through which a wave travels. (397)
medio Material a través del cual se propaga una onda.

melting The change in state from a solid to a liquid. (49)
fusión Cambio del estado sólido a líquido.

melting point The temperature at which a substance changes from a solid to a liquid; the same as the freezing point, or temperature at which a liquid changes to a solid. (49)
punto de fusión Temperatura a la que una sustancia cambia de estado sólido a líquido; es lo mismo que el punto de congelación (la temperatura a la que un líquido se vuelve sólido).

metal A class of elements characterized by physical properties that include shininess, malleability, ductility, and conductivity. (89)
metal Clase de elementos caracterizados por propiedades físicas que incluyen brillo, maleabilidad, ductilidad y conductividad.

metallic bond An attraction between a positive metal ion and the electrons surrounding it. (147)
enlace metálico Atracción entre un ión metálico positivo y los electrones que lo rodean.

metalloid An element that has some characteristics of both metals and nonmetals. (103)
metaloide Elemento que tiene algunas características de los metales y de los no metales.

microscope An instrument that makes small objects look larger. (517)
microscopio Instrumento que permite que los objetos pequeños se vean más grandes.

microwaves Electromagnetic waves that have shorter wavelengths and higher frequencies than radio waves. (467)
microondas Ondas electromagnéticas con longitudes de onda más cortas y frecuencias más altas que las ondas de radio.

mirage An image of a distant object caused by refraction of light as it travels through air of varying temperature. (506)
espejismo Imagen de un objeto distante causada por la refracción de la luz cuando viaja por el aire a temperaturas cambiantes.

mixture Two or more substances that are together in the same place but their atoms are not chemically bonded. (12)
mezcla Dos o más sustancias que están en el mismo lugar pero cuyos átomos no están químicamente enlazados.

molecular compound A compound that is composed of molecules. (141)
compuesto molecular Compuesto que tiene moléculas.

GLOSSARY

molecule A neutral group of two or more atoms held together by covalent bonds. (10, 139)
molécula Grupo neutral de dos o más átomos unidos por medio de enlaces covalentes.

momentum The product of an object's mass and velocity. (283)
momento Producto de la masa de un cuerpo multiplicada por su velocidad.

motion The state in which one object's distance from another is changing. (234)
movimiento Estado en el que la distancia entre un cuerpo y otro va cambiando.

music A set of sounds or notes combined in ways that are pleasing. (438)
música Conjunto de sonidos o notas que se combinan de una manera agradable.

N

nearsighted Having the condition in which a person can see nearby objects clearly and distant objects as blurry. (513)
miopía Condición en la que una persona ve con claridad los objetos cercanos y ve borrosos los objetos lejanos.

neutralization A reaction of an acid with a base, yielding a solution that is not as acidic or basic as the starting solutions were. (222)
neutralización Reacción de un ácido con una base, que produce una solución que no es ácida ni básica, como lo eran las soluciones originales.

neutron A small particle in the nucleus of the atom, with no electrical charge. (77)
neutrón Partícula pequeña en el núcleo del átomo, que no tiene carga eléctrica.

newton A unit of measure that equals the force required to accelerate 1 kilogram of mass at 1 meter per second per second. (263)
newton Unidad de medida equivalente a la fuerza necesaria para acelerar 1 kilogramo de masa a 1 metro por segundo cada segundo.

net force The overall force on an object when all the individual forces acting on it are added together. (264)
fuerza neta Fuerza total que se ejerce sobre un cuerpo cuando se suman las fuerzas individuales que actúan sobre él.

noble gas An element in Group 18 of the periodic table. (102)
gas noble Elemento del Grupo 18 de la tabla periódica.

node A point of zero amplitude on a standing wave. (414)
nodo Punto de amplitud cero de una onda estacionaria.

nonmetal An element that lacks most of the properties of a metal. (97)
no metal Elemento que carece de la mayoría de las propiedades de un metal.

nonpolar bond A covalent bond in which electrons are shared equally. (143)
enlace no polar Enlace covalente en el que los electrones se comparten por igual.

nuclear energy The potential energy stored in the nucleus of an atom. (355)
energía nuclear Energía potencial almacenada en el núcleo de un átomo.

nuclear reaction A reaction involving the particles in the nucleus of an atom that can change one element into another element. (107)
reacción nuclear Reacción en la que intervienen las partículas del núcleo de un átomo que puede transformar un elemento en otro.

nucleus 1. In cells, a large oval organelle that contains the cell's genetic material in the form of DNA and controls many of the cell's activities. **2.** The central core of an atom which contains protons and neutrons. **3.** The solid core of a comet. (75)
núcleo 1. En las células, orgánulo grande y ovalado que contiene el material genético de la célula en forma de ADN y que controla muchas de las funciones celulares. **2.** Parte central del átomo que contiene los protones y los neutrones. **3.** Centro sólido de un cometa.

O

objective 1. A lens that gathers light from an object and forms a real image. **2.** Describes the act of decision-making or drawing conclusions based on available evidence. (516)
objetivo 1. Lente que reúne la luz de un objeto y forma una imagen real. **2.** Describe el acto de tomar una decisión o llegar a una conclusión basándose en la evidencia disponible.

Ohm's law The law that states that resistance in a circuit is equal to voltage divided by current. (546)
ley de Ohm Regla que establece que la resistencia en un circuito es equivalente al voltaje dividido por la corriente.

opaque A type of material that reflects or absorbs all of the light that strikes it. (491)
material opaco Material que refleja o absorbe toda la luz que llega a él.

open system A system in which matter can enter from or escape to the surroundings. (175)
sistema abierto Sistema en el que la materia puede escapar a sus alrededores o entrar desde ahí.

optic nerve Short, thick nerve that carries signals from the eye to the brain. (512)
nervio óptico Nervio corto y grueso que lleva señales del ojo al cerebro.

optical axis An imaginary line that divides a mirror in half. (499)
eje óptico Recta imaginaria que divide un espejo por la mitad.

output force The force exerted on an object by a machine. (315)
fuerza desarrollada Fuerza que una máquina ejerce sobre un cuerpo.

overtone A natural frequency that is a multiple of the fundamental tone's frequency. (439)
armónico Frecuencia natural que es un múltiplo de la frecuencia del tono fundamental.

—————————— **P** ——————————

parallel circuit An electric circuit in which different parts of the circuit are on separate branches. (549)
circuito paralelo Circuito eléctrico en el que las distintas partes del circuito se encuentran en ramas separadas.

period 1. A horizontal row of elements in the periodic table. **2.** One of the units of geologic time into which geologists divide eras. (86)
período 1. Fila horizontal de los elementos de la tabla periódica. **2.** Una de las unidades del tiempo geológico en las que los geólogos dividen las eras.

periodic table An arrangement of the elements showing the repeating pattern of their properties. (82)
tabla periódica Configuración de los elementos que muestra el patrón repetido de sus propiedades.

pH scale A range of values used to indicate how acidic or basic a substance is; expresses the concentration of hydrogen ions in a solution. (220)
escala de pH Rango de valores que se usa para indicar cuán ácida o básica es una sustancia; expresa la concentración de iones hidrógeno de una solución.

photoelectric effect The ejection of electrons from a substance when light is shined on it. (463)
efecto fotoeléctrico Expulsión de electrones de una sustancia al ser iluminada.

photon A tiny particle or packet of light energy. (463)
fotón Partícula diminuta o paquete de energía luminosa.

physical change A change that alters the form or appearance of a material but does not make the material into another substance. (21, 164)
cambio físico Cambio que altera la forma o apariencia de un material, pero que no convierte el material en otra sustancia.

physical property A characteristic of a pure substance that can be observed without changing it into another substance. (6)
propiedad física Característica de una sustancia pura que se puede observar sin convertirla en otra sustancia.

pigment 1. A colored chemical compound that absorbs light. **2.** A colored substance used to color other materials. (495)
pigmento 1. Compuesto químico que absorbe luz. **2.** Sustancia de color que se usa para teñir otros materiales.

pitch A description of how a sound is perceived as high or low. (432)
tono Descripción de un sonido que se percibe como alto o bajo.

plane mirror A flat mirror that produces an upright, virtual image the same size as the object. (498)
espejo plano Espejo liso que produce una imagen virtual vertical del mismo tamaño que el objeto.

polar bond A covalent bond in which electrons are shared unequally. (143)
enlace polar Enlace covalente en el que los electrones se comparten de forma desigual.

polarization The process through which electrons are attracted to or repelled by an external electric field, causing the electrons to move within their own atoms. (533)
polarización Proceso por el cual un campo eléctrico externo atrae o repele a los electrones y hace que éstos se muevan dentro de su átomo.

GLOSSARY

polarized light Light that has been filtered so that all of its waves are parallel to each other. (462)
luz polarizada Luz que se ha filtrado de manera que sus ondas queden paralelas unas con otras.

polyatomic ion An ion that is made of more than one atom. (132)
ión poliatómico Ión formado por más de un átomo.

potential energy The energy an object has because of its position; also the internal stored energy of an object, such as energy stored in chemical bonds. (350)
energía potencial Energía que tiene un cuerpo por su posición; también es la energía interna almacenada de un cuerpo, como la energía almacenada en los enlaces químicos.

power The rate at which one form of energy is transformed into another. (312, 552)
potencia Rapidez de la conversión de una forma de energía en otra.

precipitate A solid that forms from a solution during a chemical reaction. (166)
precipitado Sólido que se forma de una solución durante una reacción química.

pressure The force pushing on a surface divided by the area of that surface. (46)
presión Fuerza que actúa contra una superficie, dividida entre el área de esa superficie.

primary color One of three colors that can be used to make any other color. (494)
color primario Uno de los tres colores que se pueden usar para hacer cualquier color.

product A substance formed as a result of a chemical reaction. (164)
producto Sustancia formada como resultado de una reacción química.

protons Small, positively charged particles that are found in the nucleus of an atom. (75)
protones Partículas pequeñas de carga positiva que se encuentran en el núcleo de un átomo.

pulley A simple machine that consists of a grooved wheel with a rope or cable wrapped around it. (331)
polea Máquina simple que consiste en una rueda con un surco en el que yace una cuerda o cable.

pupil The opening in the center of the iris through which light enters the inside of the eye. (511)
pupila Apertura en el centro del iris por donde entra la luz al ojo.

R

radar A system that uses reflected radio waves to detect objects and measure their distance and speed. (467)
radar Sistema que usa ondas de radio reflejadas para detectar cuerpos y medir su distancia y velocidad.

radiation The transfer of energy by electromagnetic waves. (379)
radiación Transferencia de energía por medio de ondas magnéticas.

radio waves Electromagnetic waves with the longest wavelengths and lowest frequencies. (466)
ondas de radio Ondas electromagnéticas con las longitudes de onda más largas y las frecuencias más bajas.

radioactive dating The process of determining the age of an object using the half-life of one or more radioactive isotopes. (111)
datación radiactiva Proceso para determinar la edad de un objeto usando la vida media de uno o más isótopos radiactivos.

radioactive decay The process in which the nuclei of radioactive elements break down, releasing fast-moving particles and energy. (107)
desintegración radiactiva Proceso de descomposición del núcleo de un elemento radiactivo que libera partículas de movimiento rápido y energía.

radioactivity The spontaneous emission of radiation by an unstable atomic nucleus. (108)
radiactividad Emisión espontánea de radiación por un núcleo atómico inestable.

rarefaction The part of a longitudinal wave where the particles of the medium are far apart. (400)
rarefacción Parte de una onda longitudinal donde las partículas del medio están muy apartadas entre sí.

ray A straight line used to represent a light wave. (496)
rayo Línea recta que se usa para representar una onda de luz.

reactant A substance that enters into a chemical reaction. (164)
reactante Sustancia que interviene en una reacción química.

reactivity The ease and speed with which an element combines, or reacts, with other elements and compounds. (91)
reactividad Facilidad y rapidez con las que un elemento se combina, o reacciona, con otros elementos y compuestos.

real image An upside-down image formed where rays of light meet. (499)
imagen real Imagen invertida formada en el punto de encuentro de los rayos de luz.

reference point A place or object used for comparison to determine if an object is in motion. (235)
punto de referencia Lugar u objeto usado como medio de comparación para determinar si un objeto está en movimiento.

reflecting telescope A telescope that uses a curved mirror to collect and focus light. (516)
telescopio de reflexión Telescopio que usa un espejo curvado para captar y enfocar la luz.

reflection The bouncing back of an object or a wave when it hits a surface through which it cannot pass. (409)
reflexión Rebote de un cuerpo o una onda al golpear una superficie que no puede atravesar.

refracting telescope A telescope that uses convex lenses to gather and focus light. (516)
telescopio de refracción Telescopio que usa lentes convexas para captar y enfocar la luz.

refraction The bending of waves as they enter a new medium at an angle, caused by a change in speed. (410)
refracción Cambio de dirección de las ondas al entrar en un nuevo medio con un determinado ángulo, y a consecuencia de un cambio de velocidad.

regular reflection Reflection that occurs when parallel rays of light hit a smooth surface and all reflect at the same angle. (497)
reflexión regular Reflexión que ocurre cuando rayos de luz paralelos chocan contra una superficie lisa y se reflejan en el mismo ángulo.

replacement A reaction in which one element replaces another in a compound or when two elements in different compounds trade places. (180)
sustitución Reacción en la que un elemento reemplaza a otro en un compuesto o en la que se intercambian dos elementos de diferentes compuestos.

resistance The measurement of how difficult it is for charges to flow through an object. (542)
resistencia Medida de la dificultad de una carga eléctrica para fluir por un cuerpo.

resonance The increase in the amplitude of a vibration that occurs when external vibrations match an object's natural frequency. (415)
resonancia Aumento en la amplitud de vibración que ocurre cuando vibraciones externas corresponden con la frecuencia natural de un cuerpo.

retina The layer of receptor cells at the back of the eye on which an image is focused. (512)
retina Capa de células receptoras de la parte posterior del ojo donde se enfoca una imagen.

rods Cells in the retina that detect dim light. (512)
bastones Células de la retina que detectan la luz tenue.

rolling friction Friction that occurs when an object rolls over a surface. (269)
fricción de rodamiento Fricción que ocurre cuando un cuerpo rueda sobre una superficie.

S

salt An ionic compound made from the neutralization of an acid with a base. (223)
sal Compuesto iónico formado por la neutralización de un ácido con una base.

satellite 1. An object that orbits a planet. **2.** Any object that orbits around another object in space. (288)
satélite 1. Cuerpo que orbita alrededor de un planeta. **2.** Cualquier cuerpo que orbita alrededor de otro cuerpo en el espacio.

saturated solution A mixture that contains as much dissolved solute as is possible at a given temperature. (207)
solución saturada Mezcla que contiene la mayor cantidad posible de soluto disuelto a una temperatura determinada.

screw A simple machine that is an inclined plane wrapped around a central cylinder to form a spiral. (325)
tornillo Máquina simple que consiste en un plano inclinado enrollado alrededor de un cilindro central para formar una espiral.

secondary color Any color produced by combining equal amounts of any two primary colors. (494)
color secundario Color producido al combinar iguales cantidades de dos colores primarios cualesquiera.

semiconductor A substance that can conduct electric current under some conditions. (103)
semiconductor Sustancia que puede conducir una corriente eléctrica bajo ciertas condiciones.

series circuit An electric circuit in which all parts are connected one after another along one path. (548)
circuito en serie Circuito eléctrico en el que todas las partes se conectan una tras otra en una trayectoria.

GLOSSARY

short circuit A connection that allows current to take the path of least resistance. (555)
cortocircuito Conexión que permite que la corriente siga el camino de menor resistencia.

simple machine The most basic device for making work easier, these are the smaller building blocks for complex machines. (323)
máquina simple Aparatos sencillos que facilitan el trabajo; son los componentes de las máquinas compuestas.

sliding friction Friction that occurs when one solid surface slides over another. (268)
fricción de deslizamiento Fricción que ocurre cuando una superficie sólida se desliza sobre otra.

slope The steepness of a graph line; the ratio of the vertical change (the rise) to the horizontal change (the run). (244)
pendiente Inclinación de una gráfica lineal; la razón del cambio vertical (el ascenso) al cambio horizontal (el avance).

solenoid A coil of wire with a current. (580)
solenoide Bobina de alambre con una corriente.

solid A state of matter that has a definite shape and a definite volume. (41)
sólido Estado en el que la materia tiene forma y volumen definidos.

solubility A measure of how much solute can dissolve in a given solvent at a given temperature. (207)
solubilidad Medida de cuánto soluto se puede disolver en un solvente a una temperatura dada.

solute The part of a solution that is dissolved by a solvent. (199)
soluto Parte de una solución que se disuelve en un solvente.

solution A mixture containing a solvent and at least one solute that has the same properties throughout; a mixture in which one substance is dissolved in another. (199)
solución Mezcla que contiene un solvente y al menos un soluto, y que tiene propiedades uniformes; mezcla en la que una sustancia se disuelve en otra.

solvent The part of a solution that is usually present in the largest amount and dissolves a solute. (199)
solvente Parte de una solución que, por lo general, está presente en la mayor cantidad y que disuelve a un soluto.

sonar A system that uses reflected sound waves to locate and determine the distance to objects under water. (448)
sónar Sistema que usa ondas sonoras reflejadas para detectar y localizar objetos bajo agua.

sonogram An image formed using reflected ultrasound waves. (449)
sonograma Formación de una imagen usando ondas de ultrasonido reflejadas.

specific heat The amount of heat required to raise the temperature of 1 kilogram of a material by 1 kelvin, which is equivalent to 1°C. (384)
calor específico Cantidad de calor que se requiere para elevar la temperatura de 1 kilogramo de un material en 1°C.

speed The distance an object travels per unit of time. (239)
rapidez Distancia que viaja un objeto por unidad de tiempo.

standing wave A wave that appears to stand in one place, even though it is two waves interfering as they pass through each other. (414)
onda estacionaria Onda que parece permanecer en un lugar, y que en realidad es la interferencia de dos ondas que se atraviesan.

static discharge The loss of static electricity as electric charges transfer from one object to another. (534)
descarga estática Pérdida de la electricidad estática cuando las cargas eléctricas se transfieren de un cuerpo a otro.

static electricity A buildup of charges on an object. (531)
electricidad estática Acumulación de cargas eléctricas en un cuerpo.

static friction Friction that acts between objects that are not moving. (268)
fricción estática Fricción que actúa sobre los cuerpos que no están en movimiento.

sublimation The change in state from a solid directly to a gas without passing through the liquid state. (53)
sublimación Cambio del estado sólido directamente a gas, sin pasar por el estado líquido.

subscript A number in a chemical formula that tells the number of atoms in a molecule or the ratio of elements in a compound. (134)
subíndice Número en una fórmula química que indica el número de átomos que tiene una molécula o la razón de elementos en un compuesto.

substance A single kind of matter that is pure and has a specific set of properties. (5)
sustancia Tipo único de materia que es pura y tiene propiedades específicas.

surface tension The result of an inward pull among the molecules of a liquid that brings the molecules on the surface closer together; causes the surface to act as if it has a thin skin. (44)
tensión superficial Resultado de la atracción hacia el centro entre las moléculas de un líquido, que hace que las moléculas de la superficie se acerquen mucho, y que la superficie actúe como si tuviera una piel delgada.

suspension A mixture in which particles can be seen and easily separated by settling or filtration. (201)
suspensión Mezcla en la cual las partículas se pueden ver y separar fácilmente por fijación o por filtración.

synthesis A chemical reaction in which two or more simple substances combine to form a new, more complex substance. (180)
síntesis Reacción química en la que dos o más sustancias simples se combinan y forman una sustancia nueva más compleja.

T

telescope An optical instrument that forms enlarged images of distant objects. (516)
telescopio Instrumento óptico que provee ampliaciones de los cuerpos lejanos.

temperature How hot or cold something is; a measure of the average energy of motion of the particles of a substance; the measure of the average kinetic energy of the particles of a substance. (26, 374)
temperatura Cuán caliente o frío es algo; medida de la energía de movimiento promedio de las partículas de una sustancia; medida de la energía cinética promedio de las partículas de una sustancia.

thermal conductivity The ability of an object to transfer heat. (90)
conductividad térmica Capacidad de un objeto para transferir calor.

thermal energy The total kinetic and potential energy of all the particles of an object. (26, 356)
energía térmica Energía cinética y potencial total de las partículas de un cuerpo.

thermal expansion The expansion of matter when it is heated. (385)
expansión térmica Expansión de la materia cuando se calienta.

thermogram An image that shows regions of different temperatures in different colors. (468)
termograma Imagen que muestra regiones de distintas temperaturas con distintos colores.

third prong The round prong of a plug that connects any metal pieces in an appliance to the safety grounding wire of a building. (555)
tercera terminal Terminal redondeado de un enchufe que conecta cualquier pieza de metal de un artefacto con el cable a tierra de un edificio.

tracer A radioactive isotope that can be followed through the steps of a chemical reaction or industrial process. (112)
trazador Isótopo radiactivo que se puede seguir mediante los pasos de una reacción química o un proceso industrial.

transformer A device that increases or decreases voltage, which often consists of two separate coils of insulated wire wrapped around an iron core. (594)
transformador Aparato que aumenta o disminuye el voltaje, que consiste de dos bobinas de alambre aislado y devanado sobre un núcleo de hierro.

transition metal One of the elements in Groups 3 through 12 of the periodic table. (93)
metal de transición Uno de los elementos de los Grupos 3 a 12 de la tabla periódica.

translucent A type of material that scatters light as it passes through. (491)
material traslúcido Material que dispersa la luz cuando ésta lo atraviesa.

transparent A type of material that transmits light without scattering it. (491)
material transparente Material que transmite luz sin dispersarla.

transverse wave A wave that moves the medium at right angles to the direction in which the wave travels. (399)
onda transversal Onda que desplaza a un medio perpendicularmente a la dirección en la que viaja la onda.

triple bond A chemical bond formed when atoms share three pairs of electrons. (140)
enlace triple Enlace químico formado cuando los átomos comparten tres pares de electrones.

trough The lowest part of a transverse wave. (399)
valle Parte más baja de una onda transversal.

GLOSSARY

U

ultrasound Sound waves with frequencies above 20,000 Hz. (447)
ultrasonido Ondas sonoras con frecuencias mayores de 20,000 Hz.

ultraviolet rays Electromagnetic waves with wavelengths shorter than visible light but longer than X-rays. (469)
rayos ultravioleta Ondas electromagnéticas con longitudes de onda más cortas que la luz visible pero mas largas que los rayos X.

V

valence electrons The electrons that are in the highest energy level of an atom and that are involved in chemical bonding. (125)
electrones de valencia Electrones que tienen el nivel más alto de energía de un átomo y que intervienen en los enlaces químicos.

vaporization The change of state from a liquid to a gas. (51)
vaporización Cambio del estado de líquido a gas.

velocity Speed in a given direction. (242)
velocidad Rapidez en una dirección dada.

vibration A repeated back-and-forth or up-and-down motion. (398)
vibración Movimiento repetido hacia delante y hacia atrás o hacia arriba y hacia abajo.

virtual image An upright image formed where rays of light appear to come from. (498)
imagen virtual Imagen vertical que se forma desde donde parecen provenir los rayos de luz.

viscosity A liquid's resistance to flowing. (44)
viscosidad Resistencia a fluir que presenta un líquido.

visible light Electromagnetic radiation that can be seen with the unaided eye. (469)
luz visible Radiación electromagnética que se puede ver a simple vista.

voltage The difference in electrical potential energy per charge between two places in a circuit. (541)
voltaje Diferencia en el potencial eléctrico que hay entre dos áreas de un circuito.

volume The amount of space that matter occupies. (17)
volumen Cantidad de espacio que ocupa la materia.

W

watt The unit of power when one joule of work is done in one second. (313)
vatio Unidad de potencia equivalente a un julio por segundo.

wave 1. A disturbance that transfers energy from place to place. **2.** The movement of energy through a body of water. (397)
onda 1. Perturbación que transfiere energía de un lugar a otro. **2.** Movimiento de energía por un fluido.

wavelength The distance between two corresponding parts of a wave, such as the distance between two crests. (404)
longitud de onda Distancia entre dos partes correspondientes de una onda, por ejemplo la distancia entre dos crestas.

wedge A simple machine that is an inclined plane that moves. (324)
cuña Máquina simple que consiste de un plano inclinado que se mueve.

weight A measure of the force of gravity acting on an object. (15, 273)
peso Medida de la fuerza de gravedad que actúa sobre un objeto.

wheel and axle A simple machine that consists of two attached circular or cylindrical objects that rotate about a common axis, each one with a different radius. (333)
rueda y eje Máquina simple que consiste en dos objetos circulares o cilíndricos unidos, de diferente radio, que giran en torno a un eje común.

work Force exerted on an object that causes it to move. (308)
trabajo Fuerza que se ejerce sobre un cuerpo para moverlo.

X

X-rays Electromagnetic waves with wavelengths shorter than ultraviolet rays but longer than gamma rays. (470)
rayos X Ondas electromagnéticas con longitudes de onda más cortas que los rayos ultravioleta pero más largas que los rayos gamma.

INDEX

Page numbers for key terms are printed in **boldface** type.

A

Absolute zero, 375
Acceleration, 246, 247–252
  due to gravity, 287
  graphing, 250–251
  and Newton's Second Law of Motion, 276–277
Acids, 213, 214
  measuring pH, 220
  neutralization, **222,** 223
  in solution, 219
Actinides, 94
Action-reaction forces, 278–279
Activation energy, 183, 184, 187
Air. *See* Atmosphere
Alkali metals, 92, 128
Alkaline earth metals, 92
Alloys, 151
Alpha particles, 109, 110
Alternating current (AC), 591
Aluminum, 94
Ammonia, 10
Amorphous metal, 157
Amorphous solids, 42
Ampere (A), 546, 553
Amplitude, 403, 404–405
  increasing and decreasing, 412–413
  of radio waves, 474
Amplitude modulation (AM), 474
Antinodes of waves, 414
Application of skills
  Apply It!, 7, 9, 18, 23, 50, 75–76, 83, 91, 98, 103, 127, 135–136, 139, 150, 164, 173, 180, 186, 199, 209, 217, 221, 236, 239, 241, 265, 270, 283, 289, 292, 295, 311, 320, 323, 325, 327, 332, 354, 359, 376, 381, 400, 411, 435, 439, 443, 448, 463, 467, 493, 501, 509, 511, 515, 534, 539, 569, 573, 581
  Do the Math!, 63, 595
    analyze data, 475, 504
    apply concepts, 177, 430
    calculate, 46, 111, 185, 206, 249, 277, 293, 313, 349, 384, 406, 417, 546, 553, 575, 595
    control variables, 61, 292
    create data tables, 287
    draw conclusions, 27, 319, 349, 384
    explain, 203, 292, 296
    graph, 61, 142, 169, 319, 585
    infer, 430
    interpret data, 93, 169, 203, 319, 475, 504, 575
    interpret tables, 384, 430

    make generalizations, 61
    predict, 142, 319, 504, 546
    read graphs, 93, 169, 203, 319
  Science Matters
    An Antiuniverse?, 35
    Can You Hear Me Now?, 454
    Channel Surfin' on the Infrared Wave, 484
    Charge It!, 368
    Discovery of the Elements, 118
    Elements of the Human Body, 119
    Forceful Fluids, 303
    Going Green, 561
    Good Things Come in Small Packages, 340
    Growing Snow, 67
    Hiding in Plain Sight, 523
    Hurricane Warning, 391
    Limestone and Acid Drainage, 228
    Long Ago in a Faraway Land, 34
    Magnetic Pictures, 600
    A New Set of Wheels, 341
    Noisy Occupations, 455
    An Operatic Superpower, 421
    Pharmacists: Chemists at Work, 156
    Power It Up!, 369
    Puny Power Plants, 485
    The Race for Speed, 256
    A Race to the Finish!, 193
    Safety Restraints, 302
    Science Athletes Let the Games Begin, 341
    Sci-Fi Metal, 157
    Scuba Diving, 66
    Seeing Double, 522
    A Shocking Message!, 601
    A Shocking State, 67
    Shrinking Storehouse, 192
    Something for Nothing, 560
    Stop Sign, 257
    The Superhero of Glues, 157
    Tornado Alley, 390
    Vinegar, 229
    Wall of Water, 420
Apply It!. *See* Application of skills
Art conservation scientist, 4
Assessment
  Assess Your Understanding, 7, 11, 13, 17, 19, 22, 25, 29, 42, 44, 47, 50, 52, 55, 57, 59, 61, 76, 79, 82, 85, 87, 91, 95, 98, 105, 108, 110, 113, 129, 133, 135, 137, 140, 142, 145, 147, 151, 165, 169, 173, 179, 181, 184, 187,

201, 203, 206, 211, 217, 221, 223, 237, 241, 243, 245, 249, 251, 263, 265, 270, 273, 275, 277, 281, 285, 287, 289, 292, 297, 311, 313, 317, 319, 321, 325, 329, 333, 335, 347, 351, 354, 357, 361, 363, 375, 377, 381, 385, 398, 401, 405, 407, 411, 413, 415, 428, 431, 433, 435, 437, 441, 445, 449, 461, 463, 465, 471, 475, 477, 479, 493, 495, 497, 501, 506, 509, 513, 517, 530, 535, 538–539, 543, 546, 551, 554–555, 567, 569, 573, 575, 578–579, 581, 583, 585, 587, 591, 593, 595
  Review and Assessment, 31–32, 63–64, 115–116, 153–154, 189–190, 225–226, 253–254, 299–300, 337–338, 365–366, 387–388, 417–418, 451–452, 481–482, 519–520, 557–558, 597–598
  Standardized Test Prep, 33, 65, 117, 155, 191, 227, 255, 301, 339, 367, 389, 419, 453, 483, 521, 559, 599
  Study Guide, 30, 62, 114, 152, 188, 224, 252, 298, 336, 364, 386, 416, 450, 480, 518, 556, 596
Atmosphere, 97
Atomic mass, 81, 83
Atomic mass units (amu), 78
Atomic number, 78, 83, 126
Atoms, 8, **10, 73,** 74–79
  Bohr's model, 75
  bonded, 139–145, 167
  cloud model, 76
  and conservation of mass, 174–177
  Dalton's atomic theory, 73
  and elements, 125–129
  and ions, 131–137
  isotopes, 79
  and metals, 146–151
  modern model, 77–79
  particle charges and masses, 77–78
  and periodic table, 80, **82,** 83–87
  Rutherford's model, 74–75
  Thomson's model, 74
  See also Molecules
Average speed, 240

INDEX

Page numbers for key terms are printed in **boldface** type.

INDEX

Page numbers for key terms are printed in **boldface** type.

INDEX

Page numbers for key terms are printed in **boldface type.**

INDEX

Page numbers for key terms are printed in **boldface type.**

ACKNOWLEDGMENTS

Staff Credits

The people who made up the *Interactive Science* team—representing composition services, core design digital and multimedia production services, digital product development, editorial, editorial services, manufacturing, and production—are listed below:

Jan Van Aarsen, Samah Abadir, Ernie Albanese, Chris Anton, Zareh Artinian, Bridget Binstock, Suzanne Biron, Niki Birbilis, MJ Black, Nancy Bolsover, Stacy Boyd, Jim Brady, Laura Brancky, Katherine Bryant, Michael Burstein, Pradeep Byram, Jessica Chase, Jonathan Cheney, Sitha Chhor, Arthur Ciccone, Allison Cook-Bellistri, Brandon Cole, Karen Corliss, Rebecca Cottingham, AnnMarie Coyne, Bob Craton, Chris Deliee, Paul Delsignore, Michael Di Maria, Diane Dougherty, Nancy Duffner, Kristen Ellis, Kelly Engel, Theresa Eugenio, Amanda Ferguson, Jorgensen Fernandez, Kathryn Fobert, Alicia Franke, Louise Gachet, Julia Gecha, Mark Geyer, Steve Gobbell, Paula Gogan-Porter, Jeffrey Gong, Sandra Graff, Robert M. Graham, Maureen Griffin, Adam Groffman, Lynette Haggard, Christian Henry, Karen Holtzman, Guy Huff, Susan Hutchinson, Sharon Inglis, Marian Jones, Sumy Joy, Chris Kammer, Sheila Kanitsch, Courtenay Kelley, Chris Kennedy, Toby Klang, Alyse Kondrat, Greg Lam, Russ Lappa, Margaret LaRaia, David Leistensnider, Ben Leveillee, Thea Limpus, Charles Luey, Dotti Marshall, Kathy Martin, Robyn Matzke, John McClure, Mary Beth McDaniel, Krista McDonald, Tim McDonald, Rich McMahon, Cara McNally, Bernadette McQuilkin, Melinda Medina, Angelina Mendez, Maria Milczarek, Claudi Mimo, Mike Napieralski, Deborah Nicholls, Dave Nichols, Anthony Nuccio, William Oppenheimer, Jodi O'Rourke, Julie Orr, Ameer Padshah, Lorie Park, Celio Pedrosa, Jonathan Penyack, Linda Zust Reddy, Jennifer Reichlin, Stephen Rider, Charlene Rimsa, Walter Rodriguez, Stephanie Rogers, Marcy Rose, Rashid Ross, Anne Rowsey, Manuel Sanchez, Logan Schmidt, Amanda Seldera, Laurel Smith, Nancy Smith, Ted Smykal, Sandy Schneider, Emily Soltanoff, Cindy Strowman, Dee Sunday, Barry Tomack, Elizabeth Tustian, Patricia Valencia, Ana Sofia Villaveces, Stephanie Wallace, Amanda Watters, Christine Whitney, Brad Wiatr, Heidi Wilson, Heather Wright, James Yagelski, Tim Yetzina, Rachel Youdelman.

Photographs

Every effort has been made to secure permission and provide appropriate credit for photographic material. The publisher deeply regrets any omission and pledges to correct errors called to its attention in subsequent editions.

Unless otherwise acknowledged, all photographs are the property of Pearson Education, Inc.

Photo locators denoted as follows: Top (T), Center (C), Bottom (B), Left (L), Right (R), Background (Bkgd)

Cover

Tony McConnell / Photo Researchers, Inc.

Front Matter

i Caitlin Mirra/Shutterstock; **vi** (TR) Nordic Photos/PhotoLibrary Group, Inc.; **vii** (TR) Michael C. York/©Associated Press; **viii** (TR) Tom Schierlitz/Getty Images; **ix** (TR) Javier Trueba/Madrid Scientific Films; **x** (TR) N A Callow/Science Source; **xi** (TR) David Doubilet/National Geographic Image Collection; **xii** (TR) Brian Snyder/Reuters Media, (TR) Liane Cary/AGE Fotostock; **xiv** (TR) Roland Weihrauch/AFP/Getty Images; **xv** (TR) Max Rossi/Reuters Media; **xvi** (TR) Nutscode/T Service/Photo Researchers, Inc.; **xvii** (TR) Corbis; **xviii** (TR) ©Associated Press; **xix** (TR) Don Carstens/Robertstock; **xx** (TR) Cloud Gate, Millennium Park, Chicago(2004), Anish Kapoor. Photo ©2008 Kim Karpeles/Kim Karpeles Photography; **xxi** (TR) Nick Suydam/Alamy Images; **xxii** (TR) Corbis; **xxiii** (TC) iStockphoto; **xxxvi** (Bkgrd) Nordic Photos/PhotoLibrary Group, Inc.

3 (BL) John Shaw/Science Source, (TL) Nigel Hicks/Dorling Kindersley/©DK Images; **4** (TCR) Nicolo Orsi Battaglini/Art Resource, NY, (CR) Scala/Ministero per i Beni e le Attività culturali/Art Resource, NY; **5** (BR) Katy Williamson/©DK Images, (BL) Nigel Hicks/Dorling Kindersley/©DK Images; **6** (B) ArabianEye/Getty Images, (BR) jlsohio/iStockphoto, (BC) Wave RF/Photolibrary Group, Inc.; **7** (C) Andy Crawford/©DK Images, (TC) Nicole Hill/Rubberball/Photolibrary Group, Inc.; **9** (BCR) ©DK Images, (CL) Ashok Rodrigues/iStockphoto, (CR) Judy Ledbetter/iStockphoto, (C) Thinkstock, (BL) webking/iStockphoto; **10** (C) Max Blain/Shutterstock; **11** (CC) Albert J. Copley/age Fotostock/PhotoLibrary Group, Inc., (C) Mark A. Schneider/Photo Researchers, Inc., (CR) Steve Gorton/©DK Images; **13** (CL) Charles D. Winters/Photo Researchers, Inc.; **14** (CR) Juergen Hasenkopf/Alamy Images, (B) Patrick Robert/Corbis; **16** (TL) Drew Hadley/iStockphoto, (R) Mark Lennihan/©Associated Press; **19** (CL) ©The Granger Collection, NY, (CR) Charles D. Winters/Photo Researchers, Inc., (BCR) Harry Taylor/©DK Images, (TR) Steve Gorton/©DK Images; **20** (B) Entienou/iStockphoto; **21** (BR) Carolyn Kaster/©Associated Press; **22** (TL) Elena Schweitzer/iStockphoto; **23** (CR) Courtesy of North Carolina State Bureau of Investigation, Raleigh NC/North Carolina State Bureau of Investigation, (B) Rich Legg/iStockphoto; **24** (TL) Anthony Upton/PA Wire URN/©Associated Press; **26** (CL) Jonathan Hayward/©Associated Press, (BR) Umit Bektas/Reuters Media; **27** (CR) John Shaw/Science Source; **28** (B) Amr Nabil/©Associated Press, (TCR) AudsDad/iStockphoto, (T) Jakub Semeniuk/iStockphoto, (C) Matthew J. Sroka/Reading Eagle/©Associated Press; **29** (C) Jim Jurica/iStockphoto; **30** (TR) Nigel Hicks/Dorling Kindersley/©DK Images, (BR) Umit Bektas/Reuters Media; **34** (L) The Art Gallery Collection/Alamy Images; **35** (CR) American Institute of Physics/Photo Researchers, Inc., (B) Lawrence Berkeley National Laboratory/Science Photo Library/Photo Researchers, Inc.; **36** (B) Michael C. York/©Associated Press; **39** (TCL) BC Photography/Alamy, (BL) Charles Winters/Photo Researchers, Inc., (BCL) SuperStock; **40** (B) James M. Bell/Photo Researchers, Inc., (BC) Ryan Pyle/Corbis; **42** (CR) Mark A. Schneider/Photo Researchers, Inc., (CL) Sue Atkinson/Fresh Food Images/PhotoLibrary Group, Inc.; **44** (TL) BC Photography/Alamy; **45** (BR) Charles D. Winters/Photo Researchers, Inc.; **47** (TL) Frits Meyst/Adventure4ever; **48** (BL) Simon Butcher/Imagestate/PhotoLibrary Group, Inc.; **49** (BR) SuperStock; **50** (TR) Winfield Parks/National Geographic Image Collection; **53** (BC) Charles Winters/Photo Researchers, Inc., (CR) Frank Greenaway/©DK Images, (B) Neal Preston/Corbis; **54** (BR) Andreas Kuehn/Getty Images, (CL) Wolfgang Weinhäupl/Westend61 GmbH/Alamy; **55** (CL) European Pressphoto Agency creative account/Alamy, (BL) Kat Fahrer/Middletown

Journal/©Associated Press, (TC) Odilon Dimier/Photolibrary Group, Inc.; **62** (CR) European Pressphoto Agency creative account/Alamy, (TR) Mark A. Schneider/Photo Researchers, Inc.; **64** (TCR) David Branch/©Associated Press; **66** (L) Sami Sarkis/Getty Images; **67** (TR) Stephen Lockett/Alamy Images, (BL) Ted Kinsman/Photo Researchers, Inc.; **68** (B) B2M Productions/Photolibrary Group, Inc.; **71** (BCL) NASA/ Photo Researchers, Inc., (TCL) Tom Schierlitz/Getty Images; **72** (BC) Nano-Tex, Inc./©Associated Press; **73** (B) Novastock/ PhotoLibrary Group, Inc.; **74** (TL) Paul Blundell Photography/ Fresh Food Images/PhotoLibrary Group, Inc.; **75** (TR) Iconotec/ Photolibrary Group, Inc., (BR) Martin Bond/Photo Researchers, Inc.; **76** (CR) Corey Radlund/Brand X Pictures/Photolibrary Group, Inc., (T) Milton Wordley/PhotoLibrary Group, Inc., (C) Steve Gorton and Gary Ombler/©DK Images, (TCR) Steve Gorton/©DK Images; **78** (L) DLILLC/Corbis, (BC) William Steinecker; **80** (C) Portrait of Dmitry Ivanovich Mendeleyev (ca. 1865). Archives Larousse, Paris, France/Bridgeman Art Library; **81** (BL, BC) Copyright ©2008 Richard Megna /Fundamental Photographs, NYC, (BR) Copyright ©2008 Richard Megna/Fundamental Photographs, NYC; **83** (BL) ©DK Images; **86** (BR, BL, BC) Charles D. Winters/Photo Researchers, Inc.; **87** (C) Charles D. Winters/Photo Researchers, Inc., (BCR) Kim Kyung Hoon/Reuters Media, (TR) PjrStudio/Alamy Images; **88** (CR) Douglas Whyte/Corbis, (CC) Luis Carlos Torres/ iStockphoto; **90** (TR) Charles D. Winters/Photo Researchers, Inc., (TL) Joel Arem/Photo Researchers, Inc., (BL) Keith Webber Jr./iStockphoto, (TC) László Rákoskerti/iStockphoto, (CL) Peter Spiro/iStockphoto; **91** (CR) Kai Schwabe/Photolibrary Group, Inc., (L) Tom Schierlitz/Getty Images; **92** (T) Bill Ross/ PhotoLibrary Group, Inc., (BL) Living Art Enterprises, LLC/ Photo Researchers, Inc.; **93** (BR) Science Source/Photo Researchers, Inc.; **94** (BL) Bullit Marquez/©Associated Press, (TC) Juerg Mueller/Keystone/©Associated Press; **95** (CR) Salvatore Di Nolfi/Keystone/©Associated Press; **96** (B) Rene Tillmann/©Associated Press; **97** (BR) Digital Art/Corbis.; **98** (CR) Charles D. Winters/Photo Researchers, Inc.; **99** (BC) Lawrence Lawry/Photo Researchers, Inc.; **100** (B) Jim W. Grace/Photo Researchers, Inc.; **101** (TR) LWA/Dann Tardif/ Photolibrary Group, Inc., (BR) Stockdisc/Photolibrary Group, Inc.; **102** (B) Julian Baum/Photo Researchers, Inc.; **103** (TR) David R. Frazier Photolibrary/Photo Researchers, Inc., (TR) NASA/Photo Researchers, Inc., (TL) Rosenfeld Images Ltd/ Photo Researchers, Inc.; **104** (L) Peter Galbraith/iStockphoto; **106** (B) European Space Agency (ESA)/©Associated Press; **108** (CL) Rue des Archives/©The Granger Collection, NY; **111** (CR) Biophoto Associates/Photo Researchers, Inc.; **114** (CR) Lawrence Lawry/Photo Researchers, Inc., (BR) Rue des Archives/©The Granger Collection, NY; **118** (L) Ed Register/Shutterstock; **119** (R) Cordelia Molloy/Photo Researchers, Inc., (Bkgrd) Photobank.kiev.ua/Shutterstock; **120** (B) Javier Trueba/Madrid Scientific Films; **123** (BCL) ©M. Claye/Jacana Scientific Control/Photo Researchers, Inc., (TCL) Giordano Cipriani/SOPA/Corbis; **124** (B) Panorama Stock/ Photolibrary Group, Inc.; **125** (BR) /©DK Images; **127** (BR) Ed Reinke/©Associated Press; **128** (B) Charles D. Winters/Photo Researchers, Inc.; **129** (TR) Edward Kinsman/Photo Researchers, Inc.; **130** (B) Jens Meyer/©Associated Press; **132** (CC) Andrew Lambert Photography/Photo Researchers, Inc., (CR) Charles D. Winters/Photo Researchers, Inc.; **134** (BL) Giordano Cipriani/SOPA/Corbis; **135** (TR) Geoffrey

Holman/iStockphoto; **136** (TL) ©M. Claye/Jacana Scientific Control/Photo Researchers, Inc.; **138** (C) Ted Kinsman/Science Source, (BL) Frank Greenaway/©DK Images, (TR) Peter Weber/ Getty Images; **139** (CR) Andrew Lambert Photography/Photo Researchers, Inc.; **141** (R) Jupiterimages/©Associated Press; **144** (B) Eric Martin/Photolibrary Group, Inc., (BL) Tom Pepeira/ Photolibrary Group, Inc.; **146** (B) OTHK/Getty Images; **147** (CR) Stephen Oliver/©DK Images; **148** (B) ©Associated Press; **150** (C, BR) ©DK Images, (BC) David H. Lewis/ iStockphoto; **151** (T) Jeff Rotman/Getty Images; **152** (BR) ©Associated Press, (CR) Eric Martin/Photolibrary Group, Inc.; **156** (L) Pictor International/ImageState/Alamy Images, (BC) Steve Cole/Getty Images; **157** (CC) Chris Johnson/Alamy Images, (BL) Jet Propulsion Laboratory/NASA, (TC) Klaus Guldbrandsen/Photo Researchers, Inc.; **158** (B) N A Callow/ Science Source; **161** (BL) Kai Schwabe/Photolibrary Group, Inc., (TCL) Martyn F. Chillmaid/Photo Researchers, Inc.; **162** (BC) Photo by Garret Savage/Courtesy Careers through Culinary Arts Program (C-CAP) and Pressure Cooker, a film from Participant Media/Careers through Culinary Arts Program; **163** (BC) Charles D. Winters/Photo Researchers, Inc., (BL) Peter Spiro/iStockphoto; **164** (CR) Christopher Pattberg/ iStockphoto, (BR, BL) Cole Vineyard/iStockphoto, (CR) Douglas Whyte/Corbis, (CC) Harun Aydin/iStockphoto, (B) Wojtek Kryczka/iStockphoto; **166** (L) Martyn F. Chillmaid/Photo Researchers, Inc.; **167** (TL) Getty Images, (B) Kevin Summers/ Getty Images, (TR) Olivier Blondeau/iStockphoto; **168** (CR) Charles D. Winters/Photo Researchers, Inc., (TL) Daniel Loiselle/iStockphoto; **170** (CL) Ho New/Reuters Media; **171** (CL) Blackpixel/Shutterstock; **172** (CR) Mike Blake/Reuters Media; **174** (CL) Rue des Archives/©The Granger Collection, NY; **176** (B) Kaminskiy/Shutterstock; **178** (L) Morgan/PA Wire/©Associated Press; **179** (T) Johnson Space Center Collection/NASA, (B) GIPhotostock/Science Source; **180** (BC) Kai Schwabe/Photolibrary Group, Inc.; **182** (C) Philadelphia Public Ledger/©Associated Press; **185** (B) Stephen Morton/©Associated Press; **188** (TR) Getty Images; **189** (CL) James Harrop/iStockphoto; **190** (CR) Amanda Rohde/ iStockphoto, (CC) Prill Mediendesign & Fotografie/ iStockphoto; **192** (Bkgrd) Brand X Pictures/Thinkstock, (CR) Maosheng Zhao and Steven W. Running/University of Montana/NASA; **194** (B) David Doubilet/National Geographic Image Collection; **197** (BCL) Eric Risberg/©Associated Press, (TL) Joe Scherschel/National Geographic Image Collection, (TCL) Stew Milne/©Associated Press; **198** (B) Sony Pictures/ Everett Collection; **200** (C) Joe Scherschel/National Geographic Image Collection; **201** (TR) Eric Risberg/©Associated Press; **202** (T) Stew Milne/©Associated Press; **204** (B) Kevin Schafer/Alamy; **207** (BR) ©DK Images, (B) Jacqueline Larma/©Associated Press; **208** (B) RDE Stock/Alamy, (TL) Sergei Kozak/Getty Images; **212** (B) Gareth Mccormack/Getty Images, (CR) Niedersächsisches Landesamt für Denkmalpflege/ ©Associated Press, (BR) Richard Ashworth/Robert Harding World Imagery; **213** (BR) Christopher Cooper/DK Limited/ Corbis, (BCR) Dimitry Romanchuck/iStockphoto, (BC) Jules Selmes and Debi Treloar/©DK Images; **214** (TL) Cristina Pedrazzini/Photo Researchers, Inc.; **215** (TR) ©DK Images, (C) Dennis DeSilva/iStockphoto, (BC) Katrina Brown/ Shutterstock, (BCL) Shutterstock; **217** (CL) ©DK Images, (TC) Scott Camazine/Science Source, (TR) Kim Taylor/Nature Picture Library; **218** (B) WaterFrame/Alamy, (TC) Gregory

ACKNOWLEDGMENTS

Ochocki/Science Source; **221** (C) Comstock/Thinkstock, (TC) Daniel R. Burch/iStockphoto, (TCL) J Semeniuk/iStockphoto, (B) Jon Schulte/iStockphoto, (CC) LuxCreativ/iStockphoto, (TL) Radu Razvan/iStockphoto, (TR) Ranplett/iStockphoto, (CR) Susan Trigg/iStockphoto, (CL) Timothey Kosachev/iStockphoto; **226** (R) Daniel R. Burch/iStockphoto, (L) J Semeniuk/iStockphoto; **228** (BL) Ron & Diane Salmon/Flying Fish Photography LLC; **229** (BC) Anthony-Masterson/Digital Vision/Getty Images, (B) Daniel Sicolo/Jupiter Images; **230** (B) Liane Cary/AGE Fotostock; **233** (TCL) Daniel Roland/ ©Associated Press, (BCL) National Geographic Image Collection, (BL) Randy Siner/ ©Associated Press, (TL) SuperStock; **234** (C) ©Paul & Lindamarie Ambrose/Getty Images, (CL) Nicolaus Copernicus Museum, Frombork, Poland/Lauros/Giraudon/Bridgeman Art Library; **235** (CR) Grant Faint/Getty Images; **236** (B) Image 100/Corbis, (BR) SuperStock; **237** (CR) Thepalmer/iStockphoto; **238** (BR) Bill Ridder/The Paris News/©Associated Press, (BL) Jillian Bauer/Newhouse News Service/Landov LLC, (CC) Liz O. Baylen/Washington Times/Zuma Press, Inc.; **239** (B) John Walton/PA Photos/Landov LLC; **240** (CL) Adam Pretty/©Associated Press, (C) Adrian Hillman/iStockphoto, (B) Daniel Roland/©Associated Press; **241** (CR) Landov LLC; **242** (BR) National Geographic Image Collection; **243** (T) Google Earth Pro/Google, Inc.; **244** (BL) Iconica/Smith Collection/Getty Images; **246** (C) Stephen Dalton/Science Source; **247** (CR) IMAGEMORE Co.,Ltd./Getty., (BR) Randy Siner/©Associated Press, (BC) The Laramie Boomerang/Barbara J. Perenic/©Associated Press; **249** (CR) John Foxx/Stockbyte/Getty Images; **250** (B) Gerhard Zwerger-Schoner/PhotoLibrary Group, Inc.; **252** (BR) IMAGEMORE Co.,Ltd./Getty, (CR) Landov LLC, (TR) Thepalmer/iStockphoto; **256** (CL) Neil Munns/©Associated Press, (T) Sam Morris/ ©Associated Press; **257** (R) Ralph Crane/Time Life Pictures/Getty Images; **258** (B) Brian Snyder/Reuters Media; **261** (BCR) Darryl Leniuk/Getty Images, (TL) Mark Humphrey/©Associated Press, (BR) Zuma Press, Inc.; **262** (B) ColorBlind LLC/Blend Images/Photolibrary Group, Inc.; **263** (BCR) Mark Humphrey/©Associated Press; **266** (B) Space Island Group; **267** (BL) Elena Elisseeva/Shutterstock, (BC) Ian Wilson/Shutterstock, (BCR) Jeff Whyte/iStockphoto, (BR) Ron Sachs/CNP/NewsCom; **270** (TR, CR) ©DK Images, (TCR) Clive Streeter/©DK Images, (TC) Steve Gorton/©DK Images; **271** (B) Darryl Leniuk/Getty Images; **273** (T) JPL/NASA; **274** (C) Georgios Kollidas/Fotolia; **275** (R) Zuma Press, Inc.; **276** (B) David Trood/Getty Images; **277** (CR) Zuma Press, Inc.; **278** (TR) Grace Chiu/UPI/UPI United Press International, (TL) Mark J. Terrill/ ©Associated Press; **279** (BC) Kim Kyung Hoon/Reuters Media, (TR) Steve Helber/©Associated Press; **282** (B) Crista Jeremiason/Santa Rosa Press-Democrat; **283** (B) Jeremy Woodhouse/Getty Images; **286** (B) Tim Platt/Getty Images; **287** (C) Richard Megna/Fundamental Photographs, NYC; **288** (T) NASA; **289** (CR) UberFoto/Alamy; **290** (B) ©Monica Schroeder/Photo Researchers, Inc.; **295** (TR) ©Ron Chapple/Corbis; **302** (BCL) Car Culture/Corbis, (B) Rick Fischer/Masterfile Corporation; **303** (Bkgrd) ©Jose Gil/Shutterstock, (BL) Karen Cochrane/©DK Images; **304** (B) Roland Weihrauch/AFP/Getty Images; **307** (TL) Javier Pierini/Getty Images, (BCL) Photolibrary Group, Inc., (BL) Yiorgos Karahalis/Reuters Media; **308** (C) John Stillwell/©Associated Press; **310** (BL) Laurie Noble/Digital Vision/Photolibrary Group, Inc.; **311** (TR) Javier Pierini/Getty Images; **313** (C) Getty Images; **314** (BL) Justine Evans/Alamy;

316 (TL) ©ThinkStock/SuperStock; **317** (TC) M. Lakshman/©Associated Press; **320** (B) John Howard/Getty Images; **321** (CL) James Shearman/Getty Images; **322** (BC) DiscountRamps; **323** (BL) Photolibrary Group, Inc.; **324** (T, CR) Seth A. McConnell/Rapid City Journal/©Associated Press; **325** (CR) ©DK Images; **326** (B) Ole Graf/Corbis; **327** (CR) Dave Sandford/Getty Images; **328** (BR) Douglas McFadd/©Associated Press, (CL) Steve Gorton/©DK Images; **330** (B) Robert F. Bukaty/©Associated Press; **333** (CR) ©DK Images, (BCR) Creatas/Photolibrary Group, Inc.; **336** (BR) Creatas/Photolibrary Group, Inc., (TR) Getty Images; **337** (CL) Javier Pierini/Getty Images; **338** (CR) Jupiter Images/Ablestock/Alamy; **340** (L) Coneyl Jay/Photo Researchers, Inc.; **341** (TC) Courtesy of MIT Mobility Lab, (BL) Dave Umberger/©Associated Press; **342** (B) Max Rossi/Reuters Media; **345** (BL) Gilbert Iundt/TempSport/Corbis, (BCL) Zuma Press, Inc.; **346** (B) Josiah Davidson/Getty Images; **347** (CR) DesignPics Inc./Photolibrary Group, Inc., (CL) PhotoLibrary Group, Inc.; **349** (BR) Zia Soleil/Iconica/Getty Images; **352** (C) ©Associated Press; **353** (B) Heinz Kluetmeier/Sports Illustrated/Getty Images; **354** (T) Zuma Press, Inc.; **355** (B) PhotoLibrary Group, Inc.; **358** (CL) Michael Goulding/Orange County Register/Zuma Press, Inc.; **360** (L) Fundamental Photographs, NYC; **361** (T) Gilbert Iundt/TempSport/Corbis; **363** (TR) Creatas/Thinkstock, (TCR) Niall Benvie/Nature Picture Library/Nature Picture Library; **364** (TR, CR) PhotoLibrary Group, Inc.; **366** (CR) Globus Brothers, NYC; **368** (BR) geopaul/iStockphoto; **369** (C) Photos to Go/Photolibrary; **370** (B) Nutscode/T Service/Photo Researchers, Inc.; **373** (TCL, BL) PhotoLibrary Group, Inc.; **374** (CL) Annette Soumillard/Corbis; **375** (CR) Martin McCarthy/iStockphoto; **376** (BL) Lisa Svara/iStockphoto; **377** (CL) Acme Food Arts/Getty Images; **378** (C) GRIN/NASA; **379** (C) PhotoLibrary Group, Inc.; **382** (CR) GRIN/NASA; **383** (B) Vincent Leblic/PhotoLibrary Group, Inc.; **384** (T) Alberto Pomares/iStockphoto; **385** (CR) Chris Mattison/Alamy Images, (TR) Mark Lewis/Alamy Images, (C) Matt Meadows/Alamy Images; **386** (BR) Mark Lewis/Alamy Images, (TR) Martin McCarthy/iStockphoto; **388** (TR) Ariel Skelley/Corbis; **389** (BR) Martin Dohrn/Science Source.; **390** (Bkgrd) Digital Stock; **391** (R) Corbis, (L) Stockbyte/Thinkstock; **392** (B) Corbis; **395** (BCL) ©Richard Megna/Fundamental Photographs, (BL) Richard Megna/Fundamental Photographs, NYC, (TL) Sami Sarkis/Getty Images; **396** (B) Wen Zhenxiao/ChinaFotoPress/Zuma Press, Inc.; **397** (BR) Adrian Lourie/Alamy; **398** (C) Sami Sarkis/Getty Images; **400** (BR) Digital Vision/Alamy; **402** (BL) Kin Images/Getty Images, (B) Martin Siepmann/Alamy, (BC) Michael Durham/Nature Picture Library; **403** (R) David Pu'u/Corbis; **404** (T) Stockbyte/Getty Images; **406** (L) Chad Baker/Digital Vision/Getty Images, (CL) Moodboard/Corbis; **407** (T) Walter Bibikow/Danita Delimont Inc./Alamy Images; **408** (B) ©AP Images, (CR) Bettmann/Corbis; **409** (BR) ©Richard Megna/Fundamental Photographs; **410** (TL) ©Matthias Kulka/Corbis, (CL) ©Richard Megna/Fundamental Photographs, (CR) Nice One Productions/Corbis, (B) Richard Megna/Fundamental Photographs, NYC; **411** (CR) ©DK Images, (TR, TL) Image downloaded from the Coastal Inlets Research Program web site, US Army Corps of Engineers, (BCR) Richard Megna/Fundamental Photographs, NYC; **412** (CL) Peter Steiner/Alamy Images, (B) Yamado Taro/The Image Bank/Getty Images; **415** (R) Special Collections Division, University of Washington Libraries; **416** (BR) ©DK Images, (CL) David Pu'u/Corbis;

418 (TR) Earl S. Cryer/UPI/Landov LLC; 420 (L) Photos 12/ Alamy Images; 421 (L) Ablestock/Alamy; 422 (T) Cheryl Gerber/©Associated Press; 425 (TCL) ©Associated Press, (TC) Aaron Haupt/Photo Researchers, Inc., (BCL) Caren Firouz/ Reuters Media, (BL) Greg Baker/©Associated Press, (TR) Michael Clutson/Photo Researchers, Inc.; 426 (C) Digital Vision/Getty Images; 427 (BC) ©Associated Press; 429 (B) Andy King/©Associated Press; 430 (TL) Harrison H. Schmitt/ Johnson space Center/NASA; 431 (TL) Jim Byrnre/QA Photos; 432 (CR) Jean Frooms/iStockphoto; 433 (CR) ©Associated Press, (CC) Clive Barda/Arena-PAL Images; 434 (B) Greg Baker/©Associated Press; 435 (TR) Caren Firouz/Reuters Media; 437 (L) ©Associated Press; 438 (CL) AlexStar/iStockphoto, (TR) iStockphoto; 439 (CR) Marc Grimberg/Getty Images; 440 (C) AlexStar/iStockphoto, (TR) Jorge Silva/Reuters Media, (BL) Mark Aronoff/Santa Rosa Press Democrat/Zuma Press, Inc.; 441 (CC) Jorge Silva/Reuters Media; 442 (CR) Clive Barda/Arena-PAL Images; 445 (TR) AJPhoto/Photo Researchers, Inc.; 446 (C) Ralph Lee Hopkins/National Geographic Image Collection; 447 (TR) Stephen Dalton/Science Source; 449 (TR) Ric Feld/ ©Associated Press; 450 (TR) ©Associated Press, (CR) iStockphoto; 454 (B) Jason Verschoor/iStockphoto; 455 (T) Chris Lemmens/iStockphoto, (B) Yevgen Timashov/ iStockphoto; 456 (B) Tom Barrick, Chris Clark/SGHMS/Photo Researchers, Inc.; 459 (BL) Don Carstens/Robertstock, (BCL) Nutscode/T Service/Photo Researchers, Inc.; 460 (C) J. A. Kraulis/©Masterfile Royalty-Free, (C) Pearson Education, (TR) Photography by Ward/Alamy Images; 462 (B) Benjamin Rondel/Corbis; 463 (T) ©DK Images; 464 (C) Arthur S. Aubry/ Getty Images, (CL) Mode Images Limited/Alamy Images; 466 (R) AbleStock/Thinkstock; 467 (TR) Dave L. Ryan/Photolibrary/ AGE Fotostock; 468 (CL) Joel Sartore/National Geographic/ Getty Images, (BR) Nutscode/T Service/Photo Researchers, Inc.; 469 (T) Goodshoot/Corbis, (BR) Tom Arne Hanslien/Alamy Images; 470 (B) Don Carstens/Robertstock; 471 (T) Stocktrek Images, Inc./Alamy; 472 (B) Brand X Pictures/Jupiter Images; 474 (BL) Fuse/Jupiter Images; 475 (TR) Ablestock/Jupiter Images, (CR) Moodboard/Corbis; 478 (BL) Dana Hoff/ Beateworks/Corbis; 480 (TR) ©DK Images, (CL) Goodshoot/ Corbis; 483 (BR) Bloomimage/Corbis; 484 (L) Ngo Thye Aun/ Shutterstock; 485 (CL) ©Peter Wynn Thompson/The New York Times/Redux Pictures, (Bkgrd) Photos to Go/Photolibrary; 486 (BC) Anish Kapoor, (B) Cloud Gate, Millennium Park, Chicago(2004), Anish Kapoor. Photo ©2008 Kim Karpeles/Kim Karpeles Photography; 489 (TCL) Corbis/Photolibrary Group, Inc., (BCL) Dick Durrance/Woodfin Camp & Associates, (TL) Glow Images/Photolibrary Group, Inc.; 490 (C) Dennis Flaherty/Getty Images; 491 (BR) Kevin Frayer/©Associated Press; 494 (TCL) ©Tom & Pat Leeson, (TL) Dmitry Kutlayev/ iStockphoto; 495 (R) Glow Images/Photolibrary Group, Inc.; 497 (CR) Eastcott Momatiuk/Getty Images; 498 (B) Corbis/ Photolibrary Group, Inc.; 501 (TR) age Fotostock/SuperStock; 502 (B) Lawrence Lawry/Photo Researchers, Inc.; 505 (TR) Lawrence Lawry/Photo Researchers, Inc., (B) AFP/AFP/Getty Images; 506 (T) Dick Durrance/Woodfin Camp & Associates; 510 (B) Stephen Alvarez/National Geographic Image Collection; 511 (BR, BCR) Adam Hart-Davis/Photo Researchers, Inc.; 514 (BL) Niels van Gijn/Getty Images; 516 (CL) John Chumack/ Photo Researchers, Inc.; 517 (CR, CL) Edward Kinsman/Photo Researchers, Inc., (CC) Markus Brunner/Imagebroker/ PhotoLibrary Group, Inc.; 518 (BL) Adam Hart-Davis/Photo Researchers, Inc.; 520 (BR) Richard Megna/Fundamental Photographs, NYC; 522 (B) David Steele/Large Binocular Telescope Observatory; 523 (B) JupiterImages/Creatas/Alamy; 524 (B) Nick Suydam/Alamy Images; 527 (TCL) Jim Ketsdever/©Associated Press; 528 (B) Moviestore Collection Ltd./Alamy; 532 (TL) Dev Carr/Cultura/Photolibrary Group, Inc., (BC) Paul A. Souders/Corbis; 533 (TL) GIPhotoStock/ Photo Researchers, Inc.; 534 (B) Jim Ketsdever/©Associated Press, (TL) Peter Menzel/Photo Researchers, Inc., (BC) Virgo Productions/Corbis; 536 (CL) Volker Steger/Photo Researchers, Inc.; 537 (B) ©2003 Universal/Everett Collection, Inc.; 538 (C) Google, Inc.; 539 (BL) Brandon Laufenberg/ iStockphoto, (CR) Franc Podgor?ek/iStockphoto, (CC) Jill Fromer/iStockphoto, (BC) jo unruh/iStockphoto, (B) Julia Nichols/iStockphoto, (BCL) Linda King/iStockphoto; 542 (CR) Alan Keohane/©DK Images; 543 (BC) Enrique de la Osa/ Reuters Media; 544 (B) Jeff Horner/ ©Associated Press; 545 (BR) iStockphoto; 549 (BR) Liquid Library/Thinkstock; 552 (C) Kim Kyung Hoon/Reuters Media; 553 (BR) Akirastock/ iStockphoto, (BL) Gualtiero Boffi/iStockphoto, (T) magicinfoto/ iStockphoto, (CR) pixhook/iStockphoto, (BC) Uyen Le/ iStockphoto; 554 (CL) Emmeline Watkins/SPL/Photo Researchers, Inc.; 555 (BL) Jill Fromer/iStockphoto; 556 (TR) Paul A. Souders/Corbis; 557 (CR) pixhook/iStockphoto; 559 (BR) iStockphoto; 560 (BR) Bettmann/Corbis, (TL) Jerry Mason/Photo Researchers, Inc., (B) Silman Snozyk/PhotoLibrary Group, Inc.; 561 (TR) Earl Roberge/Photo Researchers, Inc., (B) Michael Peuckert/Alamy Images; 562 (B) Liu Xiaoyang/Alamy Images; 565 (B) Shutterstock, (TL) Yiap Edition/Alamy Images; 566 (CL) Vikram Hoshing/Alamy; 567 (TC) /Alamy Images, (T) Galina Barskaya/Alamy, (C) Richard Baker/In Pictures/Corbis; 568 (BL, BC) Richard Megna/Fundamental Photographs, NYC, (T) Yiap Edition/Alamy Images; 569 (C) Amazing Images/Alamy; 570 (TR) Roger Harris/Science Source, (BL) DLI LLC/Corbis, (BC) Master Magnetics; 576 (BL) Novastock/Alamy Images; 581 (CR) Pictures by Rob/Alamy/Alamy; 582 (CR) Nikkytok/Shutterstock; 584 (C) Richard T. Nowitz/Photo Researchers, Inc.; 585 (TR) DreamPictures/Stone/Getty Images; 588 (B) Corbis, (CR) Peter Beck/Corbis; 591 (BR) Car Culture/Corbis, (CR) Clive Streeter/ The Science Museum, London/©DK Images, (TR) Schenectady Museum/Hall of Electrical History Foundation/Corbis; 592 (B) Shutterstock; 595 (TR) Omri Waisman/Beateworks/Corbis; 596 (TR) Amazing Images/Alamy; 600 (BCL) Living Art Enterprises/ Photo Researchers, Inc., (B) RubberBall Selects/Alamy; 601 (BL) North Wind Picture Archives, (BR) Steve Gorton/British Telecommunications/©DK Images

this is your book

you can write in it

take note

this space is yours—great for drawing diagrams and making notes

this is your book

you can write in it

this is your book

you can write in it

this is your book

you can write in it

646

take note

this space is yours—great for drawing diagrams and making notes

this is your book

you can write in it

take note

this space is yours—great for drawing diagrams and making notes

this is your book

you can write in it